AA004643

23rd Conference on Computational Linguistics and Speech Processing 2011

(ROCLING 2011)

Taipei, Taiwan
8 – 9 September 2011

Editors:

Wei-Ho Tsai
Liang-Chih Yu

ISBN: 978-1-62276-508-9

Printed from e-media with permission by:

Curran Associates, Inc.
57 Morehouse Lane
Red Hook, NY 12571

Some format issues inherent in the e-media version may also appear in this print version.

Copyright© (2011) by the Association for Computational Linguistics
All rights reserved.

Printed by Curran Associates, Inc. (2012)

For permission requests, please contact the Association for Computational Linguistics at the address below.

Association for Computational Linguistics
209 N. Eighth Street
Stroudsburg, Pennsylvania 18360

Phone: 1-570-476-8006
Fax: 1-570-476-0860

acl@aclweb.org

Additional copies of this publication are available from:

Curran Associates, Inc.
57 Morehouse Lane
Red Hook, NY 12571 USA
Phone: 845-758-0400
Fax: 845-758-2634
Email: curran@proceedings.com
Web: www.proceedings.com

Organization

Conference Chair

Yuan-Fu Liao	廖元甫	National Taipei university of Technology

Program Committee Co-Chairs

Wei-Ho Tsai	蔡偉和	National Taipei university of Technology
Liang-Chih Yu	禹良治	Yuan Ze University

Program Committee Members

Guo-Wei Bian	邊國維	Huafan University
Chia-Hui Chang	張嘉惠	National Central University
Jason S. Chang	張俊盛	National Tsing Hua University
Jing-Shin Chang	張景新	National Chi Nan University
Yi-Hsiang Chao	趙怡翔	Ching Yun University
Berlin Chen	陳柏琳	National Taiwan Normal University
Chia-Ping Chen	陳嘉平	National Sun Yat Sen University
Chien-Chin Chen	陳建錦	National Taiwan University
Hsin-Hsi Chen	陳信希	National Taiwan University
Keh-Jiann Chen	陳克健	Academia Sinica
Kuang-Hua Chen	陳光華	National Taiwan University
Sin-Horng Chen	陳信宏	National Chiao Tung University
Tai-Shih Chi	冀泰石	National Chiao Tung University
Jen-Tzung Chien	簡仁宗	National Cheng Kung University
Chih-Yi Chiu	邱志義	National ChiaYi University
Hung-Yan Gu	古鴻炎	National Taiwan University of Science and Technology
Wei-Tyng Hong	洪維廷	Yuan Ze University
Wen-Lian Hsu	許聞廉	Academia Sinica
Jeih-weih Hung	洪志偉	National Chi Nan University
Jyh-Shing Jang	張智星	National Tsing Hua University
Chih-Chung Kuo	郭志忠	Industrial Technology Research Institute

June-Jei Kuo	郭俊桔	National Chung Hsing University
Wen-Hising Lai	賴玟杏	National Kaohsiung First University of Science and Technology
Chao-Lin Liu	劉昭麟	National Chengchi University
Jyi-Shane Liu	劉吉軒	National Chengchi University
Chuan-Jie Lin	林川傑	National Taiwan Ocean University
Shou-De Lin	林守德	National Taiwan University
Richard Tzong-Han Tsai	蔡宗翰	Yuan Ze University
Yuen-Hsien Tseng	曾元顯	National Taiwan Normal University
Hsiao-Chuan Wang	王小川	National Tsing Hua University
Hsin-Min Wang	王新民	Academia Sinica
Yih-Ru Wang	王逸如	National Chiao Tung University
Chin-Sheng Yang	楊錦生	Yuan Ze University
Cheng-Zen Yang	楊正仁	Yuan Ze University
Ming-Shing Yu	余明興	National Chung Hsing University
Chung-Hsien Wu	吳宗憲	National Chen Kung University
Gin-Der Wu	吳俊德	National Chi Nan University
Jui-Feng Yeh	葉瑞峰	National ChiaYi University
Shih-Hung Wu	吳世弘	Chaoyang University of Technology

Program Overview

September 8, 2011 (Thursday) 9:10 ~ 20:00		
09:10-10:00	Registration	
10:00:10:10	Opening Ceremony	Prof. Leehter Yao Chair: Prof. Yuan-Fu Liao
10:10-11:10	Invited Talk: Machine Transliteration – Translating the Untranslatables	Speaker: Prof. Haizhou Li, Institute for Infocomm Research, Singapore Chair: Prof. Hsiao-Chun Wang
11:10-11:40	Coffee Break	
11:40-12:40	Oral Session 1: Speech Recognition and Synthesis	Chair: Prof. Chia-Ping Chen
12:40-13:30	Lunch	
13:30-14:30	ACLCLP meeting for future directions/ Poster Session 1:NSC Project reports	
14:30-15:30	Invited Talk: Opportunities and Technology Challenges for Search Engines in the mobile internet	Speaker: Dr Lee-Feng Chien, General Manager, Google Chair: Prof. Hsin-Hsi Chen
15:30-16:00	Coffee Break/ IJCLCLP editors meeting(資工系系辦公室會議室科技大樓 3 樓)	
16:00-17:00	Panel Discussion: Frontier of speech science and technology for real life	Panelists: 吳宗憲教授，簡立峰博士 郭志忠博士，沈家麟博士 Chair: Prof. Jhing-Fa Wang
17:00~18:00	Walking to banguet place (美麗信飯店)	
18:00-20:00	Banquet (美麗信飯店 buffet)	

September 9, 2011 (Friday) 9:30 ~ 16:20		
9:30-10:30	Invited Talk: Some Issues on Statistical Machine Translation Using Source and Target (or) Syntax	Speaker: Prof. Jingbo Zhu, Northeastern University, ShenYang, China Chair: Prof. Liang-Chih Yu
10:30-11:00	Coffee Break	
11:00-12:00	Oral Session 2: Machine Translation and Word Segmentation	Chair: Prof. Yuen-Hsien Tseng
12:00-13:00	Lunch	
13:00-14:30	Poster Session 2: Poster Papers	
14:30-15:00	Coffee Break	
15:00-16:00	Oral Session 3: Lexicon, Resources and NLP applications	Chair: Prof. June-Jei Kuo
16:00-16:20	Closing Ceremony and Best Paper Award	

Technical Program Details

Oral Session 1: Speech Recognition and Synthesis
Time: Thursday, September 8, 11:40-12:40

1. Empirical Comparisons of Various Discriminative Language Models for Speech Recognition
   Min-Hsuan Lai, Bang-Xuan Huang, Kuan-Yu Chen and Berlin Chen
2. Compensating the Speech Features via Discrete Cosine Transform for Robust Speech Recognition
   Hsin-Ju Hsieh, Wen-Hsiang Tu and Jeih-Weih Hung
3. 聯合語者、雜訊環境與說話內容因素分析之強健性語音辨認
   Sheng-Tang Wu, Wei-Te Fang and Yuan-Fu Liao
4. Evaluation of TTS Systems in Intelligibility and Comprehension Tasks
   Yu-Yun Chang

Oral Session 2: Machine Translation and Word Segmentation
Time: Friday, September 9, 11:00-12:00

1. 片語式機器翻譯中未知詞與落單字的問題探討
   蔣明撰, 黃仲淇, 顏合淨, 黃士庭, 張俊盛, 楊秉哲, 谷圳
2. 英文技術文獻中一般動詞與其受詞之中文翻譯的語境效用
   Yi-Hsuan Chuang, Jui-Ping Wang, Chia-Chi Tsai and Chao-Lin Liu
3. Unsupervised Overlapping Feature Selection for Conditional Random Fields Learning in Chinese Word Segmentation
   Ting-Hao Yang, Tian-Jian Jiang, Chan-Hung Kuo, Richard Tzong-han Tsai and Wen-Lian Hsu
4. 繁體中文文本中對於日文人名及異體字的處理策略
   林川傑, 詹嘉丞, 陳彥亨, 鮑建威

Oral Session 3: Lexicon, Resources and NLP applications
Time: Friday, September 9, 15:00-16:00

1. 動補結構的及物性及修飾對象
   You-Shan Chung and Keh-Jiann Chen
2. Predicting the Semantic Orientation of Terms in E-HowNet
   Cheng-Ru Li, Chi-Hsin Yu and Hsin-Hsi Chen
3. 聲符部件排序與形聲字發音規則探勘
   Chia-Hui Chang and Sean Lin
4. Frequency, Collocation, and Statistical Modeling of Lexical Items: A Case Study of Temporal Expressions in an Elderly Speaker Corpus
   Sheng-Fu Wang, Jing-Chen Yang, Yu-Yun Chang, Yu-Wen Liu and Shu-Kai Hsieh

Poster Session 2: Poster Papers

Time: Friday, September 9, 13:00-14:30

1. Probabilistic Modulation Spectrum Factorization for Robust Speech Recognition
   Wen-Yi Chu, Yu-Chen Kao, Berlin Chen and Jeih-Weih Hung
2. 應用語音辨識技術於鳥鳴聲辨識
   Wei-En Liao, Hsin-Chieh Lee and Wei-Ho Tsai
3. 使用分段式 GMM 及自動 GMM 挑選之語音轉換方法
   Hung-Yan Gu and Sung-Fung Tsai
4. 應用詞彙、語法與語料規則於中文手寫句辨識之校正模組
   Tao-Hsing Chang, Chia-Bin Chou, Shou-Yen Su and Chien-Liang Liu
5. Using Kohonen Maps of Chinese Morphological Families to Visualize the Interplay of Morphology and Semantics in Chinese
   Bruno Galmar
6. The Prior Knowledge Effect on the Processing of Vague Discourse in Mandarin Chinese
   Shu-Ping Gong and Kathleen Ahrens
7. On the Learning of Chinese Aspect Markers through Multimedia Program
   Tzu-Hui Hsieh, Yi-Chun Kuo, Shu-Chun Chung and Jiun-Shiung Wu
8. 中文文字蘊涵系統之特徵分析
   Wan-Chi Huang, Shih-Hung Wu, Liang-Pu Chen and Tsun Ku
9. 結合語言模型與網路知識源於列印前檢查
   Yu-Jui Huang, Ming-Chin Yen, Guan-Huei Wu, Yao-Yi Wang and Jui-Feng Yeh
10. Diagnosing Discoursal Organization in Learner Writing via Conjunctive Adverbials
    Tung-Yu Kao and Li-Mei Chen
11. Compositional Operations of Mandarin Chinese Verb "da3": A Generative Lexicon Approach
    Li-Chuan Ku
12. Typological Universals and Intrinsic Universals on the L2 Acquisition of Consonant Clusters
    Chin-Chin Tseng
13. 多語語碼轉換之未知詞擷取
    Yi-Lun Wu, Chaio-Wen Hsieh, Wei-Hsuan Lin, Chun-Yi Liu and Liang-Chih Yu

目 次

Keynote Speech

ROCLING 2011 Paper

Invited Speaker: Haizhou Li

Machine Transliteration - Translating the Untranslatables

Abstract

Machine transliteration is the process of automatically rewriting the script of a word from one language to another, while preserving pronunciation. The last decade has seen a tremendous progress and a growth of interests from theory to practice of machine transliteration. In this talk, I will present an overview of the fundamentals, algorithms and applications, in particular, transliteration between English and Chinese. I will also report the findings in the most recent transliteration evaluation campaigns - NEWS 2009 and NEWS 2010 Machine Transliteration Shared Tasks.

Biography

Dr. Haizhou Li is currently the Principal Scientist and Department Head of Human Language Technology at the Institute for Infocomm Research. Dr Li has worked on speech and language technology in academia and industry since1988. He taught in the University of Hong Kong (1988-1990), South China University of Technology (1990-1994), and Nanyang Technological University (2006-). He was a Visiting Professor at CRIN/INRIA in France (1994-1995), and at the University of New South Wales in Australia (2008). As a technologist, he was appointed as Research Manager in Apple-ISS Research Centre (1996-1998), Research Director in Lernout & Hauspie Asia Pacific (1999-2001), and Vice President in InfoTalk Corp. Ltd (2001-2003).

Dr Li's research interests include automatic speech recognition, natural language processing and social robotics. He has published over 150 technical papers in international journals and conferences. He holds five international patents. Dr Li now serves as an Associate Editor of IEEE Transactions on Audio, Speech and Language Processing, ACM Transactions on Speech and Language Processing, and Springer International Journal of Social Robotics. He is an elected Board Member of the International Speech Communication Association (ISCA, 2009-2013), an Executive Board Member of the Asian Federation of Natural Language Processing (AFNLP, 2006-2010), and a Senior Member of IEEE since 2001. Dr Li was the Local Organizing Chair of SIGIR 2008 and ACL-IJCNLP 2009. He was appointed the General Chair of ACL 2012 and Interspeech 2014. He was the recipient of National Infocomm Award of Singapore in 2001. He was named one of the two Nokia Professors 2009 by Nokia Foundation in recognition of his contribution to speaker and language recognition technologies.

Invited Speaker: Lee-Feng Chien

Opportunities and Technology Challenges for Search Engines in the Mobile Internet

Abstract

The web started on the PC, within the recent years it started arriving for mobile devices. It will soon arrive for many other types of devices we haven't even thought of yet. This is going to open up some pretty amazing business opportunities and technology challenges for search engine development, and online marketing that can seek to promote businesses by increasing their visibility when users access the mobile Internet. So what I'd like to do is walk you through some of the macro trends that are converging right now to set us up for explosive growth in the mobile Internet over the next couple of years and then walk you through some of the technology challenges that await those who understand and invest in -- or at least start experimenting in -- this area.

Biography

Dr. Lee-Feng Chien is working with Google as GM of Google Taiwan and engineering site director of Taiwan/Hong Kong R&D center. He is known for his work on Chinese natural language processing, has researched Chinese analysis systems, language models, speech recognition systems, and search engineering technology for many years. He has served on program committees for major conferences and journal editorial boards in the related academic areas, and is the author of a hundred of technical papers. Prior to joining Google, he was research fellow and deputy director of the Institute of information Science, Academia Sinica, Taiwan, and also jointly appointed as a professor of the Information Management Department of National Taiwan University. He received his Ph.D. in CS from National Taiwan University in 1991.

Invited Speaker: Jingbo Zhu

Some Issues on Statistical Machine Translation Using Source and (or) Target Syntax

Abstract

Machine Translation (MT) is one of the oldest sub-fields in Natural Language Processing (NLP) and Artificial Intelligence (AI). During the last decade, syntax-based approaches have received growing interests in MT community, showing state-of-the-art performance for many language pairs such as Chinese-English. In this talk, I will present our recent work on syntax-based MT, and some approaches to performing translation using source and (or) target syntax, involving string-to-tree, tree-to-string and tree-to-tree SMT paradigms. Also, an empirical study is shown to compare the strengths and weaknesses among various syntax-based SMT approaches. Furthermore, several interesting issues are further addressed to investigate what the major problems in current (syntax-based) MT paradigm are. Finally, I will spend a little time to introduce a new open-source SMT toolkit (named NEUTrans) which was developed by the NLPLab of Northeastern University, and our current efforts on incorporating syntax-based SMT paradigms into this open SMT platform.

Biography

Dr. Jingbo Zhu is a full professor of Computer Science at the Northeastern University at Shenyang, China, and is in charge of research activities within the Natural Language Processing Laboratory (NEU-NLPlab, htttp://www.nlplab.com). He received his Ph.D. degree in computer software and theory from the Northeastern University in 1999. He was a visiting researcher at the City University of Hongkong (2004) and ISI, University of Southern California at Los Angeles (2006-2007), and was selected by the Program for New Century Excellent Talents in University, Ministry of Education (2005). His research interests include machine translation, syntactic parsing, sentiment analysis and text mining. He has published 100+ papers in many high-level journals and conferences including IEEE Transactions on Affective Computing, IEEE Transactions on Audio, Speech and Language Processing, ACM Transactions on Speech and Language Processing, ACM Transactions on Asian Language Information Processing, and ACL/EMNLP/Coling, etc.

實證探究多種鑑別式語言模型於語音辨識之研究

Empirical Comparisons of Various Discriminative Language Models for Speech Recognition

賴敏軒 [1], 黃邦烜 [1], 陳冠宇 [2], 陳柏琳 [1]
[1] 國立臺灣師範大學資訊工程學系
{698470623, 699470204, berlin}@ntnu.edu.tw
[2] 中央研究院資訊科學研究所
kychen@iis.sinica.edu.tw

摘要

傳統語言模型(Language Models)是藉由使用大量的文字語料訓練而成，以機率模型來描述自然語言的規律性。*N* 連(*N*-gram)語言模型是最常見的語言模型，被用來估測每一個詞出現在已知前 *N*-1 個歷史詞之後的條件機率。此外，傳統語言模型大多是以最大化相似度爲訓練目標；因此，當它被使用於語音辨識上時，對於降低語音辨識錯誤率常會有所侷限。近年來，有別於傳統語言模型的鑑別式語言模型(Discriminative Language Model)陸續地被提出；與傳統語言模型不同的是，鑑別式語言模型是以最小化語音辨識錯誤率做爲訓練準則，期望所訓練出的語言模型可以幫助降低語音辨識的錯誤率。本論文探究基於不同訓練準則的鑑別式語言模型，分析各種鑑別式語言模型之基礎特性，並且比較它們被使用於大詞彙連續語音辨識(Large Vocabulary Continuous Speech Recognition, LVCSR)時之效能。同時，本論文亦提出將邊際(Margin)概念引入於鑑別式語言模型的訓練準則中。實驗結果顯示，相較於傳統 *N* 連語言模型，使用鑑別式語言模型能對於大詞彙連續語音辨識有相當程度的幫助；而本論文所提出的基於邊際資訊之鑑別式語言模型亦能夠進一步地提升語音辨識的正確率。

關鍵詞：語音辨識、鑑別式語言模型、邊際、訓練準則

一、緒論

在人與人的互動當中，語音是最自然且直接的表達方式之一。透過語音，人們可以彼此溝通，傳達想法、感受以及情緒。因此，我們期望能讓電腦具備與人溝通的能力，能爲生活帶來便利性。要達到此目標，我們必須先對使用者輸入的語音訊號進行辨識；待轉換成文字後，再對文字所欲表達的語意作理解，進而做出最適當的動作來回應使用者。將語音訊號轉換成文字的過程，可以透過自動語音辨識(Automatic Speech Recognition, ASR)技術來完成。在自動語音辨識的過程中，我們必須先將語音訊號做特徵擷取(Feature Extraction)，保留語音訊號中的聲學特性(Acoustic Characteristics)，並轉換成能使電腦容易處理的聲學特徵向量(Acoustic Feature Vector)；利用這些聲學特徵向量，我

們可以為不同的音素(Phoneme)分別建立聲學模型(Acoustic Model)，進而產生可能的候選詞序列(Candidate Word Sequences)。另一方面，我們也必須收集大量的文字訓練語料，用以統計自然語言中各種詞序列的出現情形，並藉此訓練語言模型(Language Model)。傳統語言模型是收集各種詞彙出現在自然語言中的詞頻數，經由最大化相似度估測(Maximum Likelihood Estimation, MLE)來建立語言模型。例如，N 連(N-gram)語言模型[1]是估測每一個詞在其前面緊鄰 N-1 個歷史詞序列已知情況下的條件機率；它可協助語音辨識器從所產生的候選詞序列中，選取機率最高(最可能)的詞序列做為最後的語音辨識結果。

利用傳統語言模型(例如N連語言模型)所選出的語音辨識結果通常是發生機率最高的詞序列，但未必是最佳(錯誤率最低)的；換句話說，在候選詞序列中其實有可能存在著其它擁有較低錯誤率的詞序列可以做為語音辨識器的輸出。於是，我們希望能透過使用更多其它語言特徵，以及候選詞序列所提供的資訊，並經適當訓練的語言模型將所有候選詞序列做重新排序(Reranking)，以輸出擁有較低錯誤率的語音辨識結果。近年來，有許多學者採用鑑別式訓練(Discriminative Training)的概念來訓練語言模型以幫助重新排序。與傳統語言模型不同，鑑別式語言模型(Discriminative Language Model)[2, 3, 4]是以最小化語音辨識錯誤率為訓練目標，藉由一組預先定義的語言特徵以及所對應的特徵權重參數，將所有候選詞序列(存在於詞圖或 M 條最佳辨識候選詞序列)重新計分(Rescoring)或重新排序(Reranking)，期望使具有最低錯誤率的候選詞序列能擁有最高的分數(排序)，並且做為最後的輸出結果。

本論文延續我們先前對於鑑別式語言模型之研究[5, 6]，探究基於不同訓練準則的鑑別式語言模型，分析各種鑑別式語言模型之基礎特性，並提出將邊際(Margin)概念引入於鑑別式語言模型的訓練準則中。本論文的安排如下：第二節將介紹近年來常見的、基於不同訓練準則的鑑別式語言模型；第三節將說明本論文所提出基於邊際資訊之鑑別式語言模型；第四節是實驗結果與分析；第五節則是結論與未來展望。

二、鑑別式語言模型介紹

(一)、鑑別式語言模型訓練之定義

一般來說，鑑別式語言模型是以最小化辨識錯誤率為訓練目標，希望對基礎語音辨識器(Baseline Speech Recognizer)所產生的候選詞序列(如前 M 條最佳辨識結果)作重新排序，使得具有較低辨識錯誤率的候選詞序列能擁有較高的排序。而重新排序的依據則是以基礎語音辨識器的辨識分數做為基礎，並加上額外定義的語言特徵向量，藉由前述兩者與其對應的特徵權重參數向量做內積後的語言模型分數來進行排序，使得前 M 條最佳辨識候選詞序列中最低錯誤率的詞序列能擁有最高的語言模型分數。以下將對鑑別式訓練所需的參數做定義：

(a) 給定一句語音訊號 x_i，其經由基礎辨識器所產生的 M 條最佳候選詞序列集合為 $GEN(x_i)=\{W_{i,j}\}$，其中 j 為1到 M 之間。

(b) 將訓練語料視為 $\{x_i,W_i^R\}$的集合，其中 i 的值介於1到 L 之間，L 為訓練語料的總句數；W_i^R 為語音訊號 x_i 在其對應 M 條最佳候選詞序列中最低錯誤率之詞序列。

(c) 對於每一條候選詞序列定義一組 $D+1$ 維的特徵向量 $f_d(W_{i,j})$，其中 d 是從 0 到 D 之間；$f_0(W_{i,j})$ 爲基礎辨識器所產生的分數，即爲聲學模型與 N 連語言模型的對數機率(Log Probability)分數總和，在此我們使用三連(Trigram)語言模型；而其它維度 d，可分別表示每一條候選詞序列 $W_{i,j}$ 中各種 N 連詞出現的次數(視爲一種語言特徵)，以 $f_d(W_{i,j})$ 來表示，本論文所定義各種可能的語言特徵爲單連詞(Word Unigram)與雙連詞(Word Bigram)。

(d) 定義一組 $D+1$ 維的特徵權重參數向量 $\lambda=[\lambda_0,\lambda_1,\ldots,\lambda_d,\ldots,\lambda_D]$，其中每一個特徵權重參數 λ_d 分別對應於每一個語言特徵 $f_d(W_{i,j})$。

因此，候選詞序列 $W_{i,j}$ 的重新排序分數可表示爲：

$$Score(W_{i,j},\lambda)=\lambda \bullet f(W_{i,j})=\sum_{d=0}^{D}\lambda_d f_d(W_{i,j}) \tag{1}$$

而經由重新排序後分數最高的候選詞序列 W_i^* 即做爲最後的輸出結果：

$$W_i^* = \mathop{\arg\max}_{W_{i,j}\in GEN(x_i)} Score(W_{i,j},\lambda) \tag{2}$$

鑑別式語言模型的訓練在於求取最佳的特徵權重參數向量 λ，期望使得測試語句的前 M 條最佳辨識候選詞序列中最低錯誤率的詞序列能在式(2)擁有最高的分數。

(二)、常見的鑑別式語言模型

鑑別式語言模型早期大多都使用在其它的應用領域上：例如，機器翻譯(Machine Translation, MT)、自然語言處理(Natural Language Processing, NLP)等。近十年來，陸續有許多學者將各種基於不同訓練準則的鑑別式語音模型介紹到大詞彙連續語音辨識(Large Vocabulary Continuous Speech Recognition, LVCSR)來使用。鑑別式語言模型的訓練可分成三個面向來探討，分別爲訓練語料、訓練準則與特徵。以下將介紹常見的各種鑑別式語言模型，並將它們依其訓練準則區分爲以下四類：最小化平方誤差、最小化錯誤率期望值、最大化對數條件機率、以及考量語句之間彼此之關係。

1、最小化平方誤差

感知器演算法(Perceptron)[7]早期是被應用在人工類神經網路(Artificial Neural Network)領域中；在 2002 年，美國學者 Collins[8]將感知器演算法應用在自然語言處理領域中。感知器演算法可視爲是最大化熵值法(Maximum-Entropy, ME)或條件式隨機域(Conditional Radom Fields, CRF)[9, 10]的一種變形。感知器演算法以最小平方誤差(Least Squared Error, LSE)[11]爲觀念，透過最小化其訓練目標函數(Training Objective) $F_{\text{Perc}}(\lambda)$ 以求得最佳的特徵權重參數向量 $\hat{\lambda}$：

$$F_{\text{Perc}}(\lambda)=\frac{1}{2}\sum_{i=1}^{L}\left(Score(W_i^R,\lambda)-Score(W_i^*,\lambda)\right)^2 \tag{3}$$

爲了求得 $\hat{\lambda}$，我們可以利用梯度下降法(Gradient Descent Method)將 $F_{Perc}(\lambda)$ 的每一個維

Initialize all parameters in the model, i.e. $\lambda_0 = 1$ *and* $\lambda_d = 0$ for $d = 1,\ldots,D$

For $t = 1\ldots T$ where T is the total number of iterations

  For each training sample $\left(x_i, W_i^R\right), i = 1,\ldots,L$

    Use current model λ to choose the W_i^* from $GEN(x_i)$

    For $d = 1,\ldots,D$

      $\hat{\lambda}_d = \lambda_d + \eta \cdot \left(f_d\left(W_i^R\right) - f_d\left(W_i^*\right)\right)$ where η is the size of the learning step

圖一、感知器演算法[12]

度特徵權重參數 λ_d 分別做偏微分，由於 $F_{\text{Perc}}(\lambda)$ 可能存在許多局部最佳解(Local Minimum Solutions)，而使用梯度下降法並無法保證可求得全域最佳解(Global Minimum Solutions)。因此，感知器演算法採取隨機近似法(Stochastic Approximation)，即對每一句訓練語句的每一維特徵權重參數分別求最佳解，求得每一維特徵權重參數的調整量：

$$\hat{\lambda}_d = \lambda_d - \eta \cdot \left(Score\left(W_i^R, \lambda\right) - Score\left(W_i^*, \lambda\right)\right) \cdot \left(f_d\left(W_i^R\right) - f_d\left(W_i^*\right)\right) \tag{4}$$

其中 η 爲學習步調常數(Learning Step Size)。除了式(4)此種特徵權重參數更新式之外，也有學者提出省略 $Score\left(W_i^R, \lambda\right) - Score\left(W_i^*, \lambda\right)$ 項，將更新式簡化爲 $\hat{\lambda}_d = \lambda_d + \eta \cdot \left(f_d\left(W_i^R\right) - f_d\left(W_i^*\right)\right)$ 來更新特徵權重參數。其演算法如圖一所示。

2、最小化錯誤率期望值

(1)、最小化錯誤率訓練(MERT)

最小化錯誤率訓練(Minimum Error Rate Training, MERT)是在 2003 年由學者 Och[13]提出，並且運用在機器翻譯(Machine Translation)領域中；在 2008 年由 Kobayashi 等學者[14]將最小化錯誤率訓練方法介紹到語音辨識領域中使用。應用於語音辨識時，其訓練準則定義成最小化基礎語音辨識器所產生的 M 條候選詞序列之錯誤率期望值，藉此找出一個最合適的語言模型特徵權重向量：

$$F_{\text{MERT}}(\lambda) = \sum_{i=1}^{L} \sum_{k=1}^{M} \frac{\omega_{W_{i,k}} \cdot \exp\left(Score\left(W_{i,k}, \lambda\right) - Score\left(W_i^R, \lambda\right)\right)^{\beta}}{\sum_{j=1}^{M} \exp\left(Score\left(W_{i,j}\right) - Score\left(W_i^R, \lambda\right)\right)^{\beta}} \tag{5}$$

其中 $\omega_{W_{i,k}}$ 爲候選詞序列 $W_{i,k}$ 的錯誤率(Error Rate)；而 β 爲一平滑化參數。透過進一步的數學推導，我們可以將式(5)中 $\exp\left(Score\left(W_i^R, \lambda\right)\right)^{\beta}$ 項提出而簡化成：

$$F_{\text{MERT}}(\lambda) = \sum_{i=1}^{L} \sum_{k=1}^{M} \frac{\omega_{W_{i,k}} \cdot \exp\left(Score\left(W_{i,k}, \lambda\right)\right)^{\beta}}{\sum_{j=1}^{M} \exp\left(Score\left(W_{i,j}, \lambda\right)\right)^{\beta}} \tag{6}$$

再將式(6)針對每一維特徵權重參數 λ_d 做偏微分，得其調整量爲：

$$\hat{\lambda}_d = \lambda_d +$$

$$\eta \cdot \sum_{i=1}^{L} \sum_{k=1}^{M} \omega_{W_{i,k}} \cdot \beta \cdot \exp\left(Score\left(W_{i,k}, \lambda\right)\right)^{\beta} \cdot \frac{\sum_{j=1}^{M} \exp\left(Score\left(W_{i,j}, \lambda\right)\right)^{\beta} \left(f_d\left(W_{i,k}\right) - f_d\left(W_{i,j}\right)\right)}{\left(\sum_{j'=1}^{M} \exp\left(Score\left(W_{i,j'}, \lambda\right)\right)^{\beta}\right)^2} \quad (7)$$

其中η爲學習步調常數。我們可以將最小化錯誤率訓練中錯誤率$\omega_{W_{i,k}}$視爲一種樣本權重(Sample Weight)資訊，用來區別每一個候選詞序列$W_{i,k}$對於鑑別式語言模型訓練時的重要性。

3、最大化對數條件機率

(1)、全域條件式對數線性模型(GCLM)

早期全域條件式對數線性模型(Global Conditional Log-linear Model, GCLM)被應用在自然語言處理領域中；2007年Roark等學者[4]以有限狀態機(Weighted Finite State Automata, WFSA)實作全域條件式對數線性模型於語音辨識結果的重新排序上，並且與感知器演算法進行比較。

全域條件式對數線性模型是希望在給定一句語音訊號x_i與所對應的M條最佳候選詞序列$GEN(x_i)$時，其中擁有最低辨識錯誤率的詞序列其對數條件機率可以越大越好，亦即最大化下列訓練目標函數：

$$F_{\mathrm{GCLM}}(\lambda) = \sum_{i=1}^{L} \log \frac{\exp\left(Score\left(W_i^R, \lambda\right)\right)}{\sum_{j=1}^{M} \exp\left(Score\left(W_{i,j}, \lambda\right)\right)} \quad (8)$$

爲了避免過度訓練(Overtraining)，我們可以在目標函數$F_{\mathrm{GCLM}}(\lambda)$中加上一個權重參數的零均值高斯事前機率(Zero-Mean Gaussian Prior Probability)項：

$$F_{\mathrm{GCLM}}(\lambda) = \sum_{i=1}^{L} \log \frac{\exp\left(Score\left(W_i^R, \lambda\right)\right)}{\sum_{j=1}^{M} \exp\left(Score\left(W_{i,j}, \lambda\right)\right)} - \frac{\|\lambda\|^2}{2\sigma^2} \quad (9)$$

因爲$F_{\mathrm{GCLM}}(\lambda)$爲一凸函數(Convex Function)，因此可以求得全域最佳解(Globally Optimal Solution)，爲求得最佳特徵權重參數向量$\hat{\lambda}$。將式(7)針對每一維特徵權重參數λ_d做偏微分，得其調整量爲：

$$\hat{\lambda}_d = \lambda_d + \eta \cdot \sum_{i=1}^{L} \left[f\left(W_i^R\right) - \sum_{k=1}^{M} \frac{\exp\left(Score\left(W_{i,k}, \lambda\right)\right)}{\sum_{j=1}^{M} \exp\left(Score\left(W_{i,j}, \lambda\right)\right)} \cdot f_d\left(W_{i,k}\right) \right] - \frac{\lambda_d}{\sigma^2} \quad (10)$$

(2)、權重式全域條件式對數線性模型(WGCLM)

不同於全域條件式對數線性模型(GCLM)，Oba 等學者[15]在 2010 年提出將樣本權重加入全域條件式對數線性模型進行改良，為每一個候選詞序列的分數加上一個不同的權重，用來表示每一條候選詞序列不同的重要程度，此方法稱為權重式全域條件式對數線性模型(Weighted Global Conditional Log-linear Model, WGCLM)。換句話說，每一個候選詞序列 $W_{i,j}$ 都會有一個相對應的樣本權重 $\omega_{W_{i,j}}$；根據不同的樣本權重來表示每一個候選詞序列對於語言模型訓練的不同重要性。其訓練目標函數可表示為：

$$F_{\mathrm{WGCLM}}(\lambda)=\sum_{i=1}^{L}\log\frac{\exp\left(Score\left(W_i^R,\lambda\right)\right)}{\sum_{j=1}^{M}\omega_{W_{i,j}}\exp\left(Score\left(W_{i,j},\lambda\right)\right)} \tag{11}$$

同樣地，為了避免在調整參數的過程中，發生過度訓練的問題，我們也可以加入一個零均值高斯事前機率項於權重式全域條件式對數線性模型的訓練目標函數中：

$$F_{\mathrm{WGCLM}}(\lambda)=\sum_{i=1}^{L}\log\frac{\exp\left(Score\left(W_i^R,\lambda\right)\right)}{\sum_{j=1}^{M}\omega_{W_{i,j}}\exp\left(Score\left(W_{i,j},\lambda\right)\right)}-\frac{\|\lambda\|^2}{2\sigma^2} \tag{12}$$

將式(12)針對每一維特徵權重參數 λ_d 做偏微分，得其調整量為：

$$\hat{\lambda}_d=\lambda_d+\eta\cdot\sum_{i=1}^{L}\left[f\left(W_i^R\right)-\sum_{k=1}^{M}\frac{\omega_{W_{i,k}}\exp\left(Score\left(W_{i,k},\lambda\right)\right)}{\sum_{j=1}^{M}\omega_{W_{i,j}}\exp\left(Score\left(W_{i,j},\lambda\right)\right)}\cdot f_d\left(W_{i,k}\right)\right]-\frac{\lambda_d}{\sigma^2} \tag{13}$$

值得一提的是，樣本權重的 $\omega_{W_{i,j}}$ 設計也是一個值得研究的議題，通常我們可以將每一個候選詞序列本身的錯誤率當成其樣本權重。

4、考量語句之間彼此之關係

(1)、輪轉雙重鑑別式模型 (R2D2)

全域條件式對數線性模型(GCLM)是期望最低錯誤率詞序列的對數條件機率能夠越大越好；Oba 等學者等針對全域條件式對數線性模型提出改良方法，在訓練目標函數中考慮了訓練語句所有候選詞序列彼此之間的關係，因而有所謂的輪轉雙重鑑別式模型(Round-Robin Dual Discrimination Model, R2D2)[16]。輪轉雙重鑑別式模型可以視為是全域條件式對數線性模型(GCLM)的一種延伸；它因為考量了兩兩候選詞序列彼此之間的關係，使得輪其擁有較好的一般化能力。同時，類似於權重式全域條件式對數線性模型(WGCLM)，輪轉雙重鑑別式模型也使用了樣本權重：

$$F_{\mathrm{R2D2}}(\lambda)=\sum_{i=1}^{L}\log\left\{\sum_{j'=1}^{M}\sum_{j=1}^{M}\frac{\exp\left(\sigma_1\omega_{W_{i,j}}\right)\exp\left(Score\left(W_{i,j},\lambda\right)\right)}{\exp\left(\sigma_2\omega_{W_{i,j'}}\right)\exp\left(Score\left(W_{i,j'},\lambda\right)\right)}\right\} \tag{14}$$

其中，σ_1與σ_2爲實驗參數。相同的，將式(14)針對每一維特徵權重參數λ_d做偏微分，得其調整量爲：

$$\hat{\lambda}_d = \lambda_d + \eta \cdot \sum_{i=1}^{L} \left\{ \frac{\left[\sum_{j'=1}^{M} \sum_{j=1}^{M} f_d\left(W_{i,j}\right) A \right] - \left[\sum_{j'=1}^{M} \sum_{j=1}^{M} f_d\left(W_{i,j'}\right) A \right]}{\sum_{j'=1}^{M} \sum_{j=1}^{M} A} \right\}, \tag{15}$$

$$\text{where } A = \exp\left(Score\left(W_{i,j}\right) - Score\left(W_{i,j'}\right) + \sigma_1 \omega_{W_{i,j}} - \sigma_2 \omega_{W_{i,j'}} \right)$$

(三)、鑑別式語言模型之特性

首先，感知器演算法(Perceptron)是以最小平方差爲其精神，希望排序分數最高的候選詞序列與最低錯誤率之詞序列(亦即參考詞序列)的分數差平方後越小越好；然而感知器演算法只考慮目前排序分數最高的詞序列與最低錯誤率詞序列之間的關係，因此其一般化(Generalization)的能力不是很好，很容易就會有過度訓練(Over-Training)的問題。

相較於感知器演算法，最小化錯誤率訓練(MERT)的精神是希望語音辨識所產生的候選詞序列其錯誤率期望值越小越好。因此，在訓練的過程中，它不僅僅考慮分數最高與擁有最低錯誤率的詞序列，更同時考慮了其它候選詞序列，故其會有較佳的一般化能力。但也因爲同時考慮了所有候選詞序列，導致在訓練的速度上相對較慢。

全域條件式對數線性模型(GCLM)的訓練目標函數則是希望最低錯誤率詞序列的條件機率越高越好；因爲全域條件式對數線性模型考慮到最低錯誤率詞序列與其它所有候選詞序列的關係，因此其一般化的能力會比感知器演算法來的好，比較不會有過度訓練的問題出現。

權重式全域條件式對數線性模型(WGCLM)是全域條件式對數線性模型(GCLM)之延伸，差別在於權重式全域條件式對數線性模型的分母項多考慮了樣本權重$\omega_{W_{i,j}}$，目的是讓每條候選詞序列對於訓練有不同的影響力。我們可以用每一條候選詞序列的錯誤率(或排序位置)來當作此樣本權重；錯誤率越高或排序越後面者，其重要程度就越重、影響力就越大。

輪轉雙重鑑別式模型(R2D2)與權重式全域條件式對數線性模型(WGCLM)類似，其目標函數期望每候選詞序列彼此之間的對數差異越小越好；輪轉雙重鑑別式模型亦考慮了樣本權重$\exp\left(\sigma_k \omega_{W_{i,j}}\right)$，不同的候選詞序列會因其本身的錯誤率(或排序位置)對於模型的訓練有不同程度的影響。因爲輪轉雙重鑑別式模型考慮了每一個候選詞序列與其它候選詞序列之間的關係，所以訓練的過程亦較其它鑑別式語言模型耗時。

三、基於邊際資訊之鑑別式語言模型(MDLM)

近年來有許多學者針對鑑別式語言模型提出了不同的觀點與做法。例如，爲了讓鑑別式語言模型的訓練更有效率，在感知器演算法中融入了訓練語句不同錯誤率程度的資訊中[17]；另外，也有學者額外地將候選詞序列的文法結構與各種詞性的出現頻率等語言特徵加入鑑別式語言模型使用，讓鑑別式語言模型在對候選詞序列進行重新排序時，可以參考詞序列所含豐富的語言相關資訊[18]。在本論文的研究裡，我們提出了考慮邊際(Margin)資訊的概念[19, 20]於鑑別式語言模型之訓練資料選取；對於每個訓練語句嘗試以其每一個候選詞序列各自的辨識錯誤率爲基礎，動態地來決定訓練資料(亦即候選詞序列)是否選取以用於模型訓練。在此，我們將先回顧邊際估測法則，接著說明本論文所提出的基於邊際資訊之鑑別式語言模型。

(一)、邊際估測法則

基於邊際資訊的資料選取方法目的是選取對於鑑別式模型訓練較具重要性的訓練資料，期望在模型訓練的過程中不僅可以降低訓練的時間，亦希望能夠得到較好的模型參數，提升辨識的正確性。例如，最大邊際估測法則(Large-Margin Estimation, LME)[19]、柔性邊際估測法(Soft-Margin Estimation, SME)[21]皆是基於邊際資訊的估測法則中典型的代表。

當最大化邊際估測法使用於鑑別式語言模型時，其基本精神是希望拉大參考(或是錯誤率最低)候選詞序列(Reference Word Sequence) W_i^R 與其它可能候選詞序列 $W_{i,j}$ 之排序分數的差異，讓參考候選詞序列 W_i^R 的分數較其它可能候選詞序列 $W_{i,j}$ 愈大愈好；通常我們將此分數的差異稱爲“分離邊際(Separation Margin)”：

$$\tau(x_i) = Score(W_i^R) - \max_{W_{i,j} \neq W_i^R} Score(W_{i,j}) \tag{16}$$

其中 $Score(W_i^R)$ 爲參考詞序列的重新排序分數； $Score(W_{i,j})$ 爲某一個候選詞序列的重新排序分數。由式(16)可知，若 $\tau(x_i) > 0$ ，表示使用目前的鑑別式語言模型對於語句 x_i 所對應的 M 條候選詞序列進行排序時，可以賦予詞序列 W_i^R 最高的排序分數，我們可以視爲沒有辨識錯誤發生(爲理想狀況)；反之，若 $\tau(x_i) < 0$ ，則表示正確(或是錯誤率最低)的候選詞序列之排序分數不是所有候選詞序列中最高的，因此經重新排序的語音辨識輸出將不是最佳的結果。在最大邊際估測法的訓練過程中，我們首先爲訓練語料 $\{x_1, x_2, \ldots, x_L\}$ 定義一組支援集(Support Set)：

$$S_{\text{LME}} = \{x_i \mid 0 \leq \tau(x_i) \leq \varepsilon\} \tag{17}$$

ε 是一個正實數，可以用來控制支援集中所包含的訓練語料個數，最大化邊際估測法的目標函數就可定義爲最大邊際估測法的訓練目標是希望最大化支援集中的最小分離邊際[19]：

$$F_{\text{LME}}(\lambda) = \min_{x_i \in S_{\text{LME}}} \tau(x_i) \tag{18}$$

由式(18)可知，訓練時所選取的訓練語料是原本使用重新排序可以正確地選出參考候選詞序列之訓練語句，而其它的訓練語句則被排除在訓練之外。在理論上，經過最大邊際估測法訓練後，對於訓練語料的分離邊際應變大，代表語言模型更具有一般化的能力。另一方面，由於大詞彙連續語音辨識系統是複雜而且其所提供辨識率尚未達完美，因此實際在鑑別式語言模型的訓練語料中，被定義於支援集裡的訓練語句個數將會是非常有限的，這會使得鑑別式語言模型調整後對整體的辨識率提升非常有限(這個問題在當最大邊際估測法被使用於聲學模型估測時，亦曾被討論過)。

爲了解決最大邊際估測法僅考慮支援集的資訊於鑑別式模型訓練的缺失，柔性最大邊際估測法則(Soft-Large Margin Estimation, S-LME)[22]被提出來改善此一問題。柔性最大邊際估測法則不在僅將重新排序可以正確地選出參考候選詞序列之訓練語句納入考量，它對訓練語句另外定義了一組錯誤集(Error Set)：

$$\varphi = \{x_{i'} \mid \tau(x_{i'}) < 0\} \tag{19}$$

結合支援集與錯誤集，柔性最大邊際估測法爲最大化下列目標函數[22, 23]：

$$F_{\text{S-LME}}(\lambda) = \min_{x_i \in S_{\text{LME}}} \tau(x_i) - \sigma \cdot \frac{1}{|\varphi|} \sum_{x_{i'} \in \varphi} \delta(x_{i'}) \tag{20}$$

也就是除了支援集所提供的鑑別性資訊外，還加入了平均錯誤估測於模型的目標函數中。在式(20)中，σ 是一個正實數，用來控制平均錯誤估測對於訓練鑑別式模型時的影響性；$\delta(\cdot)$是錯誤函數，通常被定義爲[22]：

$$\delta(x_i) = \max_{W_{i,j} \neq W_i^R} \left(Score(W_{i,j}, \lambda)\right) - Score(W_i^R, \lambda) \tag{21}$$

即分離邊際的負數。

最大邊際估測法則只考慮了“與分離邊際較近”(參照式(17))且重新排序可以正確地選出參考候選詞序列之訓練語句，如此不僅忽略了分離邊際附近的其它資訊，亦會導致訓練語句數量不足，最終使得訓練出來的鑑別式模型一般化能力不足；有別於最大邊際估測法，柔性邊際估測法(Soft Margin Estimation, SME)則是藉由考慮條件的放寬，將那些辨識錯誤(亦即參考候選詞序列之重新排序分數不是最高)在一定範圍內的訓練語句也一併列入考量，來彌補訓練語句上的不足。

柔性邊際估測法則的訓練目的如同最大邊際估測法則一樣，希望最大化訓練語料中的最小分離邊際，差別是柔性邊際估測法則在定義支援集時的條件比較彈性，加入了一個鬆弛變量(Slack Variable)ξ：

$$S_{\text{SME}} = \{x_i \mid -\xi \leq \tau(x_i) \leq \varepsilon\} \tag{22}$$

其中ξ爲一個大於零的實數，其表示那些辨識錯誤的訓練語句若其分離邊際大於$-\xi$也會在語言模型訓練時列入考量。柔性邊際估測法爲最大化下列目標函數：

$$F_{\text{SME}}(\lambda) = \min_{x_i \in S_{\text{SME}}} \tau(x_i) \tag{23}$$

(二)、基於邊際資訊之鑑別式語言模型(MDLM)

由上一節的簡介可知，過去考慮邊際概念於鑑別式語言模型時，通常只考慮參考詞序列與最佳候選詞序列之間的關係(參照式(16))。本論文嘗試將分離邊際的概念定義爲參考詞序列與每一個候選詞序列之間的關係；並且更進一步地，在定義支援集時，同時考慮每一訓練語句其參考候選詞序列與最高錯誤率候選詞序列的錯誤率差值。在多考慮每一個候選詞序列與參考詞序列的關係後，不僅可以解決訓練語料不足的問題，更可以改進鑑別式語言模型的一般化能力。我們所提出的鑑別式模型主要的目的是希望將參考(錯誤率最低)候選詞序列與其它候選詞序列彼此間的分離邊際越大越好。如此一來，可以

For $t = 1 \ldots T$ where T is the total number of iterations
For each training sample $\left(x_i, W_i^R\right), i = 1 \ldots L$
$v_j = 0,\ j = 1 \ldots N$
For $1 \le j \le k \le n$ where n is the N-best
$if\left(Score\left(W_{i,j}^R\right) - Score\left(W_{i,k}\right) < \tau\right)$
$v_j = v_j + 1$
$v_k = v_k - 1$
$\hat{\lambda}_{\mathrm{d}} = \lambda_d + \eta \cdot \sum_{j=1}^{N} v_j f_d\left(W_{i,j}\right)$

圖二、基於邊際之鑑別式語言模型演算法

降低重新排序候選詞序列時的混淆程度，進而提升鑑別式語言模型的效果。本論文所提出的基於邊際之鑑別式語言模型(Margin-based Discriminative Language Model, MDLM)的演算法如圖二所示。

首先，我們將分離邊際定義為：

$$\tau_{\mathrm{MDLM}}\left(W_{i,j}\right) = Score\left(W_i^R, \lambda\right) - Score\left(W_{i,j}, \lambda\right) \tag{24}$$

若$\tau\left(W_{i,j}\right) > 0$，表示使用目前的鑑別式語言模型可以賦予詞序列$W_i^R$有較$W_{i,j}$高的排序分數，反之，若$\tau\left(W_{i,j}\right) < 0$，則表示參考(辨識錯誤率最低)候選詞序列之排序分數較詞序列$W_{i,j}$低，因此辨識器的輸出將不會是最佳結果。接著，我們定義一組支援集(Support Set)：

$$S_{\mathrm{MDLM}} = \left\{W_{i,j} \mid \tau_{\mathrm{MDLM}}\left(W_{i,j}\right) \le \gamma_i\right\} \tag{25}$$

其中，γ_i是每一個訓練語句的判別量；在本論文中，我們將它定義為：

$$\gamma_i = \exp\left(\alpha\left(\max_j \omega_{W_{i,j}} - \omega_{W_i^R}\right)\right) \tag{26}$$

α是一個實驗常數；$\omega_{W_i^R}$為W_i^R的辨識錯誤率；$\omega_{W_{i,j}}$為候選詞序列$W_{i,j}$的辨識錯誤率；所以γ_i是隨著訓練語句的不同而有所變動，當參考候選詞序列W_i^R的錯誤率遠小於錯誤率最高的候選詞序列$W_{i,j}$時，γ_i的值應愈大。至此，不同於過去考慮邊際概念的鑑別式語言模型，本論文所提出的基於邊際之鑑別式語言模型考慮每一訓練語句其參考候選詞序列與其它所有候選詞序列的關係進行資料選取。並且在選取的過程中，考慮了訓練語句各自的辨識錯誤率。最後，結合式(24)、(25)與(26)，我們將基於邊際之鑑別式語言模型的目標函數定義為：

$$F_{\mathrm{MDLM}}(\lambda) = \frac{1}{2} \sum_{i=1}^{L} \sum_{\substack{W_{i,j} \in GEN(x_i) \\ \& W_{i,j} \in S_{\mathrm{MDLM}}}} \left(\tau_{\mathrm{MDLM}}\left(W_{i,j}\right)\right)^2 \tag{27}$$

利用梯度下降法將此目標函數對每一維權重參數λ_d做偏微分可求得其調整量，每一維特徵權重向量的更新式為：

	有無考慮樣本權重 $\omega_{W_{i,j}}$	有無考慮 W_i^R	一般化能力	訓練速度
Perceptron	無	有	差	快
MERT	有	無	佳	慢
GCLM	無	有	略佳	慢
WGCLM	有	有	略佳	慢
R2D2	有	有	略佳	很慢
MDLM	無	有	略佳	慢

表一、鑑別式語言模型之間的比較

$$\hat{\lambda}_d = \lambda_d - \eta \cdot \sum_{\substack{W_{i,j} \in GEN(x_i) \\ \& W_{i,j} \in S_{\mathrm{MDLM}}}} \left[\left(\tau_{\mathrm{MDLM}}\left(W_{i,j}\right) - \gamma_i \right) \cdot \left(f_d\left(W_i^R\right) - f_d\left(W_{i,j}\right) \right) \right] \quad (28)$$

事實上，基於邊際資訊之鑑別式語言模型(MDLM)目標函數與感知器演算法有些相似，皆是考慮最小平方誤差。然而，感知器演算法是期望排序分數最高的候選詞序列與參考詞序列之分數差異越小越好；而基於邊際之鑑別式語言模型不僅考慮排序分數最高的候選詞序列，更以分離邊際為基礎，考慮了更多參考詞序列與其它候選詞序列之間的關係，因此不會像感知器演算法會有過度訓練的問題。再者，由於我們將邊際的資料選取概念稍作改良，使得參與訓練的資料變多，因此不像先前簡介的其它各式運用邊際資訊的鑑別式語言模型，容易遭遇訓練資料太少的問題。

值得一提的是，基於邊際之鑑別式語言模型也可以如同感知器演算法一般，將式子(28)中的 $\tau_{\mathrm{MDLM}}\left(W_{i,j}\right) - \gamma_i$ 省略，將更新式子簡化成：

$$\hat{\lambda}_d = \lambda_d + \eta \cdot \sum_{\substack{W_{i,j} \in GEN(x_i) \\ \& W_{i,j} \in S_{\mathrm{MDLM}}}} \left(f_d\left(W_i^R\right) - f_d\left(W_{i,j}\right) \right) \quad (29)$$

透過此更新式以及迭代的訓練，期望能求得最佳的特徵權重向量。

利用表一來說明本論文引入的基於邊際資訊之鑑別式語言模型(MDLM)與其它鑑別式語言模型之間的比較關係。其中，考慮樣本權重的好處是能將訓練語句根據其樣本權重的不同，對於模型的訓練影響程度有不同的影響，而非每一個訓練語句都佔有相同的權重。在第四節實驗結果觀察，全域條件式對數線性模型(GCLM)與權重式全域條件式對數線性模型(WGCLM)來比較，權重式全域條件式對數線性模型多加入了樣本權重，其結果優於全域條件式對數線性模型，可推測樣本權重的考量對於模型訓練上的確是有正向幫助。

語料	句數	長度(小時)
訓練集語料	30,600	約 23
發展集語料	1,998	約 1.5
測試集語料	1,997	約 1.5

表二、實驗語料統計資訊

接著，最小化錯誤率訓練(MERT)的目標函數中沒有根據最低錯誤率詞序列W_i^R爲目標參考去做訓練，使得在訓練的過程當中訓練語句不會過度訓練去適合這些最低錯誤率詞序列，因此最小化錯誤訓練會有較佳的一般化能力；反觀感知器演算法(Perceptron)，會因爲過度訓練(Overfitting)，使得模型的一般化能力較差。

在訓練的速度上，則因爲各式方法著重的訓練目標不同，而有不同的時間複雜度。感知器演算法在訓練的過程當中，只考慮正確(或是錯誤率最低)的候選詞序列與排序分數最高的詞序列之間的關係；最小化錯誤率訓練、全域條件式對數線性模型、權重式全域條件式對數線性模型在訓練的過程中，考慮了正確(或是錯誤率最低)的候選詞序列與其它候選詞序列之間的關係；輪轉雙重鑑別式模型(R2D2)是考慮了所有候選詞序列之間彼此的關係。因此在訓練的過程中，輪轉雙重鑑別式模型所需的時間複雜度最高，相較下，感知器演算法訓練時所花費時間最少。

四、實驗結果與討論

(一)、實驗語料

本論文實驗語料取自公視新聞(Mandarian Across Taiwan-Broadcast News, MATBN)[24]。公視新聞語料是 2001 年至 2003 年間由中研院資訊所口語小組(SLG)與公共電視台(PTS)合作錄製，包含了內場新聞與外場新聞兩個部分。其中內場新聞爲主播語料，外場新聞語料包含有採訪記者(Field Reporters)語音語料與受訪者(Interviewees)語音語料。

由於內場主播語料大部分來自於同一主播所錄製，爲了避免語者相依(Speaker Dependent)現象造成實驗偏差，故不採用內場主播語料；外場受訪者語料，則是包含許多語助詞與背景音樂，所以也沒有採用；因此，本論文的實驗語料選取自外場採訪記者語料。訓練集語料、測試集語料及發展集語料皆選取自公視新聞 2001 年至 2002 年外場採訪記者，分別爲 30,600 句(約 23 小時)、1,997 句(約 1.5 小時)及 1,998 句(約 1.5 小時)。如表二所示。

背景語言模型爲三連語言模型(Trigram Language Model)，採用 Katz Back-off Smoothing 平滑化方法來解決資料稀疏的問題。其訓練語料來自 2001 年至 2002 年中央通訊社(Central News Agency, CNA)的文字新聞語料，包含了約一億五千萬個中文字，經過斷詞後約有八千萬詞。此語言模型是使用 SRI Language Modeling Toolkit(SRILM)[25]訓練所得。

我們以基礎辨識器[26]配合背景三連語言模型於完整詞圖搜尋(Word Graph Rescoring)的最佳結果做爲基礎辨識率(Baseline)，它在訓練集語料、發展集語料以及測試集語料的

各式鑑別式語言模型	訓練集(%)	發展集(%)	測試集(%)
Perceptron	8.20	14.14	14.99
MERT	10.48	14.27	15.33
GCLM	10.61	14.62	15.88
WGCLM	10.38	14.39	15.39
R2D2	8.76	13.39	14.23

表三、各式鑑別式語言模型的基礎實驗結果

辨識字錯誤率(Character Error Rate)分別爲 11.26%、15.27%與 16.39%。並且，我們挑選基礎辨識器產生的前 100 條最佳($M=100$)的辨識結果，做爲鑑別式語言模型的訓練與測試語料。

(二)、各式鑑別式語言模型的實驗結果

首先，我們比較各種不同的鑑別式語言模型應用於語音辨識結果之重新排序，各種方法的辨識字錯誤率如表三所示。我們可以由表三觀察到，如同先前提到的，感知器演算法(Perceptron)在訓練語料上的表現的確優於其它各種鑑別式語言模型，但在測試語料的表現則無法有相同的效果。而在測試語料的實驗結果，以輪轉雙重鑑別式語言模型(R2D2)的效果最爲顯著，這也說明了在訓練的過程中，考量較多有關候選詞序列彼此之間關係的資訊對模型的訓練是有正面幫助的，會使得模型有較好的一般化能力。

(三)、基於邊際資訊之鑑別式語言模型相關實驗結果

本論文所提出之基於邊際資訊之鑑別式語言模型(MDLM)於語音辨識之實驗結果如表四所示。實驗中，我們比較了四種不同支援集的定義方式：

- 動態型(MDLM-D)： $S_{\text{MDLM-D}}=\{W_{i,j} \mid \tau_{\text{MDLM}}(W_{i,j})\le \gamma_i\}$
- 正確分類動態型(MDLM-CD)： $S_{\text{MDLM-CD}}=\{W_{i,j} \mid 0\le \tau_{\text{MDLM}}(W_{i,j})\le \gamma_i\}$
- 固定型(MDLM-F)： $S_{\text{MDLM-F}}=\{W_{i,j} \mid \tau_{\text{MDLM}}(W_{i,j})\le \rho\}$，其中 ρ 是一個正實數
- 正確分類固定型(MDLM-CF)： $S_{\text{MDLM-CF}}=\{W_{i,j} \mid 0\le \tau_{\text{MDLM}}(W_{i,j})\le \rho\}$，其中 ρ 是一個正實數

其中，正實數 ρ 設定爲 5。首先，動態型的鑑別式語言模型在訓練集的辨識字錯誤率爲 6.09%，測試集的辨識字錯誤率爲 14.10%，而固定型的鑑別式語言模型在訓練集的辨識字錯誤率爲 5.18%，測試集的辨識字錯誤率爲 13.91%。因此，不論在訓練集或測試集，使用固定型的方式定義支援集似乎較考慮錯誤率資訊於資料選取的方式要好。值得一提的是，我們認爲考慮錯誤率於資料選取應該有助於挑選具鑑別性的訓練語料，但如何設

	訓練集(%)	發展集(%)	測試集(%)
MDLM-D	6.09	13.37	14.10
MDLM-CD	6.69	13.38	14.20
MDLM-F	5.18	13.25	13.91
MDLM-CF	5.49	13.17	13.98

表四、基於邊際之鑑別式語言模型實驗結果

	訓練集(%)	發展集(%)	測試集(%)
MDLM-D	5.97	13.34	13.96
MDLM-CD	7.01	13.38	14.00
MDLM-F	5.56	13.35	13.78
MDLM-CF	5.86	13.30	13.87

表五、考慮多條正確(錯誤率最低)的詞序列與樣本權重於基於邊際之鑑別式語言模型之實驗結果

計判別量γ_i，是一個值得研究的題目，也是本論文在未來將繼續研究的問題。

接著，如果我們更進一步地限制僅考慮分離邊際大於 0 的候選詞序列於模型訓練中(即正確分類動態型(MDLM-CD)與正確分類固定型(MDLM-CF))，實驗結果如表四所示。正確分類動態型的鑑別式語言模型在訓練集的辨識字錯誤率爲 6.69%；在測試集的辨識字錯誤率爲 14.20%。而正確分類固定型的鑑別式語言模型在訓練集的辨識字錯誤率爲 5.49%，測試集的辨識字錯誤率爲 13.98%。同樣地，使用固定型的方式定義支援集較考慮錯誤率資訊於資料選取的方式要好。另外，值得注意的是，僅考慮分離邊際大於 0 的候選詞序列於模型訓練，並不會得到較好的結果。分析其原因，可能由於分離邊際小於 0 的候選詞序列表示其排序分數大於參考(錯誤率最低)候選詞序列，如果我們將這些候選詞序列皆捨去不考慮，則鑑別式語言模型在訓練的過程中，可能會無法適當地調整模型參數，以使得參考候選詞序列之分數高於其它候選詞序列，如此，將會使得語言模型的鑑別性較差。

相較於其它各式語言模型(參照表三)，我們所提出的基於邊際資訊之鑑別式語言模型(包含四種不同的支援集定義方式)不論是在訓練集、發展集以及測試集皆有最低的辨識錯誤率。由此可知，使用邊際資訊於資料選取的鑑別式語言模型，的確保留了富有鑑別性資訊的訓練語句於模型訓練的過程中，並且也不會容易地遭受一般化能力不足的問題。

接著，我們更進一步的探討在訓練過程中，參考詞序列的個數對實驗的影響。在前人的研究中，使用辨識器所產生的候選詞序列中錯誤率最低的詞序列作爲訓練時的正確答案，會較使用正確的人工轉寫(Manual Transcription)詞序列有更佳的實驗結果[27]。然

而，在辨識器所產生的候選詞序列中，往往會存在數條辨識率相同且最低的候選詞序列。通常，我們會隨機選取其中分數最高的一條，當成訓練時的正確答案。在此，我們嘗試將這些擁有最低辨識錯誤率的候選詞序列皆當作參考候選詞序列，以用於模型的訓練過程中。另外，在更新特徵權重參數時，我們將詞序列的排列順序當作一種樣本權重，使得每一條詞序列對於鑑別式模型的影響程度有所不同，我們認爲，排序越前面的詞序列，應該對模型有較重要的影響性，因此我們將樣本權重定義爲詞序列排列順序的倒數之差。實驗結果如表五所示，我們可以發現，加入考慮多條正確(錯誤率最低)的候選詞序列與樣本權重後，測試集皆可以獲得更好的辨識結果，其中以固定型的支援集(MDLM-F)定義方式可以獲得 13.78%的辨識字錯誤率，是最佳的實驗結果。值得探討的是，訓練集與發展集皆沒有因爲考慮多條正確(錯誤率最低)的候選詞序列與樣本權重而獲得較佳的辨識結果。我們認爲，可能的原因是因爲模型的一般化能力增加，故雖然在訓練集上沒有正向的幫助，但當使用於測試集時，相較於先前的實驗(參照表四)，的確可以獲得較好的辨識結果。

五、結論及未來展望

語言模型不論是在機器翻譯、資訊檢索、語音辨識等領域中，都扮演一個不可或缺的重要角色。在語音辨識中，語言模型能輔助解決聲學模型的混淆，估計一段語句在自然語言中發生的可能性。N 連語言模型是最常被使用的，但它僅能捕捉到短距離的詞彙規則資訊，近十幾年來，鑑別式語言模型陸續被提出，並且廣泛的使用在於各個領域之中；在語音辨識的領域中，它提供了一個新的視野，以直接降低語音辨識錯誤率爲訓練目標。本論文針對常見的鑑別式語言模型做了一系列的討論與實驗比較，在我們的實驗中，各式鑑別式語言模型確實可以更進一步地輔助 N 連語言模型，降低辨識的錯誤率。

未來，我們將繼續研究基於不同訓練準則之鑑別式語言模型，並著重於探討各式語言特徵加入於鑑別式語言模型使用[28, 29, 30]。另外，除了加入各種語言特徵外，我們也有興趣於特徵選取對於鑑別式語言模型的影響。目前大部分鑑別式語言模型所使用的語言特徵數量皆非常龐大；面對這麼一群龐大的語言特徵，我們期望發展出一套特徵選取的方式，期望可以降低鑑別式語言模型訓練過程的時間需求，更希望進一步地改善鑑別式語言模型而獲得更好的辨識結果。

參考文獻

[1] F. Jelinek, *Statistical Methods for Speech Recognition*, the MIT press, 1999.

[2] M. Collins, and T. Koo, "Discriminative reranking for natural language parsing," *Computational Linguistics*," Vol. 31, No. 1, pp. 25-70, 2005.

[3] J. Gao, H. Suzuki, and W. Yuan, "An empirical study on language model adaptation," *ACM Transactions on Asian Language Information Processing*, Vol. 5, No. 3, pp. 209-227, 2006

[4] B. Roark, M. Saraclar, M. Collins and M. Johnson," Discriminative n-gram language modeling," *Computer Speech and Language*, Vol. 21, No. 2, pp. 373-392, 2007.

[5] J.-W. Liu, S.-H. Lin and B. Chen, "Exploiting discriminative language models for reranking speech recognition hypotheses," in *Proceedings of ROCLING XXII:*

Conference on Computational Linguistics and Speech Processing (ROCLING 2010), pp. 30-49, 2010.

[6] B. Chen and C.-W. Liu, "Discriminative language modeling for speech recognition with relevance information," in *Proceedings of the International Conference on Multimedia and Expo*, 2011.

[7] F. Rosenblatt, "The perceptron: A probabilistic model for information storage and organization in the brain," *Psychological Review*, No. 6, pp. 386-408, 1958.

[8] M. Collins, "Discriminative training methods for hidden markov models: theory and experiments with perceptron algorithms," in *Proceedings of the Conference on Empirical Methods in Natural Language Processing*, pp. 1-8, 2002.

[9] J. Lafferty, A. McCallum, and F. Pereira, "Conditional random fields: Probabilistic models for segmenting and labeling sequence data," in *Proceedings of International Conference on Machine Learning*, pp. 282-289, 2001.

[10] F. Sha, F. Pereira, "Shallow parsing with conditional random fields," in *Proceedings of the North American Chapter of the Association for Computational Linguistics on Human Language Technology*, pp. 134-141, 2003.

[11] T. M. Mitchell, *Machine Learning*. The McGraw-Hill Companies, 1997.

[12] Z. Zhou, J. Gao, F.K. Soong, and H. Meng, "A comparative study of discriminative methods for reranking LVCSR n-best hypotheses in domain adaptation and generalization," in *Proceedings of International Conference on Acoustics, Speech and Signal Processing*, pp. 141-144, 2006.

[13] F.J. Och, "Minimum error rate training in statistical machine translation," in *Proceedings of the Annual Meeting of the Association for Computational Linguistics on Computational Linguistics*, pp. 160-167, 2003.

[14] A. Kobayashi, T. Oku, S. Homma, S. Sato, T. Imai and T, Takagi, "Discriminative rescoring based on minimization of word errors for transcribing broadcast news," in *Proceedings of the Annual Conference of the International Speech Communication Association*, pp. 1574-1577, 2008.

[15] T. Oba, T Hori, and A. Nakamura, "A comparative study on methods of weighted language model training for reranking LVCSR n-best hypotheses," in *Proceedings of International Conference on Acoustics, Speech and Signal Processing*, pp. 5126-5129, 2010.

[16] T. Oba, T. Hori and A. Nakamura, "Round-robin discriminative model for reranking ASR hypotheses," in *Proceedings of the Annual Conference of the International Speech Communication Association*, pp. 2446-2449, 2010.

[17] T. Oba, T. Hori and A. Nakamura, "An approach to efficient generation of high-accuracy and compact error-corrective models for speech recognition," in *Proceedings of the Annual Conference of the International Speech Communication Association*, pp. 1753-1756, 2007.

[18] E. Arisoy, M. Saraclar, B. Roark and I. Shafran, "Syntactic and sub-lexical features for Turkish discriminative language models," in *Proceedings of the IEEE International Conference on Acoustics, Speech, and Signal Processing*, pp. 5538-5541, 2010.

[19] H. Jiang, X. Li and C. Liu, "Large margin hidden markov models for speech recognition," *IEEE transactions on audio, speech, and language processing*, Vol. 14, No. 5, pp. 1584-1595, 2006.

[20] Y.-T. Lo and B. Chen, "A comparative study on margin-based discriminative training of acoustic models," in *Proceedings of ROCLING XXII: Conference on Computational Linguistics and Speech Processing (ROCLING 2010)*, pp. 65-85, 2010.

[21] J. Li, M. Yuan and C.-H. Lee, "Soft margin estimation of hidden markov model parameters," in *Proceedings of International Conference on Spoken Language Processing*, pp. 2422-2425, 2006.

[22] H. Jiang and X. Li and C. Liu, "Incorporating training errors for large margin HMMs under semidefinite programming framework," in *Proceedings of International Conference on Acoustics, Speech and Signal Processing*, pp. 629-632, 2007.

[23] V. Magdin and H. Jiang, "Large margin estimation of n-gram language models for speech recognition via linear programming," in *Proceedings of International Conference on Acoustics, Speech and Signal Processing*, pp. 5398-5401, 2010.

[24] H.-M. Wang, B. Chen, J.-W. Kuo, and S.-S. Cheng, "MATBN: A Mandarin Chinese broadcast news corpus," *International Journal of Computational Linguistics & Chinese Language Processing*, Vol. 10, No. 2, pp. 219-236, 2005.

[25] A. Stolcke, *SRI Language Modeling Toolkit*, version 1.5.8, http://www.speech.sri.com/projects/srilm/.

[26] B. Chen, J.-W. Kuo and W.-H. Tsai, "Lightly supervised and data-driven approaches to mandarin broadcast news transcription," in *Proceedings of International Conference on Acoustics, Speech and Signal Processing*, pp. 777-780, 2004.

[27] B. Roark, M. Saraclar and M. Collins, "Corrective language modeling for large vocabulary ASR with the perceptron algorithm," in *Proceedings of International Conference on Acoustics, Speech and Signal Processing*, pp. 749-752, 2004.

[28] L. Shen, A. Sarkar and F. J. Och, "Discriminative reranking for machine translation," in *Proceedings of the Human Language Technology Conference of the North American Chapter of the Association for Computational Linguistics*, pp. 177-184, 2004.

[29] E. Arisoy, B. Ramabhadran and H.-K. J. Kuo, "Feature combination approaches for discriminative language models," in *Proceedings of Annual Conference of the International Speech Communication Association*, 2011.

[30] L. Wang, J. Lin and D. Metzler, "A cascade ranking model for efficient ranked retrieval," in *Proceedings of Annual International ACM SIGIR Conference*, pp. 105-114, 2011.

基於離散餘弦轉換之語音特徵的強健性補償法
Compensating the speech features via discrete cosine transform for robust speech recognition

Hsin-Ju Hsieh 謝欣汝, Wen-hsiang Tu 杜文祥, Jeih-weih Hung 洪志偉
暨南國際大學電機工程學系
Department of Electrical Engineering, National Chi Nan University
Taiwan, Republic of China
E-mail: s98323550@ncnu.edu.tw, aero3016@ms45.hinet.net, jwhung@ncnu.edu.tw

Abstract

In this paper, we develop a series of algorithms to improve the noise robustness of speech features based on discrete cosine transform (DCT). The DCT-based modulation spectra of clean speech feature streams in the training set are employed to generate two sequences representing the reference magnitudes and magnitude weights, respectively. The two sequences are then used to update the magnitude spectrum of each feature stream in the training and testing sets. The resulting new feature streams have shown robustness against the noise distortion. The experiments conducted on the Aurora-2 digit string database reveal that the proposed DCT-based approaches can provide relative error reduction rates of over 25% as compared with the baseline system using MVN-processed MFCC features. Experimental results also show that these new algorithms are well additive to many noise robustness methods to produce even higher recognition accuracy rates.

I. Introduction

Most of the state-of-the-art automatic speech recognition (ASR) system developed in the laboratory, in which the speech is not obviously distorted, can achieve excellent recognition performance. But in the real-world application, the recognition accuracy is seriously degraded due to so many distortions or variations existing in the application environment. Particularly speaking, the environmental distortions can be roughly classified into two types: channel distortion and additive noise, both influencing the performance of an ASR system a lot. The channel distortion occurs when the speech signal is transmitted by electronic devices or transmission lines, such as the air, the telephone line or the microphone. The additive noise is like the "shadow" or "background" existing in the environment, such as car noise and babble noise. Noise robustness techniques have thus received much attention in recent years since they are so important in the applicability of ASR.

One school of noise-robustness techniques is devoted to compensate the original speech feature to reduce the effect of noise and recover the speech feature back to its intact state. Typical examples of these techniques include cepstral mean normalization (CMN) [1], mean and variance normalization (MVN) [2], cepstral gain normalization (CGN) [3], cepstral shape normalization (CSN) [4], histogram equalization (HEQ) [5], higher-order cepstral moment normalization (HOCMN) [6], temporal structure normalization (TSN) [7] and MVN plus ARMA filtering (MVA) [8]. However, the main purpose of the above methods can be roughly divided into two parts: one is to normalize the statistics of temporal-domain feature sequence and the other is to further reduce the mismatch by enhancing some components which are not easily affected by noise. For the latter case, the discrete Fourier transform (DFT) is usually used to be an analysis tool for obtaining the modulation spectrum of temporal-domain feature sequence. Therefore, we can deal with the modulation spectrum explicitly or implicitly in order to obtain the robust temporal-domain feature sequence.

In this paper, we present two novel methods to improve the noise robustness of speech features, hoping to promote the resulting recognition accuracy. These novel methods take advantage of the discrete cosine transform (DCT) [9] to analyze and cope with the temporal-domain feature sequence, which is quite different form the conventional DFT-based methods. As we know, DCT is widely used in many fields, such as image compressing and coding. However, it is less used for robust speech feature extraction. Especially, to our knowledge, there are little research that directly uses DCT to analyze and process the temporal-domain feature sequence. Therefore, the proposed methods in this paper are both innovative and valuable.

The remainder of the paper is organized as follows: Section II describes an overview of DCT and the effect of noise on the DCT-based modulation spectrum of speech features. Then the details of our proposed feature compensation algorithms based on DCT are described in Section III. Section IV contains the experimental setup, experimental results and discussions. Finally, concluding remarks are given in Section V.

II. Brief introduction of discrete cosine transform (DCT) and the effect of noise on the DCT of the speech feature streams

Discrete cosine transform (DCT) is a Fourier-related transform similar to discrete Fourier transform (DFT), and it has been one of the most powerful analysis tools in the field of signal processing. Basically speaking, DCT expresses a sequence of finitely many data points in terms of a sum of cosine functions oscillating at different frequencies. DCT has been successfully applied in many aspects of speech analysis, like transform coding and speech feature extraction. It transforms the input signal from the time domain into the frequency domain, which highlights the periodicity of the signal. Besides, in speech feature extraction, DCT plays an important role in reducing the correlation of features and thus results in a more compact feature representation. In the following, we will make a brief introduction of DCT, and then investigate the effect of noise on the DCT of the speech feature stream, which serves as the background of the presented methods in section III.

II.1 The relationship between DCT and DFT

DCT expresses a signal in terms of a weighted sum of sinusoids, which is similar to DFT. However, DCT has some peculiar properties that are different from DFT. An obvious distinction between DFT and DCT is that, in analyzing a real-valued signal, DFT uses complex sinusoids (including the cosine and sine functions), while the latter uses only cosine functions. As a result, DFT often exhibits complex values while DCT real values only, indicating that the DCT coefficients are either 0 (positive) or π (negative) in phase.

It can be shown that the DCT of a signal $x[n]$ equals to the amplitude part of the DFT of another signal $y[n]$ given $y[n]$ is an extended version of $x[n]$ with even symmetry. According to different arrangements for the even-symmetry condition, eight DCT variants can be defined, among which the type-II DCT is probably the most commonly used form, and is often simply referred to as "the DCT". Besides, the inverse of the type-II DCT (IDCT) is just the type-III DCT.

For a finite-length real-valued sequence $\{x[n]; 0 \leq n \leq N-1\}$, its DFT $X[k]$ and DCT (type-II DCT) $C[k]$ are obtained by the following two equations, respectively:

$$\textbf{DFT:}\ X[k] = \sum_{n=0}^{N-1} x[n] e^{-j\frac{2\pi kn}{N}}, \quad 0 \leq k \leq N-1, \tag{1}$$

$$\textbf{DCT:}\ C[k] = \frac{1}{\sqrt{N}} \mu_k \sum_{n=0}^{N-1} x[n] \cos(\frac{\pi}{2N}(2n+1)k), \quad 0 \leq k \leq N-1, \tag{2}$$

where $\mu_0 = 1$ and $\mu_k = \sqrt{2}$ for $k > 0$. Besides, $X[k]$ and $C[k]$ are related by

$$\begin{cases} X[k] = 2e^{j\frac{\pi k}{2N}} C[k] & , \quad 0 \leq k \leq N-1 \\ X[2N-k] = 2e^{-j\frac{\pi k}{2N}} C[k] & , \quad 0 \leq k \leq N-1 \end{cases} \tag{3}$$

It can be shown that the inverse DFT and DCT are:

$$\textbf{IDFT:}\quad x[n] = \tfrac{1}{N} \sum_{k=0}^{N-1} X[k] e^{j\frac{2\pi kn}{N}} \quad , \quad 0 \leq n \leq N-1 \tag{4}$$

and

$$\textbf{IDCT:}\quad c[n] = \tfrac{1}{\sqrt{N}} \sum_{k=0}^{N-1} \mu_k C[k] \cos\left[\tfrac{\pi}{2N}(2n+1)k\right] \quad , \quad 0 \leq n \leq N-1. \tag{5}$$

As shown in eq. (1), the DFT $X[k]$ of a real-valued sequence is a complex sequence satisfying the conjugate symmetry condition, $X[k] = X^*[\langle -k \rangle_N]$, and thus about one-half ($\lfloor N/2 \rfloor + 1$) DFT points are in fact redundant. However, in the DCT case $C[k]$ and $x[n]$ are equal in length, and in general $C[k]$ is neither symmetric nor anti-symmetric. Therefore, DCT exhibits higher frequency resolution than DFT. In addition, eq. (3) shows DCT can be performed efficiently via the fast algorithms of DFT.

II.2 Properties of DCT

[10] shows the Karhunen Loeve Transform (KLT) gives the optimal performance in transform coding. However, KLT lacks fast algorithms in implementation. DCT compares more closely to KLT in coding performance relative to other orthogonal transforms.Therefore, DCT serves as a very good alternative of KLT for coding speech signals. Besides, DCT provides higher frequency resolution than DFT, and is more efficiently computable than discrete wavelet transform (DWT).

II.3 The impact of noise on the DCT of speech feature stream

When it comes to the analysis for the temporal characteristics of the speech feature stream, we often focus on the DFT-based modulation spectrum. In contrast, the "modulation spectrum" derived from DCT is much less considered. Since DCT possesses peculiar properties relative to DFT as described previously. Here we would like to observe the DCT-based modulation spectrum of a feature stream and investigate the corresponding response to noise.

First, Figures 1(a) and (b) depict the DCT-based and DFT-based modulation (magnitude) spectra for the MFCC c_1 feature stream of a clean utterance. We find that the DCT-based spectrum is more concentrated at low frequencies in energy than the DFT-based spectrum, and it shows higher frequency resolution.

Next, we investigate the impact of noise on the DCT-based modulation spectrum, which is separately observed in magnitude and phase (sign). Note that the DCT of an arbitrary sequence is real-valued, which can be only positive, zero or negative, corresponding a binary phase of 0 and π.

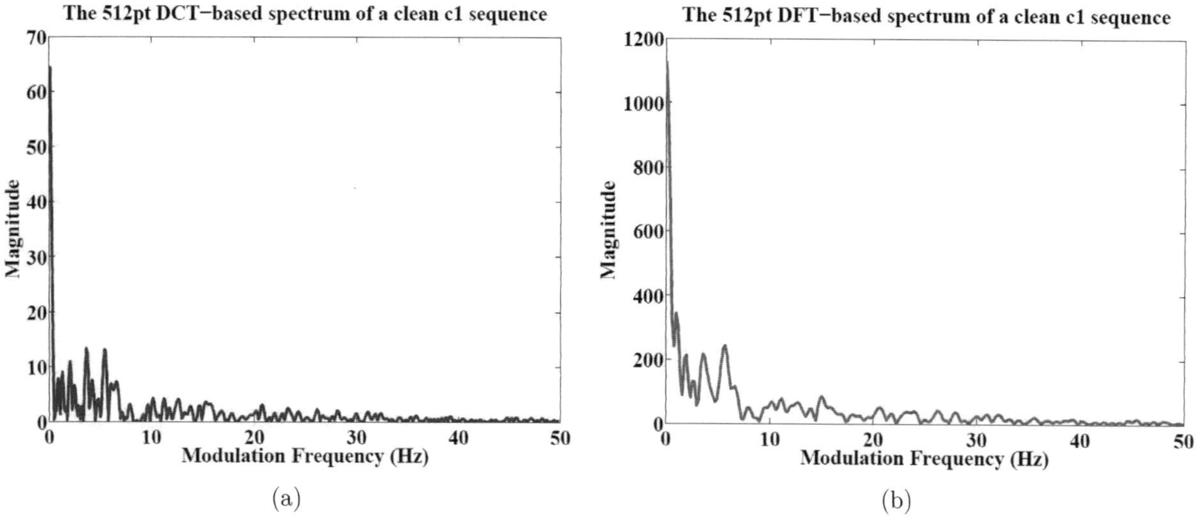

Figure 1: The modulation (magnitude) spectrum of (a) DCT-based and (b) DFT-based for the MFCC c_1 feature stream of a clean utterance.

Figures 2(a) and (b) depict the averaged magnitude and phase (sign) distortions by comparing the DCT-based modulation spectra of the MFCC c_1 streams for a set of 1001 clean utterances and its three noisy counterparts at signal-to-noise ratios (SNRs) 20 dB, 10 dB and 0 dB. From Figure 2(a), the DCT-magnitude distortions increase as the SNR get worse, and larger distortion components are mainly located in the low frequency region (roughly [0, 10 Hz]). Besides, Figure 2(b) shows that amplifying the noise level (with a lower SNR) introduces more DCT-phase (sign) distortions. However, in contrast to the case of DCT-magnitudes, DCT-phase distortions are approximately uniformly distributed over the whole frequency range, with the relatively larger phase distortions dwelling at high frequencies probably because the corresponding DCT coefficients are smaller in magnitude and easier to be changed in phase (sign).

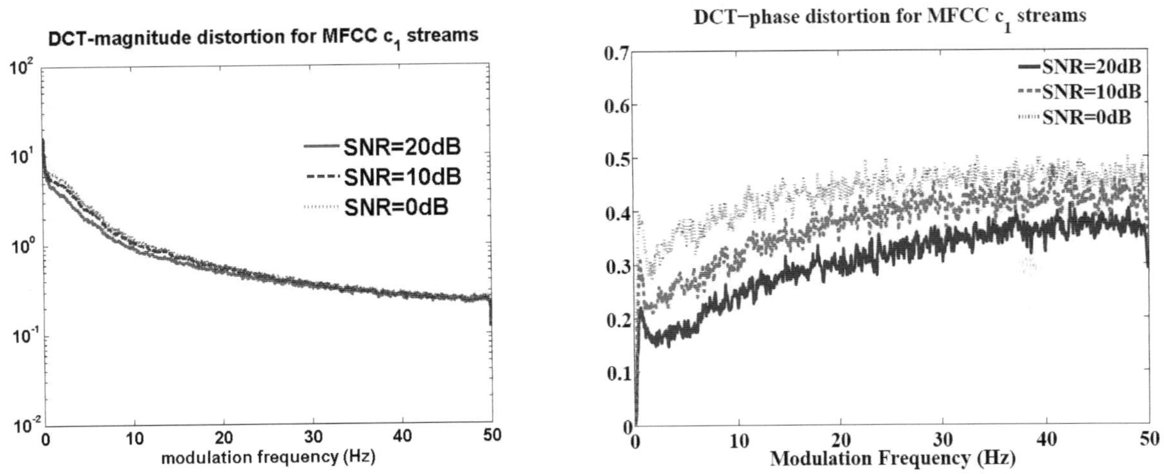

(a) (b)

Figure 2: The averaged (a) DCT-magnitude distortions and (b) DCT-phase distortions in the original MFCC c_1 streams caused by babble noise at three SNRs, 20 dB, 10 dB and 0 dB.

Moreover, here the well-known noise-robustness method, mean and variance normalization (MVN) [2], is selected to process the MFCC features used in Figures 2(a) and (b), and the corresponding DCT-magnitude and DCT-phase distortions are plotted in Figures 3(a) and (b), respectively. Comparing Figure 3(a) with Figure 2(a), DCT-magnitude distortions are significantly reduced by MVN. On the contrary, DCT-phase distortions shown in Figure 3(b) remain significant as shown in Figure 2(b). These results imply the good performance of MVN mainly comes from its capacity of reducing DCT-magnitude distortions rather than DCT-phase distortions.

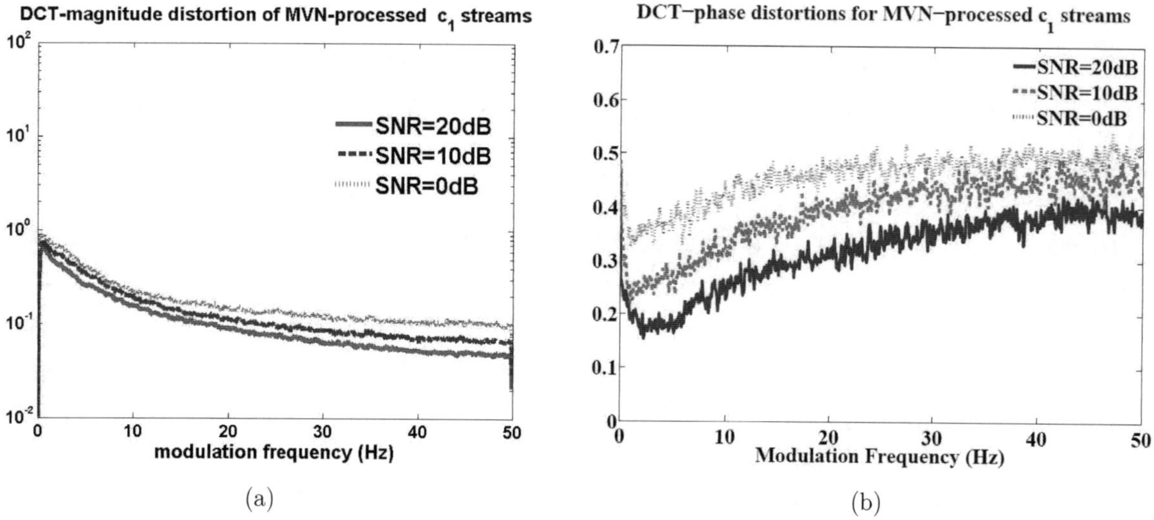

Figure 3: The averaged (a) DCT-magnitude distortions and (b) DCT-phase distortions in the MVN-processed MFCC c_1 streams caused by babble noise at three SNRs 20 dB, 10 dB and 0 dB.

III. The proposed DCT-based feature compensation approaches

This section is arranged as follows: First, we introduce two new proposed feature compensation methods based on DCT, and they are termed "DCT magnitude substitution" (DCT-MS) and "DCT magnitude weighting" (DCT-MW), respectively. Next, we introduce a variant of DCT-MS, which differs from DCT-MS primarily in the selection of processed frequency range. Finally, we examine these new methods in their capability of reducing the mismatch in the power spectral density (PSD) of feature streams.

III.1 The concepts of DCT-based speech feature compensation methods

According to the discussions in the previous section, the magnitude parts of the DCT for speech feature streams are vulnerable to noise, and properly dealing with them such as the MVN process can help a lot. Here we attempt to provide some directions to alleviate the DCT-magnitude distortions.

Let $\{x[n];\ 0 \leq n \leq L-1\}$ be the temporal-domain feature sequence of an arbitrary utterance for each channel, and its M-point DCT is represented by

$$\{C[k];\ 0 \leq k \leq M-1\}. \tag{6}$$

Then $C[k]$ corresponds to the DCT-based modulation spectrum of $\{x[n]\}$ at frequency $f = k\frac{F_s}{2M}$ in Hz, where F_s (Hz) is the frame rate of $\{x[n]\}$. Note here the DCT-size M is set to be larger than or equal to L, the length of $\{x[n]\}$, to avoid the time aliasing effect. Briefly speaking, our methods update these $C[k]$'s in its magnitude part $|C[k]|$, and leave its sign (phase) part $sgn(C[k])$ unchanged, hoping that the mismatch of $|C[k]|$ among different SNR cases can be thus reduced.

We present two types of DCT-based feature compensation methods, both of which consist of three steps:

Step 1: Obtain the DCT-magnitude reference or the DCT-magnitude weight from the training data:

Let $\{C[k];\ 0 \leq k \leq M-1\}$ be the M-point DCT of any temporal sequence in *the training set* with respect to a specific channel. Here the used DCT-size M is common to any temporal sequence in the training set, and this setting makes the DCT spectra of all training sequences (with respect to a specific channel) have the same length M. We calculate two sequences:

DCT-magnitude reference:

$$A_{ref}[k] = E\{|C[k]|\} = \frac{1}{N_{ref}} \sum_{C[k] \in training\ set} |C[k]|, \tag{7}$$

and

DCT-magnitude weight:

$$\sigma_{ref}[k] = std\{C[k]\} = \sqrt{\frac{1}{N_{ref}} \sum_{C[k] \in training\ set} C^2[k] - \left(\frac{1}{N_{ref}} \sum_{C[k] \in training\ set} C[k]\right)^2}, \tag{8}$$

where $E\{X\}$ and $std\{X\}$ denote the mean and standard deviation of X, and N_{ref} is the number of $C[k]$'s in the training set.

Step 2: Update the DCT magnitude component of the speech features currently processed:

In Step 1, the DCT-magnitude reference/weight shown in eqs. (7) and (8) are obtained from the feature sequences of **all** the clean utterances in the training set. Now we apply them to update the DCT-magnitude of **each** feature sequence in both the training and testing sets. Briefly speaking, the DCT coefficients $\{C[k];\ 0 \leq k \leq M-1\}$ of any feature sequence in the training and testing sets is updated in magnitude, and we produce the new DCT stream:

$$\tilde{C}[k] = \left|\tilde{C}[k]\right| sgn(C[k]), \qquad 0 \leq k \leq M-1. \tag{9}$$

where $|\tilde{C}[k]|$ denotes the new DCT-magnitude. That is, the original and updated DCT streams differ only in magnitude, not in phase. We propose various ways to update the DCT-magnitude, and they will be described in detail in the next subsections.

Step 3: Use IDCT to obtain the new feature sequence:

The the L-point new feature stream is obtained by

$$\tilde{x}[n] = IDCT_M\{\tilde{C}[k];\, 0 \leq k \leq M-1\}, \qquad 0 \leq n \leq L-1. \tag{10}$$

That is, the M-point inverse DCT is performed on the M-point sequence $\{\tilde{C}[k]\}$, and the resulting M-point sequence $\{\tilde{x}[n]\}$ is *truncated* and thus only the first L points in $\{\tilde{x}[n]\}$ are reserved.

III.2 The DCT-magnitude updated algorithms

In this subsection, we provide two different directions to update the DCT-magnitude of a speech feature stream as mentioned in Step 2 of sub-section III.1.

III.2.1 DCT-magnitude substitution (DCT-MS)

In DCT-MS, the DCT-magnitude of each feature stream currently processed is directly substituted by the DCT-magnitude reference shown in eq. (7). That is,

$$|\tilde{C}[k]| = A_{ref}[k], \quad 0 \leq k \leq M-1. \tag{11}$$

This operation is primarily motivated by two observations:

1. The DCT-magnitudes among different clean feature sequences look similar to one another. Using the same DCT-magnitude for different feature sequences probably causes a small amount of distortion.

2. Noise affects the DCT-magnitude very significantly, and thus the DCT-magnitude of a noisy feature stream is highly deviated from that of a clean one. Introducing a unified DCT-magnitude completely removes the effect of noise (while probably loses some speech information).

III.2.2 DCT-magnitude weighting (DCT-MW)

In DCT-MW, the DCT magnitude of each feature stream currently processed is directly multiplied by the DCT-**magnitude weight** defined in eq. (8). That is:

$$|\tilde{C}[k]| = |C[k]|\sigma_{ref}[k], \quad 0 \leq k \leq M-1. \tag{12}$$

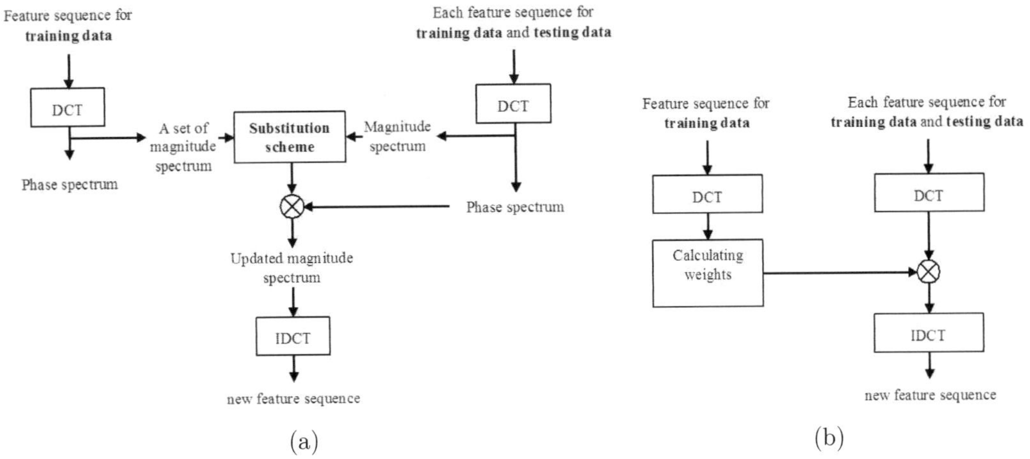

Figure 4: The flowchart of (a)DCT-MS (b)DCT-MW

The method of DCT-MW is basically from two ideas:

1. In general, the variance, or its variant such as the standard deviation, accounts for the amount of gross information contained in a random variable. Assuming most of the information corresponds to speech, to weigh the noisy DCT-magnitude with the standard deviation of the clean DCT-magnitudes probably highlights the speech components.

2. The original noisy DCT-magnitude, that is expected to contain speech information and benefit the recognition, is reserved in DCT-MW. Furthermore, DCT-MW behaves similarly to a zero-phase temporal filter, which can effectively improve the noise robustness of features if properly designed.

The flowcharts of DCT-MS and DCT-MW are depicted in Figures 4(a) and (b). Besides, the DCT-magnitude weight for DCT-MW from the MVN-processed MFCC c_1 streams is plotted in Figure 5, which shows the DCT-magnitudes at lower modulation frequencies are to be amplified in DCT-MW. This is somewhat consistent to the general idea that, the modulation frequency components within [1 Hz, 16 Hz] contain rich speech information [11], and emphasizing these components properly will improve the recognition accuracy.

III.2.3 Partial-band DCT-MS

The substitution process of DCT-MS is originally carried out on the entire DCT-magnitude stream, indicating that each modulation frequency component within the full-band range $[0, \frac{F_s}{2}$ Hz$]$ is updated, where F_s is the frame rate in Hz. Here, we propose to select the components within a specific partial-band rather than the full-band to perform DCT-MS.

This partial-band process is mainly inspired by two considerations:

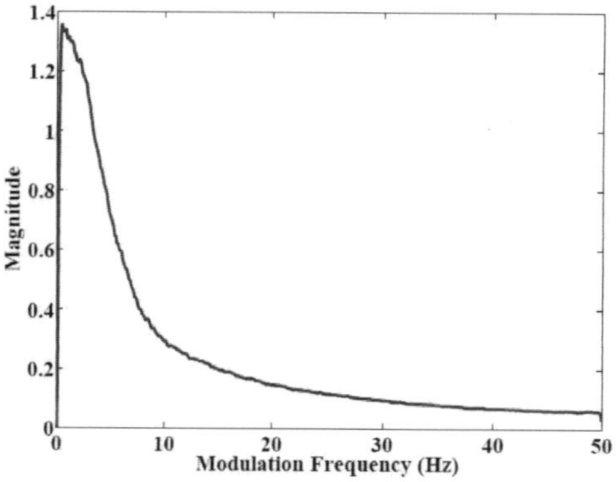

Figure 5: The DCT-magnitude weight for MVN-processed MFCC c_1 features in DCT-MW.

1. Keeping the less-distorted components unchanged:
   The deviations in the DCT-magnitudes caused by noise are in fact unequal. In particular, noise probably just contaminates a few frequency components primarily. Updating the DCT-magnitudes at all frequencies introduces another distortion, especially to those less noise-affected ones.

2. Reducing the computation complexity:
   Provided that the recognition accuracy is not degraded, decreasing the number of DCT-magnitudes necessary for an update reduces the computation complexity of the algorithms for sure.

Here, we arrange the partial-band version of DCT-MS by simply setting a cutoff frequency F_c, dividing the frequency range into two sub-bands $[0,\ F_c\ \text{Hz}]$ and $[F_c\ \text{Hz},\ \frac{F_s}{2}\ \text{Hz}]$, and performing DCT-MS for either one sub-band. Accordingly, the performance of the patial-band DCT-MS depends on the selection of the cutoff frequency F_c and the sub-band components to be updated.

Note that we do not provide the partial-band version of DCT-MW since it seems not very appropriate to weigh some DCT-magnitudes and leave the others unchanged, which behaves like a filter having a discontinuity at the cutoff frequency in magnitude response.

III.3 A preliminary evaluation of DCT-MS/DCT-MW in reducing the noise effect

We perform the proposed DCT-MS or DCT-MW on the MFCC c_1 feature streams of three utterances containing the same embedded clean speech while distorted at different SNRs: clean, 10 dB and 0 dB with subway noise. Before acting DCT-MS/DCT-MW, the feature sequence is processed by MVN to be zero-mean and unity-variance.

Figures 6(a)-(d) plot the power spectral density (PSD) curves of the c_1 feature streams for three SNR cases obtained from various processes. The corresponding detailed information and discussions are:

1. As shown in Figure 6(a), there exists significant mismatch among the PSDs of original (MVN-processed) features at different SNRs. The mismatch gets larger with increasing frequency. The PSD becomes relatively "flat" as the SNR gets worse, which agrees with the observation in [8].

2. Figure 6(b) corresponding to the features processed by DCT-MS reveals that this method successfully reduces the PSD mismatch shown in Figure 6(a). The direct substitution for the DCT-magnitudes of different feature streams with a common reference curve makes the associated PSD curves so close to each other.

3. From Figure 6(c), the PSDs of DCT-MW processed features still contain significantly mismatch as the ones from MVN in Figure 6(a). However, the scale of deviation (for the frequency greater than 10 Hz) shown in Figure 6(c) is below 10^{-2}, while the original PSD deviation shown in Figure 6(a) is roughly within the range $[10^{-1}, 10^{-2}]$. As a result, DCT-MW can reduce the PSD mismatch effectively.

4. Figure 6(d) depicts the PSDs for the "partial-band" version of DCT-MS, in which the frequency range to be updated is set to [5 Hz, 50 Hz]. That is, the first one-tenth band [0, 5 Hz] components are kept unchanged. We find that they are quite similar to the curves shown in Figure 6(b) (the "full-band" version of DCT-MS): the median/high frequency distortion is insignificant. The unprocessed band [0, 5 Hz] appears deviations among the curves. The positive or negative effect of keeping the low frequency components unchanged in recognition accuracy will be shown in section IV.

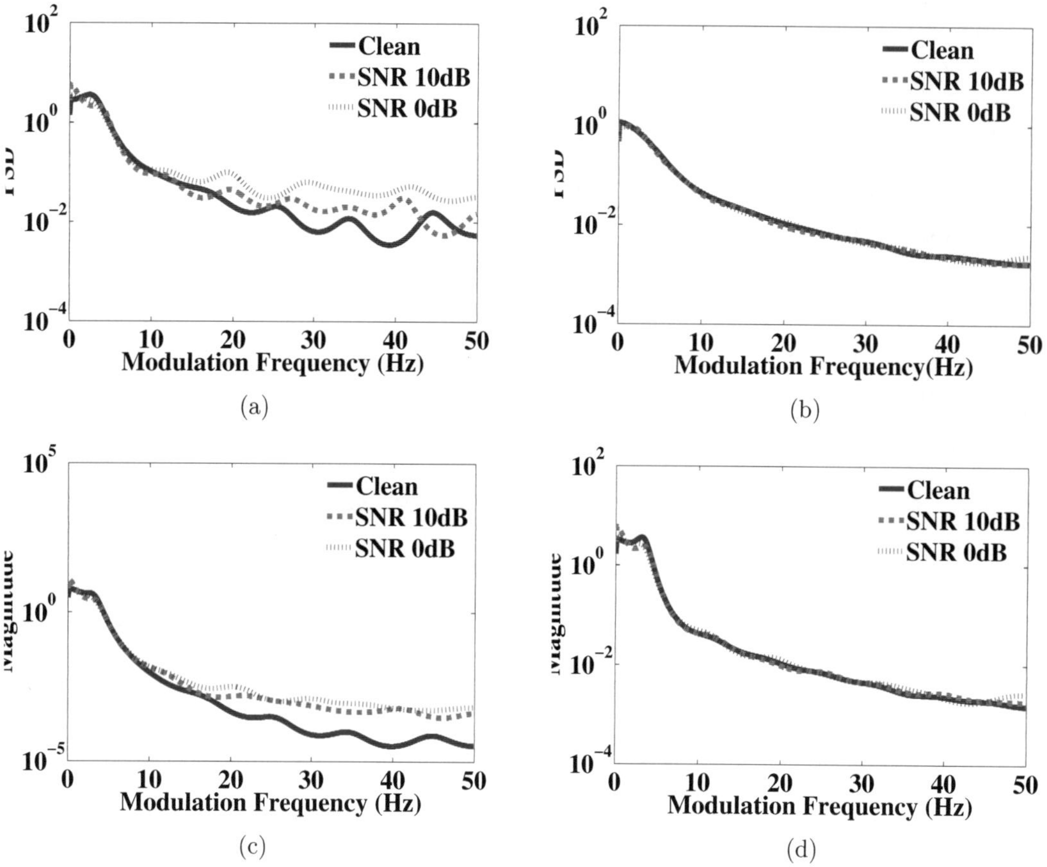

Figure 6: The c_1 PSD curves processed by various methods:(a)MVN (b)DCT-MS (c)DCT-MW (d)partial-band DCT-MS

IV. The recognition experiment results and discussions

This section is organized as follows: Firstly, sub-section IV.1 introduces the used speech database and the setup for the experimental environment. Secondly, the recognition results for the original and MVN-processed MFCC are provided in sub-section IV.2. Thirdly, we present and discuss the recognition accuracy obtained by the new DCT-based algorithms in sub-section IV.3. Finally, sub-section IV.4 briefly summarizes the recognition results of the DCT-based algorithms for the features preliminary processed by some robustness methods.

IV.1 The Experimental Environmental Setup

Our recognition experiments are conducted on the AURORA 2.0 database , the details of which are described in [12]. In short, the testing data consist of 4004 utterances from 52 female and 52 male speakers, and three different subsets are defined for the recognition experiments: Test Sets A and B are each affected by four types of noise, and Set C is affected by two types.

Each noise instance is added to the clean speech signal at six SNR levels (ranging from 20 dB to -5 dB). The signals in Test Sets A and B are filtered with a G.712 filter, and those in Set C are filtered with an MIRS filter. In the "clean-condition training, multi-condition testing" mode defined in [12], the training data consist of 8440 *clean* speech utterances from 55 female and 55 male adults. These signals are filtered with a G.712 filter. The data in Test Sets A and B are more distorted by additive noise than the training data, while the data in Set C are affected by additive noise and a channel mismatch.

With the Aurora-2 database, we performed the a series of robustness methods to compare the recognition accuracy. Each utterance in the clean training set and three testing sets is directly converted to 13-dimensional MFCC ($c0 \sim c12$) sequence. Next, the MFCC features are then updated by either noise-robustness method. The resulting 13 new features, plus their first- and second-order derivatives, are the components of the final 39-dimensional feature vector. With the new feature vectors in the clean training set, the hidden Markov models (HMMs) for each digit and silence are trained with the HTK toolkit [13] . Each digit HMM has 16 states, with 20 Gaussian mixtures per state.

IV.2 Experiment results of plain MFCCs and MVN-processed MFCCs

The recognition accuracy rates for the original MFCC are shown in Table 1. From this table, we have some observations as follows:

1. When the SNR becomes worse, the recognition accuracy rate gets lower in every noisy environment. Therefore, noise brings a significant distortion to MFCC features.
2. The averaged recognition accuracy of Set A is better than that of Set B probably because most noise types in Set A are stationary and most noise types in Set B are non-stationary.
3. Among the four noise types in Set A, "babble" and "exhibition" result in the largest and smallest accuracy degradation, respectively. In contrast, the noise types in Set B that correspond to the highest and lowest accuracy rates are "airport" and "street".
4. With the same noise type "subway", the accuracy of Set A is better than that of Set C, implying the channel mismatch in Set C further degrades the recognition performance.

Among the various noise-robustness algorithms,MVN is very widely used since implementing MVN is quite simple and significant recognition improvement can be thus achieved. Many noise-robustness techniques such as TSN [7] and MVA [8] have been developed directly on MVN-processed MFCC features and reveals very good performance. As a result, we treat the MVN-processed MFCC as the baseline features hereafter, unless otherwise mentioned.

The recognition results of the baseline experiments, using MVN-processed MFCC as features, are shown in Table 2. Comparing Table 2 with Table 1, MVN benefits the plain MFCC a lot

Table 1: The recognition accuracy rates (%) of plain MFCCs in various environments

baseline experiments (using MFCCs, including $c_0 \sim c_{12}$ plus their delta and delta-delta, totally 39 features)													
	Set A					Set B					Set C		
	subway	babble	car	exhibition	average	restaurant	street	airport	train	average	subway	street	average
clean	99.83	99.77	99.74	99.85	99.80	99.83	99.77	99.74	99.85	99.80	99.79	99.76	99.78
20dB	98.90	91.26	97.14	98.72	96.51	94.41	97.33	92.87	93.67	94.57	96.58	97.16	96.87
15dB	95.08	78.27	88.16	95.25	89.19	84.12	92.22	80.54	83.06	84.99	91.63	93.16	92.40
10dB	82.43	61.68	69.65	84.04	74.45	67.83	77.61	63.88	66.07	68.85	82.24	82.64	82.44
5dB	62.31	44.41	53.20	63.63	55.89	49.55	60.19	48.38	49.28	51.85	65.01	67.25	66.13
0dB	47.12	33.20	45.00	49.04	43.59	36.13	47.74	37.98	41.52	40.84	48.64	51.79	50.22
-5dB	43.13	30.89	42.60	43.77	40.10	33.60	42.81	35.42	40.15	38.00	43.58	45.33	44.46
average	77.17	61.76	70.63	78.14	**71.92**	66.41	75.02	64.73	66.72	**68.22**	76.82	78.40	**77.61**

Table 2: The recognition accuracy rates (%) of the baseline experiment, with the MVN-processed MFCC as the features

Baseline experiment results (with MVN-processed MFCC features)													
	Set A					Set B					Set C		
	subway	babble	car	exhibition	average	restaurant	street	airport	train	average	subway	street	average
clean	99.81	99.77	99.76	99.92	99.82	99.81	99.77	99.76	99.92	99.82	99.85	99.79	99.82
20dB	98.46	99.06	98.71	98.32	98.64	99.20	98.72	99.12	98.47	98.88	98.52	98.74	98.63
15dB	96.73	96.95	96.73	96.22	96.66	97.62	96.82	97.67	96.05	97.04	96.79	96.76	96.78
10dB	92.03	92.20	90.91	90.90	91.51	93.34	91.54	93.24	91.05	92.29	91.92	91.64	91.78
5dB	81.25	78.68	74.90	81.08	78.98	81.95	79.10	80.63	76.96	79.66	81.21	79.47	80.34
0dB	62.39	57.61	53.56	63.89	59.36	63.55	59.11	61.31	55.66	59.91	61.97	58.96	60.47
-5dB	47.84	45.63	43.72	48.64	46.46	48.17	46.44	46.98	45.30	46.72	47.58	46.74	47.16
average	86.17	84.90	82.96	86.08	**85.03**	87.13	85.06	86.39	83.64	**85.56**	86.08	85.11	**85.60**
MFCC	77.17	61.76	70.63	78.14	71.92	66.41	75.02	64.73	66.72	68.22	76.82	78.40	77.61

by enhancing the recognition accuracy rates for almost all SNR cases and all noise types, which exhibits the capability of improving noise robustness of MVN for MFCC. Furthermore, even though MVN does not eliminate the median/high (modulation) frequency distortion very well, as depicted in Figure 3(a), the low-frequency portion that contains most speech information is well treated by MVN in reducing noise effects, thus bringing about very good recognition accuracy.

IV.3 The experimental results of proposed DCT-based algorithms

IV.3.1 DCT-MS and DCT-MW

This sub-section provides the results of DCT-MS and DCT-MW. The parameter M in eq. (6) that represents the length of the common DCT-magnitude reference/weight for DCT-MS/ DCT-MW is set to 1024.

Tables 3 and 4 give the detailed recognition accuracy rates obtained from DCT-MS and DCT-MW. We have some findings from the two tables:

1. Compared with the baseline results in Table 2, both DCT-MS and DCT-MW provide better recognition accuracy, implying the two methods can enhance MVN features in noise robustness.

2. DCT-MW outperforms DCT-MS slightly,indicating that to highlight the more important DCT-components like a filtering process helps more. For example, with DCT MW, the averaged accuracy for Set B can be as high as 90%, roughly 4% better than the baseline.

Table 3: The recognition accuracy rates (%) of DCT-MS that performs on the MVN-processed MFCC

DCT-MS													
	Set A					Set B					Set C		
	subway	babble	car	exhibition	average	restaurant	street	airport	train	average	subway	street	average
clean	99.37	99.23	99.25	99.58	99.36	99.37	99.23	99.25	99.58	99.36	99.43	99.11	99.27
20dB	97.91	98.38	98.73	98.13	98.29	98.35	98.23	98.62	98.63	98.46	98.14	98.32	98.23
15dB	96.08	96.93	97.55	96.43	96.75	97.39	97.21	97.87	97.50	97.49	96.48	96.89	96.69
10dB	92.34	94.12	94.38	92.68	93.38	94.09	93.92	95.39	94.70	94.53	92.09	93.63	92.86
5dB	84.08	85.97	87.86	85.18	85.77	86.73	87.08	88.31	88.59	87.68	84.52	87.42	85.97
0dB	71.10	69.64	76.34	71.98	72.27	72.68	74.44	75.69	75.62	74.61	70.55	74.80	72.68
-5dB	56.34	52.56	61.46	57.24	56.90	55.20	59.04	58.26	60.37	58.22	56.08	59.17	57.63
average	88.30	89.01	90.97	88.88	**89.29**	89.85	90.18	91.18	91.01	**90.55**	88.36	90.21	**89.28**
MVN baseline	86.17	84.90	82.96	86.08	85.03	87.13	85.06	86.39	83.64	85.56	86.08	85.11	85.60

IV.3.2 Partial-band DCT-MS

Here we perform the partial-band DCT-MS given in sub-section III.2.3. For the sake of clarity, the notations ${}_p$DCT-MS$_u$ and ${}_p$DCT-MS$_l$ are used, where the left subscript index "p" indicates a *p*artial-band DCT-MS, and the right subscript, "u" or "l", represents the updated partial band being "*u*pper sub-band" ($[F_c$ Hz, $F_s/2$ Hz$]$) or "*l*ower sub-band" ($[0, F_c$ Hz$]$), in which F_c and F_s are the cutoff frequency and the frame rates in Hz. The averaged recognition accuracy rates achieved by ${}_p$DCT-MS$_u$ and ${}_p$DCT-MS$_l$ for five different assignments of cutoff frequency F_c are listed in Tables 5 and 6. We have the following observations from the two tables:

1. For the case of ${}_p$DCT-MS$_u$, in which only the upper sub-band magnitudes are updated and increasing the cutoff frequency narrows the upper sub-band in bandwidth, the corresponding recognition accuracy rates are always better than the baseline (with MVN-processed

Table 4: The recognition accuracy rates (%) of DCT-MW that performs on the MVN-processed MFCC

DCT-MW													
	Set A					Set B					Set C		
	subway	babble	car	exhibition	average	restaurant	street	airport	train	average	subway	street	average
clean	99.66	99.53	99.66	99.83	99.67	99.66	99.53	99.66	99.83	99.67	99.64	99.57	99.61
20dB	98.75	98.95	98.95	98.55	98.80	99.20	98.55	98.94	98.91	98.90	98.76	98.53	98.65
15dB	97.76	97.53	97.61	96.47	97.34	98.21	97.72	98.11	97.52	97.89	97.43	97.66	97.55
10dB	94.20	94.12	95.13	92.47	93.98	94.92	94.78	95.13	94.72	94.89	93.90	94.76	94.33
5dB	86.31	85.29	88.40	84.40	86.10	86.37	87.14	87.64	87.74	87.22	86.31	87.16	86.74
0dB	70.26	66.50	74.75	71.58	70.77	68.66	72.88	72.25	72.57	71.59	70.22	72.11	71.17
-5dB	53.68	48.87	56.60	55.90	53.76	50.47	54.16	54.06	55.39	53.52	53.26	54.01	53.64
average	89.46	88.48	90.97	88.69	**89.40**	89.47	90.21	90.41	90.29	**90.10**	89.32	90.04	**89.68**
MVN baseline	86.17	84.90	82.96	86.08	85.03	87.13	85.06	86.39	83.64	85.56	86.08	85.11	85.60

features). However, ${}_p$DCT-MS$_u$ outperforms the full-band DCT-MS (with the cutoff frequency 0 Hz) only when the cutoff frequency F_c is 5 Hz, and there is a performance gap when F_c is from 5 Hz to 15 Hz. This observation leads to two aspects: First, keeping the components within [0, 5 Hz] unchanged is better than updating them, probably because this frequency range has been handled well by MVN and further normalizing it in DCT-magnitude tends to attenuate the recognition information. Second, operating DCT-MS in the frequency range [5 Hz, 15 Hz] especially helps in recognition performance, which is somewhat consistent of the observation in Figure 3(a) that there remains PSD mismatch roughly above 5 Hz after operating MVN.

2. For the case of ${}_p$DCT-MS$_l$, in which only the lower sub-band magnitudes are updated and increasing the cutoff frequency broadens the lower sub-band in bandwidth, assigning a too small cutoff frequency (below 10 Hz) even worsens the recognition accuracy relative to the baseline, which supports our statements for ${}_p$DCT-MS$_u$ previously that updating the components within the frequency range [0, 5 Hz] is not a good idea. Increasing the cutoff frequency F_c in ${}_p$DCT-MS$_l$ can improve the recognition accuracy, and the best possible results for ${}_p$DCT-MS$_l$ occurs when F_c is 50 Hz, equivalent to the original (full-band) DCT-MS. As a result, partial-band DCT-MS outperforms full-band DCT-MS only when a proper *upper* sub-band is selected for update.

IV.3.3 Integrating DCT-MS/DCT-MW with other normalization techniques

In sub-section IV.3.2 the MVN-processed MFCC are treated as the baseline features and they are further updated with the presented DCT-based algorithms. Experimental results show that the DCT-based algorithms achieve higher recognition accuracy relative to the baseline,

Table 5: Recognition accuracy rates (%) averaged over all noise types different SNRs for the ${}_p$DCT-MS$_u$ method with different cutoff frequency, where AR(%) and RR(%) stand for the absolute and relative error rate reductions, respectively.

${}_p$DCT-MS$_u$ (updating the upper sub-band) with different cutoff frequencies						
Cutoff frequency F_c	**Set A**	**Set B**	**Set C**	**Average**	**AR**	**RR**
0 Hz (full-band DCT-MS)	89.29	90.55	89.28	89.79	4.44	30.31
5 Hz	90.80	91.62	90.12	90.99	5.64	38.50
15 Hz	87.51	88.03	87.95	87.80	2.45	16.72
25 Hz	86.04	86.60	86.63	86.38	1.03	7.03
35 Hz	85.57	86.14	86.24	85.93	0.58	3.96
45 Hz	85.16	85.78	85.72	85.52	0.17	1.16
50 Hz(equivalent to the baseline)	85.03	85.56	85.60	85.35	-	-

Table 6: Recognition accuracy rates (%) averaged over all noise types different SNRs for the ${}_p$DCT-MS$_l$, with different cutoff frequency, where AR(%) and RR(%) stand for the absolute and relative error rate reductions, respectively.

${}_p$DCT-MS$_l$ (updating the lower sub-band) with different cutoff frequencies						
Cutoff frequency F_c	**Set A**	**Set B**	**Set C**	**Average**	**AR**	**RR**
50 Hz(full-band DCT-MS)	89.29	90.55	89.28	89.79	4.44	30.31
45 Hz	89.13	90.50	89.16	89.68	4.33	29.56
35 Hz	88.59	89.98	88.75	89.18	3.83	26.14
25 Hz	88.27	89.70	88.46	88.88	3.53	24.10
15 Hz	85.73	87.26	86.05	86.41	1.06	7.24
5 Hz	83.78	84.71	84.53	84.30	-1.05	-7.17
0 Hz(equivalent to the baseline)	85.03	85.56	85.60	85.35	-	-

revealing that they are well additive to MVN. Here we are to investigate if the proposed DCT-MS/DCT-MW can enhance some other types of features, including the original plain MFCCs and the MFCCs processed by either of CMN, CGN, MVA, and HEQ in advance.

Tables 7, 8 and 9 list the averaged recognition accuracy rates for DCT-MS, DCT-MW and ${}_p$DCT-MS$_u$ ($F_c = 5$ Hz), respectively, for different types of features (MFCCs processed by CMN, MVN, CGN, HEQ and MVA). From the three tables, we find that

1. Similar to MVN, all the pre-processing algorithms including CMN, CGN, HEQ and MVA provide the original MFCC with improved recognition accuracy. MVA performs the best, followed by HEQ, CGN, MVN and then CMN.

2. The presented DCT-MS enhances the recognition accuracy for all the types of features shown here, including the unprocessed plain MFCCs. The resulting average accuracy rates are around 89.50% (except DCT-MS performing on the plain MFCCs). As a result,

Table 7: Recognition accuracy rates (%) averaged over all noise types different SNRs for the DCT-MS method combined with various featuer normalization methods

DCT-MS on various feature normalization methods						
Method	**Set A**	**Set B**	**Set C**	**Average**	**AR**	**RR**
MFCC	71.92	68.22	77.61	71.58	-	-
MFCC+DCT-MS	82.73	84.55	83.39	83.59	12.01	42.26
CMN	79.37	82.47	79.90	80.71	-	-
CMN+DCT-MS	89.15	90.45	89.23	89.68	8.97	46.50
MVN	85.03	85.56	85.60	85.35	-	-
MVN+DCT-MS	89.29	90.55	89.28	89.79	4.44	30.31
HEQ	87.59	88.84	87.64	88.10	-	-
HEQ+DCT-MS	88.50	90.00	89.04	89.21	1.11	9.33
CGN	87.64	88.55	87.73	88.02	-	-
CGN+DCT-MS	89.25	90.58	89.27	89.79	1.77	14.77
MVA	88.12	88.81	88.50	88.47	-	-
MVA+DCT-MS	88.93	90.20	88.88	89.42	0.95	8.24

by adopting DCT-MS, CMN and CGN become more attractive than HEQ and MVA since they are more computationally efficient.

3. Similar to DCT-MS, integrating DCT-MW with most normalization methods (except CMN and the original MFCC) provide better recognition rates than the individual component method. The optimal performance, 90.84% in averaged accuracy, occurs with the pairing of DCT-MW and CGN, better than those shown in Table 8, indicating DCT-MW behaves better than DCT-MS when combining with any of CGN, HEQ and MVA. However, since there remains significant low modulation frequency distortion in the unprocessed and CMN-processed noisy MFCC features, DCT-MW, acting as a low-pass filter, cannot benefit the two types of features in reducing the effect of noise.

4. Similar to DCT-MS and DCT-MW, ${}_p$DCT-MS$_u$ (with $F_c = 5$ Hz) is well additive to most normalization methods to make the recognition accuracy better. Comparing Table 9 with Tables 7 and 8, the partial-band DCT-MS, ${}_p$DCT-MS$_u$, outperforms the full-band DCT-MS and DCT-MW in most cases. The optimal averaged recognition accuracy shown in Table 9 is as high as 91.41%, with the pairing of ${}_p$DCT-MS$_u$ and HEQ.

IV.4 Summary

The averaged recognition accuracy rates for some methods presented in sub-section IV.3 are summarized in Figure 7 for a clear comparison. From this figure, we find that: First, among the three DCT-based algorithms, only DCT-MS can enhance the original and CMN-processed MFCC features to achieve a high accuracy rate as 89%. Second, when integrating either MVN,

Table 8: Recognition accuracy rates (%) averaged over all noise types different SNRs for the DCT-MW method combined with various featuer normalization methods

DCT-MW on various feature normalization methods						
Method	**Set A**	**Set B**	**Set C**	**Average**	**AR**	**RR**
MFCC	71.92	68.22	77.61	71.58	-	-
MFCC+DCT-MW	74.28	74.44	68.03	73.09	1.51	5.31
CMN	79.37	82.47	79.90	80.71	-	-
CMN+DCT-$MW_{(1)}$	80.02	83.05	80.60	81.35	0.64	3.32
MVN	85.03	85.56	85.60	85.35	-	-
MVN+$MW_{(1)}$	89.40	90.10	89.68	89.74	4.39	29.97
HEQ	87.59	88.84	87.64	88.10	-	-
HEQ+DCT-MW	90.24	90.80	90.85	90.59	2.49	20.92
CGN	87.64	88.55	87.73	88.02	-	-
CGN+DCT-MW	90.39	91.34	90.73	90.84	2.82	23.54
MVA	88.12	88.81	88.50	88.47	-	-
MVA+DCT-MW	89.83	90.59	90.22	90.21	1.47	15.09

Table 9: Recognition accuracy rates (%) averaged over all noise types different SNRs for the ${}_p$DCT-MS$_u$ method (with $F_c = 5$ Hz) combined with various featuer normalization methods

${}_p$DCT-MS$_u$ on various feature normalization methods						
Method	**Set A**	**Set B**	**Set C**	**Average**	**AR**	**RR**
MFCC	71.92	68.22	77.61	71.58	-	-
MFCC+${}_p$DCT-MS$_u$	70.33	68.20	75.64	70.54	-1.04	-3.66
CMN	79.37	82.47	79.90	80.71	-	-
CMN+${}_p$DCT-MS$_u$	82.69	85.18	83.24	83.79	3.08	15.97
MVN	85.03	85.56	85.60	85.35	-	-
MVN+${}_p$DCT-MS$_u$	90.80	91.62	90.12	90.99	5.64	38.50
HEQ	87.59	88.84	87.64	88.10	-	-
HEQ+${}_p$DCT-MS$_u$	91.14	92.06	90.66	91.41	3.31	27.82
CGN	87.64	88.55	87.73	88.02	-	-
CGN+${}_p$DCT-MS$_u$	90.97	91.87	90.31	91.20	3.18	26.54
MVA	88.12	88.81	88.50	88.47	-	-
MVA+${}_p$DCT-MS$_u$	90.45	91.32	90.20	90.75	2.28	19.77

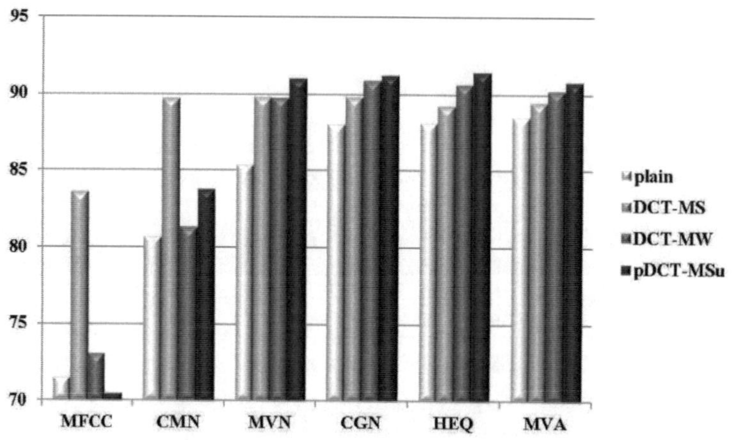

Figure 7: The recognition rates (%) averaged over all noise types and all SNRs for various DCT-based algorithms performing on various types of features

CGN, HEQ or MVA, the partial-band DCT-MS, ${}_p$DCT-MS$_u$, behaves the best, followed by DCT-MW and then DCT-MS. Finally, a relatively computationally efficient algorithm which integrates ${}_p$DCT-MS$_u$ and MVN/CGN can achieve nearly optimal recognition performance since ${}_p$DCT-MS$_u$ is the simplest among the DCT-based algorithms in implementation, and MVN and CGN need less computation complexity than MVA and HEQ.

V. Conclusion and Future Work

In this paper, we use the DCT to develop algorithms to promote the noise robustness of speech features in the temporal domain. In the presented methods, the DCT-magnitudes of feature streams are either normalized or weighted appropriately according to the information of clean speech utterances. We have shown that the two methods give rise to significant word error rate reduction when performing on the MVN-processed features, and they are also well additive to each of CMN, CGN, HEQ and MVA to provide further improved accuracy rates relative to the individual component method.

The future work will be along the following directions:

1. Performing DCT-magnitude substitution adaptively: in this paper we process the DCT-magnitude substitution by directly referring to a fixed reference magnitude curve. Although it may be the most direct and simplest approach, doing this way probably loses some important information of the original noisy speech streams for the ASR task. Therefore, we will study how to collect the information of the currently processed feature stream in order to create the reference magnitude curve in an adaptive manner.

2. Integrating the proposed new methods with some other feature normalization techniques,

such as HOCMN [6] and CSN [4], to see if further improvement can be achieved.

3. Investigating how to determine the optimal trade-off between the noise reduction and the speech distortion that always exists among the noise-robustness techniques.

References

[1] S. Furui, "Cepstral Analysis Technique for Automatic Speaker Verification," *IEEE Transactions on Acoustics, Speech and Signal Processing*, pp. 254-272, 1981.

[2] O. Viikki and K. Laurila, "Cepstral Domain Segmental Feature Vector Normalization for Noise Robust Speech Recognition," *Speech Communication*, vol. 25, pp. 133-147, 1998.

[3] S. Yoshizawa, N. Hayasaka, N. Wada, and Y. Miyanaga, "Cpestral Gain Normalization for Noise Robust Speech Recognition," *IEEE International Conference on Acoustics, Speech and Signal Processing*, vol. 1, pp. 209-212, 2004.

[4] Jun Du and Ren-Hua Wang, "Cepstral Shape Normalization (CSN) for Robust Speech Recognition," *IEEE International Conference on Acoustics, Speech and Signal Processing*, pp. 4389-4392, 2008.

[5] Ángel de la Torre, Antonio M. Peinado, José C. Segura, José L. Pérez-Córdoba, Ma Carmen Benítez, Antonio J. Rubio, "Histogram Equalization of Speech Representation for Robust Speech Recognition," *IEEE Transactions on Speech and Audio Processing*, vol. 13, pp. 355-366, 2005.

[6] C. Hsu and L. Lee, "Higher order cepstral moment normalization (HOCMN) for robust speech recognition," *Internation Conference on Acoustics, Speech and Signal Processing*, pp. 197-200, 2004.

[7] Xiong Xiao, Eng Siong Chng and Haizhou Li, "Normalization of the Speech Modulation Spectra for Robust Speech Recognition," *IEEE Transactions on Audio, Speech, and Language Processing*, vol. 16, no. 8, pp. 1662-1674, 2008.

[8] C. Chen and J. Bilmes, "MVA processing of speech features," *IEEE Transactions on Audio, Speech, and Language Processing*, pp. 257-270, 2006.

[9] S. A. Khayam, "The discrete cosine transform (DCT): theory and application," *Technical Report WAVES-TR-ECE802.602*, 2003.

[10] Rao, K. and Ahmed, N., "Orthogonal transforms for digital signal processing," *IEEE International Conference on Acoustics, Speech and Signal Processing*, vol.1, pp. 136-140, 1976.

[11] Noboru Kanedera, Hynek Hermansky and Takayuki Arai, "On properties of modulation spectrum for robust automatic speech recognition," *IEEE International Conference on Acoustics, Speech and Signal Processing*, vol. 2, pp. 613-616, 1998.

[12] H. G. Hirsch and D. Pearce, "The AURORA experimental framework for the performance evaluations of speech recognition system under noisy conditions," *Proceedings of ISCA IIWR ASR2000*, 2000.

[13] The hidden Markov model toolkit. Available from: <http://htk.eng.cam.ac.uk>.

聯合語者、雜訊環境與說話內容因素分析之強健性語音辨認

國立台北科技大學電子工程系
Department of Electronic Engineering
National Taipei of Technology

吳聖堂　Sheng-Tang Wu
t8418093@ntut.edu.tw

方偉德　Wei-Te Fang
t9418025@ntut.edu.tw

廖元甫　Yuan-Fu Liao
yfliao@ntnt.edu.tw

摘要

摘要一本論文主要研究於強健性語音辨認上，我們提出聯合語者、雜訊環境與語音內容因素分析(Joint Speaker and Noisy Environment and Speech Content Factor Analysis；JSEC)，主要是透過聯合因素分析，在特徵空間做即時語音辨認模型補償(online recognition model compensation)，使得調適出來的模型與測試環境能夠盡量匹配，進而提升辨識效果。此外，我們先將 JSEC 分解成語音和非語音二個模型做模型調適、估算影響因素，接著每個模型再利用階層式的概念，語音特性考慮之因素分成雜訊環境特徵空間、語者特徵空間、說話內容特徵空間與獨特因素空間分別估算，非語音特性考慮之因素則分成雜訊特徵空間和獨特因素空間分別估算，最後再把語音和非語音組合回辨認用的模型，用此方式來降低我們的參數量。我們使用 Aurora2 語料庫做實驗，在複合情境的訓練模式下，我們得到最佳的辨識錯誤率為 4.37%，比傳統強健性參數求取方法 MVA (Mean subtraction，Variance normalization，and ARMA filtering)[1][2]的錯誤率 4.99%低了許多，也比我們先前提出的 JSE (Joint Speaker and Noisy Environment Factor Analysis)[11]方法的錯誤率相當甚至好一點。除了辨認率之外，我們提出的方法也能使得調適模型的參數量大幅下降，JSEC 參數量約為傳統 MVA 的 4 倍，也比 JSE 方法少了十分之一的參數量，因此為更有效率的調適方法。

關鍵詞：強健性語音辨認，因素分析，Aurora2

一、緒論

語音辨認系統受雜訊環境、語者特性與通道效應等影響，導致辨識率下降。通常處理這些影響因素或環境不匹配問題，有兩種較常見的方法：強健性語音參數求取(robust speech feature extraction)與語音模型調適(speech model adaptation)。

強健性參數求取之方法，我們可以舉幾個經典的例子：倒頻譜正規化 ARMA (Auto-regression and Moving Average)濾波技術(Mean subtraction，Variance normalization，and ARMA filtering；MVA)[1][2]、分布等化法(Histogram Equalization；HEQ)[3][4]，與兩階式維納濾波器(two-stage Wiener filter)[5]等，它們的特點是有效且容易實現。

至於模型調適方法，又可分為是否需要先驗知識，不需要先驗知識的方法，主要有：最大相似度線性回歸(Maximum Likelihood Linear Regression；MLLR)[6]、最大事後機率調適法(Maximum A Posteriori；MAP)[7]調適法、平行模型結合(Parallel Model Combination；PMC)[8]等，以上皆為經典且常見之語音模型調適法，經常被應用於語音和語者辨認系統。

而需先驗知識的方法，常見的方法如雙聲源為基礎之分段線性補償(Stereo-based Piecewise Linear Compensation, SPLICE)[9]。我們也曾利用事先收集大量語者與環境先驗知識，提出基於雜訊環境參考模型內插法(Reference Model Weighting；RMW)、雜訊特徵最大相似度線性迴歸(Eigen-Maximum Likelihood Linear Regression；EMLLR)[10]，基於聯合語者與雜訊環境因素分析 (Joint Speaker and Noisy Environment Factor Analysis；JSE)[11]等方法，效果皆相當不錯。

此論文我們提出了需先驗知識的語者、雜訊環境與語音內容因素分析之強健性語音辨認(Joint Speaker and Noisy Environment and Speech Content Factor Analysis；JSEC)， JSEC 主要運用在雜訊分析處理，所考慮的影響因素及估算順序如圖一的 JSEC 架構圖。

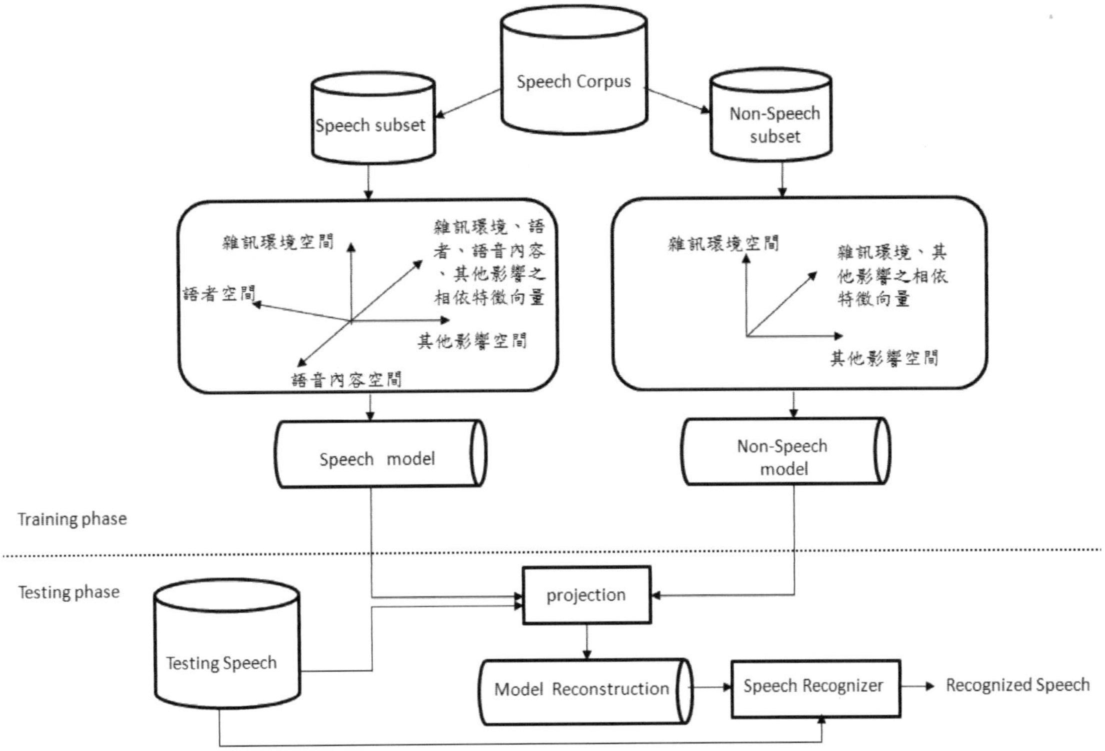

圖一、JSEC 架構圖

JSEC 在訓練端將訓練語料分成兩類，一類為左邊具有語音特性之語句做影響因素之分類，另一類為右邊非語音特性之語句做影響因素之分類，再利用階層式的概念，將語音特性分成了雜訊環境特徵空間、語者特徵空間、說話內容特徵空間與獨特因素空間分別估算，非語音特性為雜訊特徵空間與獨特因素空間分別估算，最後再把語音和非語音組合回辨認用的模型。當我們得到不同影響因素的空間後，最後在測試端，輸入測試語料後，測試語料對個別特徵空間做投影，即可對模型做即時的調適。

二、聯合語者、雜訊環境與語音內容因素分析

2.1 JSEC 模型表示

JSEC 主要考慮測試語料在辨識時，受到雜訊環境、語者、語音內容與其他因素的影響。而 JSEC 比 JSE 多考慮的語音內容影響，可分為具有語音特性的部分，以及非具有語音特性。

我們定義具有語音特性之 JSEC 模型是由古典 MAP(Classical MAP)、特徵雜訊環境、特徵語者、語音內容(zero~nine、oh、silence)四個模型結合而成：

$$M_{speech} = m_{sp} + u_{sp}x_{sp} + v_{sp}y_{sp} + g_{sp}r_{sp} + d_{sp}z_{sp} \quad (1)$$

而非語音特性之 JSEC 模型是由特徵雜訊與古典 MAP(Classical MAP)模型結合而成：

$$M_{nonspeech} = m_{non} + u_{non}x_{non} + d_{non}z_{non} \quad (2)$$

其中：

m_{sp}、m_{non}：由語音參數串接而成的超向量，模型參數串接而成的超向量。

x_{sp}、x_{non}：特徵雜訊環境空間的投影量，初始假設平均值為 0 變異數為 1 的標準高斯分佈。

y_{sp}：特徵語者特徵空間的投影量，初始假設平均值為 0 變異數為 1 的標準高斯分佈。

r_{sp}：語音內容特徵空間的投影量，初始假設平均值為 0 變異數為 1 的標準高斯分佈。

z_{sp}、z_{non}：獨特因素特徵空間的投影量，初始假設平均值為 0 變異數為 1 的標準高斯分佈。

u_{sp}、u_{non}：特徵雜訊環境特徵空間。

v_{sp}：特徵語者特徵空間。

d_{sp}、d_{non}：獨特因素特徵空間。

g_{sp}：語音內容特徵空間。

2.2 JSEC 系統架構

圖二是 JSEC 之系統流程圖，在訓練端，我們將訓練語料做 Force-alignment，變成不同語音內容的片段語句。具有語音特性的片段語句訓練一個名為 speech 的聲學模型，我們便是利用這種方式來降低最後重建模型之參數量。並且對具有語音特性的片段語句做標記分類，接著再依序估算雜訊、語者、說話內容，最後是獨特因素的特徵空間，分別以 u_{sp}、v_{sp}、g_{sp}、d_{sp} 表示。非具有語音特性的片段語句，則訓練一個 non speech 的模型，並且僅對不同雜訊做標記，同於具有語音特性的部分。接著依序估算雜訊與獨特因素特徵空間，分別以 u_{non} 與 d_{non} 表示。

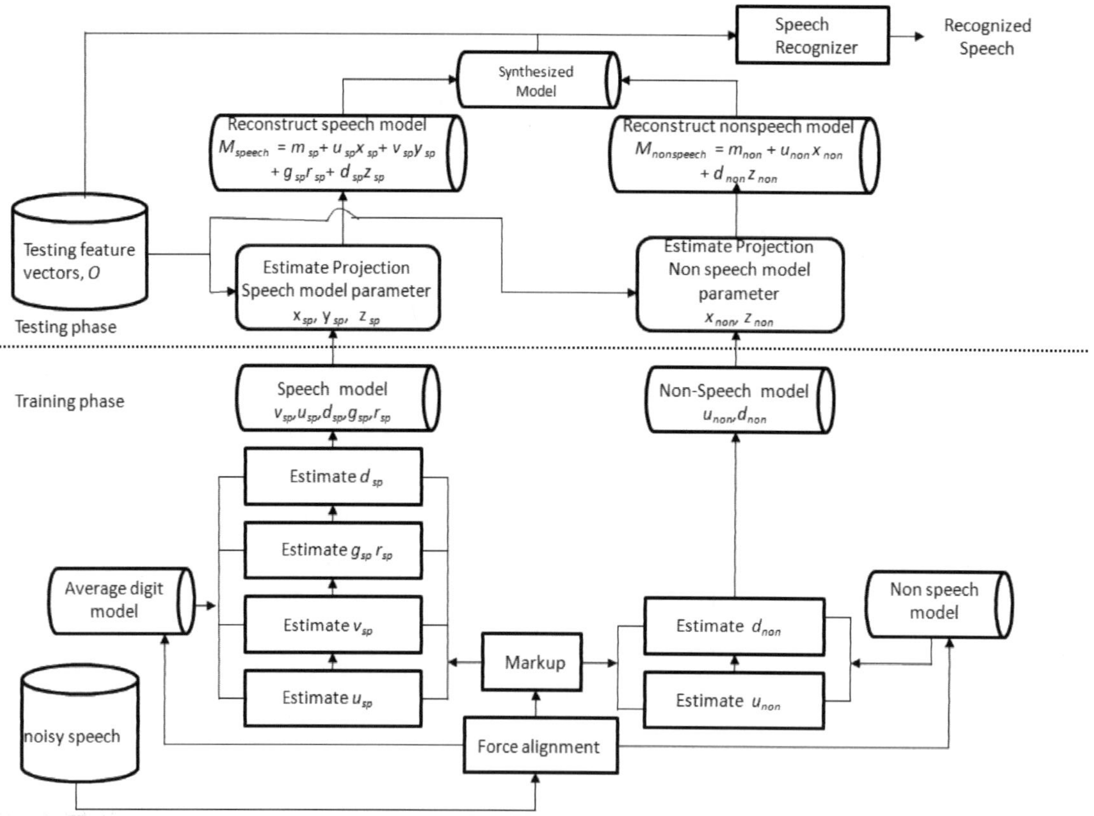

圖二、JSEC 之系統流程圖

在測試端，我們估算測試語料具有語音特性影響因素的投影量 x_{sp}、y_{sp}、z_{sp}，然後投影到建立好的 u_{sp}、v_{sp}、d_{sp}，得到偏移量 $u_{sp}x_{sp} + v_{sp}y_{sp} + d_{sp}z_{sp}$；與非具有語音特性影響因素的投影量 x_{non}、z_{non}，然後投影到建立好的 u_{non}、d_{non}，得到偏移量 $u_{non}x_{non} + d_{non}z_{non}$。得到兩者偏移量後，另外再估算訓練端具有語音特性之說話內容的偏移量 $g_{sp}r_{sp}$，用意是把單一的聲學模型，可以依照不同說話內容之影響，調適為不同語音內容特性的聲學模型，然後再加上以未切割語料訓練的聲學模型、靜音模型與停頓模型部分，即可重建出每一句測試語料獨有的模型，最後做辨識結果。

在得到所需要的轉換矩陣之後就可以進行第二步驟，也就是將原始參數向量對轉換矩陣做內積運算，就能轉換成新參數向量，然後送進模型訓練。接下來兩段將敘述主成分分析和線性鑑別分析的原理和實作的步驟。

2.3 特徵空間的估計

我們類似於參考文獻[12]之古典 MAP、特徵語者和特徵通道等方法，表示各種因素的關係。而由不同高斯混合分布(mixture)的共變異數串接而成的對角矩陣則可作為參數估測的初始值。

本文所提到的聯合因素分析是參考[13]的作法，將語音模型，利用擷取 average speech model 的平均值所構成的超向量作為基準，就像是傳統的 MAP 語者調適一樣，而由不同混合成分的共變異數$\sum_c$串接而成的對角矩陣$\sum$則可作為參數估測的初始值。在模型參數估測之前先定義系統的機率假設。

波氏統計

我們先使用波氏統計[14]主要是以average speech model的平均值、變異數以及權重來計算機率統計量。假設語者s以及語者特徵向量$\mathrm{y}_1, \mathrm{y}_2, \ldots, \mathrm{y}_\mathrm{t}$，對於每一個混合成分$c$，我們定義波氏統計如下：

$$N_c(s) = \sum_t \gamma_t(c) \tag{3}$$

$$F_c(s) = \sum_t \gamma_t(c)(Y_t - m_c) \tag{4}$$

$$S_c(s) = diag\left(\sum_t \gamma_t(c)(Y_t - m_c)(Y_t - m_c)^*\right) \tag{5}$$

其中：

$\gamma_t(c)$代表語者特徵向量於時間時落於混合成分的事後機率，而m_c代表average speech model中混合成分的c平均值。接著設$N(s)$為CF x CF的對角矩陣，其中的對角區塊是由

$N_c(s)$ (c=1,...,C)所構成。設$F(s)$為CF x 1的超向量，是由每一個$F_c(s)$ (c=1,...,C)串接而成。設$S(s)$為CF x CF的對角矩陣，其中的對角區塊是由$S_c(s)$ (c=1,...,C)所構成。

2.3.1 語者、雜訊環境、語音內容特徵空間

求得波式統計量之後，由參考文獻[13]我們可以計算出具有語音特性的語者、雜訊環境特徵空間，和非語音特性的雜訊環境特徵空間。

語者、雜訊環境、語音內容特徵空間估算方法相同，但是語音內容算出來的隱藏變數 r_{sp}，必須儲存起來給測試端使用，因為在辨認的時候並不知道要說哪些語音內容,先假設每一個 model 平均值在哪裡，再利用 ML 法重估超參數取得 g_{sp} 之後，即可將說話內容投影到對應位置。

由於 u_{sp}, v_{sp}, g_{sp}, u_{non} 其估計方法相同，以下我們以具有語音特性的特徵語者(Eigen-voice)模型為例，求取 v_{sp}。

我們利用 Expectation Maximization(EM)演算法進行 10 次的疊代，反覆更新 v_{sp}使之趨於定值：

隱藏變數y_{sp}事後分佈

先假設隱藏變數$y_{sp}(s)$是平均值為0變異數為1的標準高斯分佈，當我們輸入語音資料後就像MAP語者調適一樣會有不同的分佈。根據[12]假設，令$L_{sp,y}(s) = I_{sp,y} + V^*{}_{sp,y}(s)\sum_{sp,y}{}^{-1}(s)N_{sp,y}(s)V_{sp,y}(s)$，其中$\sum_{sp,y}{}^{-1}$為variance之超向量，而隱藏變數$y_{sp}(s)$的分佈可由平均值$L^{-1}{}_{sp,y}(s)V^*{}_{sp,y}(s)\sum_{sp,y}{}^{-1}(s)F_{sp,y}(s,m)$與共變異數$L^{-1}{}_{sp,y}(s)$去描述該機率分佈。

ML法重估超參數

初始參數 m 與$\sum$是擷取自 average speech model 的相關組合，參數 v_{sp} 則是採用隨機的初始值，假設語者為 s，定義累積的統計量如下：

$$N_c = \sum_s N_c(s) \quad (c = 1, \dots, C) \tag{6}$$

$$U_c = \sum_s N_c(s)\, E\left[y_{sp}(s)y^*{}_{sp}(s)\right] \quad (c = 1, \dots, C) \tag{7}$$

$$\mathcal{C} = \sum_s F(s)\, E\left[y^*{}_{sp}(s)\right] \tag{8}$$

$$N = \sum_s N(s) \tag{9}$$

對每一個混和成分 c =1,...,C 、每一個混合成分的元素 f=1,...,F ，設 i = (c -1)F +f，令 u_i 代表 u 的第 i 列，而 $\mathcal{C}_i$代表 $\mathcal{C}$的第 i 列，因此特徵特徵空間 v_{sp} 的更新公式可表示成：

$$v_i U_c = C_i' \quad (i=1,....,CF) \tag{10}$$

上述的表示式，可以從參考文獻[13]得到相關的表示。

2.3.2 獨特因素特徵空間

由於 d_{sp}, d_{non} 其估計方法相同，以下我們以具有語音特性的獨特因素模型為例，求取 d_{sp}。

我們利用 Expectation Maximization(EM)演算法進行 10 次的疊代，反覆更新 d_{sp} 使之趨於定值。

隱藏變數 d_{sp} 事後分佈

先假設隱藏變數 $z_{sp}(s)$ 是平均值為 0 變異數為 1 的標準高斯分佈，當我們輸入語音資料後就像 MAP 語者調適一樣會有不同的分佈。根據[12]假設，令 $L_{sp,d}(s) = I_{sp,d} + d^2{}_{sp,d}(s)\Sigma_{sp,d}{}^{-1}(s)N_{sp,d}(s)$，其中 $\Sigma_{sp,d}{}^{-1}$ 為 variance 之超向量，而隱藏變數 $z_{sp}(s)$ 的分佈可由平均值 $L^{-1}{}_{sp,d}(s)d_{sp,d}(s)\Sigma_{sp,d}{}^{-1}(s)F_{sp,d}(s,m)$ 與共變異數 $L^{-1}{}_{sp,d}(s)$ 去描述該機率分佈。

ML法重估超參數

初始參數 m 與 Σ 是擷取自 average speech model 的相關組合，參數 d_{sp} 則是採用隨機的初始值，假設語者為 s，定義累積的統計量如下：

$$N_c = \textstyle\sum_s N_c(s) \quad (c = 1, \dots, C) \tag{11}$$

$$U_c = \textstyle\sum_s diag\left(N(s)\, E\left[z_{sp}(s) z^*{}_{sp}(s)\right]\right) \quad (c = 1, \dots, C) \tag{12}$$

$$C' = \textstyle\sum_s diag\left(F(s)\, E\left[z^*{}_{sp}(s)\right]\right) \tag{13}$$

$$N = \textstyle\sum_s N(s) \tag{14}$$

對每一個混和成分 $c = 1,...,C$ 、每一個混合成分的元素 $f = 1,...,F$ ，設 $i = (c-1)F + f$，令 u_i 代表 u 的第 i 列，而 C_i' 代表 C' 的第 i 列，因此特徵特徵空間 d_{sp} 的更新公式可表示成：

$$v_i U_c = C_i' \quad (i=1,....,CF) \tag{15}$$

上述的表示式，可以從參考文獻[13]得到相關的表示。

2.3.3 投影量 x, y, r, z 的估計

當我們在訓練端得到求取出的具有語音特性的超參數 u_{sp}、v_{sp}、g_{sp}、d_{sp}，以及非語音特性的超參數 u_{non}、d_{non} 後，測試端的參數再依照具有語音特性之影響因素，經過估算而得到個別雜訊影響之投影量 x_{sp}、語者影響之投影量 y_{sp}、說話內容之投影量 r_{sp}、獨特因素之投影量 z_{sp}，非語音特性之影響因素一樣經過估算而得到投影量 x_{non}、z_{non}。

語音特性和非語音特性之投影量算法一樣，我們以估算語音部分的投影量為例：

雜訊影響之投影量 x_{sp}

假設 $L_{sp,x}(s) = I_{sp,x} + V_{sp,x}{}^{*}(s){\sum_{sp,x}}^{-1}(s)N_{sp,x}(s)V_{sp,x}(s)$ (16)

$x_{sp} = E[x(s)] = L_{sp,x}{}^{-1}(s)u_{sp,x}{}^{*}(s){\sum_{sp,x}}^{-1}(s)F_{sp,x}(s,m)$ (17)

語者影響之投影量 y_{sp}

假設 $L_{sp,y}(s) = I_{sp,y} + V_{sp,y}{}^{*}(s){\sum_{sp,y}}^{-1}(s)N_{sp,y}(s)V_{sp,y}(s)$ (18)

$y_{sp} = E[y(s)] = L_{sp,y}{}^{-1}(s)v_{sp,y}{}^{*}(s){\sum_{sp,y}}^{-1}(s)F_{sp,y}(s,m)$ (19)

語音內容影響之投影量 r_{sp}

假設 $L_{sp,r}(s) = I_{sp,r} + V_{sp,r}{}^{*}(s){\sum_{sp,r}}^{-1}(s)N_{sp,r}(s)V_{sp,r}(s)$ (20)

$r_{sp} = E[r\,(s)] = L_{sp,r}{}^{-1}(s)g_{sp,r}{}^{*}(s){\sum_{sp,r}}^{-1}(s)F_{sp,r}(s,m)$ (21)

獨特因素之投影量 z_{sp}

假設 $L_{sp,z}(s) = I_{sp,z} + d_{sp,z}{}^{2}(s){\sum_{sp,z}}^{-1}(s)N_{sp,z}(s)$ (22)

$z_{sp} = E[z(s)] = L_{sp,z}{}^{-1}(s)d_{sp,z}{}^{*}(s){\sum_{sp,z}}^{-1}(s)F_{sp,z}(s,m)$ (23)

得到 x_{sp}、y_{sp}、r_{sp}、z_{sp} 後，投影到 u_{sp}、v_{sp}、g_{sp}、d_{sp} 特徵空間，即可對模型做即時的調適，重建出每句測試語料獨有的辨認模型，而變異數、轉移機率與權重之影響很小，故暫且假設不考慮變異數、轉移機率與權重等問題。

三、實驗結果與分析

3.1 實驗設定

本論文實驗是以國際上廣泛用在雜訊環境語音辨識技術強健性的標準語料庫 Aurora 2 為主。Aurora2 是以 TIDigits 為基礎，加上不同雜訊以及通過特定的通道效應製成。Aurora2 是一個連續數字串語料庫，每句音段包含一至七個連續數字，長度最多不超過三秒鐘。

語料首先通過理想濾波器將 20 kHz 降頻為 8 kHz，此為定義的乾淨(Clean)語料，每個乾淨音段先經特定的通道效應，再依各種訊雜比(SNR20、SNR15、SNR 10、SNR 5、SNR 0 和 SNR -5dB)加上不同的加成性雜訊。

訓練語料混合各種訊雜比及不同環境雜訊的複合情境訓練訓練模式。測試語料部分則是依照原本 Aurora2 自行建立的不同通道效應與加成性雜訊，共分成 A、B、C 三種測試組合。

本論文採用梅爾倒頻譜係數，及聲學模型為連續性密度的隱藏式馬可夫模型，模型的狀態轉移只停留在原始狀態，及由左至右轉移到下一個相鄰的狀態。

數字聲學模型的單位為全詞模型，十一個英文數字聲學模型(0～9 和 oh)。每個聲學模型有 16 個狀態，每個狀態含 3 個高斯分布模型。除數字聲學模型外，還有靜音(silence)模型和停頓(short pause)模型。辨識效能評估上，採取辨識詞錯誤率，這考慮了刪除型錯誤、插入型錯誤和取代型錯誤。我們實驗分為二類：simple backend (3 mixture)和 complex backend (20 mixture)，如表一所示。

Backend	Speech model	Silence model	Short pause model
Simple	16 state, each state 3 mixture	3 state, each state 6 mixture	1 state, each state 6 mixture
Complex	16 state, each state 20 mixture	3 state, each state 64 mixture	1 state, each state 64 mixture

表一、複合情境訓練模式各種參數組合辨識結果

另外我們實驗對照需要用到我們先前提出的 JSE 方法，其模型可表示為：

$$M = m + ux(s) + vy(s) + dz(s) \qquad (24)$$

其中 m 為初始模型中所有平均值串成的超向量(super-vector)；v、u、d 分別為特徵聲音、特徵雜訊、獨特因素之特徵空間；$vy(s)$、$ux_h(s)$、 $dz(s)$分別為人聲、雜訊、獨特因素在各自特徵空間的平均偏移量。和 JSEC 最大不同在於少考慮了講話內容因素，模型的特徵向量比 JSEC 龐大。

3.2 特徵空間分析

我們想要得知此方法是否正確，能不能有效地將影響因素個別分開，所以先使用 simple

backend 分析特徵空間並畫出特徵空間投影圖，目的是讓各種不同雜訊的測試語料，能投影到正確的特徵空間上。在建構特徵空間時，我們先估算已經做好分類資訊的統計量，接著再依照 u、v、g、d 之順序，逐一估算個別之特徵空間。爲了方便分析，我們取前兩維的特徵向量作 x 軸和 y 軸，建構一個二維空間，首先以雜訊類型(地下鐵、人聲、汽車、展覽會)做分析，我們採用七種 SNR(clean、SNR20、SNR15、SNR10、SNR5、SNR0、SNR-5)做特徵空間分析，其結果如圖三、圖四所示。

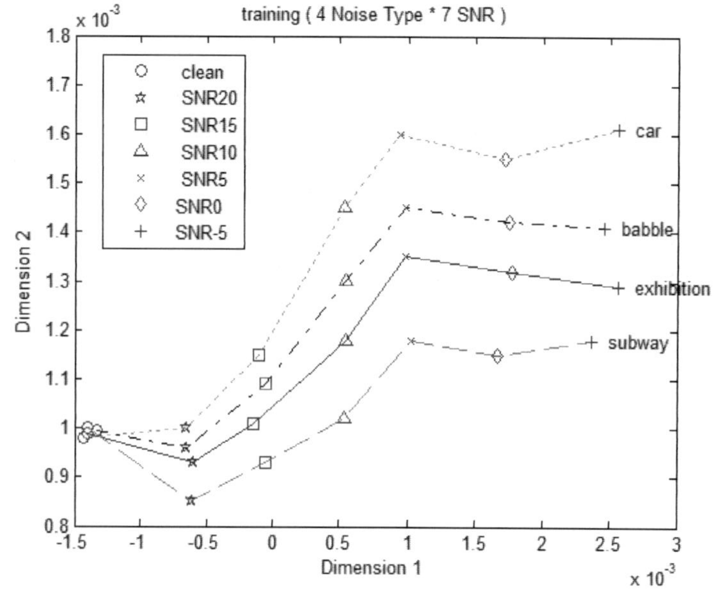

圖三、simple backend JSEC 語音特性之雜訊特徵空間投影圖

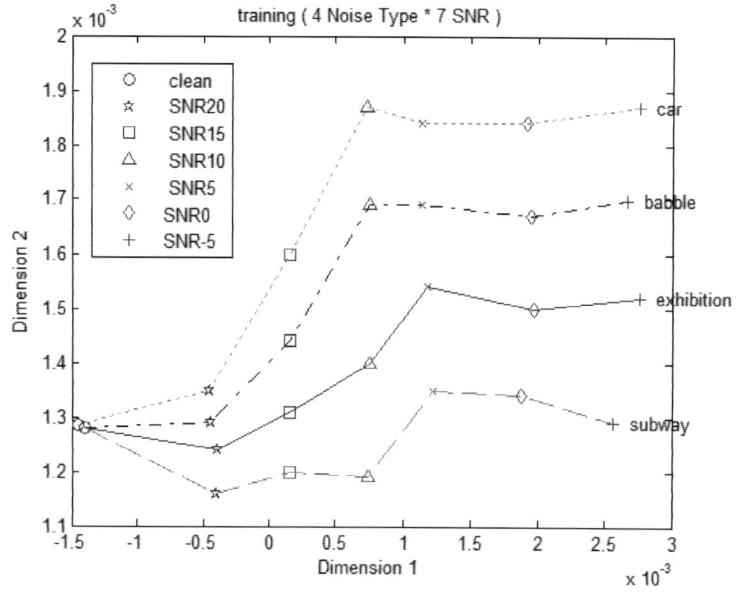

圖四、simple backend JSEC 非語音特性之雜訊特徵空間投影圖

我們可以看到圖三、圖四，在 clean 端，雜訊特性並不明顯，隨著 SNR 增加，雜訊特性

越來越明顯，而末端的線條便跟著逐漸分開。由以上之特徵空間投影圖，我們得知求出來之特徵空間能夠有效地將這些干擾因素個別分開，提升辨識效能。

接著我們要做語者特性分析，如圖五：

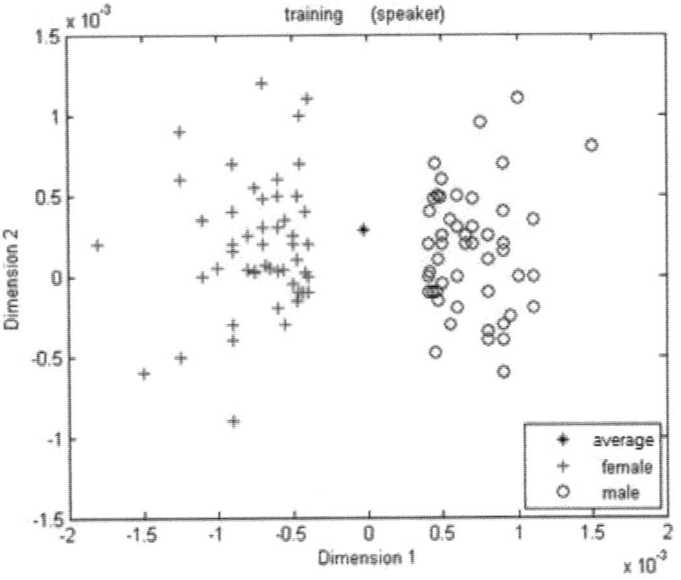

圖五、simple backend JSEC 語者特徵空間投影圖

在圖五中，我們可以看到其投影結果，很明顯依照語者的不同被分成兩邊，我們以「o」與「+」的符號分別表示男生與女生的特性。

最後是語音內容之特徵空間投影分析，其結果如圖六所示：

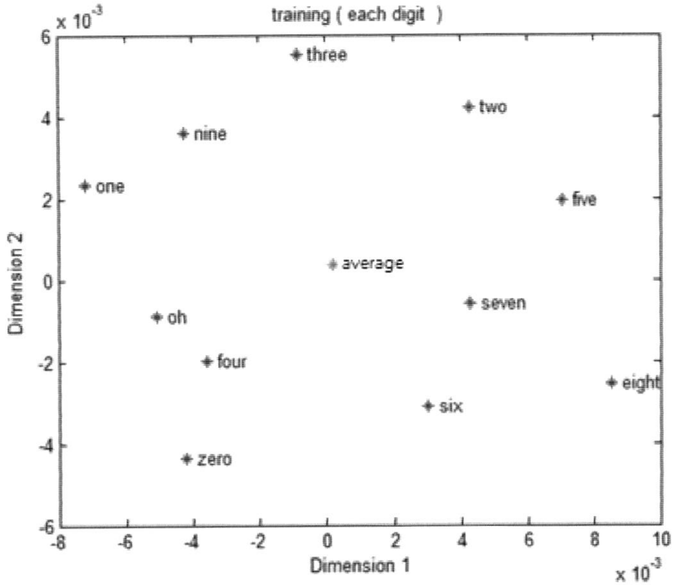

圖六、simple backend JSEC 語音內容之特徵空間投影圖

我們可以看到圖六其投影結果，依照語音內容被分開，而比較類似的音，例如 oh、four，似乎會比較靠近，而複合情境的點(digit)大約是在所有點的平均位置。由以上三種不同影響因素之特徵空間投影圖，我們預測辨識效果應當不錯。

3.3 simple backend

我們的實驗為了要有效率的找出特徵空間的最佳維度，首先固定語者(S) 55 維，語音內容(T) 6 維。雜訊(N)維度共 40 維，所以我們從 20 維開始找最佳效果，並且一次往上或往下增加 6 維(14 維、20 維和 24 維)尋找最佳維度。另外，由於調適模型中的變異數、轉移機率與權重影響很小，因此先假設與比較的 MVA、JSE 相同，並且把實驗分成 simple backend 和 complex backend 二組做維度組合分析。

辨識結果如圖七所示：

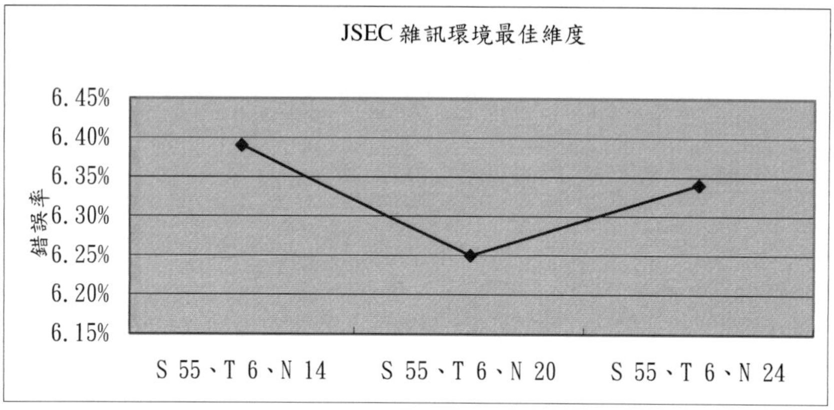

圖七、simple backend JSEC 雜訊環境最佳維度比較圖

圖七我們可以看到雜訊的最佳維度是 20 維，因此我們接著固定雜訊 20 維，語音內容一樣取 6 維，再取語者 55 維、60 維和 70 維，做測試可以得到以下結果：

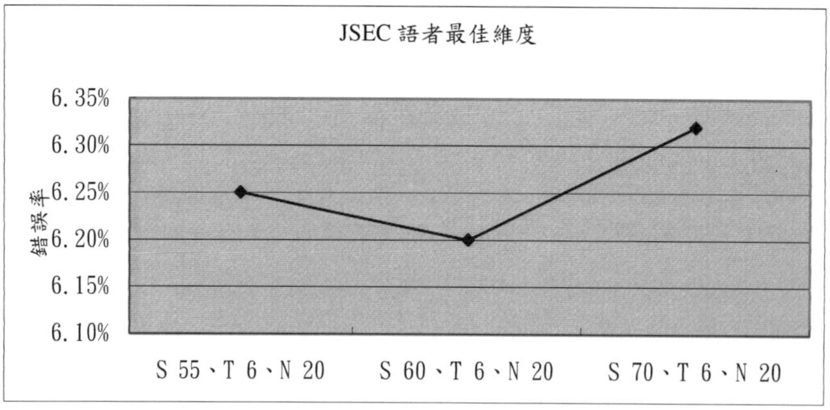

圖八、simple backend JSEC 語者最佳維度比較圖

圖八我們可以看到語者的最佳維度是 60 維，因此我們接著固定雜訊 20 維，語者取 60 維，再取語音內容 6 維、8 維和 10 維，做測試可以得到以下結果：

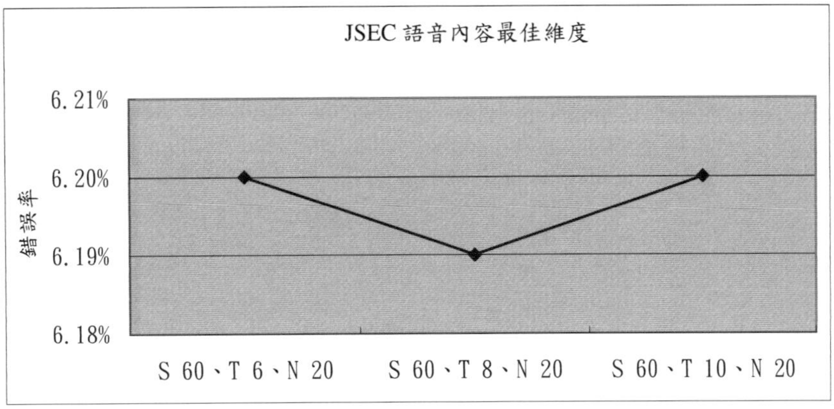

圖九、simple backend JSEC 語者最佳維度比較圖

圖九我們可以看到語音內容的最佳維度是 8 維。

3.3.2 Complex backend

由於調適模型中的變異數、轉移機率與權重影響很小，因此先假設與比較的 MVA、JSE 相同。維度測試首先固定語者(S) 55 維，語音內容(T) 6 維，雜訊(N)分別以 14 維、20 維和 24 維做測試後可得以下結果：

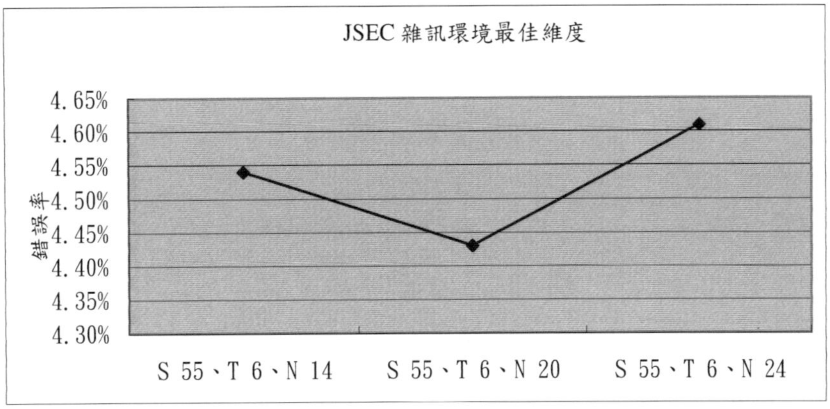

圖十、complex backend JSEC 雜訊環境最佳維度比較圖

由圖十，我們可以看到雜訊的最佳維度是 20 維，因此我們接著固定雜訊 20 維，語音內容一樣取 6 維，再取語者 55 維、60 維和 70 維，做測試可以得到以下結果：

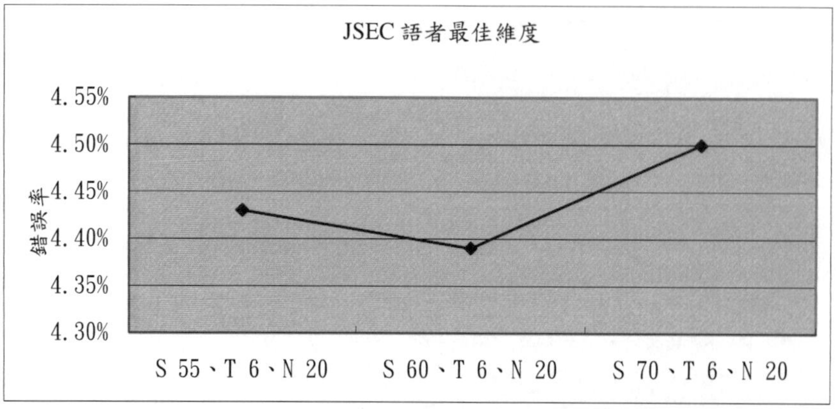

圖十一、complex backend JSEC 語者最佳維度比較圖

由圖十一我們可以看到語者的最佳維度是 60 維，因此我們接著固定雜訊 20 維，語者取 60 維，再取語音內容 6 維、8 維和 10 維，做測試可以得到以下結果：

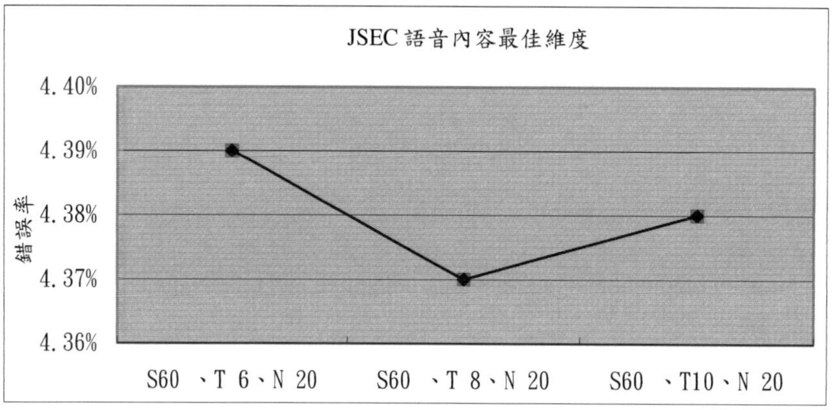

圖十二、complex backend JSEC 語音內容最佳維度比較圖

由圖十二，我們可以看到語音內容的最佳維度是 8 維。

3.4 實驗結果與討論

最後我們參數設定使用最佳的雜訊 20 維、語者 60 維、語音內容 8 維，和其他系統方法做實驗對照，並分成 simple backend 和 complex backend 二組實驗討論。

3.4.1 Simple backend

從圖十三和圖十四我們發現，JSE 與 JSEC 平均錯誤率遠優於 MVA 的 7.97%，但是 JSEC 卻略差 JSE 0.15%，我們認為 JSEC 由於聲學模型變成只有一個時，做 simple backend 的實驗，可能會導致模型不夠複雜，因此造成辨識率下降。

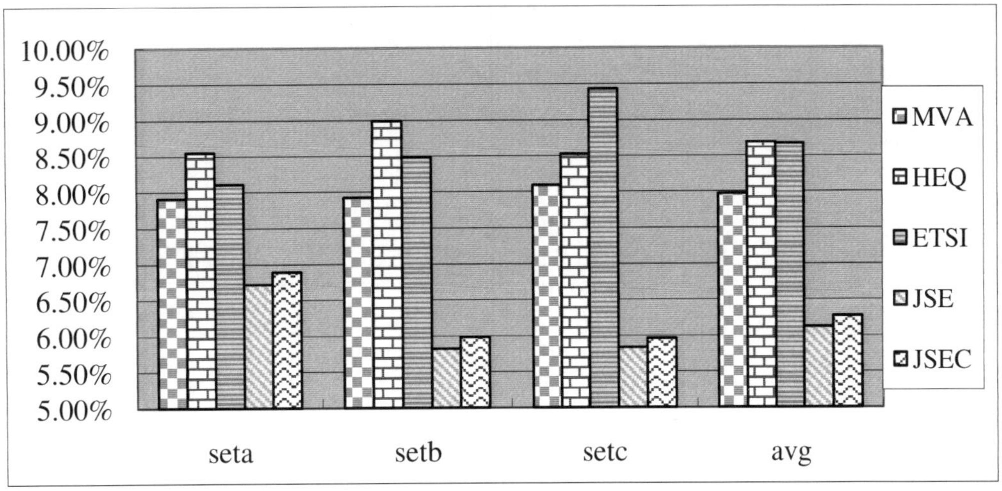

圖十三、simple backend 各系統方法不同環境之比較圖

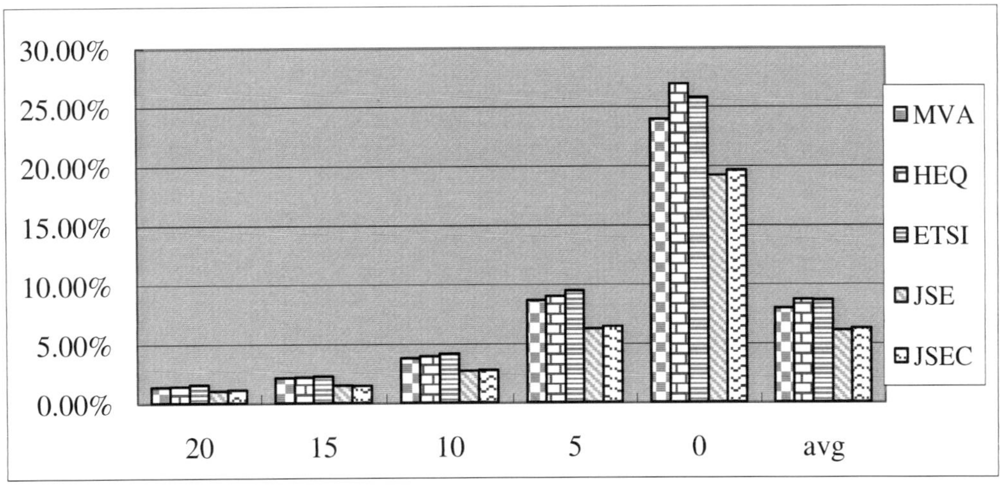

圖十四、simple backend 各系統方法不同 SNR 之比較圖

但在調適模型所需的參數量的方面，如表二和圖十五。我們可以從圖十五發現，調適模型所需的參數量明顯比原本 JSE 的方法降低很多，JSE 比 JSEC 多 9 – 10 倍的參數量，而 JSEC 只比 MVA 多了 4 倍的參數量，效能更好、運算量更小。

simple backend			
模型所需參數	MVA	JSE	JSEC
mean	21528	21528	2808
variance	21528	21528	2808
weight	552	552	72
Transition	3598	3598	358

u	–	430560	–
v	–	1291680	–
d	–	21528	–
u_{non}	–	–	14040
d_{non}	–	–	702
u_{sp}	–	–	37440
v_{sp}	–	–	112320
d_{sp}	–	–	1872
g_{sp}	–	–	14976
r_{sp}	–	–	88
總共的參數量	47206	1790974	187484
參數量的比例	1	37.94	3.97

表二、simple backend MVA 與改變參數量的 JSEC 比較表

其中 JSEC 的 mean 與 variance=(39*3*16=1872)+(39*6*3=702)+(39*6*1=234)

$$=2808 \quad (25)$$

$$\text{Transition} = 18x18 + 5x5 + 3*3 = 358 \quad (26)$$

$$\text{weight} = 3*16 + 6*3 + 6*1 = 72 \quad (27)$$

$$u_{non} = 20x702 = 14040 \quad (28)$$

$$d_{non} = 1x702 = 702 \quad (29)$$

$$u_{sp} = 20x1872 = 37440 \quad (30)$$

$$v_{sp} = 60x1872 = 112320 \quad (31)$$

$$d_{sp} = 1x1872 = 1872 \quad (32)$$

$$g_{sp} = 8x1872 = 14976 \quad (33)$$

$$r_{sp} = 11x8 = 88 \quad (34)$$

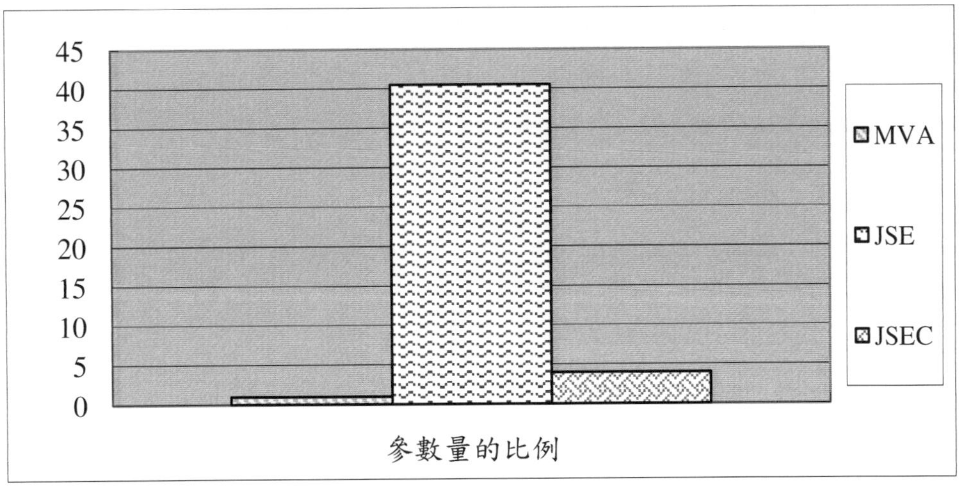

圖十五、simple backend MVA 與改變參數量的 JSEC 比例圖

3.4.1 Complex backend

我們另外做了一組 complex backend 實驗，把 mixture 數從 3 拉到 20，我們一樣使用最佳的雜訊 20 維、語者 60 維、語音內容 8 維，最後實驗數據如圖十六和圖十七。

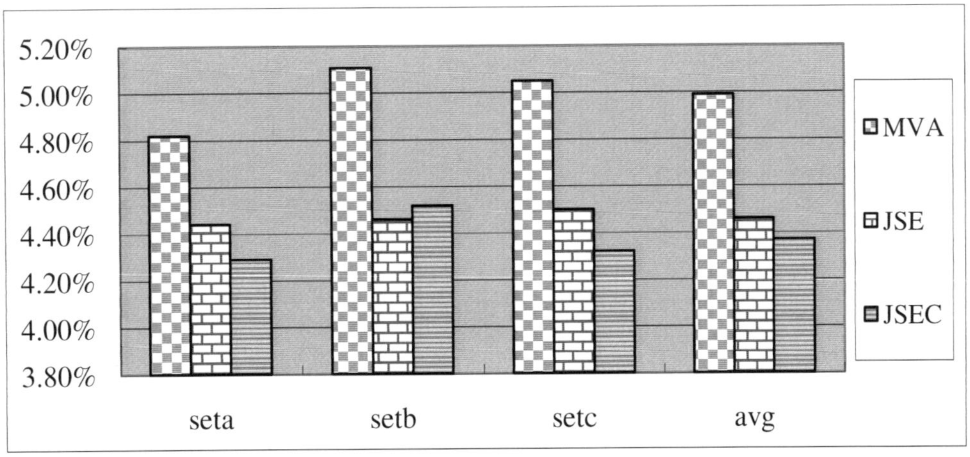

圖十六、complex backend 各系統方法不同環境之比較圖

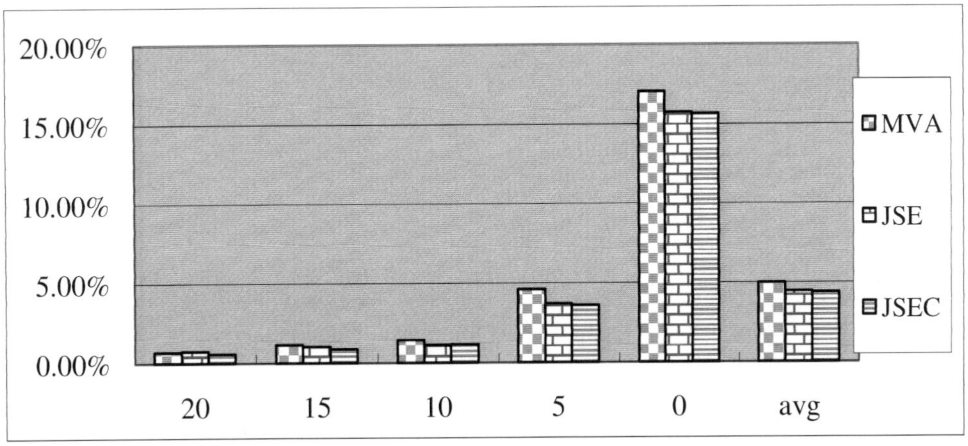

圖十七、complex backend 各系統方法不同 SNR 之比較圖

圖十六和圖十七可發現，mixture 從 3 拉到 20 之後，JSEC 錯誤率 4.37%，可以和 JSE 錯誤率 4.46%相當，甚至更低一點。

最後我們一樣統計了調適模型所需的參數量，如表三和圖十五所示：

complex backend			
模型所需參數	MVA	JSE	JSEC
mean	147264	147264	22464
variance	147264	147264	22464
weight	3776	3776	576
Transition	3598	3598	358
u	–	2945280	-
v	–	8835840	-
d	–	147264	-
u_{non}	–	-	149760
d_{non}	–	-	7488
u_{sp}	–	-	249600
v_{sp}	–	-	748800
d_{sp}	–	-	12480
g_{sp}	–	-	99840
r_{sp}	–	-	88
總共的參數量	47206	12230286	1313918
參數量的比例	1	40.51	4.35

表三、complex backend MVA 與改變參數量的 JSEC 比較表

其中，JSEC 的 mean 與 variance=(39*20*16=12480)+(39*64*3=7488) +(39*64*1=2496)

=22464 (35)

weight =20*16*11+64*3+64*1=576 (36)

$$u_{non} = 20x7488 = 149760 \tag{37}$$

$$d_{non} = 1x7488 = 7488 \tag{38}$$

$$u_{sp} = 20x12480 = 249600 \tag{39}$$

$$v_{sp} = 60x12480 = 748800 \tag{40}$$

$$d_{sp} = 1x12480 = 14800 \tag{41}$$

$$g_{sp} = 8x12480 = 99840 \tag{42}$$

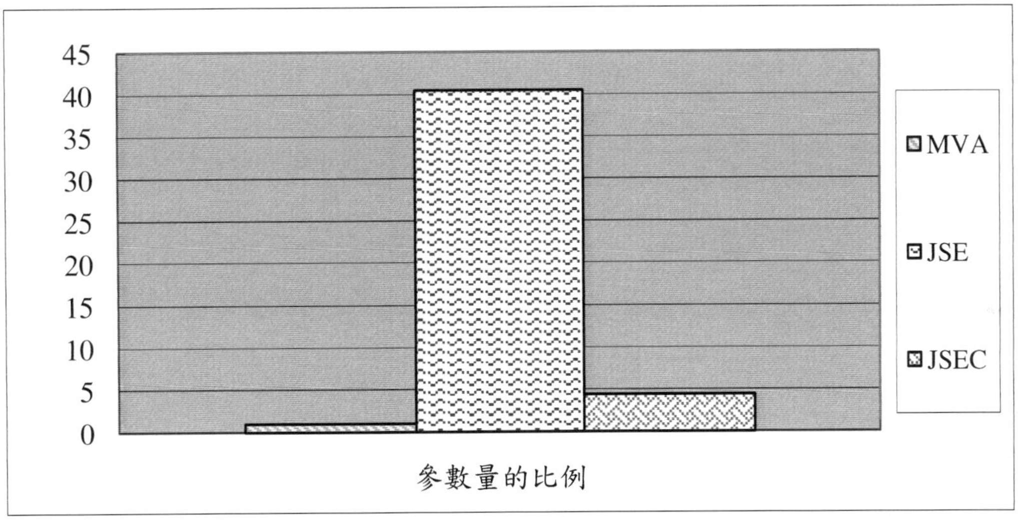

圖十八、complex backend MVA 與改變參數量的 JSEC 比例圖

從圖十八我們可以觀察出參數量依然遠小於先前的 JSE，JSE 比 JSEC 多 9 - 10 倍的參數量，而 JSEC 只比 MVA 多了 4 倍的參數量，運算量低很多。

四、結論

本論文的主要研究目標是提出新的 JSEC 方法，並且使用 Aurora2 做實驗，實驗數據最後做了總整理如圖十九和圖二十。由圖中我們提出的 JSEC 在 complex backend 的實驗當中，我們發現可以和原來 JSE 系統的錯誤率差不多，甚至可以更低一些，而且也比傳統方法 MVA 錯誤率 4.99%低了許多；除了辨認率之外，我們提出的方法也能使調適模型的參數量比原來的 JSE 降低了十分之一，JSE 的參數量是 MVA 的 40 倍，但 JSEC 只比 MVA 多了 4 倍的參數量而已，因此為更有效率的調適方法。.

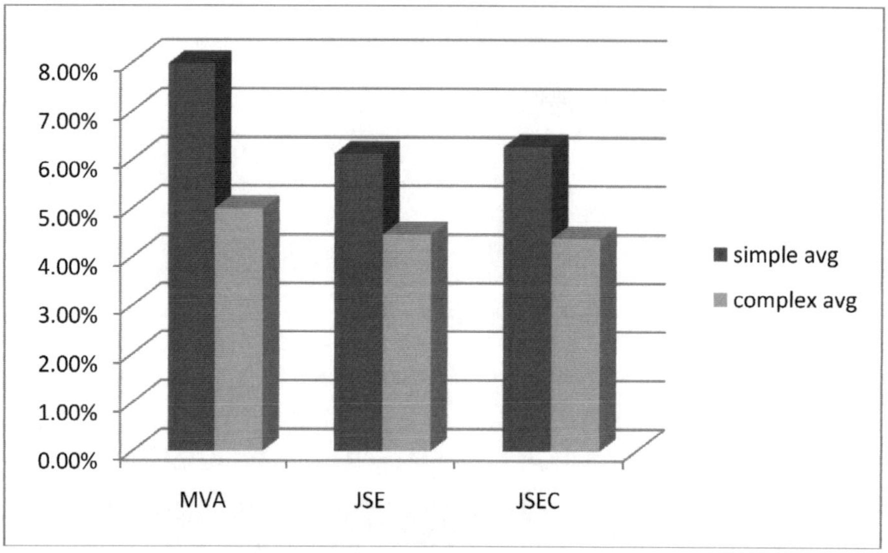

圖十九、平均錯誤率比較圖

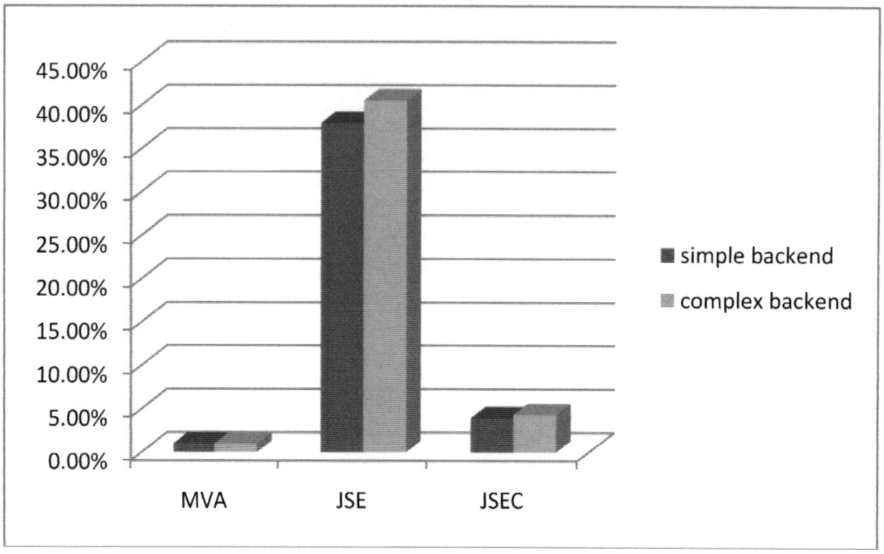

圖二十、參數量比較之比例圖

五、致謝

本論文所進行工作之成果，部分在國科會專題計畫編號 98-2221-E-027-081-MY3 和 97-2628-E-027-003-MY3 的經費補助之下順利完成，特此致謝。

參考文獻

[1] C.P. Chen, K. Filali and J. Bilmes, "Frontend Post-Processing and Backend Model Enhancement on the Aurora 2.0/3.0 Databases," in *Proc. ICSLP*, 2002.

[2] C.P. Chen, J. Bilmes and K Kirchhoff, "*Low-resource Noise-Robust Feature Post-Processing on Aurora 2.0*," in *Proc. ICSLP*, 2002.

[3] A. de la Torre, J. C. Segura, M. C. Benitez, A. M. Peinado and A. J. Rubio, "*Non-linear transformation of the feature space for robust speech recognition,*" in *Proc. ICASSP*, vol. I, 2002.

[4] A. de la Torre, A. M. Peinado, J. C. Segura, J. L. P. Cordoba, M. C. Benitez and A. J. Rubio, "*Histogram equalization of speech recognition for robust speech recognition*," *IEEE Trans. on Speech and Audio Processing*, vol. 13, no. 3, 2005.

[5] ETSI standard document, "*Speech processing, transmission and quality aspects (STQ); distributed speech recognition; extended advanced front-end feature extraction algorithm; compression algorithm; back-end reconstruction algorithm,*" ETSI Standard ES 202 212, 2003.

[6] C.J. Leggetter and P.C. Woodland, "*Maximum likelihood linear regression for speaker adaptation of continuous density hidden Markov models*," *Computer Speech Lang.*, vol. 9, 1995.

[7] J.L. Gauvain and C.H. Lee, "*Maximum a Posteriori estimation for multivariate Gaussian mixture observations of Markov chains*," *IEEE Trans.on Speech Audio Processing*, vol. 2, 1994.

[8] M. Gales and S. Young, "*Robust continuous speech recognition using parallel model combination*," *IEEE Trans. on Speech and Audio Processing*, vol. 13, no. 3, September 1996.

[9] L. Deng, A. Acero, M. Plumpe and X. Huang. "*Large-Vocabulary Speech Recognition under Adverse Acoustic Environments,*" in Proc. ICSLP 2000.

[10] M.J.F. Gales and P.C. Woodland, "*Mean and variance adaptation within the MLLR framework*," Computer Speech Lang., vol. 10, no. 3, pp. 249–264, 1996.

[11] 王瑞璟，基於聯合語者與雜訊環境因素分析之強健性語音辨認，國立台北科技大學電腦與通訊研究所碩士論文，2010 年，98 頁。

[12] P. Kenny, "*Joint Factor Analysis of Speaker and Session Variability : Theory and AlgorithmsMontreal*", Technical report CRIM-06/08-13 Montreal, CRIM, 2005

[13] Kenny, P., Ouellet, P., Dehak, N., Gupta, V., and Dumouchel, P., "A Study of Inter-Speaker Variability in Speaker Verification," IEEE Transactions on Audio Speech and Language Processing, July 2008.

[14] L. E. Baum, T. Petrie, G. Soules, and N. Weiss, "A maximization technique occurring in the statistical analysis of probabilistic functions of Markov chains", Ann. Math. Statist., vol. 41, no. 1, pp. 164–171, 1970.

Evaluation of TTS Systems in Intelligibility and Comprehension Tasks[1]

張瑜芸 Yu-Yun Chang
國立臺灣大學語言學研究所
Graduate Institute of Linguistics
National Taiwan University
june06029@gmail.com

Abstract

This paper aims at finding the relationships between intelligibility and comprehensibility in speech synthesizers, and tries to design an appropriate comprehension task for evaluating the speech synthesizers' comprehensibility. It is predicted that speech synthesizer with higher intelligibility, will have greater performance in comprehension. Also, since the two most popular used speech synthesis methods are HMM-based and unit selection, this study tries to compare whether the HTS-2008 (HMM-based) or Multisyn (unit selection) speech synthesizer has better performance in application. Natural speech is applied in the experiment as a controlled group to the speech synthesizers. The results in the intelligibility test shows that natural speech is better than HTS-2008, and HTS-2008 is much better than Multisyn system. Whereas, in the comprehension task, all the three speech systems present not much differences in speech comprehending process. This is because that the two speech synthesizers have reached the threshold of enough intelligibility to provide high speech comprehension quality. Therefore, although with equal comprehensible speech quality between HTS-2008 and Multisyn systems, HTS-2008 speech synthesizer is more recommended and preferable due to its higher intelligibility.

Keywords: speech synthesizers, intelligibility evaluation, comprehension evaluation, HTS-2008, Multisyn

1. Introduction

Recently, text-to-speech (TTS) system synthesizers have been evaluated from different aspects, such as intelligibility, naturalness, and preference of the synthetic speech, as noted by [1]. Since the final purpose of applying the synthetic speech is to make it usable to applications, it is worth carrying out experiments measuring the synthesizers' performance with human listeners. For measuring speech synthesizers, it was necessary to involve perception factors in synthetic speech evaluation, rather than merely evaluating the intelligibility, in order to better assess the speech synthesizers, as indicated by [2]. [3] also evaluated the aspect of the listener's perception on a comprehension task to learn how well the synthetic speech was created by the synthesizers could be understood by the listeners. Moreover, [2] had demonstrated that there was a strong relationship between the intelligibility and comprehension. Also, they had specified the intelligibility was one of the important factors that would affect listening comprehension. It is then worth observing the relationships between intelligibility and comprehension for speech synthesizers. Although several studies have been successfully evaluating the intelligibility of speech synthesizers, very few researchers have examined the association with comprehension. However, it is hard

[1] Acknowledgement: Thanks the people from University of Edinburgh - for the suggestions and comments offered by Simon King, and Catherine Mayo; the perception lab reserving and statistics helping supported by Rob Clark; and the HTS-2008 speech synthesizer provided by Junichi Yamagishi.

to measure comprehension, due to the fact that it involves cognitive processes which are hard to be captured and taken into account. Recent studies use post-perceptual comprehension tests to measure listeners' comprehension, but many have failed to distinguish differences between TTS systems. An appropriate strategy for evaluating the comprehension is still not found. Therefore, this research aims to design an adequate comprehension test for speech synthesis evaluation, and to try to discover the relationship between intelligibility and comprehension of TTS systems. In this study, the word "intelligibility" means the degree of each word being produced in a sentence; while the word "comprehension" means the degree of received messages being understood. This study predicts that speech synthesizers with higher intelligibility can be expected to obtain higher comprehension. In addition, this paper will also compare the most popular methods for building TTS systems in the Blizzard Challenge [4], which are unit selection [5] and hidden Markov models (HMMs) [6]. It will be interesting to find out whether the HMM-based, or unit selection approaches can better generate synthetic speech in terms of both intelligibility and comprehension.

2. Literature Review

2.1 HMM-based and Unit Selection speech synthesizers

In recent years, HMMs have been used to generate synthesized speech [7]. The basic procedures of implementing HMM-based speech synthesizers to produce synthetic speech can be grouped into two parts: a training part and a synthesis part [8]. There are two main advantages of using HMMs to generate speech synthesizers. One is that the produced synthesized speech can be smoothed and made to sound natural. The other is that, since the synthetic speech is created from HMM models with parameters [8], the characteristics of the voice can be modified easily with adequate parameter transformations. Nowadays, the latest version of the HTS (HMM-based Speech Synthesis System) used in the Blizzard Challenge is the HTS-2008. HTS-2008 used the adaptive speaker-independent approach, rather than the speaker-dependent method, to generate HMM-based synthesizers. The training database for HTS-2008 using the average voice model was 41 hours. In addition, to reduce the expensive computing time, forward-backward algorithm was introduced in the HTS-2008 [9].

As for unit selection speech synthesizers, basically, a natural speech database will be recorded by a single speaker, and then the units are extracted directly from the speech inventory and concatenated together to generate new utterances. A number of different unit sizes can be used to construct various types of unit selection speech synthesizers, such as phones, half phones, diphones, and variable sized units [10]. In recent Festival speech synthesis system, the Multisyn unit selection algorithm was introduced [5] with the diphone sized units, which could carry better acoustic features and higher level linguistic information than the phone sized units used in CHATR [11] and clunits [12]. It can produce open-domain speech voices in high speech quality, and does not need to be based on the context domain speech to produce better quality. In other words, higher quality synthesized speech can be created by using Multisyn unit selection algorithm even if the synthesized utterance is not one of the sentences in the recorded databases.

Since the Multisyn speech synthesis approach has the advantage of generating natural synthesized voices by extracting the diphone sized units straight from the speech signal with less expensive signal processing, an investigation of its distinctions from the HTS-2008 HMM-based speech synthesizer will be interesting and useful.

2.2 Evaluation of intelligibility

When evaluating the intelligibility of a speech synthesizer, the semantically unpredictable sentences (SUS) are frequently used. SUS sentences have been widely used in a dictation task and are recommended in evaluating intelligibility of speech synthesizers [13]. SUS sentences are sentences that are semantically unpredictable, but are still constructed grammatically syntactically. SUS sentences are used to prevent the process of assessing intelligibility from being influenced by linguistic cues. If semantically predictable sentences are used, listeners will learn the semantic and syntactic cues from the context, which will influence their performance in the intelligibility task [14]. [14] claimed that using SUS sentences in the intelligibility task could disrupt the predictable context. This conclusion was also supported by [15] reported that using SUS sentences could prevent from learning effect.

2.3 Evaluation of comprehension

The performance of various speech synthesizers can also be evaluated through comprehension tasks. Several researchers had indicated that comprehension evaluation is a valid way to assess intelligibility [16, 17]. This is because in intelligibility task, listeners will emphasize on recognizing individual words, rather than focusing on the meaning of sentences. However, the deeper information that lies within intelligibility cannot be examined by merely identifying each word.

There were four types of questions that had been used in previous speech synthesizer comprehension evaluation: surface structure questions, high proposition questions, low proposition questions, and inference questions. These questions were designed based on different levels of memory used during comprehension [18-20]. Surface structure questions required participants to recall specific words that occurred in the speech content; high proposition questions examined whether listeners could get a general idea from the speech content; low proposition questions asked more detailed information about the speech content than high proposition questions; finally, the inference questions measured whether the listeners could draw a conclusion from the speech. Since surface structure questions did not involve much comprehension ability, which did not meet with the purpose of present experiment, this type of question was not included in present study.

2.4 Some influential factors in intelligibility and comprehension

2.4.1 Short-term memory

The short-term memory is the biggest cognitive factor that has the greatest influence on the comprehension task. This is because short-term memory is used to store fractions of information temporarily until full information can be completely comprehended. Therefore, the technique is quite essential during the comprehension task. Furthermore, the load of short-term memory needs to be considered as well. As demonstrated from the concurrent task experiment by [21], the short-term memory had limited capacity. Goldstein [22] had identified two different levels of short-term memory, which were nominal level and supra-nominal level. He described that the nominal level short-term memory was involved in intelligibility tasks, focusing on qualitative evaluation. On the other hand, the supra-nominal level short-term memory were used in comprehension tasks, which required the information to be identified, processed, and understood. Therefore, as specified by previous researchers, it would be important to take short-term memory into account in this study.

2.4.2 Listeners' preferences

Another factor that may influence task performance is the listeners' preferences. [23] judged listeners' preferences from listeners' feedback on one natural speech and two speech synthesizers: MITalk and Votrax. The measurement was to assess the adjective words from the feedback. The researchers found that people preferred to listen to natural speech than to the two speech synthesizers, and MITalk system was preferred than Votrax system. Also, the intelligibility in MITalk system was evaluated to be higher than Votrax system. This result presented that there was a relationship between subjects' preferences and intelligibility of different speech synthesizers. Besides, [24] contended that listeners' preferences depended greatly on the quality of speech intelligibility. Moreover, [25] and [26] investigated that as the intelligibility quality got better, the degree of preference would also increase.

Therefore in this paper, HTS-2008 and Multisyn systems would be taken as the representatives of HMM-based and unit selection speech synthesizers during the evaluation. Also by modifying the evaluation approaches used in the previous studies and considering some cognitive factors, I try to design an appropriate comprehension test, which has not been found yet, rather than intelligibility test. In addition, through the newly modified comprehension test, I hope that stronger relationships between intelligibility and comprehension could be revealed.

3. Methodology

3.1 Subjects

A total of 25 native English speakers participate in the experiment, with 6 male and 19 female[2]. Table 1 shows the subjects' highest level of education status.

Table 1. Participants' highest level of education status

Degree of Education	Undergraduate	Master	PhD
Number of Subjects	5	11	9

All of the participants are students, studied at University of Edinburgh at present. There are 5 undergraduates, 11 master's students, and 9 PhD students involved in this experiment. The subjects' average age is 25.44 years old, with a standard deviation (SD) of 3.465 years old.

Table 2. Participants' English accents

English Accent	British	American	Scottish	Irish	Welsh	Indian
Number of Subjects	13	6	3	1	1	1

Table 2 above presents the survey results of the participants' English accents. In the English accent survey, 13 people have reported that they have a British accent, 6 have an American accent, 3 have a Scottish accent, 1 has an Irish accent, 1 has a Welsh accent, and 1 has an Indian accent. Only three participants have indicated that they are speech experts. No one has reported having a hearing disorder.

3.2 Materials

3.2.1 SUS sentences for intelligibility evaluation

Thirty SUS sentences are used as the material in intelligibility task. These SUS sentences are adopted from the 2008 Blizzard Challenge [27]. The structure of these sentences is "The (Determiner) + (Adjective) + (Noun) $_{\text{plural}}$ + (Verb) $_{\text{past tense}}$ + the (Determiner) + (Adjective) + (Noun) $_{\text{singular}}$". Although, this is the only structure used in the experiment, the English words in the SUS sentences are all in low frequency, in order to prevent the listeners from predicting the meanings easily. For example, one of the sentence used in the experiment is "The amicable chests became the unprepared cockroach". As the example shows, the intelligibility

2 Although the numbers of male and female participants were not balanced, the gender did not show any significance in statistical analysis. Therefore the gender difference is not considered in the paper.

task tends to make listeners hard to foretell the unheard information. In addition, listening to each sentence more than once is allowed, but are requested to keep as few times as possible.

3.2.2 News articles for comprehension evaluation

6 news articles extracted from BCC online news, which were considered to contain less story line cues, were used in the comprehension task. As in the study of [28], in order to reduce the news articles' text familiarity to the listeners, all of the topics were chosen to be research reports, which were likely to be less familiar to most of the listeners. The answers to the questions were designed with the assumption that there were no global and general knowledge to the articles. In other words, participants could not learn the answers through questions without listening. The average words in each article was about 238.8 words (SD = 21.1 words).

Each news article was attached with 10 questions. Five of the questions were designed as multiple-choice questions, while the other five questions were open-ended questions. Only the questions that required inferential skills would be arranged as multiple-choice questions with 4 multiple choices. On the other hand, factual questions with low level proposition information were assigned to open-ended questions. Below are figure 1 and 2, presenting the examples of the questions involved in the main experiment.

<u>Inferential Question</u>

Question: What would be the best topic for the news?

A. The poor quality of recent education.
B. The competition between colleges.
C. Colleges face the financial crisis.
D. Education revolution.

Figure 1. An example of inferential question in the main experiment

<u>Factual Question</u>

Question: How long would the growth of stubble usually appers?

____

Figure 2. An example of factual question in the main experiment

3.2.3 Synthesized speech and natural speech recording

HTS-2008 and Multisyn speech synthesizers were included in this experiment. Both speech synthesizers were constructed by collecting the voice from a single male speaker "roger" with British accent. Also, the male speaker's natural speech was taken as a controlled group in the experiment, to compare with the two synthesizers.

The recording was held in a Sound Lab of University of Edinburgh. The lab was equipped with a professional recording room and a control room. The voice was recorded through the MKH800 microphone, with the volume set at 60 dB. The recording wav files were all in single channel, with frequency at 16 kHz. The whole recording duration lasted approximately an hour.

The male speaker was a well-trained and professional reader, and had been cooperated with the Center for Speech Technology Research (CSTR) for a long while, participating in speech data recording. Therefore, steady and good quality of the natural speech was guaranteed.

3.2.4 Questionnaires

A questionnaire was assigned at the end of the experiment, asking for participants' basic information, whether they were a speech expert, and the average playing times of each sentence in intelligibility task. Some empty blanks were left for participants to write down their comments and suggestions to the experiment.

3.3 Procedure

There were two tasks included in the experiment. The first part was intelligibility task (listening 30 SUS sentences), and the other part was the comprehension task (listening 6 BBC news articles and answering questions). The experiment was taken place at the Perception Lab within the Informatics Forum building. The lab consisted of individual single rooms. Each room was equipped with an SAMSUNG 2043 screen monitor and a set of DT770 PRO headphones. Every participant would be arranged into one of the single rooms. The experiment was carried out by applying an online webpage. All the voices would come out from the headphones throughout the experiment, and the volume had been set into an adequate loudness to the listeners. No participants have complained about the sound volume.

3.3.1 Producing wav files

For intelligibility task and comprehension task, all wav files of SUS sentences and news passages had been produced by natural speech and the two synthesizers HTS-2008 and Multisyn. Since in intelligibility task, the wav files were generated by using every single sentence, the news passages used in the comprehension test were also synthesized into several single sentences for consistency. The sentences in the comprehension test were concatenated together into a passage afterwards, assigned with a silence interval of about 500 milliseconds between sentences.

There were some cases that needed to be carefully considered while producing synthesized speech, which the TTS systems could not identify the pronunciations as predicted in natural speech. For example, if the input text was "500MB", the synthesizers would not be able to pronounce it as "five hundred megabytes". Instead, the pronunciation turned out to be "five zero zero M B". Since the purpose of this comprehension test was to measure whether the synthesized passages were comprehensible to listeners, every word in the experiment should be made understood to listeners.

3.3.2 Pilot tests for comprehension task

Since the material used in the intelligibility test was the same as done in Blizzard Challenge, pilot tests for evaluating the intelligibility test were unnecessary. However, pilot tests were needed for the comprehension test in this study. The pilot tests for the comprehension test were done three times, measuring the length of the articles, the difficulties of the text and questions, and text familiarity. Two native English speakers were invited to do the pilot test and help evaluate the design of the comprehension task.

3.3.3 Main experiment

To make the wav files produced from HTS-2008, Multisyn, and natural speech equally distributed in the material, the wav files had been equally arranged into 6 different groups by using Latin Squares. Each group included 30 SUS sentences in the intelligibility test, and 6 news articles in the comprehension test. Then, each listener would be assigned to one of the six groups. In order to prevent the participants from having pressure on taking the exams, an announcement had been claimed beforehand indicating that they were not being tested but testing the systems.

The intelligibility task was taken first and then the comprehension task. This was done because more efforts were required while taking the comprehension task than intelligibility test, which participants needed to answer questions rather than type out what they heard. Therefore, it would be better for not depressing the listeners' patience and willingness at the first task. The listeners were informed in advance that the sentences in the intelligibility task might not be meaningful to them and were requested to try to make the listening as few times as possible. For the comprehension task, listeners were only allowed to listen to each news article once, and then answered questions without note-taking technique. Also, two extra subjective questions were followed to each news article, asking about the participants' confidence in completing the questions and their feelings of speech quality, scaling from 1 (very low) to 5 (extremely high). Finally, a questionnaire was given after completing the two tasks.

The intelligibility task of this experiment took around 15 to 20 minutes, while the comprehension test was about 25 to 30 minutes. [29] pointed out many researchers had found the participants would fail to sustain their attention after 20 to 35 minutes of doing the task. Due to the finding, participants were asked to have a 5-minute relaxing between the two tasks.

4. Results

4.1 Intelligibility task

Most of the participants specified that they only listened to each sentence once, and then typed down what they heard. For assessing SUS sentences, the measurement was based on calculating word error rates (WER) occurred in every sentence. Typos and homophones were allowed.

Table 3. Significant differences in intelligibility to the three speech systems: results of Pairwise Comparisons. ■ indicates a significant difference between a pair of systems.

	Natural	HTS-2008	Multisyn
Natural		■	■
HTS-2008	■		■
Multisyn	■	■	

In Pairwise Comparisons, as presented in Table 3, it reflects there are significant differences found between natural speech and HTS-2008 ($p = 0.005$), natural speech and Multisyn ($p < 0.001$), and also HTS-2008 and Multisyn systems ($p < 0.001$). To further verify the main effects in Pairwise Comparisons, the results in the Tests of Within-Subjects Contrasts present that there are significant main effects when natural speech compares to HTS-2008, $F(1, 249) = 10.135$, $p = 0.002$; and when HTS-2008 compares to Multisyn system, $F(1,249) = 26.685$, p

< 0.001. Therefore, it can be concluded that natural speech has significantly lower WER (M = 4.2%, SD = 10%) than the HTS-2008 (M = 6.7%, SD = 11.4%), and the HTS-2008 is even better than Multisyn system (M = 14.3%, SD = 21.6%).

4.2 Comprehension task

4.2.1 The results from news articles

A 3-point scale (0, 1, 2) had been applied in the experiment to score answers in the open-ended questions. If the responses to the comprehension questions were judged to be incorrect, 0 points are earned; if part of the answers are correct or the answers were too general and nonspecific, yet not wrong, 1 point would be given; and 2 points were given to the responses with fully correct and specific answers. A total of 10 points for 5 open-ended questions per news article could be possible. The examples of assessing the responses from open-ended questions had been provided in Table 4.

Table 4. Examples of assessing the responses from open-ended questions

Open-ended Question	Correct Answer	Listener Response	Score
What are the two new news channels that have been launched by Russia?	English and Arabic	English, Arabic	2
		English and Polish	1
		Arabic	1
		Don't know	0

The 3-point scoring system was adopted from [17]. The reason for not taking a 2-point binomial scoring scale was because in real life comprehension, it was not always an all correct or wrong situation, as described by [30]. However, since the multiple-choice questions only had one correct answer, the binomial scoring system was introduced to assess the responses. If the participants chose the correct choice, then 2 point would be earned; reversely, if choosing the wrong answer, 0 points was graded. There would be a sum of 10 points for 5 multiple-choice questions per news article. Therefore, the total score in each article was 20 points.

There is no significance found in the three speech systems; and neither in the interaction between systems and the question types. However, there is an obvious significant effect occurred in the question types, $F(1, 24) = 29.004$, $p < 0.001$. Therefore, the performance in open-ended questions is particularly worse (mean of error rate = 39.1%) than multiple-choice questions (mean of error rate = 28%). Furthermore, there is no significance found in the interactions between the systems and multiple-choice questions. However, there is a main effect observed in the interaction between systems and open-ended questions, $F(1.569, 37.649) = 7.348$, $p = 0.004$. Due to this fact, it can be interpreted that the results from open-ended questions shows the differences of the three systems.

Table 5. Significant differences in open-ended questions to the three systems: results of Pairwise Comparisons. ■ indicates a significant difference between a pair of systems

	Natural	HTS-2008	Multisyn
Natural			
HTS-2008			■
Multisyn		■	

As presented in Table 5, in the open-ended questions, a significant effect is revealed, only when the comparison between HTS-2008 and Multisyn system, $F(1, 24) = 25.939$, $p < 0.001$. Also, HTS-2008 performs a lot better (mean of error rate = 29.2%) than Multisyn system (mean of error rate = 49.8%) in answering the open-ended questions correctly.

4.2.2 A 5 point scale for subjective judgments

Two individual subjective questions were given at the end of each news articles: the confidence in making right responses to the questions (Confidence), and the feeling to the displayed speech quality (Quality). Both of the Confidence and Quality tests used a 5-point scale (from 1 to 5) in assessing the subjective questions. Higher points represented listeners with higher satisfactory, as shown below in Table 6.

Table 6. The 5-point scale measurement for the Confidence and Quality subjective tests

1 = Very low.
2 = Low.
3 = Average
4 = High.
5 = Extremely high.

Accordingly, there are main effects found in the systems, $F(1.45, 34.806) = 25.365$, $p < 0.001$, and also in the interaction between systems and the subjective tests, $F(2, 48) = 58.808$, $p < 0.001$. Nevertheless, there is no significant main effect observed in the subjective tests.

Table 7. Significant differences in the overall subjective tests performance to the three systems: results of Pairwise Comparisons. ■ indicates a significant difference between a pair of systems

	Natural	HTS-2008	Multisyn
Natural		■	■
HTS-2008	■		
Multisyn	■		

In Table 7, highly significant effects have occurred when the HTS-2008 compares to natural speech, $F(1, 24) = 24.758$, $p < 0.001$; and when Multisyn system compares to natural speech, $F(1, 24) = 37.536$, $p < 0.001$. While Quality compares to Confidence, two main effect is discovered in the interactions when the HTS-2008 compares to natural speech, $F(1, 24) =$

89.161, $p < 0.001$; when Multisyn compares with natural speech, $F(1, 24) = 73.059$, $p < 0.001$. Therefore, it can be concluded that the HTS-2008 is evaluated lower (M = 52.4%) than natural speech (M = 71.6%) in the subjective tests; and lower points is given to Multisyn (M = 52.2%) than to natural speech. Therefore, it is known that the natural speech has better results gained from the subjective tests, than the HTS-2008 and Multisyn systems.

In the Confidence test, it does not show any significant effect on the systems. This result indicates that listeners have equal confidence on natural speech, the HTS-2008, and Multisyn systems in answering the questions of each news article. As for the results from the Quality test, there is a significance discovered in the systems, $F(1.462, 35.085) = 61.249$, $p < 0.001$.

Table 8. Significant differences in Quality test to the three systems: results of Pairwise Comparisons. ■ indicates a significant difference between a pair of systems

	Natural	HTS-2008	Multisyn
Natural		■	■
HTS-2008	■		
Multisyn	■		

In the Quality test, natural speech has an extremely high score in speech quality identification (M = 82.8%), than the HTS-2008 (M = 48.8%) and Multisyn (M = 49.6%) systems. The results in Table 8 show no significance when HTS-2008 compares to Multisyn system. As a result of fact, in the subjective judgment of speech quality, natural speech is scored significantly higher than HTS-2008 and Multisyn systems. On the other hand, the HTS-2008 and Multisyn systems are rated with nearly the same synthetic speech quality by listeners. The results also demonstrate that although all the news articles are generated by concatenating the individual sentences together, natural speech still has better speech prosody than the other two speech synthesizers. This is because the recorder of natural speech knows the context and will be able to articulate the sentences with adequate prosody contours while recording. However, the news articles produced by HTS-2008 and Multisyn systems are simply synthesized into individual sentences, without considering the context prosody factor. As stated by [31], listeners preferred the speech systems with higher prosody quality. Therefore, listeners have graded natural speech with the highest score, than HTS-2008 and Multisyn systems.

5. Discussion

5.1 The discussion in the experiment results

5.1.1 The relationships between intelligibility and comprehension

In the intelligibility task, the results prove there are significant differences between the three systems. In the intelligibility performance, natural speech is better than HTS-2008, while HTS-2008 has greater performances than Multisyn system. According to the initial hypothesis in this paper, predicting systems with higher achievement in the intelligibility task would also preserve better accomplishment in the comprehension task. In this case, we can estimate the three systems in the comprehension task might have the same rankings as presented in intelligibility task. However, in the overall comprehension task performances, no significant effects are noticed within the three systems, which signify natural speech,

HTS-2008, and Multisyn all have relatively identical understandable quality for listeners. The outcomes in the comprehension task are against with the results in intelligibility task, and violate the hypothesis. Although, it seems that the comprehension task in this study has also failed to distinguish various speech systems, this is mainly because that the three systems have reached to the threshold of producing comprehensible speech quality. This can be demonstrated from the results in the Confidence test. In the Confidence test, there was no significance observed in the three systems, which meant that listeners have equivalent confidences in completing comprehension task produced by the systems. This implied that the three systems have given identical comprehension quality to the listeners. In addition, the techniques required for evaluating intelligibility and comprehension is different. In the comprehension task, the main intention is to understand and comprehend the global meanings offered in each news article, whereas, the intelligibility task is not evaluated by focusing on the meanings of the words but paying attention on every single word that can be heard. During the process of comprehending, even if some of the words are not clear to the listeners, the comprehension process will not be interrupted. Listeners can still acquire general meanings from the context of the articles. [14] had notified that with sufficient linguistic cues, it will be easy for listeners to derive learning effects and process the effects while comprehending. Thus, with sufficient cues provided from the three systems, no significant differences could be found within the three systems in the comprehension task. In other words, although natural speech, HTS-2008, and Multisyn systems are significantly different from each other in the intelligibility, they all obtain enough intelligibility quality for listeners to learn the linguistic cues and comprehend the texts. In addition, the WER of 14.3% in Multisyn system, can be taken as an intelligibility threshold reference for achieving high comprehensibility in speech synthesizers.

5.1.2 The influences of different question types used in the comprehension task

In the comprehension task, different question types used in the experiment will bring a significant effect to the systems' measurement. In this experiment, only the open-ended questions have a significant effect on the systems, rather than multiple-choice questions. This may be affected by the design purpose of each type of question. For the multiple-choice questions, they are assigned to be inferential questions, which need to be processed and comprehended before answering. Thus, this procedure is very much the same as in the real comprehension process, and presents that natural speech, HTS-2008, and Multisyn have the same comprehensibility. However, the open-ended questions are designed to be factual questions, and that make the process of answering the questions to be similar to the way in completing the intelligibility task. Both the open-ended questions and intelligibility task involve listening to the speech first, and then focus on the key words they can capture or understand. The only difference between them is the load of memory will be larger in open-ended questions, than in intelligibility task. As seen into the results of open-ended questions, the consequences are a little diverse from the results in the intelligibility task. In the open-ended questions, the performances in natural speech are identical with the HTS-2008, but are better than the Multisyn system. Whereas, the intelligibility task presents that natural speech is better than the HTS-2008, and Multisyn. In addition, even in the overall subjective tests and quality test show that natural speech has better achievement than HTS-2008. This may contribute to the reason that there were not enough participants included in the experiment (only 25 participants in this study). Therefore, it is assumed that if the number of participants increases, the significant effect between natural speech and HTS-2008 in open-ended questions might occur. Apart from the intelligibility and comprehension task, in the overall subjective tests and quality test, they are both consistent with the results specifying that the performances in HTS-2008 and Multisyn system are the same. In general, the entire experiment in present study has found that natural speech has greater consequences and performances than HTS-2008 and Multisyn systems.

5.2 Listeners' feedback and some suggestions for future studies

5.2.1 Listeners' feedback

In the intelligibility task, most of the participants found it interesting. Since the materials were all semantically unpredictable sentences, that would make up a lot of unexpected funny sentences. Still, some of the participants specified that there were a few words they seldom heard and seen in their life, and might lead to some misspelling or make up the spelling pronunciations. This problem had been solved in this study, which we allowed typos and homonyms while calculating the WER in the intelligibility task. They had also indicated that sentences with poor speech quality, it would be hard for them to recognize the words as real words.

Most of the participants reported that the second part of the experiment (comprehension task) was harder than the first part (intelligibility task). They stated that the displaying duration of news articles is a bit long for them to remember the all the information. Besides, the listeners had notified that if the article was presented with low speech quality, it would be harder for them to concentrate and follow up. In addition, they tended to focus more on the topic they were interested in, and answered more correctly on the questions. Some participants suggested that there should be an option of "do not know the answer" added into the multiple choice questions, to prevent them from guessing the answers.

Although there were comments coming from the participants, they still responded that the whole experiment was interesting, and they had a lot of fun during the process all in all.

5.2.2 Suggestions and modifications for future works.

According to the feedback received from the participants, there are some things that can be modified in the comprehension design to make the task better. Firstly, since most of the participants replied that the durations of news articles were a little bit too long, a pilot test for measuring the participants' feelings of duration need to be applied before carrying out the main experiment. Furthermore, since each news article is with different topics, there is no guarantee that the degree of text complexity and familiarity will still be the same between each article. The word "text complexity" used right here means the degree of comprehension effort that need to be devoted to listening to the article.

Due to the limitation of time, there were not enough listeners participating in each pilot test. In order to cease the individual problems and increase the results' objectivity in the test, it will be better to have at least 10 people included in the pilot test.

6. Conclusion

From the results in the intelligibility task, we find that the performance in natural speech is better than the HTS-2008, and HTS-2008 is proved to be greater than the Multisyn system. However, the results in the comprehension task present that the natural speech, HTS-2008, and Multisyn systems are with equal quality for listeners to comprehend. The explanation has been given in section 5.1.1, discussing the issue may lead to the reason that all the three systems obtain high enough intelligibility quality to be used in comprehending the news passages. Although the outcomes in the intelligibility task show that there are significant differences investigated within the three systems, their intelligibility have reached to the comprehension threshold to produce understandable high quality speech. In spite of the objective results in the comprehension task, in the overall subjective tests and the Quality test, both of them manifest that listeners consider natural speech is the best system of all, compared to the two speech synthesizers (HTS-2008 and Multisyn). Besides, the listeners feel that there is no difference between HTS-2008 and Multisyn systems.

For the design of the comprehension task, there is still one thing that needs to be mentioned. That is the comprehension task designed in this experiment could not directly evaluate the comprehension process, as stated by [2]. Since the questions are derived after listening, this kind of measurement is a post-perceptual comprehension. Therefore, the comprehension strategies involved in this study are all evaluating the products of the comprehension, rather than the process of it.

In general, from the results presented in this experiment, the HTS-2008 speech synthesizer is preferable and usable than Multisyn system in applications. Although the two systems have the same performance in comprehension, HTS-2008 is significantly better than Multisyn system in intelligibility.

7. References

[1] C. Stevens, *et al.*, "On-line experimental methods to evaluate text-to-speech (TTS) synthesis: effects of voice gender and signal quality on intelligibility, naturalness and preference," *Computer Speech and Language,* vol. 19, pp. 129-146, 2005.

[2] D. B. Pisoni, *et al.*, "Perception of synthetic speech generated by rule," in *Proceedings of the IEEE*, 1985, pp. 1665-1676.

[3] H. A. Sydeserff, *et al.*, "Evaluation of speech synthesis techniques in a comprehension task," *Speech Communication,* vol. 11, pp. 189-194, 1992.

[4] A. W. Black and K. Tokuda, "The Blizzard Challenge - 2005: Evaluating corpus-based speech synthesis on common dataset," in *Proceedings of Interspeech 2005*, Lisbon, Portugal, 2005.

[5] R. A. J. Clark, *et al.*, "Multisyn: Open-domain unit selection for the Festival speech synthesis system," *Speech Communication,* vol. 49, pp. 317-330, 2007.

[6] H. Zen, *et al.*, "The HMM-based speech synthesis system (HTS) version 2.0," in *Proceedings of ISCA SSW6*, Bonn, Germany, 2007.

[7] T. Yoshimura, *et al.*, "Simultanious modeling of spectrum, pitch and duration in HMM-based speech synthesis," in *Proceedings of Eurospeech*, 1999, pp. 2347-2350.

[8] Z. Heiga and T. Tomoki, "An overview of Nitech HMM-based speech synthesis system for Blizzard Challenge 2005," in *Proceedings of Interspeech 2005*, Lisbon, Portugal, 2005, pp. 93-96.

[9] S.-Z. Yu and T. Kobayashi, "An efficient forward-backward algorithm for an explicit-duration hidden Markov model," *IEEE Signal Processing Letters,* vol. 10, pp. 11-14, 2003.

[10] R. A. J. Clark, *et al.*, "Festival 2 - build your own general purpose unit selection speech synthesiser," in *Proceedings of 5th ISCA Speech Synthesis Workshop*,

Pittsburgh, USA, 2004, pp. 173-178.

[11] A. J. Hunt and A. W. Black, "Unit selection in a concatenative speech synthesis system using a large speech database," in *Proceedings of the ICASSP 1996*, Atlanta, USA, 1996, pp. 373-376.

[12] A. W. Black and P. Taylor, "Automatically clustering similar units for unit selection in speech synthesis," in *Proceedings of the Eurospeech 1997*, 1997, pp. 601-604.

[13] L. C. W. Pols, *et al.*, "The use of large text corpora for evaluation text-to-speech systems," in *Proceedings of the First International Conference on Language Resources and Evaluation*, Granada, Spain, 1998.

[14] C. Benoît, *et al.*, "The SUS test: A method for the assessment of text-to-speech synthesis intelligibility using Semantically Unpredictable Sentences," *Speech Communication,* vol. 18, pp. 381-392, 1996.

[15] G. A. Miller and S. D. Isard, "Some perceptual consequences of linguistic rules," *Journal of Verbal Learning and Verbal Behavior,* vol. 2, pp. 217-228, 1963.

[16] K. Yorkston, *et al.*, "Comoprehensibility of dysarthric speech: Implications for assessment and treatment planning," *American Journal of Speech-Language Pathology,* vol. 5, pp. 55-66, 1996.

[17] K. C. Hustad, "The relationship between listener comprehension and intelligibility scores for speakers with dysarthria," *Journal of Speech, Language, and Hearing Research,* vol. 51, pp. 562-573, 2008.

[18] P. A. Luce, "Comprehension of fluent synthetic speech produced by rule," Indiana University, Bloomington, IN 47405, Research on Speech Perception Progress Report 7, 1981.

[19] A. Salasoo, "Cognitive Processes and comprehension measures in silent and oral reading," Speech Research Laboratory, Indiana University, Bloomingtion, IN 47405, Research on Speech Perception Progress Report 8, 1982.

[20] D. B. Pisoni, *et al.*, "Perceptual evaluation of synthetic speech: Some considerations of the user/System interface," in *Acoustics, Speech, and Signal Processing, IEEE International Conference on ICASSP '83.*, 1983, pp. 535-538.

[21] J. V. Ralston, *et al.*, "Comprehension of synthetic speech produced by rule," Speech Research Laboratory, Indiana University, Bloomington, IN47405, Research on Speech Perception Progress Report 15, 1989.

[22] M. Goldstein, "Classification of methods used for assessment of text-to-speech systems according to the demands placed on the listener," *Speech Communication,* vol. 16, pp. 225-244, 1995.

[23] H. C. Nusbaum, *et al.*, "Subjective evaluation of synthetic speech: Measuring preference, naturalness, and acceptability," Speech Research Laboratory, Indiana University, Bloomington, IN47405, Research on Speech Perception Progress Report

10, 1984.

[24] H. Nusbaum, *et al.*, "Measuring the naturalness of synthetic speech," *International Journal of Speech Technology,* vol. 1, pp. 7-19, 1995.

[25] J. Terken and G. Lemeer, "Effects of segmental quality and intonation on quality judgments for texts and utterances," *Journal of Phonetics,* vol. 16, pp. 453-457, 1988.

[26] C. R. Paris, *et al.*, "Linguistic cues and memory for synthetic and natural speech," *Human Factors,* vol. 42, pp. 421-431, 2000.

[27] V. Karaiskos, *et al.*, "The Blizzard Challenge 2008," in *Proceedings of the Blizzard Challenge 2008 workshop* Brisbane, Australia, 2008.

[28] J. Lai, *et al.*, "The effect of task conditions on the comprehensibility of synthetic speech," presented at the CHI Letters, 2000.

[29] C. Delogu, *et al.*, "Cognitive factors in the evaluation of synthetic speech," *Speech Communication,* vol. 24, pp. 153-168, 1998.

[30] K. C. Hustad and D. R. Beukelman, "Listener coomprehension of severely dysarthric speech: Effects of linguistic cues and stimulus cohesion," *Journal of Speech, Language, and Hearing Research,* vol. 45, pp. 545-558, 2002.

[31] A. A. Sanderman and R. Collier, "Prosodic phrasing and comprehension," *Language and Speech,* vol. 40, 1997.

片語式機器翻譯中未知詞與落單字的問題探討

*蔣明撰　+黃仲淇　*顏合淨　*黃士庭　*張俊盛　++楊秉哲　++谷圳
*國立清華大學資訊工程學系
+國立清華大學資訊系統與應用研究所
++資訊工業策進會
{raconquer, u901571, fi26.tw, koromiko1104, jason.jschang}@gmail.com
++{maciaclark, cujing}@iii.org.tw

摘要

近年來，機器翻譯技術蓬勃發展並越顯重要。然而，現存的機器翻譯系統對於（系統未收錄）未知詞多採直接輸出到目標翻譯的方式。此忽略的舉動可能造成未知詞附近的選字錯誤，或是其附近的翻譯字詞順序錯置，因而降低翻譯品質或降低閱讀者對翻譯文章的理解。經過我們的初步分析，大約有 25%的系統未知詞可用重述（paraphrase）的方式來作翻譯，另外的 25%可利用組合單字翻譯來翻譯。另外，現有的片語式（phrase-based）機器翻譯系統對於落單字（singleton）的翻譯效果也未加重視。所謂的落單字是指系統在翻譯此字時必須單獨翻譯：此字沒法與前面或是後面的字組合成連續字詞片語或是文法翻譯結構。本研究將建構於片語式機器翻譯處理技術，開發未知詞翻譯模組和落單字翻譯模組。實驗結果顯示即使在不假額外的雙語資料，我們的未知詞翻譯模組仍勝出片語式翻譯系統，尤其是在包含有未知詞的句子上。

關鍵詞：未知詞，重述，片語式機器翻譯系統，落單字，機器翻譯

一、緒論

近年來，機器翻譯技術蓬勃發展並越顯重要。然而，現今先進的片語式機器翻譯系統對於（系統未收錄）未知詞與落單字（singleton）的處理仍有改進的空間。翻譯系統對於來源語（source language）未知詞採直接輸出到目標（target language）翻譯的方式，也就是說，系統並不處理未知詞。此忽略的舉動可能造成未知詞附近的選字錯誤，或是其附近的翻譯字詞順序錯置，因而降低翻譯品質或降低閱讀者對翻譯文章的理解。片語式機器翻譯系統之所以可以有令人滿意的翻譯效果在於其翻譯的過程常常是多個連續的來源語字詞一起翻譯到目標語。多個字詞一起翻譯的過程幫助了這些字詞翻譯的解歧，也就是所謂的字義解歧（Word Sense Disambiguation）亦或是字詞翻譯解歧（Word Translation Disambiguation）。以中文字「起」爲例。「起」有相當多的字義如「起床」、「上升」、「動身」、「發揮」等。不同字義的（英文）翻譯也都不盡相同。而片語式翻譯系統則會將「起」跟其周遭連續的字「的」、「很」和「早」一起看作是一個片語並翻譯成“get up very early”。換言之，解歧成「起床」字義。很少文獻針對片語式機器翻譯系統中的落單字翻譯效果進行分析。所謂的落單字是指系統在翻譯此字時必須單獨翻譯：此字無法與前面或是後面的字組合成連續字詞片語或是文法翻譯結構。落單字必然是片語式翻譯系統的自然天敵。目前系統多靠語言模型（Language Model）來選擇落單字的翻譯。但是語

言模型受限於字數限制，也不考慮像是字詞詞性等語言現象，大多數選擇最高頻的翻譯。落單字的翻譯解歧效果直接影響了翻譯之品質。

首先，我們分析了 NIST MT-08 的測試句。美國 NIST（National Institute of Standards and Technology）幾乎每年都會舉辦 MT 的比賽來促進自動翻譯研究的發展。經過我們的初步分析，大約有 25%的系統未知詞可用重述（paraphrase）的方式來作翻譯，另外的 25%可利用組合單字翻譯來翻譯。重述就是將未知詞轉換成意思相近但現於現有雙語語料中的字詞。重述的論文探討已經相當多且齊全。在這個計畫中，我們將著重在跟重述佔有相同重要角色的組合單字翻譯上。我們利用組合單字的翻譯來翻譯未知詞。我們的處理方法不假額外的雙語資料（文獻多直接藉由擴大雙語語料來減少未知詞），只利用現存的訓練資料來尋找可能的單字翻譯，也就是，系統已知字詞（in-vocabulary）翻譯。更精確的來說，我們組合排列現有的雙語訓練資料中未知詞的構成字之翻譯，並加以排序以得到較為可能的未知詞翻譯。例如：藉由雙語資料中「上」的翻譯 upper、above、rise 等，以及「肢」的翻譯 body、limbs 等可組合出 NIST MT-06 未知詞「上肢」的翻譯 upper limbs。類似的方法可以組合出形容詞-名詞複合字未知詞「韓戰」（Korean war），名詞-名詞複合字未知詞「邊貿」（border trade），動詞-形容詞複合字未知詞「成名」（become famous）之翻譯。其中，「邊貿」也是目前最尖端的翻譯系統 Google Translate 之未知詞。

另外，在針對片語式機器翻譯中落單字的翻譯時，我們發現，隨機抽樣 NIST MT-08 的五十中文句中，落單字佔全文比例高於 6%，落單字又以名詞、動詞居多，各佔 72%、21%。人工分析系統對於不同詞性字詞的翻譯品質差異很大，名詞可達五成正確率（precision），但是動詞只到兩成。分析 NTCIR 2011 年專利翻譯比賽的發展中資料，也顯示了類似比例—落單字佔全文比例約 5%。由上面幾組數據，我們知道落單字跟未知詞一樣，都是片語式機器翻譯系統急須面對處理的課題。我們預計利用「動詞-名詞」或是「動詞-副詞」搭配詞（collocation）來幫助落單字的解歧，以增加片語式機器翻譯系統之翻譯品質。畢竟，落單字要解歧就需要看稍微遠一點的字詞（context），而搭配詞往往又是幫助解歧的有用資訊（一個搭配詞一個字義 one sense per collocation）。以「起」和「打擊」這兩個多義字來作說明。它們的翻譯可能為 get up、rise、increasing、play、have 等，和 fight、combat、batting、bat 等。但是當「起」的附近有搭配詞「早」時 get up 較有可能，當附近有名詞搭配詞「作用」時 play、have 較有可能（此時的「起」有「發揮」的意思）。類似地，當「打擊」附近有搭配詞「犯罪」出現時 fight、combat 較有可能，而當其附近出現「區」,「棒球」時，則是 batting、bat 較為可能。由上面的例子，我們預期：不一定緊密相鄰的「動詞-名詞」或是「動詞-副詞」搭配詞，或稱為有彈性的搭配詞（flexible collocation），將可幫助片語式機器翻譯中落單字解歧。

本研究將建構於現有片語式機器翻譯處理技術，例如公開原始碼的 Moses 翻譯系統，開發未知詞翻譯模組和落單字翻譯模組。未知詞翻譯模組將從現存的雙語訓練資料中尋找未知詞構成字之翻譯，進而組合、排序未知詞的翻譯候選（利用雙語對應機率和單語流暢度加以排序）。排序好的翻譯候選將利用 XML 標記方法輸入片語式機器翻譯系統以作句子翻譯。落單字翻譯模組則會先利用大量的中文語料（如：Chinese Gigawords）抽取出數學統計上可能的搭配詞如「起…作用」、「打擊…犯罪」等。然後藉由這些搭配詞來為落單字解歧。解歧完後的落單字翻譯也是利用 XML 標記方法將翻譯候選提供給真正作句子翻譯的片語式機器翻譯系統。所以我們的方法除了使用雙語資料外，也會利用中文語料與英文語料（如： English Gigawords）取得中文搭配詞和英文語言模型。

二、研究方法（The Method）

本研究的範圍在於解決一般機器翻譯最常忽略的未知詞翻譯問題還有落單字的翻譯解歧問題。目標是，在現有雙語訓練語料中，爲未知詞找出翻譯並有效排序翻譯候選，另外，正確替落單字解歧，提升機器翻譯品質亦或是幫助閱讀者閱讀。我們將在以下章節詳述建構在現有片語式機器翻譯系統之上的未知詞翻譯模組和落單字解歧模組。

（一） 未知詞翻譯模組

未知詞翻譯模組針對未收錄於機器翻譯訓練語料的字詞產生並依照可能機率排列其翻譯候選。此模組可分爲兩個子模組—組成字模組和重述模組（目前我們較著重在文獻較少提到的組成字模組）。

1. 組成字模組

未知詞是系統未收錄的字詞，也就是，利用完全無誤比對（exact-match）來查詢雙語語料以得目標語翻譯必定是徒勞無功的。此模組將原本完全無誤比對（exact-match）的翻譯查詢轉換成一連串的部分比對（partial-match）查詢以先求得未知詞構成字的翻譯。接著從這些查詢回來的雙語配對（phrase pair）中，擷取出未知詞組成字的可能翻譯。最後，藉由組合組成字翻譯來翻譯未知詞，並且參考雙語字層級（character-level）翻譯機率和目標語的語言模型來排序未知詞翻譯候選。步驟大綱如下。

步驟一：我們將原本毫無所獲的字詞翻譯查詢轉換成一系列的萬用字元（wildcard）查詢以得組成字之可能翻譯。舉例來說，在不增加或是改變雙語語料的情況下，我們將對於未知詞「上肢」毫無斬獲的完全比對翻譯查詢變成「上*」和「*肢」的部分比對系列查詢，可查到翻譯配對如（上訴, appeal for）、（上升, increasing of）、（上段, upper block）等，和（四肢, the body）、（四肢, four limbs）、（義肢, prosthesis）等。

步驟二：上一個步驟得到的是來源語的字詞翻譯而不是未知詞組成字的翻譯，也就是，不是字層級（character-level）的翻譯。所以此步驟首先擷取出組成字的翻譯可能。我們是利用 N-gram 來擷取出組成字的可能翻譯。以翻譯配對（上段, upper block）和（四肢, four limbs）爲例。未知詞的組成字「上」和「肢」的可能翻譯分別是 “upper”、“block”、“upper block” 和 “four”、“limbs”、“four limbs”。値得注意的是，產生 N-gram 時，我們會考慮其變化型。這些產生的 N-gram，其實詞（例如名詞、動詞等）限定必須出現在一個大的字詞語料庫中（例如 WordNet），如果沒被此大的語料庫所包含將被剔除：畢竟一個沒被字詞語料庫包含的實詞，其 N-gram 應該也不是怎樣好的翻譯候選。最後，我們排除低頻的 N-gram。爲了公平的比較，次數是變化型的累加並共享。爲了得到原形化資訊，我們實作時，利用 NLTK 中提供的原形化器（Bird 等人, 2008）。表一呈現步驟一和步驟二的個別產物。

表一：步驟一和步驟二的輸出產物

步驟一		步驟二	
來源字詞	目標 phrase	來源字詞	目標 N-grams
四肢	the body	四肢	body
四肢	extremities	四肢	extremity
		四肢	extremities
四肢	four limbs	四肢	four
		四肢	limb
		四肢	limbs
		四肢	four limbs
義肢	prosthesis	義肢	prosthesis

表二：所有組成方法和特色組成方法所產生的雙語關聯例子。

字典中配對		雙語關聯	
source phrase	*translation*	所有組成方法 All Constituent	特色組成方法 Salient Constituent
肢	limb	(肢, limb)	(肢, limb)
手足	limb	(手, limb)	(足, limb)
		(足, limb)	
肢體	limb	(肢, limb)	(肢, limb)
		(體, limb)	
後肢	hind limb	(後, hind)	(肢, hind)
		(肢, hind)	(肢, limb)
		(後, limb)	(肢, hind limb)
		(肢, limb)	
		(後, hind limb)	
		(肢, hind limb)	

步驟三：我們利用雙語對應關係來刪除較不可能的組成字翻譯。步驟二所產生的 N-gram 有時候跟組成字的關聯是相當相當少的。為了減少計算量和增加翻譯的準確度，我們將去除比較不可能的組成字翻譯 N-gram。以針對部分比對查詢「*肢」所找出來的翻譯配對（四肢, four limbs）為例。因為 “four” 和 “limbs” 皆是常見且高頻的實詞，步驟二將會保留兩者，並視為組成字「肢」的可能翻譯。我們很明顯的知道雖然 “limbs” 是其合理的翻譯，但是中文應該是「四」才對的 “four” 顯然不是。也因此需要此步驟來檢驗存留下來的組成字翻譯和組成字的關係強弱。

首先，我們利用雙語字典如 bilingual WordNet 來建立雙語對應關係。建立關係的方式可分爲兩種方法—所有組成和特色組成方法。我們詳述如下。

- 所有組成（all-constituent）方法：針對每一個字典中的翻譯配對<*source phrase, translation*>，我們爲 *source phrase* 中的所有組成字和 *translation* 中的所有 N-gram 建立起對應關係。也就是說，一旦一個 *source phrase* 中的組成字和 *translation* 中的 N-gram 有共同出現過，他們之間就會有一個連結。以字典中的<“後肢”，“hind limb”>爲例。「後」和「肢」這兩個構成字將會和“hind limb”的 N-gram 有所連結。我們會爲此配對建立 6 個雙語關聯（請參見表二）。

- 特色組成（salient-constituent）方法：相較於上述方法，此方法只會爲 *source phrase* 中的特色組成字和 *translation* 的 N-gram 建立關聯。一個 *source phrase* 中的組成字是特色組成字如果此組成字和 *translation* 是最有相關的。嚴謹的來說，針對字典中配對<*source phrase, translation*>，特色組成字 *c** 是利用下面的公式而得

$$\arg\max_{c} Dice(c, translation) = \arg\max_{c} \frac{2 \cdot Count(c, transaltion)}{Count(c) + Count(translation)}$$

  其中 *c* 代表 *source phrase* 中的組成字，而 *Count*(·)代表字典內的頻率。以<“後肢”，“hind limb”>爲例。我們比較 *Dice*(“後”，“hind limb”）和 *Dice*(“肢”，“hind limb”）來決定特色組成字。因爲 *Count*(“後”，“hind limb”)和 *Count*(“肢”，“hind limb”)爲 1 且「後」、「肢」、和“hind limb”發生次數個別爲 1073、201、1，因此擁有較高 Dice 值的「肢」被選爲「後肢」的特色組成字，進而註冊雙語關聯(“肢”，“hind”)、(“肢”，“limb”)、和(“肢”，“hind limb”)（可參見表二）。我們可以知道特色組成方法所產生的雙語關聯將是所有組成方法所產生的子集合。

一旦建立起字典的雙語關聯，我們將可以刪除沒出現在關聯內的組成字和其上一步驟產生的 N-gram 配對。舉例來說，針對組成字「肢」所找到的翻譯配對（四<u>肢</u>, four limbs）及步驟二所允許的 N-gram（四<u>肢</u>, four）將在步驟三中被去除。因爲組成字和其 N-gram 配對（<u>肢</u>, four）沒在表二中出現。在實作上，我們首先利用所有組成方法來去除翻譯候選且保存高召回率。如果存留下來的組成字翻譯候選仍是超過門檻值（threshold），我們再使用特色組成方法來更積極作刪除以達到高準度。另外，這些雙語關聯也用作軟限制（soft constraint）而其頻率則當成是下一步驟排序的特徵（feature）。

步驟四：我們利用圖一的演算法來組合出並排列未知詞的翻譯候選。首先我們爲未知詞 *O* 的每一個組成字 *c* 從雙語翻譯對應 *TE* 中抽取出其翻譯 *SubTrans*（利用上述步驟一到三）。*SubTrans* 是一個 list 其元素像（*source word, target N-gram*），其中 *source word* 包含了 *O* 的組成字。然後（圖一步驟 1b），我們使用雙向條件機率（bidirectional conditional probabilities）來測量組成字和其翻譯的雙語關聯度，並將這樣的資訊紀錄在相對應的字層級(character-level)位置上。*CandList* 內的元素將像(*c*,(*source word, target N-gram*), P(*target N-gram*|*c*)· P(*c*|*target N-gram*))。其中雙向條件機率 P(*target N-gram*|*c*)和 P(*c*|*target N-gram*)則是由字層級（character-level）對應的平行語料（parallel corpus）訓練而來。以未知詞「上肢」爲例。我們首先爲組成字「上」和「肢」取得 *SubTrans*{(“<u>上</u>訴”，“appeal”), (“<u>上</u>策”，“policy”), …, (“<u>上</u>段”，“upper”)}和{(“四<u>肢</u>”，“limb”), (“四<u>肢</u>”，“limbs”), …, (“義<u>肢</u>”，“prosthesis”)}。然後我們計算組成字和其 N-gram 的對應強度並將這些資訊紀錄在 *CandList* 中（可參考表三）。

```
procedure GenerateAndEvaluateCandidates(O, TE, C, CT)
      for each constituent c in the OOV O
(1a)      SubTrans = RetrieveSublexicalTranslations(c, O, TE)
(1b)      CandList[position (c, O)] = BilingualInfo(SubTrans, c, C)
(2a) Straight = CandList[1]
(2b) Inverted = CandList[|O|]          // where |O| denotes the length of O
      for each constituent position cp >1 in ascending constituent positions of O
(3a)      Straight ⊗ = CandList[cp]
      for each constituent position cp <|O| in descending constituent positions of O
(3b)      Inverted ⊗ = CandList[cp]
(4a) Straight = MonolingualInfo(Straight, CT)
(4b) Inverted = MonolingualInfo(Inverted, CT)
      Candidates = Straight + Inverted
(5)   RankedCandidates = Sort Candidates in decreasing order of probability P
(6)   Return the top N RankedCandidates with probabilities P exceeding θ
```

圖一：組合並排列未知詞之翻譯候選

表三：針對未知詞「上肢」的 *CandList* 樣本

CandList	*c*	*source word*	*target N-gram*	P(*target N-gram*|*c*) · P (*c*|*target N-gram*)
CandList[1]	上	上訴	appeal	5×10^{-5} · 0.17
	上	上策	policy	1.2×10^{-7} · 1×10^{-9}
	上	上段	upper	0.02 · 0.56
CandList[2]	肢	四肢	limb	0.05 · 0.01
	肢	四肢	limbs	0.05 · 0.01
	肢	義肢	prosthesis	0.004 · 0.12

一旦我們有組成字的翻譯，我們便可產生未知詞翻譯候選。雖然未知詞的翻譯範圍遠小於翻譯一整個句子。翻譯的重組（re-ordering）仍是有可能發生。例如，「調」和「氣」的個別翻譯是“adjustment”和“air”，「調氣」的翻譯則是倒置成“air adjustment”。也因此，全順接（straight）和全反接（inverted）的情況都會被考慮。在圖一步驟 3 中，Straight 和 Inverted 會接續的涵蓋未知詞的組成字：邊收集組成字翻譯邊累乘翻譯的機率。每一個組合而成的翻譯候選 *TransCand* 的字詞翻譯分數是由雙向條件機率的乘積來推估。計算方式如下：

$$P_{trans} = \sqrt[|o|]{\prod_{c_i \in o} p(c_i \mid target\ N-gram_{ij}) \cdot P(target\ N-gram_{ij} \mid c_i)}$$

其中 c_i 代表未知詞的組成字而 *target N-gram*$_{ij}$ 代表 c_i 其中一個組成 *TransCand* 的翻譯。以未知詞「上肢」之組成字翻譯("上", ("上段", "upper"), 0.02 · 0.56)和("肢", ("四肢", "limb"), 0.05 · 0.01)爲例。我們會產生一個全順接的翻譯候選("上肢", "upper limb", $((0.02\cdot 0.56)(0.05\cdot 0.01))^{\frac{1}{2}}$)和一個全反接的("上肢", "limb upper", $((0.02\cdot 0.56)(0.05\cdot 0.01))^{\frac{1}{2}}$)。

除了利用雙語資訊外，我們也利用了單語資訊來檢測翻譯候選。每一個翻譯候選的 Mutual Information（*MI*）值將會利用下式計算出來。

$$MI(w_1, w_2) = \log_2\left(\frac{\Pr(w_1, w_2)}{\Pr(w_1)\Pr(w_2)}\right)$$

其中 w_1 和 w_2 是 *TransCand* 中的 bigram。對於 *MI* 值超過門檻值的翻譯候選我們將會算出目標語言的語言模型機率 P_{TLM}(*TransCand*)並將其乘在字詞翻譯機率上如下式（以得到評量翻譯候選的分數）

$$Score(TransCand) = P_{trans}(TransCand)^{\lambda_1} \cdot P_{TLM}(TransCand)^{\lambda_2}$$

其中 λ_i 是特徵權重值而 $\sum \lambda_i$ 等於 1。P_{TLM} 用來幫助辨識組合的翻譯候選的流暢度（fluency）。

演算法最後回傳前 *N* 個 *Score* 值超過門檻值 θ 的翻譯候選。這些候選將被當作是可能的未知詞翻譯。發動未知詞模組的門檻值 θ 和 *N* 將會利用發展中資料來尋找。

2. 重述模組

重述模組的目標在於將系統未收錄的未知詞轉換成意思相近或同義的系統已知詞（in-vocabulary）。再藉由已知詞來取得對應未知詞的翻譯。以未知詞「中餐」爲例。我們首先將其轉換成翻譯系統收錄並相似或同義的詞「午餐」、「午飯」等，再排序這些詞的翻譯當作是「中餐」的翻譯候選。

我們可以利用手工編撰辭典（thesaurus）或是機器學習（machine learning）技術來重述未知詞。手工編撰的資源如同義詞詞林或是 Sinica BOW （Bilingual Ontology WordNet）可加以利用。同義詞詞林可以直接提供高準度的未知詞同義字，而 Sinica BOW 則可利用翻譯相同或是近似來提供未知詞的重述。利用翻譯的重述，文獻上將其稱爲依賴第二語言（此例爲英文）的字詞層級（lexical-level）重述。舉例來說。在一個雙語字典或是漢英字典裡面，如果收錄翻譯條目（ "中餐", "lunch" ）和（ "午餐", "lunch" ），我們將可以知道「中餐」和「午餐」同屬一個翻譯，在某些情境下同義，可互換，互爲重述。仰賴第二語言的重述，其來源不一定是高準度的人工編撰辭典，也可能是高涵蓋率的自動字詞對應（word alignment）結果（其訓練資料通常是做好句子對應的平行語料，如 Marton 等人），亦或是混合高準度的字典和高涵蓋率的自動對應。

機器學習技術如分布相似法（distributional similarity）或是最大熵值法（maximum entropy）可推敲習得並排序未知詞的可能相似詞或是同義字。詳細地說，我們利用大量中文語料（如 Chinese Gigawords）中各字詞的前後文字（context words）來分析哪些文字附近的字詞非常接近。前後文字接近的字詞則可以視爲互爲重述。例如：互爲重述的兩詞「中餐」和「午餐」前後皆常出現「吃」和「享用」。在實作面上，模組可將重述詞限制在高頻且出現雙語語料中的數千個中文詞，以減少計算量。另外，爲了避免資料稀疏（data sparseness）問題，也許可以考慮字詞的類別而不是字的本身。手工辭典包含分類訊息如 Sinica BOW 或 E-HowNet 或是利用單語或雙語之自動字詞分類技術如（Och 1999），將可提供類別資訊。

相較於上述互爲對等的重述，Mirkin 等人在 2009 年利用推演規則（entailment rule）來重述未知詞。所謂的推演規則是：如果 A 可以推演出 B，那麼 B 就是 A 較爲一般的詞語。也就是說 A 是比較特定（specific）的詞，而 B 則比較一般（general）。舉例來說。未知詞 "skyscraper" 可以推演出 "building" ，那麼我們就可以利用 "building" 的翻譯來翻譯 "skyscraper" 。Mirkin 等人運用 WordNet 的上、下位詞資訊來取得推演規則（其重述的過程仍是有包含對等重述，利用的是 WordNet 的同義詞群組（synset））。實驗結果顯示「重述後的未知詞，有助於產生讀者更易了解原文的翻譯，潛在地，對於後處理編輯（post-editing）有所幫助」。

（二） 落單字翻譯模組

當一個單字無法與週遭字詞結合成連續片段時，我們說此單字落單存在，無法型成片語。對於這樣的落單字，片語式機器翻譯系統很難利用它前後字詞搭配解歧的優勢，爲其找出適當正確的翻譯。此模組架構在現有的片語式機器翻譯系統之上，以預處理（pre-processing）的方式爲落單字解歧（減少、限定翻譯候選），以避免片語式系統以受限的語言模型單獨翻譯落單字。

(1) 藉由單語語料取得數學統計上可信的搭配詞
(2) 從翻譯表中推衍出跳躍式 bigram 配對（skipped bigram pair）
(3) 輸出上述產物

圖二：解歧階段之前處理

圖二顯示該階段之前處理步驟。我們首先利用（Smadja, 1993）的方法從大量的單語語料庫（如：Chinese Gigawords）中抽取搭配詞。Smadja 的方法留意兩個單字是否常常一起出現、是否在某種距離下常常一起出現。舉例來說。從語料庫中我們可以發現「起」、「作用」常常距離一，因爲夾著形容詞（如：「起 極大 作用」、「起 承先啓後 作用」），也常常距離二，因爲多了副詞「了」（如：「起 了 極大 作用」、「起 了 正面的 作用」）。經過 Smadja 方法中的 *MI* 值、距離標準差、還有變異數的過濾篩選後，我們將所留下來的字詞搭配視爲數學統計上可信的搭配詞。

有了單語搭配詞後，我們還需要搭配詞的翻譯。在不增加雙語訓練資料的前提下，我們利用底層（underlying）片語式機器翻譯系統如 Moses 從平行語料中產生的翻譯表（phrase table）來推演出搭配詞翻譯。Moses 首先利用 GIZA++來作字詞對應（word alignment），接下來套用 grow-diag-final 的演算法來合併 GIZA++雙向的字詞對應結果。這樣產生的翻譯內容如集合{（"起 正面 作用"，"play a positive role"），（"起 正面 作用"，"have a positive effect"），…,（"早 起"，"get up early"），（"起 得 很早”，“get up very early”），…}。

爲了解歧落單字一它與前後字合成的片段未見於翻譯表中，我們將在翻譯表的翻譯配對中跳躍的選取來源語的字詞，並利用翻譯表中字詞對應結果來選擇這些字詞在目標語的翻譯。 以翻譯配對（“起 正面 作用”，“play a positive role”）和（“起 得 很 早”，“get up very early”）爲例。注意：字詞配對以反白還有下底線來呈現。如果我們跳躍的選擇「起」和「作用」，我們可以得到翻譯配對（“起 … 作用”，“play … role”）；如果我們跳躍的選擇「起」和「早」，我們可以得到翻譯配對（“起 … 早”，“get up … early”）。我們將這樣跳躍取得的翻譯配對稱作跳躍式 bigram 配對，因爲在中文端限制兩個字詞。

在執行時，我們首先在句子的固定範圍（window size）內尋找落單字的搭配詞。利用較爲可能的搭配詞來限定落單字的翻譯候選。例如在句子「我國警方有效打擊青少年國際犯罪」的落單字「打擊」有其名詞搭配詞「警方」、「犯罪」，形容詞搭配「國際」。利用這些搭配詞的對應翻譯如（“警方…打擊”，“the police … fight”）、（“打擊…犯罪”，“fight … crimes”）可抽取出落單字的翻譯候選 fight。以降低或直接排除「打擊」在該上下文中較不可能的翻譯如 bat 和 batting 的排序。同樣地，「起」可以分別利用「早」和「作用」解歧成“get up”、“play”和 “have”。

三、實驗設定

目前實驗專注在未知詞組合字翻譯模組上，未來也會涵蓋其他如落單字解歧模組的實驗分析。在此章節中，我們首先介紹底層的（underlying）機器翻譯系統 Moses 和我們如何將翻譯候選加入此系統（章節 3.1）。再來，我們敘述實驗中會用到的資料，包含訓練還有發展資料。章節 3.3 則是敘述我們如何根據發展中資料來更改查詢方式以取得未知詞翻譯候選。最後，我們描述微調與設定系統參數的過程。

（一）底層片語式機器翻譯系統

我們所提出的未知詞組合字模組只針對未知詞提供翻譯候選，因此必須架構再現有的翻譯系統上。在實驗時，我們選用目前先進表現優異的片語式機器翻譯系統 Moses（Koehn 等人 2007）作爲我們的底層翻譯系統。Moses 提供簡單的 XML 標記語言讓外部模組所產生的單字或是字詞組的翻譯可以輕鬆被其利用，而不會更改到像是 Moses 內部的翻譯模組（translation model）與語言模組（language model）。

（二）資料集（data sets）

我們使用 Hong Kong Parallel Text（LDC2004T08）和 ISI 中英平行語料（LDC2007T09）來訓練 Moses 的翻譯模組（translation model）和重排模組（reordering model）。這些語料的中文部分是利用 CKIP 中研院斷詞器（Ma 和 Chen, 2003）來斷詞。我們使用標準化的設定來跑 Moses：跑 GIZA++（Och 和 Ney, 2003）來取得字詞對應、grow-diagonal-final 演算法（Koehn 等人, 2005）來結合雙向字詞對應結果、和在（Koehn 等人, 2005）內介紹的方法來抽取雙語對應。至於語言模型（language model），我們使用第三版 English Gigaword 中的新華新聞部份（LDC2007T07）。大約有 800 多萬個句子利用 SRILM 工具（Stolcke, 2002）來建立 trigram 的語言模型。

另一方面，我們的未知詞組合模組使用 WordNet 3.0（Miller 等人, 1990）和 Sinica BOW（Huang 等人, 2004）來過濾限制組成字的翻譯候選（章節 2.1.1）。在計算 *MI* 值上我們利用第三版 English Gigaword（LDC2007T07）和 Web 1T fivegram（LDC2006T13）資料。我們利用與訓練 Moses 相同的平行語料還有目標語語料來分別計算雙語組成字和目標語單字機率（也就是 bidirectional conditional probabilities）和目標語流暢度。

（三）查詢形式和雙語資源

表四：未知詞長度和個數分析（發展中資料）

未知詞長度	未知詞個數	百分比(%)
1	56	4.4
2	683	53.7
3	352	27.7
4	115	9
5+	67	5.3

我們利用 NIST MT-08 的資料來分析未知詞問題。在這份總共 1,357 句資料中，有 637 個句子有未知詞（共 1,273 個未知詞）。在這些未知詞中，我們將未知詞長度和個數關係列於表四。在後續實驗中，我們專注在幫助佔超過一半比例的雙字（two-character）未知詞尋找組合式翻譯候選。爲了更進一步分析未知詞的類型、查詢組合字翻譯的形式、適合查詢的雙語資料，我們隨機抽取 100 個包含有（至少一個）二字（two-character）未知詞的句子。表五成列出我們人工針對這 100 句中的未知詞所作的未知詞類型分析。我們在作分析時，會手動的將未知詞的翻譯從 NIST MT-08 的對應參考翻譯（reference translation）中標示出來。就像是圖六中包含有「上肢」未知詞的例句。我們的組合字翻譯模組是特別設計來處理表五中佔了四分之一強的 *combination forms* 未知詞。詳細資料可參考表五。

表五：未知詞型別、其定義和例子

未知詞型別	未知詞型別之定義	例子	未知詞個數
Order Variants	Sequence of characters reversed without changing the original meaning	療治(治療) (treat)	1
Writing Variants	Replacement between simplified and traditional Chinese characters	念書 (唸書) (study)	1
Domain Specific	Domain specific terminologies	勤務 (service support) 二傳 (setter)	2

Word + Suffix	Words composed by a content character (underscored character) and a not translated function character	忙著 (busy) 爐子 (stove)	4
Informal	Used in conversation or informal writing	看頭 (worth watching) 幹麼 (what)	6
Old Use	Words rarely in use now	古稀 (60 years old) 橫流 (all over)	8
Name Entity	Name entities could be transliterated such as person, place, and organization	布希 (bush) 膠州 (jiaozhou)	12
Segmentation Error	Words erroneously split by the segmentation system	領式 (開領式) 會兒 (這會兒)	16
Rare Paraphrase	Words could be translated by replacing with its paraphrases	踐行 (practice) 訪談 (interview)	25
Combination Form	Words could be translated by combining sublexical translations	上肢 (upper limbs) 肌力 (muscle strength)	25

直覺上，針對一個雙字未知詞 c_1c_2，有四種下萬用查詢的方式以得到組合字的翻譯。表六顯示第一種和第二種查詢形式可以找出最多翻譯候選。我們的模組就採用此兩種查詢形式。以未知詞「上肢」爲例。我們將會利用「上*」和「肢*」以及「上*」和「*肢」來查詢組合字的翻譯。

另一方面，在利用上述兩種查詢形式下，我們比較了不同雙語資料尋找組成字翻譯的有效度。我們比較了下面幾種資料的翻譯擊中率（translation hit rate）：林語堂的漢英字典（http://humanum.arts.cuhk.edu.hk/Lexis/Lindict/）、LDC 翻譯字典（LDC2002L27）、字層級的翻譯表（character-based phrase table）、和字詞層級的翻譯表（word-based phrase table）。在 25 個 *combination forms* 未知詞中，他們的擊中率分別是 0.64、0.68、0.60、0.88。字詞層級的翻譯表有最高的翻譯擊中率，因此被選爲我們查詢組成字翻譯的查詢對象。

表六：針對兩字詞 c_1c_2 使用不同查詢形式可翻譯的未知詞個數

查詢形式	可翻譯的未知詞個數	例子：未知詞	例子：對應的中文字詞
「c_1*」和「c_2*」	17	上肢 (upper limbs)	(上方 肢體)
「c_1*」和「*c_2」	9	上肢 (upper limbs)	(上方 四肢)
「*c_1」和「c_2*」	2	震魔 (quake demon)	(地震 魔鬼)
「*c_1」和「*c_2」	1	鐘體 (bell body)	(時鐘 身體)

（四）參數設定

在這章節中，我們利用 50 句的發展資料來微調設定（tune）模組中的兩個參數—回傳的翻譯候選個數 *N* 還有被用來踢除較不可能的翻譯候選之門檻值 θ。這 50 句的發展資料每一句都有至少一個雙字未知詞，並且 25 句中的未知詞是型別 *combination forms*。

為了選用一個適當的 *N*，我們首先觀察那 25 句包含有 combination-form 的未知詞對於不同 *N* 值的翻譯表現。在此，翻譯表現是由 *Mean Reciprocal Rank*（*MRR*）來作評估。*MRR* 被定義為使用者在系統回傳的翻譯清單中定位第一個正確翻譯所需作的努力。*MRR* 介於 0、1 之間，1 又代表正確的翻譯總是在清單的最上頭。表七統整了不同 *N* 的涵蓋率和 *MRR* 值。在考量涵蓋率、*MRR*、和翻譯的時間複雜度（time complexity of decoding）之後，我們將 N 設為 10。

表七：*N* 和 *MRR* 之關係表

N	在 25 個未知詞中可翻譯的個數	*MRR*
5	8	0.27
10	11	0.28
20	12	0.28
40	12	0.28

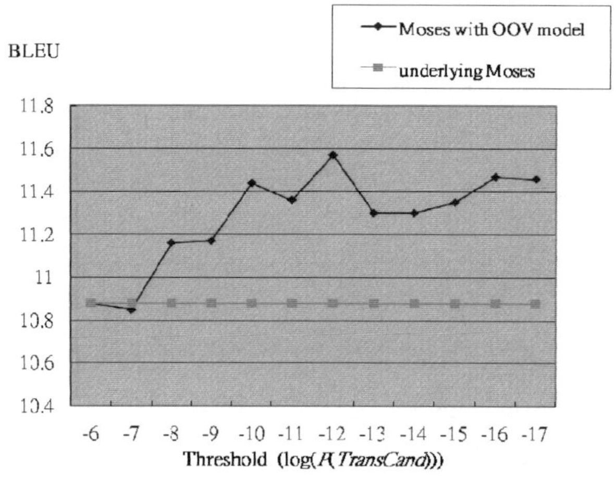

圖三：不同門檻值的 BLEU 翻譯表現

門檻值 θ 可以用來刪除候選也可以用來決定是否啓動我們的組合字翻譯模組因為畢竟有些未知詞是不適合用這樣組合方式取得翻譯候選。較高的門檻值代表較少的翻譯候選，潛在地降低涵蓋率；而較低的門檻值代表較多的翻譯候選，潛在地降低準確度。為了選用適當的 θ，我們將我們模組提供的未知詞翻譯候選用 XML 標記加入底層 Moses 系統，並且檢驗不同 θ 所得到的翻譯品質。在此，我們選用 BLEU（Papineni 等人, 2002）來當作翻譯品質的檢定標準。從圖三中可發現，當門檻值大於-8 時，相當少的翻譯候選會被考慮進去，導致翻譯品質並沒有差異太大；但是，當門檻值小於-13 時，有較多雜訊被考慮成翻譯，在翻譯的分數上就有所減少。我們選用擁有最好翻譯表現的-12 當作我們的過濾門檻值（大概在翻譯的準確度和涵蓋率取得平衡）。

四、評估

這一章節我們專注在評量未知詞組合字翻譯模組對片語式系統 Moses 帶來的影響。我們使用包含有 1,664 句的 NIST MT-06 當作是我們的測試資料。在這份資料中，共有散佈在 859 句的 933 種未知詞。細部分析顯示測試資料中未知詞個數和未知詞的長度關係和之前發展中資料是相當類似的：雙字（two-character）詞也佔了所有未知詞的一半。在這 933 種未知詞中，我們的未知詞模組為 351 句中的 170 種雙字（two-character）未知詞產生翻譯候選，進而藉由底層 Moses 產生翻譯。我們系統中的門檻值 θ 決定了我們系統的應用程度，也就是，θ 被設計來藉由機率的大小稍加檢視組合式的翻譯是否適合該未知詞。模組所產生的翻譯候選將會利用 XML 標記加入 Moses 中。

表八：系統翻譯表現（句數 1,664）

翻譯系統	BLEU	BP	翻出字詞個數
Moses	21.46	0.928	41052
CST	21.56	0.939	41707
Fixed	21.34	0.941	41805

表九：系統翻譯表現（句數 351）

翻譯系統	BLEU	BP	翻出字詞個數
Moses	17.41	0.912	10833
CST	**17.83**	**0.951**	11583

表八整理出各系統翻譯的表現。雖然底層 Moses 和有加上我們模組的 Moses（命名為系統 CST，因為 Moses with combined sublexical translations）在 BLEU 的分數上並沒有很大的差異，但是 CST 在精簡懲罰（brevity penalty，也就是 BP）上則有明顯的上升，由此可知，CST 系統所產生出來的翻譯句長和參考翻譯（reference translation）的長度較為接近。為了檢驗 CST 系統所多產生的翻譯字詞的確如 BLEU 分數所顯示的一樣一比底層 Moses 的準確度更好或是至少一樣，我們多比較了 Fixed（表八最後一列）這個系統。為了說明我們系統得到較高的 BLEU 分數除了因為精簡懲罰較大（越大越好）以外，我們所多翻譯出來的字仍維持高正確性，我們將底層 Moses 未翻譯出來的雙字未知詞都以固定（Fixed）非中文字元帶入，並觀察其翻譯表現。誠如表八，分數下降的 Fixed 系統代表著即使翻譯長度近似參考翻譯的長度，沒有翻譯的準度，BLEU 的分數是不會上升的。也反映出 CST 系統為雙字未知詞產生出不錯的翻譯。

我們更進一步來檢驗我們系統為 351 句測試句產生未知詞翻譯的 BLEU 表現（請見表九）。CST 系統為片語式翻譯系統 Moses 在 BLEU 分數上帶來的提升是數學統計上顯著的（statistically significant）。我們使用 Koehn 在 2004 年提到的 bootstrap resampling 方法來作顯著測試（significance test）。從表九翻譯分數較低（相較表八）顯示：這些句子較難翻譯，且很有可能是句子中未知詞的關係。另外，CST 系統在這些句子中的 BP 進步更大，比例（relatively）成長 4.4%之多。

總結的說，實驗數據顯示我們的未知詞組合模組可以翻譯部分的未知詞，且不會降低現存翻譯系統的表現。對於那些我們系統有產生翻譯候選的句子，翻譯表現是大幅的提升。

五、總結與未來展望

在本研究中，我們針對片語式機器翻譯系統的未知詞和落單字提出解決方案。在我們細部的分析中發現組成字（combinational form）未知詞的比例不亞於文獻較為重視的可重述之未知詞比例。另外，片語式機器翻譯系統平均而言會忽略掉 5%以上的落單字翻譯品質，而落單字又是片語式翻譯系統沒有辦法（翻譯）解歧的對象（得藉助受字數限制的語言模組來幫忙）。這次的實驗我們專注在未知詞組合字翻譯模組的貢獻。此模組包含利用萬用字元查詢取的組成字翻譯、限制且過濾較不可能的組成字翻譯、組合組成字翻譯、並藉由單雙語的資訊來排序組合出來的翻譯。我們實驗結果是相當正面的：架構在知名的片語式機器翻譯系統 Moses 之上，未知詞組成字翻譯模組產生的翻譯候選清單很有可能就包含了未知詞的正確翻譯、組合式的翻譯未知詞可以有效地降低精簡懲罰（brevity penalty）、大大提升包含有未知詞句子翻譯的品質。我們的實驗結果也暗示所謂的中文未知詞在字層級（character-level）上可能是已知的（in-vocabulary）。

未來我們也希望我們可以將組合字模組拓展到可以翻譯三字（three-character）詞或是以上。例如：「國科會」或是「電視台」。然而，我們將會需要字層級的斷詞法。例如：「國科會」應該被切成「國」（national）、「科」（science）、和「會」（council），而「電視台」被切成「電視」（television）和「台」（station）。模組中的組成字的解歧也需要加強。例如：組成字「班」可能代表「航班」（flight）、「班車」（train）、「班級」（class）、和「值班」（shift）等。除了未知詞本身，我們也許可以利用其上下文來幫忙組成字解歧。另外，我們也將結合未知詞重述模組（例如：（Mirkin 等人, 2009）和（Marton 等人, 2009））以增加翻譯的涵蓋率。最後，雖然我們針對落單字所佔的比例還有各詞性 Moses 系統翻譯的準確度作了分析並提出屬於動詞和名詞的落單字是片語式機器翻譯的弱項，我們並沒有實際實驗我們的落單字翻譯模組的效用。未來我們將專注在發展實驗此翻譯模組上，並考慮合併此論文中提出來的組合字模組、重述模組、和落單字模組。

致謝辭

本研究依經濟部補助財團法人資訊工業策進會「100 年度數位匯流服務開放平台技術研發計畫」辦理。

參考文獻

Steven Bird, Ewan Klein, and Edward Loper. 2008. Natural language processing in Python. Available online at http://nltk.org/book.html.

Chu-Ren Huang, Ru-Yng Chang, and Shiang-Bin Lee. 2004. Sinica BOW (Bilingual Ontological Wordnet): Integration of Bilingual WordNet and SUMO. In *Proceedings of the Fourth International Conference on Language Resources and Evaluation (LREC)*, pages 1553-1556.

Philipp Koehn and Kevin Knight. 2003. Empirical Methods for Compound Splitting. In *Proceedings of the 10th conference on European chapter of the Association for Computational Linguistics*, pages 187-193.

Philipp Koehn. 2004. Statistical Significance Test for Machine Translation Evaluation. In *Proceedings of the 2004 Conference on Empirical Methods in Natural Language Processing*, pages 388-395.

Philipp Koehn, Amittai Axelrod, Alexandra Birch Mayne, Chris Callison-Burch, Miles Osborne and David Talbot. 2005. Edinburgh System Description for the 2005 IWSLT Speech Translation Evaluation. In *International workshop on Spoken Language Translation*.

Philipp Koehn, Hieu Hoang, Alexandra Birch, Chris Callison-Burch, Marcello Federico, Nicola Bertoldi, Brooke Cowan, Wade Shen, Christine Moran, Richard Zens, Chris Dyer, Ondřej Bojar, Alexandra Constantin, and Evan Herbst. 2007. Moses: Open Source Toolkit for Statistical Machine Translation. In *Proceedings of the ACL 2007 Demo and Poster Sessions*, pages 177–180.

Wei-Yun Ma and Keh-Jiann Chen. 2003. Introduction to CKIP Chinese word segmentation system for the first international Chinese word segmentation bakeoff. In *Proceedings of the second SIGHAN workshop on Chinese language processing*, pages 168-171.

George A. Miller. 1995. Wordnet: A Lexical Database for English. *Communications of the ACM*, vol. 38, no. 11, pages 39-41.

Shachar Mirkin, Lucia Specia, Nicola Cancedda, Ido Dagan, Marc Dymetman, and Idan Szpektor. 2009. Source-language Entailment Modeling for Translating Unknown Terms. In *Proceedings of the 47th Annual Meeting of ACL and the 4th IJCNLP of the AFNLP*, pages 791–799.

Franz Josef Och and Hermann Ney. 2003. A systematic Comparison of Various Statistical Alignment Models. *Computational Linguistics*, vol. 29, no. 1, pages 19-51.

Kishore Papineni, Salim Roukos, ToddWard, andWei-Jing Zhu. 2002. BLEU: a Method for Automatic Evaluation of Machine Translation. In *Proceedings of the 40th Annual Meeting on Association for Computational Linguistics*, pages 311-318.

Frank A. Smadja. 1993. Retrieving collocations from text: Xtract. *Computational Linguistics*, vol. 19 (1), pages 143-177.

Andreas Stolcke. 2002. SRILM – An Extensible Language Modeling Toolkit. In *Proceedings of the International Conference on Spoken Language Processing*, vol. 2, pages 901–904.

Mei Yang and Katrin Kirchhoff. 2006. Phrase-Based Backoff Models for Machine Translation of Highly Inflected Languages. In *Proceedings of the European Chapter of the Association for Computational Linguistics*, pages 41-48.

英文技術文獻中一般動詞與其受詞之中文翻譯的語境效用

Collocational Influences on the Chinese Translations of Non-Technical English Verbs and Their Objects in Technical Documents

莊怡軒 王瑞平 蔡家琦 劉昭麟
Yi-Hsuan Chuang Jui-Ping Wang Chia-Chi Tsai Chao-Lin Liu
國立政治大學資訊科學系
Department of Computer Science, National Chengchi University
{g9804,g9916,g9906,chaolin}@cs.nccu.edu.tw

摘要

本文探索英文動詞與英文名詞的英漢翻譯中，語境資訊對於翻譯品質的貢獻度。文獻常見的研究多集中於使用英文動詞本身的各項語言特徵，或者加上與該動詞搭配的英文名詞的相關資訊來推測英文動詞的翻譯。本文探索一極端假設下的翻譯成效：如果我們也能知道英文名詞的中譯時，是否有助於英文動詞的翻譯品質？我們利用 2011 年 NTCIR 的漢英翻譯工作坊的數萬句專利語料作為實驗資料來源，同時利用七年的科學人的語料進行實驗，目前實驗顯示在所假設之情形下，增加名詞中譯的資訊，固然有助於提高翻譯品質，但是效果暫不明顯，有待更精確的實驗設計來確認英文中譯詞對於英文動詞的翻譯貢獻度。

Abstract

We investigate the potential contribution of a very specific feature to the quality of Chinese translations of English verbs. Researchers have studied the effects of the linguistic information about the verbs being translated, and many have reported how considering the objects of the verbs will facilitate the quality of translations. In this paper, we take an extreme assumption and examine the results: How will the availability of the Chinese translations of the objects help the translations of the verbs. We explored the issue with thousands of samples that we extracted from 2011 NTCIR PatentMT workshop and Scientific American. The results indicated that the extra information improved the quality of the translations, but not quite significantly. We plan to refine and extend our experiments to achieve more decisive conclusions.

關鍵詞：機器翻譯、特徵評比、自然語言處理

1. 緒論

當今的社會可視為一個地球村，即使住在不同的國家、也使用不同的語言，無論是商業貿易或是文化交流，人們互相溝通的情形相當普遍；英文更因為其容易理解及表述的語言特質成為世界上不同語言使用者通用的溝通語言。因應世界文化潮流，除了自身國家的母語，英文成為最多人學習的語言。然而許多研究指出，將英文作為第一外語的學習

者 (EFL learners: English as a Foreign Language learners) 容易受到自己國家母語的文法影響，在英文動詞及名詞的搭配組合上會產生錯誤的用法。例如，「take pills」一詞若依照中文使用者的直覺，可能會翻譯解釋為「拿藥」而非正確對應至「吃藥」。因此，我們對於英文中常用的動詞與名詞組合，與中文的對應關係感到有趣，並想透過大量正確對應的英漢平行語料庫，找尋英漢動名詞組合 (V-N-collocation) 適切的對應關係。若提到大量的語料，我們首先聯想到了專利文書。

專利文書是一種宣示並提供專利保護的重要文件。世界社會持續地進步，許多發明與技術不斷創新並被撰寫成為專利文書。當發明一項專利時，專利發明者為了讓世界各國使用不同語言者可以共同瞭解這項專利，也同時向外擴張專利的保護領域，發明者可以提出多種語言版本的專利文書以保障自己的發明跟技術。專利文書的重要性更可以從 Google Patents beta[7]提供的英文專利文書檢索服務看出，Google[6]號稱他們的專利資料庫蒐集了七百萬篇以上的專利文書，以其豐富的收藏量宣示他們強大的檢索服務。既然單語言的專利文書數量如此龐大，那麼同時具有多種語言版本的專利文書也就不在少數。如果我們將專利文句作正確解析，排除技術名詞在外，剩餘的文句結構及內容不失為一個值得運用的語文使用參考資料；特別是許多專利文書具有英漢對應的語言版本，可以當作是雙語語料使用。因此，我們可以看待跨語言的專利文書為資料量豐富的平行語料庫。本研究利用專利文書豐富的英漢對應資料，並排除技術名詞的影響，試圖挖掘一般常用英漢動名詞組合對應的用法。

除了分析英漢專利平行語料庫[9]，本研究另外以相同方式分析科學人雜誌英漢對照電子書[16]，以比較不同語料間是否有不同的特性。本研究將中英文互為翻譯的文件視為一體，將英文及中文的動名詞組合作為我們的觀察對象，建構由真實世界語料反應的語言翻譯模型。本研究對於翻譯英文動詞及名詞皆有建立翻譯模型及測試其翻譯效能，不過因受限於篇幅關係，本篇論文僅會介紹翻譯英文動詞的部分；而翻譯英文名詞的成效與翻譯英文動詞相差不多。

關於專利文書的研究，田侃文[15]使用中英文互為翻譯關係的專利文書當作主要語料，並利用動態規劃演算法進行中英文句對列，設法將中文全文文章與英文全文文章的翻譯對應，拉抬至中文句子對列到英文句子的文句對列層級；本研究亦運用該文句對列系統找尋句對關係。Lu[8]提出如何建置漢英專利文句平行語料庫。該研究從網路上蒐集優良的中英專利文書平行語料，再根據專利文書的目次結構，將專利文書拆解成多個小單位。其集結了三種作法：使用雙語辭典比對詞彙、刪除過長的句子及使用 IBM M-1 為語言模型建立文句對列，其研究結果顯示準確率最高可達 97%。

關於語言輔助教學方面，Chang[1]則針對學習英文的中文使用者製作一套英文寫作校正系統。使用者將寫好的英文文章輸入至系統，系統便會偵測動名詞片語有無誤用之處。該研究蒐集學習英文的中文使用者之英文寫作文章當作學習者語料庫，從中發現常見的錯誤用法；另外同時蒐集正確的英文語料當作正確答案的參考語料庫。該系統將錯誤的動詞翻譯成中文詞彙，將這些中文詞彙重新翻譯回英文詞彙，再把這些英文動詞替換片語中原本的動詞成為新的片語，並重新查詢共現性分數，得分高者則為系統建議的校正答案。

關於動名詞組合方面的研究，Venkatapathy[12]首先介紹了 multi word expressions (MWEs) ，即為那些從字面上看不出實際表達意義的詞彙。有很大一部分的 MWEs 是具有文法結構性但沒有語義合成的關係，而其中一個子集就是動名詞共現性 (V-N collocations)，也是該研究主要分析的目標。MWEs 很難區分是為組合性 (compositional) 或為非組合性 (non-compositional) ，早一些時間的相關研究不外乎是考慮頻率 (frequency) 、互信息或是使用 LSA 模型等相關數據作分類問題；該研究則將這些數據特色都加以考慮並列入使用。該研究聘請兩位人員進行人工標記詞彙是為組合性或是非組合性的程度，並將上述的數據當作特徵，作成向量再以 SVM 排序。最後發現合併特徵比起只單一考慮任一特徵都還要貼近人工標記的答案。

2. 語料來源介紹

2.1 專利文句

本研究使用 Patent Translation Task at NTCIR-9[9]的一百萬筆英漢對照的專利文句作為我們第一份研究語料，中文的部分為簡體中文。其使用編號標示英漢句對對應關係。由於專利文句的字數偏長、文句結構也較為複雜，如果直接使用長句進行英漢動名詞組合對列，不僅對列的時間加長，產生的對列效果也會較差。本研究認為，動名詞組合並不會跨過標點符號，因此我們把每一個長句視為一篇短文章，根據長句中暫停或結束的標點符號（逗號、分號、冒號、驚嘆號、問號及句號）作為短句的終點；一個長句可視為一篇由多句短句組合而成的短篇文章。本研究使用專利文句對列系統[15]得到英漢短句對應關係。我們設定門檻值為 0.3 取得較高對列品質的短句，作為我們的使用資料。原本一百萬組長句對中，超過本研究設定門檻值的句對有 338846 組；這三十三萬的長句對又被拆成 1148632 組短句對為本研究所使用。

2.2 科學人雜誌

田侃文[15]將科學人雜誌英漢對照電子書[16]的 1745 篇文章使用該研究的文句對列系統產出 63256 個英漢對列的高品質句對。本研究沿用這 63256 個句對作為第二份分析語料。

3. 技術名詞表建置

為了能順利排除技術名詞的資訊，我們需要有技術名詞表比對詞彙以便標記捨去。本研究從國家教育研究院學術名詞資訊網[17]取得公開的 138 個不同領域技術名詞 Excel 格式檔案，檔案大小共有 177MB 並整合為技術名詞表。在技術名詞表中，每一個英文技術名詞都有與其對應的中文技術名詞，且對應關係並不唯一，本研究將技術名詞表的翻譯詞對規列成一對一的形式。

我們發現在技術名詞表當中，英文及中文部分都有些許的技術名詞更常被當作一般用語詞彙；我們使用 E-HowNet[2][5]及 WordNet[13]來幫助刪除一般詞彙，留下技術名詞於技術名詞表。本研究認為，這兩部字典所收錄的詞彙可以代表生活中一般常用的詞彙，使用這些詞彙過濾技術名詞表是可行的方式。E-HowNet 內含 88075 個中文詞彙，共識別出技術名詞表中有 71333 個詞對更適合被當成一般詞彙而非技術名詞。我們也對稱檢驗技術名詞表中的一般英文詞彙，WordNet 內含 154754 個英文詞彙及英文短片語，

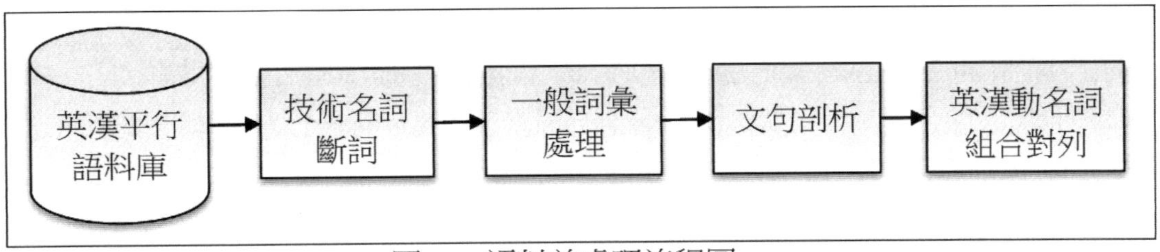

圖一、語料前處理流程圖

表一、英文及中文關係樹範例

英文句	My dog also likes eating sausage.
英文句關係樹樹狀圖	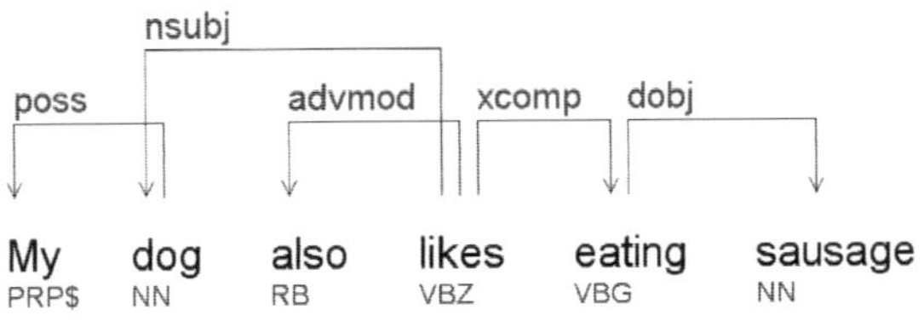
英文句關係樹結構	poss(dog-2, My-1)、nsubj(likes-4, dog-2)、advmod(likes-4, also-3)、xcomp(likes-4, eating-5)、**dobj(eating-5, sausage-6)**
中文句	我的狗喜歡吃香腸。
中文句關係樹結構	assmod(狗-3, 我-1)、assm(我-1, 的-2)、nsubj(吃-5, 狗-3)、advmod(吃-5, 喜歡-4)、**dobj(吃-5, 香腸-6)**

我們使用 WordNet 檢查共過濾了 80220 個詞對。經過以上檢測，我們的技術名詞表約略除去 14%的詞對，現存有 690640 組技術名詞詞對。我們相信這六十九萬組技術名詞詞對具有較高品質，可以降低與一般詞彙產生斷詞衝突的機率。

4. 語料前處理

本研究語料前處理的過程如圖一所示，以下逐一小節解釋各步驟流程。

4.1 技術名詞標記

技術名詞多為複合詞彙，因此我們使用長詞優先的方式，從技術名詞表比對英漢平行文句中的詞彙，一經比對成功則將技術名詞標記，並使用 Stanford Parser[11]的 TaggedWord() 函數指定詞性為名詞。本研究將技術名詞標記是為了提升文句剖析的準確率，以及處理排除技術名詞資訊。

4.2 英文詞幹還原及詞性標記

本研究使用 Stanford Parser 及其 englishPCFG.ser.gz 字典模型剖析英文文句，亦運用其 Stemmer() 函數進行詞幹還原。我們將技術名詞之外的文句部分進行詞幹還原，且令 Stanford Parser 依據字典模型斷詞及標記詞性。技術名詞在這個步驟不會被更動。

4.3 中文斷詞

標記完中文技術名詞之後，剩下的文句仍需進行斷詞，我們使用 Stanford Chinese Segmenter[10]進行斷詞，並將斷好的詞彙以空白相隔。同樣技術名詞在這個步驟不會被更動。

4.4 關係樹剖析

本研究使用 Stanford Parser 剖析文句得到關係樹結構，Stanford Parser 的關係樹剖析共含有 27 種文法關係標記。一個句子經過剖析可以得知這個句子含有幾種文法關係，上頁表一即為翻譯對應的英文及中文句關係樹範例。27 種文法關係標記中，「DIRECT_OBJECT」可以標記動詞片語的動詞及其述語對象，並以「dobj」為形式；以表一中的英文句為例，動詞「eat」的對象是名詞「sausage」，並以「dobj(eating-5, sausage-6)」標記，中文句的「dobj(吃-5, 香腸-6)」也是如此；其中數字 5 與 6 代表詞彙在文句中出現的位置次序。本研究將英文及中文的句子剖析，透過抽取「DIRECT_OBJECT」表示式得到句子中的動名詞組合。剖析英文的字典模型為 englishPCFG.ser.gz，中文剖析的部分，本研究使用 xinhuaFactored.ser.gz 字典模型處理簡體中文的專利文句，chineseFactored.ser.gz 則處理繁體中文的科學人雜誌。

5. 近義詞典建置

我們需要將互為翻譯對照的動名詞組合對列產生翻譯結果。本研究使用基於辭典資訊的機器翻譯 (dictionary-based machine translation)，採用的英漢辭典有兩部，分別為牛津現代英漢雙解詞典[3]與 Dr.eye 譯典通線上字典[4]。但是只依靠英漢辭典的資訊並不足夠，因為英漢辭典中列出與英文詞彙對應的中文翻譯詞彙有限；如果以英漢字典內的英文詞彙之中文對應詞彙為基礎找尋意義相近的中文詞彙，也就表示這些中文詞彙與該英文詞彙的意義也會近似，因此我們使用一詞泛讀[14]及 E-HowNet[5]建立近義詞典，擴充英文詞彙對應的中文翻譯詞彙，幫助英漢動名詞組合對列。

5.1 英漢辭典合併

不同辭典對於同一個英文詞彙所定義的中文對應詞彙並不完全相同；因此本研究將牛津現代英漢雙解詞典和 Dr.eye 譯典通線上字典的中文對應詞彙合併，增加英文詞彙的中文對應詞彙數量。經合併之後，本研究的「英漢合併字典」內容格式如表二所示；合併之後英文詞彙「confusion」對應的中文詞彙數量明顯增加。

5.2 使用一詞泛讀尋找近義詞彙

現代漢語一詞泛讀系統（簡稱為一詞泛讀）提供近義詞查詢服務。以表二的「confusion」為例，我們的做法為逐一將英漢合併字典一欄中的詞彙輸入至一詞泛讀，並聯集系統所傳回的近義詞群。我們認為回傳的近義詞群與「confusion」的中文對應詞彙意義相近，依照推理也與「confusion」的意思相近，因此這些近義詞群就是我們透過一詞泛讀找到的近義詞彙。

表二、英漢合併字典範例

英文詞彙：confusion	
辭典	辭典中的中文對應詞彙
牛津詞典	迷亂、惶惑、混亂、雜亂、混淆、混同
譯典通字典	混亂、騷動、混亂狀況、混淆、困惑、慌亂
英漢合併字典	混亂、混亂狀況、騷動、混淆、困惑、慌亂、迷亂、惶惑、雜亂、混同

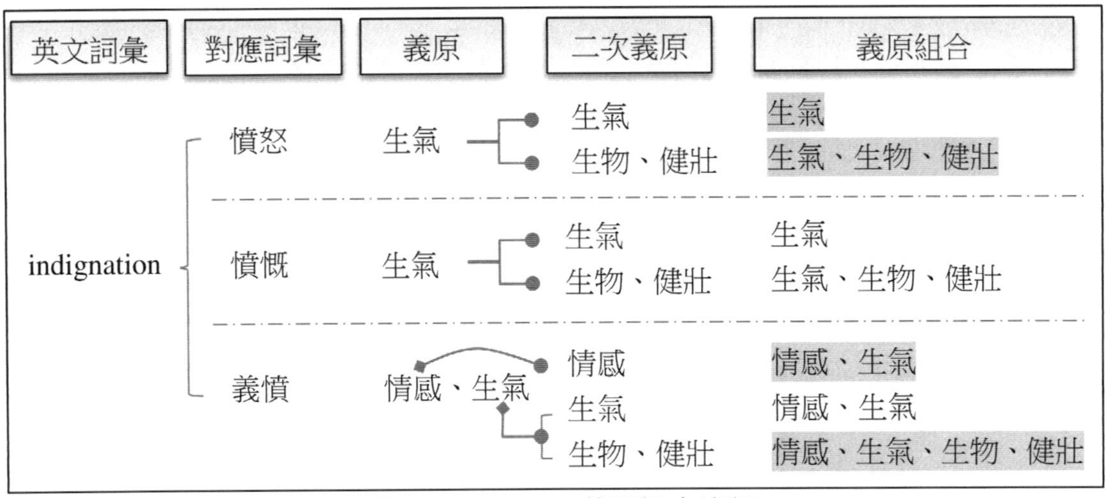

圖二、E-HowNet 義原組合流程

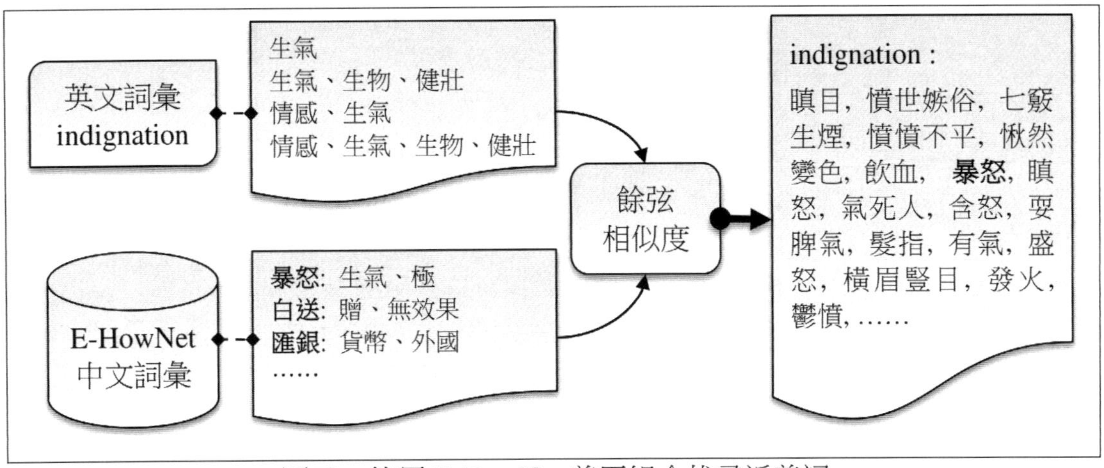

圖三、使用 E-HowNet 義原組合找尋近義詞

5.3 使用 E-HowNet 尋找近義詞彙

圖二為英文詞彙「indignation」透過中文對應詞彙至 E-HowNet 形成義原組合的過程範例。在我們的英漢合併字典中，「indignation」擁有三個中文對應詞彙，分別為「憤怒、憤慨及義憤」。而這三個中文詞彙恰巧都只有一種語意，在只有一種語意的情形之下中文詞彙的義原也只會有一群；「憤怒」及「憤慨」的義原只有「生氣」一個義原，「義憤」的義原群則由「情感」及「生氣」兩個義原組成。我們發現，E-HowNet 的義原本身同時也是一個詞彙，而且也有定義自己的義原。這種定義 E-HowNet 義原的義原，我們稱之為「二次義原」。找出中文對應詞彙的義原群及二次義原群之後，我們將義原以及各自的二次義原組合起來，形成圖二中的義原組合；排除掉重複的組合得到以灰底標示的義原組合群，即為透過中文對應詞彙找到英文詞彙可能的義原組合群。

如圖三所示，英文詞彙「indignation」有了義原組合群之後，本研究將 E-HowNet 中所有的中文詞彙依照同樣的流程組成義原組合，然後逐一取出「indignation」的每條義原組合與 E-HowNet 全部中文詞彙的義原組合作餘弦相似度 (cosine similarity) 計算並設定門檻值為 0.7。最後我們將從一詞泛讀及 E-HowNet 得到的近義詞與英漢合併字典整合，形成我們擴充英文詞彙的中文對應詞彙字典，稱之為「近義詞典」。

句對編號：54098		
英文動名詞組合	對列關係	中文動名詞組合
dobj(round-7, edge-10)		**dobj(清除-12, 部分-19)**
dobj(remove-15, portion-17)	⟷	dobj(使-24, 肩部-27)
		dobj(进-29, 圆滑-31)

圖四、英漢動名詞組合示意圖

6. 英漢動名詞組合對列

經上述步驟，英文專利文句共產生 375041 個動名詞組合，中文專利文句則產生 465866 個動名詞組合。為了確保我們使用的動名詞組合品質，本研究使用英漢合併字典內收錄的英文詞彙檢驗英文動名詞組合，只有當組合中的動詞及名詞都有出現在字典中，我們才認定這個組合是正確的，這個步驟同時排除含有技術名詞的動名詞組合，因此不會有任何技術名詞的相關資訊。經過濾之後，有 254091 個英文動名詞組合通過檢測。我們對於中文的動名詞組合也進行同等檢驗，透過近義詞典含有的中文詞彙過濾，最後有 249591 個組合通過檢測，亦排除技術名詞資訊。透過句對編號及近義詞典，本研究的對列規則為：如果英文的動詞及名詞能在近義詞典中各自的中文對應詞彙集找到中文動名詞組合，才算對列成功，如圖四所示。對列成功的英漢動名詞組合會記錄成「remove, portion : 清除, 部分」，英文動名詞組合在前、中文動名詞組合在後的資料格式。

表三、翻譯英文動詞模型公式

$\underset{CV_i}{\operatorname{argmax}} \Pr(CV_i \mid EV, EN, CN)$	(1)
$\underset{CV_i, CN_j}{\operatorname{argmax}} \Pr(CV_i, CN_j \mid EV, EN)$	(2)
$\underset{CV_i}{\operatorname{argmax}} \Pr(CV_i \mid EV, EN)$	(3)
$\underset{CV_i}{\operatorname{argmax}} \Pr(CV_i \mid EV)$	(4)
$\underset{CV_i}{\operatorname{argmax}} \Pr(CV_i \mid EV, CN)$	(5)

7. 翻譯模型建置

7.1 翻譯英文動詞公式說明

本研究提出了五種公式訓練模型翻譯英文動詞，如表三所示。我們以字母「E」代表英文、字母「C」代表中文，「V」代表動詞、「N」代表名詞；因此「EV」及「EN」各別代表英文動名詞組合中的動詞及名詞，「CV」及「CN」則為中文動名詞組合中的動詞及名詞。公式(1)至公式(4)為逐漸放寬條件的公式，公式(5)則是從另外一個觀點發想的公式。一般在考慮英漢翻譯問題時，分析英文內容的共現性 (collocation) 再對應到中文翻譯的作法較多，而本研究試想，除了考慮英文的部分，若加入中文對應翻譯的資訊是否能提升翻譯的效能。公式(1)即為我們這般考量下所提出的公式。

公式(1)除了考慮英文動名詞組合，也考慮了英文名詞的中文翻譯而推薦動詞的中文翻譯，我們想測試公式(1)會否蒐集的資訊最多而能翻譯的較為準確。對公式(1)最直覺的解釋為：若有一英文使用者在學習中文，他想把「take pills」翻譯成中文，但是他只確定「pills」可以翻譯為「藥」，則我們的公式(1)則可以透過這三個詞彙的資訊，觀察「take」跟「pills」一起使用且「pills」對應到「藥」時在語料中「take」容易被翻譯成什麼中文詞彙；如果從相反的角度解釋，則為一個中文使用者想練習英文，但是他不確定「吃藥」的「吃」該翻譯為「take」或是「eat」，但是他知道「藥」可以翻譯為「pills」，則公式(1)可以在語料中觀察「take pills」和「eat pills」跟「藥」組合在一起時哪一個的次數較多，且在公式(1)推薦的中文翻譯中可以找到「吃」這個詞彙，進而讓使用者知道該使用「take pills」或是「eat pills」。公式(1)的原理為：如果同時看見英文的動詞、名詞及英文名詞的中文翻譯，則推薦與這三者一起出現機率最高的中文動詞 CV 為英文動詞 EV 的翻譯。公式(2)及公式(3)則為許多英漢翻譯使用的方法。公式(2)的原理為：如果看見特定英文動名詞組合 EV、EN，我們的翻譯模型會從該動名詞組合所對應的中文動名詞組合中，取得出現機率最高的組合，並推薦中文動名詞組合中的動詞當作我們的推薦翻譯詞彙。公式(3)的原理為：如果看見特定的英文動名詞組合，則該動名詞組合所對應到的中文動詞群中，出現機率最高的中文動詞 CV 即為我們的翻譯推薦詞彙。公式(4)的原理則最為寬鬆：如果看到一個英文動詞 EV，則我們所推薦的翻譯詞彙即為英漢動名詞組合當中與 EV 最常一起出現的中文動詞。公式(5)的原理較特別，我們假設如果看到一個英文動詞及其受詞的中文翻譯，則我們推薦與這個組合最常一起出現中文動詞做為推薦翻譯。

除了評比這五個公式獨立運作的效果，本研究亦將這五個公式搭配成十七種公式組合，共有二十二種翻譯模型。我們讓這些公式組合「共同推薦」英文動詞的中文翻譯：組合中的公式可以各自推薦它們認為的所有可能答案，且答案順序根據答對的機率大小排列。組合中公式的排列順序即為答題順序，且回答的答案不得重複。例如，我們設定翻譯模型最多可以回答三個答案，只要三個答案中包含正確解答即算答對；則公式組合「1．2．3」即為公式(1)、(2)及(3)的組合，各自推薦了一、二和四個答案；依照公式的排列順序，公式(1)擁有最高的回答優先權，因此公式(1)推薦的答案佔掉一個回答額度，而公式(2)提供兩個答案中最佳的答案跟公式(1)的答案重複，因此公式(2)只能回答次好的答案，公式(3)提供的四個答案中，它認為前兩好的答案恰好與公式(1)及公式(2)的答案相同，因此公式(3)只能回答第三好的答案，這時候回答的答案額度已滿，所以公式組合「1．2．3」就產生了三個可能的答案。

7.2 翻譯模型評量方式

本研究將 F-measure 稍作變形，用來評量不同翻譯模型的翻譯效果。原始的 F-measure 為精確率 (precision) 和召回率 (recall) 的綜合評量。精確率可以對應為翻譯模型的答題正確率，而比起召回率，我們更著重於翻譯模型能夠回答的題目數量多寡，我們希望翻譯模型因為資訊不足而無法作答的情況越少越好，因此使用「回答率」表示翻譯模型的作答數量，並使用精確率與回答率為評量參數，本研究以「***f***-measure」代表變形後的評量方式。我們設定兩套 ***f***-measure 的係數值評量只推薦一個答案跟推薦五個答案時翻譯模型的效果，「***f***1 score」將精確率和回答率的係數平分設定為 0.5，「***f***-measure, α=0.7」則設定精確率有較高的權重 0.7，回答率的係數值為 0.3。以上說明本研究翻譯模型的原理及評量方式，接下來我們使用兩個語料庫來比較這二十二個翻譯模型的效果。

8. 使用專利語料及科學人雜誌建置翻譯模型

專利文句[9]及科學人雜誌[16]同屬於科技類文章，不過專利文句的寫作格式固定，而科學人雜誌風格較為活潑，因此本研究觀察類別相似但風格不同的兩套語料是否會造成翻譯模型的效果差異。我們利用亂數挑選的方式，將語料依據 8:2 的比例切割成訓練資料及測試資料。

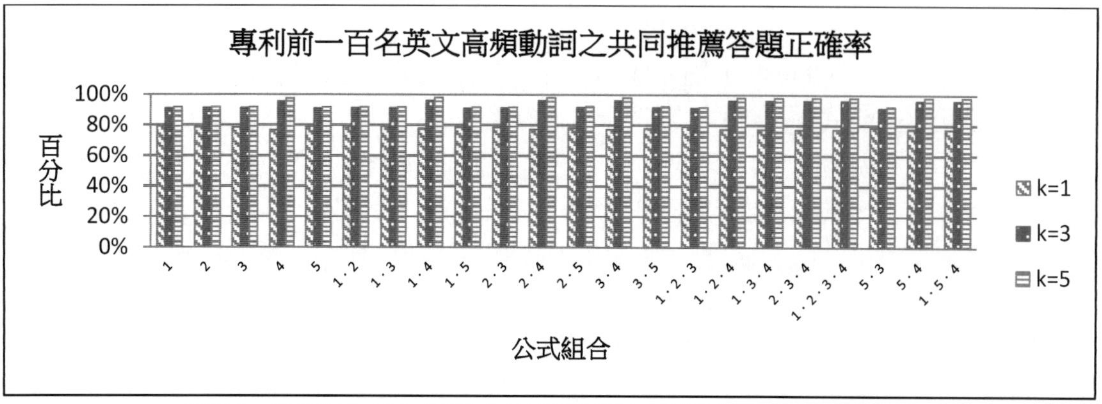

圖五、專利前 100 名英文高頻動詞之共同推薦答題正確率

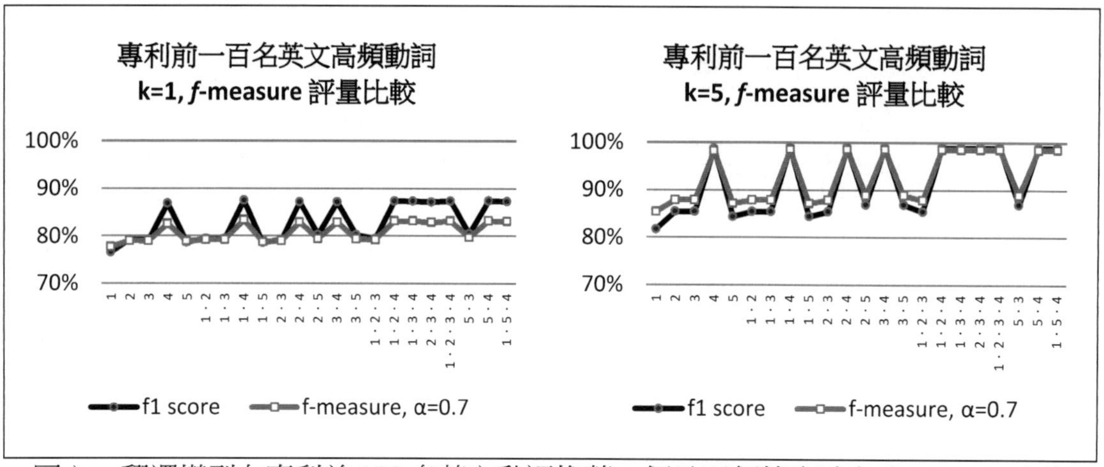

圖六、翻譯模型在專利前 100 名英文動詞推薦一個及五個答案時之 ***f***-measure 成效

8.1 使用專利文句語料建置翻譯模型

專利文句語料庫中，本研究對列成功的英漢動名詞組合共有 35811 組。

8.1.1 專利前一百名英文高頻動詞

本研究探究了在我們 35811 筆的動名詞組合資料當中，前一百名出現次數最多的英文動詞，這些動詞至少在資料中至少出現過 47 次以上，最多的出現次數則為 4530 次。這一百個英文動詞總共出現於 30376 筆資料之中，訓練資料共有 24300 筆，測試資料則有 6076 筆。

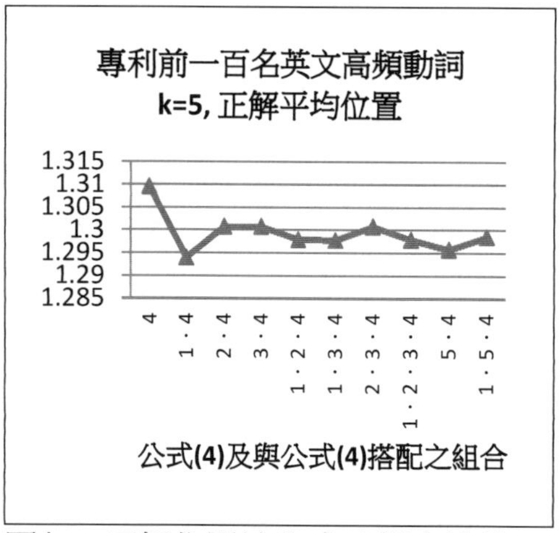

圖七、正解位置於公式(4)組合比較

圖五為翻譯模型在推薦不同數量答案時的答題正確率，圖中的 k 值為翻譯模型能夠推薦的答案數量，例如 k 設定成 5 表示翻譯模型最多可以推薦五個答案，且這五個推薦答案內如有包含正確答案即算答對。我們可以看到當推薦至三個答案跟五個答案時表現幾乎差不多，可見當我們的翻譯模型推薦三個答案時，其中幾乎都包含了正確解答。圖六為使用 ***f***-measure 評量二十二個模型翻譯專利語料中前一百名英文高頻動詞的效果比較。我們可以發現當翻譯模型只能推薦一個答案時 (k=1)，公式(4)和那些與公式(4)搭配的公式組合在 ***f***1 score 得到比較高的分數，但

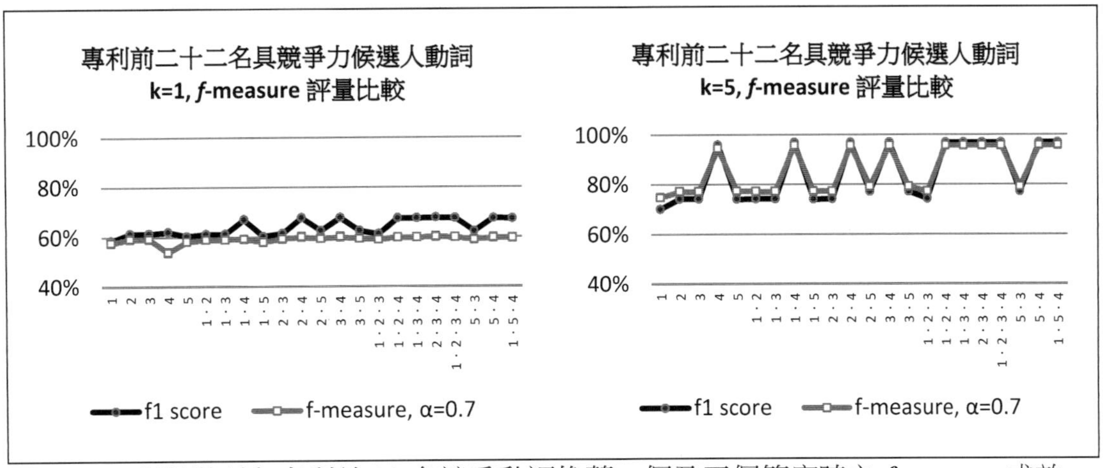

圖八、翻譯模型在專利前 22 名競爭動詞推薦一個及五個答案時之 ***f***-measure 成效

是在著重於精確率的 ***f***-measure, α=0.7 分數則往下降，其他沒有與公式(4)合作的組合及獨立運作的公式在這兩種評分機制則無差異，且分數分布略低；這是因為公式(1)、(2)、(3)及(5)都會因為測試語料中出現訓練語料所沒有的紀錄而無法作答，有回答率的問題，而公式(4)可以回答任何問題，只有答對與答錯的狀況，因為只要訓練語料有出現過的英文動詞都有其對照的中文翻譯。雖然公式(1)、(2)、(3)及(5)在圖六中只能推薦一個答案時的表現略差，但是在兩種評分機制中都維持一樣的水準；相較之下公式(4)在精確率的表現較薄弱，可以顯現出雖然公式(4)有很好的作答能力，但是僅靠著統計推薦答案效果較差，容易有答錯的情形。

翻譯模型最多能推薦五個答案 (k=5) 的情形下，每個公式組合在 ***f***1 score 及 ***f***-measure, α=0.7 的分數都有往上提升許多，特別是與公式(4)搭配的公式組合分數都相當的高；這是因為跟公式(4)搭配的公式如果有回答不出來的時候，公式(4)可以補上答案，或是當搭配的公式回答的並不是正確答案時，因為共同推薦答案不得重複的設定可以讓公式(4)更有機會補上正確解答。我們會希望當翻譯模型推薦多個答案時，正確解答能出現在推薦答案中越前面的位置越好，因此我們統計了正確答案在公式(4)及與公式(4)搭配的組合推薦答案中的排名，如上頁圖七所示。本研究發現與公式(4)搭配的公式組合中正確解答的平均位置皆比在公式(4)的平均位置還要前面；這可以證明雖然從上頁圖六公式(4)和其他與公式(4)搭配的公式組合效果近似，但是公式(1)、(2)、(3)及(5)具有把正確答案往前排名的拉提作用，特別是公式(1)效果特別明顯。

8.1.2 專利前二十二名具競爭力候選人之英文動詞

本研究由前一百名高頻動詞中選出一些英文動詞，這些動詞的特性為它們各自都不只對應到一個中文翻譯詞彙，而且出現次數最高前兩名候選人是具有競爭力的；本研究在這裡定義「競爭力」為：第一名候選人出現的次數不得多於第二名候選人出現次數的兩倍。假設英文動詞 EV 的中文翻譯候選人數依照在語料中與 EV 一起出現的次數多寡排列有 CV_1、CV_2 及 CV_3，則 CV_1 的出現次數不得多於 CV_2 的兩倍，EV 才會被我們挑選出來。根據這個門檻值的設定，我們總共找到二十二個動詞具有此特性，這二十二個動詞總共出現在 4101 筆英漢動名詞組合，訓練資料有 3280 筆，測試資料則有 821 筆。

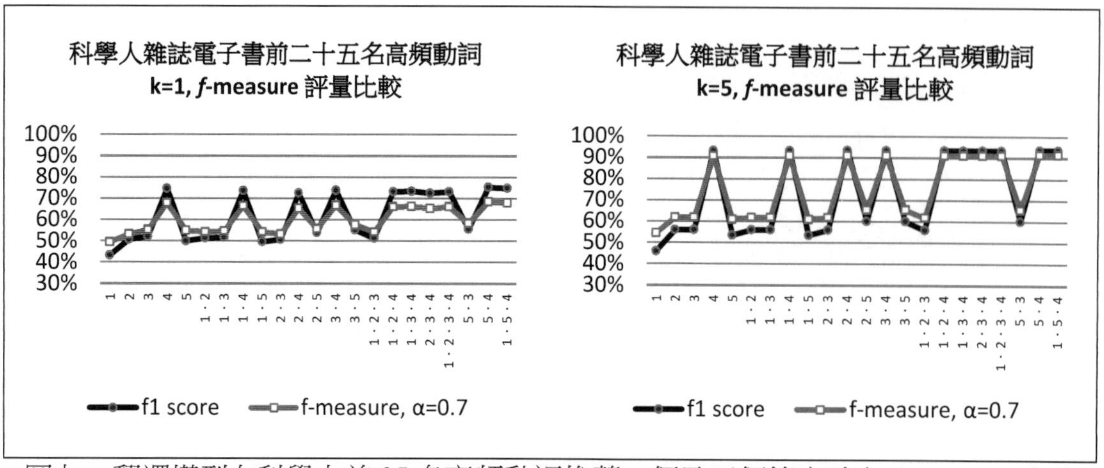

圖九、翻譯模型在科學人前 25 名高頻動詞推薦一個及五個答案時之 ***f***-measure 成效

由上頁圖八所示，當翻譯模型只能推薦一個答案時，前二十二名具競爭力候選人的動詞與前一百名高頻動詞的趨勢並不完全相同。公式(4)和那些與公式(4)搭配的組合在 ***f*1** score 得到比較高的分數，但是在著重於精確率的 ***f***-measure, α=0.7，與公式(4)搭配的公式組合分數則往下與其他沒有與公式(4)合作的公式表現相同，特別可以注意到公式(4)在 ***f***-measure, α=0.7 的表現明顯低於其他獨立公式。這是因為訓練資料量銳減，但是資料的變化性仍然不小，因此其他考慮較多資訊的公式表現就超越了資訊考慮最少的公式(4)，這也證明公式(1)、(2)、(3)及(5)所考慮的資訊是有用的。而在翻譯模型最多能推薦五個答案的情形下，***f***-measure 的趨勢走向與前一百名高頻動詞雷同，比起只能推薦一個答案時，每個公式組合的分數都有所提升，特別是與公式(4)搭配的公式組合。

8.2 使用科學人雜誌語料建置翻譯模型

科學人雜誌語料庫中，本研究對列成功的英漢動名詞組合共有 4814 組。

8.2.1 科學人前二十五名英文高頻動詞

由於科學人雜誌語料所得的英漢動名詞組合數量比起專利語料少了許多，因此本研究探究前二十五名在我們 4814 筆的動名詞組合資料當中出現次數最多的英文動詞，這些動詞在資料中至少出現過 31 次以上，最多的出現次數則為 379 次。這二十五個英文動詞總共出現於 1885 筆資料之中，訓練資料共有 1508 筆，測試資料則有 377 筆。如圖九所示，在翻譯模型推薦一個答案及推薦五個答案時的趨勢分布與圖六專利語料的前一百名高頻動詞趨勢相同；因為語料數量較少（僅有專利語料的 13%）而資料變化又較大（科學人文章風格較專利文句豐富），因此在推薦五個答案時 ***f***-measure 最高的成效落在 90% 左右。

8.2.2 科學人前九名具競爭力候選人之英文動詞

本研究由前二十五名高頻動詞中選出了具競爭力候選人的動詞，這裡的「競爭力」意義相同：第一名候選人出現的次數不得多於第二名候選人出現次數的兩倍。這九個動詞總共出現在 689 筆英漢動名詞組合，訓練資料有 552 筆，測試資料則有 137 筆。如下頁圖十所示，科學人前九名具競爭力候選人動詞在 ***f***-measure 的趨勢大致上與專利前二十二名具競爭力候選人動詞的分布相同，不過可以特別注意到公式(5)在只能推薦一個答案

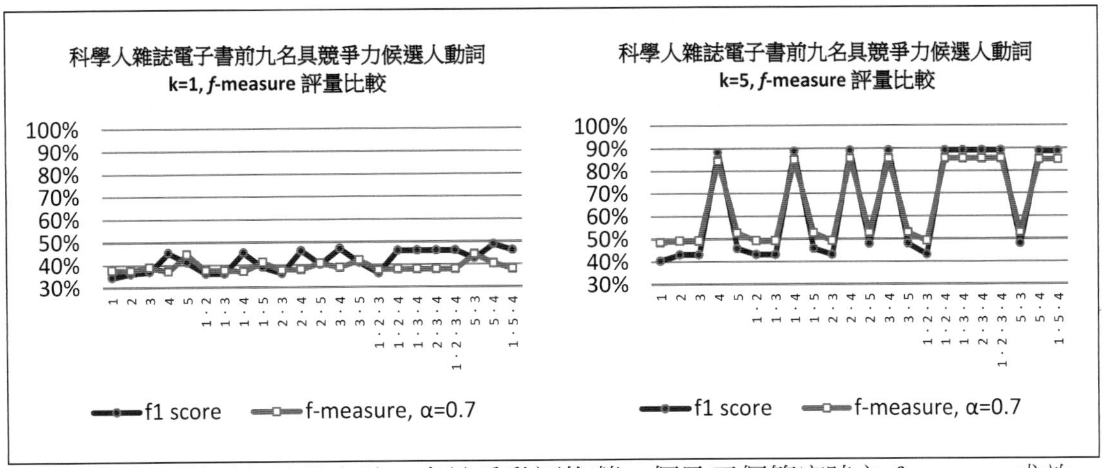

圖十、翻譯模型在科學人前 9 名競爭動詞推薦一個及五個答案時之 ***f***-measure 成效

且注重於答題正確率時，表現相對於其他獨立運作的公式突出，而與公式(5)搭配的組合也有較亮眼的表現；我們認為這是因為資料數量少而資料型態卻又豐富時，公式(5)反而可以用其獨特的觀點去猜到答案。在推薦五個答案時與公式(4)搭配的公式組合仍是表現最為亮眼。

8.3　小結

透過以上分析翻譯模型的表現，本研究提出的公式組合「共同推薦」不僅可以在推薦三個答案時幾乎就能找到正確解答，且可以透過蒐集資訊較多的公式把正確答案在推薦答案中的位置往前拉提，這對於翻譯效果都有正面的影響。

9.　受試者實驗評比

為了評比我們的翻譯模型是否能跟人類的翻譯能力競爭，我們從科學人語料中取出十句英漢對照的句子當作實驗題目，並設定三種翻譯英文動詞的實驗，邀請以中文為母語並具有資工背景的受試者參加。我們規定三種實驗的受試者不得重複跨實驗參加，每位受試者為獨立進行實驗。實驗一有 17 位受試者參與、實驗二有 19 位，實驗三則有 16 位受試者，共 52 位受試者參與實驗。我們使用公式(1)建置的翻譯模型作為參賽者，實驗題目則以公式(1)所能得到的資訊為基準，即受試者至少知道英文的動詞、名詞及中文的名詞這些資訊，不同實驗會附加其他不同程度的資訊以測試受試者會否因為附加資訊的多寡影響其答題效果。我們透過受試者的答題情況與我們的公式(1)翻譯模型作比較，驗證模型的翻譯效能。

9.1　三種實驗提供的題目資訊說明

在第一個實驗中，我們提供受試者英文及其中文翻譯的題目資訊，將題目中的英文目標動詞以灰底粗體標示，並將中文題目對應的動詞翻譯位置挖空，如下頁表四所示。為了不讓受試者只注意到英文的目標動詞及名詞而不完整閱讀題目，我們因此不將目標名詞特別標示。我們將正確答案藏在四個選項中，以表四為例，非正確答案的三個選項是從目標動詞「improving」在科學人語料對應的中文詞彙群中挑選出較高頻的三個詞彙當作誤導選項。這個實驗的目的為讓受試者在接收完整題目的資訊之下，要求受試者將目標動詞翻譯成中文詞彙，並提供選項作答。

表四、實驗一及實驗二題目範例

英文題目	Investigators are, of course, also exploring additional avenues for **improving** efficiency; as far as we know, though, those other approaches generally extend existing methods.
中文題目	當然，研究人員也在尋找其他可________效率的方法，但就我們目前所知，其他方法一般只是延伸現有的途徑罷了。
答案選項	(1) 增進 (2) 提高 (3) 改進 (4) **改善**
目標的中文翻譯群	improve={利用=1, 增加=1, 改良=1, 運用=1, 使=2, 加強=3, 提高=4, 改進=4, 增進=11, 改善=22}

表五、實驗三題目範例

題目	**improve** efficiency : ______ 效率
答案選項	(1) 增進 (2) 提高 (3) 改進 (4) **改善**

關於第二個實驗，我們提供與實驗一相同的題目資訊，唯一不同的地方在於實驗一提供了四個選項讓受試者選擇，如表四所示，而實驗二不提供虛線框起的答案選項，直接要求受試者填寫他們心目中的詞彙。

在第三個實驗中，我們不提供受試者題目的環境及提示，僅提供公式(1)翻譯模型所能得到的資訊給受試者，但是我們附加了答案選項提供選擇，如表五所示：我們僅提供英文動名詞組合及中文名詞，並將英文目標動詞以灰底粗體標記，要求受試者從我們答案選項中選出一個最適合的詞彙作答，這四個答案選項與實驗一的選項相同。

9.2 受試者與翻譯模型效能評比

下頁圖十一為三項實驗受試者平均答題正確率及本研究翻譯模型的表現比較。實驗一提供最多的資訊，受試者平均答對的題數最多，約答對 50%；實驗二雖然提供英漢的題目資訊，但是沒有提供答案選項，受試者平均答對的題數最少，約答對 30%；實驗三的受試者則平均答對了 40%。本研究的翻譯模型答對六題，因此答題正確率為 60%，贏過三項實驗受試者的平均表現。這三個實驗讓我們發現，受試者在提供答案選項的實驗表現較為良好，即使我們提供了完整題目的資訊讓受試者填空，受試者還是很難猜出正確答案；這也就代表即使是人類來答題，在只能回答一個答案時都很難答出正確解答，而我們的翻譯模型則有較好的表現。

下頁圖十二為進一步觀察三群受試者的答題情形，本研究有有趣的發現。第一題的題目在提供題目語意及答案選項的實驗一及只有提供動名詞組合及答案選項的實驗三的答題效果相似，與實驗二的填空題則有很大的差距；第三題題目的實驗二及實驗三答題效果相似；第四題則是實驗三的答題效果最差；第五題確是三個實驗的效果都相似；第六及第七題反而是實驗三效果最好，但在第八題情形卻倒轉；第九題三個實驗的表現也接近，第十題卻是實驗二的填空題效果最好。

這些作答的現象讓我們認為人類在作答的時候，在題目提供的附加資訊多寡之外，人類在閱讀到動名詞組合時應該有其特定的直覺，而且直覺的影響力可能大過實驗所提供的附加資訊，不會根據附加資訊多寡而有固定的表現，因而產生這些有趣的曲線變化。而本實驗未蒐集受試者的個人資訊失為一考量，因此沒有受試者個人特質的相關統計評估，為本實驗待改進之處。

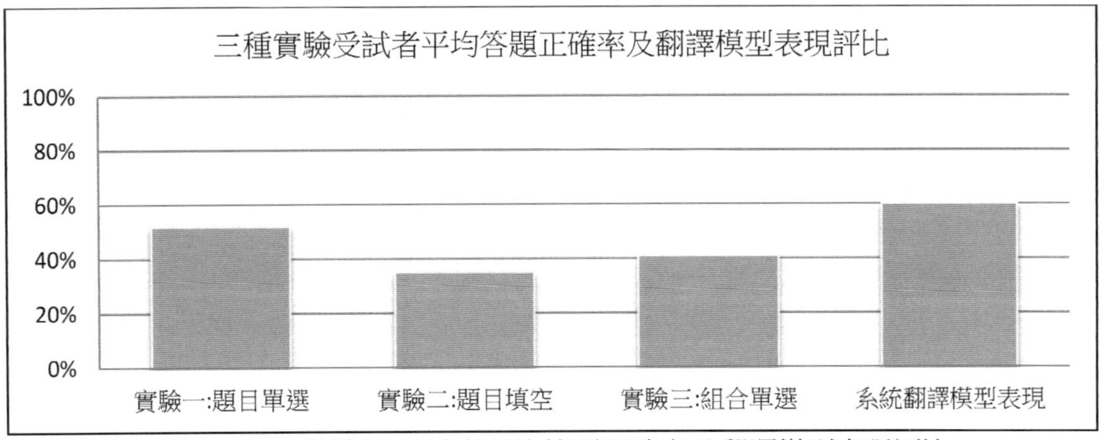

圖十一、三種實驗受試者平均答題正確率及翻譯模型表現評比

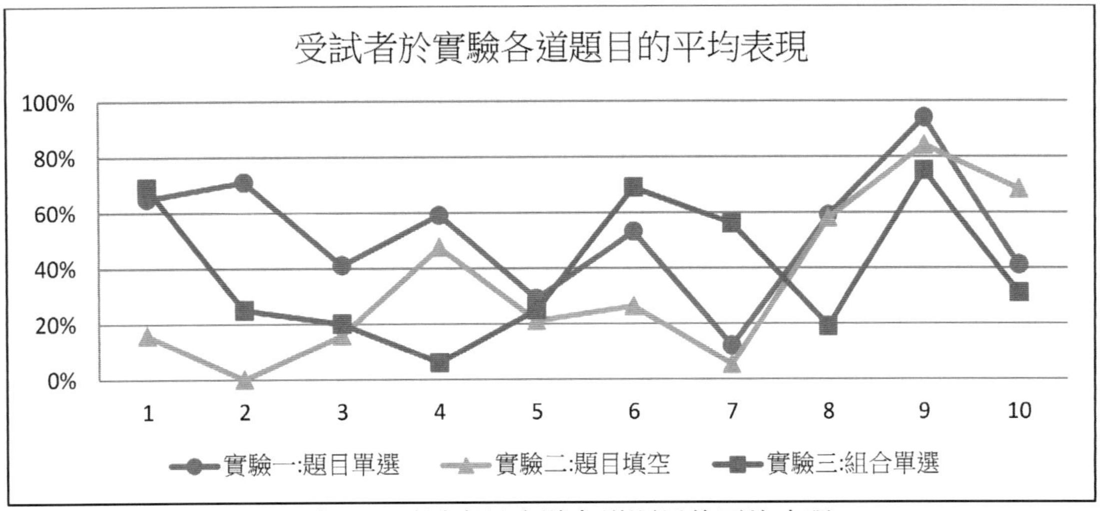

圖十二、受試者於實驗各道題目的平均表現

10. 結論

本研究使用了兩套科技技術類的英漢平行語料庫，並針對英漢動名詞組合進行英文動詞的推薦翻譯。我們分別使用了資訊蒐集程度不同的五種公式，建立針對英漢動名詞組合翻譯英文動詞的模型。我們的實驗結果顯示，將公式組合起來共同推薦能提供不錯的翻譯效果，且在 ***f***-measure 的評量下，與公式(4)搭配的公式組合效果最佳，其建置的翻譯模型推薦到三個答案時幾乎就能包含正確解答在內。蒐集資訊較多的公式(1)、(2)、(3)及(5)在與公式(4)一同搭配時，會將正確解答往前排在推薦答案中，特別是公式(1)的效果最為明顯，符合本研究對於公式(1)的期望。本研究對於英文名詞也建置了對稱的公式及翻譯模型並測試翻譯效果，因受限於篇幅的關係，我們僅描述翻譯結果，結果顯示成效與翻譯英文動詞差異不大，公式共同推薦的翻譯模型有良好的表現。

除了建置翻譯模型並比較成效，我們也設計了三項實驗讓受試者參與，並將受試者的答題正確率與我們使用公式(1)建立的翻譯模型比較表現。結果顯示三項實驗相比，本研究的翻譯模型都能贏過受試者的平均表現。

本研究透過翻譯模型的評量與分析，以及和受試者的翻譯表現作比較，可以驗證我們的翻譯模型具有不錯的推薦翻譯能力及表現。

致謝

本研究承蒙國科會研究計畫 NSC-100-2221-E-004-014 及 NSC-99-2221-E-004-007 的部份補助，僅此致謝。我們感謝評審對於本文的各項指正與指導，限於篇幅因此不能在本文中全面交代相關細節。

參考文獻

[1] Yu-Chia Chang, Jason S. Chang, Hao-Jan Chen and Hsien-Chin Liou, An Automatic Collocation Writing Assistant for Taiwanese EFL Learners: A Case of Corpus-based NLP Technology. *Computer Assisted Language Learning*, 21(3), 283-299, 2008.

[2] Wei-Te Chen, Su-Chu Lin, Shu-Ling Huang, You-Shan Chung and Keh-Jiann Chen, E-HowNet and Automatic Construction of a Lexical Ontology, *Proceedings of the Twenty Third International Conference on Computational Linguistics*, 2010.

[3] Concise Oxford English Dictionary。http://startdict.sourceforge.net/Dictionaries_zh_TW.php [連結已失效。]

[4] Dr.eye 譯典通。http://ajds.nsysu.edu.tw/learn/dict/ [Last visited on 15 June 2011]

[5] E-HowNet。http://ckip.iis.sinica.edu.tw/taxonomy/taxonomy-doc.htm [Last visited on 15 June 2011]

[6] Google。http://www.google.com.tw/ [Last visited on 15 June 2011]

[7] Google Patents beta。http://www.google.com/patents [Last visited on 15 June 2011]

[8] Bin Lu, Benjamin K. Tsou, Tao Jiang, Oi Yee Kwong and Jingbo Zhu, Mining Large-scale Parallel Corpora from Multilingual Patents: An English-Chinese Example and Its Application to SMT. *Proceedings of the First CIPS-SIGHAN Joint Conference on Chinese Language Processing*, 2010.

[9] Patent Translation Task at NTCIR-9。http://ntcir.nii.ac.jp/PatentMT/ [Last visited on 15 June 2011]

[10] Stanford Chinese Segmenter。http://nlp.stanford.edu/software/segmenter.shtml [Last visited on 15 June 2011]

[11] Stanford Parser。http://nlp.stanford.edu/software/lex-parser.shtml [Last visited on 15 June 2011]

[12] Sriam Venkatapathy and Aravind K. Joshi, Measuring the Relative Compositionality of Verb-noun (V-N) Collocations by Integrating Features. *Proceeding of Human Language Technology Conference on Empirical Methods in Natural Language Processing*, 899-906, 2005.

[13] WordNet。http://wordnet.princeton.edu/ [Last visited on 15 June 2011]

[14] 一詞泛讀。http://elearning.ling.sinica.edu.tw/c_help.html [Last visited on 15 June 2011]

[15] 田侃文，英漢專利文書文句對列與應用，國立政治大學資訊科學所，碩士論文，2009。

[16] 科學人雜誌英漢對照電子書。http://edu2.wordpedia.com/taipei_sa/ [Last visited on 15 June 2011]

[17] 國家教育研究院學術名詞資訊網。http://terms.nict.gov.tw/download_main.php [Last visited on 15 June 2011]

Unsupervised Overlapping Feature Selection for Conditional Random Fields Learning in Chinese Word Segmentation

Ting-hao Yang
Institute of Information Science
Academia Sinica
tinghaoyang@iis.sinica.edu.tw

Tian-Jian Jiang
Department of Computer Science
National Tsing-Hua University
tmjiang@iis.sinica.edu.tw

Chan-hung Kuo
Institute of Information Science
Academia Sinica
laybow@iis.sinica.edu.tw

Richard Tzong-han Tsai
Department of Computer Science & Engineering
Yuan Ze University
thtsai@saturn.yzu.edu.tw

Wen-lian Hsu
Institute of Information Science
Academia Sinica
hsu@iis.sinica.edu.tw

Abstract

This work represents several unsupervised feature selections based on frequent strings that help improve conditional random fields (CRF) model for Chinese word segmentation (CWS). These features include character-based N-gram (CNG), Accessor Variety based string (AVS), and Term Contributed Frequency (TCF) with a specific manner of boundary overlapping. For the experiment, the baseline is the *6-tag*, a state-of-the-art labeling scheme of CRF-based CWS; and the data set is acquired from SIGHAN CWS bakeoff 2005. The experiment results show that all of those features improve our system's F_1 measure (F) and Recall of Out-of-Vocabulary (R_{OOV}). In particular, the feature collections which contain AVS feature outperform other types of features in terms of F, whereas the feature collections containing TCB/TCF information has better R_{OOV}.

Keywords: Word Segmentation, Unsupervised Feature Selection, Conditional Random Fields

1. Introduction

Many intelligent text processing tasks such as information retrieval, text-to-speech and machine translation assume the ready availability of a tokenization into words, which is relatively straightforward in languages with word delimiters (e.g. space), while a little difficult for Asian languages such as Chinese and Japanese.

1.1 Background

Chinese word segmentation (CWS) is an essential pre-work for Chinese text processing applications and it has been an active area of research in computational linguistics for two decades. SIGHAN, the Special Interest Group for Chinese Language Processing of the Association for Computational Linguistics, conducted five word segmentation bakeoffs (Sproat and Emerson, 2003; Emerson, 2005; Levow, 2006; Jin and Chen, 2007; Zhao and Liu, 2010). After years of intensive researches, CWS has achieved high precision, but the issue of out-of-vocabulary word handling still remains.

1.2 The State of the Art of CWS

Traditional approaches for CWS adopted dictionary and rules to segment unlabeled texts (c.f. Ma and Chen, 2003). In recent years, the mainstream is to use statistical machine learning models, especially the Conditional Random Fields (CRF) (Lafferty *et al*, 2001), which shows a moderate performance for sequential labeling problem and achieves competitive results with character position based methods (Zhao *et al.*, 2010).

1.3 Unsupervised CRF Feature Selections for CWS

For incorporating unsupervised feature selections into character position based CRF for CWS, Zhao and Kit (2006; 2007) tried strings based on Accessor Variety (AV), which was developed by Feng *et al.* (2004), and co-occurrence strings (COS). Jiang *et al.* (2010) applied a feature similar to COS, called Term Contributed Boundary (TCB). Tsai (2010) employ statistical association measures non-parametrically through a natural but novel feature representation scheme. Those unsupervised feature selection are based on frequent strings extracted automatically from unlabeled corpora. They are suitable for closed training evaluation that any external resource or extra information is not allowed. Without proper knowledge, the closed training evaluation of word segmentation can be difficult with Out-of-Vocabulary (OOV) words, where frequent strings collected from the test data may help.

According to Zhao and Kit (2008), AV-based string (AVS) is one of the most effective unsupervised feature selection for CWS by character position based CRF. This motivates us to seek for explanations for AVS's success. We suspect that AVS is designed to keep overlapping strings but COS/TCB is usually selected with its longest-first nature before integrated into CRF. Hence, we conduct a series of experiments to examine this hypothesis.

The remainder of the article is organized as follows. Section 2 briefly introduces CRF. Common unsupervised feature selections based on the concept of frequent strings are explained in Section 3. Section 4 discusses related works. Section 5 describes the design of labeling scheme, feature templates and a framework that is able to encode those overlapping features in a unified way. Details about the experiment are reported in Section 6. Finally, the conclusion is in Section 7.

2. Conditional Random Fields

Conditional random fields (CRF) are undirected graphical models trained to maximize a conditional probability of random variables X and Y, and the concept is well established for sequential labeling problem (Lafferty *et al.*, 2001). Given an input sequence (or observation sequence) $X = x_1 \ldots x_T$ and label sequence $Y = y_1 \ldots y_T$, a conditional probability of linear-chain CRF with parameters $\Lambda = \{\lambda_1, \ldots, \lambda_n\}$ can be defined as:

$$P_\lambda(Y \mid X) = \frac{1}{Z_X} \exp\left(\sum_{t=1}^{T} \sum_{k} \lambda_k f_k(y_{t-1}, y_t, X, t) \right) \tag{1}$$

where Z_X is the normalization constant that makes probability of all label sequences sum to one, $f_k(y_{t-1}, y_t, X, t)$ is a feature function which is often binary valued, but can be real valued, and λ_k is a learned weight associated with feature f_k .

The feature functions can measure any aspect of state transition $y_{t-1} \rightarrow y_t$, and the entire observation sequence X centered at the current position t.

Given such a model as defined in Equation (1), the most probable labeling sequence for an input sequence X is as follows.

$$y^* = \operatorname*{argmax}_{Y} P_\Lambda(Y \mid X) \tag{2}$$

Equation (2) can be efficiently calculated by dynamic programming using Viterbi algorithm. The more details about concepts of CRF and learning parameters could found in (Wallach, 2004). For sequential labeling tasks like CWS, a linear-chain CRF is currently one of the most popular choices.

3. Frequent String

3.1 Character-based N-gram

The word boundary and the word frequency are the standard notions of frequency in corpus-based natural language processing. Word-based N-gram is an intuitive and effective solution of language modeling. For languages without explicit word boundary such as

Chinese, character-based N-gram (CNG) is usually insufficient. For example, consider the following sample texts in Chinese

- "自然科學的重要性" (the importance of natural science);
- "自然科學的研究是唯一的途徑" (natural science research is the only way).

where many character-based N-grams can be extracted, but some of them are out of context, such as "然科" (so; discipline) and "學的" (study; of), even when they are relatively frequent,. For the purpose of interpreting overlapping behavior of frequent strings, however, character-based N-grams could still be useful for baseline analysis and implementation.

3.2 Reduced N-gram

The lack of correct information about the actual boundary and frequency of a multi-character/word expression has been researched in different languages. The distortion of phrase boundaries and frequencies was first observed in the Vodis Corpus when the word-based bigram "RAIL ENQUIRIES" and word-based trigram "BRITISH RAIL ENQUIRIES" were estimated and reported (O'Boyle, 1993; Ha *et al.*, 2005). Both of them occur 73 times, which is a large number for such a small corpus. "ENQUIRIES" follows "RAIL" with a very high probability when "BRITISH" precede it. However, when "RAIL" is preceded by words other than "BRITISH," "ENQUIRIES" does not occur, but words like "TICKET" or "JOURNEY" may. Thus, the bigram "RAIL ENQUIRIES" gives a misleading probability that "RAIL" is followed by "ENQUIRIES" irrespective of what precedes it.

A common solution to this problem is that if some N-grams consist of others, then the frequencies of the shorter ones have to be discounted with the frequencies of the longer ones. For Chinese, Lin and Yu (2001) reported a similar problem and its corresponding solution in the sense of reduced N-gram of Chinese character. By excluding N-grams with their numbers of appearance that fully depend on other super-sequences, "然科" and "學的" from the sample texts in the previous sub-section are not candidates of string anymore. Zhao and Kit (2007) described the same concept briefly as co-occurrence string (COS). Sung *et al.* (2008) invented a specific data structure for suffix array algorithm to calculate exact boundaries of phrase-alike string and their frequencies called term-contributed boundaries (TCB) and term-contributed frequencies (TCF), respectively, to analogize similarities and differences with the term frequencies. Since we use the program of TCB/TCF for experiment within this study, the family of reduced N-gram will be referred as TCB hereafter for convenience.

3.3 Uncertainty of Succeeding Character

Feng *et al.* (2004) proposed Accessor Variety (AV) to measure how likely a string is a Chinese word. Another measurement called Boundary Entropy or Branching Entropy (BE) exists in some works (Tung and Lee, 1994; Chang and Su, 1997; Cohen and Adams, 2001;

Cohen *et al.*, 2002; Huang and Powers, 2003; Tanaka-Ishii, 2005; Jin and Tanaka-Ishii, 2006; Cohen *et al.*, 2006). The basic idea behind those measurements is closely related to one particular perspective of N-gram and information theory as cross-entropy or Perplexity. According to Zhao and Kit (2007), AV and BE both assume that the border of a potential Chinese word is located where the uncertainty of successive character increases. They believe that AV and BE are the discrete and continuous version, respectively, of a fundamental work of Harris (1970), and then decided to adopt AVS as unsupervised feature selection for CRF-based CWS. We follow their choice in hope of producing a comparable study. AV of a string s is defined as

$$AV(s) = \min\{L_{av}(s), R_{av}(s)\} \quad (3)$$

In Equation (3), $L_{av}(s)$ and $R_{av}(s)$ are defined as the number of distinct preceding and succeeding characters, respectively, except if the adjacent character has been absent because of sentence boundary, then the pseudo-character of sentence beginning or sentence ending will be accumulated indistinctly. Feng *et al.* (2004) also developed more heuristic rules to remove strings that contain known words or adhesive characters. For the strict meaning of unsupervised feature selection and for the sake of simplicity, those additional rules are dropped in this study.

4. Other Related Works

This section briefly describes the following three related works.

4.1 Frequent String Extraction Algorithm

Besides papers of TCB/TCF extraction (Sung *et al.*, 2008), Chinese frequent strings (Lin *et al.*, 2001) and reduced N-gram (Ha *et al.*, 2005) that are mentioned earlier, the article about a linear algorithm for Frequency of Substring Reduction (Lü and Zhang, 2005) also falls into this category. Most of them focused on the computational complexity of algorithms. More general algorithms for frequent string extraction are usually suffix array (Manber and Myers, 1993) and PAT-tree (Chien, 1997).

4.2 Unsupervised Word Segmentation Method

Zhao and Kit (2008) have explored several unsupervised strategies with their unified goodness measurement of logarithm ranking, including Frequency of Substring with Reduction, Description Length Gain (Kit and Wilks, 1999; Kit, 2000), Accessor Variety and Boundary/Branching Entropy. Unlike the technique described in this paper for incorporating unsupervised feature selections into supervised CRF learning, those methods usually filter out word-alike candidates by their own scoring mechanism directly.

4.3 Overlapping Ambiguity Resolution

Subword-based tagging (Zhang *et al.*, 2006) utilizes confidence measurement. Other overlapping ambiguity resolution approaches are Naïve Bayesian classifiers (Li *et al.*, 2003), mutual information, difference of t-test (Sun *et al.*, 1997), and sorted table look-up (Qiao *et al.*, 2008).

5. CRF Labeling Scheme

5.1 Character Position Based Labels

In this study, the *6-tag* approach (Zhao *et al.*, 2010) is adopted as our formulation, which achieves a very competitive performance recently, and is one of the most fine-grained character-position-based labeling schemes. According to Zhao *et al.* (2010), since less than 1% Chinese words are longer than five characters in most corpora from SIGHAN CWS bakeoffs 2003, 2005, 2006 and 2007, the coverage of *6-tag* approach should be good enough. This configuration of CRF without any additional unsupervised feature selection is also the control group of the experiment. Table 1 provides a sample of labeled training data.

Table 1. A Sample of the 6-tag Labels

Character	**Label**
反	B_1
而	E
會	S
欲	B_1
速	B_2
則	B_3
不	M
達	E

For the sample text "反而 (contrarily) / 會 (make) / 欲速則不達 (more haste, less speed)" (on the contrary, haste makes waste), the tag B_1 stands for the beginning character of a word, while B_2 and B_3 represent for the second character and the third character of a word, respectively. The ending character of a word is tagged as E. Once a word consists of more than four characters, the tag for all the middle characters between B_3 and E is M. Finally, the tag S is reserved for single-character words specifically.

5.2 Feature Templates

Feature instances are generated from templates based on the work of Ratnaparkhi (1996). Table 2 explains their abilities.

Table 2. Feature Template

Feature	**Function**
C_{-1}, C_0, C_1	Previous, current, or next token
$C_{-1}C_0$	Previous and current tokens
C_0C_1	Current and next tokens
$C_{-1}C_1$	Previous and next tokens

C_{-1}, C_0 and C_1 stand for the input tokens bound to the prediction label at current position individually. For example in Table 1, if the current position is at the label *M*, features generated by C_{-1}, C_0 and C_1 are "則," "不" and "達," respectively. Meanwhile, for window size 2, $C_{-1}C_0$, C_0C_1 and $C_{-1}C_1$ expands features of the label *M* to "則不," "不達" and "則達," respectively. According to Zhao *et al.* (2010), the context window size in three tokens is effective to catch parameters of 6-tag approach for most strings not longer than five characters. Our pilot test for this case, however, shows that context window size in two tokens would be sufficient without significant performance decreasing. We also intentionally avoid using feature templates that determine character types like alphabet, digit, punctuation, date/time and other non-Chinese characters, to stay with the strict protocol of closed training and unsupervised learning.

Unsupervised feature selections that will be introduced in the next sub-section are of course generated by the same template, except the binding target moves column by column as listed in tables of the next sub-section.

By default, CRF++ generates features not only for the prediction label at the current position, but also for combinations of the prediction label at both the previous and the current position, which should not be confused with the context window size mentioned above.

5.3 A Unified Feature Representation for CNG, AVS and TCB

To compare different types of overlapping strings as unsupervised feature selection systematically, we extend the work of Zhao and Kit (2008) into a unified representation of features. The representation accommodates both character position of a string and this string's likelihood ranked in logarithm. Formally, the ranking function for a string *s* with a score *x* counted by either CNG, AVS or TCB is defined as

$$f(s) = r, if\ 2^r \le x < 2^{r+1} \quad (4)$$

The logarithm ranking mechanism in Equation (4) is inspired by Zipf's law with the intention to alleviate the potential data sparseness problem of infrequent strings. The rank r and the corresponding character positions of a string are then concatenated as feature tokens. To give the reader a clearer picture about what feature tokens look like, a sample representation for CNG, AVS or TCB is demonstrated and explained by Table 3.

For example, judging by strings with two characters, one of the strings "反而" gets rank $r = 3$, therefore the column of two-character feature tokens has "反" denoted as $3B_1$ and "而" denoted as $3E$. If another two-character string "而會" competes with "反而" at the position of "而" with a lower rank $r = 0$, then $3E$ is selected for feature representation of the token at a certain position.

Table 3. A Sample of the Unified Feature Representation for Overlapping String

Input	**Unsupervised Feature Selection**					**Label**
	1 char	2 char	3 char	4 char	5 char	
反	*5S*	$3B_1$	$4B_1$	$0B_1$	$0B_1$	B_1
而	*6S*	*3E*	$4B_2$	$0B_2$	$0B_2$	*E*
會	*6S*	*0E*	*4E*	$0B_3$	$0B_3$	*S*
欲	*4S*	*0E*	*0E*	*0E*	*0M*	B_1
速	*4S*	*0E*	*0E*	*0E*	*0E*	B_2
則	*6S*	$3B_1$	*0E*	*0E*	*0E*	B_3
不	*7S*	*3E*	*0E*	*0E*	*0E*	*M*
達	*5S*	*3E*	*0E*	*0E*	*0E*	*E*

Note that when the string "則不" conflicts with the string "不達" at the position of "不" with the same rank $r = 3$, the corresponding character position with rank of the leftmost string, which is $3E$ in this case, is applied arbitrarily.

Although those are indeed common situations of overlapping strings, we simply inherit the above rules by Zhao and Kit (2008) for the sake of compatibility. In fact, we have done a pilot test with a more complicated representation like $3E\text{-}0B_1$ for "而" and $3E\text{-}3B_1$ for "不" to keep the overlapping information within each column, but the test result shows no significant differences in terms of performance. Since the statistics of the pilot test could be considerably redundant, they are omitted in this paper.

To make an informative comparison, we also apply the original version of non-overlapping COS/TCB feature that is selected by forward maximum matching algorithm and without ranks (Zhao and Kit, 2007; Jiang *et al.*, 2010). The following table illustrates a sample representation of features for this case.

Table 4. A Sample of the Representation for Non-overlapping COS/TCB Strings

Input	Original COS/TCB Feature	Label
反	B_1	B_1
而	B_2	E
會	E	S
欲	*-1*	B_1
速	*-1*	B_2
則	*-1*	B_3
不	*-1*	M
達	*-1*	E

Note that there are several features encoded as -1 individually to represent that the desired string is unseen. For the family of reduced N-grams, such as COS or TCB, it means that either the string is always occupied by other super-strings or simply does not appear more than once.

The length of a string is limited to five characters for the sake of efficiency and consistency with the *6-tag* approach.

6. Experiment

The version 0.54 of the CRF++ employs L-BFGS optimization and the tunable hyper-parameter, i.e. the Gaussian prior, set to 100 throughout the whole experiment.

6.1 Data Set

The corpora used for experiment are from SIGHAN CWS bakeoff 2005. It comes with four different standards including Academia Sinica (AS), City University of Hong Kong (CityU), Microsoft Research (MSR) and Peking University (PKU).

6.2 Unsupervised Feature Collection

Unsupervised feature selections are collected according to pairs of corresponding training/test corpus. CNG and AVS are arranged with the help from SRILM (Stolcke, 2002). TCB strings and their ranks converted from TCF are calculated by YASA. To distinguish the ranked and overlapping feature of TCB/TCF from those of the original version of COS/TCB based features, the former are denoted as TCF to indicate the score source for ranking, and the abbreviation of the later remains as TCB.

6.3 Evaluation Metric

The evaluation metric of CWS task is adopted from SIGHAN bakeoffs, including test Precision (P), test Recall (R), F1 measure score (F) and test Recall of Out-of-Vocabulary (R_{OOV}). Their formulae are list as follows.

$$P = \frac{\text{the number of words thatare correctly segmented}}{\text{the number of words that are segmented}} \times 100\% \quad (5)$$

$$R = \frac{\text{the number of words that are correctly segmented}}{\text{the number of words in the gold standard}} \times 100\% \quad (6)$$

$$F = \frac{2 \times P \times R}{P + R} \quad (7)$$

$$R_{OOV} = \frac{\text{the number of OOV words that are correctly segmented}}{\text{the number of OOV words in the gold standard}} \times 100\% \quad (8)$$

To estimate the differences of performance between configurations of CWS experiment, this work uses the confidence level, which has been applied since SIGHAN CWS bakeoff 2003 (Sproat *et al.*, 2003), that assume the recall (or precision) X of accuracy (or OOV recognition) represents the probability that a word (or OOV word) will be identified from N words in total, and that a binomial distribution is appropriate for the experiment. Confidence levels of P, R, and R_{OOV} appear in Table 5 under the column C_P, C_R, and $C_{R_{OOV}}$, respectively, are calculated at the 95% confidence interval with the formula $\pm 2\sqrt{([X(1\text{-}X)]/N)}$. Two configurations of CWS experiment are then considered to be statistically different at a 95% confidence level if one of their C_P, C_R, or $C_{R_{OOV}}$ is different.

6.4 Experiment Results

The most significant type of error is unintentionally segmented alphanumeric sequences, such as English words or factoids in Arabic numerals. Rather than developing another set of feature templates for those non-Chinese characters that may violate rules of closed training evaluation, a post-processing, which is mentioned in the official report of SIGHAN CWS bakeoff 2005 (Emerson, 2005), has been applied to remove spaces between non-Chinese characters in the gold standard data manually, since there are no urgent expectations of correct segmentation on non-Chinese text. Table 5 lists the statistics after the post-processing. Further discussions are mainly based on this post-processed result without loss of generality. Numbers in bold face and bold-italic style indicate the best and the second-best results of a certain evaluation metric, respectively.

Statistics show clear trends that the feature collections which contain AVS outperforms other types of unsupervised feature selections on *F*, and the feature collections containing

TCB/TCF information usually has better R_{OOV}.

Table 5. Performance Comparison After Post-processing

Corpus	Feature	C_P	C_R	F	R_{OOV}	$C_{R_{OOV}}$
AS	6-tag	±0.00125	±0.00114	.955	.726	±0.01164
	CNG	±0.00124	±0.00113	.955	.730	±0.01159
	AVS	±0.00120	±0.00109	**.958**	.738	±0.01147
	TCF	±0.00126	±0.00117	.953	**.760**	±0.01114
	TCB	±0.00123	±0.00113	***.956***	.740	±0.01145
	AVS+TCF	±0.00123	±0.00113	***.956***	***.751***	±0.01128
	AVS+TCB	±0.00120	±0.00109	**.958**	.739	±0.01147
CityU	6-tag	±0.00219	±0.00221	.948	.738	±0.01536
	CNG	±0.00207	±0.00215	.953	.760	±0.01493
	AVS	±0.00199	±0.00203	***.957***	.766	±0.01480
	TCF	±0.00208	±0.00214	.953	.767	±0.01478
	TCB	±0.00209	±0.00214	.953	***.770***	±0.01470
	AVS+TCF	±0.00197	±0.00200	**.959**	**.777**	±0.01455
	AVS+TCB	±0.00207	±0.00213	.953	.771	±0.01469
MSR	6-tag	±0.00100	±0.00105	.971	.776	±0.01405
	CNG	±0.00100	±0.00104	***.972***	.784	±0.01387
	AVS	±0.00099	±0.00099	**.973**	.764	±0.01432
	TCF	±0.00099	±0.00104	***.972***	.786	±0.01384
	TCB	±0.00099	±0.00104	***.972***	***.787***	±0.01381
	AVS+TCF	±0.00107	±0.00114	.967	**.793**	±0.01367
	AVS+TCB	±0.00101	±0.00102	***.972***	.769	±0.01422
PKU	6-tag	±0.00139	±0.00159	.939	.680	±0.01140
	CNG	±0.00139	±0.00160	.938	.671	±0.01149
	AVS	±0.00132	±0.00146	**.947**	***.740***	±0.01072
	TCF	±0.00138	±0.00155	***.941***	.701	±0.01119
	TCB	±0.00139	±0.00159	.939	.688	±0.01133
	AVS+TCF	±0.00137	±0.00155	***.941***	.709	±0.01110
	AVS+TCB	±0.00132	±0.00147	**.947**	**.743**	±0.01067

It has been observed that using any of the unsupervised feature selections could create short patterns for CRF learner, which might break more English words than using the *6-tag* approach solely. AVS, TCF and TCB, however, resolve more overlapping ambiguities of Chinese words than the *6-tag* approach and CNG. Interestingly, even for the unsupervised feature selection without rank and overlapping information, TCB successfully recognizes "依

靠 / 单位 / 的 / 纽带 / 来 / 维持," while the *6-tag* approach see this phrase incorrectly as "依靠 / 单位 / 的 / 纽 / 带来 / 维持." TCB also saves more factoids, such as "一二九 · 九 / 左右" (around 129.9) from scattered tokens, such as "一二九 / · / 九 左右" (129 point 9 around).

The above observations suggest that the quality of a string as a word-alike candidate should be an important factor for unsupervised feature selection injected CRF learner. Relatively speaking, CNG probably brings in too much noise. Non-overlapping COS/TCB seems to be a moderate choice with a lower training cost of CRF than those of other overlapping features. This confirms our hypothesis at the end of Section 1.3 that, including overlapping information as an unsupervised feature selection may help improving CWS performance of supervised labeling scheme of CRF.

7. Conclusion and Future Works

This paper provides a study about CRF-based CWS integrated with unsupervised and overlapping feature selections. The experiment results show that the feature collections which contain AVS obtains better performance in terms of F_1 measure score, and TCB/TCF enhances the 6-tag approach on the Recall of Out-of-Vocabulary. In the future, we will search for a hybrid method that utilizes information both inside and outside Chinese words simultaneously.

Acknowledgement

This research was supported in part by the National Science Council under grant NSC 100-2631-S-001-001, and the research center for Humanities and Social Sciences under grant IIS-50-23. The authors would like to thank anonymous reviewers for their constructive criticisms.

References

[1] Peter O'Boyle, "A Study of an N-Gram Language Model for Speech Recognition", PhD Thesis, Queen's University Belfast , 1993.

[2] Cheng-Huang Tung and His-Jian Lee, "Identification of Unknown Words from Corpus", *Computational Proceedings of Chinese and Oriental Languages*, vol.8, pp.131-145, 1994.

[3] Jing-Shin Chang and Keh-Yih Su, "An Unsupervised Iterative Method for Chinese New Lexicon Extraction", *Computational Linguistics and Chinese Language Processing*, vol.2, no.2, pp.97-148, 1997.

[4] Maosong Sun, Changning Huang, Benjamin K.Tsou, "Using Character Bigram for Ambiguity Resolution In Chinese Word Segmentation (In Chinese)", *Computer*

Research and Development, vol.34, no.5, pp.332-339, 1997.

[5] Lee-Feng Chien, "PAT-tree-based Keyword Extraction for Chinese Information Retrieval", in *Proceedings of the 20th Annual International ACM SIGIR Conference on Research and Development in Information Retrieval*, pp.50-58, 1997.

[6] John Lafferty, Andrew McCallum, Fernando Pereira, "Conditional Random Fields Probabilistic Models for Segmenting and Labeling Sequence Data", in *Proceedings of International Conference on Machine Learning*, pp.591-598, 2001.

[7] Yih-Jeng Lin, Ming-Shing Yu, "Extracting Chinese Frequent Strings without a Dictionary from a Chinese Corpus and its Applications", *Journal of Information Science and Engineering 17*, pp.805-824, 2001.

[8] Andreas Stolcke, *"SRILM - An Extensible Language Modeling Toolkit",* in *the Proceedings of Spoken Language Processing*, pp.901-904, 2002.

[9] Mu Li, Jianfeng Gao, Chang-Ning Huang, "Unsupervised Training for Overlapping Ambiguity Resolution in Chinese Word Segmentation", in *the Proceedings of The Second SIGHAN Workshop on Chinese Language Processing*, pp.1-7, 2003.

[10] Richard Sproat, Thomas Emerson, "The First International Chinese Word Segmentation Bakeoff", in *the Proceedings of The Second SIGHAN Workshop on Chinese Language Processing, Sapporo, July 11-12*, 2003, pp.113-143.

[11] Wei-Yun Ma, Keh-Jiann Chen, "Introduction to CKIP Chinese Word Segmentation System for the First International Chinese Word Segmentation Bakeoff", in *the Proceedings of Second SIGHAN Workshop on Chinese Language Processing*, pp.168-171, 2003.

[12] Haodi Feng, Kang Chen, Xiaotie Deng, and Wiemin Zheng, "*Accessor Variety Criteria for Chinese Word Extraction*", *Computational Linguistics*, vol.30, no.1, pp.75-93, 2004.

[13] Hanna M. Wallach, "Conditional Random Fields An Introduction", Department of Computer and Information Science, University of Pennsylvania, Tech. Rep. MS-CIS-04-21, 2004.

[14] Le Quan Ha, Rowan Seymour, Philip Hanna and Francis J. Smith, "Reduced N-Grams for Chinese Evaluation", *Computational Linguistics and Chinese Language Processing,* vol.10, no.1, pp.19-34, 2005.

[15] Thomas Emerson, "The Second International Chinese Word Segmentation Bakeoff", in *the Proceedings of the Fourth SIGHAN Workshop on Chinese Language Processing*, pp.123-133, 2005.

[16] Xueqiang Lü, Le Zhang, "Statistical Substring Reduction in Linear Time", in *the Proceedings of the 1st International Joint Conference on Natural Language Processing*, pp.320-327, 2005.

[17] Gina-Anne Levow, "The Third International Chinese Language Processing Bakeoff Word Segmentation and Named Entity Recognition", in *the Proceedings of The Fifth*

SIGHAN Workshop on Chinese Language Processing, pp.108-117, 2006.

[18]Ruiqiang Zhang, Genichiro Kikui, Eiichiro Sumita, "Subword-based Tagging for Confidence-dependent Chinese Word Segmentation", in *the Proceedings of COLING/ACL*, pp.961-968, 2006.

[19]Guangjin Jin, Xiao Chen, "The Fourth International Chinese Language Processing Bakeoff : Chinese Word Segmentation, Named Entity Recognition and Chinese POS Tagging", in *the Proceedings of The Sixth SIGHAN Workshop on Chinese Language Processing*, pp.69-81, 2007.

[20]Wei Qiao, Maosong Sun, Wolfgang Menzel, "Statistical Properties of Overlapping Ambiguities in Chinese Word Segmentation and a Strategy for Their Disambiguation", in *the Proceedings of Text, Speech and Dialogue*, pp.177-186, 2008.

[21]Cheng-Lung Sung, Hsu-Chun Yen, Wen-Lian Hsu, "Compute the Term Contributed Frequency", in *the Proceedings of The Eighth International Conference on Intelligent Systems Design and Applications*, pp.325–328, 2008.

[22]Hai Zhao, Chunyu Kit, "Exploiting Unlabeled Text with Different Unsupervised Segmentation Criteria for Chinese Word Segmentation", in *the Proceedings of The Ninth International Conference on Intelligent Text Processing and Computational Linguistics*, pp.17-23, 2008.

[23]Hai Zhao, Chang-Ning Huang, Mu Li, Lu, Bao-Liang Lu, "A Unified Character-Based Tagging Framework for Chinese Word Segmentation", *ACM Transactions on Asian Language Information Processing*, vol.9, no.2, 2010.

[24]Hai Zhao, Qun Liu, "The CIPS-SIGHAN CLP2010 Chinese Word Segmentation Backoff", in *the Proceedings of The First CIPS-SIGHAN Joint Conference on Chinese Language Processing*, pp.199-209, 2010.

[25]Richard Tzong-Han Tsai, "Chinese text segmentation: A hybrid approach using transductive learning and statistical association measures", *Expert Systems with Applications,* vol.37, no.5, pp.3553-3560, 2010.

[26]Tian-Jian Jiang, Shih-Hung Liu, Cheng-Lung Sung and Wen-Lian Hsu, "Term Contributed Boundary Tagging by Conditional Random Fields for SIGHAN 2010 Chinese Word Segmentation Bakeoff", in *the Proceedings of the CIPS-SIGHAN Joint Conference on Chinese Language Processing, Beijing, China*, pp.266-269, August 28-29, 2010.

繁體中文文本中對於日文人名及異體字的處理策略

林川傑+、詹嘉丞*、陳彥亨+、鮑建威+
國立臺灣海洋大學資訊工程學系
Department of Computer Science and Engineering
National Taiwan Ocean University
{cjlin, M98570019, M98570020}@mail.ntou.edu.tw+, jjt@cyber.cs.ntou.edu.tw*

摘要

本論文提出一個可於進行繁體中文文章斷詞時，處理非繁體中文詞彙的方法。包括以日文漢字或中文書寫的日文人名，或是以異體字書寫的同義詞等。處理人名時，我們提出了姓名組合機率模型。處理日文人名時，我們也提出一個異體字對應的方法，可將日文姓氏及名用字對應至繁體中文用字。這方法甚至可以處理同一句子中同時出現日文及繁簡中文書寫方式的情形。在加入各種特殊類別以及中日人名處理方法後，斷詞效能 F-measure 由 94.16%提昇至 96.06%。另外對 109 篇標有日文人名的中文新聞文章進行斷詞實驗，測試集裡 862 個日文人名被成功斷成詞的比例爲 83.18%。論文中亦針對以異體字書寫的中文詞提出了一套可行的處理方式。

關鍵詞：中文斷詞、日文人名判斷、異體字

Keywords: Chinese word segmentation, Japanese name identification, variant form

一、緒論

中文斷詞在中文語言處理中，是一項重要而且必須的技術。然而中文文章裡日文人名及異體字的處理卻鮮少被研究。以往繁體中文是採 BIG5 編碼的時候，要寫出一個日文人名，書寫者常以其對應的繁體中文字元來改寫。像是原本日文漢字寫做「滝沢秀明」，在繁體中文文章中就會寫做「瀧澤秀明」。Unicode 編碼計畫出現後，就可出現多種語言字元出現在同一篇文章中的情形。各地的漢字字型多有不同，像「圖」這個字，大陸簡體字做「图」，而日文則是寫做「図」。這樣書寫習慣在中文斷詞處理中有什麼影響，在過去的研究中很少被提及。本論文便想探討這些漢字對應情形的處理。

中文斷詞的研究由來已久，現有的斷詞系統多爲規則式或是機率模型的系統。常用斷詞規則像是長詞優先規則，或是少詞優先規則。機率模型則常用馬可夫模型的 unigram 模型或是 bigram 模型等等，例如[1]。斷詞候選詞的集合多爲字典詞彙，或是以大型語料庫中蒐集詞彙。有的系統會使用構詞規則來產生部份的合法詞彙 [2]，像是一個名詞後面加上 “們” 也是合法的詞 (例如 “學生們”、“家長們”)。Wu and Jiang [3] 甚至結合文法剖析來進行斷詞。

除了斷詞歧義性之外，未知詞的處理也是一個重要課題。除了罕見詞彙 (像是 “躉售”)、專門術語 (像是化學名詞 “三聚氰胺”) 以及新發明詞彙 [4] (像是 “新流感”) 之外，具名實體 (named enitiy) 如人名、地名、組織名等的辨識技術也是研究的重點之一，例如 [5]。近來斷詞研究也探討了自動機器學習的方法，支持向量機 (SVM) [6]、條件隨機域 (CRF) [7][8] 都是曾應用在斷詞研究的機器學習方法。

較少有研究提及在繁體中文文章中處理非繁體中文詞彙的議題。比較相關的研究是探討不同區域中文詞彙使用上的差異對斷詞帶來的影響，例如使用台灣地區文章做為訓練資料，拿來對大陸或是香港地區文章做斷詞的可能性，或是擴充字典來涵蓋各地域及各領域的詞彙等等 [9]。

本論文的問題定義為，當中文文章中出現非繁體中文詞彙時，例如“滝沢秀明”這類以日文漢字書寫的日文人名、以“瀧澤秀明”對應中文漢字書寫的日文人名，或是“裡面”、“裏面”這類異體同義字，甚至是繁簡中文夾雜的文本，斷詞時能將正確候選詞判斷出來，以利斷詞成功。除第二節介紹斷詞系統基本架構外，第三節為中日文人名處理模組，第四節說明中日漢字及異體字對應方式，第五節為實驗結果以及討論，第六節為結論以及未來展望。

二、斷詞策略

本文重點在探討斷詞時非繁體中文詞彙的處理策略，因此斷詞系統僅採用基本的 bigram 機率模型，旨在驗證各種策略對於斷詞效能的改善情形。候選詞除查詢已知詞列表外，另設計各種特殊類別 (如日期、數字等) 判斷規則來處理較具格式的詞彙。注意同一候選詞可能同時隸屬於多種特殊類別或是已知詞列表中的普通詞。如果在某個位置沒有找到任何長度的候選詞，系統會將該位置的字元視為單字詞做為候選詞。接著對每一種斷詞組合計算生成機率值，最高者做為最後的輸出結果。

(一) 特殊類別候選詞

許多類別例如數詞、時間、日期、人名等等，其可能詞彙非常多樣，甚至可能是無限大的集合，字典不可能收錄所有詞彙，所以我們為這些類別撰寫了判斷規則來發掘輸入句中這類候選詞。本系統所處理之特殊類別包含了地址 (可依不同國家擴增)、日期、時間、金錢、百分比、分數、網路 (IP、網址與 e-mail 地址等)、數字、外文字串及中日人名。字串中出現之英數字可為全形、半形字以及漢數字 (一二…壹貳…)。外文字串依 Unicode 碼區可任意加入其他非拉丁字母之外文字集，如韓文、希臘文、阿拉伯文等等。因為各外文多以空白為斷詞符號，便可將連續出現之同一外語字串合而為一詞。因為本論文重點不在此，各判斷規則不做說明，僅人名的判斷規則會在第三章中介紹。

(二) 二元機率模型

產生斷詞組合之後，下一步要計算各組合的生成機率值 $P(S)$。機率值的計算方法很多，本論文使用了馬可夫的 bigram 機率模型，公式為：

$$P(S = w_1 w_2 ... w_N) = P(w_1) \times \prod_{i=2}^{N} P(w_i \mid w_{i-1}) \quad (公式 1)$$

其中 $P(w_i)$ 為詞 w_i 的 unigram 機率，而 $P(w_i \mid w_{i-1})$ 為詞 w_i 出現在詞 w_{i-1} 後面的機率。為了避免機率值連乘會過小而產生 underflow 現象，習慣上以等號兩邊取其 log 值來計算：

$$\log P(S = w_1 w_2 ... w_N) = \log P(w_1) + \sum_{i=2}^{N} \log P(w_i \mid w_{i-1}) \quad (公式 2)$$

Bigram 模型訓練時因為需要兩個中文詞緊鄰出現，容易有資料稀疏 (data sparseness) 的問題，也就是說大部份的中文詞 bigram 都無法訓練得到機率值。我們採用的解決方法是 backoff 至 unigram 模型，也就是當 $\langle w_{i-1}, w_i \rangle$ 這個 bigram 不曾出現在訓練語料中時，$P(w_i \mid w_{i-1})$ 的值改由 $\alpha P(w_i)$ 來估算。

若是 bigram 中有特殊類別詞彙時，其 bigram 機率改以類別機率來計算。假設 w_i 屬特殊類別 S，則機率計算方式改爲：

$$P(w_i \mid w_{i-1})P(w_{i+1} \mid w_i) = P(S \mid w_{i-1}) \times P(w_{i+1} \mid S) \times P_G(w_i \mid S) \quad \text{(公式 3)}$$

其中 $P(S \mid w_{i-1})$ 與 $P(w_{i+1} \mid S)$表示 S 類別與其他詞彙之 bigram 機率，$P_G(w_i \mid S)$ 表示類別 S 中出現 w_i 的機率，除人名外 (請見第三節)，各特殊類別值均設爲 1。

至於類別 bigram 機率模型，地址、金錢、編號、百分比、分數、網路和外文這幾類候選詞的邊界非常明確，而且不常有歧義性出現，因此我們完全信任以這些規則所判斷出來的候選詞。這幾類詞的類別 bigram 機率值均設定爲 1，表示出現這幾類候選詞的時候就會優先採用該候選詞斷法。

數字字元倒是常出現在非數詞彙中，像是 “一切”、“萬一”，其類別機率需由訓練語料統計而得。邊界明確的日期時間，如 “中華民國九十八年六月二十一日”，類別機率可設爲 1。若是有歧義現象者，像 “三十年” 可能是指 “民國三十年” 或是 “三十個年度”，它們的類別機率也採用訓練語料統計所得者。

在訓練機率模型之前，先以特殊類別判斷規則至訓練集中找尋特殊類別詞彙的出現，將之取代爲所屬類別標籤，再用來訓練 bigram 機率模型。找尋時會佐以詞性資訊，例如數字詞性一定要是 Neu，日期時間一定是 Nd 等。地址、金錢這類在原訓練集中會被斷成好幾個詞的情形，則是採多詞合併的比對策略。

類別機率的作法和 Gao *et al.* [2] 的做法很類似，但不同的是，他們將所有字典詞視爲一個類別，由各種構詞規則所衍生出來的詞也算同一種類別。與我們各種特殊類別各有其類別機率的做法十分不同。

(三) 降低計算量之演算法

當句子長度太長、或是候選詞數目太多時，會產生太多的斷詞組合，有時會高達十萬組以上，機率計算上相當耗時甚至不可行。爲了減少計算時間，我們使用 beam search 演算法來簡化計算的步驟，演算法的精神描述如下。

令原句中有 N 個字，則建立 N 個 priority queues，表示爲 record[i]，用來記錄到目前爲止，系統所找到涵蓋輸入句前 i 個字元的斷詞組合中分數最高的前 k 名。對於每個由位置 i+1 開始的候選詞 w (令其長度爲 b)，分別與 record[i] 中 k 種斷詞方式結合，並計算 $c_1 \ldots c_{i+1} \ldots c_{i+b}$ 的斷詞機率值，再與 record[$i+b$] 佇列中各斷詞組合機率值比較。如能排進前 k 名，就將最小機率者擠出佇列 record[$i+b$]。

斷詞開始時各 priority queue 均清空，i 由 0 開始反覆進行上述步驟，直至 N 個位置候選詞均被考慮完爲止。最後儲存在 record[N] 的第一名即爲機率最高的組合，做爲輸入句的斷詞輸出結果。本論文中 k 值設爲 20。

三、中日文人名處理

本節先討論如何在繁體中文文章中找出以日文漢字書寫的日文人名候選詞，至於找出以繁體中文對應字書寫日文人名的方法則留待第四、(二)節再來討論。日文人名的斷詞策略來自於中文人名的處理經驗，因此本節會先介紹產生中文人名候選詞的方法，再說明日文人名的處理方式。

(一) 中文人名處理

產生中文人名候選詞時，任何可能的中文姓名組合都可以當作中文人名的候選詞。在計算機率時，除了估算中文字能做爲姓或名的機率外，我們還估算了各種姓名組合出現的機率值。在中文文章中可能出現的中文人名組合型式如表一所列：

表一、中文人名組合型式

組合型式	可能組合	範例	組合型式	可能組合	範例
只有姓	單姓 複姓	林　老師 諸葛　先生	姓+名	單姓+單名 單姓+雙名 雙姓+單名 雙姓+雙名 複姓+單名 複姓+雙名	陳登 王小明 張李娥 張陳素珠 諸葛亮 司馬中原
只有名	單名 雙名	慧 國雄			

辨識中文人名首先要有中文姓氏列表，本論文引用中文維基百科的兩個詞條「中國姓氏列表」[1]與「複姓」[2]，還有內政部戶政司[3]、中華百家姓[4]、千家姓[5]等網站共蒐集得 2,471 個姓氏。至於中文人名的名字部份，因爲人名可以隨便取，所以我們將所有的漢字都當成名用字的可能集合。

實際在提出可能的中文人名的候選詞時，並不考慮僅有單名而沒有姓的組合，原因是避免把每個中文單字都判斷成單字人名而大幅降低斷詞的效能。姓氏的雙姓部份也只考慮單姓+單姓的組合，不考慮複姓+單姓或是複姓+複姓這兩種組合，因爲並不曾見過。

$$P_G(w \mid S_{CHname}) = \max_{\sigma,\pi} P_\sigma(w \mid \pi) P_G(\pi \mid S_{CHname}) \qquad \text{(公式 4)}$$

一個中文字串w成爲中文姓名的機率定義如公式 4 所示，其中σ 說明和性別相關的機率模型，分別有男子名和女子名兩種。π 是w可以符合的一種姓名組合，用π = ‘xxxx’ 的格式來表示，以 ‘s’ 表示單姓，‘dd’ 表示複姓，‘n’ 表示人名裡單個字，例如雙姓+雙名的組合就表示爲π = ‘ssnn’，複姓+單名的組合就表示爲π = ‘ddn’。**姓名生成機率**$P_\sigma(w|\pi)$ 就是在性別σ 的姓名組合π 情形下生成中文人名w的機率。**姓名組合機率**$P_G(\pi \mid S_{CHname})$ 則是中文人名 (類別標爲S_{CHname}) 在文章中以π 這種姓名組合出現的機率。表二列出了各種姓名組合情形下，計算中文字串成爲中文姓名機率的算法。底下分別說明這兩種機率模型的建立方法。

計算姓名生成機率$P_\sigma(w|\pi)$ 時，我們採用Chen *et al.* [10] 的想法：假設姓名各字元之間無關，亦即姓氏與名字的選用無關，名用字間亦無相關。我們也假設姓氏出現機率與性別無關。表二中「姓名生成機率」欄定義了各種姓名組合的機率公式，其中LN_{CH}爲中文姓氏集合，FN_{CH}爲中文名用字的集合。

---

1 http://zh.wikipedia.org/wiki/中國姓氏列表
2 http://zh.wikipedia.org/wiki/複姓
3 http://www.ris.gov.tw/ch4/0940531-2.doc
4 http://www.greatchinese.com/surname/surname.htm
5 http://pjoke.com/showxing.php

表二、各種中文姓名組合機率算法

姓名組合	姓名生成機率 $P_\sigma(w\|\pi)$	姓名組合機率
單姓	$P(c_1\|LN_{CH})$	$P(\pi=\text{'s'}\|S_{CHname})$
複姓	$P(c_1c_2\|LN_{CH})$	$P(\pi=\text{'dd'}\|S_{CHname})$
單姓+單名	$P(c_1\|LN_{CH})\times P_\sigma(c_2\|FN_{CH})$	$P(\pi=\text{'sn'}\|S_{CHname})$
雙名	$P_\sigma(c_1\|FN_{CH})\times P_\sigma(c_2\|FN_{CH})$	$P(\pi=\text{'nn'}\|S_{CHname})$
複姓+單名	$P(c_1c_2\|LN_{CH})\times P_\sigma(c_3\|FN_{CH})$	$P(\pi=\text{'ddn'}\|S_{CHname})$
單姓+雙名	$P(c_1\|LN_{CH})\times P_\sigma(c_2\|FN_{CH})\times P_\sigma(c_3\|FN_{CH})$	$P(\pi=\text{'snn'}\|S_{CHname})$
雙姓+單名	$P(c_1\|LN_{CH})\times P(c_2\|LN_{CH})\times P_\sigma(c_3\|FN_{CH})$	$P(\pi=\text{'ssn'}\|S_{CHname})$
複姓+雙名	$P(c_1c_2\|LN_{CH})\times P_\sigma(c_3\|FN_{CH})\times P_\sigma(c_4\|FN_{CH})$	$P(\pi=\text{'ddnn'}\|S_{CHname})$
雙姓+雙名	$P(c_1\|LN_{CH})\times P(c_2\|LN_{CH})\times P_\sigma(c_3\|FN_{CH})\times P_\sigma(c_4\|FN_{CH})$	$P(\pi=\text{'ssnn'}\|S_{CHname})$

建立單姓、複姓與每個名用字的出現機率，也就是 $P(c_i|LN_{CH})$、$P(c_ic_{i+1}|LN_{CH})$ 以及 $P_\sigma(c_j|FN_{CH})$ 是由一個大量的語料以 maximum likelihood 的方式統計而得，即：

$P(c_i\,|\,LN_{CH})$ = 單姓 c_i 出現次數 / 所有人名個數
$P(c_ic_{i+1}\,|\,LN_{CH})$ = 複姓 c_ic_{i+1} 出現次數 / 所有人名個數
$P_\sigma(c_j\,|\,FN_{CH})$ = 名用字 c_j 出現次數 / 性別σ 所有人名名字字數總和

我們採用了收錄約一百萬個台灣地區的百萬人名表來統計姓氏與名的機率，其中男性姓名有 476,269 個，女性姓名有 503,679 個。由於百萬人名表中只有 953 個姓氏和四千多個名用字曾經出現，其他沒有統計資料的姓氏或名用字，我們也給予一個極小的機率值，以免造成姓名生成機率爲 0 的情形。多組實驗後經驗值建議爲 10^{-1000}。

接著估算姓名組合機率 $P_G(\pi\mid S_{CHname})$。由於我們希望得到的是各種姓名組合在中文文章中出現的機率，因此與百萬人名表中姓名組合分佈情形不盡相同。文章中常出現姓氏加上職稱的情形，例如“林 老師”、“諸葛 先生”。在小說、書信或是話語中，也常出現僅有名字沒有姓氏、較親密的稱呼。這些現象並無法由僅是人名列表的百萬人名表觀察而得，所以需要準備一份真實文章中人名出現情形的大量訓練語料。

人名在中研院平衡語料庫中屬於專有名詞 (詞性 Nb)。我們於是以平衡語料庫中所有符合前述中文人名組合規則的專有名詞視爲中文人名。這些人名是在真實文章中出現的，符合我們的需求。但是因爲中文姓氏太多，容易將四個字以內的專有名詞都判斷爲人名，像“中”也是一個姓氏，“中興號”這個客運名稱就會被誤判爲人名。爲了避免誤判，又希望能找出大部份的人名，我們於是只採用常見的姓氏和名用字來比對。這裡採用的是最常見單姓中出現機率 $P(c_i|LN_{CH})$ 合計 90%的 64 個姓氏 (陳林…程)、最常見男性名用字出現機率 $P_M(c_j|FN_{CH})$ 合計 90%的 467 個字 (文明…瀛)、最常見女性名用字出現機率 $P_F(c_j|FN_{CH})$ 合計 90%的 293 個字 (美淑…吉)，再加上所有已知複姓來判斷。判斷規則與優先順序如下，每個姓名只會被判斷成一種組合：

單字詞：單姓 > 單名 > 非中文人名
雙字詞：複姓 > 單姓+單名 > 雙名 > 非中文人名
三字詞：複姓+單名 > 單姓+雙名 > 雙姓+單名 > 非中文人名
四字詞：複姓+雙名 > 雙姓+雙名 > 非中文人名
五字詞：非中文人名

此外還再加入了“公孫氏”、“張姓”這類姓名組合，即姓氏加上“姓”或“氏”的組合，以π ='p' 來表示。以依照上列規則，平衡語料庫中 92,314 個專有名詞，有 39,612 個被判斷爲人名，各種姓名組合的出現頻率如表三所示。這些詞雖然有誤判或漏判爲人名的可能性，但期待由大量資料統計所得之數值仍有其準確性。本資料除了用以產生姓名組合機率外，也會用來計算中文人名類別S_{CHname}的類別bigram機率。

表三、中文姓名組合機率表

姓名組合機率	數量	機率値	姓名組合機率	數量	機率値
$P(\pi$='s'$\|S_{CHname})$	5,431	13.71%	$P(\pi$='ddn'$\|S_{CHname})$	126	0.32%
$P(\pi$='n'$\|S_{CHname})$	815	2.06%	$P(\pi$='snn'$\|S_{CHname})$	19,454	49.11%
$P(\pi$='p'$\|S_{CHname})$	487	1.23%	$P(\pi$='ssn'$\|S_{CHname})$	58	0.15%
$P(\pi$='dd'$\|S_{CHname})$	46	0.12%	$P(\pi$='ddnn'$\|S_{CHname})$	24	0.06%
$P(\pi$='sn'$\|S_{CHname})$	2,845	7.18%	$P(\pi$='ssnn'$\|S_{CHname})$	61	0.15%
$P(\pi$='nn'$\|S_{CHname})$	10,265	25.91%	總共	39,612	

舉個例子說明，計算“張德培”這個字串是否爲中文人名時，因爲“張”和“德”都是中文姓氏，所以會考慮兩種姓名組合$\boldsymbol{\pi}$={'snn', 'ssn'} 以及兩種性別$\boldsymbol{\sigma}$={M 男性, F 女性} 四種情形的機率值，取最大的值做爲“張德培”這個字串成爲中文人名的機率値。計算結果發現，以男性的單姓+雙名這種情形分數最高。

姓名：張德培		
π	σ	機率計算
snn	男	log (P(張$\|LN_{CH}$)×P_M(德$\|FN_{CH}$)×P_M(培$\|FN_{CH}$)×$P(\pi$='snn'$\|S_{CHname}$)) = (-1.26) + (-1.87) + (-2.74) + (-0.31) = -6.18
snn	女	log (P(張$\|LN_{CH}$)×P_F(德$\|FN_{CH}$)×P_F(培$\|FN_{CH}$)×$P(\pi$='snn'$\|S_{CHname}$)) = (-1.26) + (-2.89) + (-3.27) + (-0.31) = -7.73
ssn	男	log (P(張$\|LN_{CH}$)×P(德$\|LN_{CH}$)×P_M(培$\|FN_{CH}$)×$P(\pi$='ssn'$\|S_{CHname}$)) = (-1.26) + (-6.02) + (-2.74) + (-2.82) = -12.84
ssn	女	log (P(張$\|LN_{CH}$)×P(德$\|LN_{CH}$)×P_F(培$\|FN_{CH}$)×$P(\pi$='ssn'$\|S_{CHname}$)) = (-1.26) + (-6.02) + (-3.27) + (-2.82) = -13.37

(二) 日文人名處理

中文文章書寫日文人名時，會有兩種情形。以往在 BIG5 編碼的環境下，要書寫一個日本人名，都會將人名中的漢字對應回中文漢字。舉例來說，要在中文文章中提到日本藝人“滝沢秀明”，就會把他的名字改寫爲“瀧澤秀明”。然而現在已有不少文件採用 Unicode 編碼，這使得日文漢字可以和繁體中文字同時並存在一篇文章中。本斷詞系統就希望兩種書寫方式的日文人名都能被找到成爲候選詞。

日文姓名與中文姓名的組成類似，都是使用姓與名的組合，不同之處爲日文姓氏長度可爲一到三個漢字，名的部份也是一到三個漢字，甚至可以是長度不定的平假或片假名。由於本論文著重在漢字寫法的日文人名處理，含有假名的人名就暫不考慮。

因爲日文姓名的名字部份長度不固定，而且與實際讀音的音節數較有關係。在缺乏日文人名相關資料的情形下，名的部份就不分漢字個數。已知日本人名中不會有雙姓的情形，因此姓名組合只有三種情形：只有姓、只有名、姓+名，如表四所列。

表四、日文人名姓名組合

姓名組合	只有姓	只有名	姓+名
範例	木村 長谷川	理惠 新一	伊藤由奈 高橋留美子

借用中文人名判斷的經驗，要判斷日文人名時，也需要一個日文姓氏列表，還需要一個大量的人名列表，來統計各姓氏及名用字的出現機率。最後要再統計中文文章中，各日文姓名組合的機率，以及日文人名類別 S_{JPname} 的類別機率。同樣地，一個中文字串是日文人名的機率定義爲：

$$P_G(w \mid S_{JPname}) = \max_{\pi} P_G(w \mid \pi) P_G(\pi \mid S_{JPname}) \quad \text{(公式 5)}$$

公式中各符號的定義，請參見公式 4。但不同的是，因爲我們無法得到夠大量、已知性別的日文人名訓練語料，因此日文姓名生成機率暫不考慮性別。表五列出了各種姓名組合機率及其姓名生成機率的定義，其中m和n都是 1 到 3 之間的整數。而姓名組合中，‘S’表示姓氏出現，‘N’ 表示名字出現。這裡同樣地假設取名時姓氏與名用字無關，名的部份各字之間也獨立，也請注意名用字機率不分性別。

表五、各種日文姓名組合機率算法

姓名組合	姓名生成機率 $P(w\|\pi)$	姓名組合機率
只有姓	$P(c_1 \ldots c_m \| LN_{JP})$	$P(\pi=\text{‘S’} \| S_{JPname})$
只有名	$P(c_1 \| FN_{JP}) \times \ldots \times P(c_n \| FN_{JP})$	$P(\pi=\text{‘N’} \| S_{JPname})$
姓+名	$P(c_1 \ldots c_m \| LN_{JP}) \times P(c_{m+1} \| FN_{JP}) \times \ldots \times P(c_{m+n} \| FN_{JP})$	$P(\pi=\text{‘SN’} \| S_{JPname})$

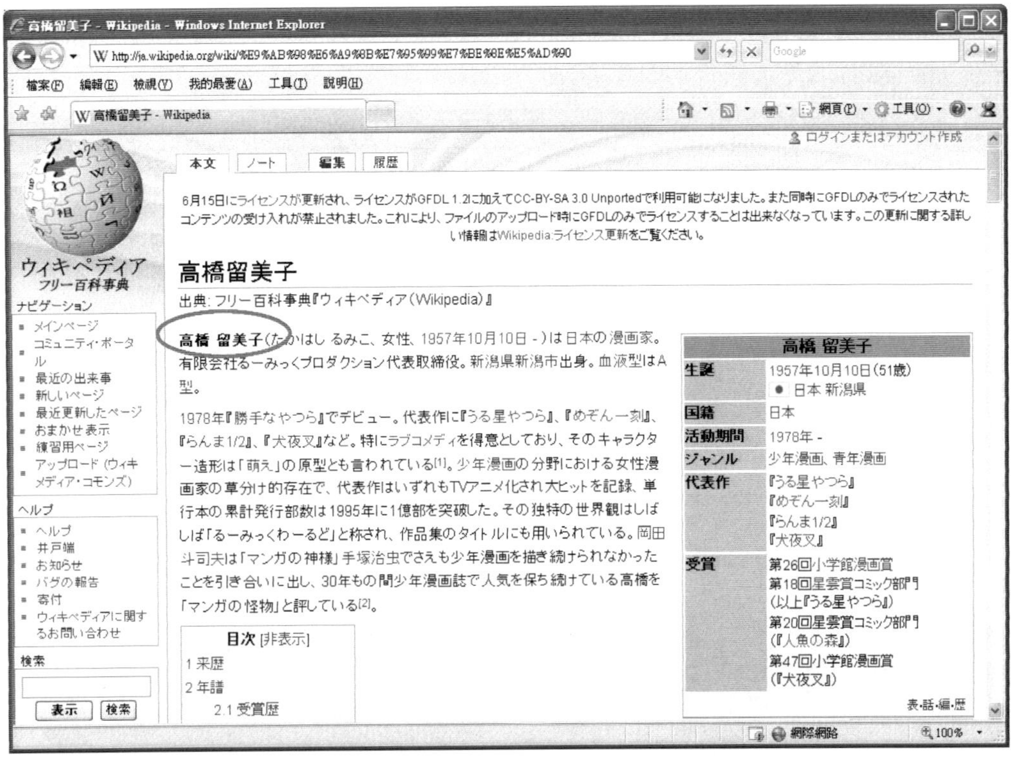

圖一、日文維基百科人名詞條範例「高橋留美子」

爲了蒐集日本姓氏，我們拜訪了一個日文網站「日本の苗字七千傑」[6]。此網站收集了8,603 個日文姓氏，並且附有各姓氏約略人口統計，統計來源是日本全國的NTT電話簿漢字記載，總共包含了約 1.17 億人口的統計資料。雖然「日本の苗字七千傑」提供了人口統計資料，正好給我們計算各姓氏的機率值。然而中文維基百科的「日文姓名」詞條[7]中提到，日文姓氏數量高達 14 萬個之多，而「日本の苗字七千傑」只提供了 8,603 個姓氏的資料，數量明顯不足。此外，「日本の苗字七千傑」裡只有姓氏統計，也沒有名用字的資訊。我們還得另覓資料才行。

我們於是決定蒐集日文維基百科裡所有的人名詞條。在日文維基百科中，成爲詞條的日文人名，都會在本文中以粗體呈現，並且會以空格斷開姓和名。圖一的「高橋留美子」詞條便是一個例子。本文中"高橋留美子"第一次出現時，是粗體字、姓名間以空格斷開的。利用這種明確的格式，我們可以很快地蒐集日文維基百科中出現的日文人名。

不過日文維基百科中也會出現台灣或是中國的名人，像是王建民、曾國藩等。爲過濾掉中文人名，凡是名在兩個字以內，姓氏是已知中文姓氏的，全部刪去不用。我們下載了 2009 年 1 月 24 日的日文維基百科完整版[8]，利用前述格式，擷取了 65,778 筆不重複並且斷好姓名的日文人名組合，包含 12,907 個姓氏以及 2,320 個不同的名用字。表六列出 2,302 個名用字的統計數據，第三欄就是姓名生成機率中名用字機率$P(c_j|FN_{JP})$。

表六、日文人名名用字統計

名用字	次數	$P(c_j\|FN_{JP})$	累積比	名用字	次數	$P(c_j\|FN_{JP})$	累積比
子	4,821	3.60%	3.60%	亨	46	0.03%	89.99%
一	3,358	2.50%	6.10%	瑞	46	0.03%	90.03%
郎	3,237	2.41%	8.52%	…	…	…	…
美	2,230	1.66%	10.18%	褒	1	0.00%	99.99%
正	1,741	1.30%	11.48%	焔	1	0.00%	100.00%
…	…	…	…	共 2,320 種，共 134,055 次			

表七、日本姓氏統計

姓氏	出現次數	所佔比例 $P(c_1..._c_m\|LN_{JP})$	姓氏	出現次數	所佔比例 $P(c_1..._c_m\|LN_{JP})$
佐藤	1928000	1.65%	高井良	760	6.49×10^{-6}
鈴木	1707000	1.46%	斉藤	111	9.47×10^{-7}
高橋	1416000	1.21%	三遊亭	106	9.05×10^{-7}
田中	1336000	1.14%	…	…	…
渡辺	1135000	0.97%	城土	1	8.54×10^{-9}
伊藤	1080000	0.92%	駒尾	1	8.54×10^{-9}
…	…	…	總共 15,702 種姓氏，117,156,792 次		

[6] http://www.myj7000.jp-biz.net
[7] http://zh.wikipedia.org/wiki/日文姓名
[8] http://download.wikimedia.org/jawiki/20090124 中的 Articles, templates, image descriptions, and primary meta-pages

蒐集自日文維基百科的 12,907 個姓氏中，有不少並未收錄在「日本の苗字七千傑」網站中。我們將這兩者合併，做爲日文人名判斷的姓氏列表，合併後得 15,702 個姓氏。計算機率時，採用「日本の苗字七千傑」所提供的人口數。未出現在「日本の苗字七千傑」中的姓氏，頻率則是採用其在日文維基百科詞條中出現的次數。最後日文姓氏統計值如表七所列，其中第三欄就是姓名生成機率中的姓氏機率。請注意在這個列表中，“佐藤” 到 “高井良” 這幾個姓氏來自網站，“斉藤” 之後的姓氏則是蒐集自日文維基百科。

接著要估算日文人名各種姓名組合的機率值$P_G(\pi \mid S_{JPname})$。同樣地，我們用規則去比對中研院平衡語料庫中所有未被判斷爲中文人名的專有名詞。因爲中研院平衡語料庫裡日文人名會以繁體中文漢字來書寫，判斷之前姓氏列表和常用名用字列表都必須先轉換成中文漢字。第四、(二)節會介紹轉換成中文漢字的做法。

比對時，採用姓氏列表裡所有的姓氏，以及表六中累積比例在 90%以內的 437 個名用字 (子一…瑞)來判斷。判斷時，組合優先順序爲 姓+名 > 只有姓 > 只有名，每個姓名只會被判斷成一種組合。依照上述規則，平衡語料庫中 92,314 個專有名詞中有 4,849 個被判斷爲日本人名。這些詞會用來計算各種姓名組合機率 (如表八所列)，也會用來計算日文人名類別S_{JPname}的類別機率。然而在實作經驗上，“只有名” 的這個組合會提出很多奇奇怪怪的候選詞，大大影響斷詞效果。因此我們不再採用只有名的姓名組合。

表八、日文姓名組合機率表

姓名組合機率	數量	機率值
$P(\pi=\text{'S'} \mid S_{JPname})$	718	14.90%
$P(\pi=\text{'N'} \mid S_{JPname})$	1,120	23.24%
$P(\pi=\text{'SN'} \mid S_{JPname})$	3,011	62.48%
總共	4,849	

最後以 “滝沢光” 的例子來說明姓名機率計算方式。“滝沢光” 有兩種可能的姓名組合方式，一種以 “滝沢” 當姓，“光” 當名，另一種是以 “滝” 當姓，“沢光” 當名。兩個機率值以“滝沢” 當姓氏的機率最高。

姓名：滝沢光	
組合	機率計算
SN	$\log(P(滝沢 \mid LN_{JP}) \times P(光 \mid FN_{JP}) \times P(\pi=\text{'SN'} \mid S_{JPname}))$ $= (-7.35) + (-5.15) + (-0.076)$ $= -12.576$
SN	$\log(P(滝 \mid LN_{JP}) \times P(沢 \mid FN_{JP}) \times P(光 \mid FN_{JP}) \times P(\pi=\text{'SN'} \mid S_{JPname}))$ $= (-10.70) + (-9.40) + (-5.15) + (-0.076)$ $= -25.326$

四、異體字處理

這個章節想要討論的主題，主要是在三種情形中出現。一是以中文漢字書寫的日文人名 (如 “滝沢秀明” 寫做 “瀧澤秀明”)，二是異體字寫法的同義詞 (如 “裡面” 和 “裏面”)，三是繁體中文文章出現的簡體字 (像是 “体育馆”)。後兩者雖然在文章中出現機率較少，尤其第三種情形要在 UTF-8 編碼的文件中才有可能出現，但爲了因應未來多語並存的可能性，此方向的研究仍有其必要。

(一) 異體漢字對應

由前面列出的三種情形來看，首先我們需要準備各種情形下異體漢字之間的對應列表。日文人名部份需要的是日文漢字和中文漢字的對應，異體字詞彙需要的是異體字對應表，而簡體詞彙部份則是要簡繁中文字元對應表。簡繁字元對應表比較容易取得，有不少軟體都提供簡繁轉換的功能。然而機率設定上要注意，這部份會在第(三)節中討論。

日中漢字及異體字對應表就沒有公定版本了。爲了產生這樣的對應表，我們使用了京都大學人文科學研究所安岡孝一 (Koichi Yasuoka) 與安岡素子 (Motoko Yasuoka) 所製作的異體字列表[9]，總共有 8,196 組異體漢字列表。每一組漢字都是在某些情形下的同義異體字，以下列範例中第一組爲例，“豊” 是日文裡的 “豐” 字，“丰” 則是簡體中文的 “豐” 字，而這兩個字本身又是合法的繁體中文字。異體字列表範例如下：

丰 豊 豐 靊 靊
秇 蓺 藝 藝
乹 乾 乾 干 漧

接下來，我們在每一組異體漢字中，找一個繁體中文字來做爲代表。若是該組中有多個繁體中文漢字，則選擇最常用的。繁體中文漢字頻率採用教育部八十七年常用語詞字頻表[10]。以第一組爲例，“丰”、“豊”、“豐” 都是繁體中文的漢字，三者中以 “豐” 字頻率最高，因此選它做爲這組代表字。如此一來，日文漢字 “豊” 可以對應至這個代表的中文漢字，異體字 “靊” 也可以對應到這個較常見的中文漢字了。

其實這個做法有不少要考慮的問題存在。首先，所謂的 “繁體中文” 字元其實不僅僅只有 BIG5 字集。Unicode 在定義字碼表時，就收錄了不少不在 BIG5 字集裡的繁體中文罕見字，像異體漢字第一組範例裡的 “靊” 字便是一例。由於我們的實驗資料集是以 BIG5 字集書寫的文章，本論文就先以 BIG5 字集做爲繁體中文字集。未來若有完整的繁體中文字元集，本章節所提做法就可再依據而調整。

另一問題是來自異體漢字的對應。在許多時候，兩個漢字會是同義的異體字，其實是基於某種特定的情形，並非百分之百同義。再以 “豊” 和 “豐” 爲例，“豊” 在繁體中文中是古代祭祀用的禮器 (參見教育部重編國語辭典[11])，與 “豐” 字完全不同義。只有在日文中 “豊” 才和中文 “豐” 同義。這可做爲未來研究主題。

(二) 日文人名用字之中文漢字對應

在第三、(二)節中曾經提到，如果要能判斷以繁體中文書寫的日文人名，需要將蒐集到的日文姓名用字轉換成繁體中文寫法才行。需要轉換的資料有兩個，一是日文的姓氏列表裡的姓氏，一是日文名用字列表裡面的漢字。

轉換日文姓氏的時候，不論姓氏字數多少，每個字都會以第(一)節介紹的方法將之轉換成對應的繁體中文字。例如 “滝沢” 就會轉換成 “瀧澤”，而 “中曽根” 就會轉換成 “中曾根”。轉換所得的中文寫法會合併至原本的日文姓氏列表中，機率就沿用原日文寫法姓氏的機率值。若是姓氏中有至少一個日文漢字沒有中文漢字對應的話，就不產

[9] http://kanji.zinbun.kyoto-u.ac.jp/~yasuoka/ftp/CJKtable/UniVariants.Z
[10] http://www.edu.tw/files/site_content/download/mandr/primary/shrest21.exe
[11] http://dict.revised.moe.edu.tw/cgi-bin/newDict/dict.sh?idx=dict.idx&cond=%E0T&pieceLen=50&fld=1&cat=&imgFont=1

生中文對應寫法。像是“古畑”的“畑”就沒有中文漢字對應。名用字列表的做法一樣，每個名用字都找到其對應的漢字，將之併入名用字列表中，機率也沿用原字機率值。

將對應漢字寫法合併至原來的列表，使得列表中同時有日文寫法和中文寫法。如此一來，即使句子中同時出現日文及中文寫法的人名，本系統皆可處理。舉例來說，若輸入句是「**滝沢聡就是瀧澤聰**」，因爲“滝沢”和“瀧澤”都在日文姓氏列表之中，“聡”和“聰”都出現在日文名用字列表中，“滝沢聡”和“瀧澤聰”都會被提出爲日本人名候選詞，而且兩者的機率值相同。

以同樣的概念，將日文姓氏名用字的繁體中文寫法再轉爲簡體中文並併入列表中的話，就可以處理「滝沢聡和泷泽聪都是瀧澤聰」這種日文、簡繁中文並存的文本了。這部份未以實驗進行驗證，僅以概念說明可行性。

(三) 對應異體詞的生成

爲了處理繁體中文文章中出現的簡字寫法以及異體字寫法，我們採用同一種策略處理：將所有已知繁體中文詞彙，轉換成各種可能的異體字寫法，包含簡體字寫法，再將這些詞彙合併回已知詞列表中。將已知詞轉換成各種異體寫法的方法，是先以第(一)節的方法找出詞中每一個字可能的異體字寫法，再去產生所有的組合。例如ABC爲一已知詞，A’、A”、B’ 與C’ 爲各別的異體字，我們會產生A’BC、AB’C、ABC’、A’B’C、AB’C’、A’BC’、A’B’C’、A”BC、A”B’C、A”BC’、A”B’C’ 這麼多種寫法。

將各異體字展開所得的異體詞，其機率值就承接原繁體詞的機率值。本論文之斷詞機率模型是二元模型，爲免機率列表過大，同一群異體詞就以同一個詞群編號來表示。斷詞時，找尋候選詞用異體展開後的已知詞列表，估算斷詞機率時則以各詞群編號之二元機率值來計算。

然而合併過程中，會遇到兩個不同的繁體中文詞彙對應至同一個異體詞的情形。這大部份是由於簡繁中文對應所造成，因爲簡繁對應是多個繁體字會對應到同一個簡體字，容易產生混淆。像是“白面”與“白麵”的簡體寫法都是“白面”，“改制”與“改製”的簡體寫法也都是“改制”。決定這情形異體字寫法機率值的設計法有三種想法，分別是取各原詞中機率最高、最低者，以及取其總和。第五、(四)節會討論這部份的實驗，最後系統採用了最高的機率值來做爲它的機率。

五、實驗

(一) 實驗資料與評估公式

中文斷詞實驗資料用的語料庫是中研院平衡語料庫 3.0 版[12]。平衡語料庫是專門針對語言分析所設計的，每個句子中各詞都以空白符號斷開，並且加註其詞性。文字爲現代漢語，涵蓋各種不同領域、不同主題的詞彙。平衡語料庫中共分成 316 個檔案，共有 743,718 個句子。

實驗評估方法是採 5-fold cross-validation。將 316 個檔案分成 5 組，當使用其中一組做爲測試集時，其他四組則作訓練集，用來產生已知詞列表、bigram機率，以及各類別bigram機率，因此五組實驗會有不同的機率值表。各組檔案與句子個數如表九所示：

---

[12] http://godel.iis.sinica.edu.tw/CKIP/20corpus.htm

表九、測試集句子資料

檔案編號	測試集	內含檔案	句子總數	已知詞	未知詞
000~065	ASBCset0	66	148,575	146,477	15675
066~129	ASBCset1	64	149,713	146,275	15877
130~183	ASBCset2	54	148,870	146,634	15518
184~244	ASBCset3	61	148,012	146,024	16128
245~315	ASBCset4	71	148,548	146,004	16148

在斷詞實驗中使用 precision、recall、F-measure，以及 BI-score 來評估系統的效能：

$$precision = \frac{\text{標準答案與系統斷出完全相同的詞彙數量個數}}{\text{系統斷出來的詞彙總數}} \quad \text{(公式 6)}$$

$$recall = \frac{\text{標準答案與系統斷出完全相同的詞彙數量個數}}{\text{標準答案的詞彙總數}} \quad \text{(公式 7)}$$

$$\mathrm{F}-measure = \frac{2 \times recall \times precision}{recall + precision} \quad \text{(公式 8)}$$

BI-score= (正確 BI 標記個數) / 總字數 (公式 9)

這裡介紹一下 BI-score 的算法。對於一個輸入句，給定一種斷詞方式之後，句中的每一個字元都標上 B 或 I 的標籤。B 表示這字元在一個詞開頭的位置，I 表示這字元在詞的中間任何位置。比對系統提出的斷詞方式的 BI 標籤序列與標準答案斷詞方式的 BI 標籤序列，就可評估有多少比例的字元的斷詞情形是正確的。

5-fold cross-validation 五組實驗在算平均的時候，我們採用 micro-average 的概念。也就是說，precision 和 recall 的分母爲平衡語料庫中所有句子的所有斷詞詞數總和，分子則爲所有正確斷詞的詞數總和。BI-score 的分母則爲所有句子裡字元數總和，分子則爲所有字元中 BI 標記正確之總數。

(二) 斷詞系統基本效能

這一節先呈現本系統在基本架構下所達到的效能。Sys1a僅採用已知詞列表及bigram機率模型，Sys1b加上了各特殊類別候選詞產生規則，包括地址、日期、時間、金錢、百分比、分數、外文、網路 (IP、網址與信箱地址等)。如第二、(二)節所談，各特殊類別所得候選詞將直接採用 (亦即機率值設爲 1)。Sys2 加入了數詞類別，包含所有以漢字或全半形阿拉伯數字所表達之數字字串。爲免冒然將所有連續數字斷成一個詞造成錯誤，這裡設計兩組實驗來探討數詞的類別機率可能估算方式。如表十所示，加入特殊類別的系統Sys1b斷詞效能大幅提昇，而考慮真正數詞類別機率的系統Sys2b效果較好。

- **Sys2a：數詞類別機率值設爲 1**
- **Sys2b：以 maximum likelihood 方式計算數詞類別機率**

表十、斷詞系統基本架構加入特殊類別實驗結果

實驗	R	P	F	BI
Sys1a	95.66	92.72	94.16	96.96
Sys1b	95.87	93.31	94.57	97.20
Sys2a	95.97	93.57	94.76	97.30
Sys2b	**96.16**	**93.68**	**94.90**	**97.38**

(三) 中日文人名處理實驗

加入中文人名判斷規則後，機率計算時採用中文人名類別機率。本論文和 Chen *et al.*[10] 不同的地方是，我們多加入了姓名組合機率的概念，也允許未提及姓的雙名組合出現。以下分別設計實驗來驗證各方法提昇的效能如何：

- **Sys3a：中文人名類別機率、無雙名組合、無姓名組合機率**
- **Sys3b：中文人名類別機率、有雙名組合、無姓名組合機率**
- **Sys3c：中文人名類別機率、有雙名組合、有姓名組合機率**

各Sys3 實驗均以系統Sys2b爲基礎，加入三種中文人名處理策略，實驗結果如表十一所示。結果發現，加入中文人名判斷、雙名組合，以及加入姓名組合機率，都能提昇效能。可見姓名組合機率幫助不小，能成功地多辨識人名，對斷詞幫助也很大。

表十一、加入中文人名處理實驗結果

實驗	R	P	F	BI
Sys3a	96.39	94.97	95.68	97.90
Sys3b	96.42	95.49	95.95	98.05
Sys3c	**96.57**	**95.53**	**96.04**	**98.10**

接著驗證加入日文人名判斷規則與其類別機率，並且引入日文姓名組合機率後，對於系統效能的影響如何。由於實驗資料所用中文字皆限定在 BIG5 繁體中文字集範圍內，這裡日文人名處理用的是進行中日漢字對應之後的姓名列表及其機率值。以系統 Sys3c 爲基礎，實驗設計如下：

- **Sys4a：日文人名類別機率、無姓名組合機率**
- **Sys4b：日文人名類別機率、有姓名組合機率**

表十二、日文人名類別實驗結果

實驗	R	P	F	BI
Sys3c	**96.57**	95.53	96.04	98.10
Sys4a	96.54	95.54	96.04	98.10
Sys4b	96.56	**95.56**	**96.06**	98.10

表十二爲加入日文人名處理的系統效能比較。可以發現僅提出日文人名候選詞而不使用姓名組合機率的方法，反而讓系統效能下降。加入了姓名組合機率後，效能與系統Sys3c相比略有提昇，但改進並不明顯。這可能是因爲測試集裡日文人名很少的關係。這可由第三、(二)節在統計日文人名類別機率時窺知一二，因爲整個語料庫 74 萬多詞中，只有 4,849 個被判斷爲日文人名。

爲了了解加入日文人名類別真正的效能，我們設計了另外一組實驗來觀察。我們準備了出現有日文人名的 109 篇新聞文章，並用人工方式標記日文人名的位置，用以觀察這些日文人名是否能被成功地斷成詞。這 109 篇文章中，出現日文人名之處共有 862 個，屬於 216 個不同的日文人名。

觀察分爲兩部份，第一部份驗證加入日文人名類別前後，日文人名能夠被正確斷成詞的比例。觀察結果在表十三。分別以系統Sys3c以及Sys4b對這 109 篇新聞文章斷詞，統計正解的 862 個日文人名，有多少比例能正確成詞。實驗結果顯示，加入日文人名判斷模組能大幅提昇正確率。

表十三、日文人名正確成詞實驗結果

實驗	日文人名正確成詞數量	正確率
Sys3c	154	17.87%
Sys4b	717	83.18%
總數量	862	

第二部份觀察則是將斷詞系統對每個候選詞所猜測的類別輸出，看看系統認爲是日文人名的詞中有多少比例確實是日文人名 (precision)，也看看正解日文人名裡，有多少比例是因爲日文人名模組而成功結合成詞 (recall)。結果在表十四。

表十四、日文人名詞性標記實驗結果

實驗	P	R
Sys4b	74.31% (648/872)	75.17% (648/862)

實驗結果顯示，recall 和 precision 都有七成五左右，已有不錯的成功率。然而比起其他類別的高準確率，仍有相當大的進步空間。這也表示日文人名辨識不是很容易的問題。

底下來觀察幾個例子，看看加入日文人名類別前後斷詞正確與錯誤的情形。比較的是系統 Sys3 與系統 Sys4b。斷詞正確的範例：

系統 Sys3c	系統 Sys4b	系統 Sys3c	系統 Sys4b
小 林恭二	小林恭二	大 前 研一	大前研一
石原慎 太郎	石原慎太郎	藥師 丸 博子	藥師丸博子

大部分的日文姓名都能夠被正確辨識出來，不過也有少部份是斷詞錯誤的情形：

系統 Sys3c	系統 Sys4b	系統 Sys3c	系統 Sys4b
麻布 和 木材	麻布和 木材	瓦斯井 原有	瓦斯 井原有
國小 林佩萱 老師	國 小林 佩萱 老師	廣島 亞運 時	廣島亞運時

(四) 異體字處理實驗

異體字轉換希望能處理的是各種不同異體字寫法的情形，然而我們找不到適合於評估的實驗資料，因爲平衡語料庫都是以繁體中文寫成，其中的異體字出現頻率又很少。

這節實驗分兩個部份，第一部份是將平衡語料庫以軟體轉換爲簡體中文，看看系統對簡體斷詞的能力，順便探討多個不同的繁體中文詞彙對應至同一個簡體中文詞彙時，詞彙機率值的選擇方式。第二個部份則以真實的簡體中文文章做爲測試集。

第四、(三)節曾提到，因爲繁體中文和簡體中文字是多對一的關係，會有多個不同的繁體中文詞彙對應至同一個簡體中文詞彙的情形。這時，簡體中文詞彙的機率值的設定方法有三種：Sys5a採用各繁體中文詞彙中機率值最大者、Sys5b採用最小機率值、Sys5c採用機率總和。因爲中文以及日文人名判斷規則也會牽涉到機率合併的問題，這裡各Sys5 系統改以未加入人名類別前的Sys2b當作基本系統。實驗結果如表十五所示，得知不管使用什麼方法對系統效能影響都不大，而把詞彙頻率加總與取最大的方式對系統效能影響較好。這也表示繁體文章中混用簡體詞彙，本系統仍會有不錯的斷詞效果，因爲三種策略效能差不多。最後選用系統Sys5a，即採用最大機率值。

表十五、多對一簡體詞機率設定實驗結果

實驗	R	P	F	BI
Sys5a	96.11	93.53	94.80	97.33
Sys5b	95.95	93.16	94.54	97.21
Sys5c	96.11	93.53	94.80	97.33

第二個實驗的測試集爲真實的簡體文章，我們使用 SIGHAN 1st Peking University Test Set 做斷詞實驗，共 380 行句子。我們沒有用它的 training set 來訓練系統，而直接使用系統 Sys5a，以及平衡語料庫的已知詞列表來進行斷詞實驗。實驗結果，precision 只有 86.56%，recall 也只有 81.47%，F-measure 值爲 83.94%，遠低於其他系統。由於 Peking University Test Set 的文章來自大陸地區，兩岸用語不同，文章中會有大陸地區才有的詞彙出現。另外，該語料的斷詞標準與中研院不同，像是人名的姓與名會被斷開 (如 "孫玉波")，所以斷詞正確率不高是可以預期的。本實驗僅在表達處理異體字詞的可能性，而不在比較效能。

六、結論

在本論文中我們提出了一個方法能夠處理在繁體中文文章中出現的日文人名及異體寫法中文詞的方法。文章爲 UTF-8 編碼，以支援各國文字同時出現。本論文建立之中文斷詞系統爲 bigram 機率模型，搭配各種特殊類別判斷規則及其機率模型。

中日文人名處理部份，我們提出姓名組合機率模型，並討論姓名機率值的訓練方法。也提出中日漢字轉換方式，因此不論以何種漢字書寫日文人名均可被判斷出來。由實驗數據可知，加入姓名組合機率確實可提昇系統效能，中日漢字對應的方式也能成功地偵測到大部份的日文人名。

實驗中所使用的日文姓氏列表僅包含了 15,702 個日本姓，與維基百科所提及之 14 萬個日本姓有相當大數量上的差距。如果有更完整的姓氏列表，可馬上合併至本系統，只要將罕見的姓氏機率值設爲極小值即可。此外，目前日文人名的判斷知識仍太粗略，未來可再試著加入讀音音節的組成機率，尋找大量日文人名訓練語料，尤其是姓名組合在文章中出現的機率訓練。

運用異體字對應表，各種異體寫法的中文詞也可成爲斷詞候選詞。對於異體字的處理方式，是以繁體轉簡體的中文測試集驗證了方法的可行性。儘管已知詞數量倍增，但在搭配雜湊表以及詞群編號的技巧下，對於處理速度影響不大。惟有多對一對應情形的機率模型需要再更仔細地研究。

參考文獻

[1] 彭載衍 and 張俊盛, "中文辭彙歧義之研究－斷詞與詞性標示", 第六屆中華民國計算語言學研討會論文集 (ROCLING-6), 1993, pp. 173-194.

[2] J. Gao, M. Li, and C.N. Huang, "Improved Source-Channel Models for Chinese Word Segmentation," In *Proceedings of the 41st Annual Meeting on Association for Computational Linguistics* (*ACL 2003*), 2003, pp. 272-279.

[3] A. Wu, and Z. Jiang, "Word segmentation in sentence analysis," In *Proceedings of the 1998 International Conference on Chinese Information Processing*, 1998 (pp. 169-180).

[4] L.F. Chien, "PAT-tree-based keyword extraction for Chinese information retrieval," In *Proceedings of SIGIR97*, 1997, pp. 27-31.

[5] J. Sun, M. Zhou, and J.F. Gao, "A Class-based Language Model Approach to Chinese Named Entity Identification," *International Journal of Computational Linguistics and Chinese Language Processing*, vol 8, no 2, pp. 1-28, 2003.

[6] X. Lu, "Combining machine learning with linguistic heuristics for Chinese word segmentation," In *Proceedings of the FLAIRS Conference*, 2007, pp. 241-246.

[7] H. Zhao, C.N. Huang, and M. Li, "An improved chinese word segmentation system with conditional random field," In *Proceedings of the Fifth SIGHAN Workshop on Chinese Language Processing*, 2006, pp. 162-165.

[8] Y. Shi, and M. Wang, "A dual-layer CRFs based joint decoding method for cascaded segmentation and labeling tasks," In *Proceedings of International Joint Conference on Artificial Intelligence* (*IJCAI '07*), 2007, pp. 1707-1712.

[9] 羅永聖, 結合多類型字典與條件隨機域之中文斷詞與詞性標記系統研究, 碩士論文, 台灣大學, 2008.

[10] H.H. Chen, Y.W. Ding, S.C. Tsai and G.W. Bian, "Description of the NTU System Used for MET2," In *Proceedings of 7th Message Understanding Conference* (*MUC-7*), 1998. Available: http://www.itl.nist.gov/iaui/894.02/related_projects/muc/index.html.

動補結構的及物性及修飾對象

鍾友珊 You-shan Chung 陳克健 Keh-Jiann Chen
中央研究院資訊所
Institute of Information Science
Academia Sinica
yschung@iis.sinica.edu.tw kchen@iis.sinica.edu.tw

摘要

動補結構〈VR〉的分析一直是中文裡一個棘手的問題。其中，動補的及物性以及 V2〈第二個動詞，表達某動作的結果 R〉是修飾主語還是賓語，更是很多理論試圖解釋的現象。本篇論文透過 V1〈第一個動詞，表達造成某結果的動作〉和 V2 本身是及物或不及物動詞以及 V1 及 V2 和主語、賓語搭配的可能性，成功預測大多數動補句型的及物性以及 V2 是修飾主語還是賓語。除了預測正確性及覆蓋率高，我們的方法在處理多數句型時只需知道 V1 和 V2 本身是否是及物動詞以及 V1 和 V2 和主語賓語搭配的可能性，因此也較其他須先辨識 V2 是修飾有生命還是無生命物體、V1 和 V2 的域外和域內論元為何的分析方法更符合自動處理的需要。

關鍵詞：動補結構，及物性，補語的修飾對象，以詞彙語義學方法分析複合詞

一、緒論

動補結構〈VR〉指的是由動作〈V1，第一個動詞〉和它造成的結果〈V2，第二個動詞〉形成的複合詞，不同學者對動補的嚴格定義有不同看法，本文所談的動補大致對應到 [1]的 resultative verb compound 和[2]的 Result RVC。因為空間有限，我們暫不討論 V2 為方向補語〈directional verb complement〉或表完成的補語〈phase/completive complement〉的動補結構。

有些研究者認為動補的語意語法是在句法層次衍生出來的，須要用到移位〈movement〉的概念才能解釋 [3]；有些研究者認為某些動補是在句法層次衍生的，某些則是組成成分本身的詞彙語意可以解釋的。例如，同樣是動補，Lin [4]認為*騎累*、*砍光*、*哭濕*等屬於詞彙語意可以解釋的"resultative compound"，而在*那瓶香檳醉倒了張三*的*醉倒*則是在句法層次衍生出來的"causative compound"。有些研究者則認為所有動補都是在詞彙層次可以解釋的〈[5]，[6]〉。Dai [6]認為動補具有複合詞的地位，而中文複合詞有自己的構詞規律，這些規律不完全等同於句法規則； Li [5]則認為單是事件結構〈event structure〉以及 V1 的及物性就足以解釋所有動補句型，不需用到句法的移位的概念。其中，Li [5]列出了所有邏輯上可能的動補句型，排除實際語言中不存在的，用事件結構成功解釋了每種可能的句型的語意語法。我們認為動補的語意語法基本上可以由組合成分的 V1 和 V2 的語意透過常識〈real world knowledge〉推導出來，但為了兼顧自動化及實用性，

我們歸納出較符合直覺的簡單規律，這些規律在處理多數句型時只須知道 V1 和 V2 本身是否是及物動詞以及 V1 和 V2 和主語及賓語搭配的可能性，因此也較其他須先辨識 V2 是修飾有生命還是無生命物體、V1 和 V2 的域外和域內論元〈external and internal argument〉為何的分析方法更符合自動處理的需要。

動補的研究常環繞兩個主題，即動補的及物性以及V2是修飾主語〈subject-control，以下簡稱SC〉還是賓語〈object-control，以下簡稱OC〉〈cf. [4], [5]〉。例如*打破*的*破*是修飾賓語，因此*打破*是OC；但*讀懂*的*懂*是修飾主語，因此*讀懂*是SC。其中，SC和OC的區分更是只有在中文才會出現，其他語言的V2通常都是修飾賓語。Lin [4]用V1的及物性及V2獨立時是修飾有生命還是無生命的物體來決定動補是SC還是OC。Li [5]也是利用V1預測整個動補的及物性以及是SC還是OC，但不考慮V2是否修飾有生命的物體。

Li [5]對 V1 採用兩種分法，第一種是依照情境類型〈situation type〉分為活動〈Activity〉和狀態〈State〉，活動和狀態各對應到兩種可能的事件結構。儘管他有提出符合各個事件結構的充要條件，但每種事件結構又各自對應到三到四種可能動補句型，要知道是哪個句型才知道是否及物以及如果是及物，是 SC 還是 OC。但是[5]似乎沒討論到如何找出適用的句型。

Li [5]的另一種分法是依照V1的及物性，分成單及物〈monotransitive〉，雙及物〈ditransitive〉以及不及物。在他的架構下，如果知道受影響者〈causee〉和影響因素〈causer〉為何，就知道動補在句子中及物與否，以及如果是及物，是SC還是OC。要知道影響因素和受影響者為何，得用規則把V1和V2的域內和域外論元對應到影響因素和受影響者，以下是這樣的規則的其中一條：“When V1 is ditransitive and V2 is monotransitive, the external argument of V1 is realized as the Causer, and the external argument of V2 is realized as the Causee and identified with the direct internal argument of V1.”[5]

依據以上的規則，若要知道影響因素和受影響者對應到哪個名詞，得先知道 V1 和 V2 的域外和域內論元，但域外和域內論元的辨識有一定的複雜度。

本篇論文和[5]同樣是採用詞彙語義學分析方法，不倚賴衍生句法來解釋不同的動補句型，接下來的章節將詳述我們所提出的規則及預測的正確性〈accuracy〉和實用性〈applicability〉。

二、判斷動補及物性及修飾方向的規則

我們判斷動補在特定情境的及物性以及 OC 還是 SC 是依據(1)V1 和 V2 獨立使用時是及物還是不及物動詞以及(2)表面主語和賓語〈surface subject and object〉和 V1 及 V2 的語義搭配性。

以下我們依照 V1 是及物動詞或不及物動詞，分別討論整個動補的及物性以及是 SC 還是 OC。

（一）V1 為及物動詞

Case 1. V1 如為及物動詞，動補通常也是及物
e.g. 張三打破了玻璃、張三教會了李四、張三賭贏了李四、張三教懂了李四
Case 2. Case1 有例外。即使 V1 為及物動詞，但若 V2 只能修飾 V1 的主語，而且 V2 是不及物動詞，VR 會是不及物[1]
e.g. 張三吃飽了、張三吃撐了、張三吃窮了

以*吃飽*為例，V1 儘管是及物，但由於*飽*這個 V2 只能修飾 V1 的主語，且*飽*又是不及物，*吃飽*在大多數情況下仍是不及物。在我們的架構下，以 V1 和 V2 本身是及物還是不及物動詞以及主語和賓語是否能當 V1 和 V2 的主語，就可決定動補是及物還是不及物，對於機器處理較方便。V1 和 V2 本身的及物性我們在廣義知網的系統已有標註〈[7]，[8]〉，主語和賓語由於純粹由名詞在句子中的位置判定，比起辨識 V1 和 V2 的域外和域內論元直接，至於主語及賓語和 V1 及 V2 語意搭配的可能性，也是電腦可以計算的。

針對及物動補是 SC 還是 OC，我們提出以下的規則：

V1 為及物動詞時

R 修飾賓語的條件〈OC(1)和 OC(2)皆須符合，或符合 OC(3)〉

OC(1)：(賓語 V1)[2]能當(主語 V2)

OC(2)：(主語 V1)不能當(主語 V2)

e.g. 打破、吃光、讀破（OC(1)和 OC(2)都符合）

OC(3)：V1 跟某個 V2 組合時的影響方向是指向賓語

e.g. 餵飽、打死、教會

R 修飾主語的條件〈SC(1)和 SC(2)皆須符合〉

SC(1)：V2 是狀態及物動詞

SC(2)：(主語 V1)能當(主語 V2)

e.g. 搶贏、打輸、讀懂（SC(1)和 SC(2)都符合）

R 修飾賓語或主語〈i.e. 兼類〉的條件〈(1)(2)(3)(4)皆須符合〉

(1) (賓語 V1)能當(主語 V2)

(2) (主語 V1)能當(主語 V2)

---

[1] 為了操作上的方便，此一規律省略了下述更精確的條件：動補的影響方向指向主語。以 V1 為*吃*、V2 為*撐*及*窮*的情形為例，影響方向一定是吃的人而不是被吃的物件。
[2] （x y）讀作「y 的 x」。

(3) V2 表達生理或心理狀態[3]

(4) (賓語 動補)能當(賓語 V1)

e.g. 張三騎累了馬、張三唸煩了李四〈(1)(2)(3)(4)皆符合〉

其他組合不是邏輯上不可能〈i.e.不可能同時符合或不符合 SC(2)和 OC(2)〉就是目前沒看到這樣的句型。

（二）**V1 為不及物動詞**

Case 1. 假如 V2 為不及物動詞，如果(主語 V1)能當(主語 V2)，動補會是不及物
e.g.冰塊化光了、畫掛偏了、小寶跳煩了、小寶哭累了
Case 2. Case1 有例外。即使 V2 為不及物動詞，且(主語 V1)能當(主語 V2)，但若 V1 和 V2 結合後的影響方向是指向賓語，仍會是及物
Case 3. 假如 V2 為不及物動詞，如果〈主語 V1〉不能當〈主語 V2〉，則會是及物
e.g. 張三跪破了草席、張三哭濕了枕頭
Case 4. 假如 V2 為及物動詞，則動補為及物的用法
e.g. 張三跪贏了李四

V1 為不及物時，當整個動補是及物時，就會是 OC。不論 V1 是及物或不及物，當整個動補是不及物時，必會是 SC。

以下我們將探討上述規律的正確性。Li [5]列出以下三個因素的所有可能邏輯組合：(1)受影響者及影響因素(2)域內及域外論元(3)V1 和 V2。他刪除掉不可能在實際語言存在的，留下了十九個動補句型。我們能正確預測所有這些句型的及物性以及是 SC 還是 OC。這些句型中，V1 是及物的有十三種，V1 是不及物的有六種。

十九個句型的例句如下，首先是 V1 是及物動詞的情形：

A) 張三追累了

<u>及物性</u>
追：及物；累：不及物，只能修飾*張三*
預測：不及物
預測是否正確：正確

<u>SC 還是 OC</u>

---

[3]表達生理狀態和心理狀態的動詞屬於廣義知網本體架構〈[7]，[8]〉的特定分支。

預測：由於動補是不及物，一定是 SC
預測是否正確：正確

B) 張三擦亮了玻璃

<u>及物性</u>
擦：及物；亮：不及物，不能修飾*張三*
預測：及物
預測是否正確：正確

<u>SC 還是 OC</u>
*玻璃*能當(主語 亮)
*張三*不能當(主語 亮)
預測：OC
預測是否正確：正確

C) 張三切鈍了刀

<u>及物性</u>
切：及物；鈍：不及物，不能修飾*張三*
預測：及物
預測是否正確：正確

<u>SC 還是 OC</u>
*刀*能當(主語 鈍)
*張三*不能當(主語 鈍)
預測：OC
預測是否正確：正確

D) 那包衣服洗累了張三

<u>及物性</u>
洗：及物；累：不及物，不能修飾*那包衣服*
預測：及物
預測是否正確：正確

<u>SC 還是 OC</u>

*張三*能當(主語 累)
*那包衣服*不能當(主語 累)
預測：OC
預測是否正確：正確

E) 衣服洗乾淨了

<u>及物性</u>
洗：及物；乾淨：不及物，只能修飾*衣服*
預測：不及物
預測是否正確：正確

<u>SC 還是 OC</u>
預測：由於動補是不及物，一定是 SC
預測是否正確：正確

F) 那塊排骨切鈍了三把刀

<u>及物性</u>
切：及物；鈍：不及物，不能修飾*那塊排骨*
預測：及物
預測是否正確：正確

<u>SC 還是 OC</u>
*三把刀*能當(主語 鈍)
*那塊排骨*不能當(主語 鈍)
預測：OC
預測是否正確：正確

G) 那把鈍鈍的刀切累了張三

<u>及物性</u>
切：及物；累：不及物，不能修飾*那把鈍鈍的刀*
預測：及物
預測是否正確：正確

<u>SC 還是 OC</u>
*張三*能當(主語 累)

*那把鈍鈍的刀*不能當(主語 累)
預測：OC
預測是否正確：正確

H) 那麼髒的水竟然洗乾淨了衣服

<u>及物性</u>
洗：及物；乾淨：不及物，不能修飾*那麼髒的水*
預測：及物
預測是否正確：正確

<u>SC 還是 OC</u>
*衣服*能當(主語 乾淨)
*那麼髒的水*不能當(主語 乾淨)
預測：OC
預測是否正確：正確

I) 張三讀懂了那首詩

<u>及物性</u>
讀：及物；懂：及物，只能修飾*張三*
預測：及物
預測是否正確：正確

<u>SC 還是 OC</u>
*懂*是狀態及物動詞
*張三*能當(主語 懂)
預測：SC
預測是否正確：正確

J) 張三教煩了李四

<u>及物性</u>
教：及物；煩：不及物，可修飾*張三*和*李四*
預測：及物
預測是否正確：正確

<u>SC 還是 OC</u>

*李四*能當(主語 煩)
*張三*能當(主語 煩)
*煩*表達心理狀態
*李四*能當(賓語 教)
預測：SC 或 OC 均可
預測是否正確：正確

K) 那個學校教煩了張三

<u>及物性</u>
教：及物；煩：不及物，不能修飾*那個學校*
預測：及物
預測是否正確：正確

<u>SC 還是 OC</u>
*張三*能當(主語 煩)
*那個學校*不能當(主語 煩)
預測：OC
預測是否正確：正確

L) 那門課教煩了張三

<u>及物性</u>
教：及物；煩：不及物，不能修飾*那門課*
預測：及物
預測是否正確：正確

<u>SC 還是 OC</u>
*張三*能當(主語 煩)
*那門課*不能當(主語 煩)
預測：OC
預測是否正確：正確

M) 張三教會了李四

<u>及物性</u>
教：及物；會：不及物，可修飾*張三*及*李四*
預測：及物

預測是否正確：正確

<u>SC 還是 OC</u>
*教*跟*會*組合時的影響方向是指向賓語
預測：OC
預測是否正確：正確

（二）**V1 為不及物的情形**

以下是 V1 為不及物動詞的六種可能句型：

N) 張三走累了腿

<u>及物性</u>
走：不及物；累：不及物；*張三*能當(主語 累)
預測：*走*和*累*組合以後的影響方向指向賓語，因此是及物
預測是否正確：正確

O) 張三餓病了

<u>及物性</u>
餓：不及物；病：不及物；*張三*能當(主語 病)
預測：不及物
預測是否正確：正確

P) 張三哭啞了嗓子
哭：不及物；啞：不及物；*張三*不能當(主語 啞)
預測：及物
預測是否正確：正確

Q) 張三病慌了李四
病：不及物；慌：不及物；*張三*能當(主語 慌)
預測：*病*和*慌*組合以後的影響方向指向賓語，因此是及物
預測是否正確：正確

R) 那件事急病了張三
急：不及物；病：不及物；*那件事*不能當(主語 病)
預測：及物

預測是否正確：正確

S) 那個幽默故事笑彎了張三的腰
笑：不及物；彎：不及物；*那個幽默故事*不能當(主語 彎)
預測：及物
預測是否正確：正確

就正確性而言，不論 V1 是及物或不及物，我們都可以做出正確的預測。Li [5]也能針對這些句型做出正確的預測，但須先辨識 V1 和 V2 的域內和域外論元。

三、規則的實用性

Li [5]的十九種句型都在我們的預測所涵蓋的範圍，我們也都能正確預測動補的及物性以及 V2 修飾的對象，然而不是每一種都能自動預測。須以「V1 和 V2 結合後的影響方向是指向主語還是賓語」為判定標準的句型，涉及常識，例如以下的 T)句〈即之前的 M)句〉：

T) 張三教會了李四

T)句的主語和賓語都是人，因此當 V1 和 V2 的主語的能力都是一樣的，所以不可能符合 OC(2)〈i.e. (主語 V1)不能當(主語 V2)〉。事實上，OC(1)和 OC(2)兩個都不符合還是有可能是 OC，例如以下的 U)句。然而，U)句卻無法用主語和賓語屬於一樣的語意類別來解釋。

U) ？？張三教會了天空

U)句不合理的原因是因為天空無法學會東西，也就是基於某種語義語法要求，*天空*而非*張三*必須被理解成*會*的主語，但*天空*又無法真的當*會*的主語，因此產生語意矛盾。值得注意的是，比起 T)，U)句連 OC(1)也沒符合，卻仍一定是 OC，但 U)的主語和賓語屬於不同語意類別，所以語意類別相近不能當作理由。事實上，*教會*不論出現在什麼情境，都只能是 OC。這種只具備一種影響方向的傾向，有時是 V1 和 V2 搭配所產生的結果。例如：

V) 張三教煩了李四
W) 張三教煩了英文
X) 張三學會了鋼琴

V1 同樣是*教*的情況下，V)的影響方向卻可以是主語也可以是賓語，但*教煩*出現在 W)

句的情境時，很自然的就只有 SC，而 U)卻無法有 SC 的解讀。但這種必為 OC 的傾向也並非由*會*所單獨造成，因為 X)是 SC。*教會*必為 OC 的原因，應該是根據常識，*教*的主語不太可能因為*教*這個動作而自己*會*了。

但有些情況下，影響方向的確似乎可單由 V2 決定：

Y)　？？牛仔褲戳破了玻璃

Y)句和 U)句有類似的語意上的矛盾。不太一樣的是，*破*當 V2 時不論跟哪個 V1 似乎一定造成 OC。例如，*打破*、*磨破*、*撞破*、*撕破*即使在 OC 的解讀違反常識的情形下，仍一定得是 OC。但 V1+破的情形又不能如 U)句解釋成「V1 的主語不可能因為 V1 這個動作而自己破了」，因為既然 V1 不限定，就常識而言，某些動作是可以使做那個動作的主體自己破掉的。例如：

Z)　？？牛仔褲磨破了玻璃

假如 Y)無法是 SC 是因為一樣東西不太可能因為戳其他東西而自己破掉，一樣東西因為磨其他東西而自己破掉卻是合理的。然而 Z)仍因為只容許 OC 的解讀，而產生語意矛盾。

綜合以上所述，我們知道有些動補及 V2 似乎天生就具備固定的影響方向，但這些詞是否可憑藉某種規律辨識，則需要進一步的考察。

四、結論

以上就(1)預測的正確性(accuracy) (2)規則的實用性(applicability)兩方面，闡述我們對動補的及物性及 V2 修飾對象〈SC 或 OC〉的預測方式。用我們的方法判斷及物性及 V2 的修飾對象只須知道 V1 和 V2 是及物還是不及物動詞以及表面主語和賓語和 V1 及 V2 搭配的可能性，不須先辨識位置不固定的句子成分，因此較實用，且都能針對動補句型做出正確的預測。因此，我們能自動處理只用 V1 和 V2 的及物性及主語及賓語和動詞搭配的能力就能解釋的情況，倚賴 V1 和 V2 結合後的影響方向才能解釋的組合則須再研究。

參考文獻

[1] C. N., Li and S. A., Thompson, *Mandarin Chinese: A Functional Reference Grammar*. Crane, Taipei, 1981.

[2] C. C., Smith, *The Parameter of Aspect*.. New York: Kluwer Academic Press, 2003.

[3] L., Shen and T.-H. J., Lin, "Agentivity Agreement and Lexicalization in Resultative

Verbal Compounding," *Paper Space*, 2005. [Online]. Available: http://ling.nthu.edu.tw/faculty/thlin/pdf/Shen_Lin.pdf. [Accessed: 2011/7/9].

[4] H. -L., Lin, *The Syntax-Morphology Interface of Verb-Complement Compounds in Mandarin Chinese*. Ph. D [Dissertation]. University of Illinois at Urbana-Champaign, Urbana-Champaign, Illinois, USA, 1998. [Online]. Available: ProQuest.

[5] C., Li, *Mandarin Resultative Verb Compounds: Where Syntax, Semantics, and Pragmatics Meet*. Ph. D [Dissertation]. Yale University, New Haven, USA, 2007. [Online]: Available: ProQuest.

[6] X. -L., Dai, *Chinese Morphology and its Interface with the Syntax*. Ph. D [Dissertation]. The Ohio State University Press, Columbus, Ohio, USA, 1992.[Online]. Available: ProQuest.

[7] K. -J., Chen, S. -L., Huang, Y. -Y., Shih and Y. -J., Chen, "Extended-HowNet- A Representational Framework for Concepts," in *Proceedings of OntoLex 2005, Jeju Island, South Korea*, 2005, pp. 1-6.

[8] 詞庫小組, "廣義知網知識本體架構線上瀏覽系統, [Online]. Available: http://ehownet.iis.sinica.edu.tw

廣義知網詞彙意見極性的預測

Predicting the Semantic Orientation of Terms in E-HowNet

李政儒 Cheng-Ru Li, 游基鑫 Chi-Hsin Yu, 陳信希 Hsin-Hsi Chen

國立台灣大學資訊工程系

Department of Computer Science and Information Engineering

National Taiwan University

#1, Sec.4, Roosevelt Road, Taipei, 10617 Taiwan

crlee@nlg.csie.ntu.edu.tw, jsyu@nlg.csie.ntu.edu.tw, hhchen@ntu.edu.tw

摘要

詞彙的意見極性是句子及文件層次意見分析的重要基礎，雖然目前已經存在一些人工標記的中文情緒字典，但如何自動標記詞彙的意見極性，仍是一個重要的工作。這篇論文的目的是為廣義知網的詞彙自動標記意見極性。我們運用監督式機器學習的方法，抽取不同來源的各種有用特徵並加以整合，來預測詞彙的意見極性。實驗結果顯示，廣義知網詞彙意見極性預測的準確率可到達 92.33%，這個結果跟人的標記準確率不相上下。

Abstract

The semantic orientation of terms is fundamental for sentiment analysis in sentence and document levels. Although some Chinese sentiment dictionaries are available, how to predict the orientation of terms automatically is still important. In this paper, we predict the semantic orientation of terms of E-HowNet. We extract many useful features from different sources to represent a Chinese term in E-HowNet, and use a supervised machine learning algorithm to predict its orientation. Our experimental result showed that the proposed approach can achieve 92.33% accuracy, which is comparable to the accuracy of human taggers.

關鍵詞：廣義知網，情緒分析，情緒字典, 語義傾向, 向量支援機

Keywords: E-NowNet, Sentiment Analysis, Sentiment dictionary, Semantic orientation, SVM

一、緒論

情緒分析（Sentiment Analysis）在現今的網路世界中，有許多實際且重要的運用，例如從網路的評論文章中分析消費者對產品的評價，或分析消費者對產品性能的關注焦點等等。不管對句子或文件層次的情緒分析，意見詞詞典都是一個重要的資源。通常意見詞詞典是用人工來收集詞彙，並用人工標記詞彙的各種情緒屬性，包括主客觀（subjective or objective）、極性（orientation/polarity)、）及極性的強度（strength）[1]。這些情緒屬性對不同的應用有不同的重要性，標記難度也各不相同，通常詞彙的極性是最容易進行標記的屬性。

標記情緒屬性時，研究者可以從零開始收集詞彙以建立意見詞詞典，如台大意見詞詞典NTUSD[2]。在另一方面，也有研究者嘗試爲自然語言處理中的許多現存的資源，添加情緒屬性，如 SentiWordNet[3]。但現有資源的語彙量通常很大，如 WordNet 3.0 就包括 206,941 個不同的英文字義（word-sense pair），要全部用人工進行標記之成本太高。因此，通常的作法是少量標記一些詞彙，再用機器學習方法，爲剩下的詞彙進行自動標記，雖然自動標記的準確率不如人工標記，但對一般應用有某種程度的幫助。

在中文自然語言處理，NTUSD 是一部重要的意見詞詞典，但此詞典只包括詞彙及極性的資訊。另一方面，董振東先生和陳克健教授所建立的知網[4]和廣義知網[5]，是重要的語意資源。對於每個詞彙，都用有限的義原給予精確的定義，但這些定義卻缺乏情緒的語意標記。因此，如何自動爲廣義知網加上情緒標記，成爲一個重要的課題，也是本研究的目的。

本研究提出爲廣義知網加上情緒標記的方法，首先利用 NTUSD 跟廣義知網詞彙的交集建立標準答案集，再由標準答案集訓練出分類器，爲其他廣義知網詞彙進行標記。如何有效的運用監督式機器學習演算法，如何爲詞彙抽取出有用的特徵，是主要的挑戰議題。在此研究中，我們有系統的嘗試抽取各種不同的詞彙特徵，最後得到跟人工標記準確率不相上下的分類器。

第二節介紹廣義知網、及英文和中文相關的情緒屬性標記研究，第三節介紹從 E-HowNet 及 Google Chinese Web 5-gram 抽取特徵的方法，第四節呈現各種實驗的結果及分析，包括跟 NTUSD 人工標記的比較，最後總結論文的成果。

二、相關研究

董振東先生於 1998 年創建知網（HowNet），並在 2003 年，跟中央研究院資訊所詞庫小組在 2003 年，將中研院詞庫小組詞典（CKIP Chinese Lexical Knowledge Base）的詞條跟知網連結，並作了一些修改，最後形成廣義知網（Extended-HowNet, E-HowNet）。詞庫小組修改並擴展知網原先的語義義原角色知識本體，建構出廣義知網知識本體（Extended-HowNet Ontology），並用這些新的語義義原，以結構化的形式來定義詞條，詞條定義式的例子如圖一。

有關情緒屬性標記的研究，我們分爲英文及中文來討論。在英文方面，最早是由 Hatzivassiloglou & McKeown[6]在 1997 年針對形容詞所做的研究，他們所用的形容詞分別有正面詞 657 個及負面詞 679 個，該論文依據不同的實驗設定，監督式機器學習的準確率（Accuracy）由 82% 到 90%。之後陸續有不同的研究，所用多爲半監督式機器學習的演算法[7-9]，效能從 67%到 88%不等，但因爲這些演算法所用的資料集並不相同，實驗過程及評估標準也不一樣，（有用 Accuracy、Precision、或 F-Measure），所以效能沒有辦法直接比較。

```
<Word item = "汽油">
  <WordFreq>15</WordFreq>
  <WordSense id="1">
    <English>gasoline</English> <Phone>ㄑㄧˋ ㄧㄡˊ</Phone> <PinYin>qi4 you2</PinYin>
    <SyntacticFunction> <POS>Naa</POS> <Freq>15</Freq> </SyntacticFunction>
    <TopLevelDefinition>{material|材料:attribute={StateLiquid|液態},telic={burn|焚燒}}</TopLevelDefinition>
    <BottomLevelExpansion>{material|材料:attribute={StateLiquid|液態},telic={burn|焚燒}}</BottomLevelExpansion>
  </WordSense></Word>
```

圖一、「*汽油*」的廣義知網定義式

在中文的情緒屬性標記相關研究，Yuen et al.[10]2004 年利用 Turney & Littman[7] 的半監督式機器學習演算法，在正面詞 604 個及負面詞 645 個的資料集上做實驗，得到最高的成績是 80.23%的精確度及 85.03%的召回率。之後從 2006 到 2010 年，陸續的研究使用不同的資料集，用不同類型的機器學習演算法來處理這個問題[11-14]，所得到的效能在不同的指標（Accuracy、Precision、或 F-Measure）下，從 89%到 96%不等。因爲基準不同，這些效能一樣沒有辦法直接比較，但相較於英文，成績則明顯提高。

三、特徵抽取及機器學習演算法

由於我們運用監督式機器學習演算法來訓練分類器，最重要的問題是爲詞彙抽取出有用的特徵。在此論文中，我們分別從 E-HowNet 及 Google Chinese Web 5-gram 這兩個來源抽取兩大類的特徵，接著將這兩個來源的特徵組合訓練分類器。此外，我們也嘗試使用組合式的監督式機器學習演算法（ensemble approach），來更進一步得到更高的效能，以下我們分別詳細介紹。

（一）、基礎義原特徵

從 E-HowNet 抽取的特徵稱之爲基礎義原特徵，也就是對每一個 E-HowNet 的詞彙 i，用一向量 $V_i = (w_{i,j}) = (w_{i,1}, w_{i,2}, \ldots, w_{i,n})$ 表示，其中 n 爲向量的維度。

由於每一詞彙的每一個語意（sense）都有一個結構化的定義式，而且定義式中都用義原來進行定義，公式 (1) 定義 V_i 中每個特徵的權重：

$$w_{i,j} = \begin{cases} 1, & \text{如果定義式 i 中出現義原 j} \\ 0, & \text{不出現義原 j} \end{cases} \quad (1)$$

以圖一「*汽油*」這個詞彙爲例，其定義式中出現了義原 material，所以它的值 $w_{汽油, material}$

就會是 1，其他沒出現的義原，值就會是 0。我們共使用了 2567 個義原來當特徵。

廣義知網的詞彙有歧異性，也就是每個詞彙可能有許多語意。而詞彙的第一個語意，是出現頻率最高的語意(除了四個詞彙例外)，所以我們用詞彙的第一個語意來抽取特徵。只從詞彙的一個語意抽取特徵，而不把該詞彙所有的語意放在一起，代表這種方法可為不同的語意給出不同的極性預測。只是由於目前 NTUSD 極性標記只到詞彙的層級，所以無法對語意的層級進行極性預測。但只要有語意層級的極性標記，我們這種做法可馬上套用。

1、基礎義原特徵加權值

除了公式 (1) 的方式外，我們可以利用更多 E-HowNet 的特性，來抽取出有用的資訊。一個可能的方式是定義式中的結構，如果把定義式展開，會得到如圖二的樹狀結構。在這樹狀結構中，義原所在的深度是一個有用的資訊，因此我們仿照劉群&李素建[15]的公式，將深度的資訊當作權重引入公式 (1)，得到公式 (2)。

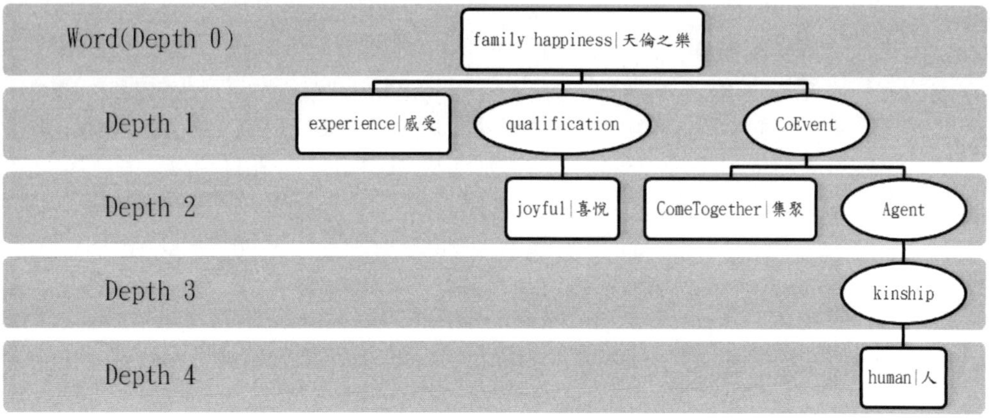

圖二、「*天倫之樂*」定義式的樹狀表示

$$w_{i,j} = \begin{cases} \dfrac{1}{1+\alpha \times d_{i,j}}, & \text{如果定義式 i 中出現義原 j} \\ 0, & \text{不出現義原 j} \end{cases} \qquad (2)$$

公式 (2) 中，α 是可調的參數，$d_{i,j}$ 是詞彙 i 跟義原 j 的距離，這可用義原 j 的深度表示。調整公式 (2) 中的 α，讓我們可以實驗那一種方式，才應給較高的權重：

（可能一）$\alpha < 0$：深度越深，表示該義原有較多資訊，應給較高權重。

（可能二）$\alpha > 0$：深度越深，表示該義原有較少資訊，應給較少權重。

由於 $\alpha < 0$ 時，$w_{i,j}$ 可能變為負值，所以最小的 α 設為 −0.05。另外，當 $\alpha = 0$，公式 (2) 會等於公式 (1)，所以我們在做實驗時，只要使用公式 (2) 即可。

2、加入否定關係調整特徵的加權值

在計算義原深度時，可能會經過帶有否定意義的關係，例如「*一事無成*」定義式中有

「{*not*({*succeed|成功*})}」，可以發現 *succeed* 被 *not* 所修飾。這時，義原 *succeed* 的權重用負值來表示可能會更好，因此我們將否定的概念引入公式 (3) 如下：

$$w_{i,j}=\begin{cases}\dfrac{Neg_{i,j}}{1+\alpha\times d_{i,j}}, & \text{如果定義式 i 中出現義原 j}\\ 0\quad, & \text{不出現義原 j}\end{cases} \tag{3}$$

其中，$Neg_{i,j}$ 表示義原 j 是否有被否定意義的關係所修飾，若有則 $Neg_{i,j}$ 爲 -1，若無則 $Neg_{i,j}$ 爲 $+1$。另外，如果樹狀結構上面的義原被否定意義的關係所修飾，這否定意義會傳遞到下面的義原。

（二）、語篇（context）特徵

廣義知網雖然有嚴謹的定義式可用以表示詞彙，但是有四個缺點，造成只用義原當特徵無法正確獲得詞彙的極性。

第一個缺點是詞彙所標的義原量太少，因爲詞彙是用人工標示義原，所以無法給予很多標示。這表示詞彙擁有的資訊量有限，會造成分類器無法有效學習。第二個缺點是義原數量太少，這會造成語義的劃分不夠精確，無法顯示出真實的語義差別，例如「*明哲保身*」跟「*見風轉舵*」的定義式都是「*{sly|狡}*」，但「*明哲保身*」是正面意見，「*見風轉舵*」卻是負面意見。第三個缺點是廣義知網定義標準的差異，例如，專有名詞在廣義知網中會用客觀的義原來定義，但該專有名詞經過使用，卻可能會引起人的正反情緒，這種差異會引入程度不等的雜訊到分類器中。第四個缺點是廣義知網尚未對所有詞彙標上定義式，例如「*乾淨俐落*」在廣義知網及 NTUSD 中都出現，但廣義知網卻沒有標上定義式。

因此我們引入語篇的特性，從該詞彙在語言中的實際使用情況，抽取出詞彙的特徵，來補償這些缺點。我們使用 Liu et al.[16] 所建立的 Google Web 5-gram Version 1，來抽取語篇特徵。Google Web 5-gram 是 Google 從網路中收集大量的簡體中文網頁，並經過處理所建立的資源。他們收集了 882,996,532,572 個字符（token），共 102,048,435,515 個句子，經過斷詞後建成 n-gram。n-gram 的 n 從 1 到 5，並且只保留頻率大於 40 的 n-gram。Google Web 5-gram 的例子如圖三所示。

```
恐吓 或 辱骂 他人 </S>  796466
恐吓 或 辱骂 他人 内容  173
恐吓 或 过度 兴奋 或    251
恐吓 或 非法 骚扰 侵犯  574
恐吓 或 非法 骚扰 有    200
恐吓 或 非法 骚扰 的    4463
恐吓 或 非法 骚扰 等    705
恐吓 或 骚扰 侵犯 他人  95
```

圖三、Google Web 5-gram 資料範例

上圖中，表示「*恐吓 或 非法 骚扰 的*」這一 5-gram 共出現了 4463 次。從圖中我們也可看到，Google Web 5-gram 是簡體中文，但廣義知網爲繁體中文，所以我們先將廣義

知網用 Microsoft Word 翻譯爲簡體中文，之後才使用 Google Web 5-gram 這一語料庫。語料庫在使用時，只用 5-gram 的部分來抽取特徵。

1、Google Web 5-gram 特徵抽取

我們使用特徵跟詞彙的同出現（co-occurrence）次數做爲特徵值，以圖三爲例，如果詞彙是「*恐嚇*」，以「*非法*」當特徵值，則同出現次數會將所有「*恐嚇*」及「*非法*」一同出現的 5-gram 次數相加。在上面的例子中，「*恐嚇*」及「*非法*」的同出現次數爲 574+200+4463 + 705=5942 次。

另外，由於廣義知網跟 Google Web 5-gram 的斷詞標準並不一致，所以在處理時把 Google Web 5-gram 的空白去掉，直接找出「*詞彙*」跟「*特徵*」這兩字串是否同時出現，來計算次數，這樣可以避免斷詞標準不一所產生的問題。例如「*一事無成*」在 Google Web 5-gram 中被斷成四個獨立的詞，將空白去掉就可以正確比對到。

因爲這裡的詞彙集合就是等待標示極性的詞，所以我們只要指定特徵的集合包括那些詞，就可算出表示詞彙 i 的向量 $V_i = (c_{i,j}) = (c_{i,1}, c_{i,2},\ldots, c_{i,\mathrm{m}})$。其中，m 是特徵集合的大小，$c_{i,j}$ 是「*詞彙 i*」跟「*特徵 j*」這兩字串同出現的次數。在我們的實驗中，共嘗試了十種不同的特徵集合，分別是廣義知網的名詞、廣義知網的動詞、廣義知網的副詞、廣義知網的形容詞、廣義知網所有詞彙、Google Web 5-gram 最常出現的 5000 詞、Google Web 5-gram 最常出現的 5000 詞（但詞彙長度最少爲 2）、Google Web 5-gram 最常出現的 10000 詞、Google Web 5-gram 最常出現的 10000 詞（但詞彙長度最少爲 2）、以及 NTUSD 完整版。

2、Google Web 5-gram 特徵值處理

用 $V_i = (c_{i,1}, c_{i,2},\ldots, c_{i,\mathrm{m}})$ 的方式來表示的缺點，是 $c_{i,j}$ 的值變化的範圍會非常大，最小爲 40，最大會到上千萬。這在機器學習中，通常需要做進一步的處理才會有比較好的結果。我們實驗了兩個不同的方法來處理這一問題：第一種是一般的餘弦標準化（cosine-normalization），將原本的向量 V_i 用公式 (4) 處理；第二種是 Esuli & Sebastiani[1] 所提的餘弦標準化 TFIDF （cosine-normalized TF-IDF），他們用該方法來處理 WordNet 中的詞彙的權重，如公式 (5) 所述。

$$CosNorm(V_i) = \frac{V_i}{\sqrt{\sum_{1\le k\le m} c_{i,k}^2}} \quad \in \Re^m \tag{4}$$

$$CosNorm(TFIDF_i) = \frac{TFIDF_i}{\sqrt{\sum_{1\le k\le m} tfidf_{i,k}^2}} \quad \in \Re^m \tag{5}$$

$$TFIDF_i = (tfidf_{i,1}, tfidf_{i,2}, \ldots, tfidf_{i,m})$$

$$tfidf_{i,j} = tf_{i,j} * idf_j$$

$$tf_{i,j} = \frac{{}_{i,j}}{\text{特徵 } j \text{ 總出現次數}} = \frac{{}_{i,j}}{\sum_{k \in D} c_{k,j}}$$

$$idf_j = \log(df_j)^{-1} = \log \frac{|D|}{|\{i : c_{i,j} > 0, \forall i \in D\}|}$$

公式 (5)中 D 表示文件的集合，此處把詞彙 i 當成文件，特徵 j 當成 term。

公式 (4) 的標準化可以讓所有詞彙的向量等長，消掉次數變化過大的缺點。公式 (5) 的想法則認爲特徵 j 的權重，應該先跨詞彙進行標準化（normalization），所以 $tf_{i,j}$ 會除以特徵 j 的總出現次數，另外再考慮特徵 j 的稀有度，所以乘上 idf_j，最後再讓所有詞彙的向量等長。我們會在後面的實驗中，比較這兩種不同權重處理方式的效能。

（三）、不同特徵的組合

我們用了基礎義原特徵 $(w_{i,1}, w_{i,2},\ldots, w_{i,\mathrm{n}}) = (w_{i,j})$，及語篇特徵 $(c_{i,1}, c_{i,2},\ldots, c_{i,\mathrm{m}}) = (c_{i,j})$ 來表示詞彙 i。如果想同時使用這兩種特徵中的資訊，一種直觀的方式，是將兩種特徵表示方式混合，用 $V_i = (w_{i,1}, w_{i,2},\ldots, w_{i,\mathrm{n}},c_{i,1}, c_{i,2},\ldots, c_{i,\mathrm{m}})$ 來表示。由於基礎義原特徵及語篇特徵都有許多不同的變形，我們無法一一嘗試所有可能的組合，所以會先分別用實驗找出最好的基礎義原特徵 $(w_{i,j})$ 及語篇特徵 $(c_{i,j})$，再把兩種特徵混合來進行實驗。我們沒有對混合後的向量做其它的處理，只是直接串接成爲 n+m 維向量。

（四）、組合式的監督式機器學習演算法（ensemble approach）

由於廣義知網詞彙的每一個意義（sense）都標有詞性，而且我們用了很多不同的特徵集合，這表示我們會有很多不同的分類器。如果依不同詞性選擇做得最好的分類器，則可以有更好的效能。例如，如果分類器 A 的總體效能不是最好，但如果它對名詞做的效能是最好的，也許拿它來預測名詞的極性會更準確，依此類推。我們把廣義知網的詞性，分爲名詞、動詞、副詞、形容詞及其他共五類，分別選在該類別預測最好的分類器來預測。這作法是一種常見的組合不同分類器的策略（ensemble approach），我們也會對此進行實驗，來觀察效能。

四、實驗與分析

（一）、實驗資料與實驗設定

本研究使用國立台灣大學意見詞詞典完整版（NTUSD）、與廣義知網的交集，作爲實驗資料，這兩個資料集的詞彙數如表一。資料集 E-HowNet∩NTUSD 會作爲標準答案集，在我們所看的相關論文中，這個答案集的大小是最大的一個。實驗使用標準答案集其中的 80% 爲訓練資料集，其餘 20%爲測試資料集，並依照實驗資料的詞性分布以及語意極性分布作分層抽樣（stratified sampling）。

表一、廣義知網、NTUSD、以及交集的資料筆數

資料集	正面	負面	總數
E-HowNet	N/A	N/A	88,127
NTUSD	21,056	22,750	43,806
E-HowNet∩NTUSD	5,346	6,256	11,602

分層抽樣詳細的作法如下：先將資料依照五種詞性以及兩種極性分成十個子集合，再針對每個子集合取其中 80%作爲訓練資料，另外 20%作爲測試資料。由於我們的資料量夠多，所以可以使用這種抽樣。這種抽樣主要的好處在於我們更容易對測試結果進行更多的分析，我們把分層抽樣的結果列於表二。

表二、訓練資料的詞性以及傾向分布

詞性		全部資料集		正面傾向	訓練資料集		測試資料集	
		正面	負面	百分比	正面	負面	正面	負面
名詞	2,040	931	1,109	45.64%	745	887	186	222
動詞	9,056	4,134	4922	45.65%	3,307	3,938	827	984
副詞	383	206	177	53.79%	165	142	41	35
形容詞	74	45	29	60.81%	36	23	9	6
其他	49	30	19	61.22%	24	15	6	4
總數	11,602	5,346	6,256	46.08%	4,277	5,005	1,069	1,251

本研究使用 Chang & Lin[17] 所發布的 LIBSVM 支援向量機，來當監督式機器學習演算法，使用 radial basis function (RBF) kernel function， RBF 的兩個手動參數 cost c 與 gamma g 以網格搜尋（Grid Search）的方式尋找最佳參數值 (c, g)，搜尋範圍 $c \in \{2^{-5}, 2^{-3}, 2^{-1},..., 2^{15}\}$、$g \in \{2^{-15}, 2^{-13}, 2^{-11}, ..., 2^{-3}\}$，總共 110 組參數，取五疊交叉驗證（5-fold cross validation）中平均準確率最高的參數。

我們使用預測準確率（accuracy）來比較分類器間的效能，這是看訓練出的分類器在測試資料集中的成績，而分類器會對測試資料集中的所有詞彙都進行極性的預測。另外，使用 McNemar 檢定[18]來測試分類器的效能差距是否爲顯著，顯著水準設定爲 0.95。

McNemar 檢定將測試資料依照兩個分類器（以下稱爲分類器 A 與分類器 B）的標記，分成四組並計數。其中測試樣本數即爲下面 $n_{1,1}$、$n_{0,1}$、$n_{1,0}$、$n_{0,0}$ 四個數字的總合，在虛無假設（null hypothesis）中，兩個分類器應具有相同的錯誤率，也就是 $n_{0,1}=n_{1,0}$ 。

$n_{1,1}$：	分類器 A 與分類器 B 皆正確標記的樣本數	$n_{0,1}$：	分類器 A 標記錯誤，但分類器 B 標記正確的樣本數
$n_{1,0}$：	分類器 B 標記錯誤，但分類器 A 標記正確的樣本數	$n_{0,0}$：	分類器 A 與分類器 B 皆錯誤標記的樣本數

McNemar 檢定建構在卡方適合度檢定 （χ2 test goodness of fit）上，整理而得的檢定值爲 $\frac{(|n_{0,1}-n_{1,0}|-1)^2}{n_{0,1}+n_{1,0}}$，此檢定值在 $n_{0,1}+n_{1,0}$ 夠大的時候會趨近於自由度爲 1 的卡方分配，因此在顯著水準（significant level）爲 0.95 時，此值若大於 $\chi^2_{1,0.95}=3.8415$，則拒絕虛無假設。我們用 (McNemar 檢定結果, p-value) 來顯示我們的檢定結果，例如檢定結果 (1.50, 0.22) 表示，McNemar 檢定結果爲 1.50 < 3.84，所以沒有通過 McNemar 檢定，p-value 爲 0.22。

（二）、基礎義原特徵的效能

圖四爲基礎義原方法在不同 α 值所得到的預測準確率，其中公式 (2) 的結果是 PBF（Prime-Based Feature）那條折線，最佳的 α 值爲 −0.02，準確率爲 89.4397%。當 PBF 中 α = 0，該結果即爲公式 (1) 的結果。公式 (3) 的結果是 PBFN（Prime-Based Feature with Negation）那條折線，最佳的 α 值爲 −0.02 及 −0.03，準確率爲 89.6121%。

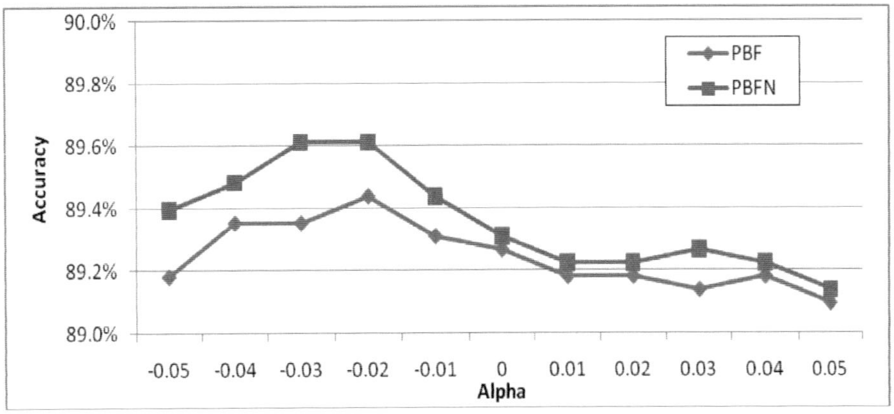

圖四、廣義知網特徵於不同 α 值的效能比較

我們從圖四可以看出，描述 PBFN 的折線在所有的 α 值下，準確率皆略高於 PBF，但是兩個最大值（α = −0.02）的差距僅 0.1724%，此差距爲不顯著，檢定結果 (1.50, 0.22)。由於 α < 0 有最佳效能，這表示深度較深給較高權重，該義原有較好的特徵，可以給分類器學習。

（三）、語篇特徵的效能

語篇特徵使用十組特徵集的名稱，以及特徵數量，如表三所示。在表中，我們使用特徵集代號來代表該特徵集。十組特徵集中，最少的是 *Adj* 的特徵集，只有 948 個詞，最多的是 *All* 的特徵集，有 86,712 個詞。

表三、語篇特徵所使用的特徵集與其特徵數

特徵集	特徵集代號	特徵數
廣義知網名詞	*Noun*	46,807
廣義知網動詞	*Verb*	37,109
廣義知網副詞	*Adv.*	2,364
廣義知網形容詞	*Adj.*	948
廣義知網所有詞彙	*All*	86,712
最常出現 5000 詞	*F5000-1*	5,000
最常出現 5000 詞（長度≧2）	*F5000-2*	5,000
最常出現 10000 詞	*F10000-1*	10,000
最常出現 10000 詞（長度≧2）	*F10000-2*	10,000
NTUSD（完整版）	*NTUSD*	42,614

我們使用三種不同的加權方式得到的預測準確率如圖五，圖中我們也把特徵集的特徵數由左至右由小到大排列。

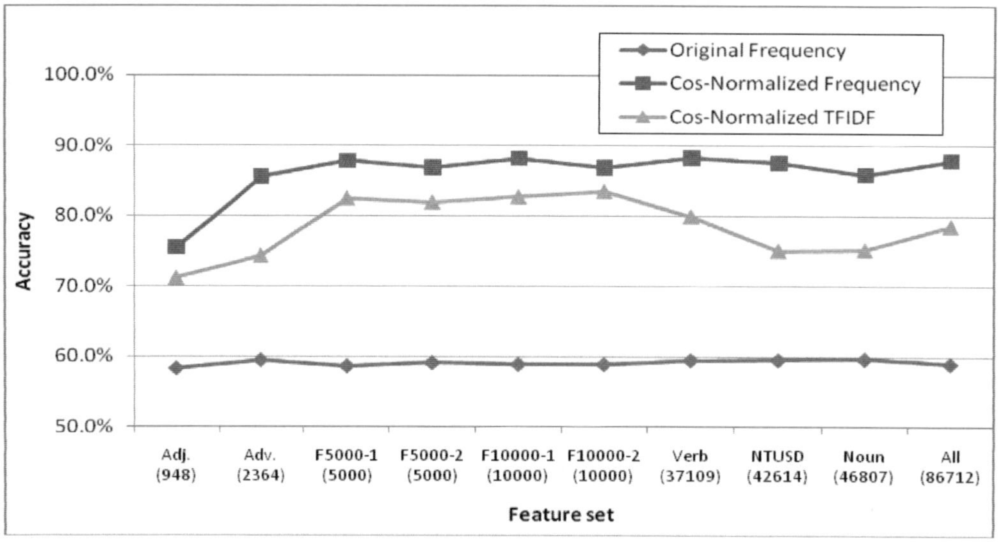

圖五、使用語篇特徵時的預測效能

從圖五可以看出，沒有標準化的原始頻率的最佳準確率為 59.70%，使用的特徵集為「廣義知網名詞」，其效能最差且差距很大。餘弦標準化 TFIDF 的效能排在中間，最佳準確率為 83.41%，使用的特徵集為「最常出現 10000 詞」。而經過餘弦標準化的特徵值則可以得到最佳效能，其最佳準確率為 88.23%，此時使用的特徵集為「廣義知網動詞」，此效能跟其他兩者的差距為顯著，檢定結果 (4.61, 0.03)。

圖五中特徵集的個數，並沒有絕對的影響，但若個數太少，如特徵個數小於 2364 個，則效能會明顯變差。圖四中的最佳值 PBFN（$\alpha = -0.02$）爲 89.61%，特徵個數爲 2,567 個，這個值比圖五中的最佳值 88.23%還要大，這表示廣義知網中的特徵比較準確，但這差距爲不顯著，檢定結果 (2.49, 0.11)。

（四）、組合不同特徵的效能

組合特徵時，因爲餘弦標準化有最好的效能，所以語篇特徵選擇餘弦標準化後的十組特徵集，分別與廣義知網特徵效能最好的 $PBFN_{\alpha=-0.03}$ 組合，來訓練分類器，分類器預測準確率如圖六。其中廣義知網特徵的特徵集效能爲固定，因此以水平直線表示（gloss 那條折線）。組合而成的特徵集，以「*語篇特徵集代碼*+$PBFN_{\alpha=-0.03}$」加以命名，例如「*F10000-2*+$PBFN_{\alpha=-0.03}$」表示「最常出現 10000 詞（長度≧2）」跟「$PBFN_{\alpha=-0.03}$」兩個特徵集的組合。

我們從圖六可以看出，將廣義知網特徵與外部語料特徵組合之後，準確率都有顯著提升，提升後的最高準確率爲 92. 3276%，使用「廣義知網所有詞彙 *All*+$PBFN_{\alpha=-0.03}$」和「最常出現 10000 詞（長度≧2） *F10000-2*+$PBFN_{\alpha=-0.03}$」爲特徵集時皆有相同的準確率。上圖中，「廣義知網所有詞彙 *All*」準確率從 88.23%提升至 92.33%時，此差距爲顯著，檢定結果 (32.14, $1.4*10^{-8}$)。

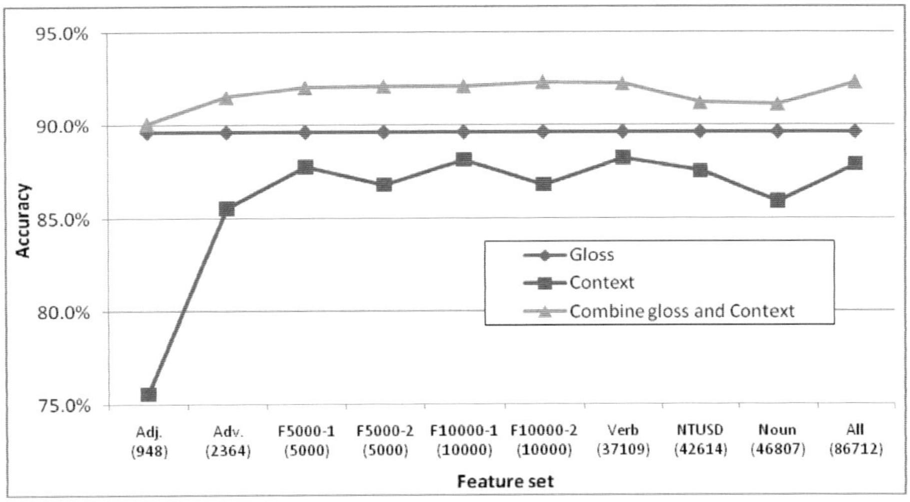

圖六、廣義知網、語篇特徵、與組合特徵的準確率比較

（五）、組合式的監督式機器學習演算法效能

在圖六中，組合出的特徵集有十個，所以共有十個分類器，每個分類器在訓練時，對不同詞性有不同的效能，我們將這十個分類器對於每個詞性的標記效能整理成表四。表四中的特徵集代號是「*語篇特徵集代碼*+$PBFN_{\alpha=-0.03}$」的簡寫，因爲使用相同的 $PBFN_{\alpha=-0.03}$，所以將其忽略。「總體效能」是指分類器訓練時的整體效能。表中，一欄中最佳的

標記效能以**粗體字**表示。

表四、訓練資料集中，組合特徵對不同詞性的標記準確率

特徵集代號	總體效能	訓練資料集中，依詞性分別計算的準確率				
		名詞	動詞	副詞	形容詞	其他
Adj.	94.3223%	95.9559%	94.2167%	89.9023%	93.2203%	82.0513%
Adv.	95.3243%	96.5074%	95.2795%	92.1824%	91.5254%	84.6154%
F5000-1	96.1000%	97.3039%	96.0110%	92.8339%	94.9153%	89.7436%
F5000-2	97.2635%	98.0392%	97.1705%	**96.0912%**	94.9153%	**94.8718%**
F10000-1	96.2400%	97.3652%	96.1767%	92.8339%	94.9153%	89.7436%
F10000-2	**97.5005%**	**98.2843%**	**97.4189%**	**96.0912%**	94.9153%	**94.8718%**
Verb	96.5632%	97.5490%	96.5079%	94.4625%	91.5254%	89.7436%
NTUSD	96.8218%	97.3039%	96.8254%	95.1140%	93.2203%	**94.8718%**
Noun	96.8541%	98.1005%	96.6460%	**96.0912%**	**96.6102%**	89.7436%
All	96.4124%	97.4265%	96.3699%	93.1596%	94.9153%	89.7436%

表四中我們可以發現，訓練時，*F10000-2*+PBFN$_{\alpha=-0.03}$有最高的總體效能，其各詞性效能除了形容詞外，多是最好；考量到資料集中形容詞的數量並不多，這表示組合多個分類器後，效能的提昇空間可能有限。表四中另一個值得注意的一點是訓練資料集的內部測試效能（inside test）*F10000-2*+PBFN$_{\alpha=-0.03}$的 97.5005% 跟實際測試效能 92. 3276% 相比，降低了 5.31%，這降低幅度並不大，顯示這分類器的 generalization 能力不錯，這也是使用 Google Web 5-gram 的優點，它可產生較強健（robust）的分類器[19]。

我們在表四中選不同詞性做得最好的分類器來組合，如果效能相同，則選特徵數量較少的那一個分類器，因爲特徵數較少通常在未看過的資料集會做得較好。組合出的分類器我們稱爲 *EnsembleClassifier*，其結果列在表五，其中 *F10000-2*+PBFN$_{\alpha=-0.03}$於各詞性的標記效能也列出來比較。

表五、組合分類器於各詞性的標記效能及比較

分類器 \ 詞性	*F10000-2*+PBFN$_{\alpha=-0.03}$分類器於各詞性的標記效能			組合分類器 *EnsembleClassifier* 於各詞性的標記效能				
	正確個數	錯誤個數	準確率	使用的分類器	正確個數	增減	錯誤個數	準確率
名詞	371	37	90.9314%	*F10000-2*	371	(+0)	37	90.9314%
動詞	1,681	130	92.8216%	*F10000-2*	1,681	(+0)	130	92.8216%
副詞	67	9	88.1579%	*F5000-2*	69	(+2)	7	90.7895%
形容詞	14	1	93.3333%	*Noun*	12	(-2)	3	80.0000%
其他	9	1	90.0000%	*F5000-2*	9	(+0)	1	90.0000%
總數	2,142	178	92.3276%		2142	(+0)	178	92.3276%

表五中，我們也列出每種詞性做錯與做對的個數，並以 *F10000-2*+PBFN$_{\alpha=-0.03}$ 分類器為基準，看組合後的分類器，在各詞性中做對做錯的次數的增減，用括號來標出增減的數量。

EnsembleClassifier 所得成績跟 *F10000-2*+PBFN$_{\alpha=-0.03}$ 相同，這表示目前的分類器組合方式，無法提升效能。

（六）、相關研究效能比較

我們總結前面各種不同的實驗結果，畫成圖七，來方便我們比較效能。其中，gloss 表基礎義原特徵 PBFN$_{\alpha=-0.03}$，最好的效能到 92.3276%。

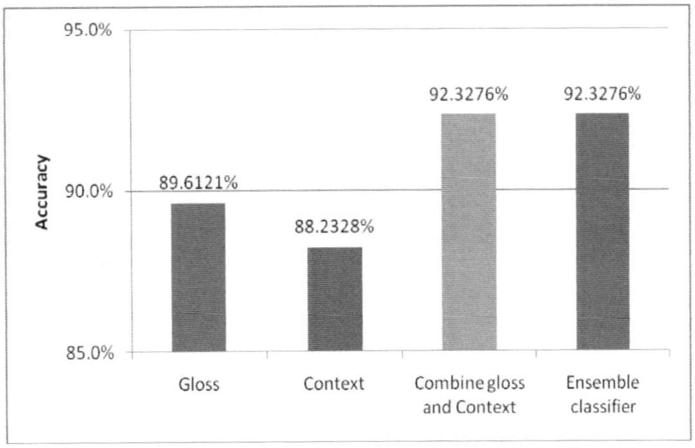

圖七、四種方法效能比較

由於我們使用 NTUSD，我們想看看 NTUSD 人類標記的效能跟我們分類器的效能有何差異。在 Ku & Chen [2]的研究中，聘請標記者對舊版 NTUSD 進行標記。舊版 NTUSD 為經過翻譯的 General Inquirer（GI）與 Chinese Network Sentiment Dictionary（CNSD）的組合，每個詞彙都有人工的意見標記。該研究中標記者的最佳標記效能與本研究的比較如表六，從表六中可以看出，本研究所產生的自動標記演算法達到了接近人類標記的效能。

表六、NTUSD 標記者與本研究標記效能比較

分類器	Recall	Precision	F-Measure
F10000-2+PBFN$_{\alpha=-0.03}$	92.36%	92.20%	92.27%
三人中最佳的人類標記者	96.58%	88.87%	92.56%

表六中，人類標記者的 Recall 及 Precision 取自 Ku & Chen [2]。*F10000-2*+PBFN$_{\alpha=-0.03}$

的預測結果為 (True Positive, False Positive, True Negative, False Negative) = (TP, FP, TN, FN) = (968, 77, 1174, 101)，其中 Positive 表正面極性。我們分別對正負面極性計算 Recall、Precision 及 F-Measure (R^+、P^+、F^+、R^-、P^-、F^-)，其中，$P^+=TP/(TP+FP)$、$R^+=TP/(TP+FN)$、$F^+= 2P^+R^+/(P^++R^+)$、$P^-=TN/(TN+FN)$、$R^-=TN/(TN+FP)$、$F^-= 2P^-R^-/(P^-+R^-)$，最後系統的 Recall=$(R^++R^-)/2$、Precision=$(P^++P^-)/2$ 及 F-Measure = $(F^++F^-)/2$ = (91.58% + 92.95%)/2 = 92.27%。由計算中我們可以看到，我們的系統對負面極性做得較好，而且因資料集有較多的負面詞彙，所以最後的準確率 92.33% 比 F^+ 高。

五、結論

本研究使用了 Google Web 5-gram Version 1 來抽取語篇特徵，並加上來自 E-HowNet 的基礎義原特徵，用監督式機器學習的方法，來預測 E-HowNet 詞彙的意見極性。雖然單獨使用不同的特徵已經可以接近 90% 的準確率，但如果把兩種特徵都加以使用，分類器的極性預測的準確率可到達 92.33%，這個結果跟人的標記準確率不相上下；以這種方式建立的分類器，可用來自動標記 E-HowNet 詞彙的意見極性。

我們希望在未來能把這種方式，往不同的方向擴展，來給予 E-HowNet 詞彙更多意見的屬性，這包括對詞彙標記主客觀的屬性及正負面傾向的強度等。除此之外，因為 E-HowNet 詞彙有許多不同的詞性，我們也希望能把我們的方法，運用詞性的層次來進行標記。藉由提供更精確的字彙意見標記資訊，來支援句子及文件層次的意見分析。

致謝

Research of this paper was partially supported by National Science Council (Taiwan) under the contract NSC 98-2221-E-002-175-MY3.

參考文獻

[1] A. Esuli and F. Sebastiani, "Determining the semantic orientation of terms through gloss classification," In *Proceedings of* CIKM-05, pp. 617–624, 2005..

[2] L.-W. Ku and H.-H. Chen, "Mining opinions from the Web: Beyond relevance retrieval," *Journal of the American Society for Information Science and Technology*, vol. 58, no. 12, pp. 1838-1850, 2007.

[3] A. Esuli and F. Sebastiani, "SentiWordNet: A publicly available lexical resource for opinion mining," In *Proceedings of the 5th Conference on Language Resources and Evaluation (LREC 06)*, pp. 417–422, 2006.

[4] Z. Dong and Q. Dong, *HowNet and the Computation of Meaning*. World Scientific, 2006.

[5] 陳克健, 黃淑齡, 施悅音, 和 陳怡君, "多層次概念定義與複雜關係表達－繁體字知網的新增架構," *漢語詞彙語義研究的現狀與發展趨勢國際學術研討會，北京大學*, 2004.

[6] V. Hatzivassiloglou and K. R. McKeown, "Predicting the semantic orientation of adjectives," In *Proceedings of ACL-97, 35th Annual Meeting of the Association for Computational Linguistics*, pages 174–181, Madrid, ES, 1997. Association for Computational Linguistics.

[7] P. D. Turney and M. L. Littman, "Measuring praise and criticism: Inference of semantic orientation from association," *ACM Transactions on Information Systems,* 21(4):pp. 315–346, 2003.

[8] J. Kamps, M. Marx, R. J. Mokken, and M. De Rijke, "Using WordNet to measure semantic orientation of adjectives," In *Proceedings of LREC-04, 4th International Conference on Language Resources and Evaluation*, vol. 4, pp. 1115–1118, Lisbon, PT,2004.

[9] A. Esuli and F. Sebastiani, "Determining term subjectivity and term orientation for opinion mining," 2006, pp. 193-200.

[10] R. W. M. Yuen, T. Y. W. Chan, T. B. Y. Lai, O. Y. Kwong, and B. K. Y. T'sou, "Morpheme-based derivation of bipolar semantic orientation of Chinese words," 2004, pp. 1008-1014.

[11] J. Yao, G. Wu, J. Liu, and Y. Zheng, "Using bilingual lexicon to judge sentiment orientation of Chinese words," 2006, pp. 38-43.

[12] D. Li, Y.-tao Ma, and J.-li Guo, "Words semantic orientation classification based on HowNet," *The Journal of China Universities of Posts and Telecommunications*, vol. 16, no. 1, pp. 106-110, 2009.

[13] Z. Han, Q. Mo, M. Zuo, and D. Duan, "Efficiently identifying semantic orientation algorithm for Chinese words," presented at the *International Conference on Computer Application and System Modeling*, 2010, vol. 2, pp. 260-264.

[14] B. Lu, Y. Song, X. Zhang, and B. Tsou, "Learning Chinese polarity lexicons by integration of graph models and morphological features," *Information retrieval technology*, pp. 466-477, 2010.

[15] 刘群 and 李素建, "基于《知网》的词汇语义相似度计算," *第三届汉语词汇语义学研讨会*, 2002.

[16] F. Liu, M. Yang, and D. Lin, "Chinese Web 5-gram Version 1." Linguistic Data Consortium, Philadelphia, 2010.

[17] C. C. Chang and C. J. Lin, *LIBSVM: a library for support vector machines*. 2001.

[18] T. G. Dietterich, "Approximate statistical tests for comparing supervised classification learning algorithms," *Neural computation*, vol. 10, no. 7, pp. 1895-1923, 1998.

[19] S. Bergsma, E. Pitler, and D. Lin, "Creating robust supervised classifiers via web-scale N-gram data," in *Proceedings of the 48th Annual Meeting of the Association for Computational Linguistics*, Uppsala, Sweden, 2010, pp. 865-874.

聲符部件排序與形聲字發音規則探勘

Pronunciation Rules Discovery for Picto-Phonetic Chinese Characters

張嘉惠　Chia-Hui Chang
國立中央大學資訊工程學系
Department of Computer Science and Information Engineering
National Central University
chia@csie.ncu.edu.tw

林書彥　Shu-Yen Lin
國立中央大學資訊工程學系
Department of Computer Science and Information Engineering
National Central University
985202041@cc.ncu.edu.tw

摘要

近年來台灣有相當多的新移民的加入，這些新移民在口語的學習上雖然有地利之變，但是在漢字的認識上則是相當弱勢。由於漢字乃是圖形文字，學習單一字的成本相對的高。如果可以讓漢字教一個字，可以學到十個字，對於漢字教學的成效應有相當的助益。本文從部件教學的概念出發，考慮聲符的發音強度、出現頻率、及筆劃數，做爲聲符部件教學順序的準則。我們利用部件發音強度 [8]，以線性加總、幾合乘積、及調和平均三種方法對部件排序。根據此部件排序學習，前五個部件便可延伸學習多達 140 個相似發音的漢字。進一步，我們應用中研院文獻處理實驗室所建立的「漢字構形資料庫」，以及標記所得之形聲字，拆解形聲字組成的部件，挖掘串連漢字之間關係的形音關聯規則。我們從 600 萬條發音規則中篩選與分群出 8 條高信賴度與兩組各約 10 條高支持度的規則，並藉由這些規則來輔助漢語發音的學習效率。

關鍵詞：形聲字、部件教學、聲符強度、機率分佈、學習曲線、關聯規則

一、簡介

漢字是世界上最古老的文字之一，也是至今仍廣爲使用一種形系文字。近年來由於中國市場的興起，以華語做爲第二外語的學習也連帶地愈來愈受到重視，華語學習者的人數也倍數成長，據 China Daily 2010 的文章指出，目前全世界超過四千萬的非華裔人士正在學習華語文。由此可見未來華語文學習市場的龐大需求；再者，台灣近年來外籍與大陸配偶的人數從 2002 年的二十三萬人成長至今四十四萬人，其中外籍配偶約十四萬六千多人，已取得國籍者約九萬人，在在顯示了漢語學習的重要性。

過去學習漢語只能靠資深的中文老師的教導或是學習者慢慢累積經驗，不僅對於海

外華語師資的培育緩不濟急，對於學習者而言更是一條漫長的路。然而，漢語字形讀音繁複，初學者並不易掌握學習要訣，尤其漢語的發音更是複雜多變。事實上華語作爲第二語言的學習，比起英文作爲第二語言的學習更是難上許多，因爲漢語的字形與音調相較拼音文字複雜，學習者要同時進行形、音、義三者的連結，如果沒有適當的聯想，將需要很大的記憶力，比起傳統的拼音拉丁文字，即使會說華語的海外華人對於漢字的認識也可能相當有限。其最主要的原因在於漢字是圖形文字(pictograph system)，無法像英文等拼音文字(alphabet system)一樣，一旦學會拼音方法(phonetic representation)，即有基本的閱讀能力。相較之下，一般漢字學習者讀寫的學習進展則會比較緩慢，而且必須搭配注音符號(Chinese phonetic symbols)或是其他拼音方法，才可知道每個漢字的發音。這樣的限制，對於漢字的學習相當不利，這也是爲什麼二十世紀初期許多專家欲將漢字拉丁化的主要原因。

漢字的構成包含象形、指事、會意、形聲、轉注、假借(總稱六書[1])。據統計資料，7000 個現代漢語通用字中，屬於「形聲」結構的有 5631 個，約佔總字數的 80.5%，這麼多的形聲字在整字的組合上，多數採用「1+1」的方式，也就是一個意符加上一個聲符。基於這樣一個語言事實，我們可以借助部件教學，充分發揮部件的組合關係強化學習者對於漢字的識記。

本篇論文中，我們應用[8]，以部件發音分佈的集中性計算聲符強度，加以部件延伸字數及筆劃數的考量，提出線性加總、幾合乘積、及調和平均三種結合方法，對部件加以排序。利用此排序做爲漢字部件教學的順序，可以幫助學習者在短時間內提高閱讀效率。我們以累計延伸字個數做爲學習成效的比較，發現有效的排序，可以在學習完前五個部件，便可藉此延伸學習多達 140 個具有高度相似發音的漢字，同時累計筆劃數也是可以接受的範圍，顯示適當排序的重要性。

除了考量聲符部件學習順序之外，我們也試圖分析漢字發音規則，做爲學習發音的參考。爲了要產出易懂的發音規則，讓中文的學習者可以應用形聲字的特性來推測漢字的發音，在本文中我們應用關聯規則探勘挖掘形聲字發音所存在的規則。我們應用中研院文獻處理實驗室所建立的「漢字構形資料庫」，拆解其組成的部件，挖掘串連漢字發音關係的形音關聯規則，來輔助學習者學習，讓漢字不是教一個字才學到一個字，而能搭配關聯規則「一舉數字」，發揮數位學習的優點。我們從 600 萬條發音規則中篩選與分群出 8 條高信賴度與兩組各約 10 條高支持度的規則，並藉由這些規則來輔助漢語發音的學習效率。

二、相關研究

最早有關漢字構造的研究，應屬中央研究院資訊科學研究所文獻處理實驗室，從 1993 年開始，陸續建構古今文字的源流演變、字形結構及異體字表，做爲記錄漢字形體知識的資料庫，也就是漢字構形資料庫[10]。漢字構形資料庫不僅銜接古今文字以反映字形源流演，也記錄了不同歷史時期的文字結構。另外也由於開發漢字部件檢字系統，得以解決缺字問題。然而漢字構形資料庫過去的研究著重在字形知識的整理，尚未涉及字音與字義的處理；因此文獻處理實驗室近年來開始文字學入口網站建置計畫[2,3]。一如其文所述："漢字構形資料庫目前只著重在字形知識的整理，尚未涉及字音與字義；建立一個形、音、義俱備的漢字知識庫，仍是我們長遠的目標"。因此本論文的目的即是以挑戰漢字的發音規則知識庫爲出發，除了了解漢字發音規則外，也希望藉由此項研究找出一套形聲字發音轉換規則，讓華語學習者可以在聲符與規則的輔助下，順利讀出字的發音出來。

與本研究最爲相關的研究計畫是淡江大學中文系高柏園、郭經華、胡映雪教授所主持之"字詞教學模式與學習歷程研究"。其概念是藉由即時回饋的寫字練習（學文 Easy Go!），比較部件拆解做爲漢字教學策略成效（洪文斌 2010），輔以線上教學平台「IWiLL Campus」（郭經華 2010），進行「以字帶詞」之詞彙學習策略（高柏園 2010）。此計畫在美國加州地區 Saratoga High School 針對 26 名修習 AP 中文課程之學生，實施四週約八堂之主題課程，用以評估漢字部件教學之學習策略對於海外華語文學習者之成效。從國科會期中報告顯示，採用多媒體自習一組的學生在認字、書寫、及字的結構上，比傳統標示筆劃順序的習字方法呈現較佳的成果，顯示以部件拆解做爲漢字教學策略的可行性。

張等人於 2010 年提出了兩種自動化判定形聲字聲符的方法[8]。第一種方法爲發音相似度比較法，由於聲符構件通常與原字的發音相似度高於非聲符構件與原字的發音相似度，因此經由語言學專家的協助，分別制訂聲母、韻母之間發音相似度。進一步，爲了提升經由發音相似度比較法判斷聲符之準確率，採用限制性最佳化技術，求得發音相似度分數。另一種爲構件發聲分佈比較法，通常做爲聲符構件的漢字，其衍生字的發聲分佈比非聲符構件的漢字發聲分佈更爲集中。因此作者利用一個可以計算兩個機率分佈差距的公式 KL divergence，來計算每個構件的發聲分佈與所有漢字的發聲分佈 KL 值做爲構件做爲聲符的強度。實驗結果顯示，發音相似度比較法在 7340 個形聲字中的判定聲符準確率爲 93.35%，而構件發聲分佈比較法則可達到 98.66%的準確率，顯示兩種方法做爲聲符判斷問題的可行性。

三、部件重要性排序

首先我們從部件教學的概念出發，希望對於聲符的教學順序，提出一個考慮聲符發音強度、出現頻率、及筆劃數的排序方法，做爲聲符部件教學順序的準則。由於構件發聲分佈比較法對於判定形聲字聲符有高達九成八的準確率，因此我們此處即採用做爲聲符發音強度。根據[8]的定義，每一個部件的聲母發音強度、韻母的發音強度、及調號的發音強度可由下列三式計算而得：

$$I(w) = KL(P_I(W) \parallel P_I(A)) \quad (1)$$

$$F(w) = KL(P_F(W) \parallel P_F(A)) \quad (2)$$

$$T(w) = KL(P_T(W) \parallel P_T(A)) \quad (3)$$

其中A表示所有漢字所成的集合，W則表示部件w所延伸的字所成的集合。函數$P_I(A)$、$P_f(A)$、$P_T(A)$分別表示A集合中漢字的聲母、韻母及調的分佈機率。KL(P||Q)則代表兩個機率分佈的KL-divergence:

$$KL(P \parallel Q) = \sum_i P(i)\log\frac{P(i)}{Q(i)} \quad (4)$$

對於聲符而言，由於發音集中度較高，因此 w 的聲母分佈 $P_I(W)$與所有漢字的聲母分佈 $P_I(A)$會有較大的差異。同理韻母分佈 $P_f(W)$與 $P_f(A)$差異，以及聲調分佈 $P_T(W)$與 $P_T(A)$差異也會較大。因此我們即可以 KL-divergence 公式對此差異值計算出其程度，換句話說我們利用公式 1, 2, 3 分別計算一個部件的聲母、韻母、及調號的 KL 值，這三種數值分別反應出此部件的聲母、韻母、及調號的發音強度。

除了部件的發音強度，在部件學習排序上，我們也必須考慮部件的頻率。因爲對於漢字學習者來說，發音強的部件，也要有一定的出現頻率，才能發揮其做爲聲符的功能。因此若單純以發音強度來決定教學順序，並不是非常適當的選擇。再者，對於學習者來說，漢字的筆畫數多寡也會影響學習的效率。因此如何將三者同時考慮於部件教學的順序，是此處最主要的挑戰。常見的結合方式是以線性加總，然而在此處並非最佳的結合方法，如圖一部件發音強度與頻率散佈圖顯示，若以線性加總發音強度與部件的頻率（部件頻率定義爲包含部件 w 的形聲字字數|W|除以全部字數），可能先找到的是頻率高但發音強度較弱的部件，或是發音強的部件但是頻率較低的部件，而非同時擁有高頻及高發音強度的部件。

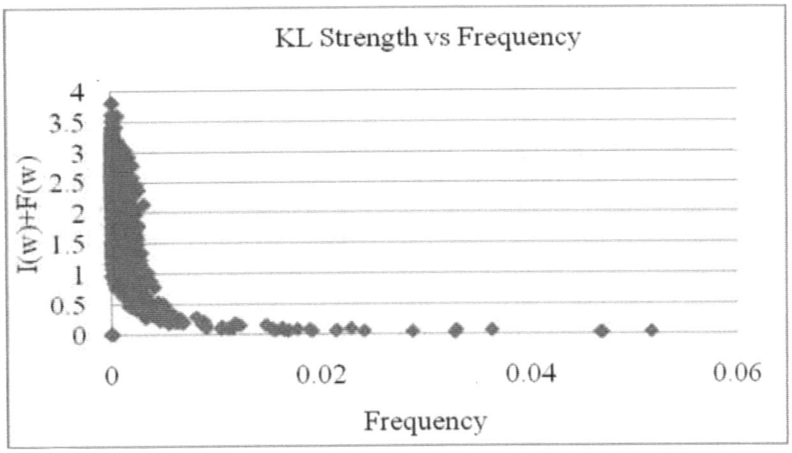

圖一、部件發音強度與頻率散佈圖

爲了找出頻率高且發音強度強的部件，且同時也希望能將筆劃數較少的部件優先排序。我們提出三種排序部件的依據：

1. 線性加總：ScoreA(w)=a*Freq(w)+ I(w)+ F(w) + b*Strokes(w)
2. 幾何乘積：ScoreG(w)= $Freq(w) * (I(w) + F(w)) / \sqrt{Strokes(w)}$
3. 調和平均：ScoreH(w)=ScoreG(w)/ScoreA(w)

其中 Freq(w)代表部件 w 的頻率，Strokes(w)爲部件 w 的筆畫數；a 與 b 則是線性加總的權重。由圖一可知發音強度約爲頻率的 a=90 倍，同理，我們求得筆畫數的權重 b=0.01，可使線性加總的三個因素間取得平衡。第二種結合方法則是三個因素的幾何乘積，最後調和平均則是取線性加總與幾何乘積的調和平均做爲部件排序的評估。

3.1 實驗評估

爲了評估三個部件排序是否能有效率地提昇學習效率，我們繪製出以幾何乘積做爲部件排序，與其累積延伸字數的關係[1]。如圖二所示，橫軸表示排序過的部件，從左而右依序是：分令丁方干包等字，縱軸淺色代表累積延伸字的個數 Y_1，縱軸深色則代表聲符能正確預測聲母個數與韻母個數的總和 Y_2，兩者分別定義如下：

$$Y_1 = \Sigma_i |W_i|\text{，} \qquad (5)$$

$$Y_2 = \Sigma_i\ (\text{Imatch}(w_i,W_i)+\text{Fmatch}(w_i,W_i)) \qquad (6)$$

其中 Imatch(w_i, W_i)代表部件 w_i 延伸字集合 W_i 中與部件 w_i 具有相同聲母的字數，同理，Fmatch(w_i, W_i)代表部件 w_i 延伸字集合 W_i 中與部件 w_i 具有相同韻母的字數。舉例來說若 w=包(ㄅㄠ)，W={炮(ㄆㄠ)、胞(ㄅㄠ)、苞(ㄅㄠ)}，那麼 w 與 W 中相同聲母的字數爲 2 {胞、苞}，相同韻母數爲 3{炮、胞、苞}。因此兩者相加後可得正確預測聲母個數與韻母個數的總和=5。

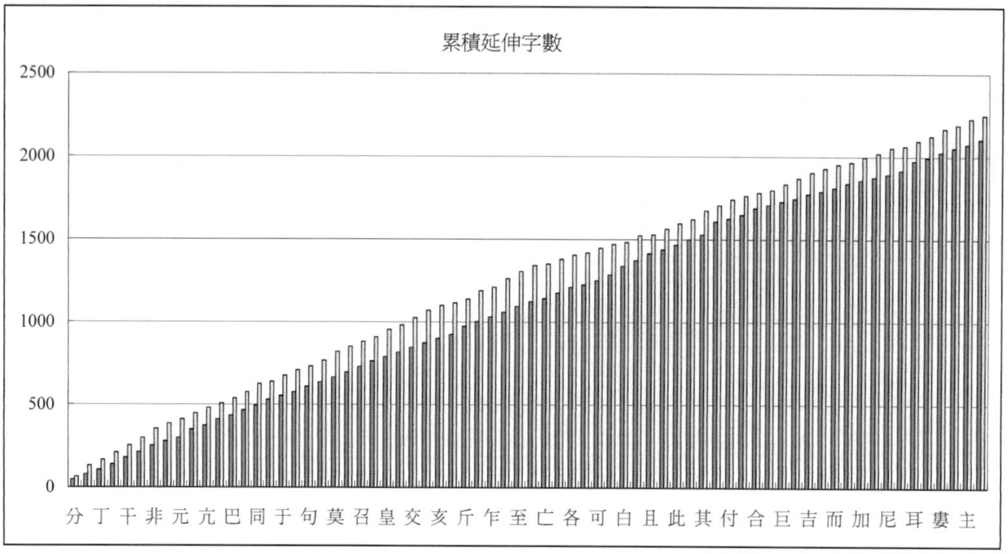

圖二、幾何乘積排序與累積延伸字關係（縱軸取對數以減少高度）

正確預測聲母個數與韻母個數的總和（Y_2）愈接近兩倍累積延伸字的個數（$2Y_1$），表示預測正確的準確率愈高，將上述兩值相除，可得準確發音比例。從圖二可以看出排序在前面的字即有相當多的延伸字，同時準確發音的比例也相當的高。表一列出排序前五個部件及其可延伸學習的形聲字，如表一所示，這些部件都具有延伸字發音高度相似、出現頻率高、筆數少的特性，益於先行學習。

接著我們比較三種排序公序的學習曲線如圖三，同樣地橫軸爲部件排序，縱軸爲正確預測聲母個數與韻母個數的總和。從圖三中可看出幾何乘積排序較線性加總法來的有效，在學到 1000 字以前幾何乘積排序呈現大幅度的成長，也就是說若我們依照乘積排序的部件順序來學習，一開始便能達到快速學習到大量的延伸字。調和平均排序採用幾何乘積與線性加總算數平均法的調和，不過其走勢幾乎與幾何乘積排序相同，這點也顯示出幾何乘積排序明顯優於線性加總。

[1] 所有漢字相關資料來源則是使用中研院所開發的漢字構形資料庫。

最後我們以累積筆畫數的學習曲線來看(圖四)，幾何乘積排序的累積筆畫數學習曲線也較線性加總排序所得來的優異。圖三的收斂點與圖四的筆劃數大增的轉折點也顯示了在學習了 2200 個部件後，累積延伸字數已呈飽和狀態，顯示接續其後的部件已是複合部件，同時筆畫數增加速度較快。也因此可判斷排序大於 2200 後的部件並不是迫切的學習對象。

表一、幾何乘積排序之部件

部件 w_i	延伸字 $\lvert W_i \rvert$	Y_1	Y_2	準確發音比例	筆劃數	累積筆劃數	延伸字
分	45	45	64	0.71	4	4	份坋坌叁吩玢枌棥棼…
令	35	80	132	0.83	5	9	伶冷坽呤囹岭狑昤泠…
丁	27	107	167	0.78	2	11	仃亭圢可叮虰宁寧玎…
方	33	140	211	0.75	4	15	仿坊彷妨枋瓬放昉防…
干	42	182	253	0.70	3	18	刊平幹杆犴旰旱汗扞…
包	32	214	298	0.70	5	23	刨匏咆庖抱胞炮怉砲…
非	38	252	353	0.70	8	31	菲啡扉緋婓腓翡徘排…
屯	26	278	386	0.69	4	35	沌盹囤鈍坉伅炖飩忳…
元	20	298	412	0.69	4	39	刓岏完妧玩杬沅忨芫…
工	51	349	448	0.64	3	42	巨仜功左巧巫差式攻…

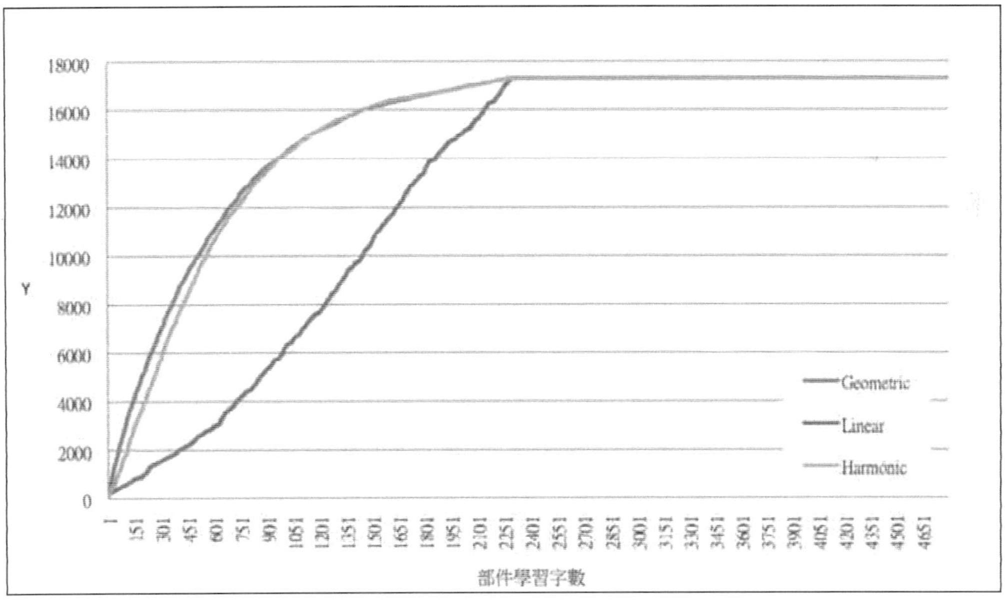

圖三、部件排序學習曲線比較圖

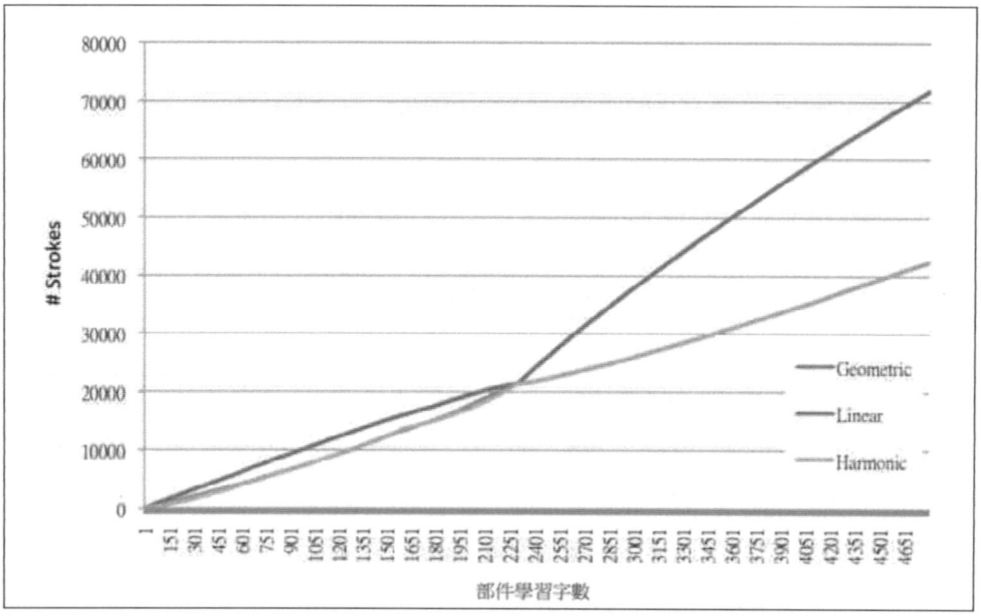

圖四、部件排序與筆畫數學習曲線比較圖

四、發音規則探勘

本文第二個重點在於形聲字發音規則的探勘，藉由已標記的形聲字聲符，找出聲符與延伸的形聲字之間是否有常見的發音規則。爲了要產出易懂的發音規則，讓中文的學習可以應用形聲字的特性來推測漢字的發音，在本文中我們將應用關聯規則探勘 Apriori 演算法做爲探勘形聲字發音規則的方法。每一條關聯規則必須符合最小支持度(support)及最小信賴度(confidence)，對於學習者才算有用。以下我們首先介紹如何準備形聲字成爲關聯規則探勘所需要的交易資料，以及規則的篩選與分群，以及最終所得的發音規則。

4.1　形聲字交易資料

關聯規則探勘原本的目的是從超市購買交易記錄的資料庫中，找出產品之間被購買的關聯程度，其主要依據爲支持度(support)及信賴度(confidence)。其中支持度代表一個規則的涵蓋率（全部交易資料中有多少百分比讓規則爲真），而信賴度則代表一個規則的準確率（前提爲真的情況下，有多少百分比資料讓結果也同時爲真）。爲了推測發音規則，我們以常用字中的 3000 個形聲字準備成 3000 筆交易資料。

形聲字的發音分成三個部份：聲母、韻母、以及調號，分別將其記爲 INITIAL、FINAL、TONE。另將形聲字的聲符(Phonetic component)，以及聲符的發音以 PC_INITIAL、PC_FINAL、PC_TONE 三個屬性標記。其次漢字的部首(Radical component)、形聲字排列方式(單體字、左右連接、上下連接、包圍式、其他)、形聲字筆劃(Stroke)、聲符筆劃(PC_Stroke)、兩者差値(diff_STROKE)等特徵都列爲表達發音規則的探勘項目之一。最後，形聲字的發音若與其聲符的發音相同，則標記成聲母發音不變(IU)、韻母不變(FU)、音調不變(TU)等項目，做爲交易資料的一部份。值得一提的部份是，由於筆劃數及數值性屬性，考慮到記憶的方便性，我們統計了漢字構形資料庫中所有的漢字的筆劃數將其平分爲三類。如此一來，若筆劃數在規則條件及以筆數是否大於或是小於某個範圍表示，降低規則的複雜性。每筆形聲字交易資料所包含的項目屬性如表二所示。

表二、漢字特徵對照表及”炮”的交易範例

符號	意義	數值範圍	範例:炮
INITIAL	聲母	{ ø ,ㄅ,ㄆ,…,ㄙ}	ㄆ
FINAL	韻母	{ø,ㄧ,ㄨ,…,ㄦ}	ㄠ
TONE	調號	{1,2,3,4,5}	4
CONNECT	形聲字的連接方法	{單體字,左右連接,上下連接,包圍式,其他}	左右
PC	聲符	形聲字	包
PC_LOCATION	聲符所在形聲字之位置	{左,右,上,下,內,其他}	右
PC_INITIAL	聲符的聲母	{ ø,ㄅ,ㄆ,…,ㄙ}	ㄅ
PC_FINAL	聲符的韻母	{ ø,ㄧ,ㄨ,…,ㄦ}	ㄠ
PC_TONE	聲符的調號	{1,2,3,4,5}	1
STROKE	形聲字筆劃數 L16 表示>=16 14-15 表示 14 與 15 s11 表<=11	{L16,14-15,s11}	s11
PC_STROKE	聲符筆劃數	{L16 ,14-15,s11 }	s11
Diff_STROKE	形聲字與其聲符筆劃差值	{s3 , 4-5 , L6}	4-5
INITIAL_UNCHANGED(IU)	形聲字與其聲符之聲母不變	{false , true}	IU=false
FINAL_UNCHANGED(FU)	形聲字與其聲符之韻母不變	{false , true}	FU=true
TONE_UNCHANGED(TU)	形聲字與其聲符之聲調不變	{false , true}	TU=false

我們使用 weka[2]來進行形聲字發音規則探勘。針對最小支持度取 0.3%、0.5%與 1%對應各種不同的最小信賴度 60%~100%，進行 Apriori 運算後，得到不同數量的規則數如表三。雖然在最小支持度 1%及最小信賴度 100%時，即可探勘出 50,054 條發音規則，然許多高支持度的規則不符合信賴度，爲避免錯失重要的發音規則，以上各項參數設定中，我們取最多規則數的參數組合(最小支持度 0.3%，最小信賴度 60%情形下)，共 6,625,518 條規則存入資料庫中，做爲進一步的篩選過濾。

表三、關聯規則探勘後規則數

sup \ conf	60%	70%	80%	90%	100%
0.3%	6,625,518	5,144,742	3,879,619	2,809,951	1,810,585
0.5%	1,573,613	1,149,779	802,029	500,708	314,523
1%	304,330	217,346	143,301	87,324	50,054

4.2 規則篩選

每條關聯規則皆是由“左邊條件[左支持度] ➔ 右邊結果[右支持度,信賴度]”組成。雖然關聯規則探勘可以取得爲數不少的發音規則，但其中有許多是不符合我們預期的規則。舉例來說：

PC_LOCATION=右 (sup=2054) ➔ CONNECT =左右 (sup=2054, conf=1)

上述這條規則表示“若聲符位置在右，則形聲字連接方式爲左右連接”。像這樣的規則對發音的推測其實並沒有幫助。又如

INITIAL=ㄅ (sup=20) ➔ PC_ INITIAL=ㄅ (sup=20, conf=1)

表四、篩選後規則數

sup \ conf	60%	70%	80%	90%	100%
0.3%	368,810	272,957	195,735	152,152	106,740
0.5%	61,171	32,089	15,243	7,561	5,190
1%	13,470	6,340	1,889	505	42

上述規則描述“若形聲字聲母發音爲ㄅ，則其聲符聲母發音爲ㄅ”。像這樣的規則也無助於推測發音，原因在於我們的本意是讓學習者在具備基礎聲符的閱讀能力下，利用對聲符的相關認知，來推測出更多尚未認識的形聲字發音。因此合法的規則應該具備: “聲

[2] http://www.cs.waikato.ac.nz/ml/weka/

符條件 或 形聲字筆劃數”➔“形聲字發音 或 形聲字發音與聲符發音的關係”。根據此一篩選原則，我們統計出最小支持度與最小信賴度不同參數下合法的規則數如表四。

4.3 規則分群

雖然在最小支持度 0.3%，最小信賴度 60%情形下，規則篩選已將的規則數減少至 368,810 筆規則，但由於規則中有許多同質性的規則散佈在資料庫中，我們需要有系統地將它們分群。以圖五條件集為例，可以發現 1、2、3 具有相同條件「聲符的聲母=ㄌ」，且這些規則均具有相近的支持度。仔細深入查看符合這些條件的字後發現，支持這些規則的字組也相當程度的重疊（如「老」、「呂」、「里」等聲符的延伸字），所以聲符的聲母條件可以是分群的重要參考因素。

1. 聲符的聲母=ㄌ，聲符的調=2，聲符所在位置=右，形聲字筆劃數=12-15 (sup=17)
2. 聲符的聲母=ㄌ，聲符的筆劃數=L16 ,漢字與其聲符筆劃差值=4-5 (sup=16)
3. 聲符的聲母=ㄌ，聲符的調=3，漢字與其聲符筆劃差值=s3 (sup=16)

圖五、發音規則條件範例

同理聲符的韻母也多涉即相同性質的規則，因此規則中若有指定相同的聲符韻母，也是我們分群的依據之一。緊接著我們繼續觀察其他規則的左方條件：

1. 部首=艸，形聲字的連接方法=上下連接，support=22
2. 部首=女，形聲字的連接方法=左右連接，support=15
3. 部首=艸，形聲字的連接方法=上下連接，support=22
4. 部首=艸，聲符所在位置=下，support=22
5. 部首=金，形聲字筆劃數=L16，support=31
6. 部首=女，形聲字的連接方法=左右連接，support=15
7. 部首=言，聲符所在位置=右，形聲字筆劃數=L16， support=28

我們發現相同部首的規則具有相近的 support 值、因此可分群成{部首=艸|1、3、4}；{部首=女|2、6}分為同群。而形聲字的連接方法在具有相同部首的狀況下通常也會有特定的連接方法如上規則{1、3、4}；{2、6}，因此形聲字的連接方法也在我們的分群條件之內。然而，有時候會出現規則中具有相同聲符與部首等條件同時出現的規則，這時我們便要設定一個判斷分群條件優先權如下：

1. 聲符
2. 聲符聲母
3. 聲符韻母
4. 部首
5. 形聲字的連接方法

根據這些分群優先條件，便可將相同性質規則分為同群。表五為篩選後合法規則數及對應上述分群後的結果。

表五、篩選後合法規則數/分群後規則數

sup \ conf	60%	70%	80%	90%	100%
IU, FU	3454/332	2004/225	1097/139	597/73	264/39
IU	9002/486	5383/383	3067/262	1758/161	809/91
FU	12171/690	8373/608	4855/470	2673/325	1392/189

4.4 結果

最後我們將規則分為兩類，高支持度(Support)與高信賴度(Confidence)。其中**高支持度**的規則可函蓋形聲字較廣泛，且需要的條件較少，但具有較多不符合規則的例外字。舉其中的規則 R1 來說，當一形聲字的聲符發音為ㄌ時，藉由它的結果"聲母發音=不變"可預測這個聲符加上其他部首或是部件時有 9 成(178/197)的比例也會發音ㄌ。像是聲符「盧(ㄌ)」+「艹」=「蘆(ㄌ)」。但由於此類規則所需條件較少，涵蓋範圍大，因此例外字也有約 197*(1-0.1)=20 字，像是聲符發音ㄌ的「立(ㄌ)」+水部=「泣(ㄑ)」。像這樣易於記憶(條件少)且含蓋範圍廣的規則就適合初次使用本系統者。由於高信賴度的規則往往需要搭配較多條件，但可以更準確的推測發音，例外字較少，如下面**高信賴度**規則中 R1 "符的聲母=ㄌ, 聲符的調=3, w 與聲符筆劃數差值=s3" ，可以看出除了上述的聲符發音ㄌ以外，加上另外兩個條件"聲符的調=3 聲符筆劃數差值=s3"便可以達到幾乎百分之百預測的效果。值得一提的是，筆劃數差值 s3(小於等於 3)也透露出聲符加上比劃數很小的部首如口、人、水...等等這樣的部首是不太影響聲符本身的發音，如里+口=哩、呂+人=侶、老+人=佬。觀察這樣的發音規則似乎也能透露出部首本身的特性。因此進階學習者較適合高信賴度的規則類別學習。[3]

高支持度規則 [Query: supp>=3% and conf>=80% and IU (聲母不變)]。共 15 規則，3 群。

1. (R1)聲符的聲母=ㄌ (supp:197) ➔聲母發音=不變 (supp:178, conf:0.9)
2. (R2)聲符的聲母=ㄇ (supp:128) ➔聲母發音=不變 (supp:105, conf:0.82)
3. (R3)w 的筆劃數=L16 , 聲符的筆劃數=L16 (supp:123) ➔聲母發音=不變 (supp:98, conf: 0.8)

高支持度規則 [Query: supp>=3% and conf>=80% and FU (韻母不變)] 。24 規則，8 群。

1. (R1)聲符的聲母=ㄌ (supp:197)➔韻母發音=不變 (supp:158, conf:0.8)

[3] 更多規則查詢請連結本系統 http://hanzi.ncu.edu.tw/picpho/pronrule.php。

2. (R2)聲符的聲母=ㄅ (supp:124)➔韻母發音=不變 (supp:100, conf:0.81)

3. (R3)聲符的聲母=ㄈ, 聲符的筆劃數=<= 11 (supp:121)➔韻母發音=不變 (supp:99, conf:0.82)

4. (R4)聲符的韻母=ㄤ (supp:111)➔韻母發音=不變 (supp:104, conf:0.94)

5. (R5)聲符的韻母=ㄨㄥ (supp:106)➔韻母發音=不變 (supp:90 , conf:0.85)

6. (R6)聲符的韻母=ㄧㄥ (supp:114)➔韻母發音=不變 (supp:93 , conf:0.82)

7. (R7)聲符的調=2, w 的筆劃數=>= 16(supp:221)➔韻母發音=不變 (supp:176 , conf:0.8)

8. (R8) 部首=艸, w 的連接符號=上下連接, 聲符的筆劃數=<= 11 (supp:113)➔韻母發音=不變 (supp:91 , conf:0.81)

高信賴度規則 [Query: conf>=100% and supp>=0.4% an IU (聲母不變) and FU (韻母不變)] 。共 34 規則， 5 群。

1. (R1)聲符的聲母=ㄌ, 聲符的調=3,w 與聲符筆劃數差値=s3 (supp:16)➔聲母發音=不變, 韻母發音=不變 (supp:16, conf:1)

2. (R2)聲符的聲母=ㄌ, 聲符的調=2, 聲符所在位置=右, w 的筆劃數=12-15 (supp:17) ®聲母發音=不變, 韻母發音=不變 (supp:17, conf:1)

3. (R3)聲符的聲母=ㄌ, 聲符的筆劃數=L16, w 與聲符筆劃數差値=4-5 (supp:16)➔聲母發音=不變, 韻母發音=不變 (supp:16, conf:1)

4. (R4)聲符的聲母=ㄒ, 聲符的調=1, w 的筆劃數=12-15, 聲符的筆劃數=s11 (supp:16) ➔聲母發音=不變, 韻母發音=不變 (supp:16, conf:1)

5. (R5)聲符的韻母=ㄤ, 聲符的調=1, w 的連接符號=左右連接, w 的筆劃數=s11 (supp:17)➔聲母發音=不變, 韻母發音=不變(supp:17, conf:1)

6. (R6)聲符的韻母=ㄥ, w 的連接符號=左右連接, 聲符的筆劃數=<= 11, w 與聲符筆劃數差値=>= 6 (supp:13)➔聲母發音=不變, 韻母發音=不變 (supp:13, conf:1)

7. (R7)聲符的韻母=ㄨㄤ, w 的筆劃數=12-15, 聲符的筆劃數=<= 11 (supp:13)➔聲母發音=不變, 韻母發音=不變 (supp:13, conf:1)

8. (R8) 聲符的韻母=ㄧ, 聲符的調=3, 聲符的筆劃數=12-15 (supp:13)➔聲母發音=不變, 韻母發音=不變 (supp:13, conf:1)

五、結論及未來研究

本論結論可分爲二個主要方向說明。第一部份，延續機率分佈比較法，考慮到部件筆劃數少、發音強度高、出現頻率高等三種因素，我們提出三種部件排序方法及兩種評量法，其中幾何平均法在筆劃數與學習字數曲線圖的表現上較爲出色。第二部份，我們藉由形聲字的特徵，運用關聯探勘法則挖掘出許多發音規則。而發音規則經由我們歸納後可分爲，高支持度與高信賴度兩大類。藉由這兩大類的規則能幫助不同程度的初學者更易於推測未知漢字的發音。

然而，仍有許多地方尙待我們改進。目前形聲字規則的演進過程不夠明朗且稍嫌不夠深入，除此之外，還欠缺有效的發音規則排序及評量方法。或者，搭配部件排序，讓重要部件的規則先行教學。另一方面，還可加強形聲字查詢介面的效率以及加入破音字作爲發音規則考據等等。最終目的，希望能充分發揮數位學習的優點，讓漢字的學習更爲生動簡易。

六、致謝

本論文的完成感謝李淑萍、廖湘美及孫致文教授，以及陳怡如、葉博榮、鍾哲宇、趙婕妤等人的幫助。

參考文獻 [References]

[1] 許慎撰，段玉裁注,《說文解字注》, 台北藝文印書館, 1988年。

[2] 莊德明、謝清俊, 漢字構形資料庫的建置與應用, 漢字與全球化國際學術研討會, 台北, 2005年。

[3] 莊德明、鄧賢瑛, 文字學入口網站的規畫, 第四屆中國文字學國際學術研討會, 山東煙台, 2008年。

[4] 董鵬程，台灣華語文教學的過去、現在與未來展望. 2007多元文化與族群和諧國際研討會，台北教育大學。http://r9.ntue.edu.tw/activity/multiculture_conference/ memoirs.html。

[5] 許聞廉、呂明蓁、胡志偉、柯華葳、辜玉旻、呂菁菁、張智凱、莊宗嚴，構建一個新移民者有機成長的多元認同平台的整合研究（期中進度報告），2009- 2011。

[6] 高柏園、郭經華、胡映雪，華語文作爲第二語言之字詞教學模式與學習歷程研究，2009-2010。

[7] 洪文斌，華語文作爲第二語言之字詞教學模式與學習歷程研究－－子計畫一：中文字部件拆解教學模式與電腦輔助學習系統之研發（期中進度報告），2010。

[8] 張嘉惠, 李淑瑩, 林書彥, 黃嘉毅, 陳志銘，《以最佳化及機率分佈判斷漢字聲符之研究》，ROCLING XXI, 2010。

[9] 萬雲英，《兒童學習漢字的心理特徵與教學》，載於楊中芳、高尙仁主編，中國人、中國心－發展與教學篇，403-448。台北：遠流。

[10] 盛繼豔，《華文教學中漢語的部件教學》。

[11] 梁彥民《漢字部件區別特徵與對外漢字教學》，《語言教學與研究》2004。

[12] 李思維、王昌茂編著，《漢字形音學》， 武漢：華中師範大學出版社，2000 年版。

[13] 中研院文獻處理實驗室，「漢字構形資料庫」網站。

Frequency, Collocation, and Statistical Modeling of Lexical Items: A Case Study of Temporal Expressions in an Elderly Speaker Corpus[1]

王聖富　Sheng-Fu Wang
國立臺灣大學語言學研究所
Graduate Institute of Linguistics
National Taiwan University
sftwang0416@gmail.com

楊靜琛　Jing-Chen Yang
國立臺灣大學語言學研究所
Graduate Institute of Linguistics
National Taiwan University
flower75828@gmail.com

張瑜芸　Yu-Yun Chang
國立臺灣大學語言學研究所
Graduate Institute of Linguistics
National Taiwan University
june06029@gmail.com

劉郁文　Yu-Wen Liu
國立臺灣師範大學英語學系
Department of English[2]
National Taiwan Normal University
Yw_L7@hotmail.com

謝舒凱　Shu-Kai Hsieh
國立臺灣大學語言學研究所
Graduate Institute of Linguistics
National Taiwan University
shukaihsieh@ntu.edu.tw

[1] Acknowledgement: Thanks Wang Chun-Chieh, Liu Chun-Jui, Anna Lofstrand, Hsu Chan-Chia, and Liu Yu-Wen for their involvement in the construction of the corpus and the early development of this paper.

[2] Graduated.

Abstract

This study examines how different dimensions of corpus frequency data may affect the outcome of statistical modeling of lexical items. The corpus used in our analysis is an elderly speaker corpus in its early development, and the target words are temporal expressions, which might reveal how the speech produced by the elderly is organized. We conduct divisive hierarchical clustering based on two different dimensions of corpus data, namely raw frequency distribution and collocation-based vectors. Results show when different dimensions of data were used as the input, the target terms were indeed clustered in different ways. Analyses based on frequency distributions and collocational patterns are distinct from each other. Specifically, statistically-based collocational analysis produces more distinct clustering results that differentiate temporal terms more delicately than do the ones based on raw frequency.

Keywords: clustering, collocation, corpus linguistics, temporal expression, gerontology

1. Introduction

The study of gerontology has gained globe wide attention as the aging population becomes a grave issue in our society nowadays. Much research has noted that aging caused not only physiological changes for elderly people, but also effects on their language production [1], cognitive load [2], context processing speed [3], language performance patterns compared to younger individuals [4], etc. To research gerontology from a linguistic viewpoint, Green [5] proposed that the phenomenon of gerontology could be studied through discourse analysis. Therefore, we collect conversations from the elderly as our speech corpus, and take the corpus as input to exemplify the procedures and usage of lexical modeling.

The social roles of elderly people may be embedded in the conversation when they share personal experience or judgment of the past [6] and the present. Thus, we presume that some temporal expressions might pervade as the anchoring points in the conversation-based aging corpus and might help us reveal a certain aspect of the speech behavior pattern the elderly have.

Statistical modeling can serve to describe a given set of data, be it diachronic subsets, register, or lexical units. Statistical models often take the so-called "bottom-up" approach which suits most corpus linguists' empirical state of mind. Moreover, nice and neat visualization is often a feat in such modeling techniques, to an extent that some of the models are called "graph models" [7]. When the proper behavior of lexical units and the structure of the lexicon are applied, statistical modeling may help us develop NLP-oriented lexicographic modules in forms of dictionaries, thesauruses, and ontologies [8].

A glimpse on relevant studies would reveal that the most prominent kind of data input is related to the distributional patterns of the lexical items in corpora, no matter whether the lexical items themselves are the target of the modeling or not. The distributional data could be in the form of words' frequencies and variability of frequencies [9] or the distribution of n-grams as a whole [10]. Distributional pattern or dependency with syntactic patterns is also a prominent source of data input [11]-[14]. Target lexical items' dependency and co-occurrence with particular word types may also be taken as the basis of lexical modeling in some studies [15]. Moreover, statistically-based collocational patterns are used for modeling similarities among lexical units of interest [16], [17].

The abovementioned different methods, or rather, different data inputs, are considered falling somewhere between raw distributional data and relational data, or between lexical items and syntactic patterns. In our study, we aim to compare the two endpoints of this methodological continuum, namely the "frequency distributional data" input and "collocation data", in order to see how these different types of input may result in different data in lexical modeling. With preliminary research like ours, we hope to make contributions to the path to full understandings of universal linguistic and cognitive patterns in the elderly's speech act.

This paper is organized as follows: Section 2 introduces the construction of the elderly speaker corpus, including data collection, guidelines for transcription, and annotation standards. Section 3 reports basic corpus information and preliminary analysis of six selected temporal expressions from the corpus. Section 4 demonstrates the methods and results of statistical modeling of temporal expressions, as well as a meta-analysis on different models. Section 5 is the summary, including some implications of our findings.

2. Corpus construction

2.1 Data collection

Speech data were collected from four pairs of elderly people. Each pair consisted of one male and one female speaker. All subjects are native speakers of Mandarin and Taiwanese Southern Min. One pair is from Changhua while the others are from Taipei. The mean age of the subjects is 65.75 years old (SD = 6.16). Each pair of speakers was asked to do a face-to-face conversation in Mandarin with each other for 30 to 40 minutes. The designated conversational topic was the speakers' life experience in the past and the present. During the recording, other participants, such as the subject's relatives or the observer, might also be involved in the talk. All files were recorded by a digit recorder in the format of WAV. The total length of the speech samples is 145 minutes.

2.2 Transcription

Speech samples collected from the elderly's conversations were then transcribed into Chinese characters, following Du Bois' transcription standards for discourse analysis [18]. Because prosodic features and vocal qualities of the intonation units (IUs) were not the main interest in this study, the aforementioned information was excluded from the transcription. A short guideline of transcription standards is provided below.

Conversation samples were manually processed into several IUs. Each IU was labeled with a number on the left, as shown in example (1).

(1)

```
34  SM: a   你   看   這   個   做工      的
        P.  you  see  this CL.  do.work   DE
35      ...(1.3) 那   個   有--
                 that CL.  have
36        有夠           重
      have.enough      heavy
```

Sometimes speech overlap happened during the conversation. These speech overlaps were indicated by square brackets, as shown in example (2). In order to indicate on the transcription when and where utterances overlap, the left brackets of the overlapping speakers' speech are aligned vertically. Double square brackets were used for more overlaps occurring in a rapid succession within a short stretch of speech, with their left brackets displaying temporal alignment.

(2)

```
70  SF: ...都  [送    人家]
          all  give  others
71  SM:        [送    人家]   [[撫養     la]]
               give  others  to raise  P.
72  SF:                      [[撫養]]
                              to raise
```

As bilinguals, the subjects might shift from Mandarin, which dominated the conversation, to another language. Such utterance of code-switching was enclosed in square brackets and labeled with *L2* as well as the code for the non-Mandarin language. Example (3) demonstrates the transcription for code-switching, where the language code TSM represents Taiwanese Southern Min.

(3)

```
268  SF: [L2 TSM  單輪車  TSM L2]
               single wheeler
```

Laughter was also marked in the transcription. Each syllable of laughter was labeled with one token of the symbol @ (see example 4a). Longer laughter was indicated by a single symbol @ with the duration in the parentheses (see example 4b). Two @ symbols were placed at each end of an IU to show that the subject spoke while laughing (see example 4c).

(4)

a. 163 F1: @@@@@

b. 200 SM: @(3.3)

c. 828 O: @沒 那麼 嚴重 la@

not that serious P.

The occurrence and duration of a pause in discourse was transcribed. Pauses are represented by dots: two dots for short pauses that are less than 0.3 seconds, three dots for medium pauses between 0.3 and 0.6 seconds, and three dots for pauses longer than 0.7 seconds with its duration specified in parentheses. Example (5) below is the instance for pauses.

(5)

40 SF: ..以前 o..是--

before P. is

41 SF: ...eh ..都 是..父母...(0.9)做 X

P. all is parents do X

Particles were transcribed in phonetic transcription to avoid disagreement on the employment of homophonic Mandarin characters, as what example (6) shows. Phonetic transcriptions for the particles included *la, hoNh, a, o, le, haNh, hioh,* and *ma.*

(6)

26 SM: hoNh.. a 我們 二十 幾 歲 結婚

P. P. we twenty more age get.married

The recorded utterances were not always audible or clear enough for the transcribers to identify what was being said. Each syllable of uncertain hearing was labeled with a capital X, as shown in example (5) above. Last but not least, truncated words or IUs were represented by double hyphens --, as shown in previous example (1) and (5).

2.3 Annotation

After all recorded samples were transcribed, the transcription would be automatically segmented and tagged with POS (part of speech) through the CKIP Chinese Word

Segmentation System provided by the Chinese Knowledge Information Processing (CKIP) group at the Academia Sinica [19]. The segmentation and POS standards were based on the Sinica Corpus guidelines [20]. The annotated language samples were then manually checked. The procedure is described below.

Firstly, every segmentation result derived from CKIP was examined, and corrected if wrong, as in the following examples. Example 7*a* is the original IU before segementation and tagging. Through CKIP, we get the result in example 7b, which is falsely processed. Example 7c shows the right segmentation after manual correction.

(7)

a. 我爸爸是他媽媽的哥哥
"My father is his mother's brother."

b. *我	爸爸	是	他媽	媽的	哥哥
I	father	is	he.mom	mom.DE	brother

c. 我	爸爸	是	他	媽媽	的	哥哥
I	father	is	he	mom	DE	brother

Secondly, POS tags were viewed as correct only if the main word classes were correct, while the details of their sub-classes were not of primary concern. For instance, in example (8), the main word class of each POS tag (in this case, *N*, *DE*, *V*, or *D*) is examined, but not the sub-class tagging, as we give less consideration for whether the POS tags should be N*a* or N*h*.

(8)

他(**N**h)	的(**DE**)	腦筋(**N**a)	動(**V**AC)	得(**DE**)	比較(**D**fa)	快(**V**H)
he	DE	brains	act	DE	more	fast

"He gets new ideas faster."

Thirdly, particles were identified as FW (for foreign word) in the CKIP system. These tags were manually corrected to *I* for IU-initial particles[3], and *T* for IU-final particles. If an IU contained nothing but particles, then the particles were tagged as *I*.

Lastly, POS tags were removed for truncations (e.g. 這--), uncertain hearing (i.e. X) and code-switching. Given that truncations were not generally viewed as lexical items, they were not suitable to be analyzed at lexical level. Considering this study targeted the elderly's Mandarin speech performance, code-switching phenomena were of less value for our analysis. Therefore, those tags were removed in these cases.

[3] According to the standards provided by Sinica Corpus, *I* represents "interjections" which usually occur in the IU-initial position.

3. Corpus information & Preliminary analysis

This corpus contains 4,982 IUs of Mandarin utterances and 22,090 word tokens produced by all speakers. Elderly people's production in Mandarin contains 3,739 IUs (male: 2,267 IUs; female: 1,472 IUs), and there are 18,076 word tokens in total (male: 11,383 word tokens; female: 6,693 word tokens).

The corpus processing tool used here is R [21], which allows us to perform tasks including preprocessing, word frequency, KWIC (KeyWord In Context) extraction, and statistical modeling .

We assume that time-related words may hold some vital clues to the elderly's speech pattern, so the following analyses will focus on the subjects' use of temporal expressions. By looking at word frequency, we first find that except for function words and pronouns, temporal expressions such as 現在 (now) and 以前 (before) are of high frequencies. This result is possibly influenced by the theme of the conversation assigned to the subjects. The term 現在 (now) expresses the speakers' concept of "the present," while 以前 (before) reveals their idea of "the past." We are interested in how elderly people use these two terms and other temporal expressions (tagged as Nd) to frame the present- and the past-related concept.

Six temporal expressions are selected for the analysis. Terms for the present-related concept are 現在 (now) and 最近 (recently); those for the past-related concept are 以前 (before), 小時候 (in one's childhood), 民國 (R.O.C. year), and 當初 (back then). Examining their frequency, we see that 現在 (now) and 以前 (before) appear most frequently, whereas other terms are seldom used by elderly speakers in this corpus. Table 1 lists the frequency of the six target temporal expressions.

Table 1. The frequency of six temporal expressions from elderly speakers in the corpus.

Term	Frequency	Ranking
現在(now)	169	1
以前(before)	169	2
小時候(in one's childhood)	12	3
民國(R.O.C. year)	11	4
當初(back then)	9	5
最近(recently)	6	6

4. Statistical modeling of temporal expressions

In this section, we will present quantitative analyses with the help of hierarchical clustering, a data-driven approach, to see how the temporal terms of interest are grouped together with the frequency data extracted from our corpus.

The clustering method employed here is divisive hierarchical clustering. It differs from agglomerative hierarchical clustering in that a group of entities is first divided into large groups and then smaller groups are classified. Such a method is useful for finding a few clusters large in size [22]. We would like to find out whether the terms for "the present" and "the past" can really be grouped into clusters different in temporality. Thus, divisive hierarchical clustering serves our need.

We execute a series of hierarchical clustering with different data input. The first analysis is run with the frequencies of the temporal terms across different files/texts in our corpus. Such an input is expected to capture the co-occurrence pattern of these temporal terms affected by individual speaker's style or idiolect, as well as by differences in the conversation topic. The output is presented in Figure 1, where 現在 (now) is separate from 以前 (before) under a major cluster on the left. Also, 最近 (recently) stands independently from any other expressions, suggesting that temporal terms within a particular time domain are more likely to occur in the same text, which is really a conversational event in our corpus.

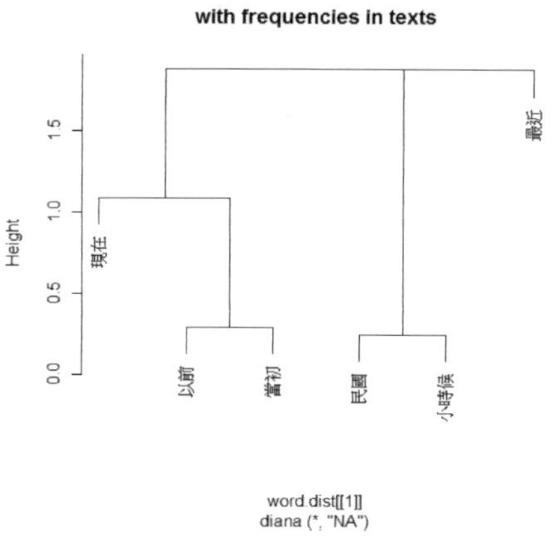

Figure 1. Clustering based on frequencies in texts

Next, four clustering analyses are made based on the frequency data across subsets of different sizes. The sizes chosen for producing subsets are 10, 50, 200, and 500 words respectively. Smaller subsets may reflect linguistic patterns in a few clauses, and larger subsets may reflect patterns in a larger unit, such as major or minor topics in the flow of conversation. The results are shown in Figure 2. As we can see in the four graphs below, 現在 (now) and 以前 (before) are classified in the same small cluster. It is worth noting that 最近 (recently) is clustered independently with a subset size up to 200, which shows only when the subset is big enough can we see it grouped with terms related to the past.

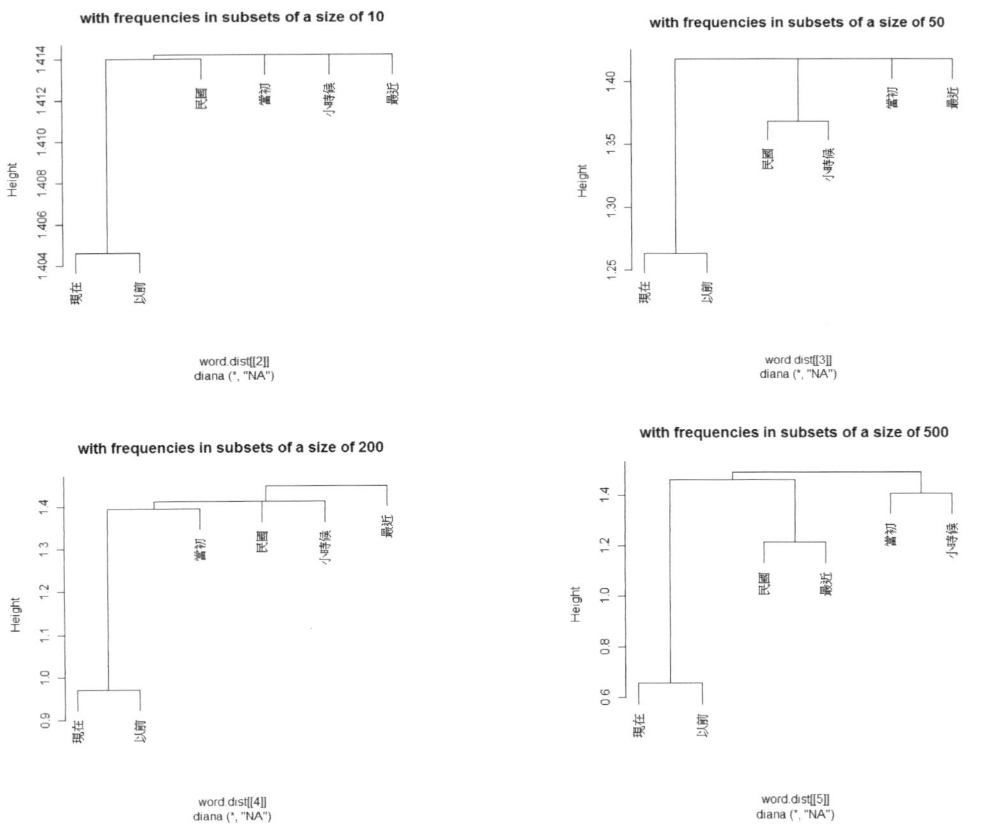

Figure 2. Clustering based on frequencies across subsets. Upper left, with subsets of a size of 10 words. Upper right, of 50 words. Lower left, of 200 words. Lower right, of 500 words.

The analyses above are obtained provided with the temporal terms' frequencies of occurrence in different parts of the corpus. In addition to this method, we can also do clustering analysis according to how these terms collocate with other words in the corpus, on the premise that collocational patterns should reveal some characteristics of lexical items. Thus, two more analyses are given based on this assumption. The first analysis is done by using each word type's collocational pattern (span = 3) with the six temporal terms as input. The second analysis is achieved through the dependency patterns of sentential particles (i.e. lah, hoNh, ah, oh, le, haNh, hioh, mah, as described by [23]), taking the temporal terms as its input. There are two reasons for the inclusion of particle collocation. Firstly, in regard to methodology, running more than one collocational test allows one to see whether collocational analyses with different approaches generate similar results. Secondly, sentential particles' dependency patterns might help us understand how the "referent" of each temporal expression is conceived and presented in discourse. The outcome is illustrated in Figure 3. Again, 現在 (now) and 以前 (before) are clustered closely, showing that their collocational patterns may be similar, regardless of the actual word types of their collocates. Noteworthily, 民國 (R.O.C. year) and 最近 (recently) are clustered together from other terms.

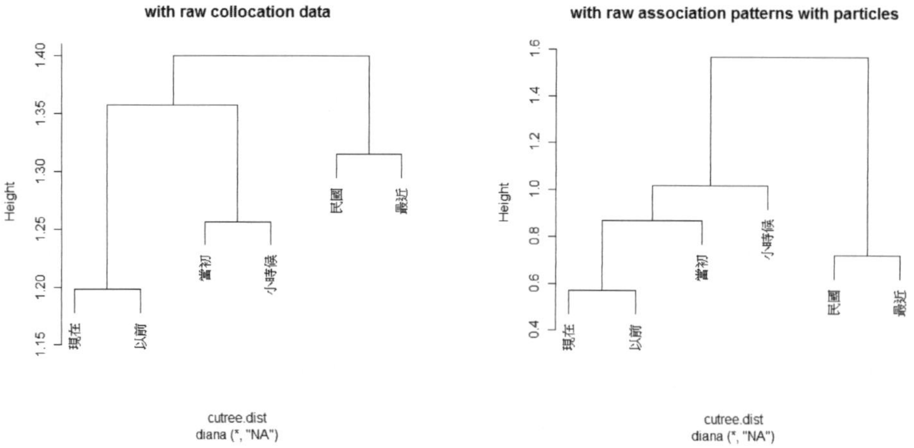

Figure 3. Clustering based on association/collocation frequencies. Left, with all word types in the corpus. Right, with particles.

Potentially, there is a problem using raw frequencies in studying collocates. Collocates with high frequencies might simply be high frequency words rather than being "exclusively close" to the terms of interest. Thus, we bring forth collexeme analysis [24], [25], a statistical method developed for finding "true collocates", that is, collocates with strong collocational strength (coll.strength hereafter). The coll.strength of each word type and particle is calculated and used as input for clustering analysis. The output is shown in Figure 4.

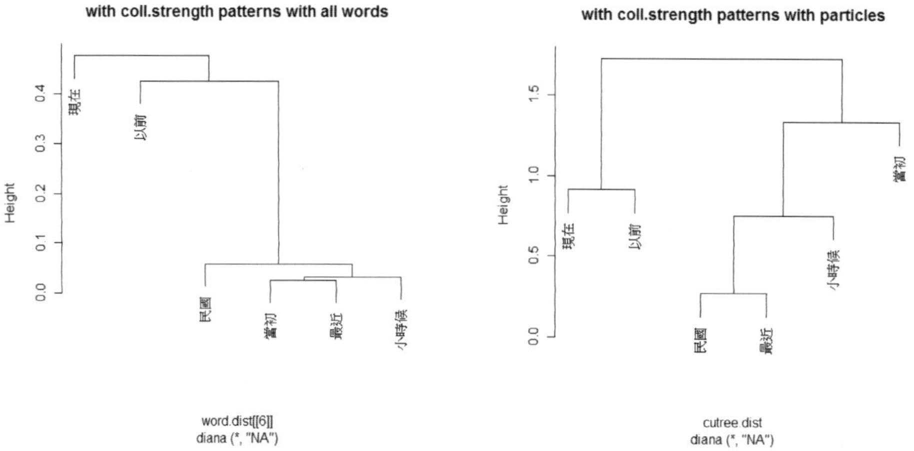

Figure 4. Clustering based on coll.strength patterns. Left, with all word types in the corpus. Right, with particles.

The next question is: How do we evaluate all these different results? The answer may not be surprising: We can do it with clustering analysis. The "clustering" package for R offers a function "cutree" for a simple quantification of different clustering: Each 'tree' is quantified in terms of which cluster an item is clustered to. We collect the data for all the trees shown above and execute clustering as meta-analysis. The outcome is shown in Figure 5.

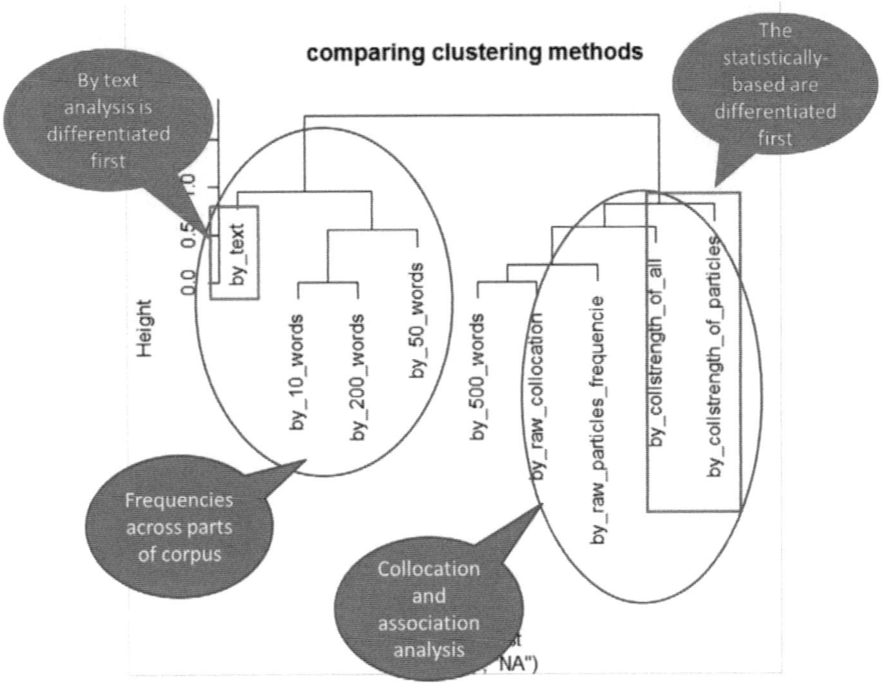

Figure 5. Clustering of various results with different types of input data

An interesting pattern shows up. There are two major clusters. The left one is based on frequency patterns of temporal terms, and the right one basically contains analyses regarding how these terms collocate or associate with other words or particles. Despite the curious occurrence of the "by-500-words" analysis in the right major cluster, the result of this meta-analysis seems to be able to characterize the major differences in terms of data input. More specifically, in the left major cluster, the "by-text" analysis is the first one being singled out. This conforms to our impression that temporal terms are clustered differently, with 現在 (now) and 最近 (recently) placed relatively away from other past-related expressions. Moreover, in the right major cluster, the analyses with coll.strength are the first ones being differentiated from the others. Again, it reflects that statistically based analyses produce different patterns from the ones based on simple frequency values. What can be inferred from the patterns in Figure 5 is that, first, different types of data input certainly influence the outcome of clustering analysis, and second, the results of quantitative analysis can also be evaluated through quantitative analysis, just as how we use hierarchical clustering to analyze and evaluate results of hierarchical clustering.

To sum up, 現在 (now) and 以前 (before) seem to intertwine concerning their occurrences in different subsets of the corpus. This may suggest that when elderly speakers talk about the past, the present follows as a contrast in time regarding the same subject matter, and vice versa. Only the by-text analysis shows a difference between the terms for the present and that for the past, suggesting that some elderly might tend to converse about the present more than the past, or vice versa. Collocational strength analysis is another approach revealing a difference between 現在 (now) and 以前 (before), showing that although usually used closely, the two terms still attract different words with different strengths. It should be noted that association patterns with particles invested in the qualitative analysis do not distinguish between the present and the past. A possible explanation for this is that such a difference in pragmatic and discourse meaning is too fine-grained to be shown with information based on quantitative data. In other words, it shows that quantitative method with corpus data has its limitation, especially when the annotation only functions at the basic POS level. Such findings of the temporal terms may in turn suggest that modeling lexical items is not a simple matter of finding any types of analyzable data input. In addition to surface frequencies, taking collocational patterns into account, especially those based on statistical analyses, seems to be a requirement to capture the nuance among lexical items.

5. Conclusion

Statistical modeling based on different types of data input does display different patterns, with modeling derived from frequencies and collocational patterns forming two major clusters as revealed in the meta-analysis, which visualizes the difference between models based on quantitative data. In the "frequency" cluster, analysis based on distributional patterns is differentiated from the ones based on arbitrarily divided subsets. In the "collocation" cluster, statistically oriented (i.e. collocation strength) analyses are distinguished from those based on surface collocational frequencies. For our present study, these findings are not overwhelmingly surprising, because it is not hard to imagine the impact of the difference in texts and subsets on research, as well as surface frequencies and statistically-calculated relational patterns. Yet, when it comes to evaluating more types of modeling methods or inputs, meta-analysis of this kind provides a valuable means of choosing adequate methods. For instance, when researchers try to model different aspects of the lexical structure, hierarchical modeling proposed here may help avoiding utilizing methods that are in fact very similar.

According to our analysis on temporal terms, the findings suggest that the core expressions of the present and the past have very similar distributional patterns, showing that elderly speakers in the corpus tend to compare the present with the past in the same textual domains. The difference between these terms is disclosed only in models based on by-text frequency and statistical collocational analysis. The former shows that different speakers or conversation events may have their own preferred usage of temporal expressions. The latter indicates that these terms are still different in terms of their collocations, yet the difference can only be revealed through statistical tests on "true collocates" proposed in [24]. These findings can be seen as a pilot result on the linguistic pattern of aging people.

6. Future work

Our prime purpose of this study is to attempt to highlight certain methodologies applicable to an elderly speaker corpus through several statistical approaches, rather than recklessly leaping to a conclusion that some universal elderly speech patterns are found in our corpus. To further explore the issue and confirm the validity of potential general linguistic patterns discovered in the current research, we must carefully conduct qualitative analyses of each temporal expression and interpret the results with the evidence from the quantitative methods we adopted previously. At the present time, the elderly speaker corpus does not yet reach a big scale, and its expansion is desirable as the outcome of our statistical modeling could be altered if the corpus size increases, which might give us other insight into our study. Furthermore, we can work on the comparisons of younger speakers' speech and that of the elderly's, and combine what we find with theories and research in other fields of study, such as sociology and cognitive science, hoping to discover the relationship between language and aging in Taiwanese society.

7. References

[1] D. M. Bruke and M. A. Shafto, "Aging and language production," *Current Directions in Psychological Science,* vol. 13, pp. 21-24, 2004.

[2] K. R. Wilson, "The effects of cognitive load on gait in older adults," Ph. D., Department of Communication Disorders, Florida State University, 2008.

[3] B. Rush, *et al.*, "Accounting for cognitive aging: context processing, inhibition or processing speed?," *Aging, Neuropsychology and Cognition,* vol. 13, pp. 588-610, 2006.

[4] M. Veliz, *et al.*, "Cognitive Aging and Language Processing: Relevant Issues," in *Revista de Lingüística Teórica y Aplicada*, 2010, pp. 75-103.

[5] B. S. Green, *Gerontolgy And The Social Construction of Old Age*. New York: Aldine De Gruyter, 1993.

[6] S.-H. Kuo, "Discourse and Aging: A Sociolinguistic Analysis of Elderly Speech in Taiwan," National Tsing Hua University, 2008.

[7] D. Widdows and B. Dorow, "A Graph Model for Unsupervised Lexical Acquisition," in *Proceedings of the 19th International Conference on Computational Linguistics*, 2002, pp. 1093-1099.

[8] O. Mitrofanova, *et al.*, "Automatic word clustering in Russian texts," in *Proceedings of the 10th international conference on Text, speech and dialogue*, 2007, pp. 85-91.

[9] S. T. Gries and M. Hilpert, "Variability-based Neighbor Clustering: A bottom-up approach to periodization in historical linguistics," To appear.

[10] S. T. Gries, *et al.*, "N-grams and the clustering of registers," *Empirical Language Research Journal,* vol. 5, 2011.

[11] P. Cimiano, *et al.*, "Comparing Conceptual, Divisive and Agglomerative Clustering for Learning Taxonomies from Text," in *Proceedings of the European Conference of Artificial Intelligence*, 2004, pp. 435-439.

[12] P. Cimiano, *et al.*, "Clustering concept hierarchies from text," in *Proceedings of LREC 2004*, 2004, pp. 1-4.

[13] D. Lin, "Automatic retrieval and clustering of similar words," in *Proceedings of the 17th international conference on Computational linguistics*, 1998, pp. 768-774.

[14] F. Pereira and N. Tishby, "Distributional Similarity, Phase Transitions and Hierarchical Clustering," Association for the Advancement of Artificial Intelligence1992.

[15] M. Redington, *et al.*, "Distributional Information and the Acquisition of Linguistic Categories: A Statistical Approach," in *Proceedings of the Fifteenth Annual Conference of the Cognitive Science Society*, 1993, pp. 848-853.

[16] C.-H. Chen, "Corpus, Lexicon, and Construction: A Quantitative Corpus Approach to Mandarin Possessive Construction," *International Journal of Computational Linguigstics and Chinese Language Processing,* vol. 14, pp. 305-340, 2009.

[17] S. T. Gries and A. Stefanowitsch, "Cluster analysis and the identification of collexeme classes," in *Empirical and Experimental Methods in Cognitive/Functional Research*, S. Rice and J. Newman, Eds., ed Stanford, CA: CSLI, To appear.

[18] J. Du Bois, *et al.*, *Outline of discourse transcription*. Hillsdale, NJ: Lawrence Erlbau, 1993.

[19] CKIP. (2004). *CKIP Chinese Word Segmentation System*. Available: Retrieved June 2, 2011, from http://ckipsvr.iis.sinica.edu.tw/

[20] CKIP, "Introduction to Sinica Corpus: A tagged balance corpus for Mandarin Chinese," Academia Sinica, Taipei, 1998.

[21] R. D. C. Team. (2010). *R: A language and environment for statistical computing*. Available: http://www.R-project.org

[22] R. H. Baayen, *Analyzing Linguistic Data. A Practical Introduction to Statistics Using R*: Cambridge University Press, 2008.

[23] C. I. Li, *Utterance-Final Particles in Taiwanese: A Discourse-Pragmatic Analysis*. Taipei: The Crane Publishing Company, 1999.

[24] S. T. Gries, *et al.*, "Converging evidence: bringing together experimental and corpus data on the association of verbs and constructions," *Cognitive Linguistics,* vol. 16, pp. 635-676, 2005.

[25] S. T. Gries. (2007). *Collostructional analysis: Computing the degree of association between words and words/constructions*. Available: http://www.linguistics.ucsb.edu/faculty/stgries/teaching/groningen/coll.analysis.r

機率式調變頻譜分解於強健性語音辨識

Probabilistic Modulation Spectrum Factorization for Robust Speech Recognition

朱紋儀 高予真 陳柏琳
國立臺灣師範大學資訊工程學系
Department of Computer Science and Information Engineering
National Taiwan Normal University
{698470075, 699470424, berlin}@ntnu.edu.tw

洪志偉
國立暨南國際大學電機工程學系
Department of Electrical Engineering
National Chi Nan University
jwhung@ncnu.edu.tw

摘要

在自動語音辨識技術的發展上，語音強健性一直都是一門重要的研究議題。在眾多的強健性技術中，針對語音特徵參數進行強化與補償為其中之一大主要派別。其中，近年來已有為數不少的新方法，藉由更新語音特徵時間序列及其調變頻譜來提升語音特徵的強健性。本論文即是從語音特徵時間序列的調變頻譜域著手，採用機率式潛藏語意分析之概念，對調變頻譜施以機率式分解並進行成分分析、進而擷取出較重要的成分以求得更具強健性的語音特徵。本方法之所有實驗皆於國際通用的 Aurora-2 連續數字資料庫進行，相較於使用梅爾倒頻譜特徵之基礎實驗，本方法能達到 62.84%的相對錯誤降低率。此外，我們也嘗試將所提方法跟一些知名的特徵強健技術做結合；實驗顯示，相對於單一方法而言，此結合法可進一步提升辨識精確率，代表所提之新方法與許多特徵強健技術有良好的加成性。

關鍵詞： 雜訊強健性、語音特徵參數強化、調變頻譜、機率式潛藏語意分析

一、緒論

大部份的自動語音辨識(automatic speech recognition, ASR)系統，在不受雜訊干擾的理想實驗室發展環境下，皆可獲得良好的辨識效果；但若應用至真實的日常環境中，卻往往因為環境中諸多複雜因素的影響，造成系統之訓練環境與測試環境存在不匹配(mismatch)的問題，使得此系統之辨識精確率大幅度降低。而以上所述造成環境不匹配問題的種種因素包含了：語者發音結構差異、語者腔調變異、加成性背景雜訊、摺積性通道雜訊及其他語者發音的干擾等。所謂的語音辨識之強健性技術，即是致力於降低上述因素所帶來之影響，進而使語音辨識系統在不匹配問題存在的環境下，仍能保有一定的辨識能力。

目前而言，針對雜訊干擾的各種語音強健技術大致可分為三種類型：第一種類型為以聲學模型為基礎之強健性技術(model-based techniques)，其概念為以不變動語音特徵為原則，主要作用於聲學模型空間，期望藉由調整聲學模型之參數而能更正確地代表含環境雜訊之語音特徵；第二種類型為以語音特徵為基礎之強健性技術(feature-based techniques)，它主要作用於語音特徵空間，期望雜訊語音與其原始乾淨語音在此特徵表

示(speech feature representation)域上能趨於一致，藉此降低環境雜訊在語音特徵上所造成的不匹配效應；最後第三個類型為綜合式強健性技術(joint technique)，它同時考慮到上述兩種類型的技術，以達到結合特徵空間與模型空間之資訊為目的。

以語音特徵為基礎之強健性技術的其中之一個研究方向，是對於語音特徵參數之統計特性加以正規化；此方向涵蓋了著名的倒頻譜平均值減去法(cepstral mean subtraction, CMS)[1]、倒頻譜平均數與變異數正規化法(cepstral mean and variance normalization, MVN)[2]與統計圖等化法(histogram equalization, HEQ)[3]等，這些方法皆是直接將時間序列域(temporal domain)上的語音特徵視作為隨機變數(random variable)的樣本(samples)，利用這些樣本估測隨機變數的各樣統計值(statistics)，進而對語音特徵時間序列做線性或非線性的轉換，使其在部分或全部統計特性上能達到正規化的目標。

值得注意的是，環境中的干擾因素不僅會改變語音特徵之統計特性，同時也會引發語音特徵之時空結構(temporal structure)扭曲；而特徵參數時間序列之調變頻譜(modulation spectrum)為一有效描繪時空結構之媒介，相對於上述之語音特徵正規化法的觀念而言，可能具有更廣泛的分析面向，因其同時考慮到了語音特徵隨時間變化的性質(即各調變頻率之成分)。特別一提的是，過去的研究[4]顯示，不同調變頻率成分對語音辨識有著不同的重要性，位於 1 Hz 至 16 Hz 之調變頻率成分包藏了最有用的語意資訊，其中又以 4 Hz 附近的頻率成分特別突出。因此，近年來已有為數不少的學者致力於正規化特徵參數之時空結構，藉此直接或間接地強化語音特徵之調變頻譜，藉此提升語音特徵的雜訊強健性；相關的技術包括了調變頻譜統計圖等化法(spectral histogram equalization, SHE)[5]、分頻式調變頻譜統計正規化法(sub-band modulation spectrum compensation)[6]與一系列資料導向(data-driven)之時間序列濾波器法[7-10]等。

綜觀上述之技術，絕大多皆是藉由正規化時間序列或調變頻譜之統計特性，以降低語句間不匹配的程度，進而提昇語音辨識系統之強健性。本論文嘗試更進一步、以一個嶄新的觀點切入，利用機率式潛藏語意分析(probabilistic latent semantic analysis, PLSA)[11]賦予調變頻譜機率的意義，其透過一組潛藏的主題機率分布，描述調變頻率與調變頻譜強度成分之間的關係。因此，此利用機率式潛藏語意分析來觀察語音特徵的時空結構，可視為一種對於調變頻譜施以機率式分解並同時進行成分分析的方法。實作上，我們藉由機率式潛藏語意分析，從乾淨訓練語音特徵中萃取出一組潛藏的主題機率分布，以利而後任一句乾淨或雜訊語句更新其強度調變頻譜時使用，進而達到強化語音特徵之調變頻譜之目的。

在一系列的語音辨識實驗上，我們發現上述的新方法可以顯著地提升原始語音特徵在雜訊環境下的精確率，其效能等同甚至超越現行許多強健性技術，足見此新方法不僅在理論上具有嶄新的意義、在應用上也有其實際顯著的價值。

二、正規化時間序列結構特性之方法

（一）語音特徵之調變頻譜受雜訊干擾之影響情形

對於一語音特徵時間序列 $\{x[n]\}$ 而言，其調變頻譜定義如下：

$$X[k] = DFT(x[n]), \tag{1}$$

其中，n 與 k 依序為音框索引與調變頻率索引，DFT 為離散傅立葉轉換(discrete Fourier transform)。式(1)之頻譜序列可視為一種對於原始語音訊號作降低取樣(down-sampled)後的調變訊號(由訊號取樣頻率轉至音框取樣率)，此序列即為所屬語音特徵時間序列之調變頻譜(modulation spectrum)。由式(1)可知，調變頻譜 $X[k]$ 之最高頻率與特徵序列 $x[n]$

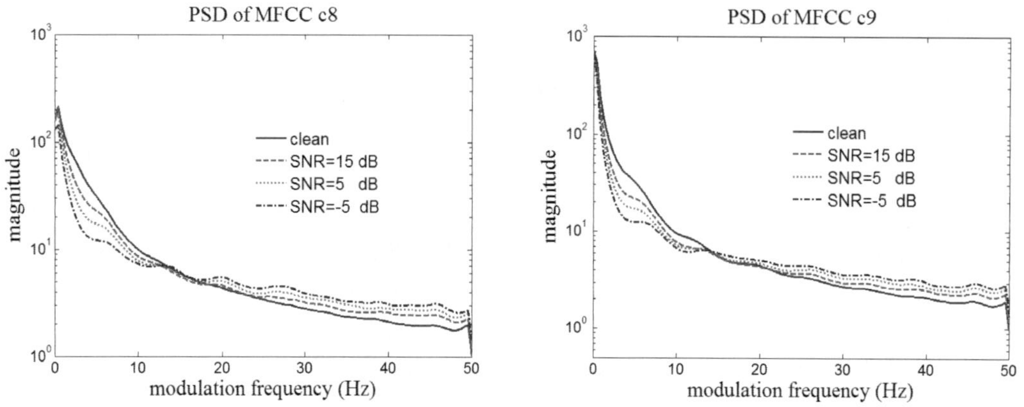

(a)c8 (b)c9

圖一、梅爾倒頻譜參數於乾淨與三種訊噪比情況之功率頻譜密度圖

之取樣頻率(音框取樣率)相關。例如，在一般設定下，音框取樣率為 100 Hz，則最高調變頻率為 50 Hz。

過去已有不少學者投注心力於語音特徵之調變頻譜特性之研究，且大多研究不約而同地顯示，調變頻譜之低頻成分(約 1 Hz 至 16 Hz)對於語音辨識精確度有顯著的關連，而其中尤以 4 Hz 的成分最為重要。有趣的是，4 Hz 也是人耳聽覺最為敏感之調變頻率[12]。此外有一假說，4 Hz 為人類大腦皮層感知之重要調變頻率[13]。當語音訊號受到噪音干擾時，不僅會使其時間特徵時間序列產生失真，同時其調變頻譜也會因而改變。在此，我們用一簡例來說明雜訊對語音調變頻譜之強度(magnitude part)產生的失真。首先，我們求取語音之梅爾倒頻譜參數(Mel-frequency cepstral coefficients, MFCC)於乾淨與不同訊噪比(signal-to-noise ratio, SNR)情況下之調變頻譜，其次，值得注意的是，因為不僅有雜訊會影響調變頻譜之值，尚有其它干擾因素，如語句之說話內容及語者特性等。因此，為降低雜訊以外的其他因素，在此我們要觀察的調變頻譜強度，是經由 1,688 句語句(出自 Aurora-2 語音資料庫[16])之倒頻譜特徵的調變頻譜強度平均而得。圖一中的曲線為梅爾倒頻譜參數於乾淨與三種訊噪比情況之平均調變頻譜強度；其中，圖一(a)對應至第八維梅爾倒頻譜參數 c8，圖一(b)則對應至第九維梅爾倒頻譜參數 c9。從圖一(a)(b)，我們首先觀察到調變頻譜之強度皆較集中於低頻，呼應了前人之發現，即語音特徵的調變頻譜強度主要都集中於低頻成分。其次，若將乾淨特徵與含雜訊特徵之調變頻譜強度加以比較，可明顯看出雜訊對整個調變頻帶都造成失真，其中低頻之強度會因此下降，而高頻之強度則反而上升，兩者之臨界約在 15 Hz 至 20 Hz 之間。最後，若比較不同訊噪比(SNR)之對應曲線，我們發現隨著雜訊的比例升高，調變頻譜強度於低頻下降與高頻上升之幅度也隨之加劇；意謂著雜訊對於調變頻譜之影響為使之整體分布趨於平坦，這與過去一些相似研究之觀點大致相同[7, 8, 17]。

（二）特徵參數之調變頻譜之強健化的相關研究介紹

目前對於調變頻譜改進其雜訊強健性(noise robustness)之技術，大多是對式(1)之 $X[k]$ 其強度成分 $|X[k]|$ 作更新，並保留其相位成分 $\theta[k]=\angle X[k]$ 不變。更新後的強度成分與原始相位成分相結合後，經由反傅立葉轉換(inverse discrete Fourier transform, IDFT)以求得新語音特徵時間序列。若上所述之調變頻譜的強度能夠被適當地更新，則將可有效降低雜訊產生的失真，進而讓使用新的語音特徵的語音辨識系統獲得較佳的辨識率。以下，我們

將簡述幾種更新調變頻譜的演算法，這些方法皆被初步驗證能有效提升語音特徵的雜訊強健性。

1、調變頻譜統計圖法(spectral histogram equalization, SHE)

此項技術[5]是將圖像辨識(pattern recognition)常用的統計圖等化演算法(histogram equalization, HEQ)應用於語音特徵調變頻譜強度的更新上，利用一非線性的轉換(nonlinear transform)，使訓練語句與測試語句的調變頻譜強度趨於同一個機率分布函數(probability distribution function, PDF)。在此方法中，新調變頻譜強度$|\tilde{X}[k]|$與原始強度$|X[k]|$之關係為

$$\left|\tilde{X}[k]\right| = F_{ref}^{-1}\left(F_X\left(|X[k]|\right)\right) \quad (2)$$

其中，$F_X(\cdot)$為單一語句$\{x[n]\}$之調變頻譜強度的機率分布，而$F_{ref}(\cdot)$則為集合所有訓練語句之調變頻譜強度所求的參考機率分布。

上述之 SHE 法可將特徵的調變頻譜強度作非線性的轉換，進而使其機率分布正規化，與其相關連的方法包括了(調變)頻譜平均正規化法(spectral mean normalization, SMN)[6]及頻譜平均與變異數正規化法(spectral mean and variance normalization, SMVN)[6]等。這兩種方法利用了線性轉換(linear transform)，分別對調變頻譜強度之平均值、或平均值與變異數加以正規化，類似 SHE 的觀念，SMN 與 SMVN 同樣可將乾淨語音特徵與雜訊語音特徵之調變頻譜強度之間的不匹配降低，進而提升特徵的雜訊強健性。

2、分頻段調變頻譜統計正規化法

前面所提到的 SHE, SMN 與 SMVN 三種方法，是將全部調變頻帶之頻譜強度值視為同一隨機變數(random variable)的樣本(samples)，進而一齊作正規化。然而，如前所述，不同調變頻率的成分在語音辨識中存在不等價的重要性，低頻成分比高頻成分相對重要。因此，文獻[6]提出將調變頻帶切割成多段的子頻段，再分別對每一個子頻段的頻譜強度作統計值(如先前所提的平均值、變異數或統計圖)正規化處理，而為了強調較低調變頻率的重要性，在低頻部分，子頻段的頻寬較細、子頻段的數目較多，高頻部分則是相反。根據文獻[6]的實驗數據顯示，分頻段正規化相對於全頻帶正規化而言，可以得到更佳的辨識率，然而，其計算複雜度與所需記憶體空間也較大。

3、時間序列結構正規化法(TSN)

時間序列結構正規化法(temporal structure normalization, TSN)[7] 是屬於一種時間序列濾波器(temporal filter)設計之技術，其藉由語音特徵序列通過一事先設計之濾波器，以達到正規化調變頻譜之目的。茲將TSN法所使用的濾波器設計步驟簡述如下：

<u>STEP 1</u>: 將訓練語料庫中，所有乾淨語音特徵序列(對單一種類之特徵而言)對應之功率頻譜密度(power spectral density, PSD)作平均，此平均視為參考功率頻譜密度，以$\{\bar{P}_{SS}[k]\}$表示，其中k為頻率索引。

<u>STEP 2</u>: 對訓練與測試語料庫中，求取個別語音特徵序列之功率頻譜密度，以$\{P_{XX}[k]\}$表示，則濾波器的頻率響應(frequency response)定為：

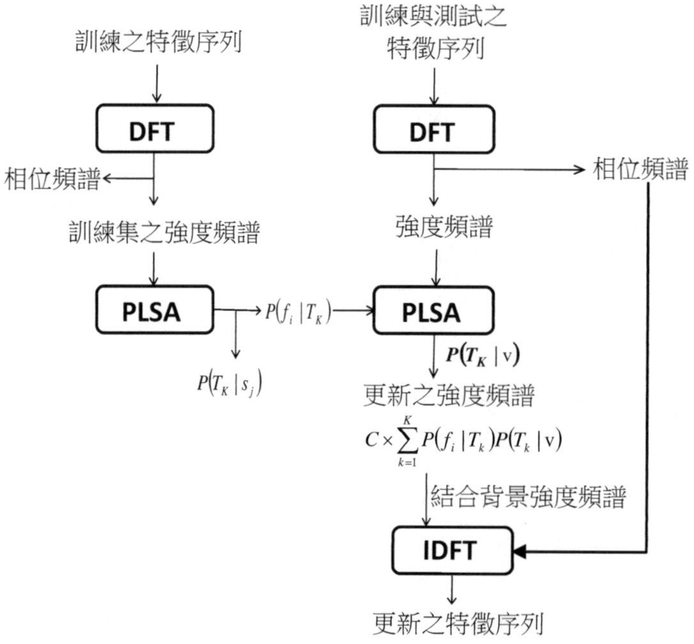

圖二、以機率式潛藏語意分析為基礎之調變頻譜正規化法之程序

$$H[k]=\sqrt{\frac{\overline{P}_{SS}[k]}{P_{XX}[k]}} \tag{3}$$

STEP 3:將式(3)做反離散傅立葉轉換(IDFT)，所得的序列先後經過窗化(windowing)與直流增益(DC gain)正規化後，最後所得的序列即為TSN所用的濾波器之脈衝響應(impulse response)，以$\{h[n]\}$表示。

值得注意的是，上述的濾波器頻率響應$\{h[n]\}$是隨不同特徵序列而改變(因為式(3)裡的$\{P_{XX}[k]\}$是個別特徵序列的PSD)，個別特徵序列通過其對應的TSN濾波器後，新特徵序列的PSD會逼近於參考PSD，由於PSD可視為平緩化後(smoothed)的調變頻譜強度平方，故TSN的目標相當於將語音特徵序列的調變頻譜強度一致化，藉以降低因雜訊干擾在調變頻譜強度造成的變異。

三、以機率式潛藏語意分析為基礎之調變頻譜正規化法

本論文嘗試機率式潛藏語意分析(probabilistic latent semantic analysis, PLSA)[11]應用於調變頻譜處理，其是一種使用機率模型的方式，找出調變頻譜強度與不同語音特徵序列之間的主題資訊。PLSA 可被視為是一種觀點模型(aspect model)的分析，其透過一組隱藏變數的機率分布，以共同預測一事件發生的可能性，而此組隱藏變數，即可被喻為一組潛藏主題。當我們使用 PLSA 來更新語音特徵時間序列的調變頻譜強度時，其流程圖如圖二所示，而詳細步驟陳述如下：

（一）藉由乾淨語音特徵序列之調變頻譜強度，求取其對應的 PLSA 生成模型

我們使用 PLSA 的觀念，為每一句乾淨訓練語句之特徵序列的調變頻譜強度建立生成模型，其透過一組共享的潛藏主題機率分布，以描繪每一語音特徵序列與其調變頻譜強度

的對應關係，首先，我們建立一關係矩陣 V，其每一行(column)是個別訓練語句特徵序列之調變頻譜強度，長度為 L，若共有 M 句訓練語句特徵序列，則 V 為 $L \times M$ 的矩陣，通常 $M >> L$，接下來，我們將矩陣 V 近似為兩個矩陣之乘積[14]：

$$\mathrm{V} \approx \mathrm{G}\mathrm{H}^{\mathrm{T}} \tag{4}$$

其中 G 與 H^{T} 分別為 $L \times K$ 與 $K \times M$ 的矩陣，而 K 即為 PLSA 中預設的潛藏主題個數。在這兩個矩陣裡：

(1) 矩陣 G 的第 i 列(row)的向量，表示為第 i 個調變頻率之強度成分(以 f_i 表示)在不同潛藏主題中生成的機率值，

(2) 矩陣 H^{T} 的第 j 行(以 s_j 表示)則是表示第 j 個語句產生不同潛藏主題的主題機率分布。更明確地說明，關係矩陣 V 中的每一個元素 $a_{i,j}$ 被近似為：

$$a_{i,j} = P(f_i \mid s_j) \approx \sum_{k=1}^{K} P(f_i \mid T_k) P(T_k \mid s_j) \tag{5}$$

即為個別序列 s_j 透過潛藏主題分布估算產生調變頻譜強度 f_i 的機率值。觀察上式可知，機率式潛藏語意分析有兩大類的模型參數需要估算，分別為每一個調變頻譜的主題機率分布 $P(T_K \mid s_j)$ 與各主題生成調變頻譜強度的機率分布 $P(f_i \mid T_K)$；而這些參數則可經由最大化訓練語句中每一個調變頻譜之對數相似度(log-likelihood)，並以期望值最大化法(expectation-maximization, EM)求得。值得一提的是，已有研究證實在適當的設定與推導下，機率式潛藏語意分析與非負矩陣分解(nonnegative matrix factorization, NMF)為等價的概念[15]，而非負矩陣分解則是一項已被廣泛運用於影像處理的演算法。藉由文獻[15]所介紹的演算法，我們可以求得上述 PLSA 的兩大類參數 $\{P(T_K \mid s_j)\}$ 與 $\{P(f_i \mid T_K)\}$ 。

（二）利用 PLSA 生成模型參數，重建語音特徵序列之調變頻譜強度

在這一步驟中，無論是測試語句或是訓練語句，其原始調變頻譜強度(以 v 表示)，皆經由上一步驟所得之機率式潛藏語意分析的兩個機率分布 $P(f_i \mid T_K)$ 與 $P(T_K \mid s_j)$，進行重新估算(新的調變頻譜強度，在此以 $\tilde{\mathrm{v}}$ 表示)。其中必須注意的是，上述之 $P(T_K \mid s_j)$ 是乾淨訓練特徵序列其調變頻譜的主題機率分布，因此對於測試特徵序列之調變頻譜 v 而言，其主題機率分布是未知的。在這裡，為了使訓練語句與測試語句皆通過相同的處理、降低可能的失真，我們對於任一調變頻譜強度 v ，利用以下公式進行估算其主題機率分布 $P(T_K \mid \mathrm{v})$：

$$P(T_K \mid \mathrm{v}) = \frac{\sum_{i=1}^{L+1} f_i \cdot h(T_k \mid f_i, \mathrm{v})}{\sum_{j=1}^{L+1} f_j} \tag{6}$$

其中

$$h(T_k \mid f_i, \mathrm{v}) = \frac{P(f_i \mid T_k) P(T_k \mid \mathrm{v})}{\sum_{l=1}^{K} P(f_i \mid T_l) P(T_l \mid \mathrm{v})} \tag{7}$$

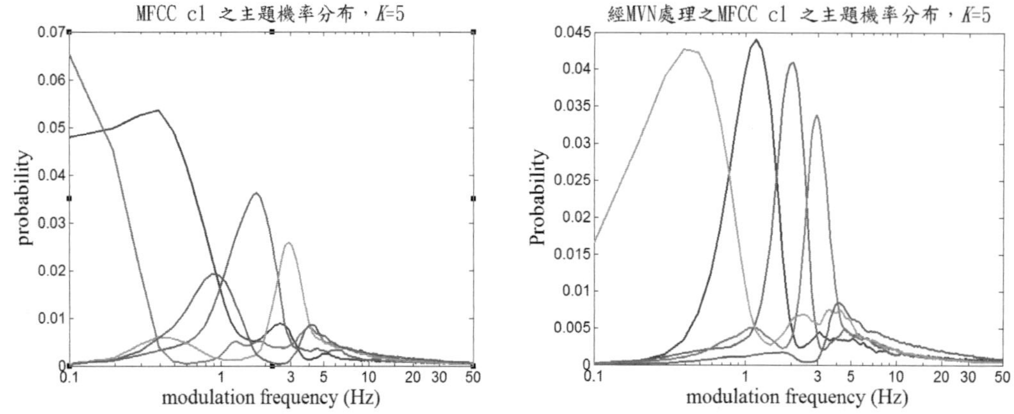

圖三、PLSA 對於(a)原始 MFCC 之 c1 (b)MVN 處理後 MFCC 之 c1 所求得的五個主題機率分布頻譜強度

在得到調變頻譜 v 的機率分布 $P(T_K \mid \mathrm{v})$，並配合原有的 $P(f_i \mid T_K)$，我們即可估算初步更新之每一維調變頻譜 $\tilde{\mathrm{v}}_i$，如下式所示：

$$\tilde{\mathrm{v}}_i = C \times \sum_{k=1}^{K} P(f_i \mid T_k) P(T_k \mid \mathrm{v}) \tag{8}$$

其中 C 為原始調變頻譜強度 v 每一維 v_i 的和，即 $C = \sum_{i=1}^{L} \mathrm{v}_i$ 。

此外，在實際操作上，由於原始機率式潛藏語意分析運用於語言模型時，皆會使用模型插補法，將其與背景模型相結合；在此我們採用相同的概念，將乾淨語音特徵之調變頻譜強度之平均作為背景調變頻譜強度(在此以 u 表示)，再利用插補法將其與式(8)之 $\tilde{\mathrm{v}}$ 做線性組合，得到最終之新的每一維調變頻譜強度 $\hat{\mathrm{v}}_i$，如下式所示：

$$\hat{\mathrm{v}}_i = \alpha \mathrm{u}_i + (1-\alpha)\tilde{\mathrm{v}}_i \tag{9}$$

其中 α 為加權值。

最後，我們將更新後之調變頻譜強度與原始調變頻譜相位做組合，並經由反傅立葉轉換(inverse DFT, IDFT)，將其轉換成新的特徵序列。

關於上述以 PLSA 為基礎之更新調變頻譜強度的演算法，有下列二項實作層面上的細節需注意，其描述如下：

(1) 儘管特徵時間序列之長度因語句而異，但是在此我們將其調變頻譜之長度(即其取離散傅立葉轉換的點數)設為定值，因此所有語句之調變頻譜長度皆相同，此外需注意的是，此定值需大於或等於任一待處理之特徵時間序列的長度，以避免時間混疊(time aliasing)的不良效應。

(2) 對更新後的調變頻譜進行反傅立葉轉換後，所得之序列長度會大於或等於原始特徵序列的長度(假設為 N)，因此我們只保留此新序列的前 N 點，作為最終的新特徵序列，此作法是根據最小化平方差(minimum mean squared error, MMSE)的最佳準則而得。

在圖三(a)與三(b)中，我們繪製了由以上 PLSA 法所得到的五個隱藏主題對應之調變頻譜強度(即等式(4)中矩陣 G 的行向量)，圖三(a)是對應原始 MFCC 之 c1 特徵，圖三(b)則是對應經 MVN 處理後 MFCC 之 c1 特徵。這兩圖都顯示了，PLSA 所得之潛藏主題調變頻譜強度都集中在低頻成分(大約 10 Hz 以下)，如前所述，這區域正是重要語音資訊匯集之處，顯示了 PLSA 可以有效將語音特徵序列重要的調變頻譜成分擷取出、並抑制不重要或容易受干擾的中高頻成分。而圖三(a)與三(b)的主要差別，在於後者的多數主題頻譜強度其極低頻之近直流成分(DC)很小，這是因為 MVN 處理後的 MFCC 特徵，其直流成分為零，PLSA 法所得的主題頻譜強度忠實地反映了這個前提。

四、實驗結果與分析

（一）實驗語料庫

本論文所使用的實驗語料庫為 Aurora-2 英文連續數字語料庫[16]，參與錄音計畫的語者皆是美國成年人。為了評估雜訊或通道對於語音的影響，測試部分的語音分別摻有八種不同來源的加成性雜訊(additive noise)和兩種不同特性的通道效應。根據不同種類的干擾，分成三個測試集：Set A, Set B 與 Set C。Set A 的語音分別含有地下鐵(subway)、人聲(babble)、汽車(car)和展覽會館(exhibition)等四種加成性雜訊與 G.712 通道效應； Set B 的語音則分別含有餐廳(restaurant)、街道(street)、機場(airport)和火車站(train station)等四種加成性雜訊與 G.712 的通道效應；Set C 分別加入了地下鐵(subway)與街道(street)兩種雜訊與 MIRS 通道效應。其中，而其中的訊噪比則有七種，分別為 clean (∞ dB)、20 dB、15 dB、10 dB、5 dB、0 dB 和-5 dB。Aurora-2 資料庫提供兩種訓練聲學模型的模式：乾淨情境訓練模式(clean-condition training)與複合情境訓練模式(multi-condition training)，本論文統一使用乾淨語料訓練模式來進行實驗，訓練集的乾淨語音共有 8,440 句，其中並無加成性雜訊，卻包含了 G.712 的通道效應，因此在三個測試集中，訓練集只與測試集 Set C 有通道上的不匹配。

（二）實驗設定

在前端處理方面，本論文的基礎實驗是採用梅爾倒頻譜係數做為語音特徵參數，其中預強調(pre-emphasis)參數設為 0.97，視窗函數為漢明窗(Hamming window)，取樣音框長度(frame length)為 25 毫秒，音框間距(frame shift)為 10 毫秒，每個音框是以 39 維特徵向量表示，其中包含 12 維的梅爾倒頻譜係數(c_1~c_{12})與第零維倒頻譜係數(c_0)，附加上其第一階差量係數(delta coefficient)和第二階差量係數(acceleration coefficient)。

在聲學模型的設定上，每個數字模型(one, two, …, nine, zero 和 oh)皆由一個由左到右(left-to-right)形式的連續密度隱藏式馬可夫模型(continuous density hidden Markov model, CDHMM)表示，其中包含 16 個狀態(state)，每個狀態則有 20 個高斯混合(Gaussian mixtures)。靜音模型則為 1 個狀態，內含 36 個高斯混合的模型。上述所有聲學特徵的建立、聲學模型的訓練與各種辨識實驗都是使用 HTK 工具套件[18]完成。

（三）辨識效能評估方式

辨識效能評估的方式是採用美國標準與科技組織(the national institute of standards and technology，NIST)[19]所訂立的評估標準，進行正確轉譯文句字串與辨識字串的比較。評估單位是以詞精確率(word accuracy)為單位，計算正確轉譯文句字串與辨識字串間的詞取代個數(substitutions)和詞插入個數(insertions)；計算公式如下所示：

$$\text{詞精確率}(\%) = \frac{\text{詞正確辨識個數} - \text{詞插入個數}}{\text{輸入詞總數}} \times 100\% \qquad (10)$$

值得注意的是，根據原 Aurora-2 資料庫的設定，每一種雜訊的平均詞精確率計算方式

表一、 PLSA 法作用於原始 MFCC 特徵的辨識結果，其中 Avg(%)與 RR(%)分別為總平均辨識精確率與相對錯誤降低率。

平均詞精確率 (%)		Clean	Set A	Set B	Set C	Avg.	RR
MFCC baseline		99.79	72.46	68.31	78.82	72.07	−−
PLSA	*K*=5	99.56	89.20	90.20	89.41	89.62	62.84
	K=10	99.59	89.05	90.25	89.25	89.57	62.66
	K=15	99.61	88.81	90.15	88.87	89.36	61.90
	K=20	99.59	88.78	90.18	88.69	89.32	61.76

是對於 20 dB 至 0 dB 的五種訊噪比(SNR)辨識率取平均，而排除掉乾淨情況和-5dB 二種極端的訊噪比的辨識率；本論文後續的所有平均辨識率皆是遵循此種呈現方式。

（四）實驗結果呈現與討論

1、PLSA 法作用於原始 MFCC 所得之辨識率

我們將所提出的 PLSA 法對於原始 39 維 MFCC 語音特徵參數時間序列做處理，其對應的平均辨識精確率詳列於表一之中；在 PLSA 法的參數設定上，我們令潛藏主題個數 K 分別為 5,10, 15 與 20，而式(9)中的加權值 α 則預設為 0.85。從表一的數據中，我們有以下幾點發現：

(1) 在匹配的乾淨環境下，相較於基礎實驗結果，PLSA 法對應的辨識精確率略為下降，但其下降程度並不顯著(最大下降率為 0.23%)，且跟選擇隱藏主題個數並無明顯關係。此現象驗證了，以 PLSA 為基礎的模型足以充分呈現語音特徵之調變頻譜強度的特性。對於調變頻譜強度而言，PLSA 為一種高效能編碼(encoding)的方式，其中只需使用少量之隱藏主題，就足以保有語音特徵之調變頻譜強度內含的辨識資訊。

(2) 在不匹配的雜訊干擾環境下，PLSA 處理後之語音特徵其表現明顯優於原始語音特徵。跟基礎實驗結果比較，在使用主題數為 5(K =5)的 PLSA 法時，辨識精確率被提升了 17.55%，相對錯誤降低率高達 62.84%，而其它主題數的 PLSA 法也有十分類似的效能。因此，我們所提出的 PLSA 法確實能有效提升原始梅爾倒頻譜特徵之雜訊強健性。此外，回顧圖三所顯示之主題機率分布對應之頻譜強度，可推知藉由 PLSA 的處理，對應至非語音成分失真之高頻調變頻譜成分會被大幅縮減，因而得到辨識精確率的進步。

(3) 相較於乾淨環境情況下，在雜訊干擾環境中增加主題機率分布數量 K，辨識精確率反而會微幅下降。然而跟乾淨環境之情形類似，不同主題數之 PLSA 其所造成的辨識精確率差距並不明顯，平均而言最大差距僅 0.30%(從 89.62%下降至 89.32%)。

2、PLSA 法結合其他強健性特徵演算法所得之辨識率

其次，我們將原始語音特徵先經過倒頻譜平均消去法(CMS)[1]或倒頻譜平均與變異數正規化法(MVN)[2]處理後，再透過我們所提出的 PLSA 法加以處理，藉此觀察 PLSA 與 CMS 或 MVN 這兩種典型的特徵序列處理技術是否有加成性，其所對應的辨識精確率分別列於表二與表三。觀察這兩個表的數據、並與表一比較，我們可知：

表二、 PLSA 為基礎之方法作用於經 CMS 處理之 MFCC 特徵的辨識結果，其中 RR_1 (%)與 RR_2 (%)分別為對比於基礎實驗與 CMS 法之辨識率之相對錯誤降低率。

平均詞精確率 (%)		Clean	Set A	Set B	Set C	Avg.	RR_1	RR_2
MFCC baseline		99.79	72.46	68.31	78.82	72.07	—	—
CMS		99.82	79.31	82.46	79.90	80.69	30.86	—
PLSA+ CMS	K=5	99.66	89.70	91.09	90.00	90.32	65.34	49.93
	K=10	99.69	89.63	91.00	89.89	90.23	65.02	49.87
	K=15	99.71	89.49	90.89	89.78	90.11	64.59	48.78
	K=20	99.73	89.38	90.92	89.70	90.06	64.41	48.52

表三、 PLSA 為基礎之方法作用於經 MVN 處理之 MFCC 特徵的辨識結果，其中 RR_1 (%)與 RR_2 (%)分別為對比於基礎實驗與 MVN 法之辨識率之相對錯誤降低率。

平均詞精確率 (%)		Clean	Set A	Set B	Set C	Avg.	RR_1	RR_2
MFCC baseline		99.79	72.46	68.31	78.82	72.07	—	—
MVN		99.82	88.58	89.32	88.28	88.82	59.97	—
PLSA+ MVN	K=5	99.66	89.98	91.01	89.72	90.34	64.70	13.60
	K=10	99.68	90.06	91.06	89.90	90.43	65.74	14.40
	K=15	99.73	90.07	91.14	89.91	90.47	65.88	14.76
	K=20	99.72	90.21	91.18	90.06	90.57	66.24	15.54

(1) 相對於使用原始 MFCC 特徵之基礎實驗而言，CMS 與 MVN 皆能改善辨識精確率，其中又以 MVN 的改進效果較好，可提供高達 17%左右的精確率提升。而我們所提的 PLSA 法，在四種潛在主題數的選擇下，皆優於 MVN 法。
(2) 當 PLSA 法與 CMS 結合時，相較於單一 PLSA 法或單一 CMS 法而言，都能使辨識精確率更有效的提升，此進步的現象也同樣發生於 PLSA 法與 MVN 的結合上。整體平均辨識率都可超過 90%，另外，在結合 PLSA 法的前提下，CMS 與 MVN 的表現差距很小(辨識精確率的差距僅有 0.5%左右)， 這代表了在 PLSA 法前置處理方法的選擇上，我們可使用簡易的 CMS 法，即可趨於較複雜的 MVN 達到的效能。
(3) 跟表一呈現的數據類似，在結合 CMS 或 MVN 後的 PLSA，其潛在主題數目的多寡與辨識精確率並無顯著的關係。而改變潛在主題數目所造成的平均精確率變化皆在 0.3%以下，這也顯示了我們可以使用很少的潛在主題(如 K=5)，也就是說在簡化運算複雜度的前提下亦不影響 PLSA 法的優異性。

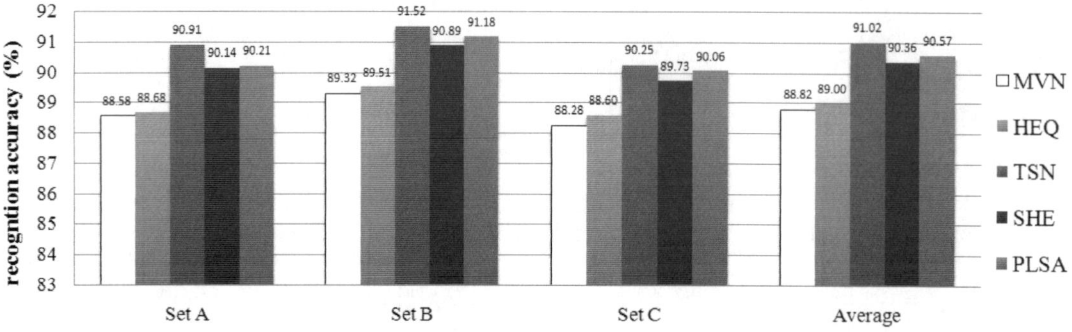

圖四、PLSA 法與其它調變頻譜更新法的效能比較(經 MVN 前置處理過)

3、PLSA 法與其他調變頻譜更新法的效能比較

在這一節中，我們將所提出的 PLSA 法，與一系列的語音特徵時間序列處理技術進行辨識精確率的比較。這些時間序列處理技術，包括了在第二章中提到的 HEQ、TSN 與 SHE 等，都是直接或間接地更新特徵之調變頻譜，進而強化雜訊強健性。由於在文獻中提及這些技術時，都是直接展示其作用於 MVN 前置處理後之特徵的辨識效果，在這裡，我們同樣先將原始語音特徵 MFCC 先經 MVN 處理後，再分別運作這些技術。

圖四中展示了上述這些技術所得之平均辨識精確率，我們提出的 PLSA 法所採用的隱藏主題數為 20。從此圖中，我們看到這裡所用的所有方法皆能提升 MVN 特徵的辨識精確率，所引用的三種方法中，又以 TSN 的效能最好，能達到 91.02%的總平均辨識率，雖然我們提出的 PLSA 法，辨識效能略低於 TSN，但也可使總平均辨識率提升至 90.57%，此初步顯示了 PLSA 法足以與現今有名的調變頻譜更新技術在效能上並駕齊驅。

4、PLSA 降低調變頻譜強度失真的效能

最後，除了辨識精確率的驗證，我們嘗試進一步藉由 PLSA 法於不同訊噪比(SNR)下所得之特徵序列調變頻譜強度，檢視其降低雜訊所產生之失真的能力。圖五(a)-(d)為單一語句其原始與經過各種處理方法後之第一維梅爾倒頻譜特徵參數 c1 於三種不同訊噪比(clean、10dB 與 0dB)之功率頻譜密度(power spectral density, PSD)。首先，觀察圖五(a)可發現，雜訊干擾所引發的不匹配效應，明顯普遍存在整個調變頻率範圍[0, 50Hz]內。圖五(b)則顯示，MVN 可有效降低低調變頻率之 PSD 失真，但是不匹配情形仍舊存在於中高調變頻率成分。圖五(c)與圖五(d)則是前述圖五(a)與(b)兩類特徵參數經過 PLSA 處理過後之 PSD 曲線；從這兩圖皆可發現，藉由 PLSA 法，可大幅降低整個頻率範圍的 PSD 失真。而相較於圖五(c)，圖五(d)中於不同訊噪比之 PSD 曲線則更為一致，顯示 PLSA 與 MVN 結合後，能更有效降低雜訊產生的失真。

五、結論與未來展望

本論文針對語音特徵時間序列之調變頻譜提出嶄新的分析與強化技術，利用機率式潛藏語意分析(PLSA)賦予調變頻譜強度其機率的意義，並透過一組潛藏的主題機率分布，以描繪語句與調變頻譜強度之關係，同時予以機率式分解與成分分析，並藉此更新調變頻譜強度以求取更具強健性的語音特徵序列。辨識實驗結果顯示，所提出的新方法能有效提升雜訊環境下語音辨識精確率，且展示了此新方法與時間序列域之正規化法能有互

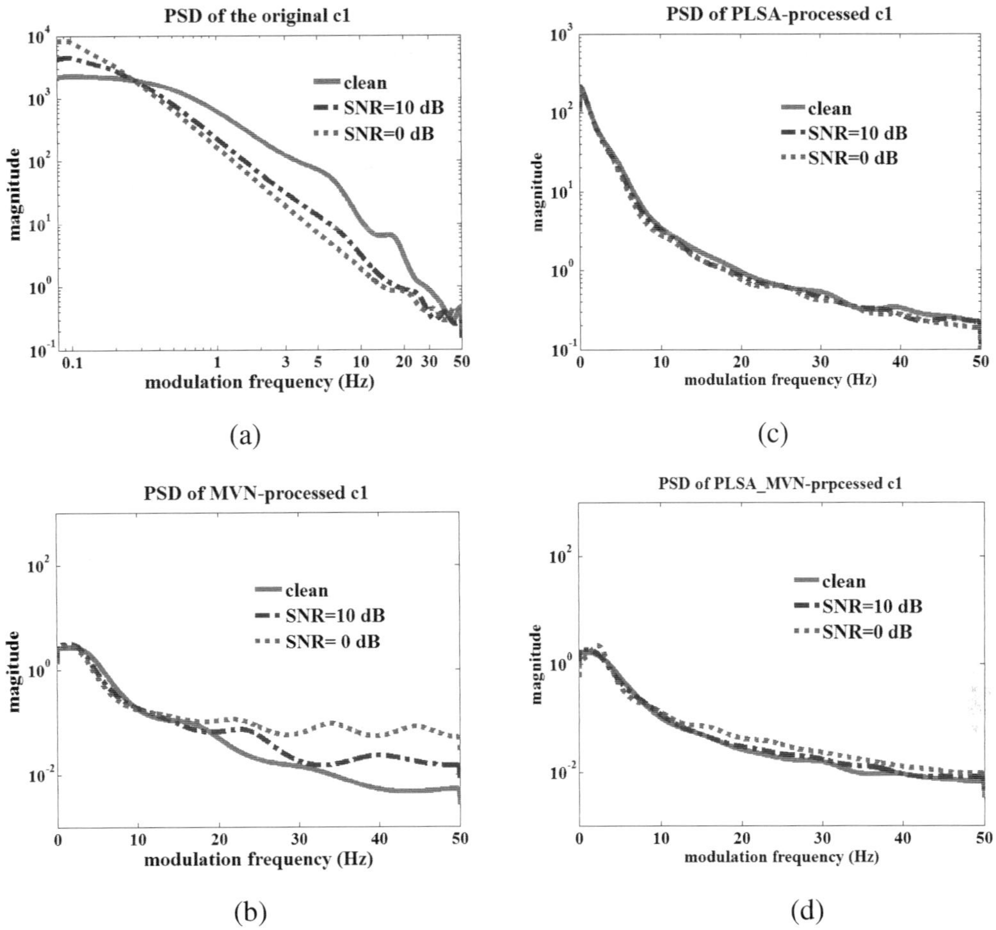

圖五、c1 特徵序列於三種訊噪比情況下之 PSD 曲線，其中(a)為原始 MFCC 特徵，(b)為 MVN 處理後之特徵 (c)為 PLSA 處理後之特徵 (d)為 PLSA 結合 MVN 處理後之特徵

補的作用。未來，我們期望能嘗試將其它資料分解(data factorization)的技術運用於調變頻譜的分析上[20]，進而比較其特性與探索優缺點。同時，將 PLSA 法與統計圖等化法及其延伸[21]作結合；並且，應用 PLSA 法探索語音訊號於其它域的特性。

參考文獻

[1] S. Furui, "*Cepstral Analysis Techniques for Automatic Speaker Verification,*" IEEE Trans. on Acoustic, Speech and Signal Processing, Vol. 29(2): pp. 254-272, 1981

[2] A. Vikki, and K. Laurila, "*Segmental Feature Vector Normalization for Noise Robust Speech Recognition,*" Speech Communication, Vol. 25: pp. 133-147, 1998

[3] A. D. L. Torre, A. M. Peinado, J. C. Segura, J. L. Perez-Cordoba, M. C. Benitez, and A. J. Rubio, "*Histogram equalization of speech representation for robust speech recognition,*" IEEE Trans. on Speech and Audio Processing, Vol. 13(3): pp. 355-366, 2005

[4] N. Kanedera, T. Arai, H. Hermansky, and M. Pavel, "*On the importance of various modulation frequencies for speech recognition,*" in Proc. European Conf. Speech Communication and Technology (Eurospeech), 1997

[5] L. C. Sun, C. W. Hsu, and L. S. Lee, "*Modulation Spectrum Equalization for robust*

Speech Recognition," in Proc. IEEE Workshop on Automatic Speech Recognition and Understanding (ASRU), 2007

[6] S-Y. Huang, W. H. Tu, and J-W. Hung, "*A study of sub-band modulation spectrum compensation for robust speech recognition*," in Proc. ROCLING XXI: Conf. on Computational Linguistics and Speech Processing, 2009

[7] X. Xiao, E. S. Chng, and H. Li, "*Normalization of the speech modulation spectra for robust speech recognition,*" IEEE Trans. on Speech and Audio Processing, 2008

[8] J-W. Hung and W-Y. Tsai, "*Constructing modulation frequency domain based features for robust speech recognition*," IEEE Trans. Acoustic, Speech, Language Processing, 2008

[9] H. Hermansky and N. Morgan., "RASTA processing of speech," IEEE Trans. on Speech and Audio Processing, 2(4): pp. 578-589, 1994

[10] J. Koehler et al., "*Integrating RASTAPLP into Speech Recognition*," in Proc. IEEE International Conference on Acoustics, Speech and Signal Processing (ICASSP), pp. 421-424, 1994

[11] T. Hofmann, "*Probabilistic latent semantic analysis.*" in Proc. Uncertainty in Arterial Intelligence, UAI, 1999

[12] H. Hermansky, "*Should Recognizers Have Ears?*" Invited Tutorial Paper, in Proc. ESCA-NATO Tutorial and Research Workshop on Robust speech recognition for unknown communication channels, pp. 1-10, 1997

[13] S. Greenberg, "*On the origins of speech intelligibility in the real world*," in Proc. ESCA-NATO Tutorial and Research Workshop on Robust Speech Recognition for Unknown Communication Channels,1997

[14] B. Chen, "*Word topic models for spoken document retrieval and transcription,*" ACM Transaction on Asian Language Information Processing, Vol. 8, No. 1, pp. 2:1-2:27, 2009

[15] J. Driesen, H. Van Hamme, "*Modeling vocabulary acquisition, adaptation and generalization in infants using adaptive Bayesian PLSA*," Neurocomputing, 2011

[16] H. G. Hirsch and D. Pearce, "*The AURORA experimental framework for the performance evaluations of speech recognition systems under noisy conditions*," in Proc. ISCA ITRW ASR 2000

[17] C-P. Chen and J. Bilmes, "*MVA processing of speech features*," IEEE Trans. on Audio, Speech and Language Processing, Vol. 15, No. 1, pp. 257-269, 2007

[18] http://htk.eng.cam.ac.uk/

[19] http://www.nist.gov/index.html

[20] W-Y. Chu, J-W. Hung and B. Chen, *"Modulation spectrum factorization for robust speech recognition,"* in Proc. APSIPA Annual Summit and Conference (APSIPA ASC), 2011

[21] B. Chen, W-H. Chen, S-H. Lin, and W-Y. Chu, *"Robust speech recognition using spatial–temporal feature distribution characteristics,"* Pattern Recognition Letters, Vol. 32, No. 7, pp. 919-926, 2011

應用語音辨識技術於鳥鳴聲辨識

廖偉恩
國立台北科技大學
電腦與通訊研究所
t8418044@ntut.edu.tw

黎欣捷
國立台北科技大學
電腦與通訊研究所
t9419004@ntut.edu.tw

蔡偉和
國立台北科技大學
電腦與通訊研究所
whtsai@ntut.edu.tw

摘要

野外賞鳥已成為大眾休閒的新趨勢，但一般民眾常只能看見鳥或聽見鳥鳴聲，卻不知其種類為何。為了協助大眾識別鳥類，本論文探討鳥鳴聲自動辨識問題，透過語音辨識相關技術，設計鳥鳴聲辨識系統。我們分別從音色及音高兩個層面進行分析，利用梅爾刻度倒頻譜係數表示鳥鳴聲的音色特徵，並搭配高斯混合模型進行特徵的參數模型化與比對；而音高層面分析則試圖求取鳥鳴聲所對應的音符，再利用雙連文模型捕捉音符的動態變化資訊，並據以比對未知鳥鳴聲。我們挑選出大台北地區常見的十種鳥類，並從商業 CD 及鳥類相關網站上收集鳥鳴聲資料，使系統訓練和測試音檔分別屬不同的來源。實驗結果發現，採用音色、音高、與結合兩者的系統辨識正確率分別為 71.1%、72.1%、與 75.04%。

關鍵詞：音色、音高、高斯混合模型、雙連文模型。

1.前言

目前全世界大約有九千七百多種鳥類，而台灣這樣一個小島就佔了約二十分之一的種類，雖然我們周遭住有許多這些可愛的鄰居，但往往都只聽到它們的叫聲，卻不知它們是誰。鳥類的鳴聲豐富且多變，我們期望藉由物種之間的鳴聲差異性，發展出一套鳥鳴聲辨識系統，讓不是鳥類專家的一般民眾，也可以從自己隨意錄製的一段鳥鳴聲音檔中，讓系統判斷所屬鳥種並獲得之相關訊息。

目前鳥鳴聲自動辨識的相關研究仍十分有限。文獻[1]中使用動態時間校正(Dynamic Time Warping，DTW)演算法，將測試聲音檔的頻譜圖（spectrogram）與事先經過專家挑選的樣板音檔作比對。文獻[2]中分別比較 DTW 和隱藏式馬可夫模型(Hidden Markov Model，HMM)在辨識鳥類聲音上的效能，其中使用 6 種特徵參數：線性預估編碼參數(Linear Predict Coding，LPC)、線性預估倒頻譜係數、LPC reflection、梅爾倒頻譜係數(Mel-frequency Cepstral Coefficients，MFCC) [3]、log mel-filter bank channel 和 linear mel-filter bank channel。實驗結果顯示，使用 DTW 的辨識效能不錯，但是對於雜訊較大的輸入聲音檔或是容易混淆的短促鳴叫聲，則需要挑選更適合的頻譜圖樣本，這道手續通常需要經驗豐富的專家反覆地試驗。對於使用 HMM，辨識效果則取決於輸入參數的鑑別度，但效能不一定比 DTW 好。而不論是 DTW 或 HMM，所使用的辨識線索皆來自於音色(timbre)特徵。本論文所提出之辨識系統，除了考慮音色特徵參數外，更加上音高(pitch)特徵參數。實驗結果發現將這兩種特徵參數進行結合後可有效提升鳥鳴聲辨識正確率。

本論文的章節組織如下：第二章描述辨識系統架構；第三章說明音色特徵參數擷取及統計模型；第四章描述音高特徵參數擷取及統計模型；第五章結合音色與音高特徵來設計辨識系統；第六章將說明本研究所使用的鳥鳴聲資料庫並呈現實驗結果；第六章進行本研究之總結。

2. 辨識系統架構

本論文所提出的辨識系統如圖 1。我們可將其分成三個單元，分別是「音色分析」、「音高分析」、與「整合決策」。各單元皆包含兩種操作模式，一為訓練、另一為測試，簡介如下：

(1) 音色分析
此單元目標是擷取各種鳥之鳴聲的音色特徵，並表示為統計模型，以便識別未知鳥鳴聲。

(2) 音高分析
此單元目標是擷取各種鳥之鳴聲的音高特徵，並表示為統計模型，以便識別未知鳥鳴聲。

(3) 整合決策
此單元整合音色與音高的判斷資訊，進行最後決策以告知使用者辨識結果。

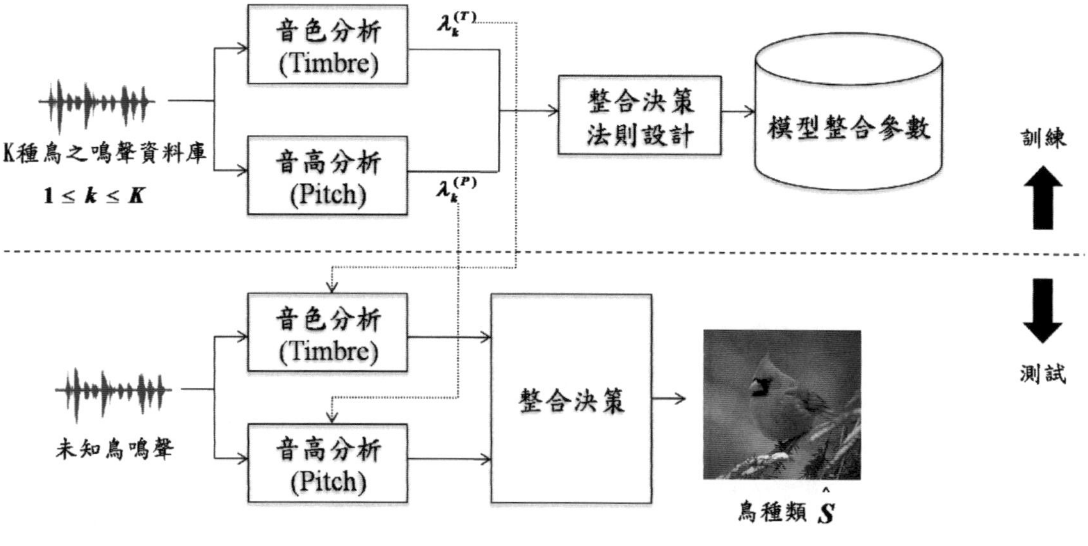

圖 1　本論文之鳥鳴聲辨識系統架構圖。

3. 音色分析

音色分析過程如圖 2 所示。主要包括預處理、特徵參數擷取、與統計模型建立及匹配。

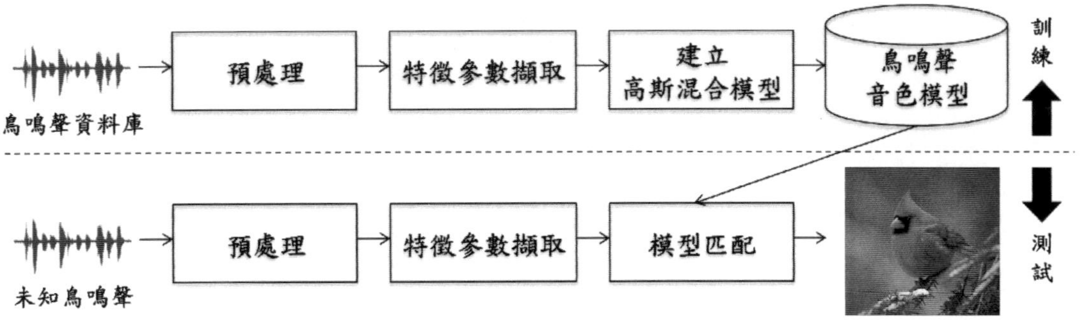

圖 2　音色分析過程。

3.1 特徵參數擷取

音色之差異如同鋼琴與吉他都彈奏相同音符，卻聽起來有不同的聲音。不同的鳥種，可視為不同的樂器一樣，音色也不相同。

首先，我們先將鳥鳴聲訊號經由短時間（short-term）快速傅利葉轉換（Fast Fourier Transform, FFT）成為一串音框頻譜序列。令 $x_{t,j}$ 為第 t 個音框訊號在第 j 個 FFT 頻率刻度上的絕對振幅頻譜（magnitude spectrum），其中 $1 \le j \le J$，而 J 為頻率刻度的總數。

再將各音框的絕對振幅頻譜送入一個「三角頻帶組」(triangular filter banks)，其中頻帶中心即是梅爾刻度值，該刻度值 mel 與頻率 f Hz 的轉換方式為 $\mathrm{mel}(f) = 2595 \cdot \log_{10}(1 + f/700)$，而頻帶的寬度為兩相鄰梅爾刻度差。接著計算各頻帶的能量值 $SG_{t,b} = \sum_{j=l_b}^{u_b} \left|x_{t,j}\right|^2$，其中 l_b 為第 b 個頻帶中最低的 FFT 頻率刻度，u_b 為第 b 個頻帶中最高的 FFT 頻率刻度，然後再將所有頻帶的對數能量值進行離散餘旋轉換(Discrete Cosine Transform, DCT)[4]，以取得倒頻譜係數（cepstral coefficients）[4]，詳細計算方式如下：

$$\mathbf{X}_t = \frac{1}{B}\sum_{b=1}^{B}\log\left(\sum_{j=l_b}^{u_b}\left|x_{t,j}\right|^2 T_b(j)\right)\cos\left(\frac{\pi i}{B}(b-0.5)\right) \qquad (1)$$

其中 B 為頻帶總數，$T_b(j)$為第 b 個頻帶的三角濾波器。

3.2 高斯混合模型**(GMM)**

為了凝聚同種鳥之不同叫聲的共有音色特徵，我們利用「高斯混合模型」[4][5]來進行 MFCC 參數統計。高斯混合模型是聲學訊號分類中最常見且最成功的模型之一。一個高斯混合模型包含若干高斯機率密度函式，每一高斯機率密度函式以期望值μ_g與變異量Σ_g所描述，其中 g 代表 G 個高斯機率密度函式中之第 g 個，另外含一加權數 w_g 將各高斯機率密度函式加總成為一機率密度。我們將模型參數記為：$\boldsymbol{\lambda}_k^{(T)} = \{w_g, \mu_g, \Sigma_g | 1 \le g \le G\}$。這些參數可經由最大化期望值法(Expectation-Maximization, EM)[4][5]估算出，此即訓練階段所須執行之工作。若資料庫中有 K 隻鳥，則我們產生 K 個模型 $\boldsymbol{\lambda}_1^{(T)}, \boldsymbol{\lambda}_2^{(T)}, \ldots, \boldsymbol{\lambda}_K^{(T)}$，代表這些鳥鳴聲的音色模型。

在測試階段，若有一未知鳥鳴聲片段之特徵向量序列為 $\mathbf{X}=\mathbf{X}_1,\mathbf{X}_2,\ldots,\mathbf{X}_T$，其中每一向量維度為 D，則我們對各模型 $\boldsymbol{\lambda}_k^{(T)}$，$1 \le k \le K$ 分別計算似然率：

$$P\left(\mathbf{X}|\boldsymbol{\lambda}_k^{(T)}\right) = \prod_{k=1} P(\mathbf{X}_t|\boldsymbol{\lambda}_k^{(T)}) \tag{2}$$

其中

$$P\left(\mathbf{X}_t\boldsymbol{\lambda}_k^{(T)}\right) = \sum_{g=1}^{G} w_g \frac{1}{\sqrt{(2\pi)^D\left|\boldsymbol{\Sigma}_g\right|}} \exp\left(-\frac{1}{2}\left(\mathbf{X}_t - \boldsymbol{\mu}_g\right)' \boldsymbol{\Sigma}_g^{-1}\left(\mathbf{X}_t - \boldsymbol{\mu}_{\backslash g}\right)\right) \tag{3}$$

則根據最大似然率決策法(maximum likelihood decision)[4]，**X** 應判斷為

$$S = \arg\max_k P(\mathbf{X} \mid \boldsymbol{\lambda}_k^{(T)}) \tag{4}$$

在實作上，考慮鳥鳴聲資料庫可能並無包含大量的聲音樣本可供精確的模型訓練，因此我們藉由模型調適技術[6]來產生個個鳥種的模型。該技術先根據EM演算法將所有訓練用之鳥鳴聲見立一個高斯混合模型當作通用模型（Universal Model），再經由最大事後機率（Maximum A Posterior, MAP）調適法進行通用模型之調整，以產生各鳥種的高斯混合模型。

4. 音高分析

音高參數與聲音的基頻（fundamental frequency, F0）有關，一連串基頻高低不同的聲音串在一起就如同不同音符被演奏出一般。本單元的基本概念是假設每種鳥都有其各自的歌聲或歌唱語言，像是音符高低相連有其獨特的規則。若我們能捕捉每種鳥的音符相連接資訊，則可據此識別未知的鳥鳴聲所屬鳥種類。如圖3所示為音高分析過程，主要包括音高特徵擷取及統計模型建立與匹配。

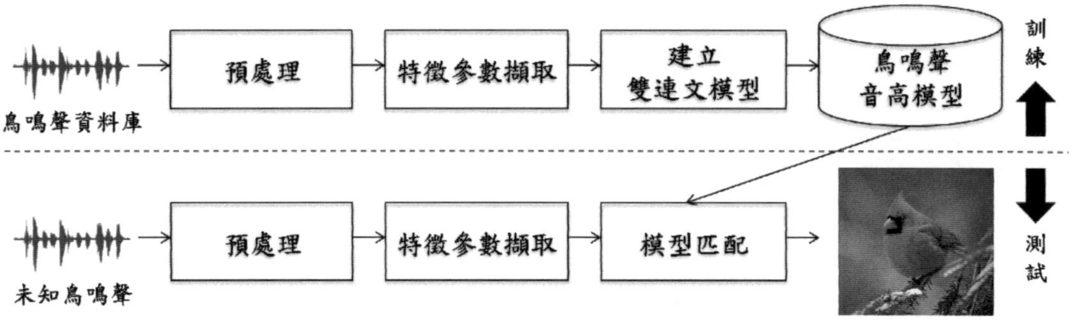

圖3　音高分析過程。

4.1 特徵參數擷取

我們採用次諧波總和法（Sub-Harmonic Summation, SHS）[7]進行音高求取。SHS的原理是根據基頻除了本身的能量較高外，其倍頻諧波（Harmonic）的能量也通常較高，若某一基頻與其倍頻諧波的能量總和明顯較高於其他頻率時，該頻率極有可能為基頻。其求取音高流程如圖4。

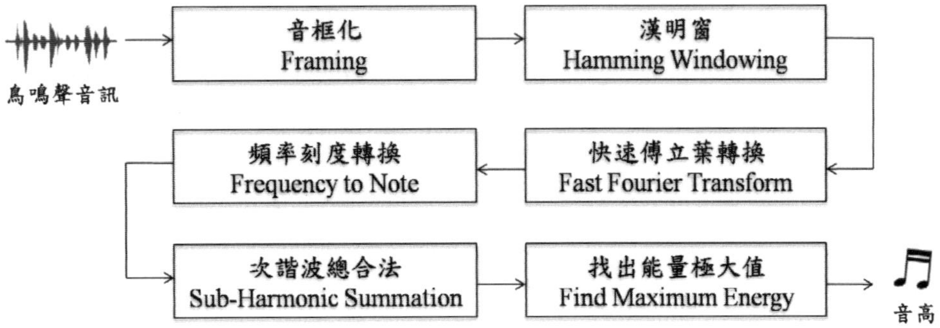

圖 4　音高求取流程圖

令 $x_{t,j}$ 為第 t 個音框訊號在第 j 個 FFT 頻率刻度上的振幅，其中 $1 \le j \le J$，而 J 為頻率刻度總數。透過方程式 5 將 FFT 刻度轉為 MIDI 音符刻度 $e_1, e_2, \ldots, e_N$

$$N(j) = 12 * \log_2\left(\frac{freq(j)}{440}\right) + 69.5 \tag{5}$$

$$y_{t,n} = \max_{\forall j, N(j)=e_n} x_{t,j} \tag{6}$$

則我們可求取訊號在 t 時間屬於音符 e_n 的能量。理想上，若在時間 t 的鳴唱音符為 e_n，則屬於音符刻度 e_n 的能量 $y_{t,n}$ 應是所有 $y_{t,1}, y_{t,2}, \ldots, y_{t,N}$ 中最大者，如(6)所示。但由於有諧波的存在，能量 $y_{t,n}$ 可能並非最大。因此為了避免誤判，可利用 SHS 的觀念檢查各音符及其若干個八度音符的加權能量和（Strength）：

$$z_{t,n} = \sum_{c=0}^{C} h^c \, y_{t,n+12c} \tag{7}$$

其中 C 是欲列入考慮的八度音符數，而 h 為小於 1 的權重。據此判定演唱音符應為

$$o_t = \arg\max_{1 \le n \le N} z_{t,n} \tag{8}$$

4.2 鳥鳴聲之模型建立

為了捕捉音符間相連的動態資訊，我們採用雙連文模型（Bi-gram Model）技術來訓練屬於鳥鳴聲的模型。

當給定一串音符序列 $o_1, o_2, \ldots o_t, \ldots$，雙連文模型可用以描述該序列中各音符前後相連接的關係，其做法是統計所有可能之兩音符組合，例如 w_1 與 w_2 的發生頻率或機率：$P(o_t = w_1 | o_{t-1} = w_2)$。若兩個音符 w_1 與 w_2 常出現於某一種鳥的鳴聲中，則機率 $P(o_t = w_1 | o_{t-1} = w_2)$ 值會較大；反之，若兩個音符幾乎不會出現於某一種鳥的鳴聲中，則機率 $P(o_t = w_1 | o_{t-1} = w_2)$ 值會較小。

在測試階段，若有一未知鳥鳴聲片段之音符序列為 $\mathbf{O = O_1, O_2, \ldots, O_T}$，則我們對各模型 $\lambda_k^{(P)}$，$1 \le k \le K$ 分別計算似然率：

$$P\left(O|\lambda_k^{(P)}\right)=\prod_{t=1}^{t=T}P(O_t|\lambda_k^{(P)}) \tag{9}$$

則根據最大似然率決策法（maximum likelihood decision）[4]，**O** 應判斷為

$$S=\arg\max_k P(\mathbf{O}\,|\,\boldsymbol{\lambda}_k^{(P)}) \tag{10}$$

5. 結合音色與音高分析之辨識系統

經實驗發現，使用音色分析與音高分析所獲得的鳥鳴聲辨識結果有許多差異與互補之處，因此嘗試結合音色與音高之辨識系統，如圖 6 所示。

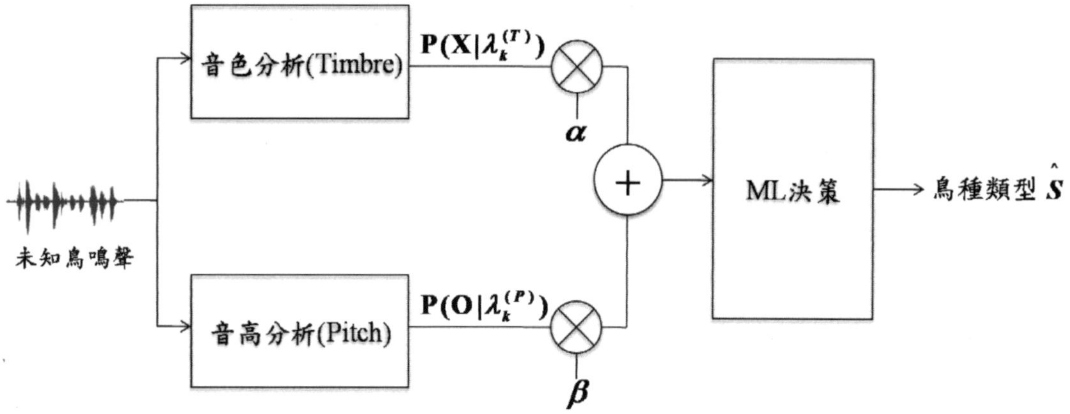

圖 6　整合音色與音高之辨識系統架構圖。

將一未知鳥種的鳴聲訊號，經由音色分析與音高分析後產生兩似然率，再將這兩似然率做加權總和，最後挑選加總後的最大似然率。據此判斷該鳥鳴聲為何種鳥，即：

$$\hat{S}=\arg\max_{1\le k\le K}[\,\alpha\cdot \mathbf{P}(\mathbf{X}|\lambda_k^{(T)})+\beta\cdot \mathbf{P}(\mathbf{O}|\lambda_k^{(P)})] \tag{11}$$

在本篇論文中，α 與 β 分別設定成 0.6 與 0.4。

6. 鳥鳴聲辨識系統

6.1 鳥鳴聲資料庫

本論文所使用的鳥鳴聲音檔有兩個來源，分別是市面上販售的商業 CD 及網路上收集來的鳥鳴聲音檔，整理如表 1、2 所示：

表 1　商業 CD 之來源。

專輯名稱	出版商
鳥-野鳥鳴唱圖鑑	風潮有聲出版有限公司
台北鳥視界	台北市政府新聞處

八仙山國家森林遊樂區常見鳥類鳴聲	行政院農業委員會林務局
大雪山國家森林遊樂區常見鳥類鳴聲	行政院農業委員會林務局

表 2　網路上收集鳥鳴聲之來源。

網站名稱	網站位置
台灣大學動物博物館	http://archive.zo.ntu.edu.tw/
國立鳳凰谷鳥園	http://www.fhk.gov.tw/
Bird Call Recordings	http://www.geocities.com/RainForest/9003/birdcall.htm
Macaulay Library	http://macaulaylibrary.org/index.do

這些商業 CD 和網站包含各種不同鳥類的鳴聲，在考慮到訓練語料量的多寡、地域的合理性、科目差異和鳴聲類型上，本篇論文共挑選了 10 種大台北地區常見的鳥種來進行實驗，分別為小卷尾、小啄木、小彎嘴畫眉、山紅頭、五色鳥、白耳畫眉、紅嘴黑鵯、紫嘯鶇、黃嘴角鴞、樹鵲。

一我們將商業 CD 音檔及網路上音檔兩種來源合併後各取一半，使得訓練音檔與測試音檔之檔案數不會差異太大。

使用商業 CD 上的音檔，原始音檔格式一律為雙聲道 44.1KHz 的 PCM WAV 檔。至於網路上收集而來的音檔，原始格式有些是經過 MP3 壓縮過的音檔，也有 PCM 格式的 WAV 檔，而取樣頻率從 8KHz 至 48KHz 不等。為了實驗的一致性及節省運算時間，我們把兩者來源的音檔皆調整為 22.05KHz 單聲道的 PCM WAV 檔。

6.2 實驗結果

6.2.1 基於音色分析之鳥聲辨識結果

首先進行不同高斯混合數的鳥鳴聲辨識實驗，結果列於表 3。從表中得知，當混合數為 64 時，其辨識率優於其他混合數。因此在本篇論文中，GMM 之混合數皆為 64。其辨識結果如表 4，總辨識率為 71.08%，其辨識率之計算方式如(12)。若僅觀察表中鳥鳴聲，僅有小彎嘴畫眉的辨識率較高，其餘的鑑別度都頗低。

$$\text{辨識率正確率} = \frac{\text{被正確辨識出的音檔數目}}{\text{總測試音檔數目}} \times 100\% \tag{12}$$

表 3　不同高斯混合數之辨識率。

高斯混合數	4	8	16	32	64	128
小卷尾	55.84%	58.44%	58.44%	59.74%	64.93%	62.33%
小啄木	59.8%	59.8%	60.78%	62.74%	62.74%	62.74%
小彎嘴	80%	81.93%	83.22%	83.22%	82.58%	81.93%
山紅頭	69.13%	69.13%	70.37%	71.6%	70.37%	69.13%
五色鳥	72.14%	73.05%	73.97%	74.42%	74.88%	74.88%
白耳畫眉	74.41%	75.58%	77.9%	77.9%	76.744%	76.74%
紅嘴黑鵯	62.42%	63.69%	64.96%	66.24%	68.78%	67.51%
紫嘯鶇	68%	72%	76%	76%	76%	76%
黃嘴角鴞	63.96%	63.96%	63.96%	63.96%	67.56%	65.76%
樹鵲	50.68%	52.05%	56.16%	57.53%	56.16%	54.79%
總辨識率	**67.12%**	**68.23%**	**69.52%**	**70.25%**	**71.08%**	**70.25%**

表 4　基於音色之鳥鳴聲辨識混淆矩陣。

	小卷尾	小啄木	小彎嘴	山紅頭	五色鳥	白耳畫眉	紅嘴黑鵯	紫嘯鶇	黃嘴角鴞	樹鵲
小卷尾	64.93%	10.38%	0%	9.09%	0%	6.49%	6.49%	0%	2.59%	0%
小啄木	9.8%	62.74%	14.7%	2.94%	3.92%	2.94%	2.94%	0%	0%	0%
小彎嘴	0%	6.45%	82.58%	0%	0%	0%	0%	6.45%	0%	4.51%
山紅頭	7.4%	3.7%	6.17%	70.37%	6.17%	3.7%	0%	2.46%	0%	0%
五色鳥	0%	0.91%	0%	0%	74.88%	0%	13.69%	0%	6.84%	3.65%
白耳畫眉	3.48%	0%	8.13%	0%	0%	76.74%	5.81%	5.81%	0%	0%
紅嘴黑鵯	0%	6.39%	0%	4.45%	8.28%	0%	68.78%	2.54%	15.92%	0%
紫嘯鶇	0%	0%	16%	0%	0%	8%	0%	76%	0%	0%
黃嘴角鴞	2.7%	13.51%	0%	9%	0%	7.2%	0%	0%	67.56%	0%
樹鵲	2.73%	0%	10.95%	0%	0%	0%	21.91%	0%	8.21%	56.16%

6.2.2　基於音高方法分析之鳥聲辨識結果

觀察現有鳥鳴聲資料庫，其基頻範圍介於 366 Hz 至 8591 Hz，對應音符為 66-120。基於音高分析之辨識結果如表 5，總辨識率為 72.09%。若僅觀察表中鳥鳴聲，僅有小彎嘴畫眉及五色鳥的辨識率高於 80%，其餘的鑑別度都頗低。

表 5　基於音高之鳥鳴聲辨識混淆矩陣。

	小卷尾	小啄木	小彎嘴	山紅頭	五色鳥	白耳畫眉	紅嘴黑鵯	紫嘯鶇	黃嘴角鴞	樹鵲
小卷尾	61.03%	19.48%	0%	10.38%	0%	5.19%	3.89%	0%	0%	0%
小啄木	2.94%	71.56%	12.74%	0%	1.96%	0%	3.92%	0%	2.94%	3.92%
小彎嘴	0%	7.74%	82.58%	0%	0%	0%	0%	7.74%	0%	1.93%
山紅頭	1.23%	0%	7.4%	75.3%	2.46%	1.23%	0%	0%	0%	0%
五色鳥	0%	1.36%	0%	1.82%	82.19%	0%	11.41%	0%	2.73%	0.45 %
白耳畫眉	0%	0%	11.62%	0%	0%	76.74%	5.81%	5.81%	0%	0%
紅嘴黑鵯	0%	6.36%	0%	2.54%	9.55%	0%	63.05%	2.54%	15.92%	0%
紫嘯鶇	0%	0%	4%	0%	12%	28%	0%	56%	0%	0%
黃嘴角鴞	7.2%	21.62%	5.4%	0%	0%	0.09%	0%	0%	64.86%	0%
樹鵲	5.4%	0%	8.21%	0%	0%	0%	24.65%	0%	2.73%	58.9%

6.2.3　將音色及音高方法結合後之鳥鳴聲辨識結果

如第 5 章介紹，我們將音色及音高兩種方法結合。在(11)式中，我們將 GMM 計算後的似然率 $\mathbf{P}\left(\mathbf{X}\,|\,\lambda_k^{(T)}\right)$ 及 Bigram 計算出的 $\mathbf{P}\left(\mathbf{O}\,|\,\lambda_k^{(P)}\right)$ 分別乘上 α 與 β 之權重，在本篇論文裡，α=0.6、β=0.4。

觀察表 6，結合後之鳴聲總辨識率達 75.04%。觀察表中鳥鳴聲之辨識率，小彎嘴畫眉、五色鳥、白耳畫眉及紫嘯鶇的辨識率皆高於 80%，且最低的辨識率也高於 60%。

表 6　整合音色、音高方法後之鳥鳴聲辨識混淆矩陣。

	小卷尾	小啄木	小彎嘴	山紅頭	五色鳥	白耳畫眉	紅嘴黑鵯	紫嘯鶇	黃嘴角鴞	樹鵲
小卷尾	67.53%	12.98%	0%	9.09%	0%	5.19%	2.59%	0%	2.59%	0%
小啄木	2.94%	75.49%	9.8%	0%	0.09%	0%	3.92%	0%	2.94%	3.92%
小彎嘴	0%	5.8%	85.16%	0%	0%	0%	0%	5.8%	0%	3.2%
山紅頭	1.23%	0%	6.17%	75.3%	2.46%	1.23%	0%	1.23%	0%	0%
五色鳥	0%	1.36%	0%	1.82%	83.1%	0%	9.13%	0%	3.19%	1.36%
白耳畫眉	0%	0%	10.46%	0%	0%	80.23%	4.65%	3.48%	0%	0%

紅嘴黑鵯	0%	6.36%	0%	1.27%	9.55%	0%	65.6%	1.27%	15.92%	0%
紫嘯鶇	0%	0%	4%	0%	4%	12%	0%	80%	0%	0%
黃嘴角鴞	7.2%	21.62%	5.4%	0%	0%	1.8%	0%	0%	63.96%	0%
樹鵲	4.1%	0%	5.47%	0%	0%	0%	21.91%	0%	2.73%	65.75%

7.結論與未來展望

本論文提出結合音色與音高線索來辨識鳥類鳴聲。實驗發現，當我們單獨用音色或音高線索來辨識十種鳥的鳴聲時，僅有 1 至 2 種鳥的鳴聲辨識率高於 80%；但若將兩種特徵結合後，將有 4 種鳥辨識率超過 80%，驗證結合使用音色及音高之方法能提升鳥鳴聲辨識效能。

由於受限於鳥鳴聲音檔的收集數量有限，所以本篇論文只挑選大台北地區常見的十種鳥種，對於系統的強健性和實用性還需要加入更多鳥種來驗證。相較於目前人聲辨識的成果來說，鳥鳴聲辨識系統還有極大的改進空間。

參考文獻

[1] S. E. Anderson, A. S. Dave, and D. Margoliash, "Template-based automatic recognition of birdsong syllables from continuous recordings," *J. Acoust. Soc. Amer.*, vol. 100, no. 2, pp. 1209–1219, Aug. 1996.

[2] J. Kogan and D. Margoliash, "Automated recognition of bird song elements from continuous recordings using dynamic time warping and hidden Markov models: A comparative study," *J. Acoust. Soc. Amer.*, vol. 103, no. 4, pp. 2187–2196, Apr. 1998.

[3] S. B. Davis and P. Mermelstein, "Comparison of Parametric Representations for Monosyllabic Word Recognition in Continuously Spoken Sentences," *IEEE Trans. on Acoustic, Speech and Signal Processing*., vol. 28, no. 4, pp. 357–366, Aug. 1980.

[4] X. Huang, A. Acero, and H. W. Hon, *Spoken Language Processing*, Prentice Hall, 2001.

[5] A. Ramalingam and S. Krishnan, "Gaussian Mixture Modeling of Short-Time Fourier Transform Features for Audio Fingerprinting," *IEEE Transactions on Information Forensics and Security*, 2006.

[6] D. Reynolds and T. Quatieri, "Speaker Verification Using Adapted Gaussian Mixture Models," *Digital Signal Processing 10*, PP. 19-41, 2000.

[7] M. Piszczalski and B. A. Galler, "Predicting musical pitch from component frequency ratios", *Journal of the Acoustical Society of America*, 66(3), pp.710—720, 1979.

使用分段式 GMM 及自動 GMM 挑選之語音轉換方法

A Voice Conversion Method Using Segmental GMMs and Automatic GMM Selection

古鴻炎 蔡松峰
Hung-Yan Gu Sung-Fung Tsai

國立台灣科技大學 資訊工程系
Department of Computer Science and Information Engineering
National Taiwan University of Science and Technology
{guhy, M9615069}@mail.ntust.edu.tw

摘要

本論文提出分段式(segmental)高斯混合模型(Gaussian mixture model, GMM)的觀念，用以改進語音轉換的效能，而爲了應用該觀念於線上(on-line)進行的語音轉換處理，我們也發展了一個基於動態規劃(dynamic programming, DP)之自動 GMM 挑選的演算法。此外，爲了使用單一高斯混合來對映(mapping)離散倒頻譜係數(discrete cepstrum coefficients, DCC)係數，我們也設計了一種高斯混合選取之演算法。關於分段式 GMM 觀念的評估，在此我們建造了三個採取不同功能組合之語音轉換系統，然後使用三個系統所轉換出的語音去作聽測實驗，實驗的結果顯示，分段式 GMM 之觀念確實可用以改進音色相似度(timbre similarity)、及語音品質(voice quality)兩方面的效能。

關鍵詞：語音轉換，離散倒頻譜，高斯混合模型，音色相似度，語音品質

一、緒論

以 GMM 爲基礎的語音轉換方法首先由 Stylianou 提出[1]，之後有許多研究者對這種方法的相關議題再作了更進一步的探討[2-5]，然而幾個棘手的問題至今仍然存在，其中一個最令人注意的是，經語音轉換得到的頻譜大多都會發生頻譜過度平滑化(over smoothing)的現象[2-4]，而使得轉換出的語音聽起來會有明顯的語音品質退化的感覺。此外，另一個也需要注意的問題是，當嘗試以最大加權值之混合來作單一高斯混合之頻譜對映時，某些相鄰音框的轉換出的頻譜，可能會發生頻譜不連續的問題，而使得轉換出的語音會時常聽到怪音(artifact sound)。

在本論文裡，我們嘗試以不同的方向來解決頻譜過度平滑的問題。在 GMM 爲基礎的語音轉換方法中，跨越多個(如 128 個)高斯混合作加權和(weighting sum)的運算，是導致過度平滑的一個重要原因。一個典型的基於 GMM 的對映函數，其公式如下[1]:

$$y = F(x;\mu,\Psi) = \sum_{m=1}^{M}\left[\frac{w_m \cdot N(x;\mu_m^x,\Psi_m^{xx})}{\sum_{m=1}^{M} w_m \cdot N(x;\mu_m^x,\Psi_m^{xx})}\left(\mu_m^y + \left(\Psi_m^{yx}\right)\cdot\left(\Psi_m^{xx}\right)^{-1}\cdot(x-\mu_m^x)\right)\right] \tag{1}$$

其中 x 表示來源語者的頻譜特徵向量，y 表示轉換後得到的頻譜特徵向量，M 是高斯混合 $N(\bullet, \bullet, \bullet)$的總數，而 μ 及 Ψ 分別表示平均向量與共變異矩陣的集合。爲了解決頻譜過度平滑之問題，我們認爲減少公式(1)中高斯混合的個數 M 是必需的，然而當直接減小 M 值時，訓練出的 GMM 所建構的機率密度函數必然會變得粗糙。因此，我們思考去對模型訓練的語句先作切割，使成爲一序列的語音片段，然後將這些語音片段作分類而分成數群，接著拿各群的語音音框分別去訓練出混合個數較少(如 16 個混合)的 GMM，而不同群的語音片段所訓練出的多個 GMM，將來就只從其中挑出一個 GMM 來對屬於同一分類的來源語音(source speech)音框作頻譜對映，如此，基於 GMM 的對映函數(如公式(1))就可使用較少的混合個數。也就是說原先一個複雜的 GMM 對映函數，現在被多個較簡單的 GMM 對映函數所取代了。

在本論文裡，我們探討國語(華語)之語音轉換，而國語是一個音節顯著的語言，因此我們決定以訓練語句裡所標示的各個音節作爲語音片段(segment)，如此一句話若有 7 個音節，就看成是由 7 個語音片段串接而成。再者，國語有 37 種不同的韻母，因此我們就依據韻母來把訓練語句的語音片段分成 37 群。由於我們使用的是平行語料，所以對於各群的平行語音片段，就可分別拿去訓練出一個對應的聯合(joint) GMM 模型，當訓練好 GMM 模型之後，就可拿這 37 個 GMM 模型去作線上的語音轉換處理。至於一個輸入的語音音框，應如何從這 37 個 GMM 中去挑選出一個正確的 GMM 來對它作頻譜轉換？對於這個問題，我們發展了一個以 DP 爲基礎的 GMM 自動挑選之演算法，該演算法將會在 3.1 節中詳細說明。

除了採取分段式的多個 GMM 來減少高斯混合的個數之外，我們更進一步採取單一高斯混合作對映的方法，來對來源語者的輸入音框作頻譜轉換，希望如此的組合式處理，能夠用以解決轉換出的頻譜包絡會變得過度平滑的問題。不過，當採取前述的組合式處理時，相鄰的兩個音框的轉換後頻譜，仍然可能發生頻譜不連續的情況，而導致怪音被產生出來。爲了避免發生頻譜不連續的情形，我們就嘗試設計一個基於 DP 的演算法，以便對一序列的音框作整體考量，即同時考慮各高斯混合被使用的似然率(likelihood)及其對頻譜連續性可能造成的危害，這個演算法的細節，我們將在 3.2 節中說明。依據前述提到的幾個作法，我們實際去製作出線上處理之語音轉換系統，然後使用這些系統轉換出的語音來作聽測實驗。

二、系統訓練階段

我們的語音轉換系統，在訓練階段的主要處理步驟如圖一所示。首先我們邀請了三位錄音者，分別到隔音錄音室來錄製 375 句之平行語料，取樣率設爲 22,050Hz，其中二位是男性，在此以 M1 和 M2 作代號，而另一位是女性，以 F1 作代號。在本研究裡，我們把 M1 當作來源語者，而把 M2 和 F1 分別作爲目標語者，也就是說我們要把 M1 的語音轉換成 M2 及 F1 的語音。

2.1 標音與分群

對於各個語者所錄的訓練語句，我們先操作 HTK (HMM tool kit)軟體，經由強制對齊(forced alignment)來作自動標音，把一個語句的各個音節的邊界標示出來。由於自動標記的音節邊界有很多是錯誤的，因此我們再操作 WaveSurfer 軟體，以人工檢查自動標記的音節邊界是否有錯，若發現錯誤則加以更正。然後，依據各音節的拼音符號標記及音節邊界標記，就可將一個訓練語句的各個音節的語音信號分別擷取、及存成獨立的音檔，再依語句編號、音節序號和音節拼音來命名該音檔。整體來說，375 個訓練語句可擷取出 2,926 個音節音檔。之後，作爲模型訓練之用的音節音檔，我們再依其檔名中的韻母拼音符號，將這些音節音檔分成 37 群。

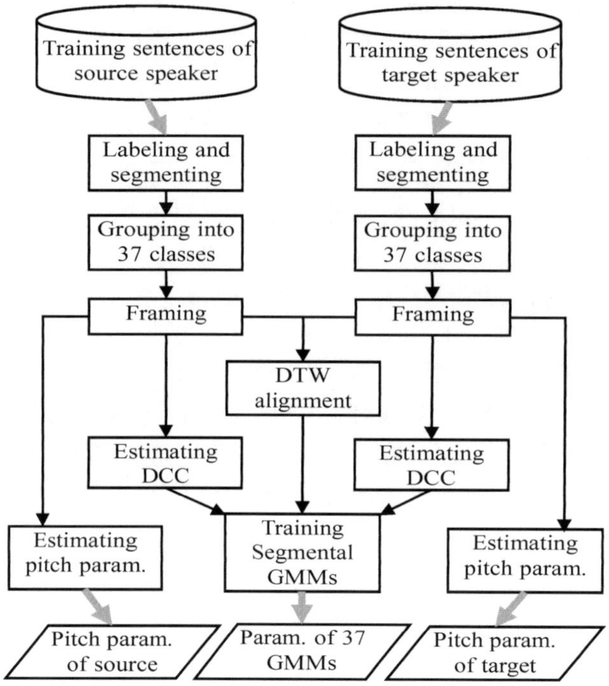

圖一、訓練階段之主要處理流程

2.2 DCC 係數計算

關於一個語音音框的振幅頻譜包絡(magnitude-spectrum envelope)的估計，過去已有一些方法被提出。雖然 STRAIGHT 法[12]可估計出相當準確的頻譜包絡，但是它需求的計算量也很大，而難以用於製作即時處理的系統。因此在本論文裡，我們採用離散倒頻譜之頻譜包絡估計方法[7, 8]，並且以離散倒頻譜係數(DCC)作爲頻譜參數。對於一個語音音框，我們使用先前發展的 DCC 估計程式[8]來計算出 40 維的 DCC 係數，在此一個音框的長度設爲 512 個樣本點(23.2ms)，而音框位移則設爲 110 個樣本點(5ms)。

2.3 分段式 GMM 之訓練

在圖一中經由方塊 "Grouping into 37 classes" 的處理之後，對於各群的音節片段，我們就分別拿去訓練出一個由 16 個高斯混合所形成的 GMM 模型，所以這樣得到的 37 個 GMM，就稱爲 37 個分段式 GMM。

由於我們使用的是平行語料，每一個來源語者音節和它對應的目標語音音節，可先以動態時間校正(dynamic time warping, DTW)作時間軸對齊的處理，這由圖一裡的 "DTW alignment" 方塊負責。然後，一個來源語音音框和它所對齊的目標語音音框，兩音框算出的 DCC 係數就可被合併成一個 80 維的頻譜特徵向量，接著我們使用基於 MLE (maximum likelihood estimate)的GMM訓練方法[9]，來對各群合併後DCC向量進行MLE訓練，如此就可得到各群的聯合機率密度之 GMM 模型。

2.4 音高參數

我們使用一種基於自相關函數及AMDF (absolute magnitude difference function)的基週偵測方法[10]，來偵測各音框的音高頻率，然後將一個語者發音中有聲(voiced)音框偵測出的音高頻率值收集起來，據以求出他們的平均值及標準差，這就是我們所需要的音高參數。

三、語音轉換階段

我們研究的語音轉換方法，其主要的處理流程如圖二所示。當一句未知內容的語句輸入後，它首先會被切割成一序列的音框，而音框長度(512 點)和位移(110 點)則和 2.2 節裡使用的一樣。然後，在圖二的左邊流程，會對各音框的音高頻率作偵測，當一個音框被偵測爲無聲時，圖二中的三個灰色方塊就被直接跳過，也就是不需作音高頻率的調整，且 DCC 頻譜參數也未被轉換。相對地當一個音框被偵測爲有聲時，我們在此採用一種簡便的音高調整公式來調整音高頻率，

$$q_t = \mu^y + \frac{\sigma^y}{\sigma^x}(p_t - \mu^x) \tag{2}$$

其中 p_t 表示偵測出的音高頻率值，μ^x 和 σ^x 分別表示來源語者的音高頻率平均值和標準查，而 μ^y 和 σ^y 是目標語者的。

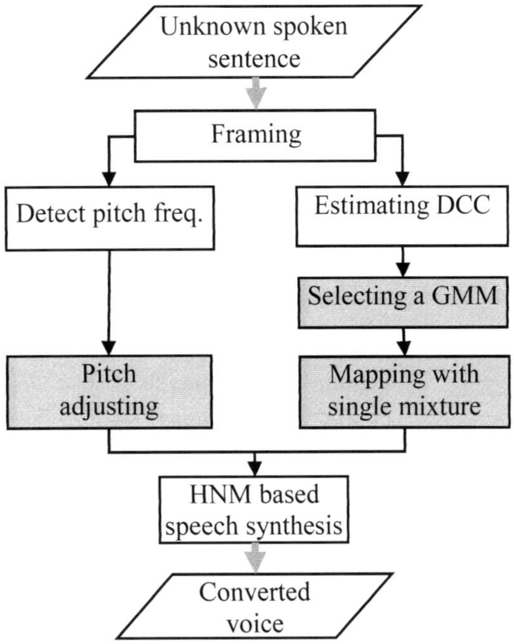

圖二、轉換階段之主要處理流程

在圖二裡的右邊流程，基本上是一個音框接著一個音框來作處理，但是在 “Selecting a GMM” 之方塊裡，我們提出一種 GMM 自動挑選之演算法，該演算法是以每 20 個有聲音框爲一個批次(batch)來作 GMM 的挑選，以便爲各個有聲音框從 37 個 GMM 中選出正確的(或鄰近的)一個 GMM。之後，在 “Mapping with single mixture” 之方塊裡，我們再從一個音框所選取到的 GMM 裡，選取出一個高斯混合來作單一高斯混合之 DCC 係數對映，以便避免頻譜曲線過度平滑的情形發生。不過，我們不能只依據加權值的大小來分別爲各個音框挑選出單一個高斯混合，因爲相鄰音框的轉換後頻譜的連續性也必需被考慮，以避免怪音被產生出來。對於單一高斯混合選取的問題，我們也發展了一個基於 DP 的演算法，該演算法和前人提出的[4]不一樣，基本上是把一序列的有聲音框(左、右兩邊被無聲音框包夾)，當作一個批次來作單一高斯混合選取的處理。接著在圖二裡左右流程合併之方塊 ”HNM based speech synthesis”，我們使用一個基於 HNM (harmonic plus noise model)的信號合成方法[8, 11]，去依據轉換出的 DCC 係數及音高頻譜，把語音信號再合成出來。

3.1 分段 GMM 之選取方法

對於一個線上處理的語音轉換系統來說，輸入語音的說話內容是事先不知道的，因此當要對一個音框的 DCC 係數作對映時，我們如何知道 37 個 GMM 當中的那一個應被選取?這樣的問題必須先被解決，而該問題是一種語音辨識的問題，不過它不需要像語音辨識那樣嚴厲地被對待，因爲選取到錯誤但近似的 GMM 是可以容忍的。

在語音辨識領域，隱藏式馬可夫模型(hidden Markov model, HMM)是最常被採用的統計模型，不過在此我們希望以所訓練出的 37 個 GMM 來取代 HMM 的角色，如此就不需另外去訓練 HMM。此外，我們觀察到一個非常接近真實的現象是，一個人不可能在一個很短暫的時間如 100ms 之內，發出多於 2 個的語音片段，在此語音片段指的是音節。所以，我們決定把每 20 個連續的有聲音框(含蓋 100ms 之時間範圍)作爲一個批次，去作 20 個音框整批的 GMM 選取之處理，如此一個批次裡就只需選出一個或二個的 GMM。本論文研發了一個 DP 爲基礎的 GMM 挑選之演算法，該演算法會依據最大似然率(maximum likelihood)去選出一個或二個 GMM。

令第 t 個輸入音框的 DCC 係數是由第 s 個 GMM 所產生的機率是 $G_t(s)$，其詳細計算公式爲

$$G_t(s) = \sum_{m=1}^{M} w_m(s) \cdot N\left(x_t;\ \mu_m^x(s),\ \Psi_m^{xx}(s)\right) , \tag{3}$$

其中 $W_m(s)$表示第 m 個高斯混合的加權，x_t 表示第 t 個音框的 DCC 向量。此外，令 $R(t, s)$表示從時刻 1 到時刻 t 的音框都是由第 s 個 GMM 所產生的似然率對數值，而令 $D(t, s)$表示從時刻 1 到時刻 t 的音框是由 2 個 GMM 所產生，並且第 t 個音框是由第 s 個 GMM 所產生的似然率對數值。依據前述的定義，我們可以推導出如下的兩個遞迴公式:

$$R(t,s) = \log\left(G_t(s)\right) + R(t-1,s) , \tag{4}$$

$$D(t,s) = \log\left(G_t(s)\right) + \max\left\{ \max_{0 \le v < 37,\, v \ne s} \left[R(t-1,v)\right],\ D(t-1,s) \right\}, \tag{5}$$

其所需設定的邊界值是，$D(1, s)$=0 和 $R(1, s)$=$G_1(s)$，s=0, 1, ..., 36。接著，依據公式(4)

和(5)，我們可得到 T 個音框整體的最大似然率爲

$$A(T)=\max\left\{\max_{0\le v<37}\left[R(T,v)\right],\ \max_{0\le v<37}\left[D(T,v)\right]\right\}\ , \tag{6}$$

其中 T 在本論文裡設爲 20。在依據公式(4)，(5)和(6)得到 $A(20)$ 之最大似然率數值之後，我們可作回溯(backtrack)處理，去找出 $A(20)$ 數值的最佳行走路徑，而得到 20 個音框各自所被指派的 GMM 編號。

3.2 單一高斯混合之對映

所謂使用單一高斯混合來對映一個輸入音框的 DCC 係數，其實際作法是把公式(1)裡的累加符號及加權項移除，如此轉換出的 DCC 向量 y 就變成以下列公式來計算，

$$y=F^{k}(x)=\mu_{k}^{y}+\left(\Psi_{k}^{yx}\right)\cdot\left(\Psi_{k}^{xx}\right)^{-1}\cdot(x-\mu_{k}^{x})\ , \tag{7}$$

其中 x 表示輸入音框的 DCC 係數，$F^{k}(x)$ 表示使用第 k 個高斯混合所建立的對映函數。

關於公式(7)裡 k 值(即高斯混合之編號)的選取的問題，我們設計了一個基於 DP 的高斯混合選取之演算法。首先令 3.1 節中爲第 t 個音框自動挑出之 GMM 編號爲 $I(t)$，接著以 $F_{I(t)}^{k}(x_t)$ 表示使用第 k 個高斯混合來對第 t 個音框之 DCC 向量 x_t 作對映，此外以 $C(t, k)$ 表示從時刻 1 到時刻 t 的累積距離，但是限定在時刻 t 時使用編號爲 k 的高斯混合，如此我們設計的遞迴公式就可寫成

$$C(t,k)=\min_{\substack{0\le m<M,\\ w_m(I(t-1))>H}}\left[dist\left(F_{I(t)}^{k}(x_t),F_{I(t-1)}^{m}(x_{t-1})\right)+C(t-1,m)\right]\ , \tag{8}$$

其中 $dist(\bullet,\ \bullet)$ 表示對兩 DCC 向量之間作幾何距離的量測，H 是一個門檻參數，我們依經驗設定它的值爲 0.3，而 $W_m(I(t\text{-}1))$ 表示第 $I(t\text{-}1)$ 個 GMM 的第 m 個混合的加權。

公式(8)的意義是，在各個時刻 t 先依 $W_m(I(t)) > H$ 之條件篩選出加權夠大的幾個高斯混合，然後從各時刻篩選出的高斯混合中，以 DP 的觀念去串接出行走的路徑，最後在結束的時刻 T 時，以下列公式找出最小的累積距離 $B(T)$，

$$B(T)=\min_{0\le k<M,\ w_k(I(T))>H}\left[C(T,k)\right]\ , \tag{9}$$

所以依據公式(8)和(9)，我們可求得最小的累積距離，然後經由回溯的程序找出行走的路徑，如此就可決定時刻 1 到時刻 T 各個音框所應選取的高斯混合。至於公式(8)裡 $C(t, k)$ 在 t=0 時的邊界數值，我們可直接設定成 $C(0, k)$=0，$0 \le k < M$。

3.3 基於 HNM 之語音信號合成

在諧波加雜音模型(harmonic plus noise model，HNM)中，一個有聲音框的頻譜被分割成低頻的諧波部分和高頻的雜音部分，而分割這兩部分的邊界頻率稱爲最大有聲頻率(maximum voiced frequency，MVF)。關於 MVF 值的偵測，在 Stylianou 的博士論文裡[11]，提出了一個對各個音框逐一作偵測的方法，不過爲了簡化語音信號合成處理的程序，在此我們把各個有聲音框的 MVF 值都直接設爲 6,000Hz。

假設第 i 和第 i+1 個音框都是有聲的，並且分別有 L^i 和 L^{i+1} 個諧波成分(harmonic partials)，L^i 的值以 MVF / q_i 作計算，q_i 表示第 i 個音框的轉換過的基頻值。當要對這兩個音框之間的第 t 個樣本點產生出信號樣本值，首先我們以線性內插來計算第 t 個樣本點上的各個諧波成分的頻率值 $f_k(t)$ 和振幅值 $a_k(t)$ ，計算方式如公式(10)所示，

$$
\begin{aligned}
f_k(t) &= f_k^i + \frac{f_k^{i+1} - f_k^i}{N} \cdot t, \quad k = 1,2,...,L, \\
a_k(t) &= a_k^i + \frac{a_k^{i+1} - a_k^i}{N} \cdot t, \quad k = 1,2,...,L
\end{aligned}
\tag{10}
$$

其中 N 表示兩相鄰音框之間的樣本點總數(在此設爲 110，即音框位移的點數)，L 表示 L^i 和 L^{i+1} 兩者的較大值，此外 f_k^i 和 a_k^i 分別表示第 i 個音框的第 k 的諧波成分的頻率值和振幅值，f_k^i 可以 $f_k^i = k \times q_i$ 作計算，而 a_k^i 則必需依據第 i 個音框對映得到的 DCC 係數，轉換成頻譜包絡後再去求取它的數值，關於 a_k^i 數值求取的細節請參考我們先前發表的論文[8]。另外，如果 L^i 小於 L^{i+1}，我們就直接設定 $a_k^i = 0$，$k = L^i + 1, \ ..., \ L^{i+1}$。然後，第 t 個樣本點上的諧波信號 $h(t)$就可以公式(11)來作計算，

$$
\begin{aligned}
h(t) &= \sum_{k=1}^{L} a_k(t) \cdot \cos(\phi_k(t)), \quad 0 \le t < N, \\
\phi_k(t) &= \phi_k(t-1) + 2\pi \cdot f_k(t) / 22,050
\end{aligned}
\tag{11}
$$

其中 $\phi_k(t)$ 表示第 k 個諧波成分在樣本點 t 時的累積相位，22,050 是取樣率。至於 $\phi_k(t)$ 的初值 $\phi_k(-1)$ ，我們可令它等於前一個音框最後一個樣本點時的累積相位(即 $\phi_k(N-1)$)，以保持相位的連續性。如果本音框是第一個音框(即沒有前一個音框)，則可令 $\phi_k(-1)$ 的值爲一個隨機值，使用隨機值是符合語音信號特性的。

四、實驗評估

爲了評估所提出的轉換方法，我們建造了三個語音轉換系統，分別以 SOG，SSG 和 SLG 作爲代號，在代號 SOG (system using original GMM for mapping)的系統裡，我們使用 350 個訓練語句來訓練出一個由 256 個高斯混合形成的 GMM，然後使用公式(1)來對各個輸入音框的 DCC 係數作對映。另外，在代號 SSG (system using single Gaussian mixture for mapping)的系統裡，我們仍然使用 350 個語句所訓練出的一個具有 256 個高斯混合的 GMM，不過在轉換階段，3.2 節裡說明的高斯混合選取方法被用來爲一序列的輸入音框選取出各音框的單一高斯混合，然後各輸入音框的 DCC 係數就使用所選出的單一高斯混合及公式(7)來作對映。至於在代號 SLG (system using selected GMM for mapping)的系統裡，我們首先以 350 個語句來訓練出 37 個分段式 GMM，而各分段式 GMM 都只有 16 個高斯混合，然後在轉換階段，我們採用 3.1 節裡說明的 GMM 選取方法，來爲每 20 個有聲音框選取出最大似然率的一個或兩個分段 GMM，接著採用 3.2 節裡的高斯混和選取方法，來爲各輸入音框選取出單一個高斯混合，再依據公式(7)作對映。

當把一個來源語者的發音檔，分別輸入到前述的三個語音轉換系統，我們就可得到三個轉換出語音檔。然後使用轉換出的音檔，我們進行了兩種類型的聽測實驗，分別是音色相似度之聽測、和語音品質之聽測。在這二類型的聽測實驗裡，我們都邀請了 25 位人士來聆聽音檔並給予相對分數，而在這 25 位人士中，有 20 位是不熟悉語音轉換之研究的。

4.1 音色相似度測試

首先我們準備了 5 個音檔，它們的代號分別是 VS(由來源語者發音)，VT(由目標語者發音)，VX1(經由 SOG 系統轉換得到)，VX2(經由 SSG 系統轉換得到)，VX3(經由 SLG 系統轉換得到)，其中 VS 與 VT 具有相同的說話內容，而 VX1、VX2 和 VX3 三者也有相同的內容，但不同於 VS 和 VT 的，這 5 個音檔可從網頁 http://guhy.csie.ntust.edu.tw/VoiceConv/去下載。在進行聽測實驗時，我們以 ABX 的次序來撥放前述的音檔，在此 A 固定爲 VS，B 固定爲 VT，而 X 則隨機由 VX1、VX2 和 VX3 三者中選出，每次以 ABX 次序播放完音檔後，受測者就被要求給一個分數。在此分數的定義是，9 分(或 1 分)表示 X 的音色確定就是 B(或 A)的音色，7 分(或 3 分)表示 X 的音色比較接近 B(或 A)的音色，而 5 分表示 X 的音色無法判斷是接近 A 或接近 B。

做完聽測實驗之後，25 位受測者所給的分數被用來計算出三個系統各自的平均分數(AVG)和標準差(STD)，所得到的分數數值就如表 1 所列出的。由表一的平均分數可知，不同性別之間的語音轉換(即從 M1 到 F1)，會比同性別之間的(即從 M1 到 M2)獲得明顯較高的分數。此外，拿三個系統的平均分數作比較，可從表一的數值得知，SLG 系統的表現明顯比 SSG 系統的好許多(7.05 vs 6.24，7.60 vs 7.24)，而 SSG 系統的表現則是比 SOG 系統的稍微好一些(6.24 vs 6.08，7.24 vs 6.92)。所以本論文提出的分段式 GMM 之觀念及自動 GMM 挑選之演算法，的確可幫忙改進所轉換出語音的音色相似度。

表一、音色相似度聽測之平均分數與標準差

		SOG	SSG	SLG
M1=>M2	AVG	6.08	6.24	7.05
	STD	1.11	1.09	0.93
M1=>F1	AVG	6.92	7.24	7.60
	STD	1.13	1.07	1.10

4.2 語音品質測試

在此我們使用三個系統轉換出的語音檔 VX1、VX2 和 VX3，來進行語音品質的聽測實驗。音檔撥放的次序爲 AX，A 固定設爲 VX1，而 X 則隨機由 VX2 和 VX3 兩者中取出，每次以 AX 次序播放完音檔後，受測者就被要求給一個分數。在此分數的定應是，9 分(或 1 分)表示 X 的語音品質明顯比 A 的好(或差)，7 分(或 3 分)表示 X 的品質比 A 的稍微好(或差)一些，5 分則表示 X 和 A 的語音品質無法分辨優劣。

作完聽測實驗之後，我們收集 25 位受測者所給的分數，來計算出 SSG 和 SLG 兩系統各自的平均分數和標準差，結果得到的數值如表二裡列出的。依據表二的平均分數可看出，同性別之間(即從 M1 到 M2)的轉換語音的品質，會比不同性別之間(即從 M1 到 F1)

的較好約 0.5 分，這顯示不同性別之間的轉換語音的品質，是比較難作改進的。此外，依據 SLG 和 SSG 兩系統的平均分數作比較，我們可看出 SLG 的分數都比 SSG 的高約 0.7 分，並且 SLG 的平均分數都高於 5 分，所以分段式 GMM 之觀念及自動挑選 GMM 之演算法，確實可用以改進所轉換出語音的語音品質。

表二、語音品質聽測之平均分數與標準差

		SSG vs SOG	SLG vs SOG
M1=>M2	AVG	5.23	6.04
	STD	1.43	1.45
M1=>F1	AVG	4.89	5.55
	STD	1.50	1.47

4.3 倒頻譜距離量測

在所錄音的 375 句平行語料中，最後 25 句並未被用於訓練 GMM 模型，因此這 25 句來源語者發音的語音檔，在此就分別被輸入到三個語音轉換系統 SOG、SSG 和 SLG，去作語音轉換的處理，以便量測轉換出語音和目標語音(目標語者發音)之間的倒頻譜距離，用以作爲轉換後頻譜和目標頻譜之間的接近程度的客觀量測。

對於轉換出的語音音檔的每一個有聲音框，我們先依先前作 DTW 時間對齊的資料，來找出目標語者發音檔中對應的音框，然後將兩對應音框的 DCC 係數，拿去計算幾何距離，接著再依所有有聲音框量測到的距離去計算出平均距離，結果對於三個語音轉換系統，我們計算出的平均距離就如表三裡所列出的。

表三、轉換後語音的平均倒頻譜距離

	SOG	SSG	SLG
M1=>M2	0.543	0.609	0.601
M1=>F1	0.598	0.634	0.612

依據表三列出的數值，可發現 SOG 系統會得到最小的平均距離，然而由聽測實驗的結果可知，SOG 系統在音色相似度方面是最差的，並且在語音品質方面也是比 SLG 系統差，如此的不一致性，其原因應是公式(1)裡的加權和運算，會導致於對映出的頻譜變得過度平滑化，而造成音質變差。另一方面，SLG 系統比起 SSG 系統所表現出的效能改進，則是有反應在所量測出的平均距離上，SLG 比 SSG 多增加了選取分段式 GMM 之處理步驟。

4.4 分段 GMM 選取之例子

當我們使用 3.1 節的方法，來爲有聲的音框序列挑選似然率最高的分段 GMM 時，有時會發生挑錯 GMM 的情況，一個例子如圖三所示，此音框序列爲/song-4/ (“送”)的發音，第一欄數字表示音框的編號，第二欄數字表示各音框偵測出的音高，第三欄數字表示各音框的對數能量值,第四欄資料則是我們的演算法爲各音框所挑選出的分段 GMM(以對應的韻母表示)。觀察第四欄的 GMM 挑選結果可以發現，在音框編號 543 時會發生韻母的切換，從韻母/ong/ (/ㄨㄥ/) 切換到韻母 /eng/ (/ㄥ/)，但是正確的答案應是不切換韻母的，即此序列的音框都要挑選到韻母/ong/。不過這兩個韻母(/ong/與/eng/)的發音，其共同點是具有相同的韻尾音素/ng/，所以我們認爲類似圖三的韻母挑選節果是可以接受的。

Frame	Pitch	Energy	Vowel
526	0	58.99	
527	0	56.65	
528	185	63.61	ong
529	185	67.59	ong
530	182	70.43	ong
531	170	71.34	ong
532	165	70.41	ong
533	160	70.83	ong
534	156	71.16	ong
535	149	70.57	ong
536	146	69.66	ong
537	141	68.95	ong
538	136	67.60	ong
539	130	64.12	ong
540	128	64.08	ong
541	125	63.74	ong
542	121	62.00	ong
543	116	61.37	eng
544	113	60.39	eng
545	113	59.01	eng
546	164	58.54	eng
547	164	56.07	eng
548	135	50.28	eng
549	0	51.49	
550	0	47.81	

圖三、語音/song-4/的有聲音框之 GMM 挑選情形

五、結論

依據聽測實驗的結果，我們可說 SLG 系統是三個系統之中效能最好的，不管是在音色相似度、還是在語音品質上都表現得最好，因此 SLG 系統所採用的處理方法，即本論文提出的分段式 GMM 之觀念及自動 GMM 挑選之演算法，經由聽測實驗的驗證，的確可用以改進 GMM 爲基礎的語音轉換機制。另一方面，依據客觀量測出的平均倒頻譜距離，可知使用原始 GMM 轉換方法之 SOG 系統，仍然可得到三個系統中最小的平均距離，不過 SOG 系統轉換出的語音，在音色相似度上卻是表現最差的，並且在語音品質上也是比 SLG 系統的差。目前我們僅根據韻母來作語音的分段與分群，將來可再考慮把有聲聲母(如/m/, /n/, /l/)的部分獨立切成語音段，這樣應可進一步改進語音轉換的效能。

參考文獻

[1] Y. Stylianou, O. Cappe, and E. Moulines, "Continuous probabilistic transform for voice conversion," *IEEE trans. Speech and Audio Processing*, vol. 6, no. 2, pp.131–142.1998.

[2] T. Toda, H. Saruwatari, and K. Shikano, "Voice conversion algorithm based on Gaussian

mixture model with dynamic frequency warping of STRAIGHT Spectrum," *Int. Conf. Acoust., Speech, and Signal Processing*, Salt Lake City, pp. 841-844, 2001.

[3] T. Toda and A. W. Black and K. Tokuda, "Voice conversion based on maximum-likelihood estimation of spectral parameter trajectory," *IEEE trans. Audio, Speech, and Language Processing*, vol. 15, no. 8, pp. 2222-2235, 2007.

[4] Z. H. Jian and Z. Yang, "Voice Conversion Using Viterbi algorithm based on Gauaaian mixture model", *Int. Symposium on Intelligent Signal Processing and Communication Systems*, pp. 32-35, Xiamen, China, 2007.

[5] Z. Yue, X. Zou, Y. Jia, and H. Wang, "Voice conversion using HMM combined with GMM", *2008 Congress on Image and Signal Processing*, Sanya, China, pp. 366-370, 2008.

[6] E. Godoy, O. Rosec, and T. Chonavel, "Alleviating the one-to-many mapping problem in voice conversion with context-dependent modeling", *Proc. INTERSPEECH*, pp. 1627-1630, Brighton, UK, 2009.

[7] O. Cappé and E. Moulines, "Regularization techniques for discrete cepstrum estimation," *IEEE Signal Processing Letters*, vol. 3, no. 4, pp. 100-102, 1996.

[8] H. Y. Gu and S. F. Tsai, "A discrete-cepstrum based spectrum-envelope estimation scheme and its example application of voice transformation," *International Journal of Computational Linguistics and Chinese Language Processing*, vol. 14, no. 4, pp. 363-382, 2009.

[9] R. A. Redner and H. F. Walker, "Mixture densities, maximum likelihood and the EM algorithm," *SIAM Review*, vol. 26, no. 2, pp. 195-239, 1984.

[10] H. Y. Kim, et al., "Pitch detection with average magnitude difference function using adaptive threshold algorithm for estimating shimmer and jitter," 20-th Annual *Int. Conf. of the IEEE Engineering in Medicine and Biology Society*, Hong Kong, China, 1998.

[11] Y. Stylianou, *Harmonic plus noise models for speech, combined with statistical methods, for speech and speaker modification*, Ph.D. thesis, Ecole Nationale Supèrieure des Télécommunications, Paris, France, 1996.

[12] H. Kawahara, I. Masuda-katsuse, and A. De. Cheveign, "Restructuring speech representations using a pitch-adaptive time-frequency smoothing and an instantaneous-frequency-based F0 extraction: possible role of a repetitive structure in sounds," *Speech Communication*, vol. 27, pp. 187-207, 1999.

應用詞彙、語法與語料規則於中文手寫句辨識之校正模組

Revision for Recognizing Chinese Handwritten Sentences Based on Lexical, Syntactical and Corpus Rules

張道行 Tao-Hsing Chang
周嘉彬 Chia-Bin Chou
蘇守彥 Shou-Yen Su
國立高雄應用科技大學 資訊工程系
Department of Computer Science and Information Engineering
National Kaohsiung University of Applied Sciences
changth@cc.kuas.edu.tw
papperkut@hotmail.com
shouyen@gmail.com

劉建良 Chien-Liang Liu
國立臺灣師範大學 資訊工程學系
Department of Computer Science and Information Engineering
National Taiwan Normal University
clliu@mail.nctu.edu.tw

摘要

離線手寫中文文字辨識有使用者書寫字跡的變異和文字書寫字體不明顯等問題，造成辨識系統難以辨識其特徵而影響正確性。本論文的研究目的是利用特定領域主題語料中呈現的詞彙、語法及語料規則提高離線手寫中文文字辨識率。本文提出了一個三階段方法來達成目標。首先、利用詞彙優先概念，從候選字中挑選語料庫中的詞彙為辨識結果。第二、查看候選字中是否出現特定的文法組合，並以該組合的候選文字為辨識結果。第三、將剩下相鄰兩個未決定的候選字集組成字串，並和事先由語料庫所產生收錄的雙字組比對，若候選字中存在雙字組則以做為辨識結果。實驗結果顯示本文所提方法可有效的提高辨識率，由單一字頻決定法的 0.45 提升至 0.85。

Abstract

Recognition of off-line handwritten Chinese character had been an important problem. Because of the variation and vagueness derived from different users' handwritings, it was hard to recognize handwriting characters via statistical features obtained from database. The purpose of this study is to use lexical, syntactical and corpus rules for increasing the accuracy mentioned above. Our methods could be divided into three phases. First, we used lexical rule "multi-syllable words priority" to predict some characters of a sentence from candidate characters. Second, neighbor several candidate characters in which particular grammar patterns appear will be treated as the characters of the sentence. Finally, two adjacent candidate characters will be regarded as a string. The strings which occur in a corpus frequently will be used to be the characters of the sentence. To contrast approach "highest frequency priority", experimental results shown that the accurate rate of Chinese handwriting character recognition could be effectively increased from 0.45 to 0.85.

關鍵詞：中文手寫辨識，離線辨識，詞彙規則，語法規則，語料規則

Keywords: Handwritten Chinese character recognition, offline recognition, lexical rules, syntactic rules, corpus rules. .

一、緒論

由於資訊科技發展，許多文件都有數位檔案的版本供資訊系統擷取使用。而如何將傳統紙張文件回溯建立可辨識內容的數位文件檔案，成為重要的問題，因為若以人工手動輸入方式將資料輸入建檔，將耗費龐大的人力和時間成本。因此許多研究提出自動轉換傳統紙張文件為數位資料的方法，其中文字辨識(Character Recognition)是自動辨識文件內容的解決方法之一。文字辨識技術主要可分成兩類：一為即時文字辨識(On Line Character Recognition , OLCR)，二為光學文字辨識(Optical Character Recognition , OCR)。即時文字辨識採用手寫過程的時間序列特性，主要用於即時的手寫輸入文字辨識。光學文字辨識則是一種離線(Off-line)文字辨識的方式，適合已存在之文件的後續數位化處理。

光學文字辨識的處理流程大略分成五個程序[8]：首先，文字文件影像輸入，將文字文件以影像檔案方式儲存。第二，影像前處理。將影像檔案做二值化、細線化、文字切割、正規化等，此階段會產生單一字的字元影像，並利用一些方法消除同字的外形變異以及影像失真所造成辨識錯誤。第三，特徵擷取。擷取影像特徵並記錄做為辨識的依據。第四，分類器與辨識模型。先經由分類器學習將已知字元影像正確分類至所屬文字，再透過辨識模型將先前記錄的字元影像特徵與分類器進行運算，找出最相似的文字。第五，輸出文字辨識結果。

其中分類器與辨識模型程序雖然已有許多不同的辨識方法[7][9][10]被提出，但由於大多採單一字元候選字機率最高者為結果的基本架構，因此仍會有發生辨識錯誤的可能。若是能利用詞彙、語法或語意關係等語言線索，設計一個有效的校正模組，或許可以進一步提升傳統文字辨識系統的效能。例如以傳統辨識模組辨識「今天」兩個手寫字，並假設辨識模組對每個字元影像都會產生三個較可能的候選字元。其中第一個影像辨識結果依機率高低分別為「金」、「今」、「會」。而第二個影像辨識結果分別為「天」、「大」、「夫」。傳統辨識模組會根據各字元最可能的候選字選出「金」和「天」。但若從詞彙的角度來看，則僅只有「今天」這組字元組合是有意義的詞彙。這說明了若運用像詞彙這類的語言線索，應可進一步提升傳統文字辨識系統的效能。

許多研究也提出類似的觀點用於提高辨識效果或是校正錯別字的方法。[1]提出一套兩階段手寫中文辨識系統，其在第二階段以一個上下文後處理器修正第一階段候選字選取的結果。[2]則提出一個判別正確字的設計來改善印刷體中文字辨識結果，這個設計主要利用詞語訊息來判別正確字是否包含在候選字集內。[3]提出一個方法來更正文件中的錯誤字，主要是利用在主題文章中某些詞彙會有重覆出現的特性(例如：主題為學校時，經常會出現學生、教室、老師…等詞彙)，更正錯誤字。[4]則發表一個錯別字偵錯與訂正建議的系統，可偵測文章中的錯誤字。

本文的基本假設是，在特定主題語料中，某些文字相鄰出現的情況相當頻繁，因此

二字元之 OCR 影像產生的候選字元可兩兩配對，由每一配對在語料中所出現的機率、或是其語法規則的合理性，可推測正確的結果。因此，本文將提出一個三階段方法，分別運用詞彙規則、語法規則與語料規則，自傳統辨識模組提供的候選字中挑選正確的字。在第一階段中，我們利用詞彙規則從可能的字元組合中挑選詞彙庫出現的詞彙做為挑選字。接著針對在第一階段中未確認的字元影像序列，尋找是否出現符合語法規則的詞性組合，並以該詞性組合所對應的字元組合作為對應字元影像的挑選字。最後針對兩個相鄰未確認的候選位置，形成一組字元組合，而以在語料中共發生機率最高的字元組合作為對應候選位置的挑選字。

二、系統架構

圖一為本論文所提方法的架構圖。首先，每一處理句內的每個字元影像會有一個代表正確字的空間，稱為候選位置，例如一個句子經掃描分析後有八個字元影像，則表示該句有八個候選位置。接著對每個候選位置都會產生一組候選字集，也就是該字元影像經辨識後產生的候選字集合。這些候選字集將先使用詞彙規則來進行詞彙挑選。詞彙規則是藉由詞彙庫提供詞彙，並以符合規則的字元組合作為對應候選位置的系統解。接著使用語法規則來找出符合規則的詞性組合，並以符合規則之詞性組合所對應的字元組合做為對應候選位置的系統解。最後使用語料規則挑選雙字組。雙字組是從語料庫中所擷取並收錄於雙字組資料庫，因此存在於雙字組資料庫的字元組合做為對應候選位置的系統解。經由三個規則的挑選流程後，最後若有候選位置仍無法確認系統解，則以語料字頻決定。經由上述流程處理，各候選位置均產生系統解，也就是每個字元影像都有系統所判斷的對應字。

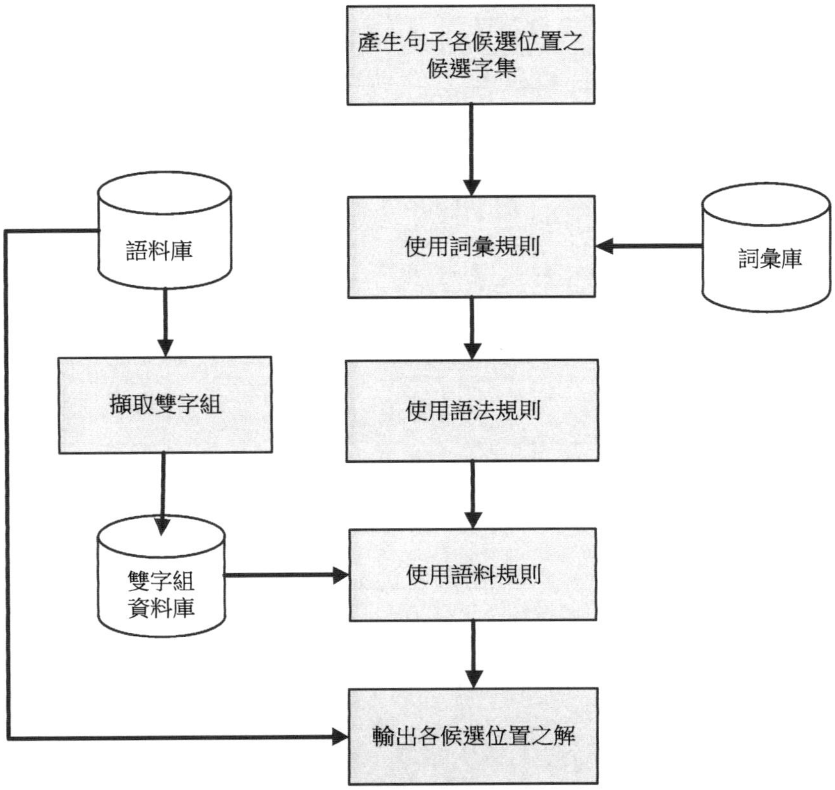

圖一、系統架構圖

三、規則使用

（一） 詞彙規則

由相鄰候選位置之候選字集內的字元產生各種字元組合，再將所有的字元組合與詞彙庫中的詞彙進行比對，若有字元組合與詞彙相同，則將此字元組合作為對應之候選位置解。此方法我們稱為詞彙規則。圖二說明如何運用詞彙規則可以找出數個連續相鄰位置的解。

圖二以一個包含七個字元影像的句子為例，有七個候選位置及其所屬候選字集，依序分別為 C1、C2、...至 C7，且假設每個候選字集內皆有六個候選字元。候選位置 W1 的候選字集 C1＝｛我、率、重、白、交、日｝，候選位置 W2 的候選字集 C2＝｛時、企、打、非、季、吃｝，以此類推。首先根據詞彙規則，在候選位置 W2 與候選位置 W3 兩個相鄰候選位置中，將 C1 與 C2 兩個相鄰候選字集內的候選字元形成 36 組字元組合，並將這 36 組字元組合與詞彙庫中的二字詞彙進行比對。在,這些字元組合中，僅有字元組「打算」可在詞彙庫中找到，因此候選位置 W2 的解為「打」、而候選位置 W3 的解為「算」。另外，根據詞彙規則，在候選字集 C5、C6、及 C7 三個相鄰候選字集中，可將相鄰的候選字元形成 216 組字元組合，並將兩百十六組字元組合與詞彙庫中的三字詞彙進行比對。在這些字元組合中，僅只有字元組「籃球場」可在詞彙庫中找到。因此分別將「籃」「球」「場」做為候選位置 W5、W6、及 W7 的解。

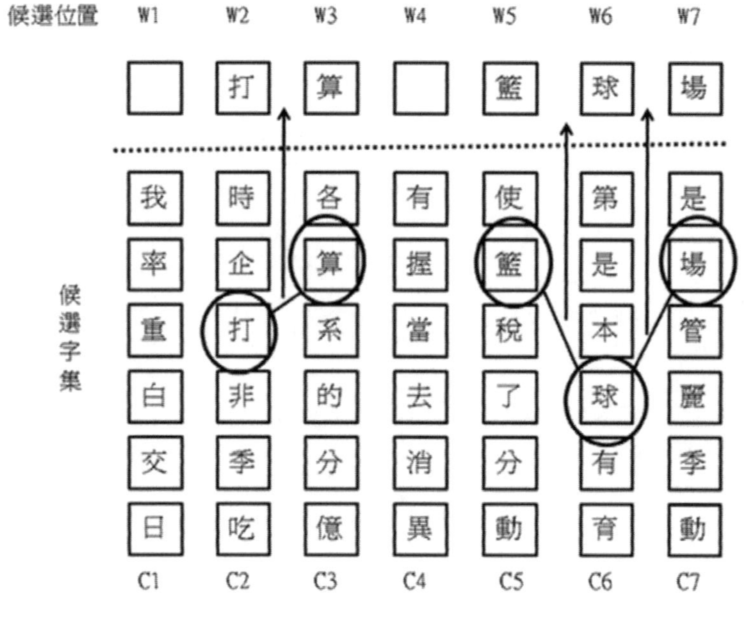

圖二、詞彙規則範例

由圖二可以發現，根據詞彙規則，可在 C5、C6 及 C7 三個相鄰候選字集挑出三字詞「籃球場」，也可在 C5 及 C6 挑出二字詞「籃球」。其中，「籃球」與「籃球場」皆為符合詞彙規則的字元組合，此時發生有兩組以上解皆符合規則、應選擇何者為解的困擾，本文稱為規則衝突。由於規則衝突有許多類型，前述衝突本文稱為詞彙包含衝突。

在詞彙包含衝突中，字數較多的詞將作為正確解。因為三個相鄰候選字集中，隨機挑選一組符合詞的字元組合的可能性，遠低於兩個相鄰候選字集中，隨機挑選一組符合詞的字元組合的可能性。換句話說，三字詞作為解的可能性遠大於二字詞隨機結合另一個單字詞的可能性。因此本文優先挑選字數較多的詞做為候選位置解。這樣的概念也被用於中文斷詞，稱為「長詞優先法」[5]。

（二） 語法規則

詞性是語法的基本單位，根據[6]的定義，中文總共有三十六種詞性。在語料中可觀察到許多詞性組合常常發生，例如詞性 Ne 是數詞(如：三、六、千...等字之詞性)，詞性 NF 代表量詞(如：個、對、片…等字之詞性)。由於描述數量的句子出現次數非常頻繁，因此若在兩個相鄰的候選字集中出現詞性組合「Ne-Nf」，則此詞性組合相對應的字元組合應該被挑選作為對應候選位置的解。本文將以兩種常見的詞性組合做為語法規則。第一種是詞性 Ne 後緊接著出現詞性 Nf 的組合，記為「Ne-Nf」規則。圖三說明了一個使用「Ne-Nf」規則的情境。

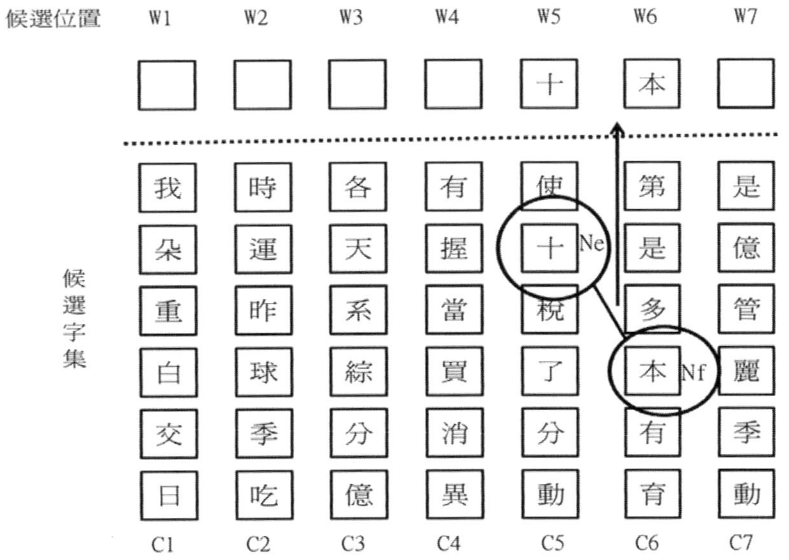

圖三、使用 Ne-Nf 規則之範例

第二種是是詞性 DE 後緊接著出現詞性 Na 的組合，記為「DE-Na」規則。在中文常見的字元「的」，其常見作用有兩類，一種是類似中文所有格的概念，例如:「我的手」；另一種是用於形容詞與名詞間，例如「藍藍的花」。前述的例句，中文「的」之詞性是 DE，「花」與「手」的詞性皆為 Na。由於這類詞性 DE 的字後緊接出現一個詞性 Na 的詞之現象在語料中非常普遍，因此在候選子集群中若出現「DE-Na」規則，則可推測候選位置的解應為詞性 DE 與詞性 Na 所對應之字元組合。圖四說明了一個使用「DE-Na」規則的情境。

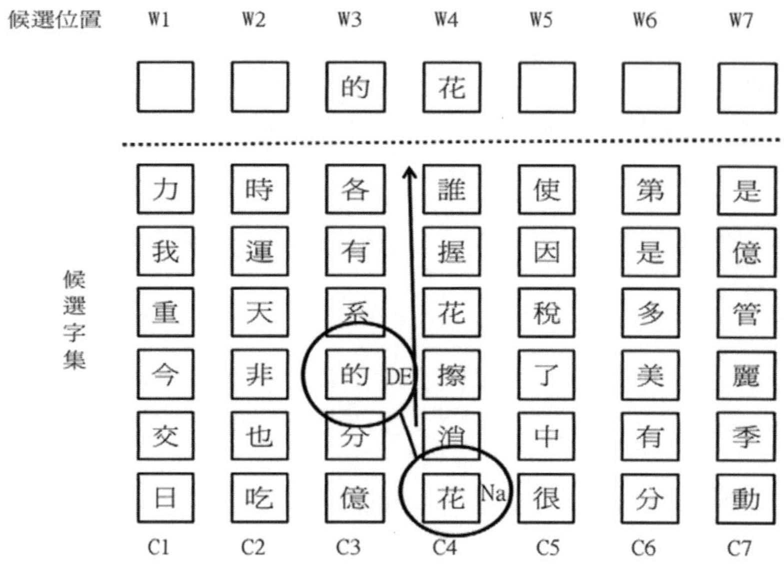

圖四、使用 DE-Na 規則之範例

（三） 語料規則

語料中可觀察到有些單一字元和另一個單一字元頻繁地一起出現，例如「那就這麼決定吧！」中的「那就」、「我是這裡主管。」的「我是」等二字元組合。此種字元組合本文稱為「雙字組」。圖五為使用雙字組「那就」挑選候選字的範例。與二字詞不同，雙字組沒有明顯的語意，只是單純地以高頻率出現在語料中的兩個單字組合。這種現象在特定主題或領域(domain-specific)的語料中特別容易出現。本文以下列程序取得雙字組。首先將語料庫中的一個句子視為一個處理單位，將句中的兩個相鄰字元形成一字組。接著統計所有字組在語料中出現頻率。最後出現頻率超過門檻設定值的字組則收錄至雙字組資料庫。若在收錄過程中發現該字組是一組二字詞或符合語法規則的字元組合，則排除收錄。

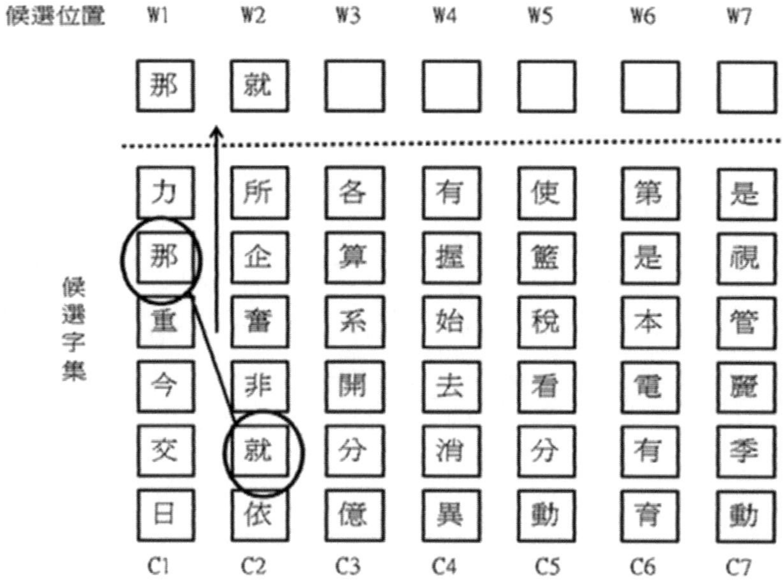

圖五、語料規則範例

有了雙字組資料庫，便可將候選字集群中兩兩相鄰候選位置之候選字集內的候選字元，形成許多字組，並將字組依序與雙字組資料庫進行比對。若該字組被收錄，則將此雙字組做為候選位置的解。

四、規則衝突處理

三之一節曾提到，在相鄰候選字集中挑選字元時若有兩組以上解皆符合規則，會發生應選擇何者為解的問題，稱為規則衝突。圖六列舉部分規則衝突的情況。在規則衝突可分「相同規則衝突」與「相異規則衝突」。相同規則衝突是指在兩個或三個相鄰候選位置之候選字集中，出現兩組或兩組以上的字元組符合同一規則的挑選條件。而相異規則衝突是指在兩個或兩個以上的相鄰候選字集中，出現兩組或兩組以上的字元組合符合兩個不同規則。若相同規則衝突或相異規則衝突在全部的位置重疊，這種情況稱為「全部位置重疊衝突」，如圖六之候選位置 W1 及 W2；若只有若干個位置重疊，這種情況則稱為「部份位置重疊衝突」,如圖六之候選位置 W5 至 W7。

由於有許多可能造成衝突的規則組合，以下三小節分別以三種規則為發生衝突的規則之一，討論規則衝突時的處理方法。

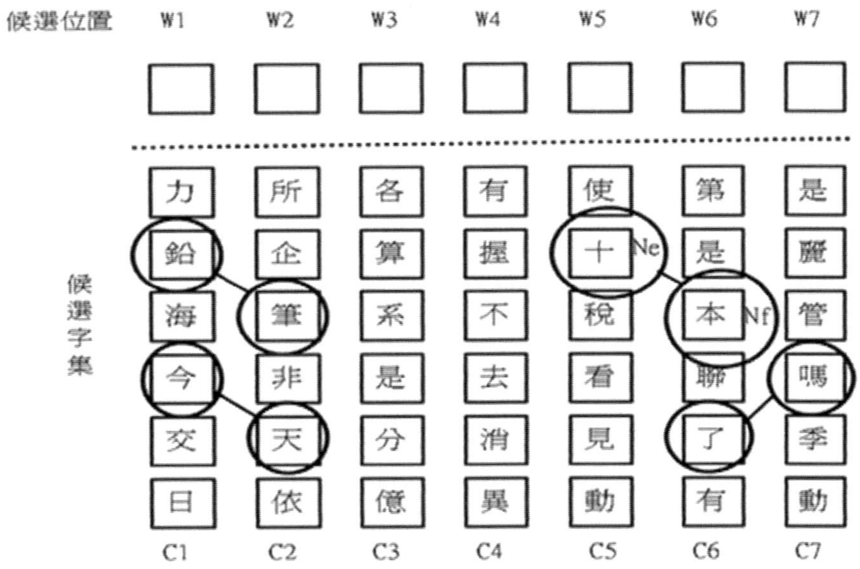

圖六、規則衝突範例

（一） 詞彙規則的衝突

在詞彙規則造成的規則衝突分為相同規則衝突與相異規則衝突。詞彙規則之相同規則衝突是指在候選字集內的候選位置出現兩組或兩組以上的詞彙組合，造成詞彙與詞彙之間衝突。在詞彙規則衝突上，不論是全部位置衝突或部份位置衝突，對詞彙規則的相同規則衝突皆採取詞頻較高的詞彙作為對應之候選位置的系統解。

詞彙規則之相異規則衝突有兩種，分別是語法規則衝突及語料規則衝突。當詞彙規則與語法規則發生衝突時，則是以詞彙規則為優先。當詞彙規則與語料規則發生衝突時，若詞彙長度大於 2，則詞彙規則優先。而一個二字詞與一個雙字組之間的衝突，其解決方式是針對二字詞及雙字組各自設定一組門檻值，以下列三種情況來判斷優先規則。首先，若二字詞的頻率超越門檻值，則使用詞彙規則。第二，若二字詞的頻率未超過所設定的二字詞門檻值，而雙字組的出現頻率超過雙字組所設的雙字組門檻值，則使用語料規則。最後，當二字詞和雙字組皆未超過各自的門檻值，則以詞彙規則為優先。

（二）語法規則的衝突

語法規則所包含的規則衝突也可以分為相同規則衝突與相異規則衝突。語法規則之相同規則衝突解決方式是比較個別衝突位置之兩個字元，以單一字頻較高的字元做為對應之候選位置的系統解。

語法規則可能與詞彙規則及語料規則發生相異衝突。與詞彙規則的衝突處理已於四章一節說明。而與語料規則之衝突解決方式是，若雙字組的發生頻率超過所設定的門檻值，則優先以雙字組做為系統解，否則以符合語法規則的字元組合做為系統解。而不論全部位置重疊及部份位置重疊衝突，皆採取相同處理方式。

（三） 語料規則的衝突

語料規則與其他規則產生的衝突已在先前兩小節討論。對於語料規則的相同規則衝突，不論相同位置衝突及部份位置衝突，皆以發生頻率較高的雙字組做為對應位置的解。在部份位置衝突情況中，有時候會出現衝突雙字組共用一個字元的現象，這種情形我們不視為規則衝突，而是同時將兩個雙字組做為三個對應位置的解。圖七以範例說明了這種情形的細節。當雙字組「我就」與「就有」在候選位置 W2 上同時與候選字「就」成為雙字組，此時不視為發生語料規則衝突，而是直接以「我就是」做為 W1 至 W3 的解。

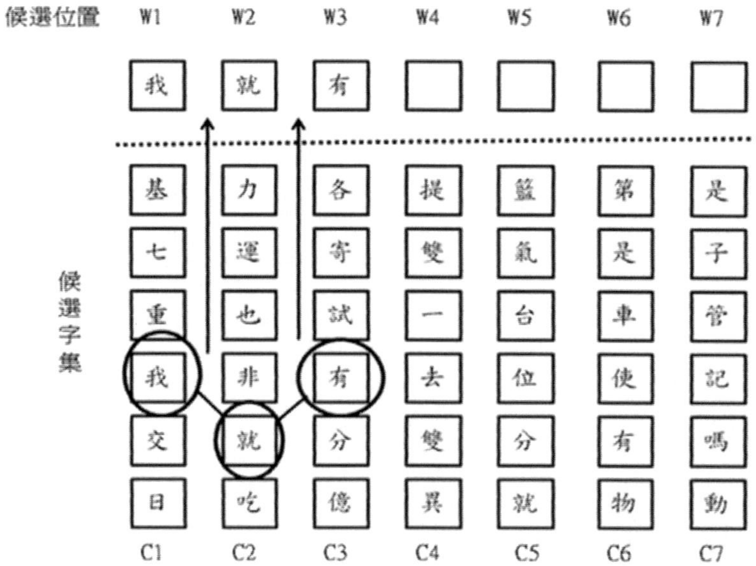

圖七、語料規則之部分衝突位置字元相同範例

五、 實驗

（一） 實驗環境

本文使用的特定主題語料是由國立臺灣師範大學心理與教育測驗研究發展中心所提供之國民中學九年級學生寫作作品。寫作篇數共計 1234 篇，寫作題目為「用餐時刻」。該語料每篇作品平均字數為 349 個字，平均每句字數為 9 個字。本實驗的測試資料是從全部寫作文本中進行 5 次隨機挑選，每次隨機挑選 200 篇寫作做為一組測試資料集。在挑選的過程中，對於先前已被挑選過的寫作文本，將不再挑選。測試資料集之後將以「資料集」簡稱之，所取得的五次資料集亦分別稱為資料集 1 至資料集 5。

本文先進行兩項實驗以便後續效能評估，第一項以純字頻挑選系統解的效能建立測試基準，第二項則測試本文所提方法必須設定的各項門檻值對正確率的影響。之後效能評估都分別對資料集 1 至資料集 5 測試，並將這 5 次測試得到的正確率取平均值做為該項效能評估之正確率。另外，本文模擬以光學辨識字元影像產生候選字集的方式進行實驗，亦即對每句中的每個已知正確字，加上隨機從字典中選取九個字形成該字之候選位置的候選字集。當之後同一個字再度出現在其他句子中，仍使用相同的候選字集，也就是本實驗不考慮正確字不在候選字集中的情形。

第一項實驗是藉由「中央研究院中文分詞詞典」所提供每個候選字元發生頻率，將每個候選字集中出現頻率最高者的字元來做為對應候選位置的解。此方法以「純字頻挑選」簡稱之，可以說明在沒有本文所提方法下，以最簡單的純字頻法可達成的正確率。表一為純字頻挑選之實驗結果。此 5 組資料集的平均正確率為 45.8%。由結果得知，若無使用任何校正方法，純字頻挑選方法的效能相當不理想。

表一、純字頻挑選方法實驗結果

	資料集 1	資料集 2	資料集 3	資料集 4	資料集 5	平均值
總測試字數	69051	63144	66155	67153	61723	65445
正確挑選字數	31796	28523	30349	30492	28873	30006
錯誤挑選字數	37255	34621	35806	36661	32850	35449
正確率百分比	46.0%	45.1%	45.8%	45.4%	46.7%	45.8%

本文的第二項實驗將設定 4 組門檻值分別對 5 個資料集進行測試。4 組門檻值分別簡稱為「設定集 1」、「設定集 2」、「設定集 3」、「設定集 4」，每個設定集包含兩個值，分別是二字詞出現次數的門檻值(以下簡稱 T 值)、以及雙字組出現次數的門檻值(以下簡稱 B 值)。設定集 1 的參數設定值為 T=212，B=106。設定集 2 的 T=106，B=52。設定集 3 的 T=920，B=52。設定集 4 的 T=52，B=920。這些數值是依據所有二字詞及雙字組在語料中出現頻率排序後，位於全體 25%、50%、75%的頻率值所設定。實驗結果如表二所示。

表二、各種門檻值組合對各資料集的選字正確率

資料集 / 門檻設定值	資料集 1	資料集 2	資料集 3	資料集 4	資料集 5	25%,
T=212, B=106	84.8	84.6	85.0	84.4	85.5	84.8
T=106, B=52	84.7	84.5	85.0	84.4	85.6	84.9
T=920, B=52	80.8	80.3	80.7	80.5	81.5	80.8
T=52, B=920	84.4	84.3	84.5	84.1	85.0	83.7

由表二可知，設定集 1 與設定集 2 的實驗結果的正確率差異並不大，代表同時調低二字詞與雙字組門檻值影響不大。經檢視資料後發現，雖然某些出現次數較少之二字詞及雙字組在調低門檻值後可以被詞彙與語料規則使用後正確校正，但較少出現次數也代表用來做為正確解的錯誤風險增加。在兩相抵消之下，其正確率差異並不大。

設定集 3 的門檻值相較於設定集 1，調高了二字詞門檻值但降低雙字組門檻值。其造成的影響為詞彙規則較少使用、而增加使用語料規則的次數，實驗結果顯示設定集 3 的正確率較低，代表使用語料規則取代詞彙規則會造成效能下降。而設定集 4 的門檻值相較於設定集 1，則是調低了二字詞門檻值但提高雙字組門檻值。其造成的影響為增加錯誤風險較高的詞彙規則的使用次數、而提高語料規則的信賴度。實驗結果顯示設定集 4 的正確率較低，但較設定集 3 為高。這說明了詞彙規則的正確性較語料規則的正確性為高，應該優先使用詞彙規則，然而適當取得兩個門檻值的平衡，才能使效能接近最佳。五之二節將採用設定集 2 的門檻值做為評估依據。

（二） 效能評估

本小節的實驗分為「單項規則效能分析」與「架構效能評估」，目的是測試個別規則對正確率的影響。單項規則效能分析是針對只使用單一規則的效能。而由於規則執行後並非全部候選位置均能得到系統解，因此未有系統解的候選位置則利用純字頻挑選法產生解。由於此實驗僅針對單一規則進行測試，在挑選文字的過程中不會發生規則衝突，因此無需設定門檻值來處理規則衝突。

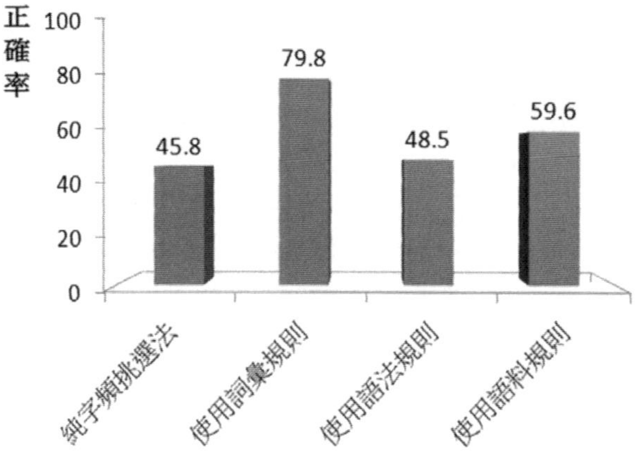

圖八、單項規則效能分析

由圖八所示，以使用詞彙規則與純字頻挑選法比較，使用詞彙規則挑選文字，其正確率可從 45.8%提升到 79.8%。使用該規則可提升 34%的正確率。在單項規則效能分析之實驗結果中，該規則提升的正確率最高，主要原因是中文句所包含的字元大多是由詞彙組成，且詞是句子的語意基本單元。因此使用詞彙規則可以有效提高正確率。

語法規則與純字頻挑選法比較，使用語法規則挑選文字，其正確率可從 45.8%提升到 48.5%。使用該規則可提升 2.7%的正確率。在此實驗中該規則所能提升的正確率最低。經檢視該規則的實驗結果發現，使用語法規則確實可以找到正確的字元組合，但由於實驗語料沒有大量出現符合該規則的句子片段，因此導致正確率提升有限。

再以語料規則與純字頻挑選法比較，使用語料規則挑選文字，其正確率可從 48.8%提升到 59.6%。相較純字頻挑選法，使用該規則可提升 13.8%的正確率。該規則對於提升正確率已有明顯效果，但低於詞彙方法的提升率。主要原因是當語料規則發生相同規則衝突，本研究是挑選出現次數較多的雙字組做為挑選字。這種解決方法並不保證所挑選的雙字組是正確解，所挑選的雙字組也可能造成挑選錯誤。本文所提之三類規則所提升的正確率差異性很大，也與本文所設計的規則優先順序相當符合。

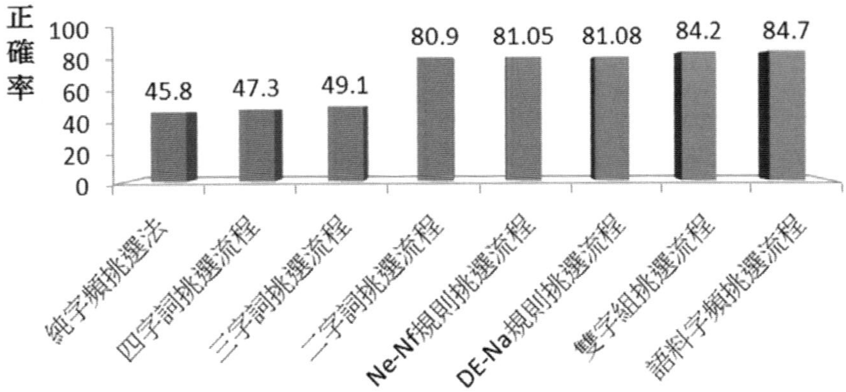

圖九、各流程執行後正確率變化

圖九則顯示依序使用第二節所述本文所提架構各階段執行結束後正確率之變化。在五之一節中已說明使用純字頻挑選法之實驗正確率為 45.8%。在各階段文字挑選處理後仍未確認的候選位置，則仍使用純挑選字頻法進行字元挑選。

詞彙規則階段因長詞優先以及詞長不同分為四字詞、三字詞及二字詞挑選流程。由圖九實驗結果可知，加入二字詞挑選程序後才會大幅提升正確率，主要原因為二字詞佔多字詞的比例相當高，相較之下四字詞與三字詞出現比例偏低，因此能處理的字數有限。特別說明的是，圖九中，使用詞彙規則的正確率比在圖 8 中要稍高，其因是圖 9 之實驗有設定門檻值解決二字詞或雙字組的規則衝突，因此正確率與圖 8 有所差異，此亦顯示使用門檻值有些微提高正確率的效果。

語法規則緊接在詞彙規則使用後加入。語法規則在圖九中也分為兩個子程序，先使用 Ne-Nf 規則再加入 DE-Na 規則，其正確率從百分之 80.9%提升至 81.8。很明顯的其正確率提升效果有限，原因如圖八之實驗討論。最後語料規則也分為兩個子程序，先使用雙字組規則再加入語料字頻挑選法，正確率由 81.08%提升至 84.7%。與圖八的實驗結果比較，此處的語料規則能提升的正確率較低，顯示最後實施的語料規則可校正的部分有許多與前兩項規則重複，因此有些語料規則可校正部分已先由前兩類規則正確校正，因此正確率提升有限，但仍具有提升正確率的效果。

六、結論

本文是利用特定領域語料特性提出三類規則做為挑選候選字依據以提高離線手寫文字辨識正確率。在詞彙規則中，由於詞是句子的語意基本單元，藉由這個特性辨識模型可以利用詞彙規則來挑選多字詞的詞彙，並做為對應位置的校正結果。而在數個連續相鄰的候選字集中，欲隨機組合出一組符合詞彙規則的字元組合之可能性相當低，因此以符合詞彙規則的字元組合做為對應之候選位置的解，較有可能正確挑選。在辨識模型辨識文字的結果中，可以使用詞彙規則來進一步校正辨識字，以提高辨識的效果。

使用語法規則可以從候選字集群中，找出符合規則的詞性組合。由於傳統辨識模型是以模型計算機率值較高的候選字做為辨識結果，因此其選出的相鄰字間並不一定符合語法規則，會出現整句不符語法的現象。加入語法規則可以在候選字集群中找出符合規則的的字元組合做為解，藉由解決整句不符語法問題改善候選字挑選流程。有別於詞彙規則與語法規則，語料規則相當依賴特定領域語料的特性，以頻繁相鄰出現的字元組合來做為對應位置的系統解。由於字元組合資訊是由語料蒐集，可表現語料使用語言的偏好，因此對於辨識準確度會有不錯的改善效果。

雖然本文已經有效提升光學文字辨識的正確率，但還有一些部分可進一步研究。首先，本文提出的詞彙規則會發生相同規則衝突與相異規則衝突。對於詞彙規則所發生的相同規則衝突，本文是以詞頻較高的詞彙做為對應候選位置的正確解，而針對詞彙規則所發生的相異規則衝突，本文是優先以較頻繁的二字詞來做為解。這種以發生頻率做為衝突解決依據的方法所造成的錯誤佔校正失敗相當大的比例。如何更有效解決規則衝突問題值得進一步研究。另外，本文所提方法可考慮提前於文字辨識的第二階段結合，提早進行候選字篩選，如此可產生更為可靠的候選字集，使得挑選正確解的可能性更高。

誌謝

作者感謝國立臺灣師範大學心理與教育測驗研究發展中心提供語料供研究使用。

參考文獻

[1] 李宜靜，2009，“中文字印刷體影像文字辨識之研究”，義守大學，碩士論文。

[2] 謝尚琳，1999，“用於辨正印刷中文字辨識結果的實用設計”，國立臺灣大學，博士論文。

[3] 曾元顯，2004，“應用於資訊檢索的中文 OCR 錯誤詞彙自動更正”，中國圖書館學會會報，72 期，頁 23~31，6 月。

[4] Yong-Zhi Chen, Shih-Hung Wu, Chia-Ching Lu and Tsun Ku, “Chinese Confusion Word Set for Automatic Generation of Spelling Error Detecting Template”, The 21th Conference on Computational Linguistics and Speech Processing , Taichung, Taiwan ,September 1-2, pp.359-372, 2009.

[5] Keh-Jiann Chen and Shing-Huan Liu, "Word identification for Mandarin Chinese sentences", In Proceedings of COLING-92, Nantes, France,pages 101-107, 1992.

[6] CKIP, "Analysis of Syntactic Categories for Chinese", CKIP Tech. Report#93-05, Sinica, Taipei, 1993,

[7] Mingrui Wu, Bo Zhang and Ling Zhang, "A neural network based classifier for handwritten Chinese character recognition", 15th International Conference on Pattern Recognition, Barcelona, Spain, September 3-8, pp.2561-2564, 2000.

[8] Zhi-guo He and Yu-dong Cao, "Survey of Offline Handwritten Chinese Character Recognition", Computer Engineering, Vol.34, No.15, pp.201-204, 2008.

[9] Feng-Jun Guo, Li-Xin Zhen, Yong Ge and Yun Zhang, "An Efficient Candidate Set Size Reduction Method for Coarse-Classifier of Chinese Handwriting Recognition", Proceedings of the 2006 conference on Arabic and Chinese handwriting recognition, College Park, MD, USA, September 27-28, pp.152-160, 2006.

[10] Hairong Lv, Wenyuan Wang, Chong Wang and Qing Zhuo, "Off-line Chinese signature verification based on support vector machines", Pattern Recognition Letters, Vol.26, Issue 15, pp.2390-2399, 2005.

Using Kohonen Maps of Chinese Morphological Families to Visualize the Interplay of Morphology and Semantics in Chinese

Bruno GALMAR
Institute of Education
National Cheng Kung University
hsuyueshan@gmail.com

Abstract

A morphological family in Chinese is the set of compound words embedding a common morpheme. Self-organizing maps (SOM) of Chinese morphological families are built. Computation of the unified-distance matrices for the SOMs allows us to perform a semantic clustering of the members of the morphological families. Such a semantic clustering shed light on the interplay between morphology and semantics in Chinese. Then, we studied how the word lists used in a lexical decision task (LDT) [1] are mapped onto the clusters of the SOMs. We showed that such a mapping is helpful to predict whether in a LDT repetitive processing of members of a morphological family would elicit a satiation - habituation - of both morphological and semantic units of the shared morpheme. In their LDT experiment, [1] found evidence for morphological satiation but not for semantic satiation. Conclusions drawn from our computational experimentations and calculations are concordant with [1] behavioral experimental results. We finally showed that our work could be helpful to linguists to prepare adequate word lists for the behavioral study of Chinese morphological families.

Keywords: Self-Organizing Maps, Computational Morphology and Semantics

1. Introduction

In this paper, we call a morphological family the set of compound words embedding a common morpheme. So, the compound words in Tab. 1 which have all the morpheme '明' as a first character belong to the morphological family of '明'.

Table 1. A subset of words belonging to the morphological family of 明 [1].

明朝	明天	明白	明確	明星	明亮
Ming Dynasty	tomorrow	to understand clear	explicit	star	bright

In Chinese, the meaning of a morpheme can be either transparent or opaque to the meaning of the compound word embedding it. For example, the common morpheme in Tab.1 "明" can mean (*clear*) or (*bright*) and is transparent to the meaning of "明星" (*star*) but rather opaque to the meaning of "明天" (*tomorrow*). If some members of a morphological family are semantically similar, one could advance as a reason for such a similarity that these members are transparent to a same meaning of the shared morpheme. Most of Chinese morphemes are polysemous [2]. Hence, in theory, *transparent members* of a morphological family could belong to different semantic clusters whose centers would be the different meanings of the shared polysemous morpheme.

This paper aims primarily at using computational linguistics methods to perform a semantic clustering of the members of the morphological families. Such a clustering is thereafter used to predict the results of a behavioral Lexical Decision Task[1] (LDT) designed by [1] to study the phenomenon of morphological satiation in Chinese.

In visual word recognition, morphological satiation is an impairment of morphological processing induced by a repetitive exposure to a same morpheme embedded in different Chinese compound words [1][3]. [1] posited that morphological satiation is due to habituation of the morphological unit of the repeated morpheme. This is represented on Fig. 1 by diagram (a).

As a morpheme is thought to be a meaningful unit, it is logical to consider whether a semantic satiation [4][5][6] - an impairment of semantic processing causing a temporary loss of the meaning of the common morpheme - would occur concomitantly with morphological satiation[2]. In other words, the satiation observed by [1] could have two loci: a morphological one and a semantic one as represented on Fig. 1 by diagram (d).

A morphological satiation could also have its loci of satiation on the links between the morphological, lexical and semantic units as represented on Fig.1 by the diagrams (b) and (c). We can quickly rule out the possibility of a locus on the link between morphological and lexical units as represented by the diagram (b). The reason is that in a LDT, this link is changing at each presentation of a new two-character word. The morphological unit of the repeated morpheme constitutes one fixed endpoint of the morphological/lexical link but the over endpoint is always changing.

The present work of semantic clustering focuses on clarifying by computational means whether morphological satiation would probably have a sole morphological locus - diagram (a) - or whether it would have both a morphological and semantic locus - diagram (d) -. [1] behavioral LDT experiment results pointed to the existence of a sole morphological locus.

---

1 A LDT is a behavioral task for which subjects have to identify whether presented visual stimuli are words or non-words.

2 If most of the members of a morphological family used in an experimental task are transparent to a same meaning of the shared morpheme, the same semantic units of the shared morpheme are repeatedly accessed and finally habituate - satiation diagram (d) -. Therefore there could be a semantic satiation in addition to morphological satiation.

Figure 1. Different possible loci of satiation for [1] morphological satiation.

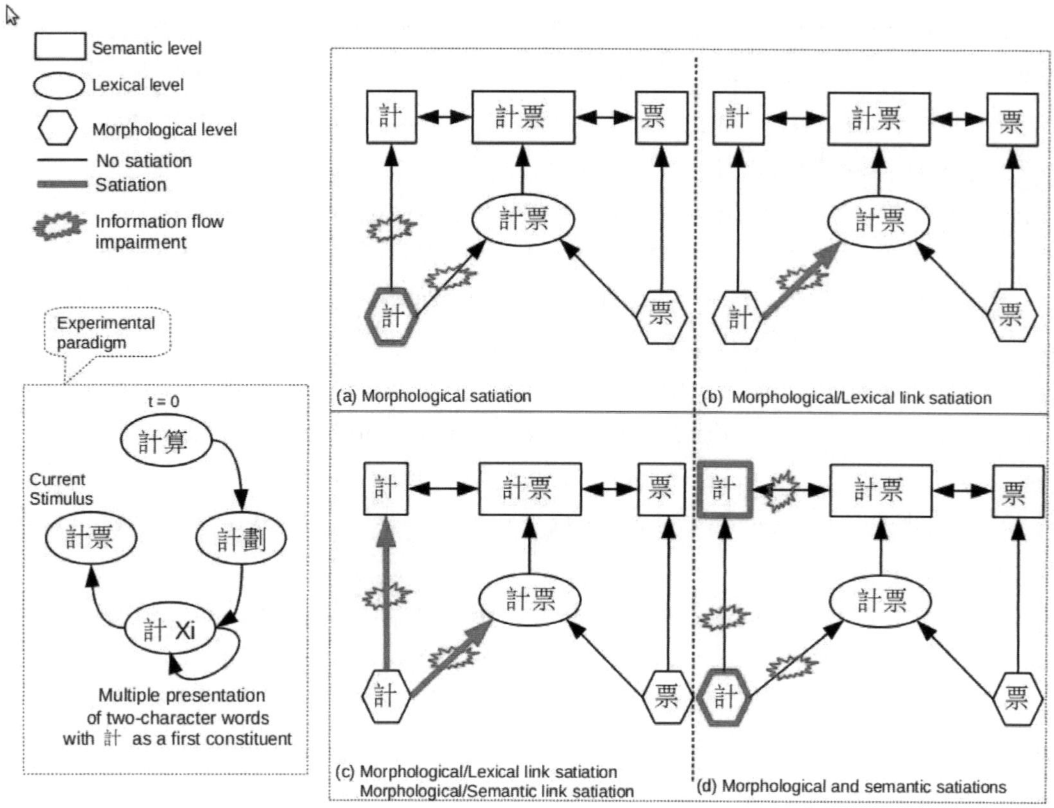

2. Rationale of our Approach

As human subjects agreement for semantic clustering tasks is low [7], computational corpus-based semantic clustering was thought to be a valuable and complementary experimental approach compared to a behavioral one with human subjects.

A corpus of written texts is a human artifact, its content is relevant to the human reader and therefore from a cognitive psychology standpoint, a corpus does embed a subset of organized human semantic knowledge and is worthy to be studied in computer simulations as a pure abstract semantic memory stripped out of sensory and motor representations.

In natural language processing, proponents of the `bag of words' approach simplify each document internal structure to a set of words, and use a whole corpus to build a matrix of co-occurrence of the words corpus [8]. Computational methods as Latent Semantic Analysis take as input such a high dimensional matrix and reduce its dimensionality to form a vector space of the documents and words [9]. This space embeds only an associative kind of semantic information[3]: words that co-occur in the same documents or which have common

[3] Semantic information can be for example also of the categorical or featural types.

co-occurrents are close associates.

For a news corpus, the association can often be of the type situational. For example, "Father Christmas" will be a close associate of "department store" as there are many news reports around Christmas about the bustling agitation in department stores full of "Father Christmas"[4]. In cognitive science and AI, it is said that the two terms "Father Christmas" and "department store" belong to a common memory frame, a frame being defined by Minsky as "*a data-structure for representing a stereotyped situation*'" [11].

In the present work, we do follow a `bag of words' approach by firstly building a term document matrix (TDM). Then, Self-Organizing Maps (SOMs) and associated unified-distanced matrices - called U-matrix thereafter - are built from the TDM. The SOMs and the U-matrices serve to visualize semantic clusters in a morphological family on a 2D hexagonal grid of bins [12].

On the SOMs, a semantic cluster is made of members of a morphological family which have been fitted into a same bin of the grid and into contiguous bins which are close neighbors - according to the U-matrix information - in the original high dimensional space. SOMs have been used successfully to capture associative semantic relationships between words in corpora. Closer to the present approach, [13][14][15][16] have used SOMs to study the developmental aspect of vocabulary acquisition in Chinese. Our study is the first one to use SOMs to study the interplay between morphology and semantics in Chinese compounds words sharing a common morpheme, i.e. to study the semantics of morphological families.

3. The Corpus and the Term Document Matrix (TDM)

3.1 The Academia Sinica Balanced Corpus

We used the Academia Sinica Balanced Corpus (ASBC), a five million words annotated corpus based on Chinese materials from Taiwan, mostly newspapers articles. The corpus is made of roughly 10000 documents of unequal length.

We removed from the corpus the foreign alphabetic words and most of the Chinese functional words. We kept POS tags information to allow differentiation between different grammatical instances of a same word[5] [10].

3.2 The Term Document Matrix (TDM)

The TDM was built by using the *TermDocumentMatrix* function of the R package *tm* [17] with a self-customized Chinese tokenizer. The TDM is a 136570 terms * 9179 documents

4 This example is borrowed from [10]

5 Some of the Chinese words can have up to 5 different POS tags [10].

matrix.

The TDM was weighted:

1. using the classical term frequency-inverse document frequency (TfIdf) weighting scheme for both local and global weighting of the terms in the TDM [8]. We used the function *weightTfIdf* of the package *tm* [17].
2. using a weighting scheme at the document level to reduce the effect of the size difference between documents:

$$\log_2\left(\frac{\text{Max\_document\_size}}{\text{Document\_size}}+1\right) \quad (1)$$

   Each document of the TDM is a genuine article of the ASBC corpus and is considered as a semantic unit. More weight is given to small documents of the ASBC corpus. A complete justification for such a decision is given in [10]. Briefly, one can say that for a human reader due to attentional capacity limitations, the gist of a news article is easier to extract from a very short article than from a very long one.

4. The Self-Organizing Maps

For a given morphological family, the rows corresponding to the members of the family in the TDM were extracted. The extracted rows constitute a submatrix of the TDM. From this submatrix, a SOM is built using the *Batch map algorithm* [12]. The U-matrix [18] is computed to assess how much members fitted to contiguous bins - bins are thereafter called units - on the SOM are close in the original high-dimensional space - thereafter called input data space -.

4.1 The batch version of the SOM algorithm

As all the data - the TDM - can be presented to the SOM algorithm from the beginning of learning, the batch version of the SOM algorithm - called "Batch Map" - is used instead of the incremental learning SOM algorithm. The batch SOM is very similar to the k-means (Linde-Buzo-Gray) algorithm [12].

Our SOM defines a mapping from the input data space $\mathbb{R}^n$ of observation samples onto a hexagonal two-dimensional grid of N_u units. Every unit *i* is associated with a *reference vector* $m_i \in \mathbb{R}^n$. The set of units located inside a given radius from unit *i* is termed *neighborhood set* N_i.

From [12, pp139-140] and [19, p1360], the Batch Map algorithm can be described as follows:

1. Initialize the N_u reference vectors by taking the first N_u observation samples.
2. For each unit i, collect a list L_i of copies of all those observation samples whose nearest reference vector belongs to N_i.

3. Update the value of each reference vector m_i with the mean over L_i.

4. Repeat from Step 2 a few times.

The Batch Map presents a main advantage over the incremental learning version of the SOM algorithm [12][20]: no learning rate parameter has to be specified. To double-check the computed batch SOM's representativeness of the input data space, we followed the recommendation of both [20] and [12] to compare organization in the Batch Map and in the incremental learning SOM.

We used the code in the R package *class* [21] for the batch SOM given by [22] to build the SOMs on a 7*8 hexagonal grid of 56 bins.

4.2 The Unified-Distance Matrix

We reused and modified the code in the R package *kohonen* [23] to build the U-matrix for the Batch Map and to plot a grey-level map superimposed to the SOM map. The U-matrix is the distance matrix between the reference vectors of contiguous units. On the grayscale SOMs, contiguous units in light shade on the SOM are representative of existing clusters in the input data space. Contiguous units in a dark shade draw boundaries between existing clusters in the input data space [18].

5. Results

We present the results for the study of the 計 (ji2) morphological family[6]. This Chinese morpheme has two main meanings: (1) to count, to calculate (2) to plan, to scheme. The study was limited to the members in the ASBC corpus embedding 計 as a first character. The SOM map of these members is noted SOM_{93} and is shown on Fig 2.

At a first level the map is divided in two zones: a dark shade one - upper part of the map - and a light shade one. Most of the words belong to the light shade zone. Among the diverse existing clusters, we note that:

- Cluster C_1 mainly gathers word sharing and other words related to meaning 1 of 計.
- Cluster C_2 gathers in a same unit three words related to the frame *taxi*.
- Cluster C_3 includes many words belonging to two contiguous units in a light shade. We decided to recompute a Batch Map SOM for the members in these two units to zoom in and have a clearer map of these members. The map is shown on Fig. 3.

---

6 Others examples are also given in the script file – available upon request - to create and plot the SOMs presented in the present paper.

Figure 4 shows only the 13 words used by [1] in one block of their LDT experiment[7]. Some of the words have two POS tags so that the total of the data points represented on Fig.4 is 17.

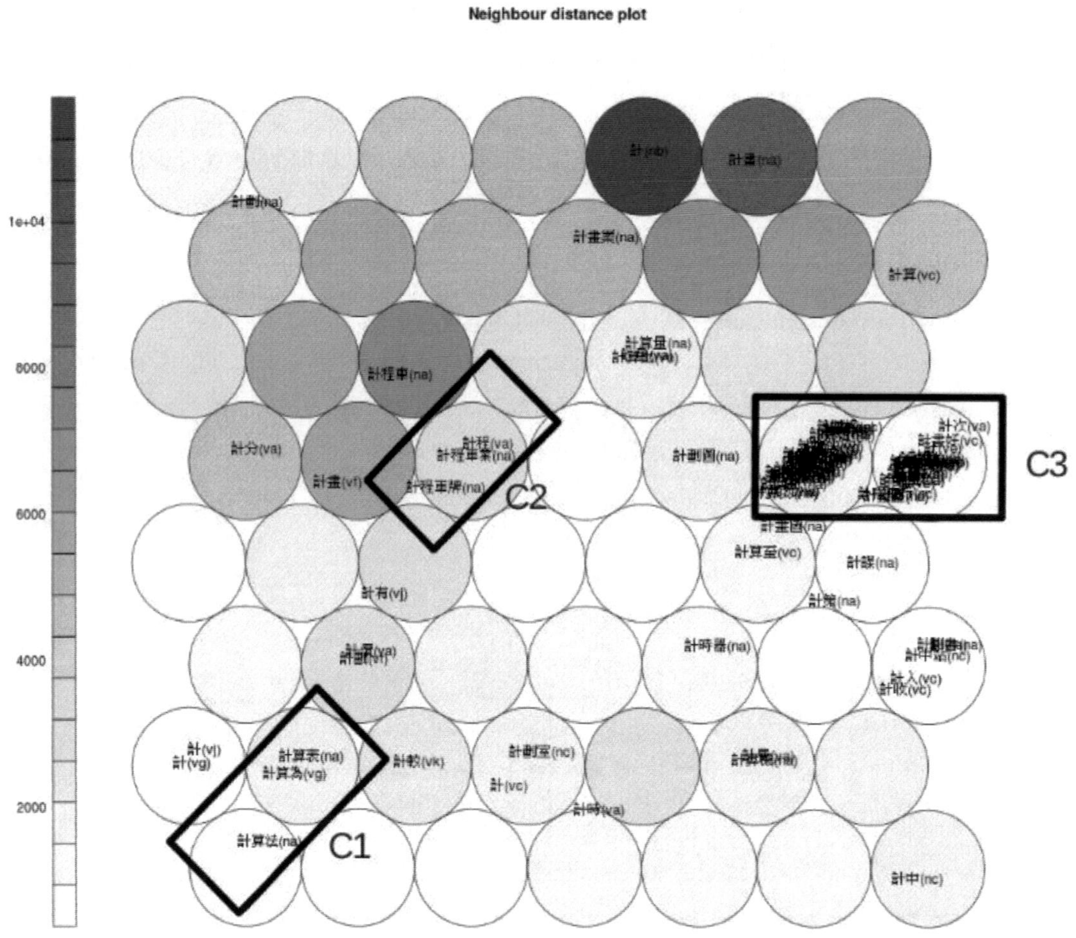

Figure 2. SOM$_{93}$ of the 計 morphological family.

7 One word of the original experiment not being in the ASBC corpus is missing here.

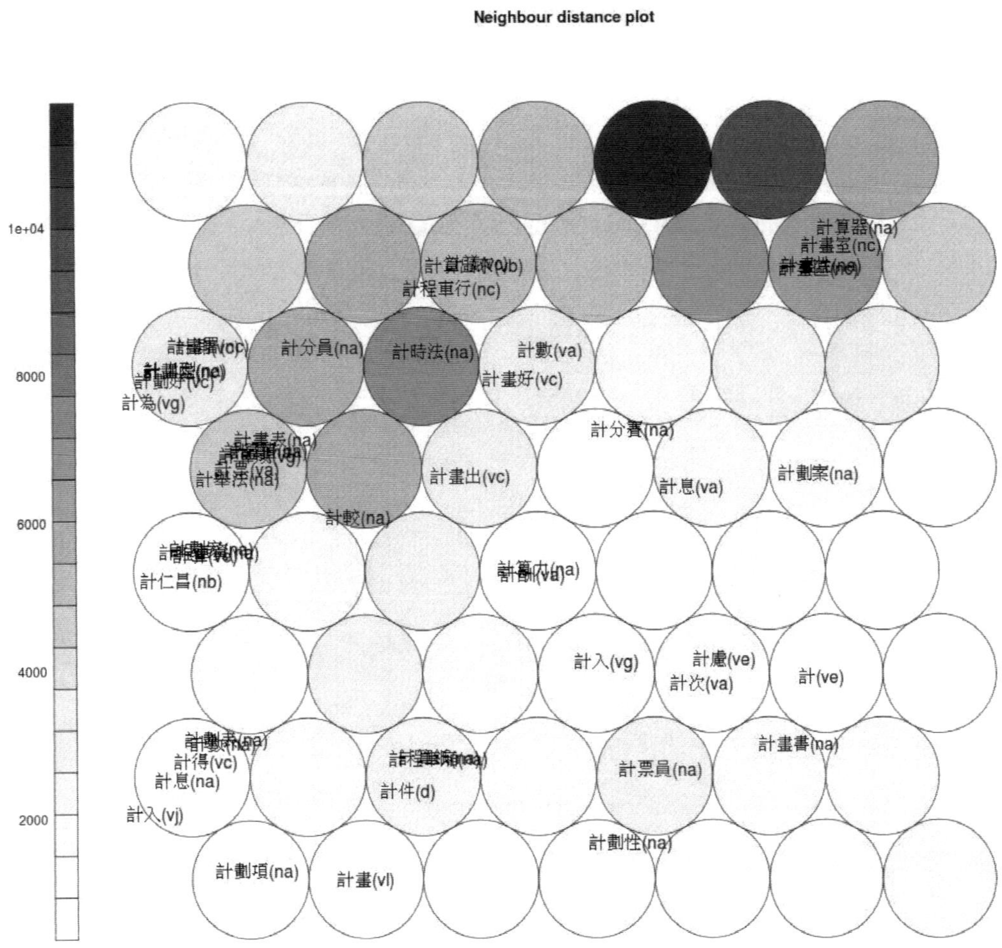

Figure 3. SOM for cluster C3 in Fig. 2

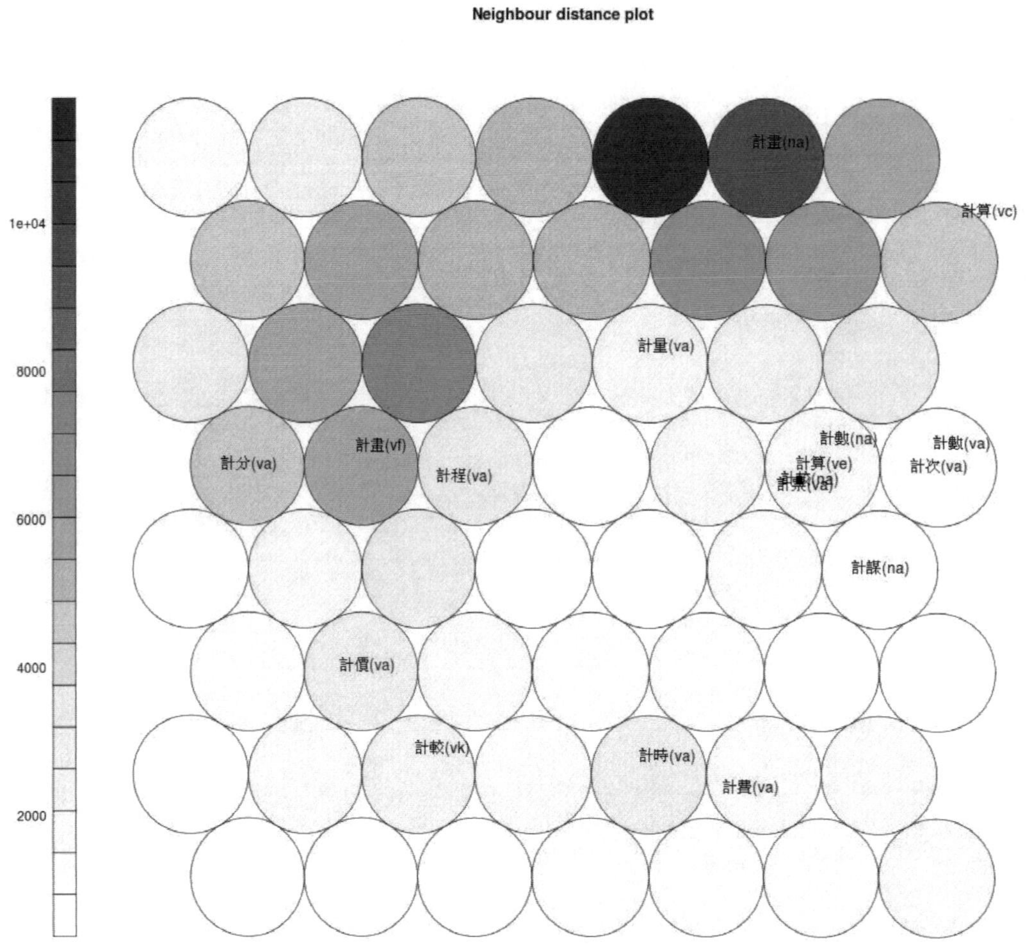

Figure 4. SOM of the members of the 計 morphological family used in [1] experiment.

Clustering is observed easily with such a few words. Three contiguous units in a light shade form the unique big cluster with a total of 6 different words. In the latest experimental research on semantic satiation, [6] found that after 5 or 7 repetitions of a given word, the word's meaning starts to be satiated. From 2 to 4 repetitions, there is semantic priming - behavioral enhancement in semantic tasks - and more repetitions are the realm of semantic satiation.

If in the [1] lexical decision task (LDT), these 6 words occur successively, there should be semantic satiation. In [1] LDT, the 13 words in Fig. 3 were randomly mixed with 13 non-words. Non-words being meaningless should not contribute to satiate significantly the semantic units of the different meanings of the shared morpheme. Therefore, from the analysis of our SOM, we predict that only in the case were the 6 members of the big cluster occur successively in the 26 words list - we call it the best case -, there could be a preliminary sign of semantic satiation.

To compute the probability of this best case, we need to calculate two numbers:

1. N_a the number of distinguishable arrangements of n=26 words of which 6 - belonging to our big cluster - constitute a first set S1 and the 20 remaining ones constitute another set S2. The order of occurrence of the 6 words of S1 does not matter and therefore the words of S1 are considered as being of a same type T1. For the same reason, words of S2 are of a same type T2, different of type T1.

$$N_a = \frac{26!}{6!20!} = 230230 \tag{2}$$

2. the number of distinguishable arrangements of 6 successive occurrences of S1 words[8] in a 26 words list: 21.

The probability *p* of the best case is given by dividing the number of distinguishable arrangements of 6 successive occurrences of S1 words by the number of distinguishable arrangements of n=26 words made of the two types T1 and T2.

$$p = \frac{21}{230230} \approx 9 * 10^{-5} \tag{3}$$

This best case has a very low probability so that subjects of [1] experiment would almost always be given a 26 words list that do not warranty - according to our analysis - elicitation of semantic satiation.

Hence, in one hand, we agree with [1] that in their experiment there were no semantic locus of satiation. On the other hand, we refine [1] conclusions by advancing that one could prepare specific experimental word lists which would maximize the probability of observing semantic satiation.

6. General Conclusion

By visualizing the SOMs augmented with neighboring distance information from the U-matrix, one can observe whether semantic clusters exist in a morphological family and how the experimental data in [1] is mapped to these clusters.

Conclusions drawn from our computational experimental results are concordant with [1] behavioral experimental results revealing the absence of a semantic satiation while morphological satiation occurs. However, we proposed that semantic satiation could theoretically be elicited with specifically arranged word lists for [1] experiment. Such lists have a very low probability of occurrence when random assignment of words is used to

[8] Order of occurrence of the S1 words does not matter.

prepare experimental word lists. Therefore, the present work showed the necessity of preparing adequate experimental word lists based on computational semantic clustering. - as shown here - or human norms of semantic similarity if available.

7. Future Directions

Alternatives to SOMs - such as GTM [24] - exist and could be used for comparison purposes with the present results.

8. Code to generate the SOMs from the ASBC corpus

The source code and R command lines are available upon request in a script file. In order to run the whole script file from the very beginning, one needs the Academia Sinica Balanced Corpus (ASBC). The ASBC has to be purchased[9].

References

[1] J.-Y. Chen, B. Galmar, and H.-J. Su, "Semantic satiation of Chinese characters in a continuous lexical decision task," in *The 21st Annual Convention of the Association For Psychological Science*, 2009.

[2] K. Chen and C. Chen, "Automatic semantic classification for Chinese unknown compound nouns," in *Proceedings of the 18th conference on Computational linguistics-Volume 1. Association for Computational Linguistics*, 2000, pp. 173–179.

[3] C. Cheng and Y. Lan, "An implicit test of Chinese orthographic satiation," *Reading and Writing*, pp. 1–36, 2009.

[4] L. Smith and R. Klein, "Evidence for semantic satiation: Repeating a category slows subsequent semantic processing," *Learning, Memory*, vol. 16, no. 5, pp. 852–861, 1990.

[5] J. Kounios, S. Kotz, and P. Holcomb, "On the locus of the semantic satiation effect: Evidence from event-related brain potentials," *Memory and Cognition*, vol. 28, no. 8, pp. 1366–1377, 2000.

[6] X. Tian and D. Huber, "Testing an associative account of semantic satiation," *Cognitive Psychology*, 2010.

[7] J. Jorgensen, "The psychological reality of word senses," *Journal of Psycholinguistic Research*, vol. 19, no. 3, pp. 167–190, 1990.

[8] T. Landauer and S. Dumais, "A solution to plato's problem: The latent semantic analysis theory of acquisition, induction, and representation of knowledge," *Psychological review*, vol. 104, no. 2, pp. 211–240, 1997.

[9] T. Landauer, D. McNamara, S. Dennis, and W. Kintsch, *Handbook of latent semantic analysis*. Lawrence Erlbaum, 2007.

[10] B. Galmar and J. Chen., "Identifying different meanings of a Chinese morpheme through

9 Contact the Academia Sinica (中央研究院語言所).

semantic pattern matching in augmented minimum spanning trees," *The Prague Bulletin of Mathematical Linguistics*, vol. 94, 2010.

[11] M. Minsky, "A framework for representing knowledge," AIM-306, 1974.

[12] T. Kohonen, *Self-Organizing Maps, 3rd Edition*, Berlin, Heidelberg, 2001.

[13] P. Li, "A self-organizing neural network model of the acquisition of word meaning," in *Proceedings of the 2001 Fourth International Conference on Cognitive Modeling*, July 26-28, 2001 George Mason University, Fairfax, Virgiania, USA. Lawrence Erlbaum, 2001, p. 90.

[14] P. Li, I. Farkas, and B. MacWhinney, "Early lexical development in a self-organizing neural network," *Neural Networks*, vol. 17, no. 8-9, pp. 1345–1362, 2004.

[15] X. Zhao and P. Li, "Vocabulary development in English and Chinese: A comparative study with self-organizing neural networks," in *Proceedings of the 30th Annual Conference of the Cognitive Science Society*, 2008, pp. 1900–1905.

[16] P. Li, "Lexical Organization and Competition in First and Second Languages: Computational and Neural Mechanisms," *Cognitive Science*, vol. 33, no. 4, pp. 629–664, 2009.

[17] I. Feinerer, "tm: Text mining package, 2008," UR L http://CRAN. R-project. org/package= tm. R package version 0.3-3.

[18] A. Ultsch and H. Siemon, "Kohonen's self organizing feature maps for exploratory data analysis," in *Proceedings of the International Neural Network Conference (INNC'90)*, 1990, pp. 305–308.

[19] T. Kohonen, E. Oja, O. Simula, A. Visa, and J. Kangas, "Engineering applications of the self-organizing map," *Proceedings of the IEEE*, vol. 84, no. 10, pp. 1358–1384, 2002.

[20] J. Fort, P. Letremy, and M. Cottrell, "Advantages and drawbacks of the Batch Kohonen algorithm," in *10th European Symp. On Artificial Neural Networks*. Citeseer.

[21] W. N. Venables and B. D. Ripley, *Modern Applied Statistics with S*, 4th ed. New York: Springer, 2002, iSBN 0-387-95457-0. [Online]. Available: http://www.stats.ox.ac.uk/pub/MASS4

[22] W. Venables, B. Ripley, and W. Venables, *Modern applied statistics with S-Plus*. Citeseer, 1998.

[23] R. Wehrens and L. Buydens, "Self- and super-organising maps in r: the kohonen package," *J. Stat. Softw.*, vol. 21, no. 5, 2007. [Online]. Available: http://www.jstatsoft.org/v21/i05

[24] C. Bishop, M. Svensen, and C. Williams, "GTM: The generative topographic mapping," *Neural computation*, vol. 10, no. 1, pp. 215–234, 1998.

The Prior Knowledge Effect on the Processing of Vague Discourse in Mandarin Chinese

Shu-Ping Gong
National Chiayi University
spgong@mail.ncyu.edu.tw

Kathleen Ahrens
Hong Kong Baptist University
ahrens@hkbu.edu.hk

Abstract

This study investigates whether prior knowledge affects the processing of vague discourse in Mandarin Chinese. Vague discourse refers to the texts using vague references and neutral descriptors (e.g. 東西 *dōngxī* "thing", 事情 *shìqíng* "item", and 物件 *wùjiàn* "object"), rather than naming the referred to items at the basic level. Three conditions of discourse were tested: one was vague texts preceded by congruent titles, another was texts preceded by incongruent titles and the third was texts preceded without titles. An on-line self-paced reading task was conducted. Participants were instructed to read the vague texts and rate the level of comprehensibility. The rating scores for the level of comprehensibility and the reading time of the whole texts were measured. The experimental results show that people read texts preceded by congruent titles significantly faster than those preceded by incongruent and no titles. However, the reading time of texts preceded by incongruent titles was also significantly shorter than those preceded without titles. We conclude that when people simply read vague idea at a discourse level, the appropriate information is useful for text integration. Inappropriate information, however, can be paid little attention during the text processing and do not increase too much processing load.

Keywords: vague texts, congruency, self-paced reading task, background knowledge

1. Introduction

There are two basic approaches to text understanding: *the top-down approach*, in which the reader starts with a preexistent structure like a schema and tries to fit the text proposition into it, and the *bottom-up approach*, in which the reader starts with the text propositions and tries to create a new structure for them.

According to the top-down approach, when no schema is explicitly given and the reader needs to determine referents and inter-relate propositions, s/he uses whatever information s/he can guess from the text. The reader may try to guess a schema at the same level of detail as that of "washing clothes"; alternatively, he may use some abstract default schema to relate propositions. We will refer to these two instances of the top-down approach as the "guessing" and "default schema" strategies, respectively [1].

With regard to the bottom-up approach to text understanding, when the reader needs to determine referents or inter-relate propositions, presumably s/he does this by using concepts that have been repeated within and between propositions. This "concept repetition" strategy is probably the best-known instance of the bottom-up approach [2].

The top-down approach predicts a schema advantage, that is, texts with schemas are processed faster than those with no schemas. There is evidence to support that people adopt the top-down approach in reading vague texts. Titles function as prior knowledge activators and allow the reader to connect existing knowledge with new information. Evidence for this effect is based on studies that show increased recall for text content when the text is preceded by a title [3, 4, 5]. Bransford and Johnson's [4] research, the classic study, examined how people comprehend and recall an unclear passage describing a series of actions. Their results showed that when the passage was preceded by a title, participants had better recall for the text context than when the passage was read without titles.

In addition, Smith & Swinney's study [6] supported the idea that the presence of schema facilitated discourse processing on-line. Participants were required to read "vague" texts and the reading time for each sentence was each text was recorded. Half the texts were preceded by a title that activated a relevant schema, whereas the other half were presented without relevant schema. Their results showed that reading time of texts without titles was substantially longer than those of texts with titles.

Moreover, research into narrative has shown the importance of narrative theme statements for the integration of narrative content. Previous studies showed that the absence of an explicit theme statement within the narrative structure reduced the reader's ability to comprehend and recall the narrative [7, 8, 9, 10].

In addition, titles can direct the readers' attention to specific information during reading. Rittschof et al. [11] found that when participants were given a written thematic prime before asking them to read a short expository text, they recalled fewer unrelated facts. The thematic prime directed the participants' attention to thematically relevant information and enhanced their ability to discount irrelevant information. Previous research has shown that thematic titles can enhance readers' ability to focus on topic information of importance or shift the focus of attention to a new integrating theme.

Furthermore, in Lee and Cheng's research [12] on Mandarin Chinese, their comprehensibility rating and recall studies provided evidence that texts with congruent titles were more comprehensible than those without titles or with incongruent titles. Participants were instructed to listen to three passages. One of texts was preceded by a congruent title, another was preceded by no titles and the other was preceded by an incongruent title. When they finished listening to the texts, they had to judge whether they could understand the texts on a 1-5 point scale, 1 indicating not comprehensible, 5 indicating very comprehensible. Their results showed that the mean comprehensibility rating scores preceded by congruent titles were higher than those preceded without titles and those preceded by incongruent titles. However, they didn't find any significant difference in rating scores between the texts preceded by incongruent titles and no titles.

Although the previous studies provided evidence that background knowledge can facilitate the discourse comprehension (i.e., the level of comprehensibility), the question of whether the title information facilitates the processing time has not been answered yet. Indeed, Lee and Cheng's [12] study used an off-line rating task, which can only measure how much people comprehend vague texts. It is not necessary that the higher level of comprehensibility for the texts preceded by congruent titles predicts the faster processing time. This unanswered question needs to be further determined.

Second, it is quite surprising that there was no significant difference in the rating scores between the vague texts preceded by incongruent titles and those without titles in Lee and Cheng's study. It is possible that the auditory presentation of vague texts affects the results. In the auditory processing, participants could easily ignore the inappropriate information since the auditory sentences went quickly. People in this situation can not memorize everything. We postulate that it is why Lee and Cheng found no significant difference between vague texts preceded by no titles and by incongruent titles. In this study, we wonder whether the significant difference in rating scores will occur between the two vague text conditions if the vague texts are presented visually and people will detect the inappropriate background knowledge.

Finally, another reason to re-conduct this experiment is that the experimental materials in Lee & Cheng's study [12] were not well-controlled, which may cause the biased results. Indeed, only three paragraphs were tested in Lee and Cheng's study, each condition involving only one paragraph. The limited numbers of materials tested in their experiment can result in unreliable results. In addition, the congruent and incongruent titles were not balanced for the character length and structure complexity, either. For example, the length of characters for the congruent titles in Lee & Cheng's study is 8.7 characters but the length for the incongruent titles is 3 characters. The longer titles could allow participants to process the vague texts with less effort. This factor could also affect how participants comprehended the vague texts.

Therefore, the goal of this current study is to determine whether the relevant background knowledge facilitate the processing time and whether the irrelevant background knowledge inhibit how much people understand vague texts when materials are presented visually. The reading time of whole texts and rating scores on the level of comprehensibility of vague texts will be recorded. In addition, we will increase the number of the vague texts and balance the length and syntactic complexity of titles in congruent and incongruent conditions. We hope that the replication of this experiment in Mandarin Chinese can bring us to understand the role of background knowledge in the text processing.

2. **Experiment: An On-line Self-Paced Reading task**

The purpose of this study is to look at the role of background knowledge in the processing of vague texts. We designed three conditions of vague texts: those preceded by congruent titles, those preceded by incongruent titles and those preceded without titles. An on-line self-paced reading task was conducted. Participants were instructed to read the three conditions of the vague texts sentence by sentence and judge how much they comprehend the texts on a 1-5 point scale. The rating scores on the level of comprehensibility of texts were recorded. In addition, the response time for comprehensibility judgment and the reading time for the whole text were recorded, too.

We predict that the appropriate background knowledge can facilitate the processing of vague texts. However, the inappropriate background knowledge will not always result in inhibitory effects in text processing. In particular, it is proposed that the inappropriate background knowledge can increase the processing load only in the situation when participants make semantic/comprehensibility judgment. But the inappropriate background knowledge will not increase the processing load when participants simply read the texts without making judgment. We think that when people simply read vague texts preceded by incongruent titles, they will not concentrate on inappropriate background information occurring between titles and contents of vague texts. Readers would like to read texts as quickly as possible in order to grasp the main idea of the vague text. So, we postulate that incongruent titles may not elicit the processing difficulty in reading time.

The absence of titles, on the other hand, does not allow one to expect what the vague texts discuss and they have to guess the themes of the vague texts until the end of texts. When people read a text without any title, they have to construct a title first. In the middle of the text, they have to keep revising the title according to the text information. The trial-and-error processing can increase the processing load and the reading time will be longer.

First, when the rating scores on the level of comprehensibility across the three conditions of vague texts are compared, we expect that the rating scores for texts preceded by congruent titles should be *significantly higher* than those preceded by incongruent titles and no titles since the appropriate background information will facilitate the processing of vague texts. Furthermore, the rating scores for texts preceded without titles should be *significantly higher* than those preceded by incongruent titles since the inappropriate background information will produce an inhibitory effect when people make comprehension judgment.

Second, when the rating response times across the three text conditions are compared, we also predict that the response time for the vague texts preceded by congruent titles should be *significantly shorter* than those preceded by incongruent titles and no titles because of the advantage of the appropriate background information. Moreover, the response time for texts preceded without titles should be *significantly shorte*r than those preceded by incongruent titles. It is the same reason that the inhibitory effects occur during the judgment task.

Finally, when the reading time of whole texts across the title condition are compared, we expect that the vague texts preceded by congruent titles will be read *significantly faster* than those preceded by incongruent titles and no titles because the relevant background information elicits facilitation effects. However, the vague texts preceded by incongruent titles will be read *significantly faster* than those preceded without titles. It is because the absence of background knowledge will cause much processing load than the inappropriate information during the reading of vague texts.

2.1 Method

2.1.1. Participants

63 undergraduate students of National Chiayi University (age range from 18 to 23 years old, mean age= 19.87 years old, SD = 1.30, 6 male and 57 female) participated in our task. They were tested individually and paid for their participation. All subjects were controlled for their language background (i.e. native speaker of Mandarin/Taiwanese).

2.1.2. Materials and Design

Our experimental stimuli consist of 51 sets of vague stories in three conditions: vague texts preceded by congruent titles, vague texts preceded by incongruent titles, and vague texts preceded without titles.

For the vague texts, each was created by using vague references and neutral descriptors (e.g. 東西 *dōngxī* "thing", 事情 *shìqíng* "item", and 物件 *wùjiàn* "object"), rather than naming the referred to items at the basic level. For instance, the example in Table 1 is a vague text discussing snowman. The content does not explicitly point out lexical items associated with these concepts "snow" or "snowman" or "winter". It uses vague descriptions or references such as 過程 *guòchéng* "procedure" and 成品 *chéngp n* "thing". In addition, the congruent title is 堆雪人 *duīxuěrén* "a snowman", which provides relevant information what a text is discussed and the incongruent one is 洗杯子 *x bēiz* "washing cups", which provides irrelevant information to the text. Both of the congruent and incongruent titles are controlled for the same syntactic structures, e.g., V+N, in this example.

Table 1: An Example of the Vague Texts in this Study

A Vague Text:

這個**過程**很簡單也很有樂趣。整個**過程**可以在任何地方發生。平均大概要花費一小時或甚至整天都有可能。**過程**中，時間長短取決於你是否要求最後**成品**要非常精緻。整個**過程**只需要一個材料。材料不但要很充足而且越新鮮越好，因為這些原因可以決定**成品**的壽命。另外，**成品**放置的位置也可以決定成品的壽命。如果你等待太久才使用材料，這種材料是會消失的。這個**過程**幾乎每一個人都可以做。

Three Conditions of Titles:

A congruent Title:	堆雪人
An incongruent title:	洗杯子
No title:	Ø

In our 51 sets of titles, the length of texts in both congruent and incongruent condition was 161 characters (range from 160 to 161 characters) and the length of titles in both congruent and incongruent conditions was 3 characters (range from 2 to 5 characters). In addition, the structures of titles involved in both title conditions were the same. There are 8 titles using the "V" structure pattern (e.g., 慢跑 *mànp o* and 洗澡 *x z o*) and 43 titles using the "V+N" syntactic pattern (e.g., 剪指甲 *ji nzh ji* and 寫報告 *xiěbàogào*).

The 51 sets of vague materials with their corresponding congruent and incongruent titles were selected from 100 vague texts via running two pretests: one title production task and one title relevance yes/no judgment task. In the production task, we instructed the 100 undergraduates (Mean age = 20.6 years old, age range from 18 to 23 years old) to read the 100 vague texts and to guess the possible titles for these texts. The titles of texts that were easily guessed by participants were filtered in our main experiment. The final 51 vague materials were controlled for the title predictability: 89 percent of participants can not guess the correct or appropriate titles for the 51 vague texts.

In addition, 100 participants were instructed to judge the level of relevance of tiles in a YES/NO force choice task. Participants saw a paragraph that was preceded by a title and had to determine whether the title was suitable for this paragraph by selecting YES or NO, YES indicating "relevant" and NO indicating "irrelevant". The purpose of this judgment task is to screen out the inappropriate titles. Congruent titles and incongruent titles were controlled for the level of relevance: the average for congruent titles on the level of relevance is 95% and for incongruent titles on the level of irrelevance is 97%.

In our self-paced reading task, the 51 sets of vague texts were counterbalanced into three lists. Each list included 51 trials in total: one third of vague texts preceded by congruent title, one third preceded by incongruent titles, and one third preceded without titles. Participants did not see the same vague text repeatedly and only saw each paragraph in one title condition once. Before the main task, participants were instructed to read 12 practice vague texts for getting familiar with the whole procedure of the self-paced reading task.

2.1.3. Procedure

The experimental stimuli were randomized in the three lists. At the beginning, participants were instructed to sit in front of a computer and gave an instruction and practice items. They were instructed to read the texts presented by titles or "XXXX" (indicating no titles). These texts were presented sentence by sentence and participants had to read them as quickly as possible but they could read them based on their reading speed. After they finished each sentence, they needed to press the button for the next sentence. The reading times from the onset of the first sentence to the button press by participants for reading the last sentence of texts were recorded by the computer. After the text reading, participants saw a 1-5 point scale on the screen and had to judge the level of comprehensibility of texts. If the text would be highly incomprehensible, they would rate 1 for "very incomprehensible". If the texts would be very comprehensible, they would rate 5 for "very comprehensible". If the texts would be partially comprehensible or incomprehensible, they could rate the number from 2 to 4 on a scale based on their intuition. The rating scores for each trial were recorded, too.

The presentation procedure of this self-paced task is as follows (Figure 1). A cross presented on the screen for 350 milliseconds and then it disappears quickly. A 150-millisecond blank followed and disappear quickly. The second cross appeared again on the screen for 350 milliseconds and disappeared immediately. The purpose of the two crosses appearing on the screen was to allow participants to concentrate their eyes on the middle of the screen and wait for the upcoming target stimuli. Then, the title of a vague text presented on the screen for 600 milliseconds and another blank slide followed for 500 milliseconds. Afterwards, the first sentence of this text appeared on the screen. Participants were asked to read and understand them based on their intuition. After reading each sentence, they pressed the button for continuing the next sentence until the last sentence of this text. After reading the whole text, the previous text was presented again with a rating scale from 1-5 point scale. Participants had to rate the level of comprehensibility of texts by pressing a button.

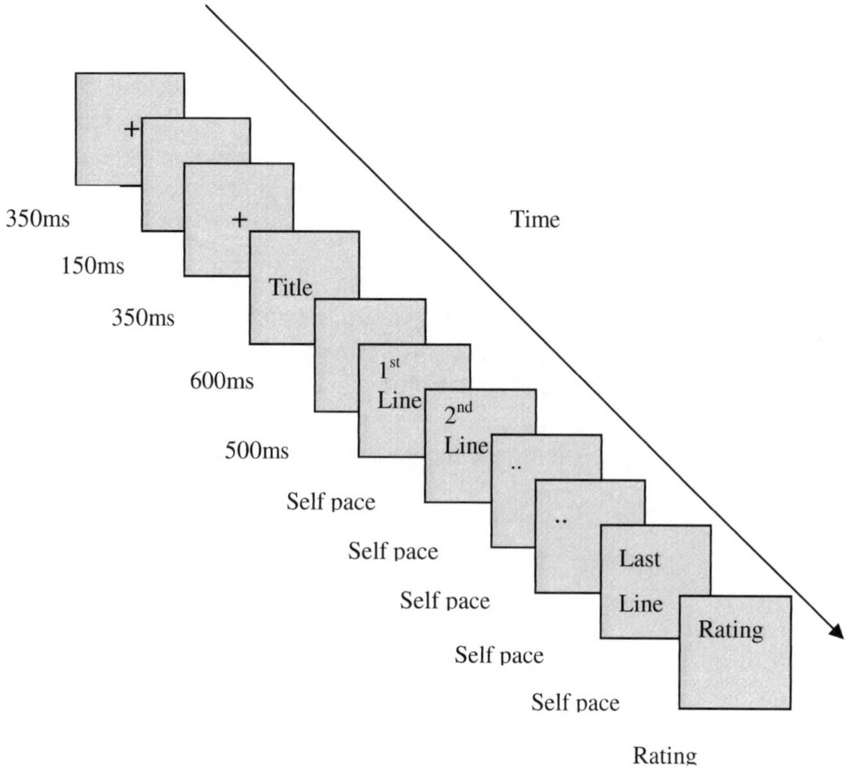

Figure 1. The procedure of the stimuli presentation

3. Results and Discussion

No data of participants were removed. The comprehensibility rating scores, the rating response time and the reading time of the whole texts were analyzed. Table 2 shows that the average rating scores on the level of comprehensibility of texts for the vague texts preceded by congruent, incongruent and no titles are 4.81, 2.27, and 3.36 scores, respectively. So, the vague texts preceded by congruent titles are the most comprehensible, followed by no title and those preceded by incongruent titles are the least comprehensible.

A one-way repeated ANOVA test for testing rating scores was conducted. The by-subject analysis shows there was significant difference in rating scores across the three conditions of vague texts (F_1 (2, 189) = 246.12, $p < .05$). The post-hoc analysis shows that the rating scores of the vague texts preceded by congruent title were *significantly higher* than those of texts preceded by incongruent titles and no titles ($p < .05$). Moreover, the rating scores of the text preceded by incongruent title were *significantly lower* than that those of the texts preceded without titles ($p < .05$). The by-item analysis also yielded consistent results as the by-subject analysis (F_2 (2, 150) = 330.97, $p < .05$). There were *significant differences* in rating scores between the texts preceded by congruent texts and those by incongruent/no titles ($p < .05$). And the vague texts preceded by incongruent titles were *significantly less comprehensible* than those of the texts preceded without titles (p < .05).

Table 2: Means of rating scores across the three conditions of discourse

Conditions of Texts	Mean rating scores
Congruent Titles	4.8 (SD= 0.24)
Incongruent Titles	2.3 (SD= 1.07)
No Titles	3.4 (SD= 0.81)

Additionally, the rating response time was analyzed. Table 3 shows that the average response times for the texts preceded by congruent title, incongruent title, and no titles are 1037.5 ms, 1809.4 ms and 1887.8 ms, respectively. The results show that the texts preceded by congruent titles were rated faster than the other two text conditions. Participants took longer time to rate the texts preceded without title than those preceded by incongruent titles.

Table 3: Means of rating response time across three conditions of discourse

Conditions of Titles	Mean reaction time
Congruent Titles	1037.5 (SD= 570.1)
Incongruent Titles	1809.4 (SD= 602.4)
No Titles	1887.8 (SD= 889.3)

A one-way repeated ANOVA analysis for testing the rating response time was conducted. The by-subject analysis shows that the rating response time was significantly different across the three text conditions (F_1 (2, 189) = 61.24, p < .05). A post-hoc analysis shows that the response time of the texts preceded by congruent title was *significantly shorter* than those of the texts preceded by incongruent titles and no titles (p < .05). However, the reaction time of the texts preceded by incongruent titles was *NOT significantly longer* than those of the texts preceded without titles (p > .05). The by-item analysis also yielded the significant difference across the three conditions of texts as the by-subject analysis (F_2 (2, 150) = 41.90, p < .05). The response time for the texts preceded by congruent titles was *significantly shorter* than that those preceded by incongruent/no titles (p < .05). Additionally, there was *NO significant difference* in reaction time between the texts preceded by incongruent titles and no titles (p > .05).

Moreover, Table 4 shows that the reading time for the texts preceded by congruent titles, incongruent titles and no title are 13976.8 ms, 15302.5 ms, and 17123 ms, respectively, which demonstrates that the vague texts preceded by congruent titles were read faster than the other two text conditions. In addition, the vague texts preceded without titles seem not to be easily read because people took the longest time to read the no-title condition.

A one-way repeated ANOVA analysis for testing reading time was conducted. The by-subject analysis shows that there are significant difference across the three text conditions (F_1 (2, 189) = 40.95, $p < .05$). A post-hoc test demonstrates that the reading time of the texts preceded by congruent titles was *significantly shorter* than those preceded by incongruent titles or no titles ($p < .05$). In addition, the reading time of the texts preceded by incongruent titles was *significantly shorter* than the one of the texts preceded without titles ($p < .05$). The by-item analysis also yielded the same results as the by-subject analysis (F_2 (2, 150) = 28.60, $p < .05$). The congruent condition was read *significantly faster* than the other two title conditions ($p < .05$). And, the vague texts preceded by the incongruent condition were read *significantly faster* than those preceded without titles ($p < .05$).

Table 4: Means of text reading time across three conditions of discourse

Type of Titles	Mean
Congruent Title	13976.8 (SD= 5052.1)
Incongruent Title	15302.5 (SD= 6486.8)
No Title	17123.0 (SD= 5401.7)

To summarize, the results of the rating scores show that the vague texts preceded by congruent titles were processed with less effort than the other title conditions. Incongruent titles, however, provide inappropriate information and make the vague texts not easily to be understood. So, the texts preceded by incongruent titles were rated as the least comprehensible. The vague texts preceded without titles served as the baseline condition and rated as the neutral one (i.e., neither comprehensible nor incomprehensible). The results of rating scores are consistent with our prediction that the relevant background knowledge facilitates the comprehensibility level and irrelevant information results in the inhibitory effects in comprehension.

On the other hand, the results of the response time show a little different from our expectation. In our experiment, the vague texts preceded by congruent titles were responded faster than the other two title conditions. This also suggests the facilitation effects of appropriate background knowledge in text processing. However, we also found that the vague texts preceded by incongruent titles were responded as fast as those preceded without titles, which is different from our prediction that there would be no difference in response time between the no-title and incongruent conditions. The possible reason may be that each vague paragraph was read twice, which allowed one not to read the texts again when the text presented at the second time and directly made responses based on the memory of their previous reading. Thus, the repeated presentation of the vague texts results in the similar response times between the incongruent titles and no-title conditions.

Furthermore, the results of reading time of whole texts show that the vague texts preceded by congruent titles were read faster than the other two conditions. In addition, the reading time of the texts preceded by incongruent titles were read faster than those preceded without titles. The results of reading time also follow our prediction that appropriate information can facilitate the reading but inappropriate information is not necessary for leading to an inhibitory effect in text reading. Even though participants thought that the no-title vague texts were much more comprehensible than the incongruent condition, participants took longer time to read the former than the latter. The reason is that participants used the different processing strategies in the reading and judgment tasks. During the reading of a vague text, participants did not suspect what we saw and tried to integrate information together to grasp the main idea for this vague text. Participants may guess the title to be problematic, they still kept reading without paying too much attention on the conflict ideas evoked between the content of the texts and the titles. Thus, the inappropriate information did not cause too much processing load.

Finally, the absence of titles can cause much effort for readers to process vague texts because the absence of titles can not allow one to construct a theme in mind. So, participants have to always postulate the possible topic from the beginning of the text to the end. If they think the postulated title is not proper, they have to revise it again and propose another possible title. This trial-and-error process costs longer time for readers to read the texts preceded without titles than those preceded by incongruent titles.

4. Conclusion

This study investigates whether the background knowledge can facilitate the processing of vague texts in Mandarin Chinese. We conducted a self-paced reading task and reading time, comprehensibility rating scores and response time were recoded. Our experimental results show that the relevant or proper background knowledge does aid the integration of vague idea together during the discourse process. However, the improper background knowledge can increase the comprehension difficulty but does not necessarily lead to an inhibition in processing. The evidence is that the reading time of the vague texts preceded without titles was longer than those preceded by incongruent titles in our experiment. The inappropriate information does not seriously interrupt how people read the vague texts even though they are considered the least comprehensible. The absence of titles can lead to a trial-and-error processing so that people take the longest time in processing this kind of texts.

Our results on rating scores are little different from Lee and Cheng's findings [12]. Lee and Cheng found that the vague texts preceded by congruent titles were more comprehensible than the other two title conditions, which is also consistent with our results of rating scores. But, Lee and Cheng did not find the significant difference in rating scores between the vague texts preceded by incongruent titles and those preceded without titles. Indeed, we found that the texts preceded by incongruent titles received significantly lower rating scores than those preceded without titles. The diverging results in rating scores between their and our studies can be attributed to the method of how to present the vague texts.

The vague texts in Lee and Cheng's study were auditory displayed but our texts were presented visually. When participants listened to the vague texts preceded by incongruent titles, each sentence went by quickly and it is not easy for listeners to detect the inappropriate information between titles and contents of texts. Therefore, they did not think the vague texts preceded by incongruent titles to be less comprehensible than those without titles. However, in our study, the texts were presented visually. The vague texts appeared on the screen until participants pressed the button to read the next sentence. The visual method can allow readers to have longer time to integrate vague idea together and can discover what information is not appropriate.

To conclude, this psycholinguistic study is to determine whether the background knowledge influences the processing of vague texts. Our results show that relevant background knowledge can aid the processing of vague texts. The irrelevant background knowledge, however, does not necessarily inhibit the processing of vague texts. The inhibitory effect only occurs in the judgment task rather than in the reading task. Finally, the absence of background knowledge leads to much processing difficulty at a discourse level.

Acknowledgments

This research was supported by grants from the National Science Council of Taiwan (NSC 96-2411-H-415 -014 -MY3). We would like to thank two anonymous reviewers of ROCLING2011 for their comments on earlier versions of this work. Remaining errors are our sole responsibility.

References

[1] D. E. Rumelhart, &, A. Ortony. "The representation of knowledge in memory". In R. C. Anderson, r. J. Spiro, & W. E. Montague (Eds.), *Schooling and the acquisition of knowledg*e (pp 99-135). Hillsadale, NJ: Erlbaum. 1977.

[2] W. Kintsch &, T. A. van Dijk (1978). "Toward a model of text comprehension and production". *Psychological Review*, 85, 363-394. 1978.

[3] J. D. Bransford, & M. K. Johnson. "Contextual prerequisites for understanding: some investigations of comprehensions and recall". *Journal of Verbal Learning and Verbal Behavior*, 11, 717-726. 1972.

[4] J. D. Bransford &, M. K. Johnson. "Consideration of some problems of comprehension". In W. G. Chase (Ed.), *Visual information processing*. New York: Academic. 1973.

[5] D. J. Dooling &, R. Lachman. Effects of comprehension on retention of prose. *Journal of Experimental Psychology*, 88, 216-222. 1971.

[6] E. Smith & D. Swinney. "The role of Schemas in reading text: a real-time examination." *Discourse Processes*, 15, 303-316. 1992.

[7] N. S. Johnson, & J. M. Mandler. "A tale of two structures: underlying and surface forms in stories". *Poetics*, 9-51-86. 1980.

[8] J. M. Mandler & M. S. Goodman. "On the validity of story structure." *Journal of Verbal Learning and Verbal Behavior*, 21, 507-523. 1982.

[9] D. E. Rumelhart. "Understanding and summarizing brief stories". In D. LaBerge & S. J. Samuels (Eds.), *Basic Processes in Reading Comprehension: Perception and Comprehension* (pp. 230-265). Hillsdale, JJ: Lawrence Erlbaum Associates, Inc. 1977.

[10] P. W. Thorndyk. "Cognitive structures in comprehension and memory of narrative discourse." *Cognitive Psychology*, 9, 77-110. 1977.

[11] K. A., Rittschof, W. A. Stock, & R. W. Kulhavy, M. P. Verdi & J. M. Doran (1994).

"Thematic maps improve memory for facts and inferences: a test of the stimulus order hypothesis." *Contemporary Educational Psychology*, 19, 129-142. 1994

[12] M-H. Lee & C-M. Cheng (1976). "Conceptual knowledge as related to language comprehension and recall." *Acta Psychologica Taiwanica* (Chinese Journal of Psychology). 18, 121-128. 1976.

模糊語境理解歷程的先前知識效應

龔書萍
嘉義大學
spgong@mail.ncyu.edu.tw

安可思
香港浸會大學
ahrens@hkbu.edu.hk

摘要

本研究探討先前知識是否會影響人處理模糊不清的脈絡文章和語境。模糊的脈絡文章是指語境使用含糊、非指涉特定物件、事件，使用中性的描述和詞彙 (例如：“東西、“事情” 、和 “物件”), 而不使用特定的名稱。本研究中，測試了三種模糊語境文章。第一是模糊語境使用了合諧 (congruent) 的標題 (titles)；第二是模糊語境使用了不合諧 (incongruent) 的標題；第三種是模糊語境但沒有標題 (no titles)。我們執行了一個「線上自主的閱讀作業」(on-line self-paced reading task) 的心理語言實驗，並測量了受試者的這三種實驗材料的閱讀時間。實驗結果顯示，受試者在處理合諧標題的模糊語境時，閱讀時間比不合諧或沒有標題的文章時，閱讀時間顯著性較短。另外，受試者在處理不合諧標題的模糊語境時，也比沒有標題的實驗材料的閱讀時間顯著性較短，這顯示由不合諧標題所引起的不相干背景知識並不會讓模糊語境處理時間較久，反而是沒有標題的文章處理時間是最長的。本研究結論為：標題的作用為背景知識的激發，可以促進理解模糊語境文章。但是，不合諧標題未必在模糊語境處理上會造成抑制效果。

關鍵字：模糊語境、合諧、自主的閱讀作業、背景知識

On the Learning of Chinese Aspect Markers through Multimedia Program*

多媒體課程對華語時貌標記學習成效之研究

謝慈惠 Hsieh, Tzu-Hui
國立嘉義大學外國語言學系
Department of Foreign Languages
National Chiayi University
ncl2008.teresa@gmail.com

郭怡君 Kuo, Yi-Chun
國立嘉義大學外國語言學系
Department of Foreign Languages
National Chiayi University
jennykuo@mail.ncyu.edu.tw

鐘樹椽 Chung, Shu-Chun
國立嘉義大學數位學習設計及管理學系
Department of E-learning Design and Management
National Chiayi University
tschung@mail.ncyu.ledu.tw

吳俊雄 Wu, Jiun-Shiung [a]
國立中正大學語言學研究所
Institute of Linguistics
National Chung Cheng University
Lngwujs@ccu.edu.tw

Abstract

* This research was funded by the National Science Council (NSC) of the Republic of China under Contract No. NSC 98-2631-S415-005. Wu Jiun-Shiung is the primary investigator of the project. Jenny Yi-Chun Kuo and Chung, Shu-Chun are the co-primary investigators. We thank to Mandarin teachers Miao-Chin Chiu and Chen-Hsuan Huang in the Division of Chinese as a Second Language, Language Center, National Chiayi University, and Xiurong Gong in Chinese Language Center of Feng-Chia University for their suggestions and comments on our teaching materials. We also thank the anonymous reviewers of the ROCLING conference for their precious comments. All remaining errors are ours.

[a] All correspondences should be directed to: Wu Jiun-Shiung, Institute of Linguistics of National Chung Cheng University, 168 University Rd., Min-Hsiung, Chia-Yi 62102, Taiwan, R.O.C.

The purpose of this study is to develop a multimedia program and examine its effects on learning Chinese aspect markers *le*, *zai*, and *zhe*. The materials in the program were based on linguistic studies of *le*, *zai*, and *zhe* (Li & Thompson, 2005; Lin, 2002; Liu, 1997; Pan, 1996; Smith, 1997; Wu & Kuo, 2003; Wu, 2003, 2005, 2007; Xiao & McEnery, 2004; Yeh, 1993). We predicted that this multimedia program with animation presenting the target sentences can significantly improve Chinese as a Foreign Language (for short, CFL) learners' acquisition of these aspect markers. The participants were totally 35 CFL beginners. Nineteen of them in the experimental group received the interactive multimedia program and sixteen of them in the control group took the computer-based grammar program. The teaching experiment is a section of twenty minutes per day for 3 days. We conduct a pretest, immediate posttest, and one-month delayed posttest, and the performances between the two groups were compared using the independent T-test. Findings indicated that the experimental group showed a significant advantage over the control group both in the immediate posttest and the delayed posttest.

摘要

本研究基於語言學對於華語時貌標記之研究，製作多媒體動畫課程，透過動畫來呈現時貌標記的語態，幫助華語爲外語學習者對「了」、「在」、「著」的習得。三十五位華語初級學習者參與實驗，其中十九位爲實驗組，用多媒體動畫課程自學;十六位爲控制組，用電腦輔助文法翻譯課程學習時貌標記，經過連續三天，每天二十分鐘的學習，以T-test來檢驗，結果顯示實驗組在後測以及延宕後測的表現，比控制組來得有顯著的進步。

Keywords: Chinese Aspect Markers, Interactive Multimedia Program, Chinese as a Foreign Language, Animation

關鍵詞：時貌標記，多媒體動畫課程，華語爲外語學習

1. Introduction

The Chinese aspect markers[1] have considered difficult for Chinese as a Foreign Language learners (Chao, 2002; Kao, 2006). Kao (2006) analyze the errors of the usage of the perfective *le* and of the imperfective *zhe* based on the corpus consisting of inter-language of Chinese produced by Chinese as a Foreign Language (for short, CFL) students abroad. Based on his study, he suggests that the interaction between aspect markers and different types of events, the comparison of the similar aspect markers and their individual characteristics should be introduced and emphasized in CFL instruction.

In this study, we develop a curriculum for three Chinese aspect markers: the perfective *le*, the progressive *zai* and the durative *zhe*. In order to eliminate the negative effect of grammar translation and possibly insufficiency of pedagogical grammar, we use the generalizations

[1] Chinese aspect markers include the perfective aspect markers *le*, the imperfective markers *zai* and *zhe*, the experiential *guo*, and verbal reduplication (Li & Thompson, 1981). In this study, we focus on the perfective marker *le*, and the imperfective markers *zai* and *zhe*.

from linguistic research on these three aspect markers, e.g. Li & Thompson, 1981; Lin, 2002; Liu, 1997; Pan, 1996; Smith, 1997; Wu & Kuo, 2003; Wu, 2003, 2005, 2007; Xiao & McEnery, 2004; Yeh, 1993, and implement the generalizations with computer animations, an instruction method along the lines proposed in Form Focused Instruction (Ellis, 1985).

According to Wu (2003, 2007), *zai* as a progressive marker goes with an event ongoing at an instant and *le* as a perfective marker presents a completed event or a terminated event. Both of *zai* and *le* can go with accomplishment[2] and activity[3] events. Thus, the comparison between them in terms of accomplishment events is stated as the following sentences (1).

(1) a. Tā **zài** xiě yì fēng xìn.
she PROG write one CL letter
"She is writing a letter."

b. Tā xiě (wán) **le** yì fēng xìn.
she write (finish) PFV one CL letter
"She finished writing a letter."

In (1), we can tell the difference between *zai* and *le* in terms of interacting with Accomplishment. For example, *xiě yì fēng xìn* 'to write a letter' gets an ongoing reading with *zai* in (1a) while it receives a completed meaning with *le* in (1b). As for Activity, the comparison between *zai* and *le* was presented in (2). As we can see, *pǎobù* 'running' gets an ongoing reading with *zai* in (2a) while it acquires a completed meaning with *le* in (2b).

(2) a. Tā **zài** pǎobù.
he PROG running
"He is running."

b. Tā pǎo **le** yí ge xiǎoshí de bù.
he run PFV one CL hour of steps.
"He ran for one hour."

Also, in our curriculum, we included the contrast between *zhe* and *le*. *zhe* as the durative aspect marker signals the durative nature of a situation (e.g. Xiao & McEnery, 2004). When it comes to Activity such as the positional verb,[4] *zhe* selects the stative reading to signal its durative posture (e.g. Li & Thompson, 2005; Xia & McEnery, 2004). For example, *dai* 'to put on; to wear' receives a stative meaning with *zhe* in (3a). In contrast, it gets a completed meaning with *le* in (3b).

[2] According to Smith (1997), accomplishment events include a process and a change of state, an accomplishment event is compatible with both durational phrases and completive phrases. For example, *xie zhe wu feng xin* 'to write these five letters' is classified as Accomplishment because it contains both a process and a natural final endpoint.

[3] Smith (1997) proposed that activity events only include a process but without a change of state; that is, they have no national final points. Since it has no natural final endpoint, Activity requires a durational phrase to signal the final endpoint. For example, *Tā kàn le yíge xiǎoshí de diǎn yǐng* 'He saw a movie for one hour.' *yíge xiǎoshí* 'one hour' terminates the activity event *kàn diànyǐng* 'to see the movie.'

[4] Positional verbs like *chuan/dai* 'to put on; wear', *na* 'take; hold', *fang* 'put' and *gua* 'hang' refer to verbs that indicate where something has been put or placed (e.g. Xiao & McEnery, 2004).

(3) a. Tā dài **zhe** yì dǐng màozi.
she wear DUR one CL hat
"She is wearing a hat."
b. Tā dài **le** yì dǐng màozi.
she wear PFV one CL hat.
"She wore a hat."

On the other hand, *zhe* can go with posture verbs[5] in addition to positional verbs and receive a stative reading as shown in (4). In (4a), the posture verb such as *zuo* 'to sit' acquires a stative meaning from the durative marker *zhe*. In addition, the V *zhe* such as that in (4a) can be used to provide a temporal background in the V *zhe* V construction (Wu & Kuo, 2003). For example, *zuo* 'to sit' in (4b) serves as a background of the main event *he kafei* 'to drink coffee'.

(4) a. Tā zuò **zhe**.
she sit DUR
"She is sitting."
b. Tā zuò **zhe** hē kāfēi.
she sit DUR drink coffee
"She is drinking coffee, while sitting.

Furthermore, locative inversion in Chinese can take either *le* or *zhe*. However, the semantics of *zhe* differs from that of *le*. (5a), a locative inversion sentence with *zhe*, focuses on the lasting of the state part of the positional verb *fang* 'to put', while (5b), with *le*, focuses on the completion of the dynamic part of the same verb.

(5) a. Zhuōshàng fang **zhe** yì pán cài.
table put DUR one CL dish
"A dish of vegetables is on the table."
b. Zhuōshàng fang **le** yì pán cài.
table put PFV one CL dish
"A dish of vegetables was put on the table."

We also include in our curriculum the comparison among the three aspect markers *zhe*, *zai*, and *le*, Take the positional verb *chaun* 'to put on; to wear' as the example, shown in (6). *zhe* signifies the stative meaning in (6a), *zai* the progressive (ongoing) meaning in (6b) and *le* the completed meaning in (6c).

(6) a. Tā chuān **zhe** wàitào.
she wear DUR coat
"She is wearing a coat."
b. Tā **zài** chuān wàitào.

[5] Posture verbs refer to verbs indicating posture or physical disposition at a location such as *zhan* 'stand', *zuo* 'sit', *tang* 'lie', *dun* 'squat', *pa* 'crouch' and *ting* 'stop; park (a car)' and they either denote an activity or the state resulting from the activity, refer to verbs indicating posture or physical disposition at a location.

she PROG wear coat

"She is putting on a coat."

c. Tā chuān **le** wàitào.

she wear PFV coat

"She wore a coat."

So far, we have addressed the interactions of the aspect markers *le*, *zai*, and *zhe* with event types. As far as second language learning is concerned, there have been studies devoted to computer-based L2 grammar instruction, such as McEnery, Baker & Wilson, 1995; Nagata, 1996; Rachel, 1995; etc. These studies show that computer-based L2 grammar instruction is more effective than traditional instruction. Ragan, Boyce, Redwine, Savenye, and McMichael (1993) also find that multimedia instruction reduces learning time by 30% compared to traditional instruction.

In the study, we focus on CFL learners' acquisition of aspect markers *le*, *zai*, and *zhe*. These aspect markers are too abstract to comprehend for CFL learners, even expressed in English translation. For example, *Ta dai zhe maozhi* "She is wearing a hat" and *Ta zai dai maozhi* "She is putting on a hat." CFL beginners may be confused why *zai* changed the verb from 'to wear' to 'to put on,' and have difficulty in distinguishing these two expressions. We predict that the animation can present the slight difference among the interaction of these aspect markers with event types and then improve CFL beginners' comprehension of the aspect markers.

However, few studies, if any, investigate the effect on the computer-based grammar instruction with animation representing the semantics of the target sentences. Hence, we address the following issue in this paper: Is a computer-based multimedia program of grammar instruction (hereafter the interactive multimedia program) more effective than a Chinese computer-based grammar translation program (hereafter the computer-based grammar program) on CFL beginners' learning of aspect markers *le*, *zai*, and *zhe*?

The remainder of the paper is organized as follows. In Section 2, we present methodology including participants, instruments, data collection and data analysis. In Section 3 we report results and discussion. Results are presented with various analyses following each of these descriptive sections. Discussion included the effect of the interactive multimedia program vs. the computer-based grammar program. Finally, Section 4 concluded this study.

2. Methodology

This study chose a quantitative method to investigate the effect of interactive multimedia program on Chinese Aspect Marker *le*, *zai*, and *zhe* learning. Based on the purpose of the study, we examined if the interactive multimedia program is more efficient and effective than the computer-based grammar program on the learning of Chinese aspect markers.

The participants were 35 CFL beginners and they were divided into two groups. One is the control group and the other the experimental group. The control group studied *le*, *zai*, and *zhe* through the computer-based grammar program and the experimental group learned through the interactive multimedia program. Both of the interactive multimedia program and the computer-based grammar program were digitalized based on our designed curriculum which included seven lessons and exercises for each lesson. The major difference between the interactive multimedia program and the computer-based grammar program lies in the presentation of the semantics of *le*, *zai*, and *zhe* with events. The interactive multimedia program presented the semantics of the target sentences with animation while the computer-based grammar program with English corresponding sentences. The following Figure 1 shows the research design.

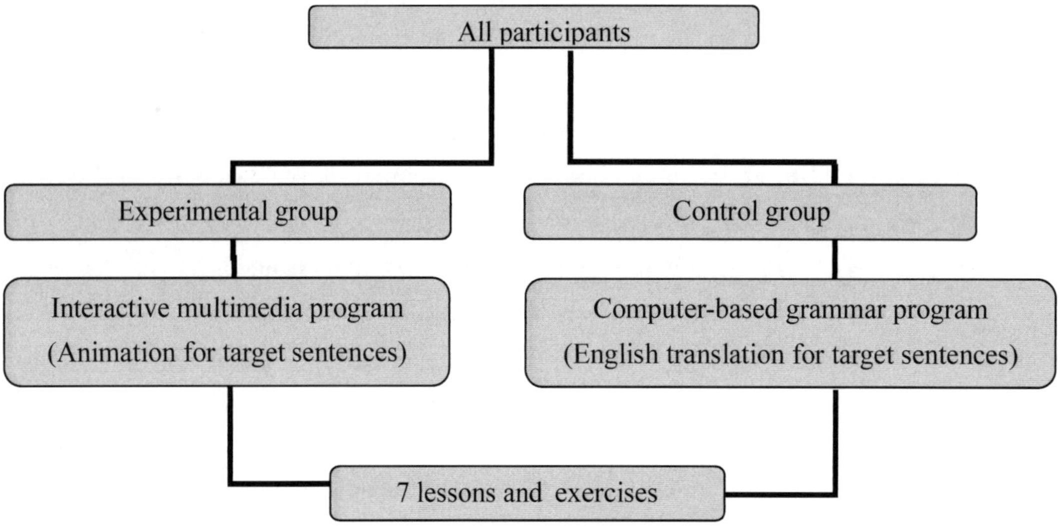

Figure 1. The research design

In addition to these two programs, a pretest, an immediate posttest, and a delayed posttest were used in the study. Performance of the experimental group who used the interactive multimedia program was compared with that of the control group who learned through the computer-based grammar program after learning an average twenty minutes of a three-day period learning. The result of the pre-test, immediate posttest, and the one-month delayed posttest were analyzed, using T-test to determine the effect of the interactive multimedia program.

2.1 Participants

Thirty-five participants for this study were selected respectively from the population of CFL beginners in National Chiayi University, National Chung-Cheng University, Chung-Yuan University and Feng-Chia University.[6] Twenty-one of them were female and fourteen were male. Their ages ranged from eighteen to fifty-five year-old. They came from various countries. As the following Table 1, eight of them come from Indonesia, seven from Korea,

[6] Among these 35 CFL beginners, four of them is from National Chiayi University, six from Chung-Yuan University, eight from National Chung-Cheng University, and seventeen from Feng-Chia University.

seven from Viet Nam, three from U.S.A, two from Mongolia, two from Russia, two from Thailand, one from Guatemala, one from India, one from Philippines, and one from Switzerland. The amount of time that the participants studied Mandarin Chinese is from half a year to one and half a year. All of them learned the perfective *le* and the progressive *zai* and half of them learned the durative *zhe*.

Table 1. Nationality of the participants in the study

Nationality	numbers of CFL beginners	Nationality	numbers of CFL beginners
Indonesia	8	Thailand	2
Korea	7	Guatemala	1
Viet Nam	7	India	1
U.S.A.	3	Philippines	1
Mongolia	2	Switzerland	1
Russia	2		

We divided these participants into two groups based on their English proficiency[7] because the control group learned the target sentences through English corresponding sentences. Participants from English speaking countries such as the U. S. A., India and Philippine and other countries Indonesia, Thailand and Switzerland were assigned to the control group. Thus, the control group and the experimental group consisted of 16 students and 19 students respectively. The homogeneity between these two groups was established by the pretest.[8] We calculated the average scores of the pretest of these two groups respectively out of a maximum score of 100 and get the mean score of the control group 68.75, and that of the experimental group 76.00, as shown in Table 2.

Table 2. Independent T-test between the two groups in the pretest

Group	*N*	*M*	*SD*	*t*
Control	16	68.75	15.75	1.557n.s.
Experimental	19	76.00	11.78	

Note: Maximum score =100, n.s.$p > .05$

Results of the independent T-test in Table 2 indicate no significant differences (t=1.557, p=0.129) between the control group and the experimental group. Therefore, these two groups are roughly the same in terms of their comprehension of Chinese aspect markers *le*, *zai*, and *zhe* before learning through our program.

2.2 Materials and Instruments

The experiment involved two parts. One is the CFL program of the perfective *le* and the imperfective *zai* and *zhe*, i.e. the interactive multimedia program and the computer-based

[7] Their English proficiency was investigated through the questionnaire about English background, also the interview with their CFL teachers.

[8] As to the details about the pretest, please see Section 2.2.2.

grammar program in our study. The other one is the test including the pretest, and the posttest. In Section 2.2.1, we indicated the design of the CFL program, and its content validity; the interactive multimedia program, and the computer-based grammar program. Then in Section 2.2.2, the pretest and the posttest were introduced. Also, their item difficulty (P) and discrimination (D) indexes and reliability were examined through a pilot study.

2.2.1 The CFL program of the perfective *le* and the imperfective *zai* and *zhe*

The CFL curriculum or program in our study shows the comparison of the interaction of *le*, *zai*, and *zhe* with event types they can go with and aims to make CFL beginners comprehend these three aspect markers in terms of syntactic structures and semantics. There are ten sentences for each lesson, and totally seven lessons. We present the comparison of *zai* and *le* from Lesson 1 to Lesson 4, that of *zhe* and *le* in Lesson 5, V_1 *zhe* V_2 structure in Lesson 6 and the comparison among *zhe*, *zai*, and *le* in Lesson 7, see Appendix I. The patterns of target sentences in every unit were based on the representative literature (Li & Thompson, 2005; Lin, 2002; Liu, 1997; Pan, 1996; Smith, 1997 Wu & Kuo, 2003; Wu, 2003, 2007; Xiao & McEnery, 2004; Yeh, 1993). Words in the CFL program came from the Mandarin 800 Words for Beginner provided by the Steering Committee for the Test of Proficiency-Hanyu (SC-TOP).[9] In order to establish content validity of the CFL program designed in our study, we invited two linguistics scholars and two senior Mandarin teachers whose inputs and feedback were useful. They were invited to review the CFL program, including the following interactive multimedia program and the computer-based grammar program. They judged the appropriateness of target sentences and their presentation. Thanks to their help, the content validity of the CFL program can be built.

2.2.1.1 The Interactive Multimedia Program

We digitalized the CFL program as above mentioned as the interactive multimedia program based on Concise Narrated Animation[10] (Mayer, 2001). In the program, the semantics of the target sentences were expressed by animation[11] and their syntactic structures were visual and audio narrated.[12] For example, in terms of the comparison between *zai*, and *le* of Lesson one, the animation expressed the progressing meaning of *zai* sentences and the completive meaning of *le* sentences; the words and voices showed their syntactic structure in Chinese Traditional Character and Hanyu Pinyin, and their pronunciation.

Besides, each lesson was followed by an interactive exercise which offered learners to do the drills. Each interactive exercise contained five to six items and most of these items were from

---

9 According to The Steering Committee for the Test of Proficiency-Huayu (SC-TOP), those who have learned Chinese more than half a year are familiar with these 800 words, shown on the following website http://www.sc-top.org.tw/download/800Words_Beginners.pdf .

10 Concise Narrated Animation (CNA), a simple principle to present multimedia, ignores the unneeded materials and shows the most important part of ready-to-learn knowledge.

11 All of the animation in the program is designed by the graduate and undergraduates in Department of E-learning Design and Management in National Chiayi University.

12 Please see the website http://web.ncyu.edu.tw/~wujs/le_zhe_zai/index.swf for the interactive multimedia program.

the target sentences of the program and they were designed based on two content objectives: (i) Users are able to comprehend the interpretation of the interaction of *zai*, *zhe*, and *le* with their compatible events. (ii) Users are able to know the collocation of these three aspect markers with events. For example, through doing the exercise 'Look at the animation and move *zai* and *le*', the users are expected to comprehend the semantics and the syntactic structure of *zai* and *le*, shown as Figure 2.

Figure 2. An example of the exercise in the interactive multimedia program.

2.2.1.2 The Computer-Based Grammar Program

Comparing to the interactive multimedia program, the computer-based grammar program[13] was also digitalized based on our designed CFL program. The difference between them lies in the presentation of semantics of the target sentences. In the interactive multimedia program, the semantics of target sentences were presented with animation as Figure 3. On the contrary, the computer-based grammar program expressed the meaning of the target sentences by English translation as Figure 4.

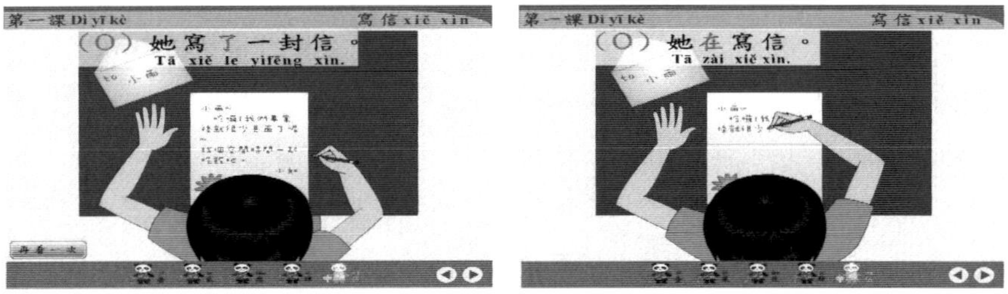

Figure 3. An example of animation in the interactive multimedia program

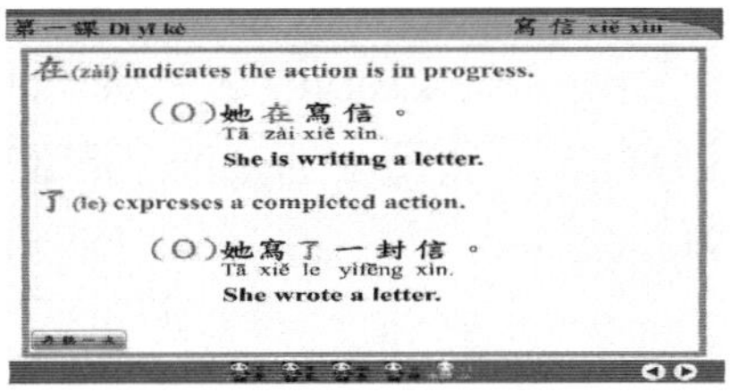

Figure 4. An example of English corresponding sentences in the grammar program

Figure 3 indicates the animation to present the semantics of *zai* and that of *le* with the event *xie xin* 'to write a letter' in the interactive multimedia program. Figure 4 shows the meaning of the target sentences expressed by their English corresponding sentences in the

---

[13] Please see the website http://web.ncyu.edu.tw/~wujs/le_zhe_zai_grammar/index1.swf for the computer-based grammar program.

computer-based grammar program. For example, 'She is writing letter' for *Ta zai xie xin* and 'She wrote a letter' for *Ta xie le yifeng xin*. Moreover, the computer-based grammar program offered the interactive exercise as the interactive multimedia program did. The interactive exercises in the computer-based grammar program are different from those in the interactive multimedia program in the presentation of the semantics of the target test items. As the following Figure 5, the meaning of the target test item was expressed by their English corresponding sentences.

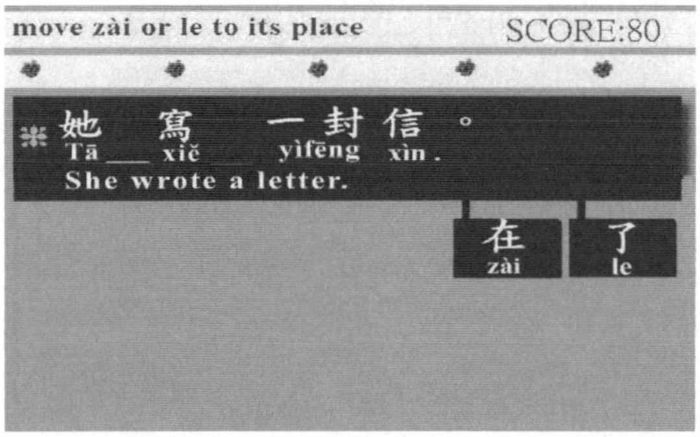

Figure 5. An example of the exercise in the grammar program

2.2.2 Pretest and Posttest

The pretest consisted of three parts for 25 questions, as shown in Appendix II. Most of these questions came from the target sentences in our CFL program and the content validity was established as a result of the review of the scholars and senior teaching CFL teachers as previously mentioned. Regarding the first part including 10 questions, the participants put words in an appropriate order. Its purpose was to test CFL beginners' comprehension of the syntactic structures of *le*, *zai*, and *zhe*. As to the second part of 10 questions, the participants choose a sentence that can best describe the clip[14] given for each question. It was to assess their understanding of the semantics of the target aspect markers *le*, *zai*, and *zhe*. In the third part including 5 questions, the participants produce a sentence by using the words provided based on the given clip. Through their production, we evaluated their comprehension of target aspect markers.

Concerning the posttest, it was formed by shifting the questions in the pretest. In order to ensure item analyses and reliability of the pretest and the posttest, we conducted a pilot study. The pilot study was given to 21 CFL learners who study Mandarin in Taiwan. They are 16 females and 5 males. The amount of time they have studied Mandarin ranged from three months to one and half a year. Their age is from 19 to 35 year-old. Most of them learned *le* and *zai* while a few of them learned *zhe*. They were asked to spend 20 minutes on our pretest without any discussion based on what they saw on the computer screen which showed questions one by one.

[14] Some of the clips were directed and performed by us, and the others were retrieved from the website http://www.youtube.com/.

After the test, the score of each participant was calculated by the percentage of correct answer out of a maximum score of 100. Then, item difficulty (P) and item discrimination (D) indexes were examined. The mean item difficulty[15] 0.63 and the mean item discrimination[16] 0.36 indicate both the pretest and the posttest are moderate for difficulty and good for discrimination. Regarding the reliability of the pretest, it was established by the Cronbach's alpha.[17] The Cronbach's alpha 0.77 of the test showed that both of the pretest and the posttest are reliable of testing comprehension of the target aspect markers *le*, *zai* and *zhe*.

2.3 Procedure

Before the experiment, all participants were given the pretest online[18] for 20 minutes. The participants were tested on their knowledge of *le*, *zai* and *zhe* in terms of their semantics and syntactic behavior. All of them were informed to do the questions without any discussion. After the pretest, participants were divided into two groups randomly. The experimental group consisted of 19 participants and the control group 16. For an average twenty minutes of a three-day period, the experimental group studied *le*, *zai* and *zhe* through the multimedia program and the control group learned these markers through the computer-based grammar program. After a three-day learning period, all participants were informed to take the 20-minute immediate posttest online[19] and a questionnaire that surveyed learner perceptions and perceived effects as well. Also, the one-month delayed posttest online was given to all of the participants.[20]

2.4 Data analysis

After the data collection, the pretest was calculated, using the percentage of correct answers out of a maximum 100. Moreover, an independent T-test was used to establish the homogeneity between the control group and the experimental group before the experiment. The result showed that there was no significant difference between these two groups before using their programs as a self-learning tool. As to the immediate posttest and the delayed posttest after the experiment, it was also computed by using the percentage of correct answers out of a maximum 100.

For Research Question, we examined if the multimedia program involved in the experimental group is more effective than the computer-based grammar program in the control group in terms of the semantics and the syntactic behavior of the target aspect markers *le*, *zai* and *zhe*. We used independent T-test to examine if any significant difference between these two groups.

---

[15] In practice, item difficulty is classified as "easy" if the index is 85% or above; "moderate" if it is between 51% and 84%; and "hard" if it is 50% or below.

[16] Generally speaking, item discrimination is identified as "good" if the index is above 30%; "fair" if it is between 10% ad 30%; "poor" if it is below 10%.

[17] The reliability of a test refers to the extent to which the test is likely to produce consistent scores. In practice, the acceptable range is from 0.70 to 0.80.

[18] Please go to the website http://web.ncyu.edu.tw/~wujs/pretest.html for the pretest.

[19] As to the immediate posttest online, please click on http://web.ncyu.edu.tw/~wujs/posttest.html.

[20] The questions in the one-month delayed posttest are the same as those in the immediate posttest.

Further, in order to increase the precision of group mean estimate and built a convincing result for this study, Analysis of Covariance (ANCOVA) was used to reanalyze the data.[21] In addition, the questionnaires collected from the participants showed their perceptions and perceived effects toward the programs.

3. Results and Discussion

In this section, we answered Research Question: In contrast with the computer-based grammar program, is the interactive multimedia program designed in the study more effective on helping CFL beginners with comprehension of the aspect markers *le*, *zai* and *zhe* ? First, an independent T-test was performed to compare performances between the interactive multimedia group and the computer-based grammar group. There was a detailed descriptive statistics in Table 3.

Table 3. Independent T-test results between two groups

Group	*N*	*M*	*SD*	*t*
Experimental	19	91.79	9.84	3.326**
Control	16	78.25	14.16	

Note. Maximum score = 100, $^{**}p = < .01$

In Table 3, the figure indicated that there was a significant difference between the mean scores of 19 experimental subjects (M = 91.79) and 16 control subjects (M=78.25, t=3.326, p=.002). The result revealed that the interactive multimedia group as a self-learning tool on 19 experimental subjects significantly outperformed the computer-based grammar program on 16 control subjects. That is to say, the answer to Research Question is positive. The multimedia program with animation for presenting the target sentences is more effective than the computer-based grammar program with English explanation.

Then, a paired T-test was used to examine performances of members within each group. The paired T-test results of 19 experimental subjects in Table 4 indicated that there was a significant difference (t=-7.414 , p=.000) between the mean scores of the pretest (M=76.00) and the posttest (M=91.79).

Table 4. Paired T-test results of 19 experimental subjects

Task	*N*	*M*	*SD*	*t*
pretest	19	76.00	11.78	-7.414***
posttest	19	91.79	9.84	

Note. Maximum score = 100, $^{***}\, p < .001$

Also, those of 16 control subjects in Table 5 showed there was a significant difference

[21] Although there was no significant difference in the performance of these target aspect markers between the experimental group and the control group before they learned through our designed program, we found the experimental group showed higher mean and lower individual difference among 19 subjects. In order to avoid the performance in the pretest as the variable of the result, ANCOVA was used to verify.

(t=-2.449, p=.027) between the mean scores of the pretest (M=68.75) and the posttest (M=78.25).

Table 5. Paired T-test results of 16 control subjects

Task	N	M	SD	t
pretest	16	68.75	15.75	-2.449*
posttest	16	78.25	14.16	

Note. Maximum score = 100, * $p < .05$

In simple terms, these results showed both of the interactive multimedia program and the computer-based grammar program are effective as a self-learning tool on the learning of the aspect markers *le*, *zai* and *zhe*.

Next, the paired T-test was employed to examine the retention phenomenon within each group. We compared the mean scores of the posttest to that of the delayed posttest within each group. The following Table 6 indicated there was no significant difference (t=-1.099, p=.286) between the posttest and the delayed posttest in the experimental group. As for the control group, Table 7 also showed no significant difference (t=-1.013, p=.327) between the posttest and the delayed posttest. As above suggested, the retention phenomenon existed in the two groups.

Table 6. Results of 19 experimental subjects between two posttests

Task	N	M	SD	t
posttest	19	91.79	9.84	-1.099 n.s.
delayed posttest	19	93.26	8.85	

Note. Maximum score = 100, n.s. $p > .05$

Table 7. Results of 16 control subjects between two posttests

Task	N	M	SD	t
posttest	16	78.25	14.16	-1.013 n.s.
delayed posttest	16	80.50	13.92	

Note. Maximum score = 100, n.s. $p > .05$

Next, in order to increase the result power for our Research Question, we laid out its results in the form of an ANCOVA summary table as Table 8, in which we considered the mean pretest the covariance. As we can see from the Table 8, the calculated value of F=7.83 is significant ($p < .05$). The figure indicated that there was a significant difference between the multimedia group and the computer-based grammar group. As a result of the adjusted mean (M = 72.69) score of the pretest, the mean score of the posttest was changed to 90.24 from 91.79 in the experimental group and to 80.09 from 78.25 in the control group based on Table 9 for the mean scores of the posttest evaluated at the covariate and Table 10 for the mean scores of the posttest. More specifically, in case of ANOVA, the significant difference existed between the experimental group and the control group.

Table 8. An ANCOVA Summary Table of these two groups.

Dependent Variable: posttest

Source	*SS*(Type III)	*df*	*MS*	*F*
covariance	1354.11	1	1354.11	12.76*
adjusted means(between-groups)	834.47	1	834.47	7.83*
adjusted error	3396.05	32	106.13	
adjusted total	6342.40	34		

Note. * $p < .05$

Table 9. Estimates of the Mean Scores of the Posttest

Dependent Variable: posttest

Group	Mean	Std. Error	95% Confidence Interval	
			Lower Bound	Upper Bound
Experimental	90.24[a]	2.40	85.35	95.14
Control	80.09[a]	2.63	74.74	85.44

a. Evaluated at covariates appeared in the model: pretest = 72.69.

Table 10. Descriptive Statistics of the Mean Scores of the Posttest

Dependent Variable: posttest

Group	Mean	Std. Deviation	*N*
Experimental	91.79	9.84	19
Control	78.25	14.16	16

On the other hand, we looked into learner perceptions and perceived effects toward these two programs from their questionnaires. For the interactive multimedia program, most students including the older participants were satisfied with it and expressed their interest in learning the abstract aspect markers through the animation expressing the semantics of the target sentences. For example, they are looking forward to the next program for the intermediate level CFL learners. Also, they identified that the comparison among *le*, *zai*, and *zhe* interacting with events helped them to comprehend their usage. One suggested that adding more target sentences interacting with *le*, *zai*, and *zhe* to the multimedia program and more test items to the interactive exercises can make them learn more about aspect markers.

On the contrary, as to the computer-based program, a few of the learners got benefit from it as a result of the curriculum comparing the usage of the target aspect markers interacting with events. However, some of them claimed that the animation or picture if adding to the English corresponding sentences of the target sentences increase their understanding of these aspect markers.

3. Conclusion

The results of the present study were summarized by pointing out that the significant effectiveness on the learning of three aspect markers *le*, *zai*, and *zhe* through the interactive multimedia program in contrast with the computer-based grammar program. The animation presenting the semantics of the target aspect markers interacting with events in the interactive multimedia program is the key point that makes the experimental group outperformed significantly the control group, in which the meaning of target sentences were expressed by English translation. The animation can express the abstract concept of aspect markers instead of English grammar translation or explanation which exist in most of the CFL textbooks. For pedagogical implication, the study provides contribution to the computer-based assisted teaching or learning tool in the classroom.

Nevertheless, the present study is not without limitations, as discussed below. The first limitation concerns the assessment of participants' language level. Only acquiring their language background from questionnaire or their CFL teachers cannot assess their actual level. The amount of time that the participants studied Chinese varies, also the familiarity with these three aspect markers. In addition, participants from 3 different institutes may receive different input and teaching methods which provide participants various bases in acquiring these three aspect markers, In this case, the generalization of the results is limited.

Next, the target sentences in the program adopted from the representative literature is limited. Learners using the program may learn small parts of target sentences with *le*, *zai*, and *zhe* which may not be proved very practical in our daily conversation although they learned their different usage. Therefore, the content of the program in our study is limited to cover all kinds of usages concerning about target aspect markers.

Regarding the future studies, we look forward to the multimedia program of aspect markers for intermediate-level CFL learners and predict its effectiveness. In order to include more practical usage of aspect markers, we will refer corpus data for the target sentences. Further, the CFL learners' proficiency will be assessed based on the approved proficiency test, such as Test of Proficiency-Huayu in Taiwan.

Reference

Ellis, Rod. (1985). *Understanding Second Language Acquisition.* Oxford: Oxford University Press.

Li, Charles, & Sandra Thompson. (2005). *Mandarin Chinese : A Functional Reference Grammar*, 5th ed., Taiwan: The Crane Publishing Co., Ltd.

Lin, Jo-Wang. (2002). Aspectual Selection and Temporal Reference of the Chinese Aspectual marker –Zhe. *Tsing Hua Journal of Chinese Studies, New Series Volume* 32(2): 257-296.

Mayer, Richard E. (2001). *Multimedia learning*. New York: Cambridge University Press.

McEnery, T., Baker, J. P., & Wilson, A. (1995). A statistical analysis of corpus based computer versus traditional human teaching methods of part of speech analysis. *Computer Assisted Language Learning* 8:259-274

Nagata, Noriko. (1996). Computer vs. workbook instruction in second language acquisition. *CALICO Journal* 14: 53-75.

Pan, Haihua. (1996). Imperfective aspect *zhe*, agent deletion, and locative inversion in Mandarin Chinese. *Natural Language and Linguistic Theory* 14: 409-432.

Rachel, J. R. (1995). Adult reading achievement comparing computer-assisted and traditional approaches: A comprehensive review of the experimental literature. *Reading Research and Instruction* 34(3): 239-258.

Ragan, T., Boyce, M., Redwine, D., Savenye, W. C., & McMichael, J. (1993). *Is multimedia worth it? : A review of the effectiveness of individualized multimedia instruction.* Paper presented at the Association for Educational Communications and Technology Convention, New Orleans, LA.

Smith, Carlota. (1997). *The Parameter of Aspect,* 2nd ed., Kluwer Academic Publishers, Dordrecht.

Wu, Jiun-Shiung. (2003). *Modeling Temporal Progression in Mandarin: Aspect Markers and Temporal Relations*. Ph.D. Dissertation. University of Texas at Austin.

Wu, Jiun-Shiung. (2005). The semantics of the Perfective LE and Its Context-Dependency: an SDRT Approach. *Journal of East Asian Linguistics* 14(4): 299-336.

Wu, Jiun-Shiung Hunter & Jenny Yi-Chun Kuo. (2003). T*he Semantics of the Durative Marker Zhe and Its Dependency on Context: A Segmented Discourse Representation Theory Account.* Paper presented at Linguistic Society of Hong Kong Annual Research Forum, Hong Kong.

Wu, Jiun-Shiung. (2007). Semantic Difference between the Two Imperfective Markers in Mandarin and Its Implications on Temporal Relations. *Journal of Chinese Linguistics* 35 (2): 372-398.

Xiao Richard & Tony McEnery. (2004). *Aspect in Mandarin Chinese: A corpus-based study.* U.S.A.: John Benjamins Publishing Co.

Yeh, Meng. (1993). The stative situation and the imperfective *zhe* in Mandarin. *Journal of Chinese Teachers Association* 23(1): 69-98.

高蕊（2006），《歐美學生漢語標記了”了”“著” “過”的習得研究》，北京:北京語言大學碩士論文。

趙立江（2002），〈外國留學生使用”了”的情況與分析〉，《第五屆國際漢語教學論文集》。北京：北京語言文化大學出版社。

劉小梅（1997），《國閩客語的動態文法體系及動態詞的上加動貌語意》。臺北市 ： 文鶴書局。

中文文字蘊涵系統之特徵分析

Feature Analysis of Chinese Textual Entailment System

黃文奇 Wan-Chi Huang, 吳世弘 Shih-Hung Wu*
朝陽科技大學資訊工程系
Department of Computer Science and Information Engineering
Chaoyang University of Technology
{s9727603, shwu}@cyut.edu.tw
*Contact author
陳良圃 Liang-Pu Chen, 谷圳 Tsun Ku
資訊工業策進會
Institute for Information Industry
{eit, cujing}@iii.org.tw

摘要

文字蘊涵(Textual Entailment)的定義是判斷兩個句子能否互相推論。推論可分爲五種類型：正向、反向、雙向、矛盾、獨立。這五種類型分別代表著不同的蘊涵關係。文字蘊涵辨識(Textual Entailment Recognition)是相當困難的自然語言處理問題。由於中文文字蘊涵的文獻較缺乏，本篇論文將中文文字蘊涵辨識提出了一個流程，提供給之後想要做這個題目的人的作爲一個參考。中文的文字處理相較於英文的文字處理有許多不同的難處，在本篇論文中，我們將介紹處理中文的文字處理遇到的難處以及處理的流程。我們的系統使用支援向量機(Support vector machine, SVM)作爲區分類型的演算法。使用的特徵分爲兩個方向：1.文字特徵 2.語意特徵。

關鍵字：文字蘊涵、tree kernel、支持向量機、語意分析

一、緒論

近幾年來，文字蘊涵受到關注，主要是因爲大家瞭解到文字蘊涵將使我們能夠更準確的去推論自然語言的語義關係[1]以及處理一些重要的應用[2]。像是檢索系統經常會檢索出成千上萬筆資料，卻難以判斷哪個句子是與問句最相關的。於是可以透過蘊涵的推論，從這些成千上萬的資料中挑選出最相關的句子。由於兩個句子中的關係有許多種，例如：蘊涵(entailment)、改寫(paraphrase)以及獨立(independence)等，語意推論的目的就是在於判斷兩個句子之間是屬於哪一種關係。可以將推論分爲五種類型：正向、反向、雙向、矛盾、獨立這五種類型。這五種類型也分別代表著不同的蘊涵關係。正向推論爲可以從 t1 句子中推論出 t2 的句子，即代表 t1 句子完整的包含著 t2 句子的資訊；而反向推論正好相反；雙向即是 t1 與 t2 兩個句子互相完全包含著彼此的資訊；矛盾即是兩個句子中提到

的資訊是互相矛盾的；獨立則是兩個句子中提到的資訊是完全不相關的。如表一。

表一中雙向蘊涵的例子比較屬於是改寫(paraphrase)，更複雜的文字蘊涵推論就像是$t_1 \rightarrow s, s \rightarrow t_2$。透過 t1 的句子可以推論出涵義 s，接著透過涵義 s 可以推論出 t2 例如：t1：小明殺了小華。t2：小華死了。從 t1 我們可以推論出的 s 有很多，如：小明是殺了小華的兇手、小華被殺了、小華死了。這種推論需要有邏輯推論以及許多背景知識才可以達成。基於中文處理的成本以及困難度考量，本篇論文主要針對改寫(paraphrase)去作分析。

表一 各種類型的例句

類型	例句
正向蘊涵 (forward)	t1：日本時間 2011 年 3 日 11 日，日本宮城縣發生芮氏規模 9.0 強震，造死傷失蹤約 3 萬多人
	t2：日本時間 2011 年 3 日 11 日，日本宮城縣發生芮氏規模 9.0 強震
反向蘊涵 (reverse)	t1：美國主權債信評級從最高的ＡＡＡ調降一級到ＡＡ＋
	t2：美國主權債信評級從最高的ＡＡＡ調降一級到ＡＡ＋，將造成美國每年的借貸成本增加約一千億美元
雙向蘊涵 (bidirection)	t1：賓拉登在巴基斯坦美軍攻擊中死亡
	t2：巴基斯坦美軍攻擊中殺死賓拉登
矛盾蘊涵 (contradiction)	t1：張學友在 1961 年 7 月 10 日，生於香港，祖籍天津
	t2：張學友生於 1960 年
獨立蘊涵 (independence)	t1：黎姿與"殘障富豪"馬廷強結婚。
	t2：馬廷強為香港"東方報業集團"創辦人之一馬惜如之子

在自然語言問答系統(Question Answering system)中。使用者輸入的是一個完整的問句。系統回傳的也是一個個完整的句子。並且連結到相對應的文章中。基本的檢索，通常會有上萬句的句子被系統挑選出來。要從這上萬個句子中，去挑選出哪一個最為相關，我們就可以透過文字蘊涵系統來輔助。例如 ntcir9 提供的範例中[3]，我們輸入 t1：「 1997 年香港回歸中國。 」，我們可以從檢索回來的句子中，挑選出 t2：「香港的主權和領土是在 1997 由英國政權歸還給中國的。」並且將它排序到較為前面的順序。因為 t1 與 t2 的關係為反向，代表著 t1 為 t2 蘊涵意義的一部分。所以我們可以認為 t2 很可能是使用者要檢索的句子。我們也可以利用其他類型，來決定這些句子排序的位置。像是語意為矛盾、獨立的句子我們就將它挑除，因為它幾乎不可能為使用者所想要檢索的句子。正向、反向、雙向我們就將之排序到較前面的位置，因為這些句子較有可能為使用者要檢索的資訊。

相較於英文中文的文字處理難度高出了許多。因為在英文的句子中，每個詞都以空白分開，且英文的文法也制定的較爲清楚，如：時態、詞性…等等，在英文中都有較爲明確的規範。中文卻是整個句子都連在一起，所以第一步必須要先斷詞，斷詞在中文處理上面就有一定的難度。因爲處理時斷詞的結果好壞都會影響到後續處理的結果。且中文的文法相較於英文，也較爲模糊，所以中文的語意判斷難度相較於英文會高出許多。

二、相關研究

其他語言到目前爲止，文字蘊涵在中文的領域較缺少相關的文獻，我們只能參考其他語言文字蘊涵處理的方法。在英文處理文字蘊涵的文獻[4]將處理英文文字蘊涵的各個方法做了分析，並且將各種方法整分成下面幾個類別。

(一)、需要透過背景知識達成之方法

1、整合背景知識與邏輯推論

由於人們在平常生活中已經很習慣使用自然語言表達意見，所以自然的有許多背景知識都已經不自覺得變成常識，判斷兩句子是否可以推論都覺得很理所當然，但是對於電腦來說並不是如此。推論是可以從邏輯蘊涵來檢查，像是使用定理證明文句對中的文本蘊涵[5][6][7][8]。有一部份的學者使用含有語意的辭典來擷取出詞彙的邏輯意義，使用 WordNet[9]或者擴展 WordNet[10]。例如於 WordNet 中"暗殺"爲"殺"的下義詞（更有具體的意義），像下面所示，x 暗殺 y 可以推論成上義詞 x 殺 y。所以像謀殺、刺殺…等等的這些都可以推論出相同的上義詞。

$$\forall x \forall y\ 暗殺(x, y) \Rightarrow 殺(x, y)$$

2、整合背景知識與向量空間模型

將每個輸入語言表達的字，對映到一個向量，可以看出用詞的分佈強度，特別是當句子其他的字也都對應到同一個語料庫中，則會明顯看出用字的分佈[11] 。例如要求共同出現的字，出現在特別的語法依存關係上[12]。在最簡單的情況下，爲每一個表達向量的總和或字詞對應的向量總和，但更複雜的方法也已提出[13]。句子可以通過測量檢測距離向量的兩個輸入表達式來判斷是否爲改寫的句子，例如，通過計算其餘弦相似性(cosine similarity)。

(二)、不需要透過背景知識達成之方法

1、透過表面文字

將文字對經過一些加工，如詞性(POS, Part of speech)標記或命名實體識別(NER, Named entity recognition) 標記。對輸入兩個字串計算字串編輯距離(edit distance)[14]，計算其共同的字數，或組合幾種字串相似度措施[15]，包括使用機器翻譯評測的方法，如 BLEU(Bilingual Evaluation Understudy) [17][18]都可能有助於文字蘊涵。

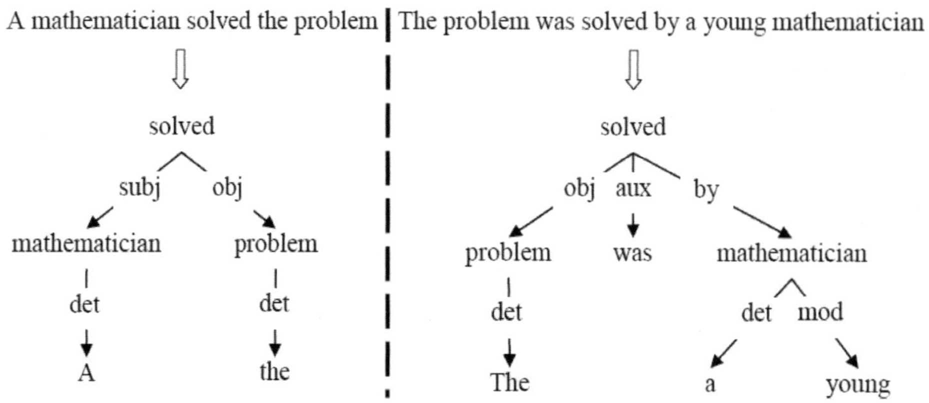

圖一 兩句非常相似句子的依存關係樹[1]

2、基於語法相似度

另一種常見的方法是在語法等級。依存語法剖析器(parser)[20][21]普遍用於文本蘊涵研究，一個句子輸出的剖析結果是一個圖(通常是一個樹狀結構) 其節點是句子的字或詞性標記，其邊緣對應詞與詞之間的句法依存關係，例如：以依賴於動詞或名詞開頭的名詞片語，或者以名詞開頭的形容詞片語。圖一顯示了兩句話的依存關係樹[1]，分析這兩棵樹可以得知這兩句句子的蘊涵關係。例如計算共同剖析樹的邊[16] [19]或使用其他樹的相似性計算方法，例如：樹的編輯距離[22][23][24]。相似性得分可以表示輸入的句子可能是改寫的程度。

3、透過機器學習

許多系統採用結合多個測量相似度的方法，在計算各種程度的相似度（表面字串，句法和語義的表示）合併使用機器學習[26][27]。每一對輸入的文句對(P1, P2)，由特徵值向量代表(f1, . . . , fm) ，我們用機器學習來判斷他們是否是一個特定的改寫或文字蘊涵。該向量包含多個相似度的特徵。前處理階段將每個輸入對轉換爲一個特徵向量[28]。前處理還包括正規化，例如，日期將轉換成一個統一的格式，個人的名稱，組織，地點等使用命名實體識別轉換爲正規化表示。代詞及指稱詞語，可能會被替換的成原本的詞[25]，構句的差異也可能標準化（例如，被動句可以轉換爲主動句）。特徵向量可以統包使用文字或部分的句法和語義表現[29] 。最後這個特徵向量，將當作支持向量機（SVM）的輸入值，去學習及區分各種文字蘊涵的類別。

三、資料處理與特徵分析：

本研究將語意蘊涵識別分爲特徵分析及機器學習兩個主要部份。本研究提出的特徵分析流程包括前置處理、背景知識的替換程序、表面文字特徵分析程序、語意句法分析程序四個部分。資料以 NTCIR-9 提供的 421 對文句對爲分析依據[3]。

(一)、前置處理

由於人們再撰寫句子的表達時可能會使用到一些替代詞以及範圍性的詞性。用程式擷取特徵，通常會遇到處理上的困難，所以我們都會必須要將資料做一些前處理，才可以程式進行運算。

1、括號選擇性替代：

一個意思可能會有兩個詞可以代表，像是音譯、中英文、代表涵義、簡寫…等等的。在撰寫文章時，爲了讓讀者可以明確的知道作者想要表達的資訊，作者會使用括號，將讀者可能聯想到的詞也都包含進來，避免造成讀者的誤會。例如：車諾比核事故(切爾諾貝利核事故)、湯姆·克魯斯(Tom Cruise)。所以在此我們將括號中的文字與前面的詞使用陣列儲存。在特徵擷取時我們將兩個詞都同時列入考量。

2、時間正規化：

在文本中時間的表達方式有很多種格式及字型，如：中文、數字全形、數字半形、數字以「-」隔開、範圍型態等，參見表二。在此將以上各種格式，統一轉換成陣列方式，以方便之後進行比對的步驟。轉換成陣列以便後續程式作比較。

3、時間運算：

在有些例子中，需要透過運算之後才能夠知道資訊是否匹配。例如：t1：「蘇哈托政權在一九九八年結束，執政卅二年。」、t2：「蘇哈托一九六六年執政，對印尼進行了卅二年的鐵腕統治。」在例子中 t1 出現時間詞「一九九八年」與「卅二年」。經過運算之後，會與 t2 的「一九六六年」符合，所以經過時間運算結果，t1 的時間將與 t2 的時間匹配。

表二 各種時間表達方式之例句

時間型態	時間表達方式
中文	一九九七年二月廿三日
數字全形	１９９７年2月２３日
數字半型	1997 年 2 月 23 日
數字以「-」隔開	1999-05-07
範圍	1999 年延長至 2001 年

(二)、背景知識的替換

在撰寫文章時，作者會使用一些簡寫或者是替代詞，好讓整篇文章可以更爲通順。由於作者已有相關的背景知識，會覺得這些事情是常識，所以並不會對於那些替代詞多做解釋。事實上往往讀者閱讀一些文章時，可能會因爲背景知識不足而需要去查閱許多資料，才可以讀懂那些文章的意思。這種人們都會遇到的事情，程式也必須處理。

1、年號統一：

在時間的表示詞中，有一些年號，是需要經過統一的，例如：乾隆 56 年等於西元 1791 年，是因爲「乾隆」等於 1735 年。昭和 57 年等於西元 1982 年，是因爲「昭和」等於 1925 年。將年號統一，以方便我們之後的分析。

2、地名正規化：

作者在書寫文件時，有時會爲了方便，而將一些詞簡寫，地名就是其中一個時常被簡寫的對象。例如：「台灣、印度、美國」這些國家的名稱，時常都會被簡寫爲：「台、印、美」。但是當我們在處理文字蘊涵分析的時候，我們必須要先將簡寫恢復成原地名。這樣在之後比對才會匹配。

(三)、表面字串特徵分析

1、時間：

許多文句對中的兩個句子都含有時間元素，當兩邊時間不符合時，可能是一個分析文字蘊含的依據。從 421 句文件集中挑出來的文句對一共有 146(34.67%)個文句對包含時間。我們將時間分析細分爲三個匹配程度，如：時間爲完全匹配、部分時間匹配、時間完全不匹配（表三）。如表三中，時間完全批配的例子，再此 t1 中含有的時間爲 2000 年，而 t2 中含有的句子也同樣爲 2000 年，所以我們將此例子視爲時間完全匹配。部分時間匹配(1)的例子，其中 t1 的時間爲「一九七八年十月十六日」，而 t2 的時間爲「1978 年」。由於「1978 年」只匹配到「一九七八年」，「十月十六日」，並沒有完全匹配。部分時間匹配(2)的例子，其中 t1 的時間爲「一九七八年十月十六日」，而 t2 的時間爲「1978 年」。由於「1978 年」只匹配到「一九七八年」，「十月十六日」，並沒有完全匹配。時間完全不匹配的例子，再 t1 的例子中時間爲「1987 年」，t2 的例子中「1988 年」。我們從這兩個時間中，明顯的看出，時間不匹配。

表三 時間批配程度之例子

批配程度	例子
時間爲完全匹配	t1：據他所知，這是查爾斯首度參加雪梨-荷芭特帆船賽，而查爾斯一向是注重安全、非常謹慎的人，他更想參加 2000 年雪梨奧運帆船賽。
	t2：2000 年奧運在雪梨舉辦
部分時間匹配(1)	t1：若望保祿二世一九七八年十月十六日被選爲教宗
	t2：若望保祿二世於 1978 年當上教宗
部分時間匹配(2)	t1：蘇哈托 1921 年 6 月 8 日出生
	t2：蘇哈托（Suharto，民間常用「Soeharto」，1921 年 6 月 8 日－2008 年 1 月 27 日）
時間完全不匹配	t1：張藝謀 1987 年以「紅高粱」拿下柏林影展金熊獎
	t2：柏林電影節應該是張藝謀的福地。1988 年，他執導的《紅高粱》贏得了最佳影片金熊獎，成爲中國電影的首個金熊獎

經過統計，這三種匹配程度所包含的類別數量如表四，可以從表中看出，完全匹配的部分，屬於 B 的機率高了很多。這是因爲當兩個句子的意義可以互相推論時，在時間上必須要完全匹配才有可能意義是一樣的。如果兩個句子都在講

同一件事情，可是日期不一樣的話，這樣就不算是完全匹配了。

表四 批配程度分佈與類別關係

	F	R	I	B	C
完全匹配	9	17	3	30	17
部分匹配	12	8	7	0	0
不匹配	1	1	2	0	7

2、句子長度：

針對句子的長度分析，將 t1 的句子長度與 t2 的句子長度做比較。即將 t1 的句子長度減去 t2 的句子長度，以用來統計各個類別中，句子長度與類別的關係。統計結果如表五所示。

表五 句子長度與類別關係

類別	F	R	I	B	C
數量	12	-19	-4	0	0

由於向前蘊涵(F)的定義爲，t1 的涵義中完全的包含了 t2 的句子，所以 t1 的文字長度，應該要比 t2 的文字長度還要長許多。相反地，如果是反向蘊涵(R)則爲反之，t2 的長度應該要比 t1 的長很多。而矛盾(C)以及雙向蘊涵(B)的涵義分別爲互相矛盾以及互相包涵，在句子中所需提到的內容都差不多。所以句子的長度也都會差不多。獨立(I)，只要兩個句子不是在談同一個內容，他們就算是獨立的句子。所以句子的長度爲不一致。

3、Bleu(Bilingual Evaluation Understudy)：

Bleu當初是被設計來測量機器翻譯(machine translation)的品質。一個良好的機器翻譯需要包含適當，準確以及流暢的翻譯[30][31]。Bleu是考量句子的相似度，經過適當修改參考，一定程度詞語的差異在選擇和語序上面。而Bleu主要的概念是使用片語匹配長度平均權重值。

4、否定詞偵測

當文句對只有差別一個否定詞時，從文字層面去計算文句對得相似度會得到很高的分數。但是從語意層面來看此文句對卻完全不相同。如：「今天天氣很好」與「今天天氣很不好」。此文句對中只有差別一個「不」否定詞。然而完全改變了此語句的語意。所以我們提出要偵測文句對中是否有否定詞，作爲特徵。

(四)、語意句法分析：

1、同義詞替換：

表達同一個意思的詞彙有許多，例如：大兒子、長男、獲得、得到…等。在人的眼中這些都是表達爲第一個兒子的意思。但是要讓程式擁有這些背景知識，是一件相當困難的事情。因爲處理中文必須事先經過斷詞系統處理，但斷詞系統有時會把詞彙斷的太細。如：「長男」會被斷成「長」與「男」兩個字。經由剖析處理後，產生的剖析樹會長得不一樣。導致計算語法相似度時產生出許多雜訊。爲解決這個問題，透過事先建立一份同義詞清單，進行同義詞的替換。但爲了減少因斷詞錯誤造成的影響，所以在此採用長詞優先來作替換。

2、語法分析(syntax analysis)：

分析句法需要透過剖析器(parser)將整個句子的句法標注，才可以計算整個句子的句法。本篇論文使用的是史丹佛剖析器(Stanford parser) [32]來剖析句子的句法。但由於史丹佛剖析器在剖析繁體中文的標注時常會判斷錯誤，所以使用的時候把資料轉換成簡體中文效果會較好。在此是透過自行開發出來的簡繁轉換系統做轉換[33]。

(1)、計算tree distance

有許多學者使用tree distance去計算兩個剖析樹的相似度[21][22][23]。所謂的tree distance主要的概念就是t1的parser tree需要經過幾次插入(insert)、刪除(delete)、替代(Substitution)才可以等於t2的parse tree。如圖二[24]中，可以看出這兩顆樹中間只有差了一個c節點，在tree distance運算中只需要刪除c節點兩個parse tree就完全mapping在一起。他們的tree distance就是2。

(2)、 Fast Tree Kernel (FTK)

FTK爲修改Quadratic Tree Kernel (QTK)[5]的演算法，QTK主要的意義爲計算兩個Tree的匹配數量。FTK爲事先將動詞爲中心點，分別跟其他的sub-tree合併成subset tree。如圖三中「張學良的父親是東北軍閥」將會以是這個動詞作爲分割點，分割出「張學良的父親是」、「是東北軍閥」這兩個subset tree。並根據每個集合計算subset tree的匹配數量，並且求出參數最大值 $t = \arg\max_{i \in S}$ [34]。

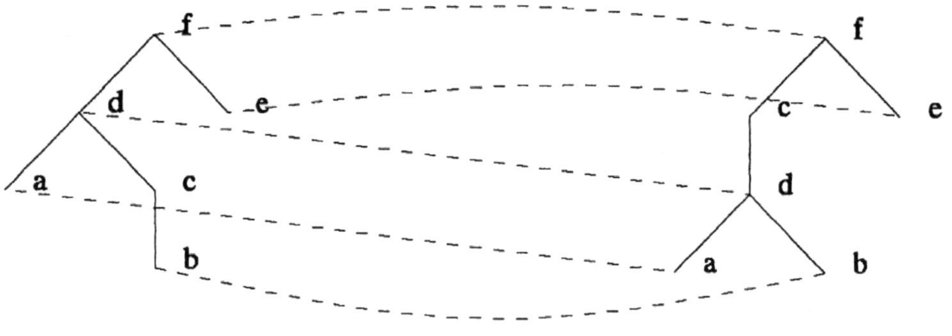

圖二 parse tree對應圖

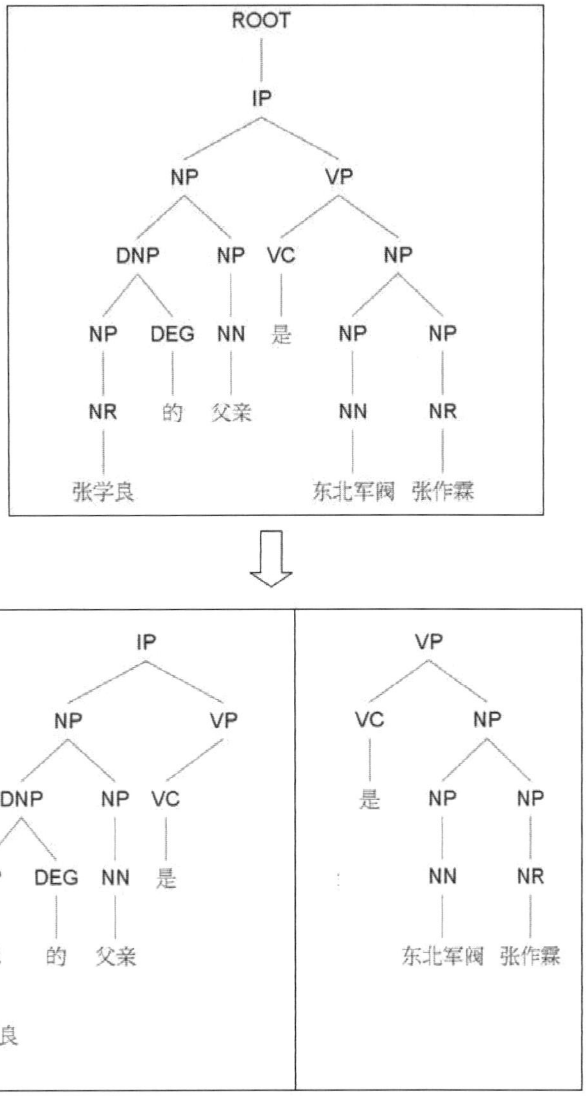

圖三 根據動詞所分解出來的sub-set tree

四、實驗

本次針對五種類別進行分析與實驗，並且使用交叉驗證的方式來實做的系統。流程如圖四所示，首先輸入文句對，進行前處理，其中前處理包括：括號選擇性替代，年號統一，以及地名正規化。之後使用 ICTCLAS 系統對句子進行斷詞，接著進行簡繁轉換才將句子使用 Stanford parser 將句子剖析，接著進行特徵擷取的動作，本次擷取的特徵如表七所示，並將擷取的特徵輸入給 SVM 進行訓練以及測試，輸出將得到判斷是否為蘊涵的結果。

(一)、資料來源：

本次研究我們的資料來源取自日本 NTCIR 第九屆中，RITE(Recognizing Inference in Text)比賽子項目的開發資料(Development Data)。而在此資料中，一共有 421 個文句對。其中向前蘊涵(F, Forward Entailment)一共有 87 個文句對，反向蘊涵(R, Reverse Entailment)一共有 97 個文句對，雙向蘊涵(B, Bidirectional Entailment)一共有 82 個文句對，矛盾(C, Contradiction)一共有 74 個文句對，獨立(I, Independence)一共有 81 個文句對如表六。

表六 每一個類別的資料數量

標籤(Label)	數量(Number)
向前蘊涵(F, Forward Entailment)	87
反向蘊涵(R, Reverse Entailment)	97
雙向蘊涵(B, Bidirectional Entailment)	82
矛盾(C, Contradiction)	74
獨立(I, Independence)	81

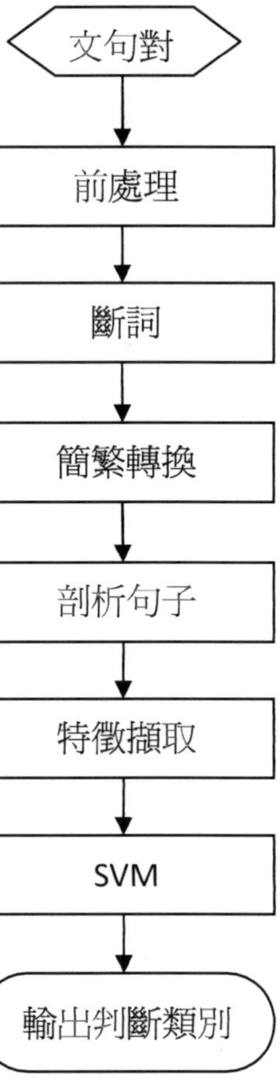

圖四 本次實驗之流程圖

(二)、使用工具：

1. ICTCLAS[35]:由於中文的句子並不像英文的句子，每個詞都以空白分開。所以要處理中文的句子首先第一個步驟需要進行斷詞，將每個詞分開。目前較爲普遍的斷詞工具有兩種：由中央研究院所研發的CKIP斷詞系統[36]，與中國科學院所研發的ICTCLAS。其中CKIP是用來處理繁體中文。ICTCLAS則是繁體與簡體中文都可以處理。所以我們的實驗選擇使用ICTCLAS。

2. Stanford parser[32]：另外一個很重要的工具就剖析器，由於要計算語意需要使用到 parser，所以在我們的實驗中使用的是 Stanford parser。因爲 Stanford parser 是依據 Chinese Treebank[37]的標準，所以 Stanford parser 能夠處理英文以及簡體中文。

3. LIBSVM [38]：由於要分類的類別一共有五類，所以採用 LIBSVM 作爲分類的分類器。因爲此分類器可以一次分多個類別，可以避免掉傳統只能分兩類對應不到類別的問題。

4.簡繁轉換系統[33]：由於 Stanford parser 只能夠處理簡體中文，於是需要透過一個簡繁轉換的系統。這次實驗所使用的系統爲自行開發的系統[33]。

(三)、使用特徵：

使用的 feature 部份是參考[16]中的特徵。因爲[16]爲參考文獻中[4]數據最好的，但由於[16]中的特徵爲處理英文時使用，所以有些特徵中文並沒有，所以只採用部份特徵。以及加入一些上面所分析的部份特徵。所使用的特徵如表七中所列。目前實驗是將分爲五種類別做四個實驗。

1.baseline 系統

其中 baseline 系統分別使用表七中 1 到 9 的特徵值，因爲這些特徵值是較容易做計算的，實驗結果如表八所示，實驗的文句對一共有 421 對其中有 220 對是判斷正確(52.25%)。

2.tree mapping 系統

相較於 baseline 系統，額外加入了第 10 個 tree mapping 的特徵值，此特徵是計算 Subset Tree mapping 的值。所以使用了 1～10 的特徵值。此實驗用來測試看看語法特徵對於文字蘊涵能夠有多大的幫助，實驗結果如表九所示，實驗的文句對一共有 421 對其中有 226 對是判斷正確(53.68%)。

3.time mapping

在我們先前的試驗分析中，可以從表七中看出時間批配是一個蠻有用的特徵，所以單獨將此特徵挑選出來做實驗看效果如何。相較於 baseline 系統中，而外加入第 11 個 time mapping 的特徵，所以使用了 1～9 的並且額外加入了第 11 個特徵，實驗結果如表十所示，實驗的文句對一共有 421 對其中有 223 對是判斷正確(52.96%)。

4. Remove length

我們可以從表五中看出本資料集的長度特徵較爲明顯，當然這有可能是本資料集才有的特色，所以在此將第 6 到 9 個關於長度特徵拿掉。用來測試這次實驗是否過度依賴長度特徵。，實驗結果如表十一所示，實驗的文句對一共有 421 對其中有 209 對是判斷正確(49.64%)。

表七 實驗所使用之特徵

1. unigram recall
2. unigram precision
3. Bleu precision
4. Bleu recall
5. Bleu F-measure
6. difference in sentence length (character)
7. absolute difference in sentence length (character)
8. difference in sentence length (term)
9. absolute difference in sentence length (term)
10. Subset tree mapping
11. Time mapping

五、結論與未來展望

本篇論文提出了一個處理中文文字蘊涵辨識的流程，可以給之後想要做中文文字蘊涵的人作爲一個參考。本次實驗只有使用部份的特徵，實驗的量也並不大，但是我們將這次的系統視爲一個 baseline。可以從實驗中看出 tree mapping 與 time mapping 確實可以略爲增加判斷文字蘊涵的效果。並且將長度的特徵拿掉之後，雖然有略爲的下降，但是幅度不至於影響太多，所以以此驗證了此系統並不是非常的依賴長度特徵。

之後我們將增加各種特徵，並且去分析出有用的特徵以改進中文文字蘊涵的效果。像是年號統一、同義詞替換、地名正規化，這一類需要事先建立出背景知識才能夠使用程式去執行。但是這要建立出這些背景知識需要花費非常多的成本，需要經過很長的時間去累積詞彙的數量。目前我只有針對語料庫中遇到需要處理的建立出來，所以未來我們希望可以將每次遇到要處理的詞，建立出越來越完整的一個可以讓電腦使用的背景知識辭典。

表八 分爲五類的 baseline 系統結果

Actual	Predicted					Total
	F	R	B	I	C	
F	60	3	9	10	5	87
R	0	68	9	15	5	97
B	5	6	56	1	14	82
I	17	35	8	16	5	81
C	11	12	21	10	20	74
Total	93	124	103	52	49	421

表九 分爲五類的 time mapping 系統結果

Actual	Predicted					Total
	F	R	B	I	C	
F	61	3	8	10	5	87
R	0	69	9	14	5	97
B	6	6	57	1	12	82
I	19	32	8	17	5	81
C	11	12	19	10	22	74
Total	93	122	101	52	49	421

表十 分爲五類的 time mapping 系統結果

Actual	Predicted					Total
	F	R	B	I	C	
F	61	3	8	10	5	87
R	0	69	9	14	5	97
B	6	6	57	1	12	82
I	19	32	8	17	5	81
C	11	12	19	10	22	74
Total	90	129	100	57	45	421

表十一 分爲五類的 time mapping 系統結果

Actual	Predicted					Total
	F	R	B	I	C	
F	54	6	12	12	5	87
R	7	58	10	10	5	97
B	8	2	59	3	10	82
I	16	37	9	16	5	81
C	18	12	18	8	22	74
Total	99	115	108	59	40	421

Acknowledgement

本研究依經濟部補助財團法人資訊工業策進會「100 年度數位匯流服務開放平台技術研發計畫」辦理。感謝國科會贊助部分研究經費，計畫編號 NSC-100-2221-E-324 -025-MY2。

六、參考文獻

[1] Gennaro Chierchia and Sally McConnell-Ginet, “Meaning and Grammar: An introduction to Semantics”, The MIT press, Cambridge, MA, 2000.

[2] Ido Dagan and Oren Glickman, Probabilistic textual entailment: Generic applied modeling of language variability, In Proceedings of the Workshop on Learning Methods for Text Understanding and Mining, Grenoble, France, 2004.

[3] NTCIR 9, Recognizing Inference in TExt task, http://artigas.lti.cs.cmu.edu/rite/Main_Page.

[4] Ion Androutsopoulos and Prodromos Malakasiotis, "A survey of paraphrasing and textual entailment methods", Journal of Artificial Intelligence Research, Volume 38, pages 135-187, 2010.

[5] Michael Collins and Nigel Duffy, " New ranking algorithms for parsing and tagging: Kernels over discrete structures, and the voted perceptron", Proceedings of the 40th Annual Meeting on Association for Computational Linguistics, 2002.

[6] Johan Bos, Katja Markert, "Recognising textual entailment with logical inference", Proceedings of the conference on Human Language Technology and Empirical Methods in Natural Language Processing, Vancouver, B.C., Canada, 2005.

[7] Marta Tatu and Dan Moldovan, "COGEX at RTE 3", In Proceedings of ACL-PASCAL Workshop on Textual Entailment and Paraphrasing, pages 22–27, Prague, Czech Republic, 2007.

[8] Marta Tatu, Dan Moldovan, "A semantic approach to recognizing textual entailment", In Proceedings of HLT/EMNLP 2005, pages 371–378, Vancouver, Canada, 2005

[9] Christiane Fellbaum, "WordNet: An Electronic Lexical Database", The MIT Press, 1998.

[10] Dan I. Moldovan and Vasile Rus, "Logic form transformation of WordNet and its applicability to question answering", In Proceedings of the 39th Annual Meeting of ACL, pages 402–409, Toulouse, France, 2001.

[11] Dekang Lin, "An information-theoretic definition of similarity", In Proceedings of the Fifteenth International Conference on Machine Learning (ICML-98) Madison, Wisconsin, 1998.

[12] Sebastian Padó and Mirella Lapata, "Dependency-based construction of semantic space models", Computational Linguistics, Volume 33, No. 2, pages 161–199, 2007.

[13] Jeff Mitchell and Mirella Lapata, "Vector-based models of semantic composition", In Proceedings of the 46th Annual Meeting of ACL: HLT, pages 236–244, Columbus, OH., 2008.

[14] Levenshtein, V, "Binary codes capable of correcting deletions, insertions, and reversals", Soviet Physice-Doklady, 10, pages 707–710, 1966.

[15] Prodromos Malakasiotis, Ion Androutsopoulos, "Learning textual entailment

using SVMs and string similarity measures", In Proceedings of ACL-PASCAL Workshop on Textual Entailment and Paraphrasing, pages 42–47, Prague, Czech Republic, 2007.

[16] Wan, S., Dras, M., Dale, R., & Paris, C., "Using dependency-based features to take the "parafarce" out of paraphrase", In Proceedings of the Australasian Language Technology Workshop, pages 131–138, Sydney, Australia, 2006.

[17] Kishore Papineni, Salim Roukos, Todd Ward and Wei-Jing Zhu, "BLEU: a method for automatic evaluation of machine translation", In Proceedings of the 40th Annual Meeting on ACL, pages 311–318, Philadelphia, PA, 2002.

[18] Liang Zhou, Chin-Yew Lin and Eduard Hovy, "Re-evaluating machine translation results with paraphrase support", In Proceedings of the Conference on EMNLP, pages 77–84 , Sydney, Australia, 2006.

[19] Prodromos Malakasiotis, "Paraphrase recognition using machine learning to combine similarity measures", In Proceedings of the 47th Annual Meeting of ACL and the 4th International Joint Conference on Natural Language Processing of the Asian Federation of Natural Language Processing, Suntec, Singapore, 2009.

[20] Igor Mel'cuk, "Dependency Syntax: Theory and Practice", State University of New York Press, 1987.

[21] Sandra Kübler, Ryan McDonald, and Joakim Nivre, "Dependency Parsing". Synthesis Lectures on Human Language Technologies. Morgan and Claypool Publishers, 2009.

[22] Selkow, S., "The tree-to-tree editing problem", The Journal of Information Processing Letters, Volume 6, No. 6, 184–186, 1977.

[23] Kuo-Chung Tai, "The tree-to-tree correction problem", The Journal of ACM, Volume 26, No. 3, 422–433, 1979.

[24] Kaizhong Zhang and Dennis Shasha, "Simple fast algorithms for the editing distance between trees and related problems", SIAM Journal of Computing, Volume 18, No. 6, pages 1245–1262, 1989.

[25] oll´a, D., Schwitter, R., Rinaldi, F., Dowdall, J., & Hess, M, Anaphora resolution in EXTRANS. In Proc. of the Int. Symposium on Reference Resolution and Its Applications to Question Answering and Summarization, pp. 23–25, Venice, Italy,2003.

[26] Mitchell, T, "Machine Learning", Mc-Graw Hill. 1997.

[27] Ethem Alpaydin, "Introduction to Machine Learning", The MIT Press, 2004.

[28] Yujie Zhang and Kazuhide Yamamoto, "Paraphrasing spoken Chinese using a paraphrase corpus", The Journal of Natural Language Engineering, Volume 11, No. 4, pages 417–434, December, 2005.

[29] Fabio Massimo Zanzotto and Lorenzo Dell'Arciprete, "Efficient kernels for sentence pair classification", In Proceedings of the 2009 Conference on Empirical Methods in Natural Language Processing, Volume 1, pages 91–100, Singapore, 2009.

[30] Eduard Hovy, "Toward finely differentiated evaluation metrics for machine translation", In Proceedings of the Eagles Workshop on Standards and Evaluation, Pisa, Italy, 1999.

[31] J.S. White and T. O'Connell, "The ARPA MT evaluation methodologies: evolution, lessons, and future approaches", In Proceedings of the First Conference of the Association for Machine Translation in the Americas, pages 193–205, Columbia, Maryland, 1994.

[32] Stanford parser, http://nlp.stanford.edu/software/lex-parser.shtml

[33] Min-Hsiang Li, Shih-Hung Wu, Ping-che Yang and Tsun Ku, "Chinese Characters Conversion System based on Lookup Table and Language Model", In Proceedings of the 22nd Conference on Computational Linguistics and Speech Processing (ROCLING 2010), pages 113-127, Nantou, Taiwan, September 2010.

[34] Alessandro Moschitti, "Making tree kernels practical for natural language learning", In Proceedings of 11th Conference of the European Chapter of the Association for Computational Linguistics (EACL2006), pages 113–120, Treato, Italy, 2006.

[35] ICTCLAS, http://ictclas.org/

[36] CKIP, http://ckipsvr.iis.sinica.edu.tw

[37] Roger Levy and Christopher Manning, "Is it harder to parse Chinese, or the Chinese Treebank?", In Proceeding of the 41st Annual Meeting on Association for Computational Linguistics, Volume 1, pages 439-446, Sapporo Convention Center, Japan, 2003.

[38] LIBSVM, http://www.csie.ntu.edu.tw/~cjlin/libsvm/

結合語言模型與網路知識源於列印前檢查

Print Pickets Combined Language Models and Knowledge Resources in Web

黃昱睿 Yu-Jui Huang
國立嘉義大學資訊工程學系
Department of Computer Science and Information Engineering
National Chia-Yi University
s0990435@mail.ncyu.edu.tw

顏明祺 Ming-chin Yen
國立嘉義大學資訊工程學系
Department of Computer Science and Information Engineering
National Chia-Yi University
s0942795@mail.ncyu.edu.tw

吳冠輝 Guan-Huei Wu
國立嘉義大學資訊工程學系
Department of Computer Science and Information Engineering
National Chia-Yi University
s0962551@mail.ncyu.edu.tw

王耀毅 Yao-Yi Wang
國立嘉義大學資訊工程學系
Department of Computer Science and Information Engineering
National Chia-Yi University
s0962576@mail.ncyu.edu.tw

葉瑞峰 Jui-Feng Yeh
國立嘉義大學資訊工程學系
Department of Computer Science and Information Engineering
National Chia-Yi University
ralph@mail.ncyu.edu.tw

摘要

人們印製文件時常會疏忽了錯字而在印製完畢後才發現內容有拼字錯誤，在這種情況下往往需要重新印製一份，但這不僅浪費紙張、墨水、印表機的電力等等資源也需花費額外的時間導致降低了工作效率。假如我們能在列印前先發現文件內容的拼字錯誤並及時阻止印表機列印，則可解決我們前面所提及的問題產生。因此，本研究使用語言模型來進行比對之外還另外增加了網路搜尋的新功能搭配一起進行檢查，以便改善拼字錯誤造成列印資源的浪費。

Abstract

People often find out spelling errors after printing the documents, therefore they need to re-print the contents of the documents. However, it is a waste of paper, ink, printer, power, other resources and so on. Even more they would need to spend extra time without efficient. This paper addresses reducing spelling errors before printing. The language model used in this research to compare and increase a new feature additionally that is a function of Internet search. Combining these research manners, this paper expect to achieve the goals of confirming, improving the spelling error, and reducing the waste of resources.

關鍵詞：拼字錯誤，語言模型，網路搜尋

Keywords: Spelling errors, Language model, Web search

一、緒論

隨著科技不斷的進步，人們的環保意識也隨之高漲，「永續發展」和「綠色運算」也逐漸被人們所重視並探討其如何實現，而在這個電子 3C 產品充斥的時代，我們每天日常生活中所消耗的電力是非常可觀的。

表一、台灣電力公司統計每戶家庭平均用電費用

台灣電力公司統計每戶家庭平均用電費用				
統計資料(年度)	2005	2006	2007	2008
家庭每月平均用電量(度)	328	322	319	308
家庭每月平均電費支出(元)	823	826	824	796

根據表一統計[1]，台灣家庭在 2005 年時的平均用電量是 328 度，每月平均用電支出則是 823 元；而在 2008 年時的平均用電量是 308 度，每月平均用電支出則是 796 元，由上表得知台灣家庭每年的平均用電量都有在逐漸減少的趨勢，可看出國人對於節能減碳觀念的重視。此外，電費支出的費用也隨著用電量減少而逐漸下滑。如此一來，即使台灣電力公司的電價每年都有小幅調漲，藉由減少用電量來降低用電支出仍有不錯的成效。儘管如此，雖然每個人的用電量都有減少，但是一大群人累積起來的大量消耗電力也間接的對環境造成了傷害。因此，如何避免無謂的電力浪費便是我們所要解決的主要課題之一。

現今觀察市面上，可以發現有「綠色印表機」產品，其大部分主要原理是使用了再生紙和對環境無害的大豆油墨等自然原料，經由減少對環境的破壞以達到地球永續的目的。縱使我們所使用的是對地球再無害的原料，列印錯誤所累積的損失對地球而言仍是一種傷害和資源的浪費，因爲使用者輸入錯誤所造成的列印錯誤是可以免除的。然而，目前電腦的周邊設備像是印表機等，其輸出設備常需要一些必要的耗材，如列印所需要

的碳粉、墨水匣、紙張等，如何降低其耗材的浪費便是我們所需要探討的問題。

首先，假如能減少紙張的用量，那勢必可以減少樹木的砍伐並維護目前森林綠地的地表覆蓋面積，間接的也能涵養土壤中的水分和維護空氣的品質。再來是墨水匣、碳粉的部分，如能夠有效的減少用量自然可以省碳且降低其他包裝材料的濫用。電能部分，一旦要使用印表機勢必要消耗一定量的電力，如果免除了因使用者輸入錯誤而需再重新印製的電力，相信可以減少部分碳的排放量。因此目前的印表機皆加入數種減紙少碳的構想於其中，像是列印時可選擇一張多頁、縮小列印、雙面列印或根據使用者的喜好減少紙張周邊的空白以增加可列印的面積，這些設計對於減紙少碳都具有一定的功效，假如能加入內容分析這項技術。相信對於節能減碳會有加分甚至是加乘的效果出現。

內容的分析我們將自然語言處理技術應用於列印前的檢查，排除因使用者的打字錯誤而導致所列印的文件無效造成資源的浪費。可以避免浪費紙張、墨水匣等，更能縮短列印時所花費的時間並提高文件的可靠度。綜合以上各點，我們決定透過文件內容分析這方面切入。一般我們會有列印錯誤的問題，有很大一部分的原因是列印前沒有確實的檢查內容，造成為數可觀的資源浪費，如果我們能在列印前將列印文件周詳的檢查一遍，經判斷正確無誤後再行列印的動作，相信將會避免掉許多不要的資源耗損，不但可以避免墨水、油墨、紙張的浪費。更可以縮短時間，提升工作效率。

二、相關研究

與印表機驅動程式相關之項目主要可以分成微軟的 WDK 開發環境、印表機驅動系統、視窗程式設計。WDK 開發環境可經由安裝 Windows 驅動程式套件-Microsoft Windows Driver Kit (WDK)且研讀 WDK 相關文件並利用其驅動程式套件進行開發，建立驅動程式[2]。而印表機驅動系統可運用前者 WDK 驅動程式套件進行客製化動作，建立所需要的印表機驅動程式。最後視窗程式設計是使用 JAVA 撰寫一個介面視窗，讓使用者在進行列印時，假如發現文章有錯誤可以出現一個提醒的視窗來提示使用者文章中哪裡有錯誤，並且詢問使用者是否要修正或是忽略錯誤直接進行列印的動作，而不僅僅是顯示文章有誤而沒有從使用者的使用習慣著想。

現今一般拼字錯誤檢查系統主要是先將文章裡的文字進行擷取並經過斷詞後，再將經過斷詞的詞彙進行分析，而這些文字擷取與斷詞的方法主要可以分成圖文分離技術(Graphic/Text Detection ASIC)、斷詞系統(Chinese Knowledge and Information Processing, CKIP)、自然語言理解(Natural Language Understanding)、語意擷取(Semantic Retrieval)、本體知識分析(Ontology Analysis)。由工業技術研究院所研發的圖文分離技術[3]，可讓圖文兩者混合的列印文件在圖形、文字中都能表現出原有的效果，簡言之，其為辨識出「文字」和「圖形」的動作，讓圖形中的文字可以與圖分離。中央研究院的斷詞系統 [4]，其系統包含了大量的詞彙庫和附加詞類、詞類頻率等資料，可用其龐大的詞彙庫來輔助列印文件中文字的切割，以確保斷詞後字詞的正確性。在自然語言方面，一般通指可以隨著文化演化的語言，像是英語、漢語、日語都可算是自然語言，而同樣的字詞在不同的句子當中又會有不同的意思。舉例來說:「我把水果拿給動物們，因為它們餓了」和「我把水果拿給動物們，因為它們熟透了」兩句有相同的句子結構，但這兩句子中的「它們」分別代表動物和水果，假如我們不了解動物和水果的屬性就無法做區分判斷。另一方面，自然語言也會隨著時間不斷的演變，再加上句法、表達上的彈性以及永無止盡的例外和變動也使得自然語言成爲一個不容易判斷的語言類別[5]。語意擷取的技術是將自然語言本中識別出其特定的詞彙、主題或關鍵字，將文件中的原始資料轉爲核心資訊，進一步的與其相關的主題內容作對應，例如人、事、時、地、物等。因此，藉由此項技術，可以依照其相關的主題進行解讀自然語言文本的動作，將原始的文件資料轉換成核心的資訊，以供程式或機器做進一步的使用[6]。本體知識分析主要是研究各名詞「存在」的問題，即探討哪些名詞是實際存在的，哪些名詞只是代表一種觀念，舉例來說:「社團」代表一群人擁有相同理念或性質的集合體，「幾何」表示一種特殊知識的集合。討論此相關問題並分析在各種不同領域的名詞，並描述各領域中實際的特性即爲本體(Ontology) [7]。

在語言模型與網路搜尋的技術，可分爲自動分析網路內容、N-gram 語言模型、文句自動產生、智慧型輸入法、文句自動分析。近年來大陸針對互聯網成功研製了互聯網信息採集分析系統[8]，可針對特定的網絡內容進行採集、跟蹤、預警、監控，目前在國內多個權威機構已經獲得實際應用，取代了國外同類系統，被應用單位評價爲是「融合了最新的人工智能、信息檢索、文本挖掘和互聯網技術的研究成果」，在實際應用中取得了良好的效果。N-gram 語言模型是一種文字斷詞方法，分成 Tri-gram、Bi-gram 和 Uni-gram。Tri-gram 是以 3 個字爲一組的方式來進行文字切割、Bi-gram 是以 2 個字爲一組的方式來進行文字切割而 Uni-gram 則以 1 個字爲一組的方式來進行文字檢查。近年來由美國麻省理工學院蘇波和芭茲萊發表的自動產生維基百科文章的研究[9]，他們事先收集維基百科中有關美國電影明星以及疾病的文章。然後利用這些資料來訓練電腦自動分析文章結構、擷取各段落資料、選擇文章主題文句以及透過文句組合來撰寫文稿。並且透過學界常用的自動化評估方法，得出依照此方式讓電腦自動生成文章的資訊與品質，非常接近真人寫出的文章。智慧型輸入法(網際慧智)是指接受使用者輸入注音符號與音韻，再依據上下文、使用者以往的輸入習慣，依據機率多寡或特定的挑選策略，列出並過濾使用者期望的字詞，例如自然輸入法、倚天忘形輸入法，或是微軟的新注音輸入法等。在網路上收集詞彙資料庫是件很容易的事，但單純根據辭彙頻率，並無法推得操作者的真正需求。因爲辭彙頻率是眾人的累計，對於個人的效果並不明顯。個人除了有用詞習慣、還有專業領域、輸入時期等因素會影響到同音詞的判斷。因此一個拼音注音型的輸入法，無法單憑一個很大的詞庫就搞定一切，爲了提高同音詞的正確率，互動學習是智慧型輸入法的關鍵。透過中研院的斷詞系統(CKIP)與 YAHOO 的斷章取義 API 皆可提供使用者進行自動化的文字語意分析與處理，將文章裡的文字進行切割，並且也能將詞性列出。

三、系統介紹

本研究之系統流程圖如下圖一所示：

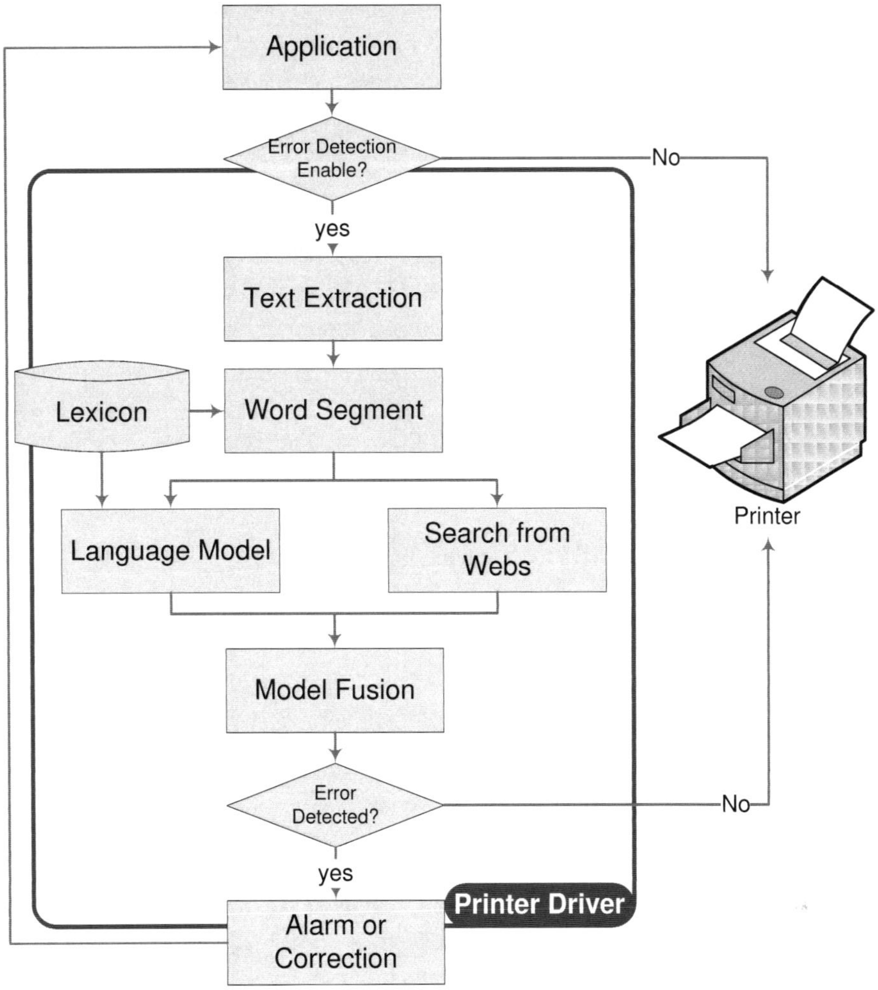

圖一、系統流程圖

根據上述之系統流程圖，我們將原本的列印驅動程式(Printer Driver)加上拼字檢查模組，完成印表機驅動程式的加值功能。因此，列印文件時若使用者選擇不進行文件偵錯功能(Error Detection Enable)，那程式會立即將文件列印出來，假使選擇進行列印偵錯的動作，將會進行以下的檢查步驟：

(一)文字抽取 (Text Extraction)

首先我們要對列印的文件進行文字正確性的判斷，所以我們只抽取文字部分來做處理。然而文件中的內容格式可能包含了各種的文字大小與各類型的文字格式，因此，我們需要將要列印的文件抽取出純文字(Plain Text)以便進行後續處理的動作。這邊使用 Zan Image Printer 這個工具來幫助我們對一份含有圖文的文件進行文字抽取的動作，最後輸出一個只有文字的文件檔[10]

(二)文字切割 (Word Segmentation)

我們將文件中抽取出來後的純文字進行切割的動作，由於這些純文字內容可能包含許多詞彙或專有名詞，所以要對如何這些名詞如何做正確切割的動作，是一件相當龐大的工作。於是本模組利用中研院斷詞系統(CKIP)來進行輔助，我們利用其龐大的詞彙庫來完成更精確的斷詞，如：我把水果拿給動物們，經過斷詞後的結果可以得到，我、把、水果、拿給、動物、們，使我們在斷詞部分的處理準確性提高。

(三)語言模型(Language Model)

將切割完畢後的文字進行第一次的拼字檢查，我們使用中文十億詞語料庫(Chinese Gigaword Corpus)訓練出的語言模型進行與詞彙庫的交叉比對檢查，利用了 n-gram 中的 tri-gram、bi-gram、uni-gram 一層層的進行分析檢查[11]，假如文件中有新的詞彙或無法判讀的字詞出現，那我們將會使用網路搜尋(Web search)進行檢查，更進一步的判讀字詞的正確性以求更精確的拼字矯正。本研究將 N 值提高，精確度會提升，可是效果不明顯，且效能會由於搜索字串增加而降低，因此本研究只使用到 tri-gram。

(四)網路搜尋(Web Search)

如果使用語言模型做拼字檢查但出現無法解讀的詞彙時，將透過網路搜尋引擎進行判斷，向 Google AJAX Search API 提出要求並利用其所回傳之 JSON 編碼結果，其結果包含了搜尋字串的網站、網址、搜尋筆數等，我們取其中的搜尋筆數作判斷，如果這個詞的搜尋筆數相當高，也就能間接證明這個詞是存在的是有意義的，從另外一個角度來看也等同於將網路變身為一個超大型資料庫，可以不斷的更新詞彙增加詞彙的數目。

舉例來說：像「阿凡達」這個詞在幾年前沒有出現，在一般的詞彙字典中更是找無此字，是一個不存在直到最近幾年才創出來的新詞彙，不過利用網路來搜尋的特性，如果能找到相關資訊且搜尋筆數不少的話，那也就可以幾乎肯定「阿凡達」這個詞是存在且有意義的[12][13]，用這樣的方法可大幅提升拼字檢查的正確性，並與一般的拼字檢查相比有了較低的錯誤率，而印出來的文件錯誤率降低，效率自然提高，也能使資源能有效的利用不會浪費無謂的資源，進一步的達到節能減碳、地球永續的理念。

(五)模型融合(Model Fusion)

在此步驟我們將上述的語言模型(Language Model)和網路搜尋(Search From Web)以線性組合方式進行整合，並根據兩者最後的綜合計分和結果來進行錯誤偵測，假如判別文件無誤，則將列印訊號傳至印表機進行列印的動作，相反的假如判別文件有誤，則出現提醒(Alarm)或進行修正(Correction)，直到文件全面檢查無誤就可以將文件正確的印製完成。

經過以上的五個步驟，我們就可進行文件的拼字檢查的動作，透過這些動作將文件中有誤的字詞挑選出來，提醒使用者作修改的動作，進而達到減少錯誤列印發生的機率。

綜合以上所述，我們可以將列印程序簡化成如下圖二所示：

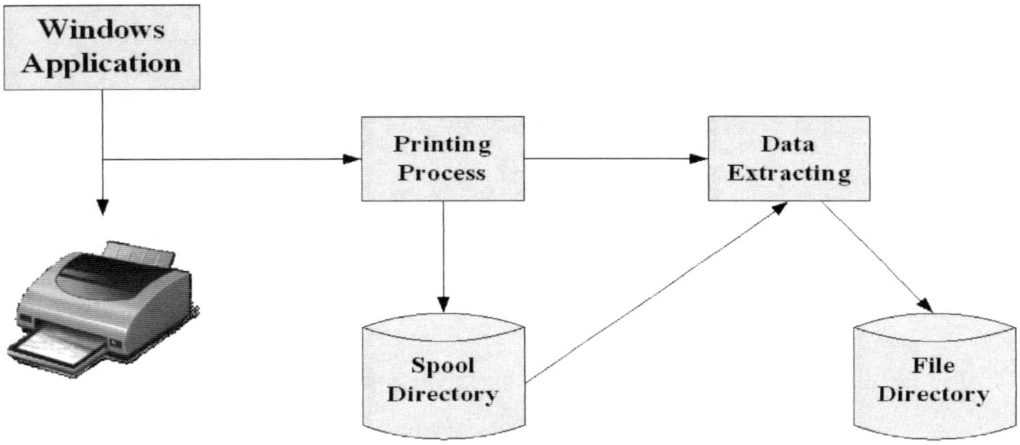

圖二、印表機列印程序示意圖

當列印的動作產生時，其中會有三個執行程序(Process)被啓動，包括使用者接觸使用的視窗應用程式(Windows Application)、列印處理程序(Printing Process)以及資料擷取程序(Data Extracting)。在資料擷取上可以著力在由列印處理程序(Printing Process)與經過列印後暫存列印緩衝區的 Spool Directory 中的檔案兩部分。但在 Spool Directory 中的檔案必須是經過轉譯成印表機語言像是 Printer Command Language (PCL)、ECL 的檔案，若從 Spool Directory 處理勢必引入許多來自印表機的語言的問題。因此本研究優先由列印處理程序中將文字擷取出來，這樣的處理程序會比在列印緩衝區的資料存取速度來的較快，可靠度(Reliability)也較高。而資料擷取出來後可以直接進行處理或者暫存至另一個緩衝區(File Directory)。

四、實驗結果與討論

(一)評估標準

精準度(Precision)和召回率(Recall)常常用來衡量一個系統的效能，尤其是在資訊檢索或資料探勘的領域中，我們常常會想知道當我們在檢索或搜尋系統中進行一個查詢(query)時，其回傳的結果是不是使用者需要的，還有其回傳的效率好不好等問題。因此計算出 Precision 和 Recall 這兩個值便可以解決前面所提的問題，運用量化的方式將數值呈現出來，便能使我們能更清楚的了解其系統的效能。而 Precision 和 Recall 其定義如下[14]

1. 精準度(Precision)定義：Relevant Documents Retrieved / Total Retrieved Documents
   (1) Relevant Documents Retrieved：系統判為錯誤中實際錯誤的個數
   (2) Total Retrieved Documents：系統判為錯誤的個數

2. 召回率(Recall)定義：Relevant Documents Retrieved / Total Relevant Documents
   (1) Relevant Documents Retrieved：系統判為錯誤中實際錯誤的個數

(2) Total Relevant Documents：文章中實際錯誤的個數

(二) Precision 與 Recall 的定義象限表說明

表二、Precision 和 Recall 之象限表

	相關	不相關
回傳	**Tp (true positive)**	**Fp (false positive)**
未回傳	**Fn (false negative)**	**Tn (true negative)**

Tp：代表回傳(系統判斷為錯誤)文字與query(實際錯誤文字)相關，系統判斷正確並回傳

Fp：代表回傳(系統判斷為錯誤)文字與 query(實際錯誤文字)無關，系統判斷錯誤並回傳

Fn：代表回傳(系統判斷為錯誤)文字與 query(實際錯誤文字)相關，系統判斷錯誤並無回傳

Tn：代表回傳(系統判斷為錯誤)文字與 query(實際錯誤文字)無關，系統判斷正確並無回傳

精準度與召回率的公式如下：

1. 精準度(Precision)：Tp / Tp + Fp
2. 召回率(Recall)：Tp / Tp + Fn

(三)實驗說明

在我們的實驗中總共使用三種拼字檢查模式，經由這三種模式的比較可以得知本研究的拼字錯誤檢查系統應該使用哪一種檢查模式才可以得到較好的效率及偵錯能力，下列針對該三種模式做一個概略說明：

1. 網路+語言模型(tri-gram+bi-gram)：此模式運用了語言模型的 tri-gram 和 bi-gram，而 uni-gram 因為是經由 CKIP 斷詞後之結果，大致上都是屬於有意義之詞彙，因此在這邊不列入考慮當中。除此之外，還搭配網路搜尋的功能進行檢查，而這裡 tri-gram 的網路搜尋的判斷筆數設定為 1 筆，假如查詢筆數結果大於 1 筆則將該詞彙視為正確；而 bi-gram 的網路搜尋判斷筆數設定為 10 筆，假如查詢筆數結果大於 10 筆則將該詞彙視為正確。
2. 網路+語言模型(bi-gram)：此模式運用了語言模型的 bi-gram，並搭配網路搜尋功能，bi-gram 的網路搜尋判斷筆數設定為 10 筆。
3. 語言模型(tri-gram+bi-gram)：此模式運用了語言模型的 tri-gram 和 bi-gram，此外此模式無搭配網路搜尋的功能。

本研究所使用的語言模型是由「十億詞中文語料庫」（Chinese Gigaword Corpus）訓練而成的，其內容分別來自台灣與大陸，1990-2002 年的完整通訊社新聞語料。

本研究的實驗文件是從網路上抓取新聞稿，總共分爲 10 大類，分別是政治、科技、教育、旅遊、社會、生活、財經、國際、運動和影劇，每一類分別有 20 篇，實驗新聞稿總計 200 篇，並且將每篇文件內容手動設定 5 個錯誤字，經由我們的拼字錯誤檢查系統後，將其檢查結果分別依照上述 Precision 和 Recall 的公式計算出表三和表四的數據。表五爲根據 Precision 和 Recall 計算出的 F1 值，表中的生活類別之網路+語言模型得出最高的 F1 值，因爲此類別的測試不只有語言模型還有加入網路搜尋的支援，所以得出的結果最高；而財經類別之語言模型的部分，由於只有語言模型的檢查，所以財經新聞中可能有許多未知的字詞，所以才會得出最差的結果。
注意：每一格所代表的數值爲 10 大類別，各 20 篇新聞稿共同實驗後所得的平均值。

表三、精準度(Precision)實驗數據

Precision (%)	政治	科技	教育	旅遊	社會	生活	財經	國際	運動	影劇
網路+語言模型 (tri-gram+bi-gram)	**63.70**	**72.70**	**65.09**	**57.71**	**55.77**	**60.91**	**47.55**	**47.02**	**9.95**	**59.01**
網路+語言模型 (bi-gram)	**43.06**	**50.61**	**41.18**	**42.52**	**33.00**	**37.07**	**30.58**	**37.93**	**9.37**	**5.99**
語言模型 (tri-gram+bi-gram)	**6.94**	**7.75**	**7.34**	**8.22**	**8.08**	**2.60**	**3.36**	**7.88**	**3.95**	**4.05**

表四、召回率(Recall)實驗數據

Recall (%)	政治	科技	教育	旅遊	社會	生活	財經	國際	運動	影劇
網路+語言模型 (tri-gram+bi-gram)	**61.00**	**52.00**	**59.00**	**63.00**	**65.00**	**68.00**	**66.00**	**63.00**	**58.00**	**68.00**
網路+語言模型 (bi-gram)	**61.00**	**52.00**	**62.00**	**65.00**	**64.00**	**66.00**	**67.00**	**64.00**	**66.00**	**65.00**
語言模型 (tri-gram+bi-gram)	**96.00**	**96.00**	**97.00**	**94.00**	**95.00**	**51.00**	**54.00**	**61.00**	**69.00**	**66.00**

表五、F1 值(F1-score)實驗數據

F1-Measure (%)	政治	科技	教育	旅遊	社會	生活	財經	國際	運動	影劇
網路+語言模型 (tri-gram+bi-gram)	62.32	60.63	61.90	60.24	60.03	64.26	55.28	53.85	16.99	63.19
網路+語言模型 (bi-gram)	50.48	51.30	49.49	51.41	43.55	47.47	41.99	47.63	16.41	10.97
語言模型 (tri-gram+bi-gram)	12.94	14.34	13.65	15.12	14.89	4.95	6.33	13.96	7.47	7.63

圖五和圖六則是將表三和表四分別做成長條圖，依照下面 2 張圖所示可得知網路+語言模型(tri-gram+bi-gram)其 Precision 和 Recall 的平均值比其他兩者的 Precision 和 Recall 平均還要高，因此我們可以知道網路+語言模型(tri-gram+bi-gram)在文字檢查上擁有較高的效能表現。

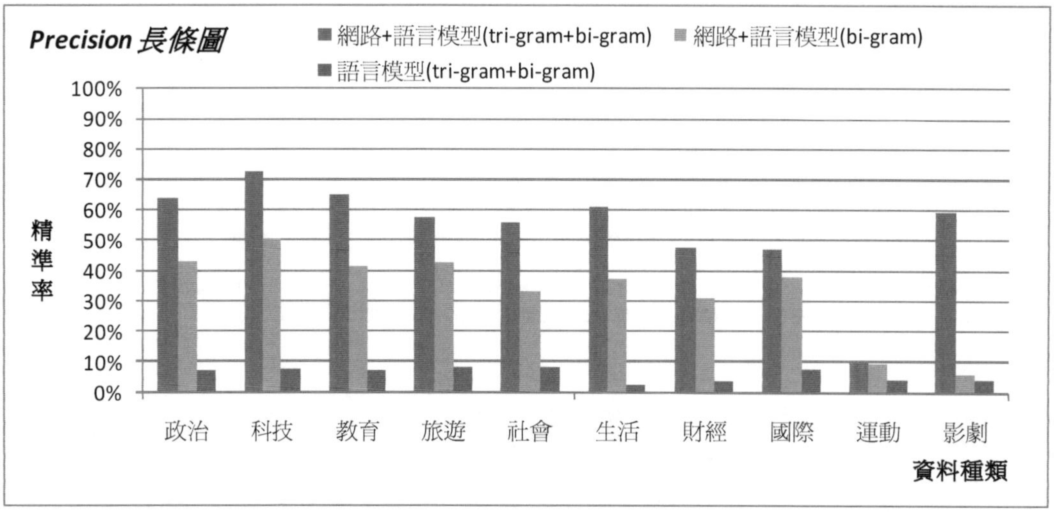

圖五、精準度(Precision)長條圖

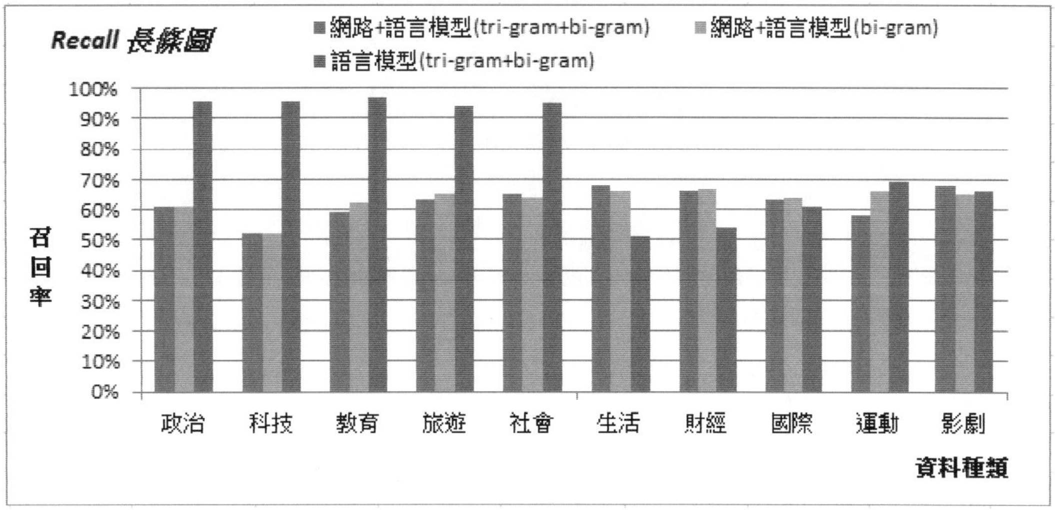

圖六、召回率(Recall)長條圖

五、結論與未來研究方向

本研究經過不斷的測試後發現中研院的 CKIP 系統會將錯字分別斷詞為單一字詞，而這些單一的字詞經過語言模型與網路搜尋後幾乎會判為正確，這也使的整個模組的檢測會疏忽這一類的錯字，因此我們將斷詞結果長度為一的詞進行不同的組合，以期填補這類的缺失，使的整個模組更加完善，辨錯率提高並落實完善檢查的功能。

在本研究中加入網路搜尋是在拼字檢查模組中應用網路搜尋技術，將檢查的誤判率大幅減低，並且藉由網路上龐大的資料作為拼字檢查的輔助，將網路資源當作一個大型的動態資料庫，其資料能隨著時間不斷的更新，除了涵蓋過去所有的詞彙還包含了列印當下所有的流行詞語或新創的詞彙等，使得本拼字檢查模組的正確率可以高於其他一般的拼字檢查。以及增加人性化提示訊息，常見的拼字檢查(如 Microsoft word)，在文件內容有錯誤時，雖然在該部分字詞會有特殊顏色的標記，但不會在列印時提醒使用者有錯誤，而列印了錯誤的文件，造成列印資源的浪費。而本模組在列印的時候如發現文件有錯誤，即會跳出一個提醒的視窗警告使用者需要更正，同時也可以讓使用者自行選擇是否要進行修正或是忽略錯誤直接將文件列印出來，以此模式進行文件檢查的最後一步把關。

本研究的可行性相當高，虛擬列表機的建立可以利用原有的 windows driver 改寫後作為檢查用途，知識經濟可以分為文字擷取與錯誤判斷兩部分。利用中研院的 CKIP 系統依照詞性種類進行斷詞，而後將斷詞後得到的結果透過模組內的語言模型(Language Model)和網路搜尋(Search From Web)來校正。語言模型中使用 N-gram 並分成三種方式來進行檢查，分別為三字為一組的 Tri-gram、二字為一組的 Bi-gram 以及一字為一組的 Uni-gram。網路搜尋使用 Google AJAX Search API，依照其傳回搜尋字串的網站內容、網址、搜尋筆數等進行判別。將以上各種功能結合，並給予人性化的操作介面讓使用者可以容易的使用本模組，達到列印前文件內容校正的目標。

本研究可帶來環保性或節能減碳效益，如：避免紙張浪費，印刷的主要原材料是紙張和油墨，而其中紙張就占印刷總成本的 60%～70%[15]，而造成印刷錯誤的主要原因是文件內容有誤，因此減少文字錯誤是為重要課題之一。以及減少油墨消耗，根據估計[16]台灣有超過六十萬台雷射印表機，每年約使用 300 萬支以上的碳粉匣，若能增加文字正確性，將避免重複列印而大幅降低碳粉夾的消耗量。還有可以節約能源，印刷業的能源消費(CO2 排放)占工業部門 0.13 %[17]，在總工業部門中排名 22，若能避免文字錯誤而減少重複列印，將可有效節約能源。

本研究在拼字檢查模組上結合網路搜尋技術，在檢查拼字正確的效果明顯高於只使用語言模型，但正確的拼字不代表在特定情境下是正確的用字，未來擬將情境納入拼字檢查，來改善這方面的問題。

致謝

本研究係國科會研究計劃「應用語言模型與網路知識源之列印拼字錯誤偵測驅動模組之開發(NSC100-2622-E-415-001-CC3)」之成果，承蒙. 國科會提供經費上的支援，特此申謝。

參考文獻

[1] 台灣電力公司電價查詢
http://www.rod.idv.tw/fastfood/electricity0001.html

[2] ACULIST'SBLOG Available:
http://miraculist.blogspot.com/2009/08/windows-driver-kit-wdk.html

[3] Industrial Technology Research Institute – Graphice/Text Detection ASIC. Available:
http://www.itri.org.tw/chi/tech-transfer/04.asp?RootNodeId=040&NodeId=041&id=2353

[4] Academia Sinica – Chinese Knowledge and Information Processing. Available:
http://ckip.iis.sinica.edu.tw/CKIP/publication.htm

[5] Bates, M. (1995). Models of natural language understanding. Proceedings of the National Academy of Sciences of the United States of America, Vol. 92, No. 22 (Oct. 24, 1995), pp.9977–9982.

[6] R. K. Srihari, W. Li, C. Niu and T. Cornell,"InfoXtract: A Customizable Intermediate Level Information Extraction Engine",Journal of Natural Language Engineering, Cambridge U. Press , 14(1), 2008, pp.33-69.

[7] Eldred, Michael, Social Ontology: Recasting Political Philosophy Through a Phenomenology of Whoness ontos, Frankfurt 2008 xiv + 688 pp.ISBN 978-3-938793-78-7

[8] 互聯網內容的海量信息自動分析技術

http://www.ilib2.com/A-cstaID~CG2008435623.html

[9] 科學人雜誌網站-語言研究維基化
http://sa.ylib.com/circus/circusshow.asp?FDocNo=1448&CL=95

[10] Zan Image Printer. Available:
http://www.zan1011.com/index.htm

[11] Christopher D. Manning, Hinrich Schütze, Foundations of Statistical Natural Language Processing, MIT Press: 1999. ISBN 0-262-13360-1

[12] Jaime Teevan, Eytan Adar, Rosie Jones, Michael Potts.History repeats itself: Repeat Queries in Yahoo's query logs. Proceedings of the 29th Annual ACM Conference on Research and Development in Information Retrieval (SIGIR '06). 2005: pp. 703-704.

[13] Amanda Spink, Dietmar Wolfram, Major B. J. Jansen, Tefko Saracevic. Searching the web: The public and their queries. Journal of the American Society for Information Science and Technology. 2001,52(3): 226-234.

[14] Precision and Recall. Available:
http://en.wikipedia.org/wiki/Precision_and_recall

[15] 如何減少商業輪轉印刷機的紙張消耗
http://www.hkprinters.org/news/news.asp?sub_id=560

[16] 優彩環保再生碳粉匣
http://www.ucolor.org.tw/

[17] 台灣綠色生產力基金會-節能服務網
http://www.ecct.org.tw/print/52_3.htm

診斷學習者英語寫作篇章結構：以篇章連接副詞爲例

Diagnosing discoursal organization in learner writing via conjunctive adverbials

高東榆 Tung-yu Kao
國立成功大學外國語文學系（所）
Department of Foreign Languages & Literature
National Cheng Kung University
dodofishletter@hotmail.com

陳麗美 Li-mei Chen
國立成功大學外國語文學系（所）
Department of Foreign Languages & Literature
National Cheng Kung University
leemay@mail.ncku.edu.tw

Abstract

The present study aims to investigate genre influence on the use and misuse of conjunctive adverbials (hereafter CAs) by compiling a learner corpus annotated with discoursal information on CAs. To do so, an online interface is constructed to collect and annotate data, and an annotating system for identifying the use and misuse of CAs is developed. The results show that genre difference has no impact on the use and misuse of CAs, but that there does exist a norm distribution of textual relations performed by CAs, indicating a preference preset in human cognition. Statistic analysis also shows that the proposed misuse patterns do significantly differ from one another in terms of appropriateness and necessity, ratifying the need to differentiate these misuse patterns. The results in the present study have three possible applications. First, the annotate data can serve as training data for developing technology that automatically diagnoses learner writing on the discoursal level. Second, the founding that textual relations performed by CAs form a distribution norm can be used as a principle to evaluate discoursal organization in learner writing. Lastly, the misuse framework not only identifies the location of misuse of CAs but also indicates direction for correction.

Keywords: conjunctive adverbial, textual relation, misuse pattern, learner corpus.

1. Introduction

Due to much interest in learning English around the globe, many tools are developed, or wanted to be developed, to facilitate learners to learn English better. One of many wanted tools is probably a tool that can automatically diagnose a piece of learner writing and provide direction for improvement of the writing. The need results from the fact that only by constantly revising process can learners keep polishing their writing skill but that there is just not enough manpower to help learners recognize the defects in their writing. Therefore, much software is developed to satisfy the need, such as the two famous online writing platforms, *My Access!* and *Criterion*, and the two popular writing software packages, *StyleWriter* and *White Smoke*.

However, after evaluating the above mentioned tools aiming to automatically diagnose learner writing, it is found that the diagnosis is mainly a grammar check at the sentence level yet fails to generate revising suggestions on the discourse level. In other words, the existing tools may help learners compose a piece of writing free from grammatical mistakes, but poor organization of sentences and anomaly in coherence may still lead to failure in comprehension. Therefore, a writing-facilitating tool that can automatically diagnose learner writing on the discourse level is further wanted. To do so, a further investigation of existing learner corpora is made to seek if they fit as training data for developing such tools in question. The result shows that all the three corpora under investigation, Taiwanese Learner Corpus of English (TLCE) [1], Chinese Learner English Corpus (CLEC) [2], and International Corpus of Learner English (ICLE) [3], are only annotated with linguistic information at the sentence level, which limits further development on the discourse level. In light of the investigation, the first goal of the present study is to construct a learner corpus that provides annotated discoursal information as a basis for developing technology that can automatically diagnose learner writing in terms of discoursal organization.

With the goal in mind, the correct use and misuse of conjunctive adverbials are selected as the discoursal information that is used to annotate the targeted learner corpus. In terms of correct use, many writing textbooks introduce conjunctive adverbials (hereafter CA) as explicit linguistic features that organize textual relation among sentences in a coherent order, and contend that CAs performing certain textual relation would be more prominent in certain genre [4] [5] [6] [7] [8]. For instance, the words or phrases, such as *firstly*, *next*, and *in addition*, are thought to appear more in the process genre, indicating progressive relations in the text. Yet, after reviewing literature [9] [10] [11] [12] [13] [14], it is found that the textual relations performed by CAs present a norm distribution no matter which genre the writing belongs to, which is contrary to what writing textbooks usually suggest.

In terms of misuse of CAs, [15] regulates three common misuse patterns, *non-equivalent exchange*, *connective overuse*, and *surface logicality*, that often occur in learner writing. However, after trying applying the misuse framework of CAs to classify the mistakes found in learner writing, the framework is found insufficient in doing so. Based on the review of literature on CAs, the second goal of the present study aims to empirically examine if writing genres play a role in the use of CAs, and to propose a framework that can better describe the misuse patterns of CAs found in learner writing.

In short, the present study is two-fold. One is to compile a learner corpus annotated with discoursal information, to be specific, information on CAs, which can serve as training data of developing technology that automatically diagnoses learner writing on the discoursal level, while the other is to investigate genre influence on use and misuse of CAs and to construct a misuse framework for CAs.

2. Annotating system of CAs

The annotating system developed in the present study is used to annotate learner writing in terms of the use and misuse of CAs that organize textual relation among sentences. The set of annotations that indicates textual relations performed by CAs is based on the taxonomy in [16], whereas the set concerning misuse patterns of CAs is on the classification in [15].

2.1 Annotation for textual relations by CAs

According to the taxonomy in [16], there are seven types of CAs that organize seven textual relations among sentences, which include *Listing*, *Transitional*, *Appositive*, *Summative*, *Resultive*, *Inferential*, and *Contrastive*. In the present study, two textual relations, *Resultive* and *Inferential*, are collapsed into one since both indicate the cause-effect textual relation, and one additional textual relation, *Corroborative*, is supplemented. As a result, seven types of textual relations performed by CAs are used to annotate learner writing, which are *Listing*, *Transitional*, *Appositive*, *Summative*, *Resultive/Inferential*, *Contrastive*, and *Corroborative*. Table 1 lists all the textual relations with their definitions and the possible language items performing these relations. Notice that Table 1 also shows that one language item may serve more than one textual relation, for example, the language item *then* is in both *Listing* and *Resultive/Inferential* relations. In other words, the semantic annotation must depend on the relation performed by the CA, not on certain fixed language items.

Table 1. The Set of Textual Relations Indicated by CAs

Textual relation	Definition	Example
Listing	Mark the next unit of discourse with or without relative priority or temporal sequence.	first, moreover, then, in addition
Transitional	Serve to shift attention to another topic that does not follow directly from the preceding event.	meanwhile, in the meantime, now
Appositive	Provide an example or an equivalent of the preceding text.	in other words, for example
Summative	Conclude or sum up the information in the preceding discourse.	in conclusion, to summarize

Resultive/ Inferential	Mark the second part of the discourse as the result or consequence of the preceding discourse.	accordingly, then, as a result, so
Contrastive	Show incompatibility between information.	however, on the contrary, anyhow
Corroborative	Express writers' attitudes toward and comments on the text.	in fact, of course, actually

Another issue regarding the annotation of the textual relations is register. Register refers to the fact that CAs performing the same textual relation are further classified into written register and spoken register, with the latter is considered informal and suggested to be avoided in formal writing. Take *moreover* and *plus* for example. While both CAs indicate the *Listing* textual relation, the use of the latter is sometimes seen as a misuse for its informal nature in writing. Given the distinction in CA register use, the annotating system also differentiates CAs performing the same textual relation in terms of register to examine the influence genre difference has on register use in CAs.

2.2 Misuse Patterns of Conjunctive Adverbials (CAs)

In contrast with the set that annotates learner writing with textual relations performed by CAs, the other set in the annotating system is to indicate the misuse of CAs when they fail to logically connect sentences or do not appropriately fit the context. With the three misuse patterns proposed in [15], there are six misuse patterns in total generalized in the present study, which are *Non-equivalent Exchange*, *Connective Overuse*, *Surface Logicality*, *Wrong Relation*, *Semantic Incompletion*, and *Distraction*. Table 2 showcases the six misuse patterns with their definitions and examples.

Table 2. The Set of Misuse Patterns of CAs

Misuse Pattern	Definition & Example
Non-equivalent Exchange	Use CAs conveying the same textual relation in an interchangeable manner when they are not • Those are the images of the UK that the Communists want to impose on the local Chinese. <u>*On the contrary*</u>, they describe the communists as patriotic Chinese who did not show the slightest fear.

Connective Overuse	Use CAs with high density in short texts, making texts fragmental and readers unable to expect where texts are going to lead. • The communicative approach proves not only practicable for juniors, but also for senior. <u>*However*</u>, only the junior forms were observed. <u>*Nevertheless*</u>, the study in juniors is essential for this is the stage when students establish the right ways of learning English.
Surface Logicality	Use CAs to impose logicality to texts or bridge the gap among propositions when there exists no deep logicality in texts. • This question means the same as 'Evaluate the degree to which Japanese imperialism was a result of militarism.' <u>*So*</u> this question requires an independent argument about them. <u>*So*</u> the student must think critically if Japanese imperialism was a result of militarism.
Wrong Relation	Use a CA to express certain textual relation that it does not express. • Many studies have showed that it would be better for the hearing disabled to have the cochlear implant at an early age. <u>*Also*</u>, if implanted the cochlear implant at the age one to two, their language learning could come out of great improvement.
Semantic Incompletion	The context where CAs are used needs more elaboration to make the CAs functional. • After finishing the competitive entrance exam, you enter the college. <u>*However*</u>, nowadays, graduating from college not necessarily guarantees you future.
Distraction	The context would be coherent itself without the use of the conjunctive adverbial or that the use is redundant. • Statistics that four countries had higher averages of education than Taiwan. <u>*For example*</u>, the percentage to get admitted to college of Finland and South Korea is 90 percent, New Zealand with 86 percent and Sweden with 84 percent.

2.3 Annotating system in electronic format

In total, there are 20 labels, 14 for identifying textual relations and 6 for recording misuse patterns, in the developed coding scheme, as presented in Table 3.

Table 3. The Complete annotating system

Textual relations			Misuse Patterns	
Register	Type	Abbreviation	Type	Abbreviation
Y / R	Listing	Y/R Lis	Non-equivalent Exchange	N NE
Y / R	Transitional	Y/R Tra	Connective Overuse	N CO

Y / R	Appositive	Y/R App	Surface Logicality	N SL
Y / R	Summative	Y/R Sum	Wrong Relation	N WR
Y / R	Resultive/Inferential	Y/R Res	Semantic Incompletion	N SI
Y / R	Contrastive	Y/R Con	Distraction	N DI
Y / R	Corroborative	Y/R Cor		

Then, to make the annotating system applicable to computational development, the system is converted into digital tags that preserve the linguistic information on the text. Table 4 presents the 20 digital tags.

Table 4. The digital tags in the annotating system

Textual relations (Written Register)	<tag Y Lis anno=" "> </tag>	<tag Y Res anno=" "> </tag>
	<tag Y Tra anno=" "> </tag>	<tag Y Con anno=" "> </tag>
	<tag Y App anno=" "> </tag>	<tag Y Cor anno=" "> </tag>
	<tag Y Sum anno=" "> </tag>	
Textual relations (Spoken Register)	<tag R Lis anno=" "> </tag>	<tag R Res anno=" "> </tag>
	<tag R Tra anno=" "> </tag>	<tag R Con anno=" "> </tag>
	<tag R App anno=" "> </tag>	<tag R Cor anno=" "> </tag>
	<tag R Sum anno=" "> </tag>	
Misuse Patterns	<tag N NE anno=" "> </tag>	<tag N WR anno=" "> </tag>
	<tag N CO anno=" "> </tag>	<tag N SI anno=" "> </tag>
	<tag N SL anno=" "> </tag>	<tag N DI anno=" "> </tag>

The tag design include a pair of pointed brackets delimit the text it annotates. In the tag, there are four layers separated by space. The first layer uses the word *tag* to ratify the other words in the first bracket as supplemented linguistic information. The letters, Y, R, and N, on the second layer refer to written register use, spoken register use and misuse pattern. The third layer specifies which use of misuse of the enclosed CA is. The last layer, shown as anno=" ", allows researchers to supplement other information if necessary. The following is an illustrative example.

<tag **Y Lis anno=" "**>First</tag>, children who have nasal allergy always have some mental problems to some extent.

3. Corpus compiling and application with CA annotation

The learner corpus compiled in the present study is based on the OLAC Metadata Set via the developed Perl-based online interface, accessible at http://awta.csie.ncku.edu.tw/. In total, 2290 pieces of English compositions by Chinese speakers, approximately one million words, are collected over three years. These compositions belong to 13 different genres, including *process*, *summary*, *essay question*, *cause-effect*, *comparison-contrast*, *definition*, *description*, *narration*, *classification*, *multiple strategies*, *argumentation*, *problem solving*, and *research article*.

Among the collected data, 65 pieces of writing, with 5 pieces a genre and 28941 words in total, are further selected for the investigation into the use and misuse of CAs. The selected data are annotated via the online tagger, as seen in Figure 1. Part A is the raw text, Part B shows the annotating system, and Part C presents how the raw text is annotated with CA information.

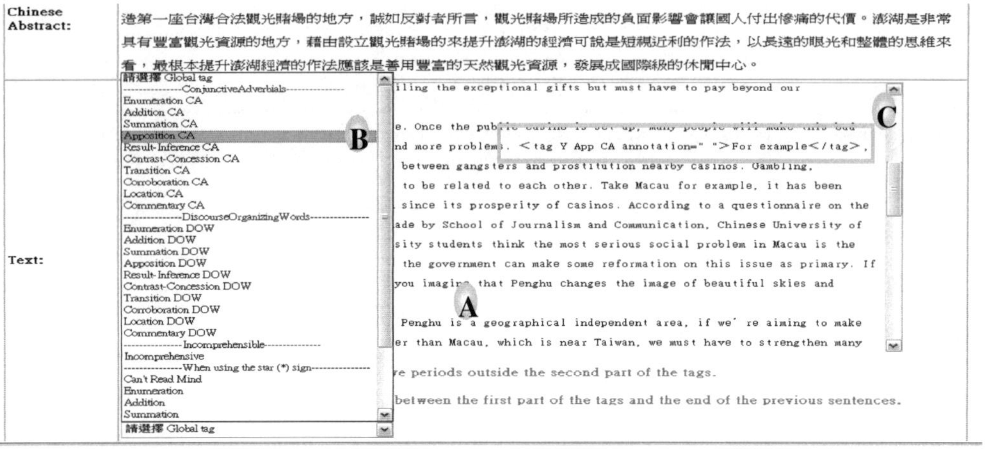

Figure 1. Tagger page

Each annotation of CA is made through a four-step procedure, shown in Figure 2. The first step identifies the CA. The second step is to judge whether or not the CA is correctly used. If the CA logically connects the context, the use of the CA is viewed as correct and the judgment goes to Yes. If not, the use is incorrect and the judgment goes to No. Lastly, if the use is correct yet the language form is stylistically improper, the judgment goes to Spoken Register. The third and last steps complete the annotation. If the judgment of the procedure goes to Yes or Spoken Register, then decide which textual relation the CA conveys, and select a tag from the bottom list. Likewise, if the judgment goes to No, select a misuse pattern tag from the bottom list to annotate the CA.

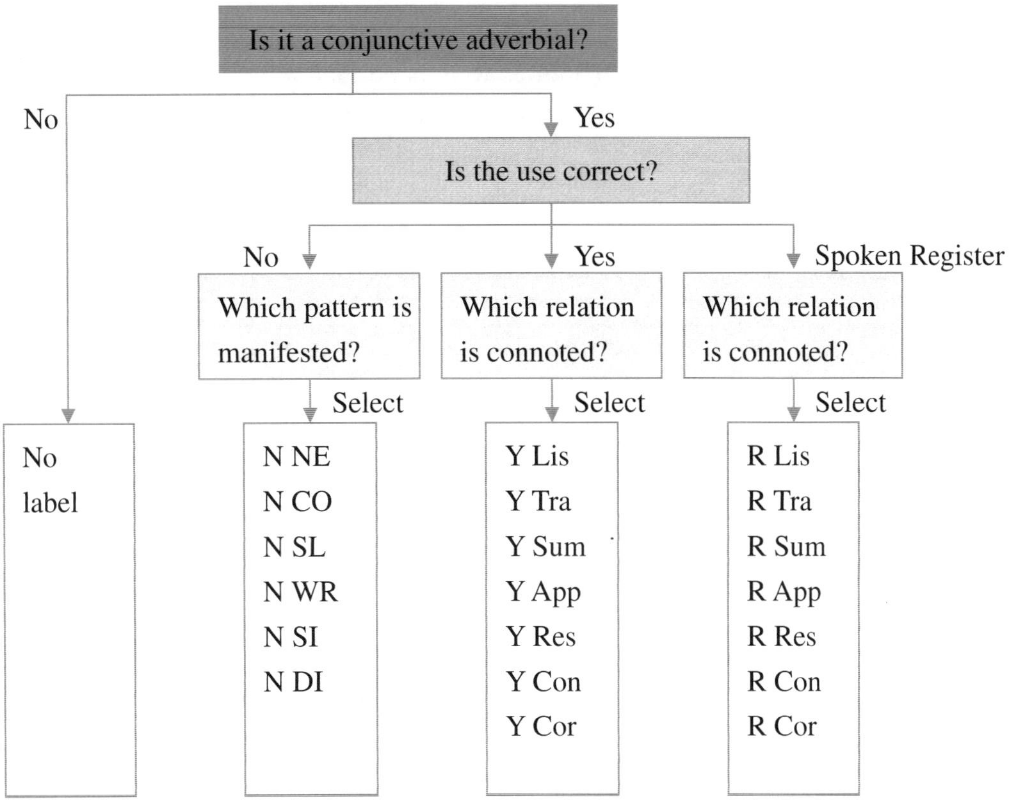

Figure 2. The annotating procedure

After annotating the selected data and tallying the counts, all the obtained figures were further analyzed via inferential statistical measurements on SPSS to investigate on the use and misuse distribution of CAs across genres.

To investigate the use distribution of CAs across genres, a two-way within-subjects analysis of variance (hereafter ANOVA) is designed, with two independent variables being textual relation and genre while the dependent variable is the counts of CAs. To further examine the effect of register, the ANOVA design would be calculated again, with the independent variable, textual relation, replaced with textual relation performed by CAs in written register. Lastly, to investigate the misuse distribution of CAs across genres, a two-way within-subjects ANOVA is employed again, with the two independent variables being misuse pattern and genre while the dependent variable is the counts of CAs. A significant level of $p<.05$ was chosen.

4. Results

In the investigation of the use distribution of CAs across genres, the raw counts of CAs show that regardless of genre difference, there is a tendency that the listing and contrastive relations are the two most frequently occurring types performed by CAs while the summative and transitional relations are the two least frequently occurring types. The rest of the textual relations are in the middle. In addition, the ANOVA analysis to examine the effect of textual relation and genre shows that there is no interaction between textual relation and genre ($F(48, 192)=1.070$, $p=0.366$) as well as no main effect from genre ($F(8, 32)=1.697$, $p=0.137$). However, there does exist a main effect from textual relation ($F(6, 24)=10.476$, $p<0.05$). Table 5 shows the statistic results.

Table 5. ANOVA results for the effect of textual relation and genre

Source	DF	SS	MS	F	P
Textual Relation	6	3005.681	500.947	10.476	0.000*
Genre	8	111.234	13.904	1.697	0.137
Textual RelationxGenre	48	64.977	1.354	1.070	0.366

*p<.05

In the follow-up investigation of the use distribution of written-register CAs across genres, the raw counts of written-register CAs show that regardless of genre difference, the listing and contrastive relations are the two most frequently occurring types performed by written-register CAs while the summative and transitional relations are the two least frequently occurring types. The rest of the textual relations are in the middle. After applying ANOVA analysis, as presented in Table 6, it is found that there is no interaction between textual relation performed by written-register CAs and genre ($F(48, 144)=0.969$, $p=0.537$). However, there does exist the main effect from textual relation ($F(6, 18)=8.585$, $p<0.05$). Meanwhile, Due to the scarce occurrence of spoken-register CAs, the row counts of spoken-register CAs are too small to decide the frequency order of occurrence and to run an ANOVA analysis.

Table 6. ANOVA results for the effect of textual relation via written-register CAs and genre

Source	DF	SS	MS	F	P
Textual Relation	6	1968.256	328.043	8.585	0.000*
Genre	8	99.374	12.422	2.062	0.082
Textual RelationxGenre	48	49.831	1.038	0.969	0.537

*p<.05

Lastly, in the examination of the misuse distribution of CAs across genres, ANOVA analysis shows, as seen in Table 7, that there is no interaction between misuse pattern and genre ($F(40, 160)=1.031$, $p=0.432$) as well as no main effect from genre ($F(8, 32)=1.857$, $p=0.102$) while there exists the main effect from misuse pattern ($F(5, 20)=3.210$, $p<0.05$). Although the raw counts of misuse patterns seem to show a norm distribution, it is just coincidence for most misuse patterns have no significant difference with others. However, some misuse patterns do differ from each other on a significant level. The misuse pattern, *Wrong Relation*, significantly differs from *Semantic Incompletion* and *Non-equivalent Exchange*, whereas *Surface Logicality* differs from *Conjunctive Overuse* and *Distraction.*

Table 7. ANOVA results for the effect of CA misuse and genre

Source	DF	SS	MS	F	P
CA Misuse	5	49.857	9.971	3.210	0.027*
Genre	8	25.239	3.155	1.857	0.102
Misuse Pattern×Genre	40	24.100	0.603	1.031	0.432

*p<.05

5. Discussion

The present study aims to achieve two goals. The first goal is to compile a learner corpus annotated with linguistic information on textual relation performed by CAs, which can serve as training data of developing technology that automatically diagnoses learner writing on the discoursal level. The second goal is to investigate genre influence on use and misuse of CAs and to construct a misuse framework for CAs.

In terms of the first goal, the compiled learner corpus fulfills the expectation. Researchers can use the annotated data as training data to develop automatically discourse-diagnosing technology and conduct pilot studies based on the rest of the corpus. Meanwhile, the annotated data are based on XML format, which bestows the data with great compatibility for all operating systems and extensibility to other possible alteration [17] for other application.

In terms of the second goal, it is found that, contrary to what most writing textbooks suggest that CAs performing certain textual relation are more prominent in certain genre, genre has no role in impacting the distribution of textual relations performed by CAs. In effect, the textual relations performed by CAs form a norm distribution regardless of genre difference. That is, *Listing* and *Contrastive* are the most frequent. *Resultive/Inferential*, *Appositive* and *Corroborative* are the second most frequent. *Summative* and *Transitional* are the least frequent, which corresponds to what is found in [9] [10] [11] as well as [12] [13] [14]. The same is true of the distribution norm performed by written-register CAs.

The lack of genre influence may result from the fact the genres are not mutually exclusive. That is, different genres may share many similar characteristics, which, in some sense, makes different genres one general superordinate genre without distinct differences. Consequently, a distribution norm of textual relations would be discovered, because the distribution norm of textual relations performed by CAs across genres, in fact, is the distribution of textual relations of the general superordinate genre.

To account for the formation of the distribution norm among textual relations performed by CAs, two explanations are proposed. One lies in the nature of different textual relations. For example, the transitional and summative relations occur least frequently at a significant level. This is understandable in that the two relations serve opening and closing functions which only appear at the beginning and at the end no matter how long a textual unit is. The other explanation is that there is a preference preset in human cognition for employing CAs to convey certain textual relations. Take the contrastive relation as example. The relation is relatively complicated because it requires the action to analyze two events and to locate the contrastive points, which would take more energy to describe the relation compared with writing in the common temporal sequence. Due to the extra energy required, Economy Principle, to minimize the energy consumption [18], is applied in human cognition, which is to use CAs to convey the contrastive relation explicitly, rather than describe the relation in context. Ultimately, the contrastive relation becomes one of the textual relations most frequently performed by CAs.

Lastly, although no genre influence on the misuse patterns of CAs is found, nor is a distribution norm of CA misuse, the proposed misuse framework is proved meaningful in differentiating CA misuse patterns. According to ANOVA analysis, *Wrong Relation* significantly differs from *Non-equivalent Exchange* and *Semantic Incompletion*, while *Surface Logicality* from *Connective Overuse* and *Distraction*. The results suggest that the causes of these misuse patterns are fundamentally different, and that the distinction and recognition of them are necessary. Also, the six misuse patterns can be divided into two groups based on the significant difference among them, with one group being *Wrong Relation*, *Non-equivalent Exchange*, *Semantic Incompletion*, while the other group being *Surface Logicality*, *Connective Overuse* and *Distraction*. To explain the division, the principles of appropriateness and necessity are proposed. The former group refers to the situation in which the use of the CA is required to signify the textual relation between sentences but the use is not correct, or inappropriate. In contrast, the latter group refers to the situation in which the use of the CA is not necessary and sentences themselves can form a unit of text with the CA.

6. Conclusion

The present study contributes in three aspects. First, a learner corpus annotated with textual relations via CAs is compiled, which can serve as training data for developing technology that automatically diagnoses learner writing on the discoursal level. Second, it is found that genre difference plays no role in impacting either textual relations via CAs or the misuse of CAs, and that there exists a norm distribution of textual relations performed by CAs across genres. The found norm distribution can be used to examine whether or not a piece of learner writing conforms to proper discoursal organization. Deviation from the norm distribution may be a signal, suggesting learners to re-organize their text. Third, the proposed misuse framework can help learners locate the misuse of CAs, and provide direction for correction by evaluating whether the misuse is inappropriate or not necessary.

Nevertheless, there is still room for further research. For a starter, the annotated data only account for a small amount of the compiled corpus. More data are expected to be annotated in the future, which can further validate the study and provide more training data to develop automatized technology. Moreover, although no genre influence is found in textual relations performed by CAs or in the misuse of CAs, as the anonymous reviewer suggests, the results may be still subject to other factors, such as age, educational background, English proficiency, or even L1 transfer. If the interaction between the use of CA and these factors can be made clear in future studies, non-native writers can receive a different angle in terms of learning CA use and organizing their English writing.

References

[1] H. H. Shih, Compiling Taiwanese Learner Corpus of English. *Computational Linguistics and Chinese Language Processing, 5*(2), 87-100, 2000.

[2] S. C. Gui, and H. Z. Yang, *Chinese Learner English Corpus*, Shanghai: Shanghai Foreign Language Education Press, 2003.

[3] S. Granger, International Corpus of Learner English - ICLE. Retrieved November 23, 2008, from http://www.fltr.ucl.ac.be/fltr/germ/etan/cecl/Cecl-Projects/Icle/icle.htm#heading1

[4] M. Connelly, *Get writing: Sentences and paragraphs*, Australia: Thomson Higher Education, 2006.

[5] J. M. Lannon, *The writing process: A concise rhetoric, reader, and handbook*, New York: Longman, 2007.

[6] M. Morenberg, and J. Sommers, *The writer's options: Lessons in style and arrangement*, New York: Pearson Longman, 2008.

[7] J. M. Reid, *The process of composition*, White Plains, NY: Longman, 2000.

[8] R. L. Smalley, M. K. Ruetten, and J. R. Kozyrev, *Refining composition skills: Rhetoric and grammar*, Boston: Heinle & Heinle, 2001.

[9] Y. Field, and L. Yip, A comparison of Internal conjunctive cohesion in the English essay writing of Cantonese speakers and native speakers of English. *RELC Journal,*

23, 15-28, 1992.
[10] M. Liu, and G. Braine, Cohesive features in argumentative writing produced by Chinese undergraduates. *System, 33*, 623-636, 2005.
[11] W. Y. C. Chen, The use of conjunctive adverbials in the academic papers of advanced Taiwanese EFL learners. *International Journal of Corpus Linguistics, 11*(1), 113-130, 2006.
[12] G. Tankó, The use of adverbial connectors in Hungarian university students' argumentative essays. In J. M. Sinclair (Ed.), *How to Use Corpora in Language Teaching* (pp. 157-181). Amsterdam: John Benjamins B. V, 2004.
[13] B. Altenberg, and M. Tapper, The use of adverbial connectors in advanced Swedish learners' written English. In S. Granger (Ed.), *Learner English on Computer* (pp. 80-93). London: Longman, 1998.
[14] T. C. Shen, *Advanced EFL Learners' Use of Conjunctive Adverbials in Academic Writing*. MA Thesis, Taiwan: National Taiwan Normal University, 2006.
[15] W. J. Crewe, The illogic of logical connectives. *ELT Journal, 44*(4), 316-325, 1990.
[16] R. Quirk, S. Greenbaum, G. Leech, and J. Svartvik, *A Comprehensive Grammar of the English Language*, London: Longman, 1985.
[17] A. Møller, and M. I. Schwartzbach, *An introduction to XML and Web technologies*, New York: Addison-Wesley, 2006.
[18] F. Ungerer, and H. J. Schmid, *An Introduction To Cognitive Linguistics*, UK: Pearson Education Limited, 2006.

Compositional Operations of Mandarin Chinese Verb "da³": A Generative Lexicon Approach

Li-Chuan Ku
Department of English
National Taiwan Normal University
lchnku@gmail.com

Abstract

The compositional operations of Mandarin Chinese predicates are very complex. In a highly analytic language such as Mandarin Chinese, a verb can often choose from a wide range of nouns/nominal compounds as its arguments. This paper hopes to capture a different picture of such an operation through investigating authentic corpus data of Chinese verb "打" (da³, *to hit*). In this study, we'd like to show that the qualia structure and type system proposed by Pustejovsky's (1995) the *Generative Lexicon* can affect the interpretation of verb-argument composition of "da³", and to examine whether the compositional operations of "da³" varies under different senses with its own type selection preference. Our results show that, given that Wang and Huang (2010)'s similar investigation on the perceptual verb "kàn" (look at) indicates diverse mechanisms, the compositional operation patterns of "da³" are much like those proposed by Pustejovsky's (2008). In view of this, we also provide some limitation and future direction of this study in the last section.

Keywords: verb-argument composition, accommodation, introduction, selection

1. Introduction

The compositionality of a verb and its arguments differs from one to another. Traditionally, although distributional analysis can provide us a glimpse of how a lexical word patterns across different surface structures of propositions, it is more intriguing to explore how a verb selects its arguments based on deeper decomposition of the lexical item, namely, the verb and argument itself. One of the ways to analyze the verb-argument composition is to consider that by word sense enumeration, a verb can potentially have several polysemous senses contributing to multiple meanings in the lexicon. Take *want* in the following sentences for example.

(1) a. Mary wants another cigarette.
b. Bill wants a beer.

c. Mary wants a job.

To capture each use of *want*, we can explicitly refer to the manner of the wanting relation in different contexts and have the following correspondent word sense enumeration, rendering the word *want* a selectional polysemy [3].

(2) a. $want_1$: to want to smoke;
b. $want_2$: to want to drink;
c. $want_3$: to want to have

However, enumeration is unable to exhaustively list all the senses that verbs assume in new contexts [1]; that is, it cannot characterize all the possible meanings of the lexical item in the lexicon. Instead of adopting this approach, Pustejovsky [3] proposes that the way how verbs are combined with arguments can fit into more finely grounded compositional operations, extended from the type theory and qualia structures he developed in *Generative Lexicon* [2][3], as shown in Table 1.

Table 1: Verb-Argument Composition

Argument is	Verb selects		
	Natural	Artifactual	Complex
Natural	Selection/Accommodation	Qualia Introduction	Dot Introduction
Artifactual	Accommodation	Selection/Accommodation	Dot Introduction
Complex	Dot Introduction	Dot Introduction	Selection/ Accommodation

In view of this, we aim to capture a full description of the composition between Mandarin Chinese verb "da^3" (hit) indicating hand motions and its arguments collected from authentic corpus data, including Academia Sinica Balanced Corpus of Modern Chinese[1] and Plurk data as a complement in this paper. Since there are over one-hundred different senses of the word "da^3" listed in Chinese Wordnet[2], we will re-categorize the senses of "da^3" by referring to Huang's definition [5] in the following sections in order to process the later analysis of the compositional operations, and provides the characteristics of such operations under the frame of Generative Lexicon (GL). We further predict that, due to the complexity of the senses of "da^3", the verb-argument composition will yield different results from those suggested by Pustejovsky [3] in Table 1.

1 http://db1x.sinica.edu.tw/kiwi/mkiwi/
2 http://cwn.ling.sinica.edu.tw/

2. Theoretical Framework

In the GL model, Pustejovsky [1] proposes that a lexical item is given an explicit type for a word positioned within a type system for the language, where qualia can be unified to create more complex concepts out of simple ones. The lexical typing structure and the qualia structure (modes of explanation, composed of FORMAL, CONSTITUTIVE, TELIC, and AGENTIVE roles) mentioned above, together with the event (defining the event type of a lexical item or a phrase) and argument (specifying the number and type of the arguments to a predicate) structure, comprise a richer and deeper decomposition of a lexical item. According to Pustejovsky [2], he divides the type structure into the following three levels:

(1) Natural Types: Concepts of natural kind made up of reference only to Formal and Constitutive qualia roles such as *dog*, *man*, and *bird*;

(2) Artifactual Types: Concepts consisting of reference to Telic (purpose or function), or Agentive (origin) qualia roles such as *pet*, *doctor*, and *plane*;

(3) Complex Types: Concepts making reference to an inherent relation between types from the other levels such as *book*, *picture*, or *sign*.

In addition, there are three mechanisms at work in the selection of an argument by a predicative expression [3]. These are, as pointed out by Pustejovsky [2]:

(1) Pure Selection (Type Matching): the type a function requires is directly satisfied by the argument;

(2) Accommodation: the type a function requires is inherited by the argument;

(3) Type Coercion: the type a function requires is imposed on the argument type. This is accomplished by either:

a. Exploitation: taking a part of the argument's type to satisfy the function;

b. Introduction: wrapping the argument with the type required by the function.

Under the three mechanisms, Pustejovsky argues that the ability to assign more than one interpretation to a lexical or phrasal expression is a result of type coercion and this is when polysemy arises in grammar.

3. Basic semantic analysis of "da^3"

In Huang's thesis [5], nominal arguments of the verb "da^3" are thoroughly analyzed under GL framework. There are eight semantic components in "da^3" as follows: *to make contact with*, *to make use of*, *to cause a displacement*, *to change the internal state of*, *to move outward*, *learnability*, *by media*, and *with company*. Based on the existence of these semantic components, nine basic senses of the verb "da^3" can be distinguished and derived as shown in Table 2. These are:

(1) to make contact with sth.

(2) to get sth.

(3) to make sth.

(4) to deal with sth.

(5) to have skills of sth.

(6) to make use of sth.

(7) to exclude/depart from sth.

(8) to participate in sth.

(9) to trigger physical/mental activities

Furthermore, these nine senses can derive richer meanings in the lexicon by the mechanism of metonymy and metaphors. Through co-composition, which describes a structure allowing, superficially, more than one function application, "da^{3}" can create new senses with a variety of different nominal arguments to form a verbal polysemy.

On the other hand, Chinese Wordnet also lists 121 senses of "da^{3}" in total. Since it does not group together those senses with basically similar semantic components, in this paper we adopt the nine categories of senses in "da^{3}" proposed by Huang [5] to avoid word sense enumeration analysis and demonstrate a more general pattern of its argument combination.

Table 2: The Semantic Components and Senses of "da3"

Senses	Semantic Components
(1) to make contact with sth.	[+to make contact with] [-to make use of] [-to cause a displacement]
(2) to get sth.	[+to make contact with] [-to make use of] [+to cause a displacement] [-to move outward]
(3) to make sth.	[-to make contact with] [+by media]
(4) to deal with sth.	[+to make contact with] [-to make use of] [+to change the internal state of]
(5) to have skills of sth.	[+to make contact with] [+to make use of] [+learnability]
(6) to make use of sth.	[+to make contact with] [+to make use of] [-learnability]
(7) to exclude/depart from sth.	[+to make contact with] [-to make use of] [+to cause a displacement] [+to move outward]
(8) to participate in sth.	[-to make contact with] [-by media] [+with company]
(9) to trigger physical or mental activities	[-to make contact with] [-by media] [-with company]

4. Analysis and Discussion

In this section, we take a closer look at how the Mandarin Chinese verb "da^{3}" combines with its nominal arguments under the three compositional operations.

4.1 "da^{3}": to make contact with sth.

The most basic sense of "da^{3}" is *to make contact*, which is a broader sense of the common interpretation of this verb, *to hit*. Under this sense, it can combine with any physical objects as its arguments. The compositional operations of different types of arguments thus are provided as follows.

4.1.1 "da^{3}"+Natural Types

(1) Selection/Accommodation

Many natural type arguments can be combined with "da^{3}". For example, they can be human, animals, or body parts such as "人" (people), "小孩" (children), "耳光" (ears), "穴" (acupuncture points), or "蚊子" (mosquitoes). Furthermore, they can be accommodation as shown in the following example. In this case, the subject may hit the child on his/her partial body, namely, the face, not the whole part of the child. All these arguments are similar in that they are physical objects (phys).

(3) 他 打 了 小孩 一 個 耳光。
He hit ASP child one CL ear
"He hit the child on the face."

4.1.2 "da^{3}"+Artifactual Types

(1) Accommodation

As argued in Pustejovsky [1], an artifactual type can be further decomposed into a head type and a tail type. The head type (the FORMAL quale role) need not be an atomic type (natural), but can be arbitrarily complex itself. If the head alone is exploited, the operation is type accommodation [3]. For instance, in Mandarin Chinese, "da^{3}" can take "鼓" (drums), "桌球" (table tennis), "靶" (targets), or "鐘" (alarms) as arguments and the head *physical object* is exploited. In a more extended sense, "da^{3}" can also take "前鋒" (forward) as its artifactual type arguments to indicate a player need to *reach* a specified location to play in a basketball game.

4.2 "da^{3}": to get sth.

4.2.1 "da^{3}"+Natural Types

(1) Selection

Under this category, "da^{3}" can be combined with natural resources or creatures like "水"

(water), “柴” (firewood) and “魚” (fish) to express *to get/retrieve*. All the arguments are physical objects.

(2) Qualia Introduction

On the other hand, there are some more abstract resources accessible to us like “天下” (world) or “江山” (river and mountain). Since they are originally features of places, by introducing the FORMAL value “something that can be owned” to these words, we can say “打江山” (to get and own the country) as if the argument itself is concrete.

geographical features $\otimes_{\text{formal}}$ something that can be owned: “江山” (river and mountain)

4.2.2 “da^3”+Artifactual Types

(1) Accommodation

Instances in this category are the arguments including “飯菜” (rice and vegetable), “香腸” (sausage), or even “回票” (return tickets). Likewise, the head *physical object* is exploited so that they can be combined under the accommodation operation.

4.3 “da^3”: to make sth.

4.3.1 “da^3”+Artifactual Types

(1) Accommodation

The third sense of “da^3” is to make or produce something which is represented in the arguments such as “地鋪” (sleeping places with bedding on the floor), “毛衣” (sweaters), “井” (wells), “結” (knots), “洞/孔” (holes), “全壘打” (homerun), “空包彈” (blank cartridges), “項鍊” (necklace), and “根基” (foundation). Again, the head *physical object* is exploited so that they can be combined with “da^3”.

(2) Artifactual Exploitation

There are some arguments denoting marks, rates, symbols, or numbers. Often when they are combined with “da^3”, the intended meaning is to provide the information of thoughts, opinions, or evaluations towards things. For example, “字” (words), “成績” (scores), “鉤” (checks), “問號” (question marks), and “知名度” (prestige/popularity) can serve as artifactual type arguments. In these cases, the tail type is either an agentive or telic role as demonstrated and according to Pustejovsky and Jezek (2008), if the tail of an artifactual type is exploited, then it is artifactual exploitation.

number, rate $\otimes_{\text{telic}}$ show information: “成績” (scores), “知名度” (prestige/popularity)
mark $\otimes_{\text{telic}}$ show information: “鉤” (checks), “問號” (question marks)

symbol ⊗ $_{telic}$ show information: “字” (words)

4.3.2 “da^3”+Complex Types: Dot Exploitation

Complex type arguments can have more than one meaning facets. A common example is *book* with the complex type (phys•info). It can both refer to the physical book or the information provided in the book. When they are combined with verbs, either one or two meaning facets can be exploited.

(1) Only one meaning facet can be exploited.
Some examples in this case (phys•info) are: “報告” (reports), “電報” (telegrams), and “草稿” (drafts). When they are combined “da^3”, only the information aspect can be exploited.

(2) Both meaning facets can be exploited.
Some examples in this case (event•info) are: “手語” (sign languages), “手勢” (gestures), and “暗號” (secret signals). When these words are the arguments of “da^3”, each of the two facets of meaning is likely to be exploited.

4.4 “da^3”: to deal with sth.

“da^3” with this sense can be combined with artifactual type arguments like “折扣” (discount), and natural type ones such as “蛋” (egg), “火” (fire) and “奶泡” (milk foam). In the former condition, an accommodation operation happens while in the latter, selection occurs, both leading to the meaning of dealing with something and rendering a resultative status.

4.5 “da^3”: to have skills of sth.

“da^3” can also be combined with various artifactual type arguments which indicate to carry out something such as “領帶” (tie), “牌” (cards), “麻將” (mahjong), “電動玩具” (video games), “電腦” (computers), “針” (needles), “蠟” (wax), “算盤” (abaci), “彈珠” (marbles), “禪” (meditation), and “陀螺” (top). In these cases, subjects must have the skills or ability of manipulating the following physical objects; otherwise, they need to learn to understand how to deal with them. All the arguments go through an accommodation operation.

4.6 “da^3”: to make use of sth.

4.6.1 “da^3”+Natural Types

(1) Selection
There are few instances in this category concerning the natural type arguments to be combined with “da^3”: “石膏” (casts), and “光” (light). Under this operation, the words

denoting a physical material which is utilized can be selected as the verb's arguments.

4.6.2 "da^3"+Artifactual Types

(1) Accommodation

A variety of artifactual type arguments can be combined with the verb "da^3" such as "籃球" (basketball), "燈籠" (lantern), "傘" (umbrella), "電話" (telephone), "粉底" (foundation), "方向盤" (steering wheel), "口號" (slogans) , "比方" (analogy), "官腔" (bureaucratic tone) , "快攻" (fast break), "馬賽克" (mosaic) and "啞謎" (riddle). In these cases, either the head *physical object/appliance* or *abstract object* can be exploited so that the accommodation operation still works.

(2) Artifactual Exploitation

Under this category, "卡" (card) is found to be combined with "da^3" to indicate the retrieval of temporal or spatial information of a specific moment by machines. The tail of this artifactual type exploited here is:

physical object $\otimes_{telic}$ record information: "卡" (card)

4.6.3 "da^3"+Complex Types: Dot Exploitation

(1) Only one meaning facet can be exploited.

The example arguments involving the dot exploitation are "擂台" (arena for contests) (phys•<u>loc</u>), "廣告" (advertisement) (<u>event</u>•info), and "半/全場" (half-/full- court)[3] (phys•<u>loc</u>) with the complex type specified in the second parenthesis and the only exploited facet underlined

4.7 "da^3": to participate in sth.

Instances in this category are all artifactual arguments including "零工" (odd jobs), "仗" (war), "招呼" (greeting), "照面" (seeing each other), "官司" (lawsuits), "總決賽" (final) and "交道" (principles of interpersonal contact). In these cases, the head *event* is exploited so that they can be combined with "da^3" under the accommodation operation.

4.8 "da^3": to trigger physical or mental activities

4.8.1 "da^3"+Natural Types

"拳" (fist), "光腳" (bare foot), "赤膊" (shirtless), and "雷" (thunder) are several examples

[3] It refers to playing a basketball game according to the area/court size defined by the arguments.

of natural type arguments which can be combined with "da^3". The selection operation occurs to make these physical objects or activities carried out with one's own will.

4.8.2 "da^3"+Artifactual Types

Other examples under this category are "寒顫" (cold shiver), "盹" (nap), "哈欠" (yawn), "瞌睡" (doze), "噴嚏" (sneeze), "鼾" (snore), "主意" (plan) or "拍子" (tempo). By accommodation operation, the head *event* is exploited. Besides, there are two extended usage of "da^3" in this category, "先鋒" (vanguard) and "頭陣" (first array), which indicate one becomes/belongs to a certain role. In this case, the head *human* is exploited under the accommodation operation.

4.9 "da^3": to exclude/depart from sth.

A typical instance of "da^3" combined with natural type arguments to indicate removing of specific substances or objects is "胎" (fetus). By selection, all physical objects including animate beings can serve as the argument of "da^3".

A summary of the above analysis can be shown in the following table:

Table 3: Mechanisms of compositional operations of "da^3"

Sense	Natural Types	Artifactual Types	Complex Types
make contact with	selection/accommodation	accommodation	-
get	selection/ qualia introduction	accommodation	-
make	-	accommodation/ artifactual exploitation	dot exploitation
deal with	selection	accommodation	-
have...skills	-	accommodation	-
make use of	selection	accommodation/ Artifactual Exploitation	dot exploitation
participate in	-	accommodation	-
trigger physical/mental activities	selection	accommodation	-
exclude	selection	-	-

As indicated in Table 3, we find that the sense "to make use of something" is rather active among all the senses concerning "da^3". It can go through three different kinds of composition with all three types of arguments, which signals the highest compositional ability. Other senses owning a high compositional ability include "to make contact with", "to get something", and "to make something"; however, they have fewer argument type choices compared with the sense "to make use of something". On the other hand, how the Mandarin Chinese verb "da^{3}" selects its argument types is also demonstrated in Table 3. For example, a verb has to choose a typical type, either natural types, artifactual types or complex types as indicated in Table 1. Yet, in Table 3, only the senses "to have…skills", "to participate in" and "to to exclude/depart from" have this trait. Except for that, it is surprising that the overall patterns of the compositional operations show the correspondence with what Pustejovsky [3] proposes in Table 1 with regard to the abundant senses of the word. But it perhaps is due to our lack of focus on the usage of fixed phrases, idioms, and a variety of other metonymic or metaphorical expressions of "da^{3}" springing up recently in online resources such as "打屁" (chat leisurely), "打牙祭" (enjoy a feast) or "打高空" (unrealistic attitudes or speeches). Though the result of this preliminary study differs from what Pustejovsky and Jezek [3] pointed out after investigating *listen* that "how difficult it is to map each context into the appropriate slot" in Table 1, which is further evidenced by Wang and Huang [4] with the verb "kàn" (look at), it can still provide an elaborative description of the compositional operations exerted on verbs other than perceptional ones and clarify the characteristics of argument selection patterns between different verb types in Mandarin Chinese.

Reference

[1] J. Pustejovsky, *The Generative Lexicon*, Cambridge MA: MIT Press, 1995.

[2] J. Pustejovsky, "Type theory and lexical decomposition," *Journal of Cognitive Science*, vol. 6, pp. 39-76, 2006.

[3] J. Pustejovsky, and E. Jezek, "Semantic Coercion in Language: Beyond Distributional Analysis," *Italian Journal of Linguistics/Rivista Italiana di Linguistica*, vol. 20, no. 1, pp. 181-214, 2008.

[4] S. Wang, and C.-R. Huang, "Compositional Operations of Mandarin Chinese Perception Verb "kàn": A Generative Lexicon Approach," in *the 24th Pacific Asia Conference on Language, Information and Computation*, 2010, pp. 707-714.

[5] 黃苕冠, *現代漢語徒手動作動詞<打>字的語義、語法探析*, 國立臺灣師範大學華語文教學研究所碩士論文, 2001.

Typological Universals and Intrinsic Universals on the L2 Acquisition[1] of Consonant Clusters[2]

Chin-Chin Tseng
National Taiwan Normal University
tseng@ntnu.edu.tw

Abstract

This study is to examine if typological universals built upon primary languages are applicable to interlanguage data in SLA. Implicational universal is considered the classic example of a typological universal by Croft (2003). Thus, the Interlanguage Structural Conformity Hypothesis, which consists of two implicational universals proposed by Eckman (1991), were tested against data from an interlanguage. The interlanguage data reconfirms that syllable structure plays a key role in the Fricative-Stop Prinicple. However, the Fricative-Stop Principle is sensitive to the position which clusters occur in a syllable. This typological universal is only applicable to final consonant clusters only. The test results do not conform with the Resolvability Principle. The Resolvability Principle claims that if a language has a consonantal sequence of length m in either initial or final position, it also has at least one continuous subsequence of length m-1 in this same position. Taiwanese[3] speakers' interlanguage data show that they can produce a consonantal sequence of 3 [spr-], but fail to produce a consonantal sequence of 2 [bl-], which violates the proposed typological universal. Thus, intrinsic universals are proposed to explain the interlanguage data in this study, i.e. the position that a consonant cluster occurs in a

[1] I am hesitating to use the word "acquisition", because this study is not a longitudinal study, and its scope is limited to the production form only. Although I think "production" is a more appropriate word to use here, however, in order to conform with the word choice by Eckman, I shall use "acquisition" instead of "production".

[2] acknowledgment to Aim for the Top University Plan, Ministry of Education, Taiwan, R.O.C. and anonymous reviewers of ROCLING2011.

[3] Taiwanese is a South-Min variety of Chinese spoken in Taiwan. This language does not allow consonant clusters.

syllable and its articulatory components all contributed to the intrinsic universals.

Keywords: structural conformity hypothesis, typological universals, second language acquisition, consonant clusters

1. Introduction

The acquisition of consonant clusters has been a popular issue in SLA. If a language does not allow consonant clusters, what would happen when a speaker of that language tries to acquire English consonant clusters. Eckman (1987) and Karimi (1987) have found that final obstruents devoicing, vowel insertion, and consonant deletion are common strategies employed by L2 learners.

One implicational universal has been posited by Greenberg (1978), which is possession of property *Pi* implies possession of *Pj*--but not vice versa. Lass (1989:131) made a comment on implicational universals. He said:

> *It is uncertain whether a large and interesting set of such statements can be made; steps have been taken, but we're nowhere near knowing yet if the goal is attainable.*

Lass (1989:132) further pointed out that the implicational universals were usually under the heading of 'markedness'. He listed several criteria for defining a marked segment. They are: (i) less common cross-linguistically than its unmarked counterpart; (ii) tends not to appear in positions of neutralization; (iii) generally has lower text-frequency; (iv) is later in appearing during language-acquisition, (v) tends to undergo phonemic merger; (vi) tends to be less stable historically; (vii) tends to imply the existence of its unmarked counterpart.

Despite the dispute about implicational universals, Eckman (1991) posited a Structural Conformity Hypothesis, attempting to explain the difficulty and the developmental sequence in acquiring English consonant clusters. He proposed that universal generalizations of primary language also apply to interlanguage. He strived to test two implicational universals in interlanguage. One was the *Fricative-Stop Principle*; the other was the *Resolvability Principle*.

In this study, three problems regarding Eckman's Structural Conformity Hypothesis were identified. One is that Eckman overlooked one important variable, the voicing of a consonant cluster. All the words he used for his study were consonant clusters of voiceless obstruents. He did not provide an explanation for why he chose to do so. Our study indicates that clusters of voiced obstruents acquire later than their voiceless counterparts, because voiced obstruents are more difficult to produce intrinsically. The oral constriction impedes the airflow required by voicing

(Stampe 1979:7), that can explain the devoicing phenomena observed in native English speakers' word-initial and word-final voiced consonant and consonant clusters.[4]

The second problem was how Eckman determined the presence or absence of a target consonant cluster. The criteria for the presence of a consonant cluster was 80% of occurrence of that consonant cluster. However, Eckman did not go into details on how he determine the occurrence of a consonant cluster. How did he determine if a consonant is deleted or pronounced unreleased? To what extend would he consider an epenthetic vowel present? Edge (1991) studied the production of word-final voiced obstruents in English by L1 speakers of Japanese and Cantonese,. He found that the voicing-devoicing decision was the most troublesome. If both consonant deletion and vowel epenthesis were both found in native English speakers' speech, how would he define a target form? All the questions mentioned above may affect the choice of a target form, and the judgment call of the presence or absence of a consonant cluster.

The third problem was the applicability of implicational universals as a prediction of second language behavior. Because implicational universals are structurally based, while second language behavior has more than one attribute.

2. Application of Implicational Universals

Not all implicational universals can be applied directly to predict second language behavior. Implicational universals which are phonetically motivated can better explain the interlanguage phenomena. Our study is to bring up this issue by comparing our test result with the two implicational universals proposed by Eckman. Here are two intrinsic universals (phonetically motivated principles) proposed in this study.

(i) Word-initial consonant clusters are easier to acquire than word-final consonant clusters. This principle is motivated by the fact that word-initial consonant clusters can be released through the following nucleus (vowel), while word-final consonant clusters cannot.

(ii) Clusters of voiced obstruents acquire later than the voiceless consonant clusters, because their oral constriction impedes the airflow required by voicing. Therefore, they are more difficult to produce than voiceless consonant clusters.

---

[4] Ladefoged (1982) stated that English word-final voiced consonants are partially voiceless. Lisker & Abramson (1964) also pointed out that English initial voiced stops should be transcribed as voiceless unaspirated.

3. Method

Subjects

The subjects for this study were ten Taiwanese speakers. Two native American English speakers, mean age 25, served as the control group. Appendix 1 gives a profile of the participants. The Taiwanese speakers, mean age 30.6, all had six years of high-school English and college English in Taiwan. Their English speaking proficiency level ranged from intermediate to advanced. Eight of them had extensive exposure to English speaking environment, 5.9 years on the average.

Materials and Procedures

In order to compare Taiwanese interlanguage data with the native English speakers' pronunciation under the same context, a sheet of words which contains English initial and final consonant clusters were listed (Appendix 2). Each word was read twice by a subject. Initial consonant clusters test items are listed in Table 1. Final consonant clusters test items are listed in Table 2. Phonetic environment, familiarity and frequency of the test words were taken into consideration, but not strictly controlled.

Table1. Initial Consonant Cluster Test Items

bl-(1) blue	br-(1) bring	kl-(2) class climb	kr-(2) cream crisp	tr-(1) tree	dr-(2) dreams dry	dw-(1) dwarf	fl-(1) flag	fr-(1) friend	gl-(1) glass	gr-(2) grow groups	pl-(1) play	pr-(1) pray
qw-(2) question quilt	sk-(1) sky	sl-(1) slow	sp-(1) spilt	ʃr-(1) shrimp	θ r-(1) three	skr-(1) scream	sp-(1) speak	spr-(1) spring	st-(3) stamped stand stands	str-(1) street	tw-(1) twenty	N/A

Table2. Final Consonant Cluster Test Items

-rm (1) arm	-nt (1) aunt	-rn (1) barn	-gd (1) begged	-rf (1) dwarf	-kt (1) fact	-nd (2) friend stand	-dz (1) beds	-lp (1) help	-rp (1) harp	-zd (1) buzzed	-rb (1) orb	-md (1) seemed
-mz (1) dreams	-st (1) last	-nz (1) pens	- ŋdʒ (1) orange	-rk (1) park	-sk (1) risk	-ndz (1) stands	-rd (1) hard	-lpt (1) helped	-ps (2) lips groups	-lθ (1) health	-bz (1) Bob's	-sp(1) crisp

-rmz (1) arms	-nst (1) balanced	-rnz (1) barns	-ndʒd (1) changed	-rks (1) parks	-ks (1) six	-ʃt (1) pushed	-rt (1) short	-lt (2) quilt spilt	-rps (1) harps	-lz (1) walls	-rbz (1) orbs	-ŋk (1) thank
-mp (1) Jump shrimp	-nts (1) aunts	-ts (2) seats sits	-rv (1) carve	-kts (1) collects	-kst (1) next	-ft (1) shift	-rz (1) years	-lvd (1) solved	-nθ (1) month	-lb (1) bulb	-gz (1) legs	-ŋz (1) sings
-mpt (2) jumped stamped	-mps (1) jumps	-rnt (1) arn't	-rvd (1) carved	-rkt (1) parked	-sts (1) beasts	-tʃt (1) watched	-rts (1) hearts	-ld (1) world	-nθ s (1) months	-lf (1) wolf	-bd (1) webbed	-ŋks (1) thanks

Ten native speakers of Taiwanese were instructed to read the word list. Two native American English speakers served as the control group. Subjects were instructed to read each word twice, as naturally as possible, i.e. not to make an extra effort to adjust their accent. Subjects were given time to skim through the word list. Their pronunciation was recorded with a AIWA stereo cassette recorder (Model No. HS-J303) with an external microphone.

4. Analysis

The recordings were used as the input for the acoustic analysis[5] to verify the transcription. With the visual information of spectrogram, the researcher was able to make a more consistent and objective judgment call on the voicing distinction.[6] It also helped to identify if an epenthetic vowel was present.[7]

A list of subcategorization tags of position in a syllable and consonant clusters types can be found in Appendix 3. For example, **i** stands for word-initial, **f** stands for word-final, **pf** stands for a voiceless stop followed by a voiceless fricative, **bb** stands for a voiced stop followed by a voiced stop, etc.

There were four variables involving in the analysis of the consonant clusters: the position of the consonant cluster in a word, the number of consonants in a cluster, the voicing and the manners of articulation in a consonant cluster, and the categorization of the consonant cluster in terms of target-like and native-like[8]

[5] The spectrograms were done on the DSP Sono-Graph: model 5500

[6] If a segment is voiced, a low frequency dark stripe will show on the spectrogram.

[7] If there exists an epenthetic vowel, the vowel formants can be detected on the spectrogram.

[8] Target-like refers to the form which is predicted by the pronunciation rules of standard English. Native-like refers to the form which is deviant from the pronunciation rules of standard English, yet conforms to the way the two native speakers of English pronounced.

dimensions. For instance, if *-rnt* is pronounced as [rnt], it will be categorized as f|3|lnp|t, f satnds for word-final, 3 stands for a consonant cluster of three, lnp indicates that this is a sequence of a liquid + a nasal + a voiceless stop, and 't' stands for target-like forms. Appendix 3 lists all the subcategorization tags used in the current study.

If the two tokens were not pronounced in the same category by a subject, they would be marked by a question mark "?". Each consonant cluster was classified into one of the following four categories: target (t), non-target (n), target-but-non-native (N), and non-target-but-native (T). A target form is predicted by the pronunciation rules of Standard English. For example, the *-s* in *arms* should be pronounced as [z]. However, both the native English speakers pronounced it as [s]. Therefore, [z] will be considered target-but-non-native (N), while [s] will be considered as non-target-but-native (T). Non-target forms are those which involve deletion, devoicing, epenthesis, or other strategies that adult native English speakers do not usually use. For example, r --> w is a process of increasing sonority, i.e. making r less consonant like and easier to produce; therefore, r --> w, w is considered a non-target form.

5. Interrater Reliability

Two Taiwanese subjects' recordings were used for comparing interrater reliability. The researcher had one native English speaker and one Taiwanese speaker as raters of the researcher's transcriptions. This is to see how difference in rater's language background would effect the interrater reliability. Raters were told to circle one transcription that he or she agreed upon. If what they hear on the tape does not match either one of the given transcriptions, they can write down their own transcription in the blank space. We found the agreement rate between the researcher and the native English speaker was 91% for subject 1's interlanguage data and 73% for subject 2's interlanguage data. The agreement rates between the researcher and the Taiwanese rater were 85% and 67% respectively, and the agreement rates between the two raters were 85% and 71%. The difference in the interrater reliability shown in the data may be correlated with the accuracy in the two subjects' interlangauge pronunciation. Subject 1's pronunciation had higher accuracy rate.

6. Instrumentation

I used CHILDES[9] (Child Language Data Exchange System) to process the

---

[9] CHILDES is a software package originally designed to analyze L1 acquisition data. Here I am applying it to analyze L2 data.

subcategorized data. Each word was represented by three tiers in CHILDES. Each begins with a percent sign %. The first tier listed the code for the subject and the target word. For example, the following representation tells us that the speaker is PSZ, and the target word is *arm*.

%PSZ: arm

The second tier is the phonetic tier, which listed the expected target form and the actual pronunciation. For example, the following representation tells us that "pho" stands for the phonetic tier, rm is the expected target form, and the actual pronunciation was [rm].

%pho: rm=rm

The third tier is the quality tier, which coded the four variables previously mentioned. For example, the following representation tells us that "qua" stands for the quality tier, 'f' satnds for word-final, 3 stands for a consonant cluster of three, 'ln' indicates that this is a sequence of a liquid + a nasal, and 't' stands for a native-like target form.

%qua: f|2|ln|t

The format of each entry in CHILDES would look like the following:

%PSZ: arm
%pho: rm=rm
%qua: f|2|ln|t

7. Results

Graph 1 shows that the target-like percentage is significantly higher at the word-initial position than at the word-final position. This is true for all ten Taiwanese subjects' interlanguage data (Appendix 4). It is also true for a consonant cluster of two or three segments (see Table 3).

Graph 1. **target-like consonant clusters of word-initial and word-final**

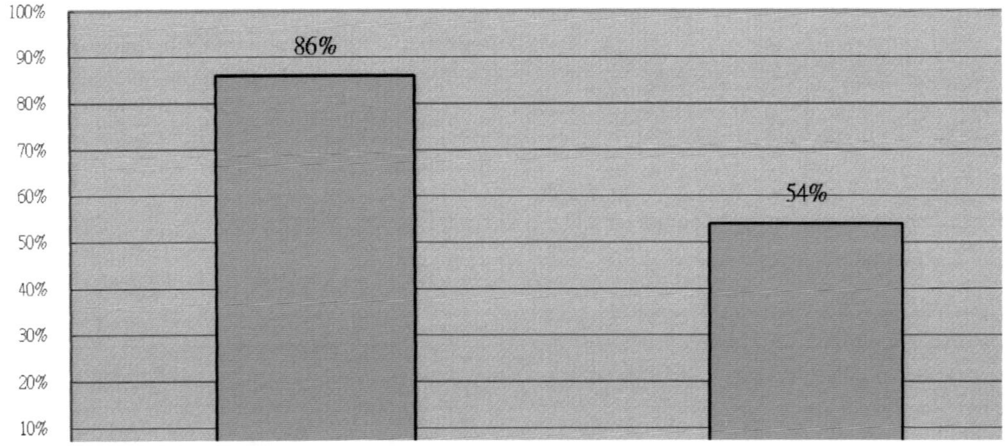

Table 3. Percentage of target-like consonant clusters in terms of number of consonants

	2 consonants in a cluster	3 consonants in a cluster
initial	86%	85%
final	61%	42%

Graph 2 shows that the target-like percentage is significantly lower for consonant clusters of voiced segments than for those of voiceless segments. This is true for all interlanguage data (Appendix 5). It is also true for a consonant cluster of two or three segments (see Table 3).

Graph 2. target-like consonant clusters of voiced vs. voiceless segments

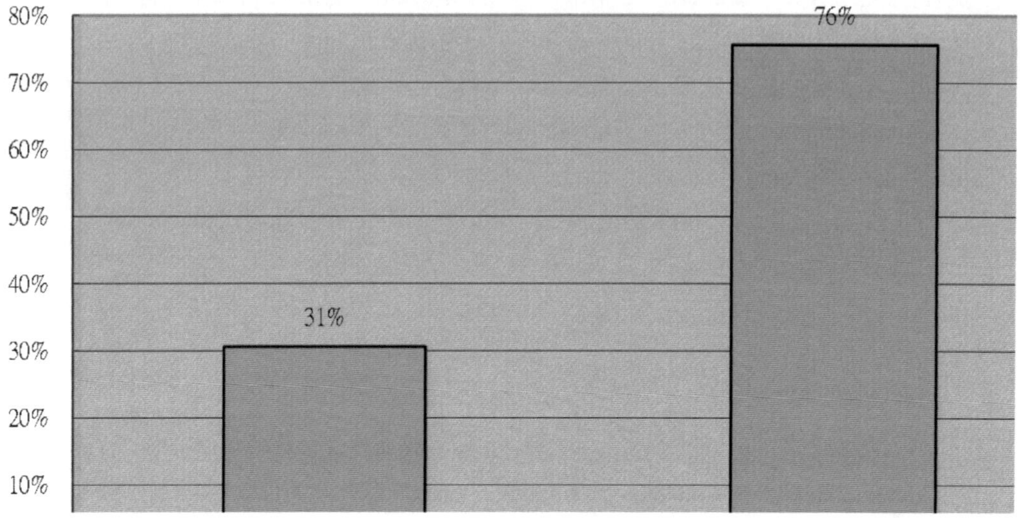

Table 4 shows that the target-like percentage is consistently higher at word-initial position. Word-final 2 consonants in a cluster achieves higher percentage of target-like forms than 3 consonants in a cluster. However, four subjects does not conform to the Resolvability Principle at word-initial position, i.e., 2 consonants in a cluster does not necessarily achieves the higher percentage of target-like forms than 3 consonants in a cluster for all subjects.

Table 4. Percentage of target-like consonant clusters in terms of position and number

	i2	i3	f2	f3	i	f
PSZ	92%	100%	83%	71%	93%	79%
CSH	96%	75%	75%	71%	93%	74%
PXJ	92%	75%	56%	50%	90%	54%
KJR	80%	75%	46%	33%	79%	42%
CJL	96%	100%	79%	75%	97%	78%
HZX	80%	100%	71%	54%	83%	65%
ZSY	80%	50%	56%	21%	76%	44%

RMY	84%	100%	42%	8%	86%	31%
LX	76%	75%	54%	17%	76%	42%
WMQ	84%	100%	46%	17%	86%	36%
avg	86%	85%	61%	42%	86%	54%

i2=initial consonant cluster of 2; i3= initial consonant cluster of 3; f2= final consonant cluster of 2; f3=final consonant cluster of 3; i=initial consonant; f=final consonant

Table 5 shows that the initial and final voiced consonant clusters may be pronounced devoiced even by native speakers. The target-like percentage is consistently higher for voiceless counterpart consonant clusters in both word-initial and word-final positions. The data in Table 5 suggest an intrinsic universal favor voiceless consonant clusters.

Table 5. Percentage of native-like consonant clusters in terms of position and number

trg = target-like
ntv = native-like

initial	Tw(trg)	Eng(trg)	Tw(ntv)	Eng(ntv)
bl-	68%	75%	82%	100%
pl-	77%	100%	77%	100%
bw-	90%	100%	90%	100%
pw-	100%	100%	100%	100%
final	**Tw(trg)**	**Eng(trg)**	**Tw(ntv)**	**Eng(ntv)**
-bb	10%	75%	15%	100%
-pp	90%	100%	90%	100%
-bv	27%	33%	27%	100%
-pf	84%	100%	84%	100%
-vb	20%	50%	40%	100%
-fp	84%	100%	84%	100%
-lbv	10%	0%	0%	100%
-lpf	37%	100%	37%	100%
-lb	13%	67%	20%	100%
-lp	50%	100%	50%	100%
-lv	15%	50%	20%	100%
-lf	35%	63%	35%	100%
-nG	40%	0%	90%	100%
-nC	100%	100%	100%	100%
-nb	43%	100%	43%	100%

-np	80%	100%	80%	100%
-nv	0%	0%	77%	100%
-nf	95%	100%	95%	100%
-npf	63%	100%	63%	100%
-npp	55%	100%	55%	100%

Table 6 and Table 7 were results of the partial replication and extension of Eckman's two implicational universals. Table 6 shows that 3 out of 10 subjects violated Eckman's Fricative-Stop Principle, which says if a language has at least one final consonant sequence consisting of stop + stop, it also has at least one final sequence consisting of fricative + stop.

Table 6. Interlanguage Varification Result for Eckman's Fricative-Stop Principle

+ = presence of a consonant cluster
- = absence of a consonant cluster
N = presence of a native-like but non-target consonant cluster
? = uncertain

	PSZ	CSH	PXJ	KJR	CJL	HZX	ZSY	RMY	LX	WMQ
-kt	+	+	+	+	+	+	+	-	+	+
-sp	+	+	+	+	+	+	+	-	-	+
-st	+	+	+	+	+	+	-	+	?	+
-sht	+	+	+	+	+	+	+	+	+	+
-sk	+	+	+	+	+	+	-	+	?	+
-ft	+	+	+	+	+	-	+	+	-	+
-gd	-	+	+	-	-	-	-	-	-	-
-bd	N	-	-	-	-	-	-	-	-	-
-zd	-	N	N	-	+	-	-	+	-	-
FS	for	for	for	for	for	against	against	for	against	for

Table 7 shows that 14 out of 230 tokens (6%) clearly violated the Resolvability Principle, which says if a language has a consonantal sequence of length m in either initial or final position, it also has at least one continuous subsequence of length m-1 in this same position.

Table 7. Interlanguage Varification Result for Eckman's Resolvability Principle

+ = for Resolvability Principle 90%
- = against Resolvability Principle 6%
? = uncertain 4%

	PSZ	CSH	PXJ	KJR	CJL	HZX	ZSY	RMY	LX	WMQ
-rnt	+	+	+	+	+	+	+	+	+	?
-rmz	+	+	+	+	?	+	+	+	+	+
-nts	+	+	?	-	+	?	+	+	+	+
-nst	+	+	+	+	+	+	+	+	+	+
-rnz	+	+	-	-	+	+	+	+	+	+
-sts	+	+	?	?	+	+	+	+	+	+
-rvd	+	+	+	+	+	+	+	+	+	+
-kts	+	+	?	?	+	+	+	+	+	+
-rps	+	+	+	+	+	+	+	+	+	+
-rts	+	-	-	+	+	+	+	+	+	+
-lpt	+	+	+	+	+	+	+	+	+	+
-mps	+	+	+	+	+	+	+	+	+	+
-kst	+	+	+	+	+	+	+	+	+	+
-rbz	+	+	+	+	+	+	+	+	+	+
-rkt	+	+	+	+	+	+	+	+	+	+
-rks	+	+	+	+	+	+	+	+	+	+
-ndz	+	+	+	-	?	+	+	+	+	+
-ngks	+	+	+	+	+	+	+	+	+	-
-mpt	+	+	+	+	+	+	+	+	+	?
spl-	+	+	-	-	+	+	+	+	+	+
str-	+	+	-	-	+	+	+	+	+	+
spr-	+	+	+	+	+	-	+	+	+	-
skr-	+	+	+	+	+	-	+	+	+	+

8. Discussion

In this section, two main points will be discussed: (a) the applicability of implicational universals; (b) intrinsic universals (phonetically motivated) can best explained the interlanguage phenomena.

The difference between typological universals and intrinsic universals is that we can always find counterexamples to the typological universals, but not to intrinsic universals. Not only interlanguage data but also first language data would conform to intrinsic universals. Typological universals are general statements about the tendency observed in documented language structures. People can always find counterexamples to typological universals no matter in primary language or in interlanguage. As the results shown in the study, we do find counterexamples to Eckman's principles. In fact, Eckman also observed counterexamples in his own study. However, he tried to explain the counterexamples with the lack of enough tokens to evaluate the result. However, we should not ignore counterexamples simply because the number is small. On the contrary, intrinsic universals can be explained by the phonetic laws of natural language, such as ease of production. There will be no exception to the intrinsic universals.

Another important issue relating to the proposed intrinsic universals is that second language researchers were trying to employ the typological universals to explain the phenomena observed in interlanguage data. I will quote Lass's (1989: 132-33) comment on this particular issue. He says:

> *It is debatable, however, if these observations can be pushed much further, i.e. given a non-formal, non-statistical interpretation, and used as the basis for an explanatory (predictive) theory. ... But it is not clear that the predictive power of any form of markedness theory is enough to make it interesting--as anything but a set of inductive generalizations about the distributions of properties in the world's languages. In particular there seems to be no good way to accounting for the 'failures' of markedness predictions.*

9. Conclusion

Eckman's (1991) Structural Conformity Hypothesis would have been a valid hypothesis, if he had applied intrinsic universals rather than typological universals. Position in a word and the voicing quality turn out to be the critical factors for the acquisition of consonant clusters rather than the number of a cluster sequence nor the stop-fricative difference.

The results of the current study not only sort out the intrinsic factors that is essential to the acquisition of consonant clusters, but also raise an important issue for SLA, i.e., what can be used as an explanatory theory for SLA? SLA is considered as an applied science, which means it is heavily dependent upon other disciplines of science. This study suggests that the L2 acquisition should be based on cognitively-induced intrinsic universals rather than structurally-based typological universals.

Appendix 1. Subject profile

Name	NL	Age	Sex	Exposure to English-Speaking Env.
JY	Eng	28	M	Native English speaker
DA	Eng	24	F	Native English speaker
PSZ	Tw	25	F	*1 year*
CSH	*Tw*	*34*	*F*	*2.5 years*
PXJ	*Tw*	*26*	*F*	*5 years*
KJR	*Tw*	*26*	*M*	*9 months*
CJL	*Tw*	*25*	*F*	*2 years*
HZX	*Tw*	*43*	*F*	*20 years*
ZSY	*Tw*	*21*	*F*	*None (reside in Taiwan)*
RMY	*Tw*	*32*	*M*	*6 years*
LX	*Tw*	*51*	*F*	*10 years*
WMQ	*Tw*	*23*	*M*	*None (reside in Taiwan)*

Appendix 2. A Word List of consonant clusters

accidental	day	magazine	spilt
aren't	dish	month	six
arm	dreams	months	sky
arms	dry	necessarily	slow
aunt	during	next	solved
aunts	dwarf	no	speak
balanced	fact	orange	spring
barn	flag	orb	stamped
barns	friend	orbs	stand
beasts	garage	park	stands
beautiful	give	parked	street
beds	glass	parks	television
begged	groups	peas	thank
blue	grow	pens	thanks
Bob's	hard	play	this
bring	harp	pray	three
bulb	harps	pure	tree
butter	health	pushed	tune
buzzed	hearts	question	twenty
carve	help	quilt	vacation

carved	helped	risk	walls
chair	inch	scream	watched
changed	international	seats	webbed
class	jump	seemed	why
climb	jumped	shift	with
collects	jumps	short	wolf
comparative	language	shrimp	world
cream	last	since	years
crisp	legs	sings	yes
cute	lips	sits	zero

Appendix 3. List of Subcategorization Tags

i = word-initial

f = word-final

2 = a consonant cluster of two

3 = a consonant cluster of three

t = target

n = non-target

N = non-target but native-like

T = target but non-native-like

? = the utterances can not be classified into one category

Cp = voiceless affricate + voiceless stop

bb = voiced stop + voiced stop

bl = voiced stop + liquid

bv = voiced stop + voiced fricative

bw = voiced stop + [w]

fl = voiceless fricative + liquid

fpf = voiceless fricative + voiceless stop + voiceless fricative

fpl = voiceless fricative + voiceless stop + liquid

fp = voiceless fricative + voiceless stop

lbv = liquid + voiced stop + voiced fricative

lb = liquid + voiced stop

lf = liquid + voiceless fricative

llb = liquid + liquid + voiced stop

lnp = liquid + nasal + voiceless stop

lnv = liquid + nasal + voiced fricative

ln = liquid + nasal

lpf = liquid + voiceless stop + voiceless fricative
lpp = liquid + voiceless stop + voiceless stop
lp = liquid + voiceless stop
lvb = liquid + voiced fricative + voiced stop
lv = liquid + voiced fricative
nC = nasal + voiceless affricate
nGb = nasal + voiced affricate + voiced stop
nG = nasal + voiced affricate
nbv = nasal + voiced stop + voiced fricative
nb = nasal + voiced stop
nff = nasal + voiceless fricative + voiceless fricative
nfp = nasal + voiceless fricative + voiceless stop
nf = nasal + voiceless fricative
npf = nasal + voiceless stop + voiceless fricative
npp = nasal + voiceless stop + voiceless stop
np = nasal + voiceless stop
nv = nasal + voiced fricative
pfp = voiceless stop + voiceless fricative + voiceless stop
pf = voiceless stop + voiceless fricative
pl = voiceless stop + liquid
ppf = voiceless stop + voiceless stop + voiceless fricative
pp = voiceless stop + voiceless stop
pw = voiceless stop + [w]
vb = voiced fricative + voiced stop

Appendix 4. Percentage of target-like consonant clusters of the ten subjects

	S1	S2	S3	S4	S5	S6	S7	S8	S9	S10	average
initial	93%	93%	90%	79%	97%	83%	76%	86%	76%	86%	86%
final	79%	74%	54%	42%	78%	65%	44%	31%	42%	36%	54%

Appendix 5. **Percentage of target-like consonant clusters in terms of voiced and voiceless components**

	bl-	bw-	-bb	-bv	-vb	-lbv	-lb	-lv	-nG	-nb	-nv	average
voiced	68%	90%	10%	27%	20%	10%	13%	15%	40%	43%	0%	31%
voiceless	77%	100%	90%	84%	84%	37%	50%	35%	100%	80%	95%	76%

References

[1] Croft, William. 2003. 2nd ed. Typology and Universals. New York: Cambridge University Press.

[2] Eckman, Fred R. 1991. The structural conformity hypothesis and the acquisition of consonant clusters in the interlanguage of ESL learners. SSLA 13.23-41.

[3] Eckman, Fred R. 1987. The reduction of word-final consonant clusters in interlanguage. Sound patterns in second language acquisition, ed. by Allan James and Jonathan Leather,143-62. Dordrecht: Foris.

[4] Karimi, S. 1987. Farsi speakers and the initial consonant cluster in English. Interlanguage phonology, ed. by Georgette Ioup and Steven H. Weinberger,305-18. Cambridge: Newbury House Publishers.

[5] Greenberg, Joseph, H. 1978. Universals of Human Language. California: Stanford University Press.

[6] Lass, Roger. 1989. Phonology: An introduction to basic concepts. Cambridge: Cambridge University Press.

[7] Stampe, David. 1979. A dissertation on natural phonology. New York: Garland Publishing, Inc.

[8] Ladefoged, Peter. 1982. A course in phonetics. 2nd ed. Los Angeles: Harcourt Brace Jovanovich, Inc.

[9] Lisker, Leigh, and Arthur S. Abramson. 1964. A cross-language study of voicing in initial stops: acoustical measurements. Word 20.384-422.

[10] Carlisle Robert S. 2001. Syllable structure universals and second language acquisition. International Journal of English Studies 1.1-19.

[11] Edge, Beverly A. 1991. The production of word-final voiced obstruents in English by L1 speakers of Japanese and Cantonese. SSLA 13.377-93.

[12] Edwards, Jette G. Hansen, & Mary L. Zampini (Eds.). 2008. Phonology and second language acquisition. Philadelphia: Benjamins.

[13] Major, Roy C. 1987. The natural phonology of second language acquisition. Sound patterns in second language acquisition, ed. by Allan James and James Leather,207-24. Dordrecht: Foris.

[14] Sato, Charlene J. 1985. Task variation in interlanguage phonology. Input in second language acquisition, ed. by Susan M. Gass and Carolyn G. Madden,181-96. Rowley: Newbury House Publishers, Inc.

多語語碼轉換之未知詞擷取

Unknown Word Extraction from Multilingual Code-Switching Sentences

吳依倫 Yi-Lun Wu
元智大學資訊管理學系
Department of Information Management
Yuan Ze University
s986301@mail.yzu.edu.tw

謝佼彣 Chaio-Wen Hsieh
元智大學資訊管理學系
Department of Information Management
Yuan Ze University
s971641@mail.yzu.edu.tw

林瑋軒 Wei-Hsuan Lin
元智大學資訊管理學系
Department of Information Management
Yuan Ze University
s971636@mail.yzu.edu.tw

劉君毅 Chun-Yi Liu
元智大學資訊管理學系
Department of Information Management
Yuan Ze University
s971647@mail.yzu.edu.tw

禹良治 Liang-Chih Yu
元智大學資訊管理學系
Department of Information Management
Yuan Ze University
lcyu@saturn.yzu.edu.tw

摘要

在多語環境下，一段語句可能發生由一種語言轉換到另一種語言的現象，也就是說，語句由兩種或兩種以上的語言所組成，此即爲語碼轉換(code-switching)現象。以我國語言使用的情況來說，國語夾雜台客英短語的現象在日常生活中已相當普遍，這些語言混用現象也造成了語言處理上的重大挑戰。有鑑於此，本論文收集中英、國台及國客夾雜之文字語料，並分析以國語爲主要語言之中英、國台及國客夾雜現象，接著提出以交互資訊(mutual information)與熵(entropy)爲基礎之未知詞擷取演算法，自動從多語夾雜語料中找出未知詞。實驗結果顯示本論文所提出的方法可藉由過濾無關的新詞提升未知詞擷取之精確度。

關鍵詞：語碼轉換、未知詞擷取、交互資訊、熵

一、緒論

語音及語言處理在人機介面應用中扮演相當重要的角色。近年來，在國內外研究學者共同努力下，語音及語言處理技術已有顯著的進步並逐漸實現在許多應用之中，如：語音辨識與合成(speech recognition and synthesis)、口語對話系統(spoken dialog system)及語音查詢與檢索(speech query and retrieval)等。然而，全球共有超過 6,900 種語言[1]，加上全球化趨勢與國際交流日益頻繁，人們對於多語(multilingual)服務的需求也逐漸增加，例如：出國旅遊時即可能需要多語點餐、導覽甚至緊急醫療服務；國際化企業亦可藉由多語電話客服系統協助其全球客戶解決問題。因此，現行系統如何支援多種語言便成爲目前語音及語言處理技術重大的挑戰之一。

在多語環境下，一段語句中可能發生由一種語言轉換到另一種語言的現象，也就是說，語句由兩種或兩種以上的語言所組成，此即爲語碼轉換(code-switching)或語言混合(language mixing)現象[2][3]。這種現象較常發生在使用雙語或多語的地區，一般語者受其文化及教育的影響，在全球化及現代化的過程中對於本地方言及外來語接受較高而成爲雙語或多語使用者，因此在使用語言時，常會因爲不同的習慣、場合及對象而產生多語夾雜或混用的語句。這些多語夾雜語句的特性之一就是以一種語言爲主要語言(primary language)，而其他次要語言(secondary language)以字詞或片語等短語的形式夾雜其中。以台灣地區來說，除了一般通行的國語(Mandarin)外，國人對於台語(Taiwanese)甚至是客語(Hakka)的使用也很普遍，加上中英雙語教學的推行及教育水準不斷提高，學習英語早已成爲全民運動，因此，日常生活中常會出現國語夾雜台語、客語及英語等混用現象，這些現象亦常出現在新聞媒體、報章雜誌及網路文件中。下列句子即是以國語爲主要語言，夾雜英語(E)、台語(T)及客語(H)短語之範例句 (資料來源：網路新聞與搜尋結果)。

(E1) 兩岸 **ECFA** 即將進入正式協商。
(E2) 享受樂活舒壓的 **SPA** 活動。
(T1) 選情緊繃，候選人四處**趴趴走**拜票。
(T2) 這裡有一家很傳統的柑仔店。
(H1) 客家對於天穿日非常重視。
(H2) **四炆四炒**是客家菜的代表菜色之一。

在語碼轉換相關研究中，大部分仍著重從語言學或社會學的角度探討語碼轉換現象，對於自動處理語碼轉換語音及語言的相關研究並不多見，而國內近年來已有部分研究團隊積極朝此領域發展。在語料庫方面，有台師大、清大、交大、成大及台大共同錄

製的 EAT (http://www.aclclp.org.tw)語料庫，其中即包含中英夾雜句，而長庚大學亦有錄製國台客多語語音資料庫 ForSDat (Formosa Speech Database) [4]；在語音辨識方面，成大在中英混合語音辨識上已有成果發表[5][6]，長庚及元智大學亦有從事國台、國客混合語音辨識之研究[7][8]；其它地區則有學者針對廣東語-英語混合句進行語音辨識[9][10]，中英日等六種語言之聲學模型[11]，或是中英混合句的語音合成[12][13]。

上述多語語碼轉換相關研究著重於語料庫建立、語音辨識與合成之研究，對於詞典擴增(lexicon augmentation)、語言模型(language modeling)及語音辨識後語言理解(spoken language understanding)等語言處理層面的議題較少探討，然而這些議題在語音處理技術上亦扮演重要的角色，例如：在詞點擴增的議題中，(E1)中的 ECFA 即無法在英文詞典找到，(T1)與(T2)中的"趴趴走"與"柑仔店"也無法從台語字典找到，這些未知詞都會影響後續語言模型及語音理解的效果。有鑑於此，本論文收集中英、國台及國客夾雜之文字語料，並分析以國語爲主要語言之中英、國台及國客夾雜現象，接著提出以交互資訊(mutual information)與熵(entropy)爲基礎之未知詞擷取演算法，自動從多語夾雜語料中找出未知詞。本論文章節安排如下：第二章簡介多語夾雜語料庫及分析結果；第三章說明未知詞擷取演算法；第四章爲實驗結果；第五章爲結論。

二、多語夾雜語料收集與分析

(一) 多語夾雜語料收集

本論文所探討的語碼轉換現象限定於國台客英四種語言，並且以國語夾雜台語、客語及英語短語的混用現象爲主，分析這些現象可進一步瞭解多語夾雜語料庫的特性，包括容易發生夾雜現象的句型或語法結構等，亦有助於後續未知詞擷取、語言模型及語言理解模組之設計。中英及國台夾雜語料較爲常見，透過網路 BBS、Blogs、討論區等收集有關新聞時事、旅遊、美食等主題即可取得語料，至於國客夾雜語料收集上較爲困難，但網路上仍有部分專業網站提供客語學習等相關資源，例如：行政院客家委員會推動的「哈客網路學院」 (http://elearning.hakka.gov.tw/)，站內提供一系列的客語能力認證教材，並可超連結至「臺灣客語詞彙資料庫」(http://wiki.hakka.gov.tw/)，該資料庫將客語詞彙區分爲 30 大類，並提供四縣、饒平、六堆、海陸、美濃、詔安及大埔等七種腔調之字典檔，總計 35,605 個詞彙，每個客語詞彙均有音標以及國語及英語辭義解釋，更重要的是有提供客語造句範例及對應的國語譯句，例如：海陸腔詞彙檔中編號 01-013 的詞彙「風搓」，代表第一大類天文地理中的第十三個詞彙，其國語解釋爲颱風，客語例句及國語譯句如下。

人講：「一雷壓三搓」，𠊎看這擺个風搓怕毋會登陸咧。　　　(客語例句)
俗話說：「一雷壓三颱」，我看這次的颱風可能不會登陸了。　　(國語譯句)

由於所謂國客夾雜語句係指以國語爲主要語言夾雜客語短語之語句，因此可將客語詞彙取代國語譯句中意義相同的詞彙得到國客夾雜語料，例如：上例中，若將客語詞彙風搓取代國語譯句中的颱風即可得到一國客夾雜句子，不過當字典檔中國客詞彙相同時，這種詞彙取代的方法將失效，因此，我們初步從海陸字典檔 4,959 個詞彙之例句中，扣除國客詞彙相同的例句，再以詞彙取代的方法產生共 1,275 句國客夾雜語料。

(二) 語碼轉換現象分析

在多語夾雜語句中，雖然台客英等短語可能出現在國語語句內任何位置，但在實際使用上並非完全沒有規則可循，目前已有學者針對中英夾雜語句分析英語短語出現的語法結構及樣式(pattern)[2][3]，我們依其整理出的樣式分析從網路收集到的國台客英夾雜語料，部分結果如表一所示。爲了進一步分析這些夾雜短語的詞性與型態，我們隨機選取 500 份網路新聞以人工方式找出夾雜的台語及英語短語，其詞性與型態分佈情形如表二及表三所示。由表二的統計結果發現，中文語句中所夾雜之英語短語約有 90%是名詞，並以人名、地名及組織名較爲常見，而動詞僅佔了約 10%，這顯示了在表達動詞時一般較常使用母語，而表達名詞時，因爲許多公司、餐廳及地方等名稱本來即是英文，直接以英文表達並不會造成溝通的不便，因此並不常翻譯成中文使用，甚至有些情形下直接以英文表達反而比翻譯更容易理解。至於國語語句中夾雜台語短語的分佈情形，由表 3 的統計結果可發現動詞約佔 70%，名詞僅佔約 24%，結果與英語短語的分佈相反，這顯示了以台語表達動詞較爲常見，例如：挫著等, 阿莎力, 趴趴走等，原因除了說話者個人的習慣之外，使用這些詞彙較能以通俗的方式表達語意也是可能的原因之一，至於名詞較少使用台語短語可能是使用台語命名的地名、組織名較少的原因。另一方面，不論是台語的名詞或動詞短語其型態較不一定，較難呈現分類上的趨勢，不像英語名詞短語較集中分佈在人名、地名及組織名，因此表三並未進一步細分台語短語各詞類之型態。

表一、國語夾雜台客英短語之句型樣式

編號	句型樣式	範例句
1	程度副詞(Dfa) + 短語(Adj) (e.g., 很、非常、相當、最)	這道料理**非常 smooth** 入口即化 這家餐廳的老闆**很阿莎力** 隔壁的小孩一點也不瘦，反而很**大箍** (客)
2	短語(Adj) + 的(DE)	這裡都沒有可以 **shopping 的**地方 終於體驗到甚麼是**足感心的**服務了 小孩子什麼都不肯吃，所以餵養得**瘦夾夾的** (客)
3	的(DE) + 短語(Noun)	紐約**的 pizza**，單片就幾乎比臉大 好想念劉文聰**的番仔火**跟雞蛋糕啊！ 媽媽**的黃瓠粄**做得很好吃 (客)
4	1. + 2. 2. + 3. 1. + 2. + 3.	介紹你一家我**很尬意的**火鍋店 哪一間 **hotel 的 view** 最棒？ 這附近有一些**很古早的柑仔店** 他是**很擁人的**小孩，總愛耍無賴 (客)
5	數量定詞(Neqa) + 短語(Noun) (e.g., 很多、許多、一些)	我們還有**一些 issue** 要解決 這夜市有賣**很多賊仔貨** 吃飯前不要吃那麼多**零嗒** (客)
6	短語(Noun) + 位置詞(Ncd) (e.g., 上、下、內、裡、旁)	我們約在 **lobby 旁**的水池見面 **烘爐地上**有一尊超級大的土地公神像 晚飯後，祖父常在**天墀坪裡**唱山歌 (客)

表二、中英夾雜語料英語短語之詞性與型態分佈

詞性		數量	比例		範例
名詞	人名	89	25.14%	**90.4%**	John Culver, Kobe, Paul Hertz
	地名	80	22.60%		Boston, London, Paris
	組織	70	19.77%		NASA, NIKE, NHK, LV, Sony
	單位	14	3.95%		cm, GHz, kg
	食物	13	3.67%		bagel, coffee, salad
	其他	54	15.25%		cartoon, CPR, I-phone, MSN, MVP
動詞	—	34	9.6%	**9.6%**	call-in, DIY, po, shopping
合計		**354**	**100%**		

表三、中英夾雜語料台語短語之詞性與型態分佈

詞性	數量	比例	範例
名詞	17	23.61%	咱, 阮, 月娘, 運將, 囝囡, 代誌, 天公伯, 古早厝
動詞	50	69.44%	尬意, 讀冊, 拍謝, 假仙, 挫著等, 阿莎力, 趴趴走
副詞	2	2.78%	攏, 嘛
疑問詞	3	4.17%	安怎, 蝦米, 衝啥
合計	**72**	**100%**	

三、未知詞擷取

多語夾雜語料庫中夾雜的短語有些並未出現在目前的字典中，因此可能無法正確的斷詞，例如：”趴趴走”即無法被 CKIP 斷詞系統(http://ckipsvr.iis.sinica.edu.tw)[14]斷成一個詞，因此本年度另一項工作就是從多語夾語料庫中找出未知詞，尤其是夾雜短語的部分。我們提出的未知詞擷取演算上做法上是先對語料庫進行斷詞，此時未知詞將被切成數個單字詞或較短的詞，因此兩相鄰詞是否經常在語料中重複出現就成為偵測新詞的重要依據。我們使用文獻中常用的點式交互資訊(Pointwise Mutual Information, PMI)[15]來衡量兩詞的內聚力，並以閥值(threshold)篩選有較大 PMI 值的相鄰詞為候選新詞。由於 PMI 只考慮兩個詞是否經常相鄰出現，但經常相鄰出現的字合併後未必是新詞，有鑑於此，我們除了使用 PMI 之外，亦將使用前後文脈之 entropy 來過濾無關的新詞以提升精確度[16]，流程如圖一所示。

(一) CKIP 斷詞

我們收集的多語夾雜語料庫經過國台客英字典及 CKIP 斷詞，此時未知詞將以單字詞或短語的形式出現，而英文單字將被 CKIP 標記為 FW。

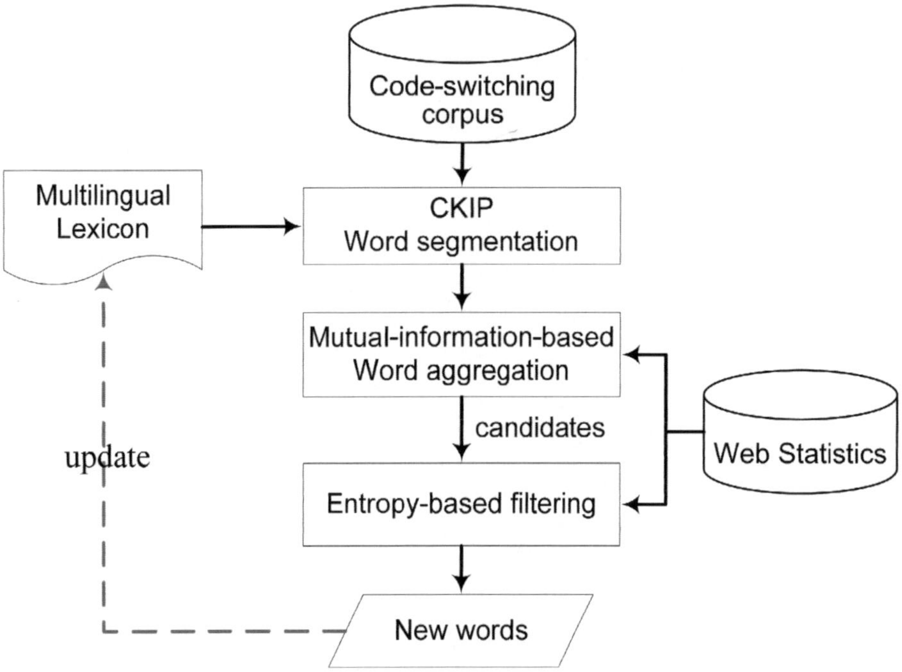

圖一、未知詞擷取流程圖

(二) 以交互資訊爲本的聚合機制(Mutual-information-based word aggregation)

針對語料庫中斷完詞的句子，從左至右計算任兩相鄰詞的 PMI 分數，定義如下。

$$PMI(w_i, w_j) = \log\frac{P(w_i, w_j)}{P(w_i)P(w_j)} = \log\frac{C(w_i, w_j)\bullet N}{C(w_i)C(w_j)}, \quad (1)$$

其中 $C(w_i, w_j)$ 表示 w_i 與 w_j 在語料庫中相鄰出現的次數，而 N 代表語料中的字數且爲常數，在此我們取 Google 查詢所回傳的文件數做爲 $C(w_i, w_j)$、$C(w_i)$ 及 $C(w_j)$，由於無法知道正確的 N 值，我們以 10^{12} 代替之 (N 值大小並不影響 PMI 的排序結果)。當所有相鄰詞的內聚力計算完後以 PMI 值遞減排序，接著即可篩選有較大 PMI 值的相鄰詞爲新詞候選者。

(三) 以 Entropy 爲本的過濾機制(Entropy-based filtering)

前一個階段產生的候選新詞可能包含無關的新詞，其主要原因在於 PMI 只考慮詞與詞的內聚力，並未考慮該詞是否爲一個語意完整的單元。一般來說，統計式方法較難直接評估一個詞語意的完整性，不過一個語意完整的詞在語用的表現上卻有其特徵，也就是它可與許多其它的詞搭配使用形成更大的單元，因此，若某個詞與之相鄰的詞較少且集中在少數幾個時，即表示它與這些詞的相依性高，較有機會合併成爲新詞。根據上述特性，一個詞的語意完整性便可用與之相鄰詞的數量及分散程度間接衡量，原則如下所示。

相鄰詞數量多且分佈平均 → 語意完整性高 → 單獨使用

相鄰詞數量少且分佈集中 → 語意較不完整 → 適合與其相鄰詞合併成爲新詞

表四、“趴趴”之左右文脈情形(取前五個最常出現的詞)

趴趴			
詞頻	左文脈	右文脈	詞頻
8	愛	走	336
5	軟	GO	42
5	台灣	造	23
2	【	熊	21
1	「	照	19

舉例來說，”趴趴走”使用 CKIP 斷詞的結果為“趴趴”　“走”，因此，我們以“趴趴”為例查詢 Google，並從回傳結果中擷取 999 筆含有“趴趴”的標題，分析緊鄰其左右的詞彙分佈情形，如表四所示。由結果可以發現，“趴趴”的左邊及右邊分別出現 212 及 58 個不同的詞，並且其右邊文脈分佈相當集中，“走”就佔了 336 次，而左文脈的分佈則較為平均，這顯示“趴趴”與“走”的相依性高，較有可能向右合併形成為新詞。

為了以系統化的方法分析每個詞左右文脈分佈的集中程度，我們可用左右文脈的詞頻除以總詞頻的方式將左右文脈轉換為機率表示法，再以 entropy 表示左右文脈分佈的集中程度。假設 $RC(w_t)=\{w_1,...,w_n\}$ 表示某個詞 w_t 的右文脈(right context)，也就是語料庫中緊鄰出現在 w_t 右邊的字詞集合，則 w_t 右文脈的 entropy 可定義為

$$H_{RC}(w_t) = -\sum_{w_i \in RC(w_t)} P(w_i)\log_2 P(w_i), \quad (2)$$

其中 $H_{RC}(w_t)$ 為 w_t 右文脈的 entropy，而 $P(w_i) = C(w_i)/N$ 為 w_t 右文脈中某個詞出現的機率，其中，$C(w_i)$ 為語料庫中 w_i 緊鄰出現在 w_t 右邊的次數，N 為語料庫中所有緊鄰出現在 w_t 右邊的總次數。同理，$H_{LC}(w_t)$ 表示 w_t 左文脈的 entropy，計算方法同上。根據上述 entropy 的計算方式，文脈分佈愈集中，則 entropy 愈小表，而文脈分佈愈平均，則 entropy 愈大。因此，以 entropy 來衡量一個詞的語意完整性，其原則如下。

Entropy 大 → 語意完整性高 → 單獨使用

Entropy 小 → 語意較不完整 → 適合與相鄰詞合併成為新詞

表五即為趴趴走等詞左右文脈的 entropy。由表五可發現”趴趴”右文脈的 entropy 較低，表示其語意較不完整，適合與其右邊的詞”走”合併成為一個新詞，至於”是”與”的”這兩個詞左右文脈的 entropy 都很大，表示這些單字詞已經是完整的語意單元，不需要與其它詞合併。由此觀察可發現當兩個詞要合併時，如果其中一個詞的左邊或右邊不完整時，便是一個良好的合併候選者，因此，我們定義兩個詞 w_i 與 w_j 合併前的 entropy 為 w_i 右文脈與 w_j 左文脈 entropy 的最小值，如下所示。

$$H_{before}(w_i, w_j) = min(H_{RC}(w_i), H_{LC}(w_j)), \quad (3)$$

表五、合併前後左右文脈 entropy — 以趴趴走、是的爲例

	$H_{LC}(w_t)$	$H_{RC}(w_t)$		$H_{LC}(w_t)$	$H_{RC}(w_t)$
趴趴	6.07	**2.75**	是	7.17	8.24
走	4.85	5.56	的	8.34	7.72
趴趴走	6.07	5.56	是的	7.17	7.72

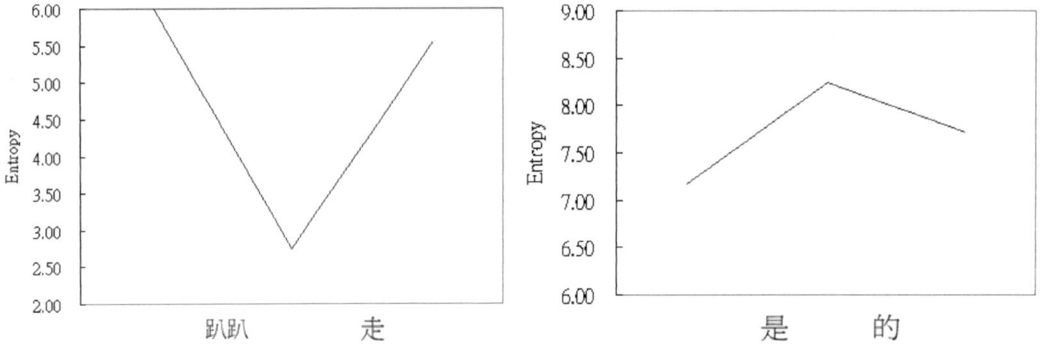

(1) (2)

圖二、兩詞合併前後 entropy 變化情形

表五的另一個發現爲兩詞合併後其左右文脈的 entropy 會變大，這是因爲合併後的新詞語意較爲完整之故，例如：趴趴走合併前的 entropy 爲 2.75，合併後若取”趴趴”的左文脈爲合併後的左文脈，”走”的右文脈爲合併後的右文脈，則合併後左右文脈的 entropy 分別變大爲 6.07 與 5.56，如圖二(1)所示，反之，兩個語意完整不需合併的詞如果合併，則合併後的 entropy 並不會明顯變大，甚至可能變小，如表五及圖二(2)中”是”與”的”的範例所示。由此可知，兩個詞合併前後 entropy 的變化便是判斷是否爲新詞的重要依據，因此，我們定義兩詞合併前後的 entropy 比值(ratio)，如下所示。

$$\lambda_{w_iw_j}^{LC} = \frac{H_{after}^{LC}(w_i, w_j)}{H_{before}(w_i, w_j)}, \tag{4}$$

$$\lambda_{w_iw_j}^{RC} \frac{H_{after}^{RC}(w_i, w_j)}{H_{before}(w_i, w_j)}, \tag{5}$$

其中 $\lambda_{w_iw_j}^{LC}$ 與 $\lambda_{w_iw_j}^{RC}$ 分別爲 w_i 與 w_j 兩個詞合併後左右文脈 entropy 與合併前的比值，其中 $H_{after}^{LC}(w_i, w_j) = H_{LC}(w_i)$，也就是取 w_i 的左文脈做爲 w_i 與 w_j 合併後的左文脈，同理，$H_{after}^{RC}(w_i, w_j) = H_{RC}(w_j)$，因此，當 $\lambda_{w_iw_j}^{LC}$ 與 $\lambda_{w_iw_j}^{RC}$ 皆大於 1 時代表合併後 entropy 較合併前大，可考慮將兩詞合併成爲新詞。

四、實驗結果

(一) 實驗設計

在實驗設計上，我們從雅虎新聞中隨機挑選 500 篇新聞，接著以人工的方式找出國台夾雜的句子，再以 CKIP 斷詞系統進行斷詞，如果某句所夾雜的台語短語無法被正確的斷詞，則表示該短語為台語新詞，反之，可以被正確斷出的台語短語將不列入本實驗中。依此原則，本實驗共挑選出 40 句包含台語新詞的國台夾雜測試句，句中任兩相鄰詞皆爲合併候選者，共計 200 個，其中僅有 41 個台語新詞，即爲本實驗的標準答案。測試時，給定一斷完詞的測試句，首先透過 Google 的回傳結果從左至右計算句中任兩相鄰詞的 PMI 分數及左右文脈 entropy，接著針對有較高 PMI 的相鄰詞以合併前後的 entropy 比值，即 $\lambda^{LC}_{w_i w_j}$ 與 $\lambda^{RC}_{w_i w_j}$ 做爲閥值來評估是否合併成爲新詞，最後以召回率(recall)、精確率(precision)與 F-measure 來評估未知詞擷取演算法的效果，其中召回率是用來評估系統能從正確的 41 個新詞中找出幾個，精確率則是評估系統所建議的新詞中有多少是正確的，而 F-measure 則是召回率與精確率的綜合評估，即 2 * recall * precision / (recall+precision)。一般說來，調高 PMI、$\lambda^{LC}_{w_i w_j}$ 與 $\lambda^{RC}_{w_i w_j}$ 等閥值將可提系統的精確率，但召回率卻可能下降，反之，若閥值太低則可以找出更多新詞，但也會降低系統的精確度。

(二) 結果

表六即爲部分候選新詞之 PMI 及合併前後左右文脈 entropy 之比值。結果顯示調高 PMI 等閥值可過濾許多不爲新詞的候選詞，但也可能損失如"破糊糊"(PMI 太小)與"皮皮挫"($\lambda^{LC}_{w_i w_j}$ 太小)等正確的新詞。本實驗藉由調整閥值(PMI=3，$\lambda^{LC}_{w_i w_j}$ =1.15，$\lambda^{RC}_{w_i w_j}$ =1.05)得到的最佳結果爲 F-measure=68.49%，Recall=60.98%，Precision =78.13%，如表七所列之部分結果，圖三即爲同時調整 $\lambda^{LC}_{w_i w_j}$ 與 $\lambda^{RC}_{w_i w_j}$ (0.75 ~ 1.25)之實驗結果。

表六、候選新詞之 PMI 及合併前後左右文脈 entropy 之比值

候選詞	PMI	$\lambda^{LC}_{w_i w_j}$	$\lambda^{RC}_{w_i w_j}$
瞭解 甚麼	12.69	1.11	1.00
碎碎 念	12.33	4.14	5.29
皮皮 挫	11.42	0.92	1.07
囝 囡	11.07	1.29	1.38
才 發生	3.90	0.79	0.96
好 山	0.80	1.13	1.18
破 糊糊	-2.14	1.33	1.14
就 是	-2.87	1.13	1.27

表七、不同閥值未知詞擷取效果之影響 (PMI=3)

$\lambda_{w_i w_j}^{LC}$	$\lambda_{w_i w_j}^{RC}$	Recall	Precision	F-measure
1.15	0.75	0.6585	0.6000	0.6279
1.15	0.80	0.6585	0.6136	0.6353
1.15	0.85	0.6585	0.6136	0.6353
1.15	0.90	0.6585	0.6136	0.6353
1.15	0.95	0.6341	0.6341	0.6341
1.15	1.00	0.6098	0.6757	0.6410
1.15	**1.05**	**0.6098**	**0.7813**	**0.6849**
1.15	1.10	0.5610	0.7667	0.6479
1.15	1.15	0.5366	0.8148	0.6471
1.15	1.20	0.4390	0.9000	0.5902
1.15	1.25	0.4390	1.0000	0.6102

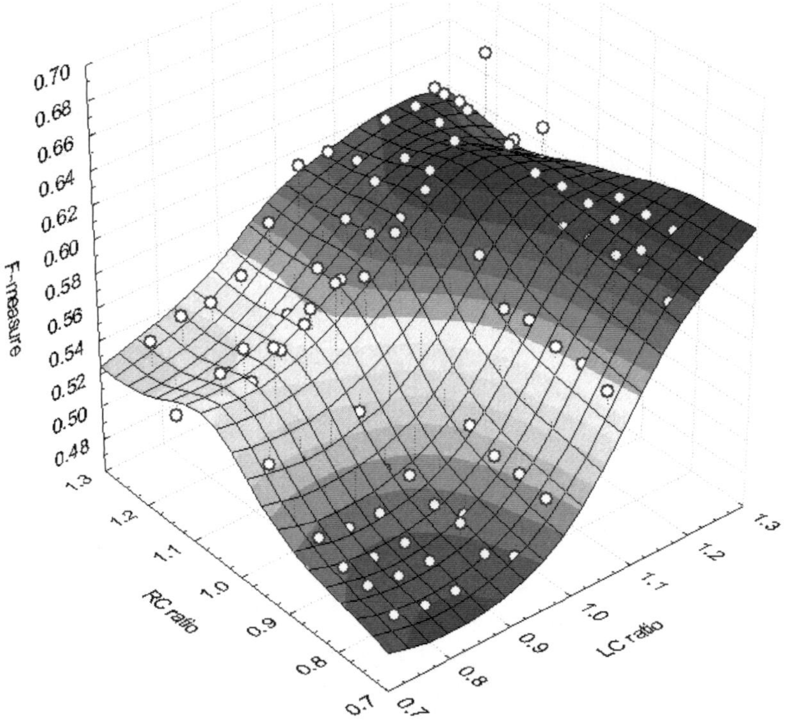

圖三、兩詞合併前後 entropy 變化情形

五、結論

本論文提出結合交互資訊與熵之未知詞擷取演算法，自動從多語夾雜語料中找出未知詞，使用交互資訊之目的在計算詞與詞的內聚力並挑選較高者爲候選新詞，接著使用以熵爲基礎的過濾機制，根據候選新詞左右文脈的分佈情形過濾無關的新詞，實驗結果顯示本論文所提之以熵爲基礎的方法可藉由過濾無關的新詞提升未知詞擷取之精確度。未來，我們將研究機器學習的方法以期達到更精確的結果。

誌謝

本研究感謝王政欽及粘書豪同學在先期工作上所做的努力。此外，本研究承蒙國科會 NSC 99-2221-E-155 -036 -MY3 費補助特此致謝。

參考文獻

[1] P. Fung and T. Schultz, "Multilingual Spoken Language Processing," *IEEE Signal Processing Magazine*, 25(3), pp. 89-97, 2008.

[2] L. Ge, "An investigation on English/Chinese Code-switching in BBS in Chinese Alumni's Community," Master thesis, University of Edinburgh, 2007.

[3] Y. Liu, "Evaluation of the Matrix Language Hypothesis: Evidence from Chinese-English Code-switching Phenomena in Blogs," *Journal of Chinese Language and Computing*, 18(2), pp. 75-92, 2008.

[4] R. Y. Lyu, M. S. Liang, and Y. C. Chiang, "Toward Constructing a Multilingual Speech Corpus for Taiwanese (Min-nan), Hakka, and Mandarin," *International Journal of Computational Linguistics and Chinese Language Processing*, 9(2), pp. 1-12, 2004.

[5] C. H. Wu, Y. H. Chiu, C. J. Shia, and C. Y. Lin, "Automatic Segmentation and Identification of Mixed-language Speech using Delta-BIC and LSA-based GMMs," *IEEE Trans. Audio, Speech, and Language Processing*, 14(1), pp.266-276, 2006.

[6] C. L. Huang and C. H. Wu, "Generation of Phonetic Units for Mixed-Language Speech Recognition Based on Acoustic and Contextual Analysis," *IEEE Trans. on Computers*, 56(9), pp. 1225-1233, 2007.

[7] D. C. Lyu, R. Y. Lyu, Y. C. Chiang, and C. N. Hsu, "Speech Recognition on Code-switching among the Chinese Dialects," in *Proc. of ICASSP-06*, pp. 1105-1108, 2006.

[8] W. T. Hong, H. C. Chen, I. B. Liao, and W. J. Wang, "Mandarin/English Mixed-Lingual Speech Recognition System on Resource-Constrained Platforms," in *Proc. of ROCLING-09*, pp. 237-250, 2009.

[9] J. Y. C. Chan, P. C. Ching, T.Lee and H. M. Meng, "Detection of Language Boundary in Code-switching utterances by Bi-phone Probabilities," in *Proc. of ISCSLP-04*, pp. 293-296, 2004.

[10] J. Y. C. Chan, P. C. Ching, T.Lee and H. Cao, "Automatic Speech Recognition of Cantonese-English Code-mixing Utterance," in *Proc. of Interspeech*, pp. 113-116, 2006.

[11] C. M. White, S. Khudanpur, and J. K. Baker, "An Investigation of Acoustic Models for Multilingual Code-Switching," in *Proc. of Interspeech*, 2008.

[12] Y. Zhang and J. Tao, "Prosody Modification on Mixed-Language Speech Synthesis," in *Proc. of ISCSLP-08*, pp. 1-4, 2008.

[13] Y. Qian, H. Liang, and F. Soong, "A Cross-Language State Sharing and Mapping Approach to Bilingual (Mandarin–English) TTS," *IEEE Trans. on Audio, Speech, and Language Processing*, 17(6), pp. 1231-1239, 2009.

[14] W. Y. Ma and K. J. Chen, ""Introduction to CKIP Chinese Word Segmentation System for the First International Chinese Word Segmentation Bakeoff," in *Proc. of ACL, Second SIGHAN Workshop on Chinese Language Processing*, pp. 168-171, 2003.

[15] K. Church and P. Hanks. "Word Association Norms, Mutual Information and Lexicography," *Computational Linguistics*, vol. 16, no. 1, pp. 22-29, 1991.

[16] Z. Luo, and R. Song, "An Integrated Method for Chinese Unknown Word Extraction," in *Proc. of the Third SIGHAN Workshop on Chinese Language Learning,* pp. 148-155, 2004.